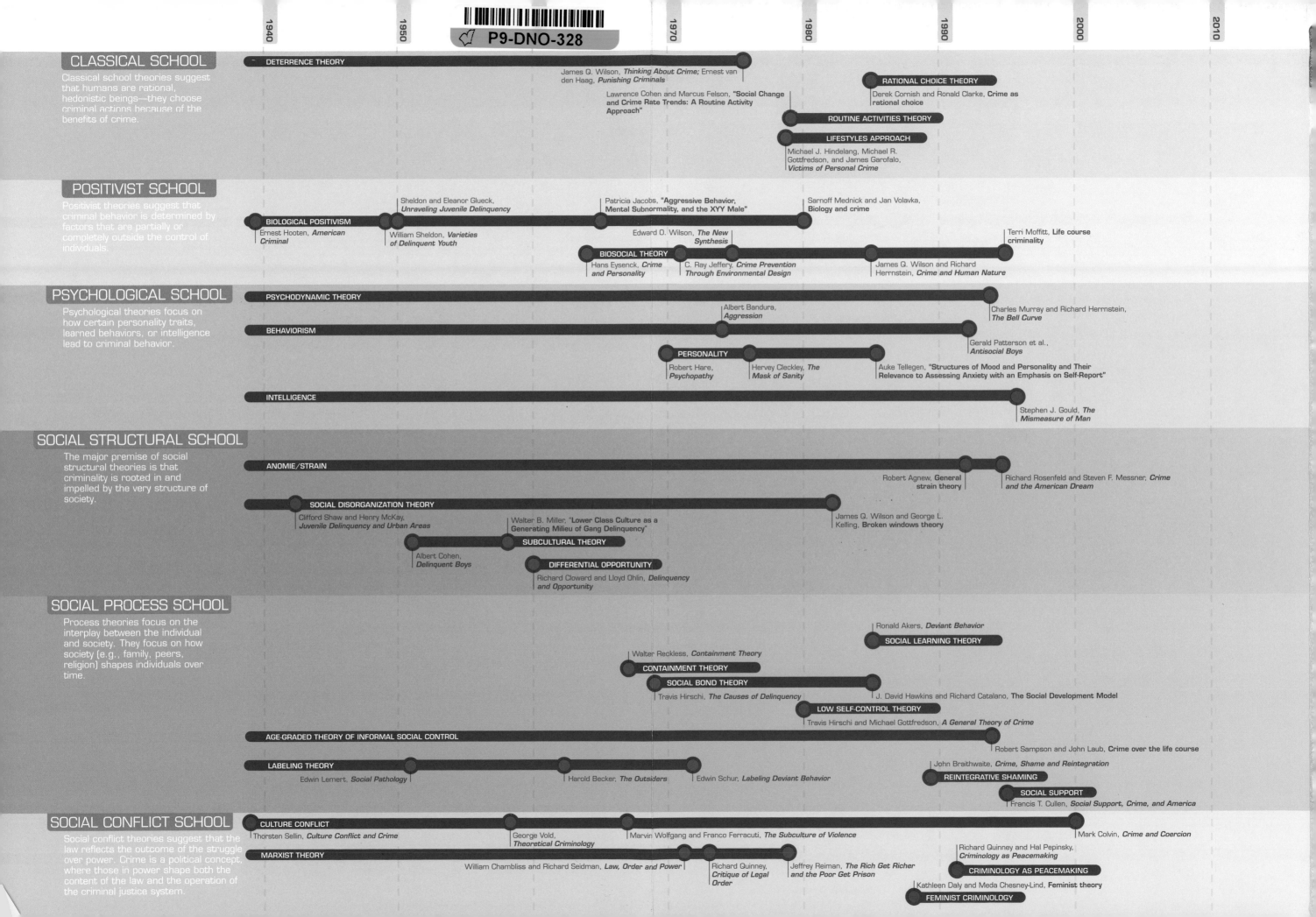

CLASSICAL SCHOOL

Classical school theories suggest that humans are rational, hedonistic beings—they choose criminal actions because of the benefits of crime.

DETERRENCE THEORY
James Q. Wilson, *Thinking About Crime*; Ernest van den Haag, *Punishing Criminals*

RATIONAL CHOICE THEORY
Derek Cornish and Ronald Clarke, **Crime as rational choice**

Lawrence Cohen and Marcus Felson, **"Social Change and Crime Rate Trends: A Routine Activity Approach"**

ROUTINE ACTIVITIES THEORY

LIFESTYLES APPROACH
Michael J. Hindelang, Michael R. Gottfredson, and James Garofalo, *Victims of Personal Crime*

POSITIVIST SCHOOL

Positivist theories suggest that criminal behavior is determined by factors that are partially or completely outside the control of individuals.

BIOLOGICAL POSITIVISM
Ernest Hooten, *American Criminal*

Sheldon and Eleanor Glueck, *Unraveling Juvenile Delinquency*

William Sheldon, *Varieties of Delinquent Youth*

Patricia Jacobs, **"Aggressive Behavior, Mental Subnormality, and the XYY Male"**

Sarnoff Mednick and Jan Volavka, **Biology and crime**

Edward O. Wilson, *The New Synthesis*

Terri Moffitt, **Life course criminality**

BIOSOCIAL THEORY
Hans Eysenck, *Crime and Personality*

C. Ray Jeffery, *Crime Prevention Through Environmental Design*

James Q. Wilson and Richard Herrnstein, *Crime and Human Nature*

PSYCHOLOGICAL SCHOOL

Psychological theories focus on how certain personality traits, learned behaviors, or intelligence lead to criminal behavior.

PSYCHODYNAMIC THEORY

BEHAVIORISM

Albert Bandura, *Aggression*

Charles Murray and Richard Herrnstein, *The Bell Curve*

Gerald Patterson et al., *Antisocial Boys*

PERSONALITY
Robert Hare, *Psychopathy*

Hervey Cleckley, *The Mask of Sanity*

Auke Tellegen, **"Structures of Mood and Personality and Their Relevance to Assessing Anxiety with an Emphasis on Self-Report"**

INTELLIGENCE
Stephen J. Gould, *The Mismeasure of Man*

SOCIAL STRUCTURAL SCHOOL

The major premise of social structural theories is that criminality is rooted in and impelled by the very structure of society.

ANOMIE/STRAIN
Robert Agnew, **General strain theory**

Richard Rosenfeld and Steven F. Messner, *Crime and the American Dream*

SOCIAL DISORGANIZATION THEORY
Clifford Shaw and Henry McKay, *Juvenile Delinquency and Urban Areas*

Walter B. Miller, **"Lower Class Culture as a Generating Milieu of Gang Delinquency"**

James Q. Wilson and George L. Kelling, **Broken windows theory**

Albert Cohen, *Delinquent Boys*

SUBCULTURAL THEORY

DIFFERENTIAL OPPORTUNITY
Richard Cloward and Lloyd Ohlin, *Delinquency and Opportunity*

SOCIAL PROCESS SCHOOL

Process theories focus on the interplay between the individual and society. They focus on how society (e.g., family, peers, religion) shapes individuals over time.

Ronald Akers, *Deviant Behavior*
SOCIAL LEARNING THEORY

Walter Reckless, *Containment Theory*
CONTAINMENT THEORY

SOCIAL BOND THEORY
Travis Hirschi, *The Causes of Delinquency*

J. David Hawkins and Richard Catalano, **The Social Development Model**

LOW SELF-CONTROL THEORY
Travis Hirschi and Michael Gottfredson, *A General Theory of Crime*

AGE-GRADED THEORY OF INFORMAL SOCIAL CONTROL
Robert Sampson and John Laub, **Crime over the life course**

LABELING THEORY
Edwin Lemert, *Social Pathology*

Harold Becker, *The Outsiders*

Edwin Schur, *Labeling Deviant Behavior*

John Braithwaite, **Crime, Shame and Reintegration**
REINTEGRATIVE SHAMING

SOCIAL SUPPORT
Francis T. Cullen, *Social Support, Crime, and America*

SOCIAL CONFLICT SCHOOL

Social conflict theories suggest that the law reflects the outcome of the struggle over power. Crime is a political concept, where those in power shape both the content of the law and the operation of the criminal justice system.

CULTURE CONFLICT
Thorsten Sellin, *Culture Conflict and Crime*

George Vold, *Theoretical Criminology*

Marvin Wolfgang and Franco Ferracuti, *The Subculture of Violence*

Mark Colvin, *Crime and Coercion*

MARXIST THEORY
William Chambliss and Richard Seidman, *Law, Order and Power*

Richard Quinney, *Critique of Legal Order*

Jeffrey Reiman, *The Rich Get Richer and the Poor Get Prison*

Richard Quinney and Hal Pepinsky, *Criminology as Peacemaking*

CRIMINOLOGY AS PEACEMAKING

Kathleen Daly and Meda Chesney-Lind, **Feminist theory**
FEMINIST CRIMINOLOGY

1860　1870　1880　1890　1900　1910　1920　1930

Immanuel Kant, *Philosophy of Law*

Cesare Lombroso, *The Criminal Mind*

Raffaele Garofalo, *Criminology*

Enrico Ferri, *Criminal Sociology*

Richard Dugdale, *The Jukes*

Charles Goring, *The English Convict*

Henry H. Goddard, *The Kallikak Family: A Study in the Heredity of Feeble-Mindedness*

PSYCHODYNAMIC THEORY

William Healy, *The Individual Delinquent*

Sigmund Freud, *General Introduction to Psychoanalysis*

August Aichhorn, *Wayward Youth*

BEHAVIORISM

Ivan Pavlov, *Conditioned Reflexes*

H.H. Goddard, *Feeble-mindedness*

Alfred Binet, *A Method of Measuring the Development of Intelligence in Young Children*

INTELLIGENCE

ANOMIE/STRAIN

Emile Durkheim, *Suicide*

Robert K. Merton, *Social Structure and Anomie*

SOCIAL DISORGANIZATION THEORY

Frederick Thrasher, *The Gang*

LAWS OF IMITATION

Gabriel Tarde, *Penal Philosophy*

Edwin Sutherland, *Criminology*

DIFFERENTIAL ASSOCIATION

Edwin Sutherland, *The Professional Thief*

AGE-GRADED THEORY OF INFORMAL SOCIAL CONTROL

Sheldon and Eleanor Glueck, *500 Criminal Careers*

LABELING THEORY

Frank Tannenbaum, *Dramatization of Evil*

Wilhelm Bonger, *Criminality and Economic Conditions*

Georg Rusche and Otto Kirchheimer, *Punishment and Social Structure*

Criminology
Theory, Research, and Policy

SECOND EDITION

Gennaro F. Vito, PhD
University of Louisville

Jeffrey R. Maahs, PhD
University of Minnesota-Duluth

Ronald M. Holmes, EdD
University of Louisville

JONES AND BARTLETT PUBLISHERS
Sudbury, Massachusetts
BOSTON   TORONTO   LONDON   SINGAPORE

World Headquarters
Jones and Bartlett Publishers
40 Tall Pine Drive
Sudbury, MA 01776
978-443-5000
info@jbpub.com
www.jbpub.com

Jones and Bartlett Publishers Canada
6339 Ormindale Way
Mississauga, Ontario L5V 1J2
Canada

Jones and Bartlett Publishers
International
Barb House, Barb Mews
London W6 7PA
United Kingdom

Jones and Bartlett's books and products are available through most bookstores and online booksellers. To contact Jones and Bartlett Publishers directly, call 800-832-0034, fax 978-443-8000, or visit our website www.jbpub.com.

Substantial discounts on bulk quantities of Jones and Bartlett's publications are available to corporations, professional associations, and other qualified organizations. For details and specific discount information, contact the special sales department at Jones and Bartlett via the above contact information or send an email to specialsales@jbpub.com.

Production Credits
Chief Executive Officer: Clayton E. Jones
Chief Operating Officer: Donald W. Jones, Jr.
President, Higher Education and Professional Publishing: Robert W. Holland, Jr.
V.P., Sales and Marketing: William J. Kane
V.P., Production and Design: Anne Spencer
V.P., Manufacturing and Inventory Control: Therese Connell
Publisher, Public Safety Group: Kimberly Brophy
Acquisitions Editor: Stefanie Boucher
Editor: Christine Emerton
Production Editor: Jenny L. McIsaac
Photo Research Manager/Photographer: Kimberly Potvin
Director of Marketing: Alisha Weisman
Interior and Cover Design: Anne Spencer
Composition: Group 360
Cover Image: © AbleStock
Text Printing and Binding: Courier Kendallville
Cover Printing: John P. Pow Company

ISBN-13: 978-0-7637-3001-7
ISBN-10: 0-7637-3001-7

Library of Congress Cataloging-in-Publication Data

Vito, Gennaro F.
   Criminology / Gennaro F. Vito.— 2nd ed.
       p. cm.
   Includes bibliographical references and index.
   ISBN 0-7637-3001-7 (hardcover)
  1. Criminology. I. Title.
   HV6025.V57 2006
   364—dc22
                                     2005024823

6048

Printed in the United States of America
10 09 08 07 06   10 9 8 7 6 5 4 3 2 1

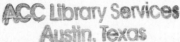

This book is dedicated to the Vito, Maahs, and Holmes families.

BRIEF CONTENTS

CONTENTS

Chapter 8

Chapter 9

Chapter 10

Chapter 15

Crimes of the Powerful: Organized and
White-Collar Crime   398

Chapter 16

The Future of Criminal Justice
and Criminology   432

Criminology: Theory, Research, and Policy, Second Edition provides students with comprehensive coverage of the leading criminological theories using sociology, psychology, biology, and ecology to explain how and why crime occurs. The text explores contemporary crime issues within the framework of criminological theory.

Features that reinforce and expand on essential information include:

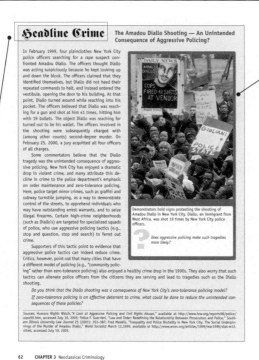

Full-Color Photos Critical thinking questions accompany photographs of recent cases and criminals relevant to chapter topics.

Headline Crime Recent high-profile crimes or policy issues are highlighted and pose discussion questions relating to relevant theories.

Links Connect the current topic to related subjects in other chapters.

You Are the Criminologist Realistic case studies and accompanying discussion questions challenge readers to think like a practicing criminologist.

Theory in Action Relate theoretical premises to real-world cases and events.

End of Chapter Material Each chapter concludes with a chapter review, critical thinking questions, a glossary of key terms, and a bibliography for further reading on chapter subjects.

Instructor Resources

Instructor's ToolKit CD-ROM
ISBN: 0-7637-4374-7
Preparing for class is easy with the resources found on this CD-ROM, including:

- **PowerPoint Presentations,** providing you with a powerful way to make presentations that are both educational and engaging. Slides can be modified and edited to meet your needs.
- **Lecture Outlines,** providing you with complete, ready-to-use lesson plans that outline all of the topics covered in the text. Lesson plans can be edited and modified to fit your course.
- **Electronic Test Bank,** containing multiple-choice and scenario-based questions, allows you to originate tailor-made classroom tests and quizzes quickly and easily by selecting, editing, organizing, and printing a test along with an answer key that includes page references to the text.

The resources found on the Instructor's ToolKit CD-ROM have been formatted so that you can seamlessly integrate them into the most popular course administration tools. Please contact Jones and Bartlett Publishers technical support at any time with questions.

Student Resources

Student Workbook
ISBN: 0-7637-4385-2
This resource is designed to encourage critical thinking and aid comprehension of course material through:

- Case studies and corresponding questions
- Matching questions
- Fill-in-the-blank questions
- Short answer questions
- Multiple-choice questions

Technology Resources

Essential components to the teaching and learning system are interactivities and additional resources that help the students grasp key concepts in criminology.

www.criminology.jbpub.com
Make full use of today's teaching and learning technology with www.criminology.jbpub.com. This site has been specifically designed to complement *Criminology: Theory, Research, and Policy, Second Edition.* Some of the resources available include:

- Interactivities
- In the News
- Key Term Explorer
- Web Links

ACKNOWLEDGMENTS

Reviewers

Christopher D. Bader
Baylor University
Waco, Texas

Stephen Brodt
Ball State University
Muncie, Indiana

Peter Conis
Iowa State University
Ames, Iowa

John Galliher
University of Missouri-Columbia
Columbia, Missouri

Michael Givant
Adelphi University
Garden City, New York

Heather C. Melton
University of Utah
Salt Lake City, Utah

Paul J. Munson
Winona State University
Winona, Minnesota

Lawrence F. Travis III
University of Cincinnati
Cincinnati, Ohio

Contributors

Special thanks to the following people for their contributions to the text:

Lee Ayers-Schlosser
Southern Oregon University
Ashland, Oregon

Dale J. Brooker
Saint Joseph's College of Maine
Standish, Maine

B. Keith Crew
University of Northern Iowa
Cedar Falls, Iowa

Jennifer L. Gossett
Indiana University of Pennsylvania
Indiana, Pennsylvania

Heather C. Melton
University of Utah
Salt Lake City, Utah

ABOUT THE AUTHORS

Gennaro F. Vito is a Professor and a Distinguished University Scholar in the Department of Justice Administration at the University of Louisville. He also serves as a faculty member in the Administrative Officer's Course at the Southern Police Institute, Vice Chair, and Graduate Program Coordinator. He holds a PhD in Public Administration from The Ohio State University. Active in professional organizations, he is a past president and fellow of the Academy of Criminal Justice Sciences. He is also the recipient of the Educator of the Year Award from the Southern Criminal Justice Association (1991) and the Dean's Outstanding Performance Award for Research and Scholarly Activities from the former College of Urban and Public Affairs at the University of Louisville (1990), the Dean's Award for Outstanding Research from the College of Arts and Sciences, and the President's Distinguished Faculty Award for Excellence in Research (2002).

Jeffrey R. Maahs received a BA in psychology from the University of Wisconsin-Eau Claire in 1993, an MA in criminal justice from Sam Houston State University in 1997, and a PhD in criminal justice from the University of Cincinnati in 2001. Dr. Maahs has been on the faculty at the University of Minnesota-Duluth since 2000. His research interests include corrections (probation outcomes, drug courts, prison privatization) and criminological theory, and he has authored numerous articles, book chapters, and agency reports in these areas.

Ronald M. Holmes is an Emeritus Professor in the Department of Justice Administration at the University of Louisville where he continues to teach classes on the topics of serial murder, sex crimes, and criminal profiling. A world-renowned author and expert on these subjects, Dr. Holmes presently serves as the Coroner for Jefferson County, Kentucky (Louisville). He received his doctorate in Education from Indiana University. Dr. Holmes has completed more than 500 psychological profiles for police departments across the United States.

OBJECTIVES

Define criminology and understand how this field of study relates to other social science disciplines.

Understand the meaning of scientific theory and its relationship to research and policy.

Recognize a "good" theory of crime, based on criteria such as empirical support, scope, and parsimony.

Know the criteria for establishing causation and identify the attributes of good research.

Understand the politics of criminology and the importance of social context.

Define criminal law and understand the conflict and consensus perspectives on the law.

Describe the various schools of criminological theory and the explanations that they provide.

Crime and Criminology

> "
>
> Crime and the fear of crime have permeated the fabric of American life.
>
> — Warren E. Burger, Chief Justice, U.S. Supreme Court[1]
>
> "

> "
>
> "We don't seem to be able to check crime, so why not legalize it and then tax it out of business?"
>
> — Will Rogers[2]
>
> "

YOU ARE THE CRIMINOLOGIST

A Research Project

You have several friends who spend a considerable amount of time every day on the Internet and they refer to themselves as "hackers." Hackers gain illegal access into computer networks to gain information (e.g., credit card numbers) to use for their profit or interest. From your criminological studies, you know that hackers engage in activities that are illegal. Many of your friends, however, do not see their activities as a problem because they just "look around" the network and do not take any important information. You begin to wonder how many people engage in hacking, and thus, you conduct an Internet search on the term *hacker* to see what information is available. You discover that there are an abundance of Web sites dedicated to various hacker groups. You begin to think about why some people, including your friends, engage in hacking and others do not, even though they may have the same computer skills and ability to access private or confidential information.

As a criminologist, where would you start in researching the reasons why some people hack and others do not?

What ethical issues would arise if you were to use your friends as research subjects to answer your question?

Which school of criminological thought might assist you in explaining why hackers engage in illegal behavior and in developing policies to stop this crime?

Introduction

Crime is a social phenomenon that commands the attention and energy of the American public. When crime statistics are announced or a particular crime makes national headlines, the public demands that "something be done." American citizens are concerned about the safety of their families and their possessions. In 2003, for example, 49% of the public "avoided going into certain places or neighborhoods."[3] Because of the public's concern about the safety of their communities, crime is a perennial political issue that candidates for political office are compelled to address.

Dealing with crime commands a substantial portion of the country's tax dollars. In fiscal year 2001, the criminal justice system cost taxpayers over $167 billion. Between 1982 and 1992, these costs rose by over 360%.[4] Much of this cost is due to the rise in the prison population that resulted from the "get-tough" strategies popular in the 1980s and 1990s (e.g., mandatory minimum sentences, the "war" on drugs, three-strikes legislation). In 1987, the number of sentenced prisoners under the jurisdiction of state and federal correctional authorities stood at 560,812. The 1987 rate of incarceration was 231 per 100,000 citizens. By the year 2000, the number of prisoners was 1,381,892 — a

146% increase over the 1987 figure. In addition, the incarceration rate in 2000 more than doubled in comparison to the 1987 rate (478 per 100,000).[5] In addition, this rising trend shows little indication of slowing down. If rates of first-time incarceration remain the same, population estimates indicate that about 7% of all persons born in the United States in 2001 will go to state or federal prison in their lifetime.[6]

As these statistics indicate, crime is an important social issue. Further, *how* policymakers deal with crime (via crime policy) can have enormous social and financial implications. A basic tenant of this text is that a combination of theory and research can help provide direction to crime policy. The chapters in this book attempt to organize ideas in order to explain criminal behavior. This includes the factors that contribute to crime and the social reactions (including proposed and actual policies) to crime. In short, this book explores the field of criminology.

Defining Criminology

Simply put, criminology is the scientific study of crime. More broadly, Edwin Sutherland identified criminology as the study of law making, law breaking, and the response to law breaking.[7] Some scholars further distinguish *criminal justice* from criminology. Here, Sutherland's definition is subdivided into two related fields, where criminology focuses on law breaking (i.e., the nature, extent, and causes of crime) and criminal justice focuses on the response (i.e., policing, courts, and corrections) to criminal behavior. Scholars interested in criminal justice, for example, may study the causes and consequences of prison crowding or the effectiveness of different policing models. Of course there is a relationship between criminology and criminal justice. The response to crime depends largely on one's view of the causes of crime. For this reason, many criminologists dabble in both of these areas.

Another field that overlaps with criminology is the study of *deviance*. A "deviant" is anyone who violates social norms. *Norms* are simply guidelines that define for members of a society the types of behaviors that are appropriate or inappropriate in certain situations. Norms are classified as folkways, mores, and laws, based largely on the response to their violation.[8] *Folkways* are norms against actions that may evoke a snicker or some teasing as a response (e.g., nose picking). Violations of a society's *mores* evoke a more serious response from others (e.g., having a child outside of marriage). *Laws* are norms that have been codified, and the response to violations comes from formal government agencies. Therefore, although some deviant behavior is criminal, deviance can also include acts (e.g., cross-dressing, membership in a motorcycle gang) that are not defined as crime. Deviance scholars are often interested in how deviant behaviors come to be criminalized; that is, they focus on the "law-making" aspect of Sutherland's definition.

Criminology and Academics

Until recently, people with an academic interest in criminal behavior sought degrees in social science disciplines such as anthropology, psychology, economics, law, political science, ethics, and sociology; thus, a student might earn a degree in sociology with an emphasis on deviance and crime. Although some people still study crime through other disciplines, most universities now offer degrees in criminology or criminal justice. Moreover, many universities have separate criminology departments, divisions, or schools. In that sense, crimi-

nology has recently emerged as a distinct social science field.

This emergence has been partial, however, and a bit awkward. In part, this is because unlike other social science disciplines, criminology is organized around a class of behaviors (crime) rather than a particular way of understanding these behaviors. Social science disciplines tend to be organized around common assumptions, guiding insights, and specific research methodologies.[9] For example, psychologists generally seek to understand the mental processes that explain human behavior, while sociology emphasizes the role of social institutions and processes. Within any social science discipline, "crime" is only one type of human behavior that attracts interest. A psychologist might also be interested in intelligence, a political scientist in voting behavior, and a sociologist in explaining social movements. One might expect, therefore, that criminology would be multidisciplinary in nature. To some extent, this is indeed the case; many disciplines have made contributions to the scientific study of crime. Some of the earliest scientific theories of crime came from biologists and psychologists. Few would dispute the fact, though, that sociology has had the largest impact on the study of crime.

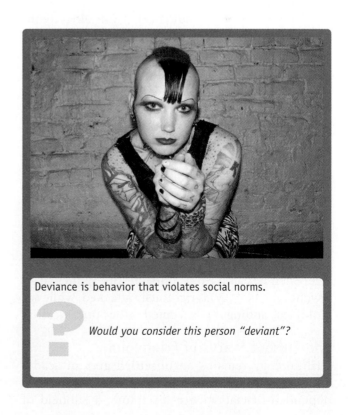

Deviance is behavior that violates social norms.

? *Would you consider this person "deviant"?*

The Dominance of Sociology

Throughout most of the 20th century, sociologists dominated scientific discourse about criminal behavior. The roots of this dominance can be traced to members of the sociology department at the University of Chicago. Ernest W. Burgess, W. I. Thomas, and a host of other sociologists created a body of research methodology, research findings, and theory related to crime that came to be called simply the "Chicago School of Crime."[10] During the 1930s, Edwin Sutherland, a student of the Chicago School sociologists, became the dominant advocate of a sociological criminology. At about the same time, Robert K. Merton, a Columbia University sociologist, developed the sociological theory of *anomie* to explain crime. Sociological dominance during the 1900s was such that criminology came to be considered a "child" to the "parent" discipline of sociology. As one commentator notes, the two-word term *sociological criminology*, until recently, was redundant.[11]

The sociological dominance of criminology continues to have implications for the study of crime. Even where universities have separate criminology departments, many of the criminologists in these departments were trained as sociologists. Also, the shift toward independent criminology departments is relatively recent and not complete. Many universities still offer criminology degrees through sociology departments.

Supporters of a sociological criminology point to the importance of the "sociological imagination."[12] Humans tend to see causes of people's behavior (including crime) as the result of individual traits and choices. The sociological imagination helps reveal the sometimes subtle social and historical influences on an individual's behavior. Sociology is also committed to a "debunking motif" by challenging taken-for-granted assumptions about human behavior, social institutions, and society.[13]

Individuals from other disciplines are sometimes (understandably) less enthusiastic about the dominance of sociology. For example, psychologists D. A. Andrews and James Bonta point out that the "debunking" within sociology can become destructive when research from "outside" disciplines (e.g., psychology, biology) is rigorously attacked, while sociological findings are accepted rather uncritically.[14]

The Current Status of Criminology

Criminology remains an unsettled area in academia. Different scholars consider criminology an independent social science discipline, a subfield of sociology, or a general field open to all disciplines. Currently, many universities have distinct criminology or criminal justice departments. In other colleges, criminology or criminal justice degrees are still offered through sociology, political science, or other disciplines. A common theme in the growth of criminology has been a call to make the study of crime truly interdisciplinary.[15] Readers of this book will find the disciplines of psychology, biology, and sociology well represented. Sociological theory, however, does receive more attention, primarily because sociologists have generated more theories of criminal behavior than other disciplines.

The Role of Criminologists

If criminology includes the study of law making, law breaking, and the response to law breaking, then the role of the criminologist is to study these areas. Most criminologists hold advanced degrees in sociology, criminology/criminal justice, psychology, or other social science fields. Criminologists with a doctoral degree use their research expertise to study various aspects of criminal behavior and law-breaking dynamics. Persons earning a doctorate typically teach in colleges and universities, but they may also manage large research projects for federal agencies (i.e., the National Institute of Justice) and private think tanks that specialize in research and policy issues.

Most university-based criminologists carry a teaching load and are also expected to engage in scientific research. This research can be basic (e.g., creating and testing theories of crime) or applied (evaluating a criminal justice program to see whether it works as intended). Criminologists who have a master's degree tend to hold positions in state and federal agencies and administrative or management positions within the criminal justice system.

There are numerous local, national, and international professional organizations for criminologists of all degree levels and experiences. At the national level, two primary organizations are the American Society of Criminology and the Academy of Criminal Justice Sciences. Among other things, these organizations host annual conferences where criminologists present their most recent research findings.

People who earn a bachelor's degree in criminology or criminal justice typically obtain entry-level positions within state and federal agencies related to the criminal justice system. For example, criminology/criminal justice graduates work as police officers, probation and parole agents, correctional officers within prisons, juvenile detention officers, and caseworkers within treatment and rehabilitation programs.

A Primer on the Criminal Law

Criminologists do not typically receive extensive training in law; the foundation of the law is primarily philosophy (rather than science), and law degrees (Juris Doctor, or J.D.) involve little if any scientific training. Despite this fact, criminologists must have some understanding of the criminal law because, simply put, crimes are violations of the criminal law. It is also worth noting that some criminologists hold both a doctorate in criminology and a J.D., which allows them to apply scientific methods in order to study the law.

A Brief History of the Criminal Law

The criminal law has a long history, dating back over 2000 years. The first acknowledged set of laws (dated 1792 BC), the Code of Hammurabi, established the precept that the punishment should fit the crime. This code was adopted from Babylonian and Hebrew laws that existed as early as 2000 BC. The Mosaic Code of the Israelites (1200 BC) developed the laws of the Old Testament, which include the Ten Commandments.[16]

The root of American law is English common law. Common law developed from English "circuit" courts, where judges traveled from community to community hearing cases. Judges kept written records of their court decisions and initially decided cases based on prevailing community standards. Over time, these judges began to unify and standardize the legal code across different communities. To accomplish this, they used past decisions as precedents (regardless of community) for new legal disputes. Eventually this web of legal decisions evolved into a national unified set of codes or *common law*.[17]

The English colonies followed common law, and after the revolution, the new governments of the United States (federal and state) adopted many of these laws by passing specific legislation — statutes. For this reason, most of the U.S. criminal code is considered <u>statutory law</u>. Even here, judges must interpret laws and apply them to specific circumstances; this creates <u>case law</u>. Also, where laws

do not cover a particular circumstance, U.S. courts still rely on common law. Finally, the federal government and each state have separate, written constitutions that define the general organization and the powers (or limits of power) of the government. <u>Constitutional law</u> is expressed within these documents and is the supreme law of the land (the U.S. Constitution for the country and state constitutions for their respective states).[18]

Defining the Criminal Law

The substantive criminal law consists of prohibited behaviors and the possible sanctions for these behaviors. As noted previously, each state has its own criminal code, as does the federal government. Federal and state codes (as well as constitutions) are readily available on the Internet. The Legal Information Institute at Cornell Law School maintains a site that features links to all federal and state statutes.[19]

Crimes are defined by two components: the specific act (*actus reas*) and the criminal intent (*mens rea*). *Actus reas* includes the act and the circumstances under which the act occurs (e.g., the common law crime of burglary includes the breaking and entering of another's dwelling, at night, without consent). Although most crimes require the commission of some act, in some cases involving special relationships (e.g., parent and child or lifeguard and swimmers), crime is defined by the failure to act. *Mens rea* refers to a person's mental state. There are different levels of criminal intent, defined by the elements of purpose, knowledge, negligence, and recklessness[20]:

- A person *purposely* commits a criminal act when they desire to engage in criminal conduct to cause a particular criminal result.

- To *knowingly* commit a criminal act, a person must know, believe, or suspect that an action is criminal.

- Criminal *negligence* occurs when a person grossly deviates from a standard that a reasonable person would use under the same circumstances — the person is accused of taking a substantial and foreseeable risk that resulted in harm.

- Criminal *recklessness* is the conscious disregard of a substantial risk — a person accused of recklessness is viewed as more blameworthy than someone accused of negligence.

Some offenses (e.g., traffic offenses) do not require criminal intent. These are considered *strict liability* offenses. Criminal behavior carries a variety of formal punishments, including imprisonment, death, fine, or probation.

There are various ways to classify crimes within the criminal law. Among the oldest is the distinction between crimes that are *mala in se* and *mala prohibita*. <u>Mala in se</u> crimes, considered "evil in themselves," encompass the core of the criminal code, including acts such as homicide and robbery. <u>Mala prohibita</u> crimes are "wrong because they are prohibited." These crimes represent a particular society's attempt to regulate behavior, such as drug abuse, gambling, and prostitution, that offends their moral senses. *Mala prohibita* offenses are likely to vary over time and across jurisdictions. For example, casino gambling is legal in several states, and many states have state-sanctioned lotteries. Similarly, the use of alcohol has shifted from legal to illegal and back to legal over time in the United States.

Another common way to classify crimes is according to the seriousness of the offense. On a general level, jurisdictions distinguish between felonies (serious crime) and misdemeanors (petty crimes). Criminal codes further categorize felonies according to degree (e.g., first-, second-, or third-degree felony offenses).

In addition to the substantive criminal law, <u>procedural law</u> dictates what actions actors within the criminal justice system may legally take. Procedural law dictates, for example, how police may interact with citizens (e.g., search-and-seizure law) and how criminal trials proceed (e.g., the admissibility of evidence). The criminal law can also be distinguished from civil law. Civil law includes (among other things) contract law, property law, and tort law.[21] Among the various forms of civil law, tort law bears the strongest resemblance to the criminal law. In a tort case, an individual or group seeks compensation to redress some wrongdoing or harm. Violations of the criminal law can result in both a criminal and tort trial. For example, a person can be tried in criminal court for homicide and (regardless of how the criminal trial turns out) also in civil court for wrongful death.[22]

Laws are dynamic and greatly influenced by current events, politics, economics, and numerous other external factors. Criminal law continues to change, as judges have to interpret situations with the emergence of new technology (e.g., computers) and new threats (e.g., terrorism). For example, the September 11, 2001, terrorist attack in the United States had a substantial impact on the law. The USA Patriot Act was passed on October 24, 2001, just six weeks after the events of 9/11. Although the Patriot Act amended numerous laws, the primary intent of the act was to relax the procedural laws that restrict law enforcement investigation and surveillance powers.

The U.S. Department of Justice hails the Patriot Act as an effective tool for counterterrorism efforts.[23] Critics contend that the law grants sweeping search and surveillance powers to domestic law enforcement without proper judicial oversight.[24] One of the most controversial provisions of the law is a "sneak-and-peek" search warrant, which authorizes law enforcement officers to enter private premises without the occupant's permission or knowledge and without informing the occupant that such a search was conducted.[25] The act also expanded the government's ability to view records on an individual's activities that are held by third parties (e.g., libraries, doctors, Internet service providers). Key provisions of the Patriot Act were set to expire on December 31, 2005. Amid debate about whether the act sacrifices too many civil liberties, Congress approved an extension to February 3, 2006, making the future of this legislation uncertain at the time of this writing.

Perspectives on the Criminal Law

Criminal law serves several functions in society. First, criminal law discourages revenge because the government, rather than the victim, is responsible for punishing law violators. Second, the law serves to express public opinion and morality; this is especially apparent for *mala prohibita* offenses. Third, the punishment meted out according to criminal law also serves as a warning to other citizens who may be thinking of committing the same crime.[26]

LINK In Chapter 3, deterrence theory is presented. Deterrence theory assumes that punishments will prevent crime. Rational people will think about the pain of the punishment and will not commit the crime, if the punishment outweighs the pleasure or gain of committing the offense.

Typically, criminal law also attempts to make the punishment fit the crime. The aim is to match the severity of the offense and the harm that it creates to the punishment; thus, the punishment balances the damage caused by the crime. However, the punishment does not always fit the harm of the crime. For example, white-collar offenses often involve large sums of money and affect great numbers of people but typically result in shorter (if any) prison sentences than robbery or burglary. Another area to consider is illicit drugs relative to alcohol. By most measures, alcohol is more dangerous or harmful than marijuana. Despite this fact, marijuana is illegal while alcohol is legal. If criminal laws and the punishments for law violators do not directly reflect the harm caused to society, then what determines how a crime is punished? How do some acts come to be criminalized while others do not? Criminologists approach such questions within the framework of two general perspectives.

LINK In Chapter 15, the various forms of white-collar crime are analyzed. White-collar crimes are typically committed by high-status individuals during the course of their legitimate business operations. They fit the definition of *mala prohibita* in that they are recognized as harmful with penalties defined by law.

The **consensus perspective** illustrates the belief that laws are set in place to keep people from harming others and society as a whole by engaging in behaviors that the majority of society believes to be hurtful. *Consensus* is defined as a general agreement, and thus, this perspective sees society as having come to terms with specific behaviors classified as wrong or immoral. This consensus comes from a society's culture, which includes its beliefs, values, attitudes, and behaviors. From this perspective criminologists would argue that laws are in place to be fair to all members of society.

In contrast to the consensus view, the **conflict perspective** portrays the law as the result of a continuous competition or "conflict" among members of society. Here, the law reflects the interests, values, and beliefs of whatever group has power. Power can come from a variety of sources such as group size or wealth. For example, Karl Marx portrayed capitalist societies as riddled with constant competition that breeds continued conflict among its members. In Marx's analysis, conflict stems from a system of inequality that allows the wealthy elite to rule or control all other members of society. On a smaller scale, the conflict perspective sheds light on how political interest groups try to shape laws (e.g., gun control, abortion) in a way that is consistent with their beliefs and values. The preceding discussion of the controversy surrounding the USA Patriot Act also illustrates the conflict perspective in action.

These general perspectives on the law influence the research questions that criminologists ask and also help determine how they go about answering such questions. Following the consensus model generally leads criminologists to ask, "Why do some in society violate laws that exist to benefit all members of society?" The conflict perspective generally leads to questions regarding the content and enforcement of the law, such as, "Why is marijuana illegal and how did it come to be criminalized?" Each of these perspectives appears to have some credence within a specific realm of behavior. Laws against *mala in se* offenses such as homicide and robbery are backed by widespread consensus. *Mala prohibita* offenses, such as gambling, prostitution, and illicit drug use are more relevant to the conflict perspective.

Theories of Crime

Theory represents the foundation on which all discussion of crime is built. Unfortunately, students of criminology often struggle to understand the various theories of crime or simply find them to be boring, useless, and confusing. The premise of this section is that when properly understood, theory can be exciting, thought provoking, and useful. This section covers basic information on theory that will allow students to understand and evaluate the discussions on crime that follow in later chapters.

Defining a Scientific Theory

There is no shortage of opinions regarding the roots of criminal behavior; news articles, movie dialogue, politicians, relatives, and friends all offer opinions on the causes of crime. Often these sources point to a single factor: drugs, violent movies, poor parenting, or bad companions. Such theories are often based on speculation or hunches. Scientific theories of crime include many of these common-sense explanations, yet unlike a "hunch," a theory of crime must explain in a logical and clear manner how such factors relate to crime.

A theory is nothing more than a set of principles or statements that attempts to explain how concepts are related. In the case of crime theory, these statements typically explain how one or more factors lead to criminal behavior. A *scientific* theory must also be testable, meaning that it must be stated in such a way that other scientists can go out into the real world, collect information, and test the theory's validity. If a theory is too vague or if the central concepts cannot be measured, it is essentially useless to science.

Consider, for example, the following statement: "Little green creatures that live inside peoples' minds cause them to engage in crime." Furthermore, suppose that one argues that science is unable to detect little green creatures through brain scans or other technology and that people are generally unaware of their existence. How could one test this theory? Of course, the little green creature theory is rather absurd. However, what if the words "little green creatures" were changed to "a lack of conscience" and the theory becomes that a lack of conscience causes crime? Unless researchers devise a way to measure conscience, this is still a theory with no scientific value, even though it may sound more credible.

A theory may also be impossible to test if it is based on circular reasoning. Scientists refer to this kind of reasoning as *tautological*. Literally, a tautological theory of crime would argue that "crime causes crime." Of course, tautological statements are usually not as obvious as that and can therefore be more difficult to detect. Let us stick with the example of "a lack of conscience" as the cause of crime and think about how one might test that theory. One could argue that people who do bad things must not have a conscience. In doing so,

however, one is engaging in circular reasoning: People who do "bad things" engage in criminal behavior (bad things), which is like arguing that crime causes crime.

In order to be useful then, one must be able to subject a theory to empirical tests. Assuming that a theory meets this minimal standard (and most do), what next? What makes one scientific theory better than others?

Evaluating Theory

A number of useful criteria are presented here for evaluating theory. An important fact to keep in mind, however, is that not all criteria are equally important. **FIGURE 1-1** illustrates how different criteria relate to one another. Testability has already been covered; the remaining criteria include empirical support, scope, and parsimony.

Empirical Evidence

After a theory is determined to be testable, the next step in the evaluation process is establishing whether those tests support the theory. In other words, when this theory is applied to the real world, does it work? Does the research support this theory? The importance of this criterion cannot be overstated; if tests fail to support a theory, that theory is *incorrect*. It makes little sense to look at other

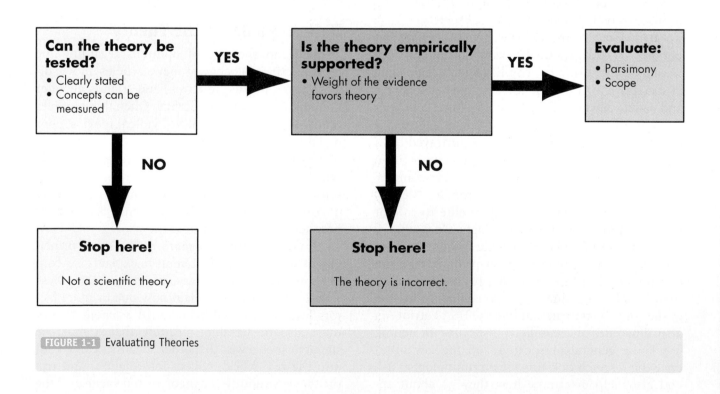

FIGURE 1-1 Evaluating Theories

aspects of the theory if it fails to work in the real world.

Unfortunately, most theories of crime are never completely supported or refuted. Some empirical tests may support the theory; others might offer partial support, and still others may refute the theory. For this reason, those who examine theories must consider the "weight of the evidence."[27] To do so, ask questions such as these:

- Do the majority of tests appear to support the theory?
- Are certain aspects of the theory supported more than others?
- Do studies with high-quality research designs support the theory?

The final question suggests that not all empirical tests are the same. How much weight to put on an individual study depends on how confident the researcher is in the research design. Some research designs are better at demonstrating cause-and-effect relationships than others.

Demonstrating Cause and Effect A number of ways are available to test theories of crime. Because most theories predict cause-and-effect relationships (e.g., poverty causes crime), a good empirical test tries to establish that certain factors have a *causal* relationship with crime. To clarify this point, an example may be useful. Start with a simple theory: Hanging around with criminal friends causes criminal behavior. To establish causation, a test needs to demonstrate three things:

1. Having criminal friends is *related* to criminal behavior.
2. Having criminal friends happens *before* engaging in criminal behavior.
3. The relationship between criminal friends and criminal behavior is not spurious.

The first point would be rather easy to demonstrate. Ask a group of people to report how many of their closest friends have been arrested for a crime. Also ask them to report their own criminal behavior. If those with criminal friends are more likely to engage in crime themselves, a relationship was established (mathematically, this is called a *correlation*). The second point, called *time ordering*, is a little more difficult to verify. The researcher must demonstrate that these individuals had criminal friends before they engaged in crime (i.e., the factor that does the causing must happen before the

effect). Demonstrating this is important because the relationship between criminal friends and criminal behavior might be the result of criminals wanting to hang out together. In other words, engaging in criminal behavior might cause people to seek out other criminals. One way to demonstrate time ordering is to conduct a *longitudinal study*. The researcher could measure criminal friends at one point in time and then measure criminal behavior six months later and then further on in time. Assuming that the researcher can establish time ordering, they can move to the third point.

A relationship is considered spurious when, even though two things are related, one does not cause the other. For example, suppose that a survey of residents in a city revealed that "time spent in the past week riding a bicycle" was correlated (related) to engaging in vandalism. People who reported riding a bicycle were more likely to have also engaged in vandalism. Does this mean that the act of riding a bicycle *caused* people to vandalize property? A more plausible explanation is that younger people were more likely to ride bikes (because they do not yet have a driver's license) and vandalize property. Isolating causes of crime (and excluding spuriousness) is the most difficult challenge of doing

If a researcher finds a relationship between bicycle riding and vandalism, can she conclude that riding a bike causes people to engage in vandalism?

? *What third factor might explain her finding?*

research in criminology. How spuriousness is dealt with depends largely on research methods.

Experimental Designs Experimental research designs are the most efficient way to establish cause-and-effect relationships and exclude spuriousness. Although there are many variations, the basic experimental design is illustrated in FIGURE 1-2 . The key to the experimental method is the *random assignment* of subjects to a control and experimental group. If the sample is large enough, random assignment leads to groups that are equivalent on all factors, measured or not. For example, one would expect roughly the same number of males, overweight individuals, people with high IQs, and so forth, in each group. The experimental group receives some form of treatment, whereas the other group, known as the *control,* does not.

In drug studies, participants in the control group are often given a *placebo* (typically a sugar pill) to exclude the possibility that subjects would report improvement simply because they received some treatment. The power of the experimental design is that the only thing that could cause differences between the two groups is the experimental treatment. Thus, if a pill designed to reduce headaches does so in the experimental group, but not the control group, this is very persuasive evidence that the pill works. Unfortunately, many of the factors of interest to criminologists cannot be assessed through experiments. A criminologist cannot, for example, randomly assign children to "poverty" and "no-poverty" conditions and assess their criminality.

Nevertheless, some criminologists do use experimental methods to study crime. One way to test a theory is to follow its policy implications and see whether the policy that was developed reduces crime. For example, many sociological and psychological theories of crime identify "targets" (e.g., procriminal attitudes, delinquent friends) for rehabilitation programs. If changing these targets reduces crime, the theory behind the target is supported. Researchers can randomly assign offenders to either a rehabilitation program or a control group and see whether the rehabilitation program reduces future criminal behavior or <u>recidivism</u>. Criminologists have also manipulated policing practices, using random assignment to dictate how police respond to a domestic violence dispute or how they patrol cities. Finally, researchers sometimes capitalize on natural experiments, where conditions in the environment naturally allow comparisons between two similar groups.

Nonexperimental Designs

Despite the many examples of experimental research in criminology, most research on theories of

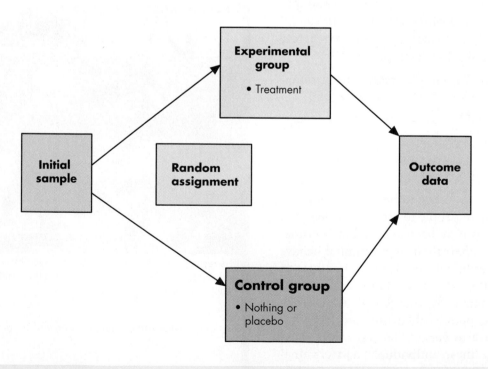

FIGURE 1-2 The Experimental Design

crime continues to involve nonexperimental methods. Typically, a sample of individuals are surveyed and asked questions relevant to a particular theory. For example, they may be asked to report on their attitudes, behaviors (including criminal behavior), and/or social circumstances. Sometimes researchers also have people complete tasks to measure such constructs as "impulsivity" or IQ. Criminologists also use information collected by government agencies, such as arrest records or census data. Regardless of how the information is obtained, nonexperimental methods share a common problem. Although they are useful in establishing whether two things are related (correlation), they are not very efficient at excluding spuriousness.

To demonstrate cause-and-effect relationships in a nonexperimental design, the researcher must (1) identify and measure those factors that might render a relationship spurious and then (2) control for these factors in a mathematical model. For example, recall the hypothetical relationship between bicycling and vandalism. A criminologist could statistically control the effects of age. If the relationship between vandalism and bicycling disappears after this control, the relationship is spurious. The major limitation of this approach is that the researcher must identify, measure, and control for many factors that might make a relationship spurious. This limitation often leaves an empirical study open for criticism, because someone can point to an important factor that was not statistically controlled.

However, that is not to say that nonexperimental research is unworthy of consideration. Indeed, as pointed out earlier, many theoretical concepts cannot be studied experimentally. Furthermore, to the extent that many empirical studies (each controlling each for different factors) find nonspurious relationships, one can gain confidence that the studies have identified a true cause-and-effect relationship.

Scope and Parsimony

Assuming that a theory has generated a good amount of empirical support, other criteria can be applied to identify "good" theories. The related concepts of *parsimony* and *scope* are two such criteria.[28] A theory that uses only a few concepts to explain crime is better than a theory that uses many concepts. This is the principle of parsimony — a more concise explanation is preferable. *Scope* refers to what a particular theory can explain. A theory

that explains "criminal behavior" is better than a theory that explains only "burglary committed by youth gangs." This is the principle of scope. <u>Grand theories</u> (wide scope) strive to explain all types of criminal behavior. For example, Gottfredson and Hirschi argue that their general theory of crime explains all forms of criminal behavior, in addition to similar behaviors (adultery, cigarette smoking) that are noncriminal. Combining scope and parsimony, a good theory is one that explains a lot (scope) with very few concepts (parsimony).

Organizing Theories of Crime

Students' first exposure to scientific theories of crime is often less than pleasant. Some of this frustration stems from the sense that there is evidence both for and against most theories. As seen, however, not all research studies are equal. Throughout the theory chapters, those studies with strong research designs are highlighted to give a sense of where the "weight of the evidence" lies. Another maddening aspect of theory is the sheer number of theories and authors. To help students cope with this issue, the following sections outline a number of ways to classify theories into meaningful categories.

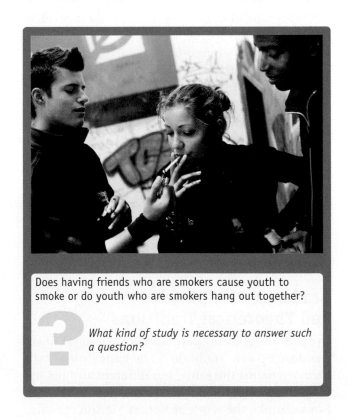

Does having friends who are smokers cause youth to smoke or do youth who are smokers hang out together?

? *What kind of study is necessary to answer such a question?*

Theories of "Law Making, Law Breaking, and Reaction to Law Breaking"

As noted earlier, Edwin Sutherland identified criminology as the study of law making, law breaking, and the response to law breaking.[29] This definition of criminology is also a useful way to categorize the theories covered in this text. Theories of "law breaking" are the most common and obvious. These theories seek to answer questions such as, "Why do people commit crimes?" or "What makes some countries more prone to crime than others?" Theories of law making attempt to explain why some acts are outlawed, whereas others are not, or why legal acts become illegal over time. Theories of the response to law violations concern the criminal justice system's reaction to crime. Many "critical" theories focus on these latter two issues. Such theories might question why police arrest certain offenders and not others or why certain laws are enforced more stringently than others.

LINK Chapter 8 presents a discussion of social conflict theories. These theories generally attempt to explain the content of the criminal law and the operation of the criminal justice system, rather than crime.

Macro- and Micro-Level Explanations

Theories can also be classified by their level of analysis. Some theories operate at the individual or *micro level*. A micro-level theory explains why some individuals engage in crime and others do not. In contrast, a *macro-level* theory attempts to explain differences in groups. For example, a macro-level theory might offer an explanation for why some neighborhoods have higher crime rates than others or why some countries have higher crime rates than others. A simple trick to identify whether a theory is macro or micro level is to look at what the theory predicts. If crime is expressed in "rates," then it is a macro-level theory (only a group has a rate). Most theories of crime (especially those in biology and psychology) operate at the micro level.

Academic Disciplines and Theoretical Traditions

In some disciplines (particularly sociology), theories develop as a "tradition." The basic thrust of the theory remains the same, but different authors update, revise, and change the particulars of a theory. For example, the work of Robert Merton spawned several related "strain" theories that revised or changed some of his original ideas but maintained the same core theme. These theoretical traditions are another important tool for organizing theories of crime — where relevant, how these traditions unfold is highlighted. Of course, the academic disciplines themselves offer a useful way to classify theories; for example, two of the chapters in this text are organized around the specific disciplines of psychology and biology. On a much broader scale, students can locate theories of crime in one of two historical theoretical traditions: the classical and positive school crime.

LINK Chapter 4 presents biological theories of crime and Chapter 5 relates psychological explanations of criminal behavior.

The Origins of Criminological Theory

When did humans first begin to devise theories to explain criminal behavior? The answer depends greatly on what qualifies as a "theory." **TABLE 1-1** illustrates the major schools of thought regarding the causes of crime. Throughout much of Western history, the "demonic perspective" dominated thinking about crime and punishment.[30] Although the specifics differed according to the particular society and time, the gist of this perspective is that supernatural forces caused criminal behavior. Quite literally, people believed that the devil (or other demons) made people commit crimes. In primitive societies, crimes were viewed as acts, aided and abetted by evil spirits, against the gods.[31] In that context, punishment was often designed to placate the gods.

Throughout the Middle Ages (1200–1600) in Europe, people who engaged in deviant, sinful, or criminal behavior (especially if they were women) were labeled "witches" and burned at the stake.[32] Brutal methods were often used to determine guilt or innocence. Trial by ordeal involved subjecting the accused to some form of painful torture — only God's intervention could demonstrate their innocence. For example, the suspected witch would be tied up and thrown into a body of water. If God allowed the individual to float, he or she was innocent; if not, the unfortunate person was presumed guilty and allowed to drown.[33]

Corporal punishments (e.g., gibbeting, ear clipping, drawing and quartering, dismembering, blinding, burning, and branding) were frequently used

TABLE 1-1

Major Schools of Thought in Criminology

School of Thought	Cause of Crime	Implication for Criminals
Demonic Perspective	Demonic possession, God's will, or other supernatural forces cause crime.	Brutal corporal punishments designed to placate the gods, cleanse the community, and identify individuals as deviant.
Classical School	Crime is the result of a rational decision based on a calculation of costs and benefits.	Swift, certain, severe punishment within the framework of a rational legal system will deter criminal behavior. Punishment should fit the crime.
Positive School	Criminal behavior is determined by biological, social, or psychological factors outside of a person's control.	Advocate a medical model (and reject the importance of punishment). Individuals are "treated" based on the set of factors that caused them to engage in crime. The punishment (rehabilitation) should fit the individual.

in Europe and America as late as 1700. Powerless members of society (e.g., slaves, women, and children) were often the targets of corporal punishment.[34] Mutilation and branding identified offenders and sent a message to others. The punishments also were designed to purge the body of the offender of evil and restore the community to its proper relationship with God.[35] Again, the idea here is that crime was caused largely by demonic influence. Although the "devil made me do it" is certainly an explanation of criminal behavior, it is not a *scientific theory*. Supernatural forces cannot be observed, and the demonic perspective (like our "little green creature" example) is therefore not testable. Toward the end of the 1700s, the demonic perspective was challenged by a group of philosophers who came to be called *classical school criminologists*.

The Classical School of Crime

The Age of Enlightenment burned hot in Europe during much of the 18th century. Enlightenment thinkers such as John Locke and Jean-Jacques Rousseau challenged the prevailing belief that human behavior was directly determined by God (or demons). Rather, they believed that God instilled in humans the capacity to exercise free will and the ability to choose a course of behavior through reason. Several scholars — chief among them Cesare Beccaria and Jeremy Bentham — used this general platform to argue for legal reform. In doing so, these penal reformers also articulated a scientific theory of criminal behavior.[36]

To appreciate the importance of the legal reforms advocated by Beccaria and Bentham, one first needs to understand the state of the legal system at the time in which the two men wrote. Laws were vague and judges often interpreted them to suit their own interests. Those accused of crimes had few legal protections. The state provided neither legal assistance nor access to family and friends and commonly used torture to obtain confessions. Witnesses testified against the accused in secret proceedings. Punishments for those found guilty included whipping, branding, mutilation, and death by various means.[37]

Rebelling against the brutal and arbitrary nature of the legal system, Beccaria argued that the function of law was to promote justice.[38] In his 1764 essay *On Crimes and Punishments,* he formulated the following principles, which represented a dramatic departure from the way in which criminal law had previously been conceived:[39]

- Prevention of crime is more important than punishment for the crime committed. Punishment is desirable only as it helps to prevent crime and does not conflict with the ends of justice.
- The purpose of punishment is to deter persons from the commission of crime, not to give society an opportunity for revenge.
- Desirable criminal procedure calls for the open publication of all laws, speedy trials, humane treatment of the accused, and the abolishment of secret accusations and torture. Moreover, the accused must have every right and facility to bring forward evidence.
- The criminal code should be written with all offenses and punishments defined in advance.
- The criminal law should be restricted in its scope because it can result in the curtailment of freedoms.

- The presumption of innocence should be the guiding principle at all stages of the justice process. Individual rights must be protected.

Beccaria deserves much credit for "pulling together many of the most powerful 18th century ideas of democratic liberalism" and connecting them to issues of criminal justice.[40] His ideas directly influenced the American Bill of Rights as well as the Declaration of the Rights of Man and Citizen, the precursor to the French constitution of 1791.[41] The linchpin that holds together all of Beccaria's legal reforms was the argument that a properly designed legal system had the potential to prevent or *deter* criminal behavior. Beccaria believed that because humans were rational, they would consider the consequences of their behavior before acting. Swift, certain, and sufficiently harsh punishment should therefore deter a rational actor from engaging in crime. Beccaria argued that punishment should only be severe enough to deter crime and denounced the use of the death penalty.[42]

Another influential scholar and reformer of the classical school of criminology was Bentham, who embraced Beccaria's ideas and made contributions to his deterrence theory. Specifically, Bentham described human decision making as a <u>hedonistic calculus</u>. In other words, people will act in ways that maximize positive outcomes and minimize negative ones. Naturally, a person commits a crime because of the perception that the benefits of the act are greater than the costs of punishment. The corollary to this is that punishment should be painful enough to outweigh the pleasure of the criminal act.

Like Beccaria, Bentham believed that the purpose of punishment should be crime prevention and that punishment must be proportional to the severity of the crime to have a deterrent effect. Moreover, the severity of punishment should be directly proportionate to the number of persons injured by the crime. Although some of their ideas are taken for granted today, classical theorists were liberal reformers who sought to restate the definitions of crime and to reformulate punishments. Their proposed legal reforms were revolutionary — a complete break with customary practices. As a theory of crime, the classical school idea of deterrence is relatively simple: People will refrain from crime if punishment is swift, certain, and sufficiently severe. Because empirical tests of this proposition are possible, however, it represented a dramatic departure from the demonic perspective. Classical school theory dominated criminological thought into the late 1800s, until it was challenged by a new group of theorists.

The Positive School of Crime

The influence of the classical school of criminology began to wane in the late 1800s. One reason for this decline was that changes in the legal system based on classical theory failed to reduce crime (i.e., crime rates continued to increase).[43] More importantly, the underlying assumption of the classical school — that behavior was the result of rational calculation — was criticized for being too simplistic. Throughout the 1700s, scientists such as Galileo and Newton made great discoveries about the workings of the physical world. These demonstrations of cause-and-effect relationships were made through careful observation and analysis of natural events. It was not long before scholars applied this scientific method beyond the physical world to the social world.

Auguste Compte, the 19th century scientist considered the "father of sociology," argued that human behavior was caused, or *determined,* by forces outside of human control. Compte believed that societies progressed through various stages, moving from a primitive understanding of the world (recall the demonic perspective) to a more rational, scientific understanding. He referred to this last rational/scientific stage as *positivism,* and those who continued this line of inquiry were subsequently called *positivists.*[44]

The history of scientific inquiry into criminal behavior is uneven — several pioneers in scientific criminology predate Compte's positivism. For example, Benjamin Rush (United States) and Philippe Pinel (France), writing in the late 1700s, argued that serious, repeat criminal behavior was caused by "moral insanity," a mental disease.[45] Despite these early efforts to scientifically study crime, positivism did not gain wide acceptance until the mid 1800s. During this time, for example, Charles Darwin's *Origin of Species* (1859) outlined the theory of evolution.

Influenced by Darwin's theory of evolution, the first widely acknowledged positive theories of crime focused on biology. For example, phrenologists like Franz Joseph Gall studied the pattern of bumps on the skull and attempted to correlate them to criminal behavior. Cesare Lombroso, building off Darwin's theory of evolution, argued that some criminals were evolutionary throwbacks to a more primitive species. Over time, biology gave way to a psychology/psychiatry focus on "feeble-mindedness" and mental disease. During the 20th century, sociological positivism dominated criminology and found causes of crime in social factors such as learning experience and poverty.

Regardless of the particular discipline or historical timeframe, positive theories share some commonality. Positivists are committed to the use of the scientific method to study the causes of crime. They emphasize methodological issues such as proper data collection, statistical sampling, and the validity and reliability of measurement.[46] Criminologist C. Ray Jeffrey outlines several other precepts of positivist criminology and contrasts them with the classical school. According to Jeffrey, the positive school advocates[47]:

- A rejection of punishment and its replacement with treatment based on the medical (rehabilitation) model
- A rejection of free will and its replacement with scientific determinism
- A rejection of the study of criminal law and its replacement with a study of the individual offender and his or her medical, psychological, and social characteristics

The positive school of crime, like the classical school, had a great deal of influence on the operation of the criminal justice system. In the United States, rehabilitation (the medical model) emerged as a primary goal of the justice system during the early 1900s. The underlying assumption of the medical model is that the factors that make a criminal can be identified and treatment plans can be formulated and administered to rehabilitate them. In the medical model, the offender is viewed as a patient to be treated, not an evildoer to be punished. The "rehabilitative ideal" involved isolating and correcting, within each individual, the specific deficits that led to his or her criminal behavior. In that sense, the punishment must fit the offender, rather than the offense.[48]

Although rehabilitation remained the dominant goal of corrections throughout much of the 1900s, the medical model was never fully realized. The seriousness of the crime (and not the nature of the criminal), for example, remained the primary determinant of the punishment. In other words, the punishment still tended to "fit the offense." Still, the rise of rehabilitation produced a number of innovations that remain part of the current criminal justice system. For example, many states embraced *indeterminate sentencing,* where offenders were incarcerated without a firm release date (e.g., 20 years to life). Parole boards emerged as a way to judge when offenders, based on their treatment progress, should be released.

The Classical and Positive School — Where Do We Stand Now?

The positive school of criminology has dominated theorizing since it replaced the classical school. Classical school theorizing, however, made a comeback in the 1970s. A number of theories derived from the classical school (called *neoclassical theories*) now compete with positive theories for acceptance.

Crime Policy

A tenet of this book is that theory and policy are intimately related. To be sure, criminology is an "applied" social science. In other words, criminologists investigate crime in order to generate practical solutions to the problem. Theory and research on the causes of crime and criminal behavior can provide information that can be used either to prevent crime from occurring or to lessen its impact on society.

The applied nature of criminology is illustrated by the research questions that are addressed in criminological research. Gibbs identified four major questions that criminologists traditionally attempt to answer[49]:

1. Why does the crime rate vary?
2. Why are crimes committed by certain individuals and not others?
3. Why is there variation in reactions to alleged criminality?
4. What are the possible means of controlling criminality?

The fourth question specifically deals with crime policy. Note, though, that the answer to the fourth question depends largely on responses to the first two questions. In other words, if one knows what causes crime, one is better able to develop effective policies.

Theory, coupled with sound research, should help guide policy making throughout the criminal justice system. Empirically supported theory can provide clues for the passage of legislation and the sound operation of social programs. To proceed without theoretical guidance is to take a shot in the dark — there is no logical basis to assume that a particular program will work. Policy prescriptions based on theories that are not supported empirically are also unlikely to work. Unfortunately, crime policy often violates these principles; programs with little theoretical guidance emerge time and again.

Policy Without Theory — The Case of Intensive Supervision

To illustrate the need to link theory with policy, consider the highly praised <u>intensive supervision</u> programs (ISP). These programs reflect the belief that the probation/parole officer can do a better job of monitoring and supervising high-risk offenders if the officers' caseloads are smaller. ISP programs emerged in the 1980s as a potential solution to the crowding problem in U.S. jails and prisons. Therefore, one attractive feature of intensive supervision is that it pleases people with conflicting views. ISPs promise to increase surveillance (protect society), provide more treatment, and reduce the size of jail and prison populations — yet, the emergence of intensive supervision took place in "the absence of any true theory that more supervision will lead to lower recidivism rates."[50]

Research on intensive supervision initially found that it led to higher rates of probation revocation and had little influence on recidivism (repeat offending).[51] In fact, had ISP supporters reviewed research from the 1960s, they would have discovered that lowering probation caseloads did not reduce recidivism.[52] Although research on ISPs was largely negative, it did provided information that suggested conditions under which these programs might be more successful. In particular, the rehabilitative aspects of the program (providing better services and referrals) have proven effective.[53] There is evidence that ISPs that implemented the suggested changes achieved reductions in recidivism rates.[54]

> **LINK** In general, programs that emphasize only supervision and punishment do not reduce recidivism. "Scared Straight," discussed in Chapter 3, is another example of a punishment-based program that has proven to be ineffective.

Theoretically Informed Policy — The Case of Multisystemic Therapy

In contrast to ISPs, multisystemic therapy (MST) is based explicitly on well-known and empirically supported theories of crime. Developed by psychologist Scott Henggeler and his associates, MST is a community-based treatment program that targets many known causes of delinquency and crime. The targets of MST are drawn from several empirically supported theories of crime, including social learning theory, social control theory, and cognitive theory. Examples of treatment targets include parental supervision and discipline, antisocial attitudes, association with delinquent peers, and the mix of rewards and punishments for both antisocial and prosocial behavior.[55] MST has accumulated a track record of success, reducing crime substantially among serious/chronic offenders, including inner-city juvenile delinquents, adolescent sex offenders, and abusive parents. This track record has led some scholars to conclude that MST is perhaps the best treatment option available to reduce recidivism.[56]

How has MST achieved this success? Part of the answer lies in the structure of the program — MST therapists receive extensive training and support and are held accountable for the progress (or lack thereof) of offenders. Also, treatment plans are individualized to the needs/problems of each offender and each treatment has multiple targets for change. A central reason for success, however, is that MST identifies known (from theory and empirical research) causes of delinquency and targets these factors for change. For example, parental discipline is a key factor in several theories of crime, and empirical research consistently demonstrates that lax supervision and harsh/inconsistent punishment promote delinquency. Therefore, theory dictates that improving the disciplining skills of the parents of delinquents should lead to a reduction in recidivism.

> **LINK** MST, and the theories of crime that underlie this program, are discussed in more detail in Chapter 5.

Limitations of Criminological Research

One purpose of research is to validate or test the accuracy of theories, yet the most common conclusion of criminological research is that more information on a given subject is needed before any definite conclusions can be drawn. There are at least three reasons for this.

First, criminology is a part of the research tradition in sociology. One norm of sociological research, established primarily by German sociologist Max Weber (1864–1920) is that the research and its results should be **value free**. Weber contended that if researchers sought definite conclusions, their work could be biased by that desire to achieve certain results. The primary aim of sociological research was to generate accurate, unbiased, and objective data — not to draw conclusions. As a result, some criminological studies do not contain policy recommendations on crime.

Second, most criminological studies are based on limited data. Because all statistical analyses of a given sample reflect probabilities, a small sample increases the chance of drawing erroneous conclusions. The possibility always exists that the conclusions based on a single study are wrong and that the patterns found in the sample under study may not truly exist in the general population. The possibility of inaccurate findings causes criminologists to be cautious.

Third, criminological studies are not always methodologically sound. For example, Robert Martinson reviewed studies and research reports published between 1945 and 1967 on the effectiveness of correctional treatment. He included only those studies that met the following methodologic criteria: "[They] had to employ an independent measure of the improvement secured by that method, and [they] had to use some control group, some untreated individuals with whom the treated ones could be compared."[57] Reviewing over 20 years of research, Martinson found only 231 studies that met these basic standards of research. Based on this information, the "Martinson report" reached this now-famous conclusion: "With few and isolated exceptions, the rehabilitative efforts that have been reported so far have had no appreciable effect upon recidivism."[58]

A related research problem is **overgeneralization**.[59] Overgeneralization is a problem related to the researcher's interpretation of the research results. Martinson's own pessimistic conclusion on offender rehabilitation ("Nothing works!") is an example of an overgeneralization — one that he later recanted.[60] Recent reviews of rehabilitation programs have shown success in the treatment of

offenders.[61] Unfortunately, overgeneralization is far from uncommon — two additional examples include research on felony probation and domestic violence.

Studies of Felony Probation

A classic example of overgeneralization is the study by Rand Corporation researchers of felony probation in California.[62] They reached the widely publicized conclusion that these offenders represented a threat to public safety. Rand reported that 65% of felony probationers (offenders placed on probation based on a felony-level offense) were rearrested within two years of their release. What the media neglected to report was that the sample under study was not representative of the California felony offender population. Moreover, the results could not reflect felony probation recidivism rates across the nation. Indeed, replications of this study reported much lower rearrest rates, ranging from 22% to 43%.[63] Replication helps determine whether research findings and their policy implications are stable over time and place. Despite these replications, the Rand study was used to justify the creation of intensive supervision programs.

Experiments on the Impact of Mandatory Arrest in Domestic Violence Cases

A third example of overgeneralization occurred with domestic violence experiments. Lawrence Sherman has conducted several studies on the impact of arrest in domestic violence cases. In the first study, suspects in Minneapolis were randomly assigned to one of three potential responses by the police: (1) arrest, (2) threat of arrest (with the suspect leaving the home), and (3) a "talking to" by the police (with the suspect left at the scene).[64] The results supported the use of arrest in domestic violence cases as a way to protect the victim. The suspects who were arrested had the lowest rate of recidivism.[65]

This study had a dramatic impact on policing in domestic violence cases. Although the authors were careful to recommend against the passage of mandatory arrest laws until further research was conducted, the results of the Minneapolis experiment contributed to the passage of such laws in 15 states by 1991.[66] The study was replicated (repeated with the same method in a different location) in

Omaha,[67] Charlotte,[68] and Milwaukee[69] with dissimilar results. Arresting domestic violence suspects in both Omaha and Charlotte was no more effective than other methods of handling the case (e.g., citation or advisement).

In Milwaukee, Sherman and his colleagues specifically examined the impact of arrest on domestic violence cases in poverty-stricken inner-city areas. The authors concluded that short-term arrest might even cause harm by increasing anger at society without increasing the fear of rearrest.[70]

Sherman and Berk have been severely criticized for the impact of their studies on public policy in domestic violence cases. Critics have chastised the researchers for failing to acknowledge that the use of arrest in domestic violence cases failed to achieve the desired result upon replication. They also note that the Minneapolis study resulted in a "dramatic change in public policy with potentially substantial negative effects on many people and an unwarranted large expenditure of public monies."[71] Sherman[72] and Berk[73] countered these objections by noting that three of the six experiments provided some evidence of deterrence and that they always fully listed the policy limitations of the findings of the studies.

As these examples suggest, criminological studies must be interpreted with caution. Sound policy should only follow accurate research. Research should be replicated in other locations to be certain that results generated in one area apply to others. For these reasons, criminologists are often reluctant to reach definite conclusions based on their studies.

Theory Versus Streetwise Criminology

Students are often frustrated by the failure of criminology to provide certain and clear-cut answers to the crime problem. This frustration also promotes the view that theory is both illogical and impractical. Jeffery has accurately portrayed this attitude[74]:

Theoretical courses are characterized as useless. "I want some course material that is relevant," is the usual student response to the curriculum. When one asks, "What is relevance?" it turns out to be vocational training in being a police [officer] or a corrections officer.

Clearly, these students are saying that "street smarts" are more valuable than "book knowledge" of criminal behavior.

One exemplar of this type of thinking is the student who has worked or is working in the criminal justice system and who believes that the only legitimate source of knowledge is experience. The argument is summarized by Carter[75]:

Nothing personal, but most professors don't know what they are talking about. They sit on campus putting out all this good shit about rehabilitation and causes of crime. Most of them haven't ever been on the street and if you want to know what's happening, you have to be on the street. Instead of telling us about crime, we ought to be telling them. If they would spend a couple of days with us, they might find out what's happening. No, they don't want to do that. It might upset all their theories.

Indeed, this belief is not limited to students. In academia, one of its most vocal and visible adherents is George Kirkham. His experience as "the professor who became a cop" led him to first gently admonish his colleagues to observe firsthand the problems of police officers before criticizing them.[76] He later turgidly stated that a "criminologist would not know a criminal if one bit him on the ass."[77]

Another source of the street-smarts bias stems from what Carter calls the Dick Tracy Mentality. This mindset is characterized by several beliefs[78]:

- The crime fighter is no mere mortal but, rather, a SUPER crime fighter.
- The criminal is distinctive, unique, readily identifiable, and different (from "normal" people).
- There are two kinds of people in society — good guys and bad guys.

A corollary view holds that theoretical statements represent attempts to provide a defense for criminals. The reality, however, is that criminological theory attempts to *explain* rather than *excuse* criminal behavior.

Still another version of this mentality can be bluntly called the "asshole theory" of crime by which police officers guide their actions in specific situations. "Assholes" commit crimes that are motiveless, completely senseless, or otherwise irrational. Carter relates this statement by a police officer/student[79]:

I've heard all the theories of crime. Let me tell you, crime is caused by assholes. That's the asshole theory. If you want to check that, come out on the street. See it like it is.

Readers of this text, however, will discover that theory does not always clash with street knowledge. In fact, theory is often verified by experience. Students will find within many theories examples of commonsense, streetwise factors that influence crime.

Politics: The "Left" and "Right" of Criminal Justice Policy

Although scientists often attempt to offer "value-neutral" theories and research, the reality is that science occurs within the political landscape of society. Crime has been a major campaign issue in almost every presidential election since 1964 and most victors have made criminal justice policy a central theme in their administrations. For example, consistent with his aim of creating a "Great Society" through civil rights legislation and a war on poverty, Lyndon Johnson made fighting crime an integral part of his programs. Democrats Johnson and later Jimmy Carter were guided by the promise of **distributive justice**: that increased economic opportunity is the best defense against crime. President Bill Clinton emphasized community policing — an approach that attempts to foster closer relationships between police and citizens. In contrast to this liberal tradition, Republicans such as Richard Nixon, Gerald Ford, Ronald Reagan, and George Bush generally took the more conservative law-and-order stance against crime, emphasizing individual responsibility, deterrence, and retribution.[80]

Each president was aware of the political capital that could be generated by addressing the crime problem and each dealt with the issue in ways that reflected his own political ideologies. For example, as part of his campaign to promote a new federalism, Nixon cut the strings attached to the Law Enforcement Assistance Administration funds, allowing state and local governments to decide spending priorities. Ford established career criminal prosecution programs. In accord with his populist views, Carter stepped up federal efforts to apprehend and prosecute white-collar criminals. Reagan denounced liberal spending programs as destructive to individual values and made the fight against violent crime a priority of his administration. Bush derailed Democratic nominee Michael Dukakis' bid for the presidency with his infamous Willie Horton ads that painted Dukakis as a liberal who was more

Convicted killer Gary Sampson is escorted into court where he pleaded guilty to killing Robert Whitney in New Hampshire. Sampson is already facing execution for the murder of two men in Massachusetts.

? *What might a liberal or conservative say caused such horrendous crimes?*

concerned with the rights of criminals than their victims (Horton was a convicted murderer who committed a violent rape and murder while on furlough from a Massachusetts prison). During his presidency, President George Bush continued the Reagan administration's war on drugs. After the September 11, 2001 tragedies, President George W. Bush made terrorism his crime priority through the creation of the Department of Homeland Security.

For all of the rhetoric, however, crime policy is not a distinct entity. Criminal justice policy does not drive any administration's programs; rather, it follows the same themes as other social policies — it fits within a political ideology.[81] *Ideology* is a set of relatively unquestioned assumptions about how the world works. Walter Miller outlined the "crusading issues and general assumptions" of both conservatives and liberals regarding crime.[82] Conservative politicians tend to view crime as a "bad choice" made freely by an offender. Conservatives therefore view the criminal as directly responsible for his or her own behavior. Their ideology is consistent with the classical school of crime.

Furthermore, traditional conservative values include discipline and respect for authority. Therefore, they see the following as the most important causes of crime[83]

- Excessive leniency toward lawbreakers
- Emphasis on the welfare and rights of lawbreakers at the expense of the welfare and rights of victims, law enforcement officials, and law-abiding citizens
- Erosion of discipline and respect for authority
- Excessive permissiveness in society

In contrast, liberals are generally dissatisfied with the present social order and emphasize dysfunctional elements of the criminal justice system such as the following[84]:

- Overcriminalization
- Labeling and stigmatization
- Overinstitutionalization
- Overcentralization of authority
- Discriminatory bias, especially racism and sexism

The schism between left and right is reflected not only among politicians but among criminologists as well. On the right, the neoclassical school has

a common interest in dealing with predatory crimes and substantially less interest in the "root causes" of crime which have entertained the more liberal social determinists for so long. The neoconservatives are concerned more with dealing with the symptoms and intermediate correlates of social problems than in affecting major changes in the social fabric of society.[85]

As noted previously, the neoclassical school has influenced criminal justice policy in several areas, particularly with respect to career criminal laws and incapacitation.

LINK In Chapter 3, the theories of the neoclassical school are presented. Deterrence and incapacitation (preventing crime through incarceration of active offenders) are discussed. Chapter 9 presents theories of criminal careers and examples of how the policy of incapacitation has been implemented.

One leading advocate of this point of view is James Q. Wilson. In the provocative book *Thinking About Crime*, Wilson argues that the typical causal analysis of sociologists has nothing to do with policy analysis[86]:

Causal analysis attempts to find the source of human activity in those factors which themselves are not caused, which are, in the language of sociologists, "independent variables." Ultimate causes cannot be the object of policy efforts precisely because, being ultimate, they cannot be changed.

Policy analysis considers only the condition that the government wishes to create. Its focus is on current circumstances and its purpose is identifying the forces the government can marshal to bring the desired state into being.

In fact, Wilson declares that there is no reason for criminologists to be policy analysts.[87] He believes the policy analyst should ignore the study of the causes of crime and instead focus on the manipulation of objective conditions because "the only instruments society has by which to alter behavior in the short run require it to assume that people act in response to the costs and benefits of alternative courses of action."[88] Thus, Wilson advocates such policies as the incapacitation of career criminals, a return to foot patrols by police, and the continued criminalization of drugs.

Left-leaning criminologists identify with the positive school of crime and seek the root causes of criminal behavior. Liberal criminologists also attempt to debunk the assumptions that inform the conservative law and order ideology in the United States."[89] A leading critic of conservative criminology is Elliot Currie. He considers crime a symptom of such social problems as child poverty and abuse/neglect, inadequate public services, and economic inequality. As a result, Currie calls for the following reforms[90]:

- We should move to reduce inequality and poverty.
- We should move toward crime prevention rather than incapacitation. Prevention priorities include preventing child abuse, enhancing children's intellectual and social development, and providing support to vulnerable adolescents.
- We should work toward a genuinely supportive national family policy.
- We should begin assuming greater responsibility for the economic and social stability of local communities.
- We need to learn more about how to create comprehensive strategies for high-risk communities and understand why some societies have lower crime rates than others.[91]

Clearly, politics cannot be divorced from policy making. Ideas from the left and right will always shape criminology research, theories of crime, and crime policy. The value of science, however, is that theories of crime from both the left and right are subject to the same empirical scrutiny. There is much to be learned, however, about how policy is made and implemented within a political context.[92]

The Influence of Social Context — The "Martinson Report" as a Case Study

As the preceding discussion of ideology and politics makes clear, science does not operate in a completely objective, value-neutral environment. Social context shapes scientific research, theory, policy, and the law. The previously discussed "Martinson report" provides an illustration of how social context can shape the interpretation of research results. As noted, Martinson concluded that few, if any, rehabilitation programs appeared to work. Many credit this report with ending rehabilitation as a goal of corrections and ushering in a conservative get-tough approach to crime. Did the Martinson report, through a scientific review of the literature, persuade lawmakers and scholars to abandon rehabilitation? A careful analysis suggests otherwise.

First, Martinson was not the first scholar to review the rehabilitation literature and conclude that rehabilitation programs appeared to be ineffective. Between 1950 and 1966, several scholars reached equally pessimistic conclusions about scientific evaluations of rehabilitation programs. The response, however, was a call to find better programs, conduct better research, and enhance funding for rehabilitation. Also, few people are even aware that Martinson recanted his original statements. If the Martinson report led to the demise of rehabilitation, then why didn't the recant have a similar influence? Finally, positive findings in reviews of rehabilitation efforts in the 1980s and 1990s have been met with a great deal of skepticism.[93]

Why did the Martinson report generate such interest and why was it interpreted as the death knell of rehabilitation? The answer lies largely in the social context of the late 1960s and early 1970s. This was a period of great social change in America — events such as the Vietnam war, the Watergate scandal, civil rights protests, the Kent State University shootings, and the Attica prison riot shaped the social context. For liberals, government responses to civil rights marchers and the Watergate scandal signified that the government could

not be trusted at any task, including rehabilitation. To conservatives, the "hippie movement" was evidence of a decaying social disorder that a "get-tough approach" might correct. Thus, by the time the Martinson report appeared, many criminologists and other commentators had already concluded that rehabilitation was a failed endeavor.[94]

Apart from corrections policy, social context impacts which theories of crime gain popularity, how research findings are interpreted, and indeed, what areas within criminology are deemed important enough to study. For this reason, readers are encouraged to keep in mind the social context of research and theory; social context is discussed explicitly on a number of occasions throughout the remaining chapters.

Crime as a Normal Phenomenon

A common belief is that crime is something that can and must be eliminated from society. President Lyndon Johnson's War on Crime in the 1960s and, more recently, President George Bush's War on Drugs represent large-scale efforts to reduce crime. These much-trumpeted campaigns notwithstanding, one needs to consider what French sociologist Emile Durkheim (1858–1917) wrote about crime through the course of history[95]:

> Crime is present not only in most societies of one particular species but in societies of all types. There is no society that is not confronted with the problem of criminality. What is normal is the existence of crime. Crime is normal because a society exempt from it is utterly impossible. Even a community of saints will create sinners.

Clearly, Durkheim did not mean that it was desirable or even acceptable to kill one's neighbor. Rather, he was pointing out that wherever there is conformity, there is also deviance — and some deviance will inevitably be deemed criminal.

Durkheim also noted that deviance is a prerequisite for social change. Without deviance, a society stagnates. Cohen followed up on this observation by outlining seven ways the deviant may make positive contributions to the success and vitality of societies[96]:

1. Deviance cuts through "red tape." The deviant rebels against the categorical and stereotypical

nature of the rules, often violating the rules to accomplish organizational tasks.

2. Deviance acts as a "safety valve" for societal pressures. The deviant prevents the excessive accumulation of discontent and reduces strain on the legitimate order.

3. Deviance clarifies the "rules." The deviant enables other members of society to learn what deviance is and how far one may safely venture.

4. Deviance unites the group (against the deviant). The deviant provides society with a common enemy.

5. Deviance unites the group (for the deviant). The deviant gives society an opportunity to save and reclaim or rehabilitate the deviant.

6. Deviance accents conformity. The deviant serves as a reference point against which conformity can be measured and gives others a feeling of self-satisfaction for adhering to the rules.

7. Deviance acts as a "warning signal." The deviant alerts others to the defects in an organization or society.

Of course, there is a point at which crime becomes dysfunctional. If a high level of crime becomes "normalized" or considered inevitable, the consequences can be devastating for a community,[97] yet crime and deviance are not always threatening. Although Durkheim and Cohen were writing about deviant behavior such as political protest and not murder, the message is that the elimination of crime cannot be accomplished.

How to Study Crime

Knowledge about crime stems from several sources, including personal experience and studies by oth-

ers. Each source, however, has its own problems and limitations. Commonsense observations about crime may be limited to an individual's own experience and not reflect broader trends. Such a limited perspective impedes one's ability to understand the nature of crime. As noted previously, scientific studies also may have problems with generalizability, and interpretations of findings are always subject to the influence of social context. However, the construction of theory, the development of **hypotheses**, and empirical testing provide the best promise of understanding the crime problem. Such careful study both generates and organizes data in a meaningful way.

Where do these limitations leave the student? This book offers several suggestions on how the reader should approach criminology. First, keep an open mind. One student probably will enthusiastically agree with certain theories about the nature of criminal behavior and the causes of crime; another may violently disagree with others (this is ideology at work). Keep in mind, however, that the readers' task here is to learn the components of each theory no matter what their personal feelings may be. Only then can the student compare and contrast theories, see how they interact, and synthesize them. Remember, too, that each theory is a product of and is influenced by its social, intellectual, and historical context.[98]

Second, students are cautioned against discounting a theory based on the "exceptional case." Students often cite the one instance, example, or individual that the theory fails to explain. There are always exceptions to the rule, but they are just that — exceptions beyond the average. For example, many people know a person who smoked cigarettes their whole life and did not die of cancer. Does this mean that cigarettes do not cause cancer? Try to examine the strengths and weaknesses of each theory in its own context. In other words, apply another of Max Weber's sociological concepts, *verstehen,* or empathetic understanding. To examine a theory properly, the student must understand it on its own terms.

Third, learn not to expect easy answers and do not accept them without reservation. Finckenauer cautions against settling for simple solutions to the delinquency problem, but his words apply to any aspect of criminology[99]:

> The highway of delinquency prevention history is paved with punctured **panaceas** [emphasis added]. First, a certain approach is posed as a cure-all or becomes viewed and promoted as a cure-all — as an intervention which will have universal efficacy and thus be appropriate for nearly all kids. Unfortunately, the approach, no matter what it is, almost always fails to deliver; fails to live up to the frequently unrealistic or unsound expectations raised by the sales pitch.

If easy answers were readily available, criminologists would have delivered them long ago, and the crime problem would not exist today.

Criminological theory often cannot provide literal answers to the crime problem. Nevertheless, when studying a social problem like crime, researchers are trying to explain it and figure out its causes. Explanations do more than describe what has happened. They give reasons for what has occurred — the "how" and the "why." To be of practical value, explanations should improve the ability to predict events more accurately than through common sense alone. As noted, each criminological theory provides a set of causes.

Good theory should be linked to reality through research: The empirical testing of theory confers relevance — and criminological theory is no exception. This text presents the latest research on the various theories and reviews the policy implications of this research, but it will become clear that the "doctors don't always have the cure." In other words, physicians can often find the *causes* of an illness (e.g., AIDS), but they cannot develop a *cure.* This is also frequently the case in criminology. Knowledge of the nature of the problem is no guarantee that a solution will be found. Unfortunately, such knowledge is also no consolation to the victims of crime. Approaches to the crime problem, however, should have a firm foundation — one provided by both theory and research, not guesswork.

Conclusion

Crime should be viewed not as a single phenomenon but as one in which many kinds of behavior occur in different situations and under different conditions. No single theory can provide all the explanations for — let alone answers to — the crime problem. Again, criminological theory attempts to explain the causes of criminal behavior, not to excuse crimes or the people who commit them.

The next several chapters discuss theories of crime across several disciplines, including biology, psychology, and sociology. The reader is encouraged to organize them in some meaningful way as they are encountered. This chapter provided a number of ways to accomplish this task. Theories can focus on law breaking (crime) or the criminal justice system response to crime. They can operate at the micro or macro levels; they are generally part of an academic discipline, and they are often part of a specific theoretical tradition within a discipline. Although virtually all of the theories encountered are positivistic, a few theories are grounded firmly in the classical school of crime.

WRAP UP

A Research Project

A criminologist would start any research project by locating existing information and research studies on the area in question. Studies may already exist that attempt to answer the same question. The value of reviewing the existing literature on hacking (or any research area) is in exploring if the question has been answered and how, so that if you wanted to further the study of hackers you could do so by changing the research question and/or using a different research method.

You might consider using your friends to conduct a scientific study of why people are or are not hackers, but you would encounter problems with this approach. Asking someone whether he or she would commit a crime could also make you liable to contact the authorities with this information. If the research participants are your friends, you may be less likely to contact the police, which in turn holds you accountable for knowing about a crime. The problem of bias would also be present because you are friends with the research subjects and you may be less inclined to follow the scheduled questions that should be asked of all participants. Moreover, you may bias the interpretation of the information you receive from your friends.

A researcher from the classical school perspective might argue that people engage in hacking because current laws are not severe enough to deter people from this activity. In addition, various news accounts have shown that some hackers who are caught actually get hired by the federal government and large corporations instead of receiving fines or incarceration for their illegal acts. When rational individuals weigh the costs and benefits of hacking, the benefits may outweigh the costs.

The positive school approach to the question of why some people hack relates to understanding their behaviors. Individuals are influenced by inherent abnormalities (e.g., biological and psychological) and by their environment (e.g., upbringing and community). Hackers may engage in illegal behaviors because of internal and/or external factors.

Chapter Spotlight

- Edwin Sutherland defined criminology as the study of law making, law breaking, and the response to law breaking. Modern scholars often distinguish criminology (the study of law breaking) from criminal justice (the study of responses to law breaking). The study of deviance also overlaps with criminology.

- Within academia, criminology is currently in a state of flux. Some consider criminology an independent discipline, while others view it as a general field open to all social science disciplines. Historically, sociology has had the largest impact on the study of crime, and sociologists tend to view criminology as a subdiscipline of sociology.

- The substantive criminal law is a codification of prohibited behaviors and the possible sanctions for these behaviors. The definition of a criminal act has two components, the *mens rea* (criminal mind) and the *actus reas* (criminal act).

- Criminal laws can be classified in a number of ways. *Mala in se* (evil in themselves) crimes, including homicide, robbery, rape, and burglary make up the core of the legal code. *Mala prohibita* (wrong because they are prohibited) crimes such as gambling and illicit drug use tend to vary across societies and over time.

- Two general perspectives on the law exist. The consensus perspective views the law as the result of widespread societal agreement about what acts should be illegal. The conflict perspective suggests that the legal code is the end result of a power struggle among competing interest groups.

- A scientific theory is a set of principles or statements that attempt to explain how concepts are related. In the case of crime theory, these statements typically explain how one or more factors lead to criminal behavior. A scientific theory must also be testable, meaning that it must be stated in such a way that other scientists can go out into the real world, collect information, and test the theory's validity.

- A good theory of crime is supported by empirical tests. In other words, it appears to "work" in the real world. Aside from empirical support, a good theory is also parsimonious (concise) and wide in scope (explains a wide range of phenomena).

- Historically, the first explanations of criminal behavior invoked spirits and gods to explain crime. The *scientific* study of crime is dated to the classical school of crime. Classical school theorists argued that humans were rational, hedonistic beings — they choose criminal actions because of the benefits of crime. Accordingly, humans could be *deterred* from crime if the legal system was properly structured. The positive school of crime suggests that criminal behavior is *determined* by factors that are partially or completely outside the control of individuals. Different social science disciplines (e.g., psychology, sociology, biology) highlight different factors that cause criminal behavior.

- Criminology is an applied science. Theory, coupled with sound research, should help guide policy making throughout the criminal justice system. To proceed without theoretical guidance is to take a shot in the dark — there is no logical basis to assume that a particular program will work. Intensive supervision programs are an example of a policy implemented with little theoretical guidance, while multisystemic therapy (MST) is theoretically grounded.

- Although science generally strives to be "value free," criminology is heavily influenced by ideology. Liberal (left) criminologists tend to associate with the positive school of crime and to focus on social causes of crime. Conservative (right) criminologists lean toward the classical school of crime and to focus on deterrence.

Putting It All Together

1. What is "criminology?" How does criminology relate to other social science disciplines?

2. What is a scientific theory? How can you tell whether or not a theory is good?

3. What is the substantive criminal law? Describe the two main perspectives on the criminal law, and give an example of a crime that is consistent with each perspective.

4. Describe the history of theorizing about crime. How does the classical school of crime differ from the positive school of crime?

5. Discuss the linkage between theory and policy.

6. What does it mean to be a "liberal" or "conservative" criminologist? How does ideology impact the study of crime?

Key Terms

case law Law that is created when judges interpret constitutional provisions, statutes, or regulations created by administrative agencies.

conflict perspective View that criminal law is the result of constant clashes between groups with different levels of power. Those groups that win the clashes define the legal code in a manner consistent with their values.

consensus perspective View that criminal law is the result of widespread agreement among members of society as to what should be legal and illegal.

constitutional law The law as expressed in the U.S. Constitution, as well as the constitutions of individual states. Constitutions are the supreme law of the land.

distributive justice Campaign theme of liberal Democrats that increased economic opportunity is the best defense against crime.

grand theories Sweeping theories that attempt to explain all types of criminal behavior.

hedonistic calculus Jeremy Bentham used this term to describe human nature — humans seek pleasure (hedonism) in a rational, calculating manner.

hypotheses Testable statements about the relationship between variables in a scientific study.

intensive supervision Practice based on the assumption that probation/parole officers with reduced caseloads can better monitor and supervise high-risk offenders more effectively. This practice has also been touted as a potential solution to jail and prison-crowding problems.

law and order Campaign theme of conservative Republicans that a "hard line" is the best defense.

mala in se Crimes that are considered as "evil in themselves" (e.g., homicide).

mala prohibita Crimes that are forbidden by laws that attempt to regulate behavior (e.g., drug abuse, gambling, prostitution).

overgeneralization Jumping to sweeping conclusions based on the results of a single study.

panaceas Cure-alls. Applied to criminology, the term refers to the search for simple solutions to the crime problem.

policy analysis Focuses on the condition the government wishes to create, rather than on the root causes of crime.

procedural law The portion of the criminal law that dictates the type of behaviors in which criminal justice actors can legally engage.

recidivism Repeat offending.

statutory law Criminal code created by legislatures and governing bodies.

value free The belief that researchers should keep their personal views out of their study and the interpretation of its findings. Objectivity is the goal.

Notes

1. *Simpson's Contemporary Quotations,* available at http://www.bartleby.com/63, accessed January 2, 2006.
2. *Brainyquote,* available at http://www.brainyquote.com/quotes/quotes/w/willrogers106272.html, accessed January 2, 2006.
3. Bureau of Justice Statistics, *Sourcebook of Criminal Justice Statistics Online,* 30th ed., available at http://www.albany.edu/sourcebook/index.html, accessed December 2, 2005.
4. Ibid.
5. Allen J. Beck and Paige M. Harrison, *Prisoners in 2000* (Washington, DC: Bureau of Justice Statistics, 2001): 1.
6. Thomas P. Bonczar, *Prevalence of Imprisonment in the U.S. Population, 1974–2001* (Washington, DC: Bureau of Justice Statistics, 2003): 1.
7. Edwin Sutherland and Donald Cressey, *Principles of Criminology,* 6th ed. (Philadelphia: J.B. Lippincott, 1960).
8. William Sumner, *Folkways* (Boston: Gin, 1906).
9. Joachim J. Salvelsberg and Robert J. Sampson, "Introduction: Mutual Engagement: Criminology and Sociology?" *Crime, Law, and Social Change* 37 (2002): 99–105.
10. James F. Short, Jr. "Criminology, the Chicago School, and Sociological Theory," *Crime, Law, and Social Change* 37 (2002): 107–115.
11. Steven E. Barkan, *Criminology: A Sociological Understanding* (Upper Saddle River, NJ: Prentice Hall, 2006).
12. C. Wright Mills, *The Sociological Imagination* (London: Oxford University Press, 1959).
13. Barkan, 2006, 8.
14. D.A. Andrews and James Bonta, The Psychology of Criminal Conduct, 2nd ed. (Cincinnati, OH: Anderson, 1998).
15. Margaret A. Zahn, "Thoughts on the Future of Criminology — The American Society of Criminology 1998 Presidential Address," *Criminology* 37 (1999): 1–16.
16. Larry J. Seigel, *Criminology: Theory Patterns, and Typologies,* 8th ed. (Belmont, CA: Wadsworth, 2004): 27.
17. Ibid., 29–31.
18. Larry K. Gains and Roger L. Miller, *Criminal Justice in Action,* 2nd ed. (Belmont, CA: Wadsworth, 2004): 54.
19. Cornell Legal Information Institute, "Constitution and Codes," available at http://www.law.cornell.edu/, accessed January 10, 2006.
20. Gains and Miller, 2004, 62–63.

21. Seigel, 2004, 33.

22. Ibid.

23. U.S. Department of Justice, "Preserving Life and Liberty," available at http://www.lifeandliberty.gov/highlights.htm, accessed January 2, 2006.

24. Electronic Freedom Foundation, "The USA Patriot Act," available at http://www.eff.org/patriot, accessed January 2, 2006.

25. Ibid.

26. Seigel, 204, 35–36.

27. Ronald L. Akers and Christine S. Sellers, *Criminological Theories: Introduction, Evaluation, and Application* (Los Angeles: Roxbury, 2004): 141–147.

28. Akers and Sellers, 2004, 5–6.

29. Edwin Sutherland and Donald Cressey, *Principles of Criminology,* 6th ed. (Philadelphia: J.B. Lippincott, 1960).

30. Harry E. Barnes, *The Story of Punishment* (Montclair, NJ: Patterson-Smith, 1972).

31. Barnes, 1972.

32. William E. Burns, *Witch Hunts in Europe and America: An Encyclopedia* (Westport, CT: Greenwood Press, 2003).

33. J. Robert Lilly, Francis T. Cullen, and Richard A. Ball, *Criminological Theory: Context and Consequences,* 3rd ed. (Thousand Oaks, CA: Sage, 2002): 11.

34. Graeme Newman, *The Punishment Response* (Philadelphia: Lippincott, 1985).

35. Stephen J. Pfohl, *Images of Deviance and Social Control: A Sociological History* (New York: McGraw-Hill, 1985): 25.

36. Lilly, Cullen, and Ball, 2002, 13–15.

37. Ibid., 14.

38. David Young, "Let Us Content Ourselves with Praising the Work While Drawing a Veil Over Its Principles: Eighteenth Century Reactions to Beccaria's *On Crimes and Punishments,*" *Justice Quarterly* 1 (1984): 155–170.

39. Lilly, Cullen, and Ball, 2002, 14–15; George B. Vold, *Theoretical Criminology* (New York: Oxford University Press, 1970): 18–22.

40. Lilly, Cullen, and Ball, 2002, 15.

41. Ysabel F. Rennie, *The Search for Criminal Man: A Conceptual History of the Dangerous Offender* (Lexington, MA: Lexington Books, 1978): 18.

42. Elio Monachesi, "Cesare Beccaria," in Hermann Mannheim, ed., *Pioneers in Criminology* (Montclair, NJ: Patterson-Smith, 1960).

43. Francis T. Cullen and Robert Agnew, *Criminological Theory: Past to Present* (Los Angeles: Roxbury, 2003): 18.

44. Larry J. Seigel, *Criminology,* 8th ed. (Belmont, CA: Wadsworth, 2003): 6.

45. Nicole Rafter, "The Unrepentant Horse-Slasher: Moral Insanity and the Origins of Criminological Thought," *Criminology* 42 (2004): 979–1008.

46. Gideon Fishman, "Positivism and Neo-Lombrosianism," in Israel Barak-Glantz and C. Ronald Huff, eds., *The Mad, the Bad, and the Different: Essays in Honor of Simon Dinitz* (Lexington, MA: Lexington, 1981): 17.

47. C. Ray Jeffrey, "The Historical Development of Criminology," in Hermann Mannheim, ed., *Pioneers in Criminology* (Montclair, NJ: Patterson-Smith, 1960): 468.

48. Francis T. Cullen and Karen E. Gilbert, *Reaffirming Rehabilitation* (Cincinnati, OH: Anderson, 1982).

49. John P. Gibbs, "The State of Criminological Theory," *Criminology* 25 (1987): 821–840.

50. Lawrence A. Bennett, "Practice in Search of Theory: The Case of Intensive Supervision — An Extension of an Old Practice or a New Approach?" *American Journal of Criminal Justice* 12 (1988): 293.

51. Joan Petersilia and Susan Turner, "Evaluating Intensive Supervision Probation/Parole," *Research in Brief* (Washington, DC: National Institute of Justice, 1993).

52. Robert M. Carter, James Robison, and Leslie T. Wilkins, *The San Francisco Project: A Study of Federal Probation and Parole* (Berkeley: University of California Press, 1967).

53. Edward J. Latessa and Gennaro F. Vito, "The Effects of Intensive Supervision on Shock Probationers," *Journal of Criminal Justice* 16 (1988): 319–330.

54. James M. Byrne, Arthur J. Lurigio, and Christopher Baird, "The Effectiveness of the New Intensive Supervision Programs," *Research in Corrections* 2 (1989): 1–48; Betsy Fulton, Edward J. Latessa, Amy Stichman, and Lawrence F. Travis, "The State of ISP: Research and Policy Implications," *Federal Probation* 61 (1997): 65–76.

55. Scott W. Henggeler, Phillippe B. Cunningham, Susan G. Pickrel, Sonja K. Schoenwald, and Michael J. Brondino, "Multisystemic Therapy: An Effective Violence Prevention Approach for Serious Juvenile Offenders," *Journal of Adolescence* 19 (1996): 47–61.

56. Francis T. Cullen and Paul Gendreau, "Assessing Correctional Rehabilitation: Policy, Practice, and Prospects," in *Criminal Justice 2000* (Washington, DC: National Institute of Justice, 2000).

57. Robert M. Martinson, "What Works? Questions and Answers About Prison Reform," *The Public Interest* Spring (1974): 24.

58. Ibid., 10.

59. Michael G. Maxfield and Earl Babbie, *Research Methods for Criminal Justice and Criminology* (Belmont, CA: Wadsworth, 2005): 10.

60. Robert M. Martinson and Judith Wilks, "Save Parole Supervision," *Federal Probation* 41 (1977): 23–27; Robert M. Martinson, "New Findings, New Views: A Note of Caution Regarding Sentencing Reform," *Hofstra Law Review* 7 (1979): 242–258; Jose E. Sanchez, "The Use of Robert Martinson's Writings on Correctional Treatment: An Essay on the Justification of Correctional Policy," *Journal of Contemporary Criminal Justice* 6 (1990): 127–138.

61. Paul Gendreau and Richard R. Ross, "Revivication of Rehabilitation: Evidence from the 1980s," *Justice Quarterly* 4 (1987): 349–407; Craig Dowden and D.A. Andrews, "The Importance of Staff Practice in Delivering Effective Correctional Treatment: A Meta-Analytic Review of Core Correctional Practice," *International Journal of Offender Therapy and Comparative Criminology* 48 (2004): 204–214; Craig Dowden and D.A. Andrews, "Effective Correctional Treatment and Violent Reoffending: A Meta Analysis," *Canadian Journal of Criminology* 42 (2000): 449–467.

62. Joan Petersilia, Susan Turner, J. Kahan, and J. Peterson, "Executive Summary of Rand's Study: 'Granting Felons Probation: Public Risks and Alternatives,'" *Crime and Delinquency* 31 (1985): 379–392.

63. Johnny McGaha, Michael Fichter, and Peter Hirschburg, "Felony Probation: A Re-examination of Public Risk," *American Journal of Criminal Justice* 11 (1987): 1–9; Gennaro F. Vito, "Felony Probation and Recidivism: Replication and Response," *Federal Probation* 50 (1987): 17–25; John Whitehead, "The Effectiveness of Felony Probation: Results from an Eastern State," *Justice Quarterly* 9 (1991): 525–543; Patrick A. Langan and Mark A. Cunniff, *Recidivism of Felons on Probation, 1986–89* (Washington, DC: Bureau of Justice Statistics, 1992); W. Reed Benedict and Lin Huff-Corzine, "Return to the Scene of the Punishment: Recidivism of Adult Male Property Offenders on Felony Probation, 1986–1989," *Journal of Research in Crime and Delinquency* 34 (1997): 237–252; Barbara Sims and Mark Jones, "Predicting Success or Failure on Probation: Factors Associated with Felony Probation Outcomes," *Crime and Delinquency* 43 (1997): 314–327.

64. Lawrence W. Sherman and Douglas A. Smith with Janell D. Schmidt and Dennis P. Rogan, "Crime, Punishment, and Stake in Conformity: Legal and Informal Control of Domestic Violence," *American Sociological Review* 57 (1992): 680–690.

65. Lawrence W. Sherman and Richard A. Berk, "The Specific Deterrent Effects of Arrest for Domestic Assault," *American Sociological Review* 49 (1984): 261–272; Richard A. Berk and Lawrence W. Sherman, "Police Responses to Domestic Violence Incidents: An Analysis of an Experimental Design with Incomplete Randomization," *Journal of the American Statistical Association* 83 (1988): 70–76.

66. Sherman and Smith, 1992, 680.

67. Franklyn W. Dunford, David Huizinga, and Delbert S. Elliott, "The Role of Arrest in Domestic Assault: The Omaha Police Experiment," *Criminology* 28 (1990): 183–206.

68. J. David Hirschel, Ira W. Hutchison, and Charles W. Dean, "The Failure of Arrest to Deter Spouse Abuse," *Journal of Research in Crime and Delinquency* 29 (1992): 7–33.

69. Lawrence W. Sherman, Janell D. Schmidt, Dennis P. Rogan, Patrick R. Gartin, Ellen G. Cohen, Douglas J. Collins, and A.R. Bacich, "From Initial Deterrence to Long-Term Escalation: Short Term Custody Arrest for Poverty Ghetto Domestic Violence," *Criminology* 29 (1991): 821–850; Sherman and Smith with Schmidt and Rogan, 1992.

70. Sherman, Schmidt, et al., 1991, 846.

71. Arnold Binder and James W. Meeker, "Implications of the Failure to Replicate the Minneapolis Experimental Findings," *American Sociological Review* 58 (1993): 887.

72. Lawrence W. Sherman, "Implications of the Failure to Read the Literature." *American Sociological Review* 58 (1993): 888.

73. Richard A. Berk, "Policy Correctness in the ASR," *American Sociological Review* 58 (1993): 889.

74. C. Ray Jeffery, *Crime Prevention Through Environmental Design* (Beverly Hills, CA: Sage, 1977): 331.

75. Robert M. Carter, "The Police View of the Justice System," in Malcolm W. Klein, ed., *The Juvenile Justice System* (Beverly Hills, CA: Sage, 1976): 123.

76. George L. Kirkham, "From Professor to Patrolman: A Fresh Perspective on the Police," *Journal of Police Science and Administration* 2 (1974): 137.

77. George L. Kirkham, *Signal Zero: The Professor Who Became a Cop* (Philadelphia: Lippincott, 1976): 206.
78. Robert M. Carter, "Where Have All the Crime Fighters Gone?" *Gunsmoke Gazette* 1 (1972): 9.
79. Carter, 1976, 124.
80. James O. Finckenauer, "Crime as a National Political Issue, 1964–76," *Crime and Delinquency* 24 (1978): 10–19.
81. Gennaro F. Vito, "The Politics of Crime Control: Implications of Reagan Administration Pronouncements on Crime," *Journal of Contemporary Criminal Justice* 2 (1983): 1–7.
82. Walter B. Miller, "Ideology and Criminal Justice Policy," in Norman Johnson and Leonard D. Savitz, eds., *Justice and Corrections* (New York: John Wiley, 1978).
83. Ibid., 8–9.
84. Ibid., 9–10.
85. Richard R.E. Kania, "Conservative Ideology in Criminology and Criminal Justice," *American Journal of Criminal Justice* 13 (1988): 80.
86. James Q. Wilson, *Thinking About Crime* (New York: Vintage Books, 1985): 46.
87. Ibid., 49.
88. Ibid., 50–51.
89. Robert M. Bohm, "Crime, Criminal and Crime Control Policy Myths," *Justice Quarterly* 3 (1986): 194. See also Samuel Walker, *Sense and Nonsense About Crime and Drugs* (Belmont, CA: Wadsworth, 2000); Jeffrey Reiman, *The Rich Get Richer and the Poor Get Prison: Ideology, Class and Criminal Justice* (Boston: Allyn and Bacon, 2003); Gregg Barak, Jeanne M. Flavin, and Paul S. Leighton, eds. *Class, Race, Gender and Crime: Social Realities of Justice in America* (Los Angeles: Roxbury, 2001).
90. Elliot Currie, "Confronting Crime: Looking Toward the Twenty-First Century," *Justice Quarterly* 6 (1989): 16.
91. Ibid., 21. See also Elliot Currie, *Confronting Crime: An American Challenge* (New York: Pantheon Books, 1985); Elliott Currie, *Crime and Punishment in America* (New York: Henry Holt, 1998).
92. Lawrence F. Travis III, Edward J. Latessa, and Gennaro F. Vito, "Agenda Building in Criminal Justice: The Case of Determinate Sentencing," *American Journal of Criminal Justice* 10 (1985): 1–21.
93. Cullen and Gendreau, 2000, 119–122.
94. Ibid.
95. Emile Durkheim, "Crime as Normal Phenomenon," in Leon Radzinowicz and Marvin E. Wolfgang, eds., *The Criminal in Society: Crime and Justice,* Volume 1 (New York: Basic Books, 1971): 391–392.
96. Albert K. Cohen, *Deviance and Control* (Englewood Cliffs, NJ: Prentice Hall, 1966): 6–10.
97. Daniel P. Moynihan, "Defining Deviancy Down," in Richard C. Monk, ed., *Taking Sides: Clashing Views on Controversial Issues in Crime and Criminology* (Guilford, CT: Dushkin, 1996): 11.
98. Franklin P. Williams III and Marilyn McShane, *Criminological Theory* (Englewood Cliffs, NJ: Prentice Hall, 1988): 7.
99. James O. Finckenauer, *Scared Straight! and the Panacea Phenomenon* (Englewood Cliffs, NJ: Prentice Hall, 1982): 5–6.

WWW.CRIMINOLOGY.JBPUB.COM

Interactivities
In the News
Key Term Explorer
Web Links

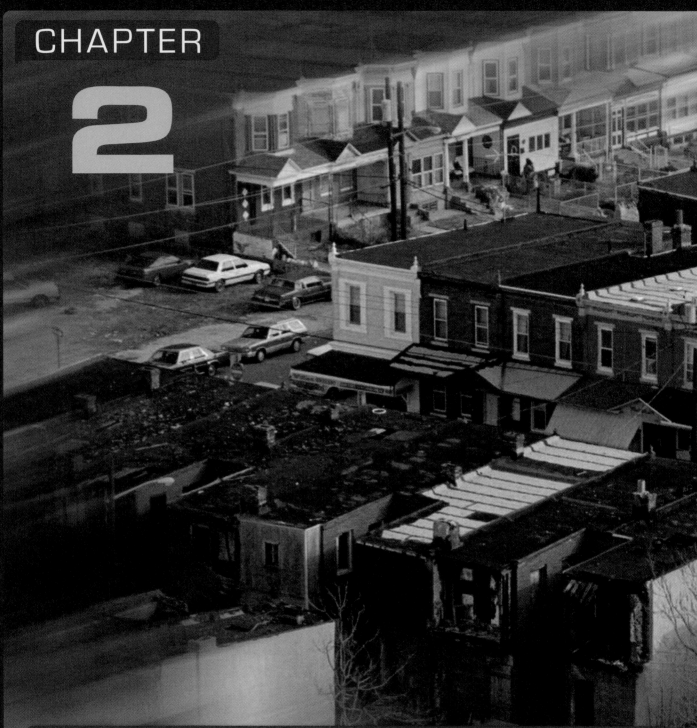

CHAPTER

2

OBJECTIVES

Define the elements of the Uniform Crime Report (UCR) and identify its strengths and weaknesses as a crime data source.

Define the elements of the National Crime Victimization Survey (NCVS) and identify its strengths and weaknesses as a crime data source.

Define the elements of the National Incident-Based Reporting System.

Understand what patterns are present in the UCR and the NCVS and what they tell about crime.

Summarize what data sources tell about the criminal justice system.

The Incidence of Crime

If we knew more about the character of both offenders and victims, the nature of their relationships and the circumstances that create a high probability of crime conduct, it seems likely that crime prevention programs could be made much more effective.

—The President's Commission on Law Enforcement and the Administration of Justice (1967)[1]

YOU ARE THE CRIMINOLOGIST

Introduction

Like many other human activities, crime is difficult to measure. The total amount of crime in the United States is unknown. Typically, one depends on official figures and on activities of the criminal justice system to indicate the volume of crime in society. Each of these sources has its strengths and weaknesses, however. In this chapter, several sources of crime data are reviewed and a number of findings presented. In wading through the sea of data in this chapter, keep in mind that it is more important to remember the conclusions based on the statistics than the numbers themselves.

Crime statistics are viewed as one indicator of societal health. A high crime rate causes alarm, while a low crime rate spurs feelings of security. For example, each year Morgan Quitno Press calculates rankings for "America's Safest (and Most Dangerous) Cities." **TABLE 2-1** includes the list of the safest and most dangerous cities in the United States for 2005.[2] Information such as this affects the life choices that citizens make. There is some evidence that reductions in the crime rate of New York City were related to that city's real estate

boom in the mid-1990s.[3] It was also reported that crime rates had no direct effect on housing prices in Jacksonville, Florida, but homes were highly discounted in high crime areas.[4] Crime rates (especially violent crime) also had an impact on mortgage default rates.[5]

It is also important to collect accurate crime statistics for operational purposes. How can the police, courts, and correctional system handle the crime problem if the statistics about crime are inaccurate? How does a person know where crimes are committed, the methods used to carry them out, and just how great the problem actually is? Without valid crime data, it is impossible to address these questions.

Many problems relate to the collection of crime data. For starters, it is difficult to determine just how much crime there is in society, because not all crimes are reported to the police. Perhaps the victim feels that the police will do nothing about the crime because it is not very serious, just a theft of property of little value or that the offender is a powerful person beyond the reach of the law. Victims may be embarrassed by their victimization — that they fell for an Internet fraud or other scam,

TABLE 2-1

Morgan Quitno's 12th Annual America's Safest (and Most Dangerous) Cities, 2005

Rank	Safest 25 Cities	Rank	Most Dangerous 25 Cities
1	Newton, MA	1	Camden, NJ
2	Clarkstown, NY	2	Detroit, MI
3	Amherst, NY	3	St. Louis, MO
4	Mission Viejo, CA	4	Flint, MI
5	Brick Township, NJ	5	Richmond, VA
6	Troy, MI	6	Baltimore, MD
7	Thousand Oaks, CA	7	Atlanta, GA
8	Round Rock, TX	8	New Orleans, LA
9	Lake Forest, CA	9	Gary, IN
10	Cary, NC	10	Birmingham, AL
11	Colonie, NY	11	Richmond, CA
12	Fargo, ND	12	Cleveland, OH
13	Irvine, CA	13	Washington, DC
14	Orem, UT	14	West Palm Beach, FL
15	Dover Township, NJ	15	Compton, CA
16	Warwick, RI	16	Memphis, TN
17	Sunnyvale, CA	17	Dayton, CA
18	Hamilton Township, NJ	18	San Bernardino, CA
19	Parma, OH	19	Springfield, MA
20	Canton Township, MI	20	Cincinnati, OH
21	Greece, NY	21	Oakland, CA
22	Simi Valley, CA	22	Dallas, TX
23	Coral Springs, FL	23	Newark, NJ
24	Port St. Lucie, FL	24	Hartford, CT
25	Centennial, CO	25	Little Rock, AR

Source: Morgan Quitno Awards, "12th Annual America's Safest (and Most Dangerous) Cities," available at http://www.morganquitno.com, accessed December 5, 2005.

were "dumb" enough to leave the door to the house unlocked or their car unsecured, or were attacked by a friend, family member, or date. Companies are often too concerned to report embezzlements and frauds because the negative publicity could harm their business. Victims of violent crime such as assault and rape may not report the crime because they fear retaliation by the offender.

Other crimes seem "invisible" because the evidence of the crime has been hidden and thoroughly concealed. This applies not only to violent crimes such as homicide but also to white-collar crimes such as embezzlement where the crime scene is not out in the open and may be under the control of the offender.

LINK Chapter 15 presents information on "crimes of the powerful" — organized crime and white-collar offenders.

Crimes such as drug abuse are unlikely to be reported because there is no obvious victim. Drug abusers harm only themselves, unless of course their drug use leads to other crimes. For instance, drug addicts may commit a crime to obtain funds to buy drugs, or the drugs may spark violent behavior and lead to assault or other violent offenses.

Sources of Crime Statistics

To study the incidence of crime, it is helpful to compare the findings from two data sources: the **Uniform Crime Report (UCR)**, which lists crimes reported to the police, and the **National Crime Victimization Survey (NCVS)**, which documents the extent of victimization. The public is often concerned with whether crime is up or down, but the main point regarding these data sources is that they are intended to measure different aspects of crime.[6] The problem is that most crime is not directly observable: "No one measure is capable of providing all the information about the extent and characteristics of crime."[7]

In 1929, the International Association of Chiefs of Police called for the development of a uniform crime reporting program. In 1930, the Federal Bureau of Investigation (FBI) began to compile nationwide crime statistics. The FBI's famous director, J. Edgar Hoover, recognized the potential of such a program to generate positive publicity for his agency as the leader in the fight against crime.

The Uniform Crime Report

The UCR is based on the number of crimes reported to the police, is the major source of crime information in this country, and is completely voluntary. Typically, police agencies report the number of crimes uncovered within their jurisdiction over the previous year to a centralized state clearinghouse (e.g., the state police), which passes the data on to the FBI. Thus, the annual report (entitled *Crime in the United States*) consists of both crimes reported (by complainants or victims) to the police and those uncovered (as a result of investigation) by the police. Because the UCR contains information from most jurisdictions, it is the major source of nationwide crime data. This makes it possible to examine the crime rate for a particular area, as well as to compare crime rates across regions.

The UCR format features standardized definitions of crime. Thus, the term *uniform* really is a synonym for *standardized*. If legal codes were used, the difference between legal definitions across the states would lead to confusion, with similar events counted and classified as different crimes. *Crime in the United States* highlights the most serious crimes, which are called Part I or **index offenses**: murder, rape, assault, burglary, larceny-theft, motor vehicle theft, and arson. These crimes were selected because their seriousness made them more likely to be reported to the police.[8] Thus, the crime index is an indicator of the level of serious crime in the United States.

The UCR presents crime rates, or the incidence of crime per 100,000 citizens. The use of this rate makes it possible to compare the number of crimes reported in cities, towns, and states of different sizes. FIGURE 2-1 presents the national UCR crime rates for 2003. Note that property crimes such as larceny-theft, burglary, and motor vehicle theft are most common, while violent crimes such as assault, robbery, and rape occur less often. Rape, however, presents a particular problem because the seemingly low rate may actually reflect a reluctance to report the crime. Rape victims are traumatized

Timothy Mobly, known as the "Internet Rapist," is escorted out of the courtroom after being sentenced to three consecutive life terms in a Washoe County, Nevada, courtroom. He confessed to assaulting two women that he met online in Internet chat rooms.

? *Is this type of crime likely to be reported to the police and show up in crime statistics?*

by the offense and often feel that reporting the crime only extends their victimization, causing them to relive the event.

FIGURE 2-2 depicts the rate of violent and property crimes reported to the police from 1984 to 2003. Note that the property crime rate was fairly constant over this time period; however, the violent crime rate peaked in the early 1990s, declined sharply, and now appears to have leveled off. The change in the violent crime rate has been the subject of some controversy among criminologists who are attempting to determine the reasons for it. They consider such variables as police programs, changes in drug abuse rates, the availability of firearms, stricter sentencing, changes in the age of the population, family structure, the economy, the political system, and religious makeup.[9] Such analyses are the heart of criminology.

Limitations of the UCR

As with all crime statistics, these crime figures must be carefully considered. Typically, the follow-

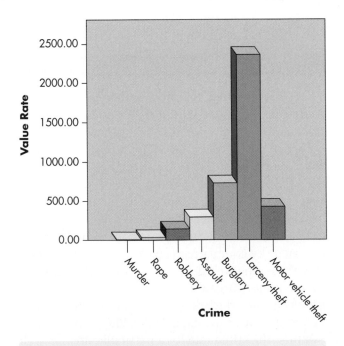

FIGURE 2-1 UCR Index Crimes, 2003

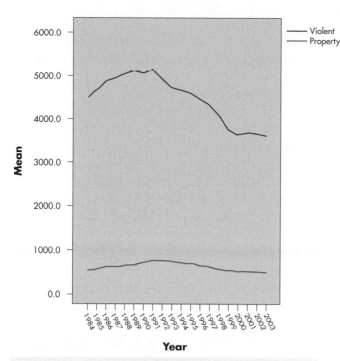

FIGURE 2-2 UCR Violent and Property Crime Rates, 1984–2003

Source: Federal Bureau of Investigation, *Crime in the United States, 2003* (Washington, D.C.: U.S. Department of Justice, 2004), available at http://www.fbi.gov/ucr/03cius.htm.

ing four factors affect the accuracy of UCR figures[10]:

1. **UCR figures reflect only the volume of crime reported to the police.** A number of reasons exist why victims would not report a crime. For example, victims may feel that the crime is not serious or may be embarrassed by their victimization (e.g., a man robbed by a prostitute). Rape victims may not report the crime because they know the offender (e.g., incest or date rape) or because they fear the consequences of reporting (e.g., testifying in court if an arrest is made).

2. **UCR figures are affected by the recording practices of the police.** For instance, the police may report crimes in such a way that presents them (the police) and the community in the best light. Consider the crime figures for the safest and most dangerous cities. Would law enforcers want their city to be known as the "most crime-ridden" city in the country?

3. **The UCR emphasizes street crime.** These crime figures represent only part of the crime problem. The focus on street crime obscures the impact of crimes of the powerful, those known as organized and white-collar crimes.

4. **Crimes reported to the police mainly reflect the results of their style of work.** The major problem in crime measurement is the source of the information. Official statistics reflect the actions of the criminal justice system itself. For example, if the police "crack down" on a certain type of crime (e.g., prostitution), then the rate of that particular crime will certainly rise.

For these reasons, UCR figures are not representative of the actual level of crime in the United States; still, it has some obvious strengths. As previously mentioned, the UCR is the major source of crime statistics in this country and has been since 1930. Thus, it has a certain tradition and prestige that is also enhanced by the FBI involvement in the data collection and reporting process. In addition, it presents data from every region of the country. If someone wants to know about crime in a particular city, town, or state, the UCR is the best source of information.

The National Incident-Based Reporting System

In 1991, those with the UCR program began to change its system of data collection to generate more information to conduct crime analysis. This new system is known as the National Incident-Based Reporting System (NIBRS). This system is

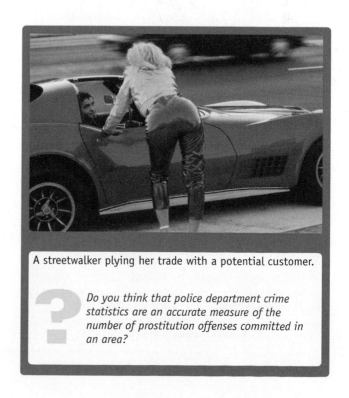

A streetwalker plying her trade with a potential customer.

? *Do you think that police department crime statistics are an accurate measure of the number of prostitution offenses committed in an area?*

designed to collect a great number of details about crimes reported to the police, such as where and when the offense occurred and victim information (on the harm caused by the crime); if arrests are made, it will also include data on the offenders. The NIBRS will contain information on reported crime and arrests, all elements that were missing from the UCR system. The NIBRS will eventually replace the UCR as the official source of crime information from police departments as reported to the FBI.

The NIBRS will contain information on 46 Group A offenses that represent 22 categories, rather than concentrate on the eight index offenses from the UCR. Unlike the UCR, NIBRS will:

- Make a distinction between attempted and completed crimes.
- Provide more inclusive definitions of crime (i.e., the definition of rape has been expanded to include male victims).

- Count all offenses that occur during an incident rather than concentrating only on the most serious crimes. For example, if an offender held up a liquor store and shot and killed the person working there, the UCR would count the homicide but not the robbery. In the NIBRS, both offenses will be tallied.

The major distinction is the focus on the crime incident itself.[11] A list of the differences between UCR and NIBRS is presented in **TABLE 2-2**.

Although the system is not fully in place across the country, reports based on NIBRS data have been conducted. For example, the following are some findings based on homicide data trends through 2002[12]:

- Homicide rates stabilized after declining to levels last seen in the late 1960s, about 5.6 homicides per 100,000 people in 2001 and 2002. Therefore, from this data, one can conclude that murders are not increasing.
- In 2002, males were 10 times more likely than females to commit murder. Typically, more males than females are involved in all types of criminal activity, especially violent crimes.
- According to data, in 2002, blacks were six times more likely to be homicide victims and seven times more likely than whites to commit homicides. Thus, the risk of violent victimization is not spread equally across the population. Some groups are more at risk, depending on the type of crime.
- According to data for the time period 1976 through 2002, homicides were usually not interracial: 86% of the white murder victims were killed by whites and 94% of the black victims were killed by blacks. Again, crime typically occurs within, rather than across, racial groups.
- From 1976 to 2002, the number of law enforcement officers killed in the line of duty declined. The danger of the job to police officers may be declining.
- Arguments remain the most frequently cited circumstance in homicides. This finding provides some indication of how NIBRS can tell something about the circumstances of an offense. In turn, this information could lead to ways to prevent the crime.
- In 2002, the homicide victimization rate for cities with a population of 1 million or more

TABLE 2-2

Differences Between UCR and NIBRS

UCR	NIBRS
Consists of monthly aggregate crime counts for eight index crimes	Consists of individual incident records for the eight index crimes and 38 other offenses with details on: offense, offender, victim, property
Records one offense per incident as determined by the hierarchy rule (counts only the most serious offense). Hierarchy rule suppresses counts of lesser offenses in multiple-offense incidents.	Records each offense occurring in the incident
Does not distinguish between attempted and completed crimes	Distinguishes between attempted and completed crimes
Records rape of females only	Records rape of males and females Restructures definition of assault
Collects weapon information for murder, robbery, and aggravated assault	Collects weapon information for all violent offenses
Provides counts on arrests for the eight index crimes and 21 other offenses	Provides details on arrests for the eight index cimes and 49 other offenses

Source: Ramona R. Rantala, *Effects of NIBRS on Crime Statistics* (Washington, DC: Bureau of Justice Statistics, 2002): 1.

reached the lowest level since 1976. Again, homicide is apparently not on the rise.

- Homicide rates were higher in the southern United States and lower in the New England, Mountain, and West North Central regions of the United States. NIBRS gives an indication of differences by region. This information directs one's attention to the areas where crime is more likely to occur and leads to more research to learn the reasons why these concentrations occur.

- 64% of all homicides were cleared in 2002 compared with 79% in 1976. Homicide investigations are less effective than in the past.

These findings are also important because homicide is the most reliable indicator of violent crime. Because it is so serious, it is the crime that is most likely to be reported to the police. It is very difficult to conceal a body.

National Crime Victimization Survey

A second source of crime information is the National Crime Victimization Survey (NCVS), which has been conducted by the Bureau of Justice Statistics since 1972. The purpose of the survey is to uncover crime that has not been reported, enlighten the "dark figure of crime," and thus learn the actual level of crime in the country (i.e., if the victim does not report it, if it goes unseen or undetected by the police or others, it will not be reported and thus will not show up in crime figures). It attempts to eliminate the middle person (the police) by going directly to the victim. The survey is based on the premise that citizens may report to the NCVS the crimes that they did not report to the police.

The NCVS is a scientifically designed annual survey of a representative sample of some 60,000 U.S. households. Information in this report is also presented as a population rate: the number of victims per 1,000 households. As an estimate of the risk of crime victimization, the NCVS is an improvement over UCR for two reasons. First, the survey presents information taken directly from victims whether they report the crime to the police or not. Second, it collects background information on victims, making it possible to decide which groups have the highest rates of victimization for particular types of crime. By contrast, the data from the UCR may lead a person to incorrectly assume that every individual has an equal chance of becoming a crime victim.

TABLE 2-3 shows that the NCVS does uncover more crime than is reported in the UCR. In 2003, approximately 5 million more crimes were uncovered by the NCVS. The difference was apparent for every crime classification. The greatest difference was for larceny-theft and was smallest for rape. Motor vehicle theft was the only crime for which the UCR had a higher figure than the NCVS.

Although the UCR measures only the crimes reported to the police and the NCVS captures both reported and unreported crime, these two sources of crime statistics often present similar patterns. **FIGURE 2-3** presents the NCVS rates per 1,000 households for 2003. Note that the pattern of victimization is identical to that reported in the UCR (see Figure 2-1): The rate of property crime victimization (larceny-theft, burglary, motor vehicle theft) is the highest, followed by violent crime victimization (assault, robbery, rape). In addition, the victimization trends over the past decade, presented in **FIGURE 2-4**, are comparable to those detailed by the UCR (see Figure 2-2).

Several studies have noted a high level of correspondence between UCR and NCVS crime rates.[13] The NCVS victimization rates between 1993 and 2003 also note the steep decline in violent crime during the 1990s. Property crime rates apparently peaked in 1994 and then leveled off. In fact, since 1972, changes in the violent crime rate from both the UCR and the NCVS have moved in the same

TABLE 2-3		
UCR and NCVS Crime Rate Figures, 2003		
Type of Crime	**UCR**	**NCVS**
Rape	93,433	91,330
Robbery	413,402	434,680
Assault	857,921	769,370
Burglary	2,153,464	2,987,020
Larceny-theft	7,021,588	11,380,360
Motor vehicle theft	1,260,471	948,710
Total	**11,800,279**	**16,611,470**

Sources: Federal Bureau of Investigation, *Crime in the United States, 2003* (Washington, D.C.: U.S. Department of Justice, 2004); Bureau of Justice Statistics, *Criminal Victimization 2003* (Washington, D.C.: U.S. Department of Justice, 2004).

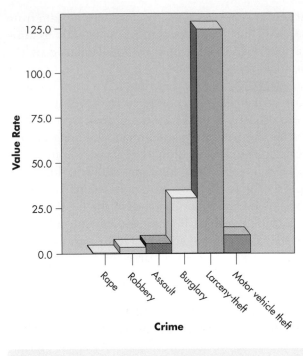

FIGURE 2-3 NCVS Victimization Rates per 1000 Households, 2003

- **Marital status:** Persons who were never married experienced higher overall violent victimization rates than any other grouping.
- **Region:** In 2003, Western residents experienced assault at significantly higher rates than residents in the Northeast and South.
- **Residence:** Urban residents were victimized at higher rates than suburban and rural residents.
- **Victim-offender relationship:** Females were most often victimized by someone they knew and males were more likely to be victimized by a stranger.
- **Weapons in violent crimes:** 24% of all violent crime incidents were committed by an armed offender.

Of course, the bottom line or reason for the existence of this survey is the rate of reporting to the police. During 2003, 48% of all violent victimization and 38% of all property crimes were reported to the police. Motor vehicle theft (77%) has consistently been the crime that is most likely to be reported to the police by victims.

direction 60% of the time, and property crime rates moved in the same direction about 75% of the time.[14]

Attributes of Victimization Patterns, 2003

The NCVS gives specific information about crime by focusing on the attributes of the victim. Thus, criminologists can examine who is likely to be the victim of a particular type of crime. The following findings on victimization rates by victim attributes were reported for 2003[15]:

- **Gender:** Males were more likely than females to be the victims of every type of violent crime except rape/sexual assault.
- **Race:** Violent victimizations have fallen substantially since 1993. Hispanic rates have fallen the most (45%) followed by blacks (38%) and then whites (29%).
- **Age:** Persons age 12 to 19 had the highest rates of violent crime. These rates decrease as people age.
- **Household income:** Persons in households with an annual income under $7500 were more likely to be victims of robbery and assault than households with higher incomes.

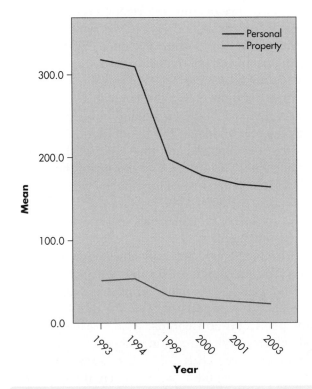

FIGURE 2-4 NCVS Victimization Rates per 1000 Households, 1993–2003

Source: Patsy A. Klaus, *Crime in the Nation's Households, 2003* (Washington, D.C.: Bureau of Justice Statistics, 2004), available at http://www.ojp.usdoj.gov/bjs/abstract/cnh03.htm.

Categories of Victims and Victimization

The NCVS has generated data that has led to special analyses of crime victimization by type of crime. Summaries of several of these studies follow.

Intimate Partner Violence, 1993–2001

Intimate partner violence (i.e., victimizations committed by current or former spouses, boyfriends, or girlfriends of victims) is a significant category of crime victimization. Between 1993 and 2001, the following patterns emerged for this type of crime[16]:

- The number of violent crimes by intimate partners against females dropped by nearly half (49%). They also declined for male victims (42%).

- Intimate partner violence accounted for 20% of the total violent crime victimization against women in 2001.

- Simple assault was the most common type of violent crime involving intimate partners.

- Between 1976 and 2000, the number of men murdered by intimates dropped 68%. During this same period, the number of females killed by intimates declined 22%.

Given the recent laws and programs devoted to the prevention of domestic violence and increased public awareness of this type of crime, the decline in intimate partner victimization is encouraging.

Violent Victimization of College Students, 1995–2000

The following patterns emerged from 1995–2000 for comparisons made between the victimization rates for college students and other persons age 18–24[17]:

- From 1995 to 2000, violence against college students decreased 40%, while violence against nonstudents of similar ages fell 44%.

- College students experienced overall violence, robbery, aggravated assault, and serious violent crime at rates lower than those for nonstudents.

- Among women, college students had lower violent crime victimizations than nonstudents. However, the rate for rape was nearly identical.

- Rape and sexual assault were the only violent crimes against college students more likely to be committed by a person the victim knew.

- Among men, college students had lower victimization rates for robbery and slightly higher rates for simple assault than nonstudents.

- For both blacks and whites, students were victims of violent crime at rates lower than that of nonstudents. Hispanic students had similar rates of violent crime as nonstudents.

- In 41% of all violent crime experienced by college students, the offender was perceived to be under the influence of drugs and/or alcohol.

- Firearms were used in 9% of all violent crimes, 7% of the assaults, and 30% of the robberies against college students.

- The number of off-campus victimizations of college students was over 14 times greater than the number of on-campus victimizations.

- College students were less likely to report violent victimizations to the police (34%) than nonstudents (47%).

The best news was that most college student victims were not injured as a result of the violence against them — only 24% reported an injury as a result of the crime. Studies of campus victimizations have also revealed that the risk of violent crime was enhanced by partying at night with high levels of drugs.[18] To prevent criminal victimization, college students should avoid or at least be wary of the danger associated with these behaviors. In other words, there are things that people can do to avoid or limit the risk of victimization.

School Crime and Safety

What are the patterns of victimization in schools, from elementary to high school? The NCVS has long provided direct information on this subject. Again, the aim of presenting this information is to determine who is at risk and how to prevent crime from occurring. Here are some selected findings on school crime victimization[19]:

- **Age:** In 2002, students 12–18 were more likely to be the victims of nonfatal, serious violent crime *away from school*. However, younger students (ages 12–14) were more likely to be victims of such violent crime *at school* than older students. Therefore, the age of the student affects the place of violent crime victimization.

- **Use of a weapon:** The percentage of students in grades 9–12 who have been threatened or injured with a weapon on school property fluctuated between 1993 and 2003. Seven percent to 9% of these students were threatened with a weapon (gun, knife, or club) on school property in the year prior to the survey. In short, despite what appears in the media, being threatened with a weapon on school grounds is not a common, everyday occurrence.

- **Fighting:** It appears that fighting at school is declining. Between 1993 and 2003, the percentage of students in grades 9–12 who reported being in a fight on school property declined from 16% to 13%.

- **Bullying:** Between 1999 and 2003, the percentage of students age 12–18 who reported being bullied at school increased from 5% to 8%. There was no significant difference in the rates of bullying between public and private and urban, suburban, and rural schools. Bullying has been cited as a contributor to violent crimes in school.

LINK Chapter 5 presents a Headline Crime feature on the Columbine Massacre, where bullying was identified as a factor in the event.

Thus, it appears that, although schools are not immune from crime and safety problems, victimization rates are declining and serious events are not commonplace.

Violence in the Workplace, 1993–1999

Media reports give the impression that workplace violence is on the rise and becoming a major prob-

Still frame from a video made by Eric Harris (left) and Dylan Klebold before their assault on Columbine High School that led to the death of 12 students and one teacher.

 Do you think it is likely that students will admit to being victims of bullying in a survey?

lem. Again, yearly examinations by the NCVS have made long-term comparisons possible. The following patterns have emerged[20]:

- **By incidence:** Between 1993 and 1999, violent crime in the workplace declined even more than the overall violent crime rate (44% vs. 40%). Therefore, according to these figures, the rate of violent crime in the workplace is not increasing. Who are the most likely victims of workplace violence? By profession:

  1. Police officers had the highest rate of workplace violence victimization (261 per 1000) and college professors the lowest (2 per 1000).

  2. Elementary school teachers (17 per 1000) had lower rates of workplace violence victimization than junior high (54 per 1000) and high school teachers (38 per 1000).

  3. Whites had the highest rate of workplace violence victimization (13 per 1000), compared to blacks (10 per 1000) and all other races (8 per 1000).

- **By race:** Most workplace violent victimizations were intraracial. About 6 in 10 white and black victims perceived their assailant to be of the same race.

- **By gender:** The violent crime victimization rate for males was 56% higher than the female rate during the period 1993–1999.

- **By most common type of crime:** Although homicide attracts the greatest amount of publicity, the simple assault victimization rate was more than four times the rate of all other categories of workplace violent crime. Workplace homicide data show:

  1. **Victim/offender relationship:** During the period 1993–1999, the majority (84%) of workplace homicides (899 total) were committed by offenders who were strangers to their victim. Coworkers or former coworkers accounted for 7% and customers or clients 4% of workplace homicides for this time period.

  2. **Weapon used:** Shooting accounted for more than 80% of all workplace homicides between 1993 and 1999.

In addition, the authors of the study examined NCVS workplace data from 1992–1996 for gender differences in violent victimization in the workplace. They determined that more robberies were committed against females who were employed at teaching institutions, in law enforcement, and in retail business than their male counterparts. More simple assaults were committed against females than males in law enforcement and the transportation business. When injuries did occur, females lost more time from work than males.[21] Therefore, although men are more likely to be victims of workplace violence, these crimes often have a more severe impact on female victims.

Overall, these analyses reveal the tremendous information potential generated by the NCVS. Such specific analyses would not be possible if this survey were not routinely conducted. The NCVS provides valuable crime information that is not available from other sources.

Limitations of the NCVS

Although data for the NCVS is obtained directly from victims, there are some problems with the data of which criminologists must be aware. In sum, five factors can affect the accuracy of NCVS data[22]:

1. **Respondents are not always reliable.** Because the NCVS asks respondents to recall events from a specific time period, forgetting and telescoping (moving a crime event from the past forward or pushing a victimization backward to be included) is a problem.[23]

2. **Respondents may not be truthful.** People may conceal victimization because of embarrassment or report crimes to please the interviewer. In addition, they may report trivial incidents as crime.

3. **The NCVS asks questions about rape in an indirect fashion.** Respondents are never asked whether they have been the victims of an attempted or completed rape. Rather, after the other crime victimizations are addressed, they are asked whether they have been attacked "in some other way."[24]

4. **Problems administering the survey or coding the data.** The accuracy of any survey depends on the way it is conducted. If the questions are unclear or if sample members are not reached, the validity of the results is compromised. If responses are not recorded accurately, the results will be imprecise.

5. **The survey does not contain specific information on particular areas.** There are breakdowns by

Police lead family members of workplace shooting victims away from the Con Agra plant in Kansas City, Kansas. The shooting left seven dead and three injured.

? *Does this shooting fit the pattern presented by other workplace violence shootings in the United States?*

geographic region, but the UCR remains the sole source of detailed regional crime information. In addition, the survey concentrates on large cities and may not adequately represent victimization patterns in other areas.

To some extent, these problems occur with any type of survey. In short, the truthfulness of the respondent and the skill of the survey researcher affect the quality of the data. Despite these weaknesses, the NCVS provides vital, detailed information about crime victimization — and because it collects information from victims, it can be used to direct crime prevention efforts.

TABLE 2-4 compares the UCR and the NCVS. Again, the important thing to remember is that both sources represent different aspects of crime.

Criminal Justice System Statistics

Another crime indicator is the size of the population being served by the different parts of the criminal justice system. These figures give long-term trends about how the system operates but this does not always mean that the results are clear indicators of the nature of crime. They are indicators of how the system operates and what type of enforcement has been a priority. For example, if the police

TABLE 2-4

Comparison of the UCR and NCVS

	UCR	NCVS
Basic Counting Unit	The Offense	The Victimization: "a specific criminal act that affects a single victim, whether a person or a household."
Offenses Measured	Murder Rape Robbery (personal and commercial) Assault (aggravated) Burglary (commercial and household) Larceny (commercial and household) Motor vehicle theft Arson	Rape Robbery (personal) Assault (aggravated and simple) Burglary (personal) Larceny (personal and household) Motor vehicle theft
Scope	Crimes reported to the police in most jurisdictions; considerable flexibility in developing small-area data.	Crimes reported and not reported to the police; all data are for the nation as a whole; some data are available for large geographic areas.
Collection Method	Police department reports to the FBI. The program is voluntary.	Survey interviews; periodically measures the total number of crimes committed by asking a national sample of 60,000 households representing 135,000 persons over the age of 12 about their experience as victims of crime during a specified period.
Kinds of Information	In addition to offense counts, provides information on crime clearances, persons arrested, persons charged, law enforcement officers killed and assaulted, and characteristics of victims.	Provides details about victims (such as age, race, sex, education, income, and relationship to perpetrator) and about crimes (such as time and place of occurrence, reported or unreported, use of weapons, occurrence of injury, and economic consequences).
Sponsor	Department of Justice, Federal Bureau of Investigation	Department of Justice Bureau, of Justice Statistics

Sources: Bureau of Justice Statistics, *Report of the Nation on Crime and Justice: The Data* (Washington, DC: U.S. Department of Justice, 1983): 6; Michael R. Rand and Callie M. Rennison, "True Crime Stories? Accounting for Differences in Our National Crime Indicators," *Chance* 15 (2002):48–49.

and courts decide to crack down or go after methamphetamine dealers, this crime will "increase" in the crime statistics and thus will be noted in the UCR. In addition, if rural whites are more likely to be arrested and convicted for this crime, these statistics would lead to the conclusion that they are more involved in this offense. However, one cannot be sure of that. Whites in rural areas may be more likely to be caught, while others are not apprehended, arrested, and convicted.

Therefore, criminal justice system statistics specifically reflect who is in the system. They do not necessarily demonstrate what is going on in society regarding a particular type of offense. They are production figures and reflect who is processed by the criminal justice system for various crimes. Like the NCVS, these reports are conducted and maintained by the Bureau of Justice Statistics.

Jail Population

An annual survey of the nation's jails is conducted each year. Jails are local facilities that primarily hold inmates sentenced to short terms (generally under 1 year), receive individuals pending arraignment, and hold persons awaiting trial, conviction, or sentencing as well as housing inmates for federal, state, or other authorities because of crowding to their facilities.[25] Jail population figures can help to determine how to manage jail space and avoid overcrowding. At midyear 2003, the following patterns were revealed in the analysis of the national jail population[26]:

- **Jail population size:**
  1. A total of 691,301 persons were housed in local jails. This figure represented an increase of 3.9% over the previous year.
  2. Since 1995, the national jail incarceration rate has risen from 193 to 238 inmates per 100,000 resident population.

- **Gender:** Male inmates made up 88% of the jail population. Yet, on average, the adult female jail population has grown 6.4% annually in the past 10 years, while the adult male inmate population has grown 3.9%.

- **Race:** Nearly 6 in 10 persons in local jails were racial or ethnic minorities. Blacks were five times more likely than whites, nearly three times more likely than Hispanics, and over nine times more likely than persons of other races to have been in jail. However, this does

Inmates at the Dade County, Florida, jail.

? *What do the official statistics say about the availability of jail and prison space in the Unites States?*

- **State versus federal prisons:** State prisons were estimated to be at 16% above capacity. Federal prisons are even more crowded — 39% above capacity.
- **Age:** The U.S. prison population is aging. Inmates between 40 and 54 accounted for more than 46% of the total growth in the inmate population since 1995.
- **Race and gender:**
  1. Blacks represent an estimated 44% of all inmates with sentences of more than 1 year; whites account for 35% and Hispanics 19%.
  2. Among black males age 25 to 29, 9.3% were in prison compared with 2.6% of Hispanic males and 1.1% of white males of the same age group.
  3. Black females (incarceration rate: 185 per 100,000) were more than twice as likely as Hispanic females (84 per 100,000) and nearly five times more likely than white females (38 per 100,000) to be in prison.

not mean that blacks and Hispanics are more likely to commit crimes. The figure represents the activities of law enforcement rather than who actually commits crime. Persons of other races may have committed the same crimes but simply were not apprehended.

- **Jail space:** At midyear 2003, 94% of all jail capacity was occupied.

Prison Population

Of course, jail figures represent only one aspect of the incarceration figures for the country. Prisoners held in federal and state adult correctional institutions are another part of the picture. In 2003, the following patterns were present in the prison inmate population[27]:

- **Prison population size:**
  1. The total number of prisoners held in state and federal institutions was 1,470,045 at year end 2003 — an increase of 2.1% over 2002.
  2. The incarceration rate was 482 sentenced inmates per 100,000 U.S. residents — up from 411 per 100,000 in 1995.
  3. One in every 140 U.S. residents was either in prison or jail at year end 2003.
- **Gender:** The number of female prisoners increased 3.6% while the number of male prisoners went up 2% in 2003.

Probation and Parole Figures

The final piece of the adult correctional system picture is probation and parole. Probation is an alternative sentence that is served in place of incarceration. Parole is a form of early conditional release from incarceration. If the conditions of probation or parole are violated, the offender can be sent to prison to complete the remainder of the sentence.

At year end 2003, the following patterns were present in the probation population[28]:

- **Size of the probation population:** The adult probation population was 4,073,987 in 2003 — an increase of 1.2% and less than half of the average annual growth of 2.9% since 1995. It appears that the use of probation is declining.
- **Type of offense:** Of these probationers, 49% had been convicted of a felony, 49% of a misdemeanor, and 2% of other violations. Twenty-five percent were on probation for a drug law violation and 17% for driving while intoxicated.
- **Sex and race:** One in five probationers was a woman; one in three were black.

The parole population in 2003 had the following attributes[29]:

- **Size of the parole population:** 774,588 persons were on parole in 2003 — an increase of 3.1%, which is almost double the average annual growth of 1.7% since 1995. Mandatory releases from prison as a result of a sentencing statute or good-time provision accounted for 51% of those entering parole in 2003. In 1995, they accounted for 45% of the parole population.

- **Gender:** Women accounted for one of every eight adults on parole in 2003 — a figure that has increased steadily since 1995.

- **Recidivism rates:**

  1. About two of every five parolees (40%) discharged from supervision returned to prison.

Forty-seven percent successfully met the conditions of parole — a success rate that has been fairly stable since 1995.

2. Of the parolees discharged in 2003, 38% had been returned to prison for either a rule violation or a new offense. Nine percent had absconded and 1% failed to successfully meet the conditions of parole but were discharged without incarceration.

Again, it must be emphasized that these figures represent who is processed by the system, not necessarily who commits crime or how much crime is present in society. However, they are important indicators of how the system handles the crime process. They demonstrate the volume of people present in the criminal justice system and for what crime. In summary, it is important management information that can inform the operation of the various parts of the criminal justice system.

Conclusion

The actual volume of crime is difficult to estimate. Not all crimes are reported to or uncovered by the police. The reporting behavior of victims is affected by several considerations. Similarly, the figures collected from criminal justice agencies are more accurate reflections of their own operations than of the true rate of crime in society. Nevertheless, the figures presented in this chapter collectively indicate the incidence of crime in recent years.

WRAP UP

Lying with Statistics—Police Style

As mentioned in the text, the recording practices of the police affect the figures in the Uniform Crime Report. The police control the data collection and reporting in the Uniform Crime Reporting system. How they classify the crime and count it affects the results. If police "cheating" on crime figures is widespread, the crime rates for the city are inaccurate. Thus, a false picture of crime safety (or a crime wave) is presented. If citizens feel safe when in fact they are not, they will fail to take the precautions necessary to prevent victimization. They will also be less wary of crime and be less apt to be on the lookout for crime and act as information sources for the police.

Chapter Spotlight

- Crime statistics are key indicators of societal health and provide information for the operation of the criminal justice system to prevent crime and victimization and provide justice. Therefore, the quality and accuracy of crime statistics are important.

- It is difficult to estimate the amount of crime committed in America. For various reasons, not all crimes get reported to the police: The victim may feel that nothing will be done about the crime, or they may be reluctant to call the police because the offender is someone they know and they fear retaliation. They may also be embarrassed by their victimization. Other crimes go unreported because they are victimless or hidden from public view.

- There are several sources of crime information:

- The Uniform Crime Reports, compiled and published by the Federal Bureau of Investigation, consists of crimes reported to the police. It is the primary source of information on national, state, and local crime rates.

- The National Crime Victimization Survey, conducted by the U.S. Bureau of Justice Statistics, surveys the public about their crime experiences whether they have reported the incident to the police or not. It also provides information about certain types of crime and special categories of victims.

- Several other sources of information exist that present the amount and number of persons processed by the criminal justice system, including jail and prison populations and probation and parole figures.

Putting It All Together

1. What is the level of crime in this country? How can this question be answered?

2. What do the crime figures tell about the level of crime in the United States? What conclusions can be drawn from this data?

3. What conclusions can be drawn from the NCVS results and the special topic reports?

4. Do the figures on the criminal justice system show that the United States is "soft on crime"?

5. Can the statistics cited in this chapter be used to make the case that crime is worse than ever?

6. Go on the World Wide Web and find current data from the UCR and the NCVS. Have crime patterns changed compared with those presented in this chapter? If so, how?

Key Terms

index offenses The most serious crimes in the Uniform Crime Report: murder, rape, assault, burglary, larceny-theft, motor vehicle theft, and arson.

National Crime Victimization Survey (NCVS) A survey conducted since 1972 by the U.S. Bureau of Justice Statistics that attempts to uncover unreported crime by seeking victims. The NCVS is a representative sample drawn of about 60,000 U.S. households that is renewed every year.

National Incident-Based Reporting System (NIBRS) A system designed to collect a greater number of details than the UCR about crimes reported to the police. The NIBRS will contain information on both reported crime and arrests. It will eventually replace the UCR as the official source of crime information from police departments as reported to the FBI.

NIBRS will contain information on 46 Group A offenses that represent 22 categories, rather than concentrate on the eight index offenses from the UCR. Unlike the UCR, NIBRS will:

- make a distinction between attempted and completed crimes
- provide more inclusive definitions of crime (i.e., the definition of rape has been expanded to include male victims)
- count all offenses that occur during an incident rather than concentrating on only the most serious crime

Uniform Crime Report (UCR) An annual report, published by the FBI since 1930, consisting of crimes reported to and uncovered by the police. Currently, the UCR is the major source of nationwide crime data, containing information from most U.S. jurisdictions.

Notes

1. President's Commission on Law Enforcement and the Administration of Justice, *Task Force Report: Crime and Its Impact — An Assessment* (Washington, DC: U.S. Department of Justice, 1967).

2. Morgan Quitno Awards, "12th Annual America's Safest (and Most Dangerous) Cities," available at http://www.morganquitno.com, accessed December 12, 2005.

3. Amy E. Schwartz, Scott Susin, and Ioan Voicu, "Has Falling Crime Driven New York City's Real Estate Boom?" *Journal of Housing Research* 14 (2003): 101–136.

4. Allen K. Lynch and David W. Rasmussen, "Measuring the Impact of Crime on House Prices," *Applied Economics* 33 (2001): 1981–1989.

5. David B. Nickerson and Robert M.Feinberg, "The Impact of Crime Rates on Residential Mortgage Default." May 4, 1998, available at http://ssrn.com/abstract=141593, accessed December 5, 2005.

6. Michael R. Rand and Callie M. Rennison, "True Crime Stories? Accounting for Differences in Our National Crime Indicators," *Chance* 15 (2002): 47.

7. Ibid., 48.

8. Ibid.

9. John E. Conklin, *Why Crime Rates Fell* (Boston: Allyn and Bacon, 2003); Alfred Blumstein and Joel Wallman, eds., *The Crime Drop in America* (Cambridge, UK: Cambridge University Press, 2000).

10. Gennaro F. Vito, Edward J. Latessa, and Deborah G. Wilson, *Introduction to Criminal Justice Research Methods* (Springfield, IL: Charles C. Thomas, 1988).

11. Brian A. Reaves, *Using NIBRS Data to Analyze Violent Crime* (Washington, DC: Bureau of Justice Statistics, 1993): 1–2.

12. James A. Fox and Marianne W. Zawitz, *Homicide Trends in the United States: 2002 Update* (Washington, DC: Bureau of Justice Statistics, 2004): 2–3. See also *Homicide Trends in the United States,* available at http://www.ojp.usdoj.gov/bjs/homicide/homtrnd.htm.

13. Scott H. Decker, "Official Crime Rates and Victim Surveys: An Empirical Comparison," *Journal of Criminal Justice* 5 (1977): 47–54; John E. Eck and Lucius J. Riccio, "Relationship Between Reported Crime Rates and Victimization Survey Results," *Journal of Criminal Justice* 7 (1979): 293–308; Michael J. Hindelang, "The Uniform Crime Reports Revisited," *Journal of Criminal Justice* 2 (1974): 1–17;

Anne L. Schneider, "Differences Between Survey and Police Information About Crime," in Robert G. Lehnen and Wesley G. Skogan, eds., *The National Crime Survey: Working Papers, Volume I* (Washington, DC: U.S. Government Printing Office, 1981).

14. Rand and Rennison, 48.
15. Shannan M. Catalano, *Criminal Victimization, 2003* (Washington, DC: Bureau of Justice Statistics, 2004): 9–10.
16. Callie Marie Rennison, *Intimate Partner Violence, 1993–2001* (Washington, DC: Bureau of Justice Statistics, 2003): 1–2.

17. Timothy C. Hart, *Violent Victimization of College Students* (Washington, DC: Bureau of Justice Statistics, 2003).
18. Bonnie S. Fisher, John J. Sloan, and Francis T. Cullen, et al., "Crime in the Ivory Tower: The Level and Sources of Student Victimization," *Criminology* 36 (1998): 671–710.
19. Jill F. DeVoe, Katharin Peter, Phillip Kaufman, Amanda Miller, Margaret Noonan, Thomas D. Snyder, and Katrina Baum, *Indicators of School Crime and Safety: 2004* (Washington, DC: National Center for Education Statistics and Bureau of Justice Statistics, 2004): iv.
20. Detis T. Duhart, *Violence in the Workplace, 1993–99.* (Washington, DC: Bureau of Justice Statistics, 2001).

21. Bonnie S. Fisher and Elaine Gunnison, "Violence in the Workplace: Gender Similarities and Differences," *Journal of Criminal Justice* 29 (2001): 145–155.

22. Joseph P. Levine, "The Potential for Crime Overreporting in Criminal Victimization Surveys," *Criminology* 14 (1974): 307–330.

23. Anne L. Schneider and David Sumi, "Patterns of Forgetting and Telescoping: An Analysis of LEAA Survey Victimization Data," *Criminology* 19 (1981): 400–410.

24. Helen M. Eigenberg, "The National Crime Survey and Rape: The Case of the Missing Question," *Justice Quarterly* 7 (1990): 657.

25. Paige M. Harrison and Jennifer C. Karberg, *Prison and Jail Inmates at Midyear 2003* (Washington, DC: Bureau of Justice Statistics, 2004): 7.

26. Ibid., 7–11.

27. Paige M. Harrison and Allen J. Beck, *Prisoners in 2003* (Washington, DC: Bureau of Justice Statistics, 2004).

28. Lauren E. Giaze and Seri Palla, *Probation and Parole in the United States, 2003* (Washington, DC: Bureau of Justice Statistics, 2004).

29. Ibid.

WWW.CRIMINOLOGY.JBPUB.COM

Interactivities
In the News
Key Term Explorer
Web Links

CHAPTER
3

OBJECTIVES

Understand the social context of neoclassical theories and their rise to prominence in America during the 1970s.

Grasp the central concepts in deterrence theory, including specific, general, and marginal deterrence.

Understand what the various empirical tests indicate about the empirical status of deterrence theory.

Know the central concepts in the routine activity and lifestyle approaches to criminal behavior.

Understand rational choice theory and its relation to deterrence.

Understand the policy implications of rational choice theory, including criminal justice policies and situational crime prevention.

Neoclassical Criminology

> If you want to know why crime proliferates in this nation, don't look at statistics on income and wealth; look at statistics on arrests, prosecutions, convictions, and prison populations . . . The primary problem is in a criminal justice system that seems to have lost much of its capacity to determine the truth, prosecute and punish the guilty, and protect society.
>
> —Ronald Reagan, 1975[1]

> Crime has tripled in two decades because crime pays. It is the nation's growth industry because it is an exciting, enjoyable profession where the criminal element runs little risk of being forced to pay an unacceptable price. In a decade, tens of thousands of men, women, and children have been murdered. In retaliation, our defender, the state, has executed exactly one killer.
>
> —Pat Buchanan, 1977[2]

Can Drunk Driving Be Deterred?

It was the middle of the summer: July 25, 2003. Melanie, 13, had a birthday party to go to after spending the previous night at a friend's house. Later, walking to the beach with friends, Melanie was hit by a car and died of her injuries. It was the second drunken driving arrest for the driver, Pamela Murphy, age 49.

James Broadbent Jr. and his fiancée, Lisa Squillacioti, loved to do volunteer work. They were also looking forward to getting married and raising children. As they drove home from a charity golf tournament in September 2001, they were killed by a drunk driver. Police reported that Russell Curran, the driver, had been drinking for hours that night. Curran pleaded guilty, and he was sentenced to three to four years in prison.

As these stories illustrate, drunk driving can have tragic results. Can these tragedies be averted by increasing legal penalties? Mothers Against Drunk Driving (MADD) and legislators across the country make this argument. MADD was established by a group of women in California outraged after the death of a teenage girl killed by a repeat-offender drunk driver. Since 1980, MADD has pressured government officials to increase penalties for driving under the influence. MADD's lobbying has resulted in the passage of thousands of federal and state anti–drunk driving laws.

A police officer administers a sobriety test to a driver.

? *If this person is arrested, what impact will it have on his future behavior?*

On May 27, 2005, Governor Mitt Romney of Massachusetts filed legislation he dubbed "Melanie's Bill," a new proposal that cracks down on repeat drunk driving offenders. Romney said the legislation is necessary to preserve federal funding and protect the lives and safety of Massachusetts citizens. The bill increases penalties for drunk driving–related offenses, particularly with regard to individuals who repeatedly drink and drive.

Will increasing penalties for drunk driving reduce this behavior?

Do individuals considering driving after having consumed alcohol think about the consequences (including legal sanctions) of their actions?

What effect does increasing punishment have on other kinds of criminal offenses?

Sources: Janice Lord, "Really MADD: Looking Back at 20 Years," available at http://www.madd.org/aboutus/0,1056,1686,00.html, accessed July 9, 2005; *The Patriot Ledger*, "Victim Profiles. Lives Lost: Some Victims of Drunken Driving Accidents on the South Shore," available at http://www.southofboston.net/specialreports/drunkendriving/2c.shtml, accessed July 2, 2005; Massachusetts Registry of Motor Vehicles, "Legislation Stiffens Penalties for Repeat Offenders, Preserves Federal Funding," May 27, 2005, available at http://www.mass.gov/rmv/rmvnews/2005/melanie.htm, accessed July 9, 2005.

Introduction

The quotations on the previous page illustrate the fact that, toward the latter part of the 1970s, politicians, commentators, and scholars started to revive classical school ideas. As rehabilitation came under attack as the dominant goal of corrections, so too did the sociological and psychological theories of crime that supported this model. Throughout the 1980s and 1990s, the federal government and individual states passed legislation (e.g., mandatory minimum sentences, longer prison terms, "three strikes" laws) designed to deter people from criminal behavior by increasing punishment. One result of this effort has been a massive increase in the number of prisoners held in jails and prisons — but — have these laws and prison expansions reduced crime? Do stricter legal penalties deter offenders from engaging in future crimes? Does capital punishment deter homicide?

As the name suggests, neoclassical theory builds on the work of classical school theorists. The emphasis is therefore often on the role of the criminal justice system in preventing crime. In this chapter, two complementary theories that place emphasis on punishment are discussed: Deterrence theory suggests that swift, certain, and severe punishment reduces crime, while the rational choice perspective holds that human beings calculate both the costs and benefits of criminal behavior before they decide whether to engage in crime. Additionally, routine activities theory is discussed in this chapter because it also assumes that criminals behave in a rational manner. Before getting to the individual theories, it is important to consider how and why neoclassical theory emerged.

The Rise of Neoclassical Theory

As noted in Chapter 1, the popularity of the classical school of crime diminished toward the end of the 1800s, and the positive school gained popularity. Throughout most of the 1900s then, sociological, biological, and psychological theories of crime dominated the landscape. Because positive theories identify potential causes of criminal behavior (e.g., poverty, personality, delinquent peers), they naturally fit with the corrections goal of rehabilitation. In essence, such theories provide the "targets" of rehabilitation efforts. During the early 1970s, however, the corrections goal of rehabilitation was attacked and labeled as a failure by both liberal and conservative commentators.[3] When rehabilitation faltered as a goal of corrections, many scholars called for a return to the use of prisons to punish and deter, rather than rehabilitate, offenders. These commentators recommended punishments such as lengthy prison terms, corporal punishment,[4] and the death penalty.[5]

The so-called "get-tough" movement also included calls to make prison itself more painful. Indeed, some jurisdictions reinstituted "chain gang

Sheriff Joe Arpaio, the self-proclaimed "toughest sheriff in the country."

Do pink underwear, chain gangs, and camera-equipped dogs make the jail experience so miserable that inmates will refrain from future criminal behavior?

crews" and old-time striped uniforms. Perhaps nobody has taken this trend further than Sheriff Joe Arpaio of Maricopa County, Arizona. Arpaio has cultivated a reputation as the "toughest sheriff in the country" through his management of the county jail. Some of the sheriff's policies are[6]:

- Inmates are issued pink underwear and striped uniforms.
- Cigarettes and coffee are prohibited.
- Inmates are housed in tents outside of the jail (the jail is located in a desert).
- Inmates are allowed no recreation.
- Television is generally limited — those allowed to watch television can choose from CSPAN, the Disney channel, and cooking shows.
- Inmates in chain gangs pick up garbage on city streets.

- Camera-equipped dogs roam the jail.
- Inmates are served only two cold meals per day (at a total cost of 62 cents per day per inmate).

The "get-tough movement" brought together several different perspectives that emphasized the importance of punishment, including retribution, just deserts, incapacitation, and deterrence. The concept of <u>just deserts</u> suggests that punishment rightfully reflects the pain caused and thus earned by the criminal. Punishment also serves as a collective expression of society's disapproval for criminal acts.[7] The goal of punishment, then, is sentences that are commensurate with the seriousness of the crime, the extent to which it adversely affects society, and the culpability of the offender. Moreover, persons who commit the same type of crime should receive the same sentence.

<u>Retribution</u> is similar to just deserts and implies that criminals deserve to be punished because they have violated a legal system from which everyone benefits.[8] They have taken unfair advantage of the law-abiding citizens in society. Punishing offenders restores the social balance and reaffirms social bonds — it sends a message that crime will not be tolerated. According to Earnest van den Haag, "Retribution must be paid because it is owed, because it has been threatened, and a threat is a (negative) promise."[9]

The idea of <u>incapacitation</u> is simple — someone who is incapacitated (through death, prison, or some other method) can no longer commit crimes against the public. Thus, the goal of incapacitation is to prevent crime by locking up criminal offenders. Like retribution and just deserts, incapacitation is a theory of punishment that does not rest on any particular theory of crime. Unlike them, however, incapacitation is designed to reduce future criminal behavior. A substantial body of literature addresses whether and how incapacitation affects crime. See the **Theory in Action: Lock 'em Up — Incapacitation as Goal of Corrections** for more information.

In addition to retribution, incapacitation, and just deserts, some scholars emphasize the deterrent value of punishment; that is, punishment has the potential to reduce criminal behavior by sending a message to both the offender and society that crime "doesn't pay." It is this link that clearly ties the get-tough movement with the classical school. In this case, a deterrence theory of punishment rests on an explicit theory of criminal behavior.

Deterrence Theory

Drawing on the work of classical school theorists such as Beccaria and Bentham, deterrence theorists portray humans as rational, pleasure-seeking, pain-avoiding creatures. This assumption leads to a relatively simple theory of crime: People will engage in criminal behavior when it brings them pleasure (generates rewards) and carries little risk of pain.

LINK In Chapter 1, we discussed the emergence of the classical school. Leaders in this school were legal reformers — they argued that penalties that were proportionate to the offense would deter potential offenders.

Consequently, formal punishment has the potential to reduce crime in two ways. One objective of punishment is to send "a message addressed to the public at large. The punishment of an offender deters others by telling them: 'This will happen to you if you violate the law.'"[10] In other words, punishing offenders broadcasts to society that there is a substantial amount of "pain" associated with criminal behavior. The idea that punishing offenders will deter the rest of society is termed <u>general deterrence</u>. Of course, punishing offenders might also have an effect on the offenders themselves; that is, offenders who feel the pain of punishment should be less likely to reoffend in the future. This is the principle of <u>specific deterrence</u>. A summary of the elements of deterrence theory is provided in **TABLE 3-1**.

Deterrence theorists, again drawing from the classical school, point out that punishment is most effective when it is swift, certain, and severe enough to outweigh the potential rewards of criminal behavior. In essence, neoclassical theorists restated and refined classical school statements about deterrence, rather than making any major changes. The main contribution of deterrence theorists was to generate empirical tests of deterrence theory.

Empirical Tests of Deterrence Theory

The basis of deterrence theory — that formal punishment reduces criminal behavior — is very straightforward. Testing deterrence theory, however, is more complex. Researchers have studied both specific and general deterrence. Further, they have tried to gauge the relative importance of the certainty and severity of punishment (very few look at swiftness). To help organize this research, the different tests of both general and specific deterrence

TABLE 3-1
Key Elements of Deterrence Theory
Assumptions: Deterrence theory assumes that humans are rational and hedonistic.
Levels of Deterrence: Deterrence can take place on two levels that differ in the purpose of the punishment. Specific deterrence focuses on the individual offender. It seeks to teach criminals a lesson, so that they will learn from experience and "go straight" in the future. General deterrence is concerned with society as a whole. Here, individual punishment is aimed at sending a message to everyone — the punishment demonstrates what will happen to them if they violate the law.
Effective Punishment: Deterrence theorists argue that effective punishment is swift, certain, and severe. Deterrence may also be **conditional**; that is, legal threats deter only persons who have a stake in conformity and are tied to conventional society in such a way that they will suffer from the stigma of punishment. Finally, deterrence may be **marginal**, which refers to the inhibiting effect of one punishment as compared with another.

police and prisons would have no effect on crime. Marginal deterrence addresses whether incremental (marginal) increases in punishment produce decreases in crime. For example, does doubling the prison sentence for robbery lead to reductions in that particular crime? Almost all empirical tests of deterrence theory test marginal deterrence rather than absolute deterrence.

General Deterrence

General deterrence is the proposition that increases in the certainty, severity, or swiftness of punishment produce decreases in criminal behavior for the population at large. Most researchers test either the certainty or severity of punishment. The severity of punishment is relatively easy to measure. One could look, for example, at the average prison sentence for crimes in different jurisdictions. Studies on capital punishment (the ultimate in severity), though, are by far the most common tests of this aspect of deterrence theory.[11] Obviously those who are executed will never commit another crime (this is incapacitation rather than deterrence). The issue is whether the death penalty serves as a general deterrent against homicide. Concerning the

discussed are outlined in **TABLE 3-2**. Prior to discussing this research, it is important to distinguish between absolute and **marginal deterrence**. Absolute deterrence is the notion that having a formal system of punishments deters criminal behavior. Indeed, few would argue that a complete absence of

TABLE 3-2	
Empirical Tests of Deterrence Theory	
Specific Measures/Tests	**Findings**
General Deterrence	
Death penalty research (Severity)	Most studies find that the death penalty has no effect on homicide rates. A small minority of studies find a brutalization effect, a deterrent effect, or both.
Clearance rate studies (Certainty)	Most studies find that the clearance rate has no effect on crime. A minority of studies find that a deterrent effect emerges when the clearance rate reaches a certain tipping point. Even here, the effect is limited to small cities.
Police experiments	The Kansas City Preventative Patrol experiment found that doubling police patrols had no effect on crime. Later experiments using directed patrols, saturation patrols, and zero-tolerance policing produced reductions in crime. These deterrent effects tend to be short lived.
Perceptions research (Certainty and Severity)	Those who believe that the punishment for crime is severe and that their likelihood of apprehension is high are less likely to engage in crime. However, this is mostly because offenders, over time, lower their estimates of severity and certainty (the experiential effect).
Specific Deterrence	
Police arrest experiments	An initial experiment found that arresting domestic violence perpetrators reduced later calls for service more than other options (e.g., warning, separating). Later studies suggest that this finding applies only to those who have conventional ties to society (e.g., employment).
Comparison of probation versus intensive programs	Intermediate sanctions (e.g., intensive probation, shock probation, boot camps) do not appear to reduce recidivism more than regular probation.
Scared Straight	Numerous experiments indicate that scared straight programs have no positive effect on criminal behavior. The weight of the evidence suggests that they actually increase crime.

Lock 'em Up — Incapacitation as Goal of Corrections

The basic premise of incapacitation, that "A thug in prison cannot mug your sister," is simple to grasp. When offenders are in prison, they no longer have the opportunity to engage in crime. If society locks up enough offenders, crime should decline. Scholars identify two types of incapacitation. *Collective incapacitation* refers to the reduction in crime achieved through a change in sentencing (e.g., mandatory minimum sentences) that affects a large proportion of offenders. *Selective incapacitation* attempts to control crime by sentencing individual offenders. Here, offenders who are thought to pose the greatest risk of future crime receive longer sentences. This policy provides for the identification and removal of chronic offenders from society so that crime can be controlled.

Incapacitation came to be a primary goal of corrections (especially prisons) in the 1980s largely by default. Rehabilitation was attacked as a failure, and evidence emerged that neither specific nor general deterrence was likely to have a great impact on crime. During this period, scholars began to argue that incapacitation, if done ruthlessly, could have a substantial impact. The promise of selective incapacitation, in particular, was seductive. James Q. Wilson argued that, if much serious crime is committed by repeaters, isolating these repeaters from society would produce major reductions in crime rates. In other words, long-term incarceration of the career criminal will lower the crime rate because a small, hard-core group of chronic offenders is responsible for a vastly disproportionate share of serious crimes.

In the past 25 years, the United States has in many ways conducted an experiment in incapacitation. According to the U. S. Department of Justice, the number of individuals in secure confinement has increased from under 200,000 in 1980 to over 2 million in 2003. During that same time, the incarceration rate increased from roughly 150 prisoners per 100,000 citizens to almost 500 prisoners per 100,000 citizens. The rate of secure confinement (which includes jail populations) was 718 per 100,000 people at the end of 2003. What has been the effect of such massive increases in the use of prison and jail? Has incapacitation worked?

Evaluations of Incapacitation

Critics of incapacitation often point out that throughout the 1980s and early 1990s, when many states were dramatically increasing their prison populations, crime rates continued to rise. Incapacitation supporters contend that crime rates would have risen even higher without the increased use of prisons, and they point to the recent decline in crime as evidence that incapacitation works. Researchers have tackled this issue in a number of ways, including:

- Surveying inmates as they enter prison to assess how much crime they committed in the past year. This is then used as an estimate of how many crimes they would commit in the future if they were not incarcerated.
- Comparing states that dramatically increased their prison population with states that did not during the same time period.
- Using statistical models to estimate "crime saved" through incapacitation in a single state.
- Studying the crime committed by offenders who were released from prison early due to court-imposed prison population caps.
- Studying offenders who were sentenced to death, but had their sentence commuted, and were eventually released.

Although different studies reach somewhat different estimates of the incapacitation effect, a common theme runs through the research — large increases in prison population produce moderate decreases in some forms of criminal activity. For example, a study by researchers Thomas Marvell and Carlisle Moody Jr. sought to assess the impact of state increases in prison population in the 1970s and 1980s on serious crimes. The researchers found that the increases had little or no impact on the crimes of rape, murder, or assault. There were moderate effects, however, for robbery, larceny, and burglary. Adding roughly 300,000 inmates over the course of the 1980s, for example, decreased robbery by about 18%.

Frank Zimring and his associates examined the effects of California's huge prison increase in the 1980s. They first estimated what the crime rate would have been without any prison increase and then compared these figures with the actual crime rate to get an estimate of the incapacitation effect. They found that each "person year" (incarcerating one person for a year) of prison prevented roughly 3.5 crimes per year. Virtually all (93%) of the reduction, however, was due to reductions in burglaries and larcenies.

The general finding then is that huge increases in the use of prison produced moderate reductions in offenses such as robbery, larceny, and burglary, but had little impact on assault, homicide, or rape. This finding makes sense because the former crimes tend to be high-rate offenses, while the latter do not. A single person might commit many burglaries or robberies over the course of a year. A crime like homicide, however, is extraordinarily rare — very few individuals ever commit more than one in their lifetime.

For example, several recent studies have traced the recidivism rates of former death-row inmates who had their sentences commuted because of the 1972 *Furman v. Georgia* ruling. Because many of these offenders were eventually paroled, these studies test the argument that the death penalty, through incapacitation, prevents future murders. A study that followed the entire cohort (558 inmates, of whom 233 were paroled) learned that only one committed murder following release from prison.

Criticisms of Incapacitation

Although this evidence offers some support for incapacitation, the massive increase in prison rates in the United States did not produce the type of reductions anticipated by supporters of this theory. Several factors may impede the incapacitation effect:

- By the time some offenders are incarcerated for a lengthy period, they may already be aging out of criminal activity.

- Selective incapacitation has proved elusive, because one cannot predict who will be a "chronic offender" with the necessary accuracy.

- Locking up drug offenders, because they are readily replaced in society, yields no reduction in drug crime.

Further, even those who support incapacitation recognize that further increases in imprisonment will generate even smaller reductions in crime. As states lock up a greater proportion of offenders, the remaining pool of offenders is inevitably a less serious and chronic group. Thus, while doubling the prison population might initially produce a 15% to 20% reduction in some crimes, doubling it again will not have the same effect. For this reason, even John DiIulio, a noted and vocal supporter of incapacitation, argued recently that the country has "maxed out" on the benefits of prison.

Elliot Currie points out an even greater flaw in the incapacitation literature: The question, "Does incapacitation work?" is not a very good question. The better question is "How well does incapacitation work compared with other strategies?" Reframing this issue recognizes that building and maintaining prisons generates huge costs. Could the money spent on prisons have created more crime reduction if spent elsewhere? A 1996 cost-benefit analysis suggests that is the case. The researchers compared early prevention programs with an incapacitation program (California's three-strikes law) and found that prevention generated similar crime reductions at a fraction of the cost. Those who support prevention and early intervention programs point out that while a thug in prison can't shoot your sister, he *already* shot somebody's sister to wind up in prison.

Over the past decade, support for the strategy of incapacitation has waned, but not because of scientific evidence or ideological arguments. Instead, the enormous cost of this strategy has caught up with many states. Indeed, corrections costs are the fastest growing items in many state budgets. With recent budget shortfalls, some states have closed prisons, delayed the opening of new prisons, and/or reduced sentences for some criminal acts. It may be fiscal limitations, rather than scientific evidence, that end the great incapacitation experiment.

Sources: Cristy A. Visher, "Incapacitation and Crime Control: Does A 'Lock 'Em Up' Strategy Reduce Crime?" *Justice Quarterly* 3 (1987): 513–533; Peter W. Greenwood, *Selective Incapacitation* (Santa Monica, CA: Rand Corporation, 1982); James Q. Wilson, *Thinking About Crime* (New York: Random House, 1975); Paige M. Harrison and Allen Beck, "Prisoners in 2003," *Bureau of Justice Statistics Bulletin* (Washington, D.C.: U.S. Department of Justice, 2004); Anne Morrison Piehl and John J. DiIulio Jr., "Does Prison Pay? Revisited," *Brookings Review* 13 (1995): 20–25; Steven D. Levitt, "The Effect of Prison Population Size on Crime Rates: Evidence from Prison Overcrowding Litigation," *Quarterly Journal of Economics* 3 (1996): 319–351; James W. Marquart and Jonathan R. Sorensen, "Institutional and Postrelease Behavior of Furman-Commuted Inmates in Texas," *Criminology* 26 (1988): 677–693; James W. Marquart and Jonathan R. Sorensen, "A

National Study of the Furman-Commuted Inmates," *Loyola of Los Angeles Law Review* 23 (1989): 5–28; Thomas B. Marvell and Carlisle E. Moody Jr., "Prison Population Growth and Crime Reduction," *Journal of Quantitative Criminology* 10 (1993): 109–130; John J. DiIulio Jr., "Two Million Prisoners Are Enough," *The Wall Street Journal* (March 12, 1999). A-14; Elliott Currie, Crime and Punishment in America: Why the Solutions to America's Most Stubborn Social Crisis Have Not Worked and What Will (New York: Henry Holt, 1998): 65; Peter W. Greenwood, C. Rydell, and J. Chiesa, Diverting Children from a Life of Crime: Measuring Costs and Benefits (Santa Monica, CA: RAND, 1996); Fox Butterfield, "Tight Budgets Force States to Reconsider Crime and Penalties," *New York Times* (January 22, 2002): A1.

death penalty, the most common research strategies focus on a comparison of homicide rates (1) between states that have the death penalty and those that do not and (2) before and after executions within the same jurisdiction.

Among the studies of the first type, the vast majority of studies find that there is little difference in homicides between states that have or do not have the death penalty.[12] One study used a matching technique to compare the murder rates of death penalty states with nondeath-penalty states for the years 1920–1955 and 1920–1962.[13] The research discovered no difference between the two — executions appeared to have had no effect on homicide rates.

Many of the studies looking at the same jurisdiction over time also fail to find a relationship between executions and homicide rates. These studies take advantage of the moratorium on capital punishment that resulted from the 1972 Supreme Court *Furman v. Georgia* ruling. This decision stated that the capital sentencing system was arbitrary and discriminatory and that it violated the defendant's right to due process of law. McFarland examined the pattern of homicide rates in the United States following the first four executions after the death penalty was reinstated in 1976.[14] He failed to find significant evidence, nationally or locally, of a deterrent effect for executions. This study also found that executions and the amount of television coverage given to them did not affect the number of felony homicides committed in the United States between 1976 and 1987.[15]

A small minority of studies do find that capital punishment has an effect on homicide rates. These findings, however, cut both ways. Some research documents a deterrent effect, while other studies find an increase in homicide. One study examined the national data on the relationship between the homicide rate and executions for 1943–1969.[16] In particular, the study examined the "execution risk": the ratio of the number of executions to the number of homicides. The central hypothesis was that higher execution rates would produce lower homicide rates. The study found that a 1% increase in the execution rate accounted for 6% decrease in the homicide rate. Although the methodology and results of this study have been severely criticized,[17] it is still cited by supporters of capital punishment.

Two pieces of research examined the results of Oklahoma's 1990 return to the use of capital punishment after a 25-year moratorium.[18] In each study, using different methodologies, weekly homicide figures were tracked for 1 year before and after the execution. Little or no evidence of deterrence emerged from these studies. Both studies, however, found that certain types of homicides actually increased following the execution — a **brutalization effect**. Scholars suggest that the state's execution legitimizes the use of violence, demonstrating that it is appropriate to kill people who have gravely offended.[19]

An analysis of California's resumption of executions (again, after a lengthy moratorium) revealed a more complex pattern.[20] The authors categorized homicides as stranger/nonstranger and felony/nonfelony. Felony murders occur when an offender commits homicide to further another felony (e.g., an armed robbery that results in homicide). Because the underlying felony is rationally planned, the offenders might be deterred by the existence of the death penalty. The analysis revealed a small but significant deterrent effect for felony murder, but only when it involved nonstrangers. This effect, however, was overshadowed by a much larger brutalization effect for homicides resulting from arguments among strangers.

In sum, most studies of the death penalty find that they have no effect on homicides. The small minority of studies that document a relationship between the death penalty and homicide find a mix of brutalization and deterrent effects. Research on the deterrent effect of nonlethal penalties (e.g., length of prison terms) is no more encouraging to deterrence advocates. Again the most common

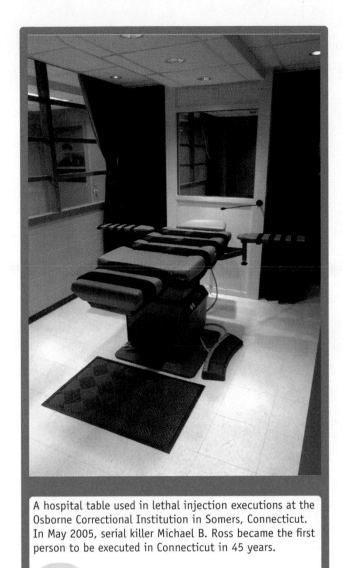

A hospital table used in lethal injection executions at the Osborne Correctional Institution in Somers, Connecticut. In May 2005, serial killer Michael B. Ross became the first person to be executed in Connecticut in 45 years.

? *According to available research, what happens to homicide rates when states return to the death penalty after such a moratorium?*

finding for these studies is that the length of prison terms has no effect on crime rates.[21]

Evidence regarding the deterrent effect of the certainty of punishment is perhaps a bit more promising. Clearance rate, the proportion of total crimes cleared by arrest, is a common measure of certainty. A high clearance rate means that offenders' odds of getting caught are also high. Deterrence theory predicts that crime should be lower when the clearance rate is high. Like death penalty studies, researchers compare different jurisdictions to see whether clearance rates predict arrest rates. Although some early studies found that high clearance rates were associated with lower crime rates, recent studies (using better methodology) have failed to replicate these findings. Again, the most

common finding among these studies is that clearance rates are not related to crime rates.[22]

A couple of studies, however, appear to have identified an exception to the general finding that clearance rates do not predict crime. A study of Florida cities discovered that when the clearance rates reached a certain "tipping point" (roughly 30%), a modest deterrent effect emerged.[23] A later study of Pennsylvania cities documented the same pattern, but with a higher (about 40%) tipping point.[24] In both studies, however, the deterrent effect was limited to small cities. Unfortunately, small cities with high clearance rates are rare — this limits the importance of the tipping point finding.

Researchers have also tested whether the certainty of punishment reduces crime by experimentally manipulating policing practices. Evidence that increased police presence (which increases the certainty of detection) reduces crime would support deterrence theory. The most famous study in this realm is the **Kansas City Preventative Patrol Study**. In this experiment, conducted in the early 1970s, police beats were randomly assigned to one of three conditions.[25] In the reactive beats, police only entered the area to respond to calls for service. In the second group, police doubled or tripled the normal level of patrol. The final group of beats was patrolled as usual. The researchers discovered that neither increasing nor reducing police presence had any effect on the crime rate. Some have criticized the study, however, primarily because police cars left the normal or preventative beats to answer calls for service in the other beat.[26]

The effect of certainty is more apparent in studies of directed or saturation patrols. This research suggests that increasing police presence in high crime areas can lower crime. Cities tend to have a few hot spots of criminal activity, which generate most of the calls for police service. Directed patrols focus police attention toward these areas, during times when criminal activity is highest (typically at night). For example, in an experiment in Minneapolis, patrol was doubled for 55 hot spots by taking patrols away from low crime areas. Normal patrol levels were continued in an additional 55 hot spots. Analyses of crime-related calls for police service revealed that the additional patrols produced a moderate reduction in crime.[27]

Saturation patrols, as well as zero-tolerance policing, and other forms of police crackdowns raise police presence further. Typically, police target certain offenses (drunk driving, drug dealing)

Headline Crime

The Amadou Diallo Shooting — An Unintended Consequence of Aggressive Policing?

In February 1999, four plainclothes New York City police officers searching for a rape suspect confronted Amadou Diallo. The officers thought Diallo was acting suspiciously because he kept looking up and down the block. The officers claimed that they identified themselves, but Diallo did not heed their repeated commands to halt, and instead entered the vestibule, opening the door to his building. At that point, Diallo turned around while reaching into his pocket. The officers believed that Diallo was reaching for a gun and shot at him 41 times, hitting him with 19 bullets. The object Diallo was reaching for turned out to be his wallet. The officers involved in the shooting were subsequently charged with (among other counts) second-degree murder. On February 25, 2000, a jury acquitted all four officers of all charges.

Some commentators believe that the Diallo tragedy was the unintended consequence of aggressive policing. New York City has enjoyed a dramatic drop in violent crime, and many attribute this decline in crime to the police department's emphasis on order maintenance and zero-tolerance policing. Here, police target minor crimes, such as graffiti and subway turnstile jumping, as a way to demonstrate control of the streets, to apprehend individuals who may have outstanding arrest warrants, and to seize illegal firearms. Certain high-crime neighborhoods (such as Diallo's) are targeted for specialized squads of police, who use aggressive policing tactics (e.g., stop and question, stop and search) to ferret out crime.

Supporters of this tactic point to evidence that aggressive police tactics can indeed reduce crime. Critics, however, point out that many cities that have a different model of policing (e.g., "community policing" rather than zero-tolerance policing) also enjoyed a healthy crime drop in the 1990s. They also worry that such tactics can alienate police officers from the citizens they are serving and lead to tragedies such as the Diallo shooting.

Demonstrators hold signs protesting the shooting of Amadou Diallo in New York City. Diallo, an immigrant from West Africa, was shot 19 times by New York City police officers.

Does aggressive policing make such tragedies more likely?

Do you think that the Diallo shooting was a consequence of New York City's zero-tolerance policing model?

If zero-tolerance policing is an effective deterrent to crime, what could be done to reduce the unintended consequences of these policies?

Sources: Humans Rights Watch, "*A Look at Aggressive Policing and Civil Rights Abuses,*" available at http://www.hrw.org/reports98/police/uspo99.htm, accessed July 10, 2005; Felice F. Guerrieri, "Law and Order: Redefining the Relationship Between Prosecutors and Police," *Southern Illinois University Law Journal* 25 (2001): 353–387; Fred Mazelis, "Inequality and Police Brutality in New York City: The Social Underpinnings of the Murder of Amadou Diallo," *World Socialist* March 12, 1999, available at http://www.wsws.org/articles/1999/mar1999/dial-m12.shtml, accessed July 10, 2005.

in certain geographical areas, and saturate these areas with police. The idea of zero-tolerance policing is that in addition to simply patrolling, police aggressively pursue even small infractions (e.g., loitering, panhandling, traffic violations). Policing crackdowns have had some success in lowering certain offenses (drunk driving, robbery), but appear to be less effective for drug-related crimes. Further, the deterrent effect of such crackdowns tends to be short-lived and may sometimes shift crime to neighboring areas. Zero-tolerance policing, targeted traffic enforcement, and other aggressive policing strategies might also produce some negative consequences. In particular, massive increases in arrests for minor (traffic, loitering, etc.) offenses may alienate residents, lower police legitimacy, and cause other long-term problems. Many commentators point, for example, to the New York City police shooting of Amadou Diallo as the result of aggressive police tactics. The Diallo shooting is discussed in more detail in the **Headline Crime** box.

In addition to looking at objective official measures (e.g., death penalty, clearance rate) and conducting experiments in policing, investigators also use survey research. These researchers raise the issue of whether the average citizen (or criminal) can identify with any accuracy the clearance rate or specific punishment for a particular crime. In that sense, peoples' *perceptions* about the severity and certainty of punishment are more important than the actual levels. People are asked survey questions such as, "If you committed auto theft on 10 different days, on how many of those days do you think you would be caught?" Similarly, to gauge estimates of severity, one might ask a question such as, "What punishment do you think you would receive if you got caught stealing an automobile?"

These "perceptual" measures of deterrence yield findings that are fairly consistent with research using objective measures. First, the studies suggest that perceptions of certainty are better predictors of crime than perceptions of severity. Second, even the effects of certainty perceptions on crime are modest.[28]

There is evidence, however, that the relationship between perceptions and criminal behavior may not reflect deterrence. Individuals who engage in more crime may become likely to lower their estimate of the certainty or severity of the punishment. Because experience with crime causes people to change their perceptions (and not the reverse, as deterrence theory suggests), researchers have dubbed this an *experiential* effect.[29]

Specific Deterrence

Specific deterrence, also called *special deterrence*, refers to the effect that punishment has on the offender. Deterrence theory predicts that offenders who are punished swiftly and severely will be less likely to engage in future crime. The available empirical evidence concerns mostly the effect of severity. One simplistic way to look at specific deterrence is to ask how often those who are imprisoned commit new offenses upon release. Follow-up studies of those released from prison consistently indicate that 60% to 75% are rearrested within three years — hardly comforting to advocates of specific deterrence.[30]

A more sophisticated approach would be to compare groups of similar offenders who are punished differently. The emergence of intermediate sanctions in the 1980s allowed researchers to conduct just such an experiment. Intermediate sanctions are designed to be more painful than traditional probation, but less severe than prison. The two most popular types are <u>intensive supervision probation (ISP)</u> and correctional boot camps. ISP, which includes increased contact with the probation officer, curfews, drug testing, and other enhancements, was designed to "turn up the heat on probationers."[31] In a very rigorous (random assignment of subjects, multiple program sites) experiment, however, researchers discovered that ISP programs did not reduce arrests for new offenses when compared with traditional probation.[32]

<u>Correctional boot camps</u>, sometimes called *shock incarceration*, are also designed to be more painful that traditional sanctions. Following the military boot camp model, these programs emphasize physical training and military drill.[33] Although the research here is less conclusive, there is little evidence that boot camps reduce recidivism.[34] In a review of intermediate sanctions, Francis Cullen and his associates note that, although these programs are perceived by offenders as more "painful" than regular probation, they are no more effective at reducing recidivism.[35]

Even Sheriff Joe Arpaio's jails, discussed earlier, appeared to have little effect on inmates' behavior once they were released. In a study commissioned and paid for by Arpaio comparing jail inmates under his tenure with inmates who served time prior to his arrival, researchers found no differences in recidivism rates.[36] In other words, wearing pink underwear and sleeping out in the desert heat

Youth offender at a correctional boot camp.

? *Is there any evidence that boot camp graduates are less likely to engage in crime?*

man refers to arrest as "the aspirin of criminal justice, the most widely dispensed incarceration 'drug' in the United States."[38] Important here is the fact that police have a great deal of discretion in choosing whether or not to arrest an offender. Deterrence theory would predict that those who are arrested would be less likely to engage in future crime than those whom the police choose not to arrest.

An analysis of data from the 1948, Racine, Wisconsin birth cohort revealed that arrest appeared to serve as a specific deterrent.[39] Among novice offenders, arrest was somewhat more likely to end a criminal career. Among more hardened offenders, arrest significantly reduced future rates of crime. Other studies suggest, however, that arrest and formal processing either have no effect on, or actually increase, future criminal activity.[40] These mixed findings probably reflect the difficulty in untangling cause-and-effect relationships using nonexperimental data.

Given this difficulty, a series of experiments focusing on police response to domestic violence may shed more light on the effect of arrest. In the first study, suspects in Minneapolis were randomly assigned to one of three potential responses by the police: (1) arrest, (2) threat of arrest (with the suspect leaving the home), and (3) a "talking to" by the police (with the suspect left at the scene). The results supported the use of arrest in domestic violence cases as a way to protect the victim — the suspects who were arrested had the lowest rate of recidivism. Arrest appeared to have a specific deterrent effect upon domestic violence.[41]

This study had a dramatic impact on policing in domestic violence cases. Although the authors were careful to recommend against the passage of mandatory arrest laws until further research was conducted, the results of the Minneapolis experiment contributed to the passage of such laws in 15 states by 1991.[42] The study was replicated (repeated with the same methodology in a different location) in Omaha (Nebraska), Charlotte (North Carolina), and Milwaukee (Wisconsin) with dissimilar results.

Sherman and his colleagues specifically examined the impact of arrest on domestic violence cases in ghetto areas. The Milwaukee experiment was conducted in inner-city, crime-ridden neighborhoods. Suspects were randomly assigned the same potential police responses as in the Minneapolis experiment. Although interviews with victims in such cases revealed that arrest had a short-term

was no more of a deterrent than the normal jail experience.

Some programs attempt to increase delinquents' perceptions of the severity of prison. The most widely recognized example is "Scared Straight," a program featured in two separate television specials, one of which won an Academy Award. In this type of program, youth are brought into a prison where inmates aggressively confront them and graphically describe the horrors of prison life. Although both television specials portrayed these programs as a success, scientific evaluations consistently show that at best, the programs have no effect on criminal behavior. There is some evidence that Scared Straight programs actually increase criminal behavior.[37] (A more detailed analysis of the Scared Straight phenomenon is presented in **Theory in Action: And the Oscar Goes to . . .** *Scared Straight!*)

Researchers have also examined and manipulated police behaviors to test the principle of specific deterrence. In particular, they have examined the consequences of police officers' decision to arrest. Arrest can be considered punishment because it leads to booking and in most cases to at least some short-term incarceration. Indeed, Lawrence Sher-

In 1978, the Academy Award for best documentary film went to *Scared Straight!*, a film that followed a group of 17 juveniles through the Juvenile Awareness Program. In the movie, juveniles are confronted by the "lifers," a group of inmates serving lengthy sentences at the maximum security Rahway Prison in New Jersey. The inmates describe prison life in graphic detail (e.g., rapes, murder) and physically confronted the youth. The theory of deterrence is clearly the rationale for this program. It is an attempt to increase juveniles' fear of punishment by emphasizing the nastiness of prison life. In the documentary, the program is described as extremely successful, having a success rate of 80% for the more than 8,000 youth that attended the program.

Given the social context of the late 1970s (the attack on rehabilitation and the start of the get-tough movement), this film, which aired on television in 1979, captured the imagination of the public and policymakers alike. Not surprisingly, similar programs spread across the United States and the rest of the world, and the phrase "scared straight" is now used to describe them generically. Unfortunately, scientific research on these programs indicates that they do not reduce criminal behavior and may in fact have a negative effect. Anthony Petrosino, Corly Turpin-Petrosino, and James Finckenauer reviewed seven of the most methodologically sound evaluations of scared straight programs. The programs under evaluation varied on the level of inmate confrontation (from very aggressive to an educational-type approach), whether females participated, and the average age of participants. Despite these differences, a consistent finding emerged: In none of the seven studies did the scared straight group do better than a control group. Indeed, these programs under study actually *increased* delinquency anywhere from 1% to 30%.

Because these studies were all conducted between 1967 and 1983, one might think that the scared straight type of programs would have vanished from the earth. While enthusiasm for such programs did wane throughout the 1980s, many of them are still operating. In 1999, "Scared Straight: 20 Years Later" aired in the United States. Hosted by Danny Glover, the program followed up on the 17 kids from the original documentary and claimed that only one became a serious criminal. At the same time, MTV aired a new scared straight documentary, again showing a group of juveniles being confronted by inmates and portraying the intervention as successful.

In August 2003, the governor of Illinois signed into law a bill that requires the Chicago public school system to set a program called "Choices." This program would identify children at risk for committing crime and give them tours of a state prison. Chicago Mayor Richard M. Daley supported the measure, saying, "As a freshman at De La Salle, they brought us down to Stateville. It shows you how harsh life is."

Why do scared straight programs continue to draw support and funding from policymakers in the face of evidence indicating they actually increase delinquency? Anthony Petrosino and his colleagues identify a number of reasons. Chief among them is the belief that, as Mayor Daley put it, "If you save one child, it's worth it." The problem with this statement is that it ignores that fact that on balance, scared straight programs are doing more harm than good. A good analogy would be producing a new seatbelt that, when activated during crashes, killed more people than it saved. If the seatbelt saved just one life (but ended more lives than it saved), would anyone want it installed in their car? Apart from faulty logic, Petrosino and his colleagues identify a number of other reasons that contribute to the staying power of scared straight programs, including:

- Public appeal — The program does make intuitive sense. Many in the public respond to the film by saying, "Well, it scared the hell out of me." This is a powerful incentive for policymakers to support the program.

- Institutional staying power — Once a program is started, it sometimes takes on a life of its own and becomes difficult to dismantle.

- "It's good for the inmates." — Some defenders of scared straight point out that although it may not benefit the juveniles, it may benefit the inmates by giving them something positive to work toward.

- The "true believers" — Some people believe so strongly in the program that they are simply not persuaded by scientific evidence of failure. Indeed, the policy response to findings from one experiment was to end the evaluation rather than the program.

Sources: Arnold Shapiro, *Scared Straight!* (Santa Monica, CA: Pyramid Films, 1978); Anthony Petrosino, Carolyn Turpin-Petrosino, and James Finckenauer, "Well Meaning Programs Can Have Harmful Effects! Lessons From Experiments of Programs Such as Scared Straight," *Crime and Delinquency* 36 (2000): 353–379; Al Swanson, "Scared Straight," United Press International, available at http://newsmax.com/archives/articles/2003/8/22/225025.shtml, accessed August 23, 2003.

deterrent effect, analysis of calls to police revealed no difference among the three sanctions. The authors concluded that short-term arrest may even cause harm by increasing anger at society without increasing the fear of rearrest. Thus, "a little jail time can be worse than none."[43]

A subsequent analysis of the Milwaukee experiment suggested that suspects without a stake in conformity were less likely to be deterred by arrest. They found that unmarried, unemployed, and black subjects were more likely to become involved in domestic violence again. The authors believe that the results confirm that the effectiveness of legal sanctions (e.g., arrest) is dependent on informal controls (e.g., employment, marriage).[44] A second replication of the domestic violence experiment was conducted in Dade County, Florida. Here, evidence of the influence of social bonds was also registered. Arrest had a significant deterrent effect on employed suspects and the opposite effect on unemployed suspects. The study's authors felt that these results highlighted the interrelationship between formal and informal sanctions.[45] Policies should take into account that arrest seems to deter only those who have something to lose (e.g., a job).

Finally, researchers synthesized the findings of these three domestic violence experiments with a fourth in Colorado Springs.[46] They found that overall, arrest appeared to do little to either increase or decrease the likelihood of repeat offending in domestic violence cases. In all four locations, however, arrest seemed to have a deterrent effect on employed suspects but to increase the risk of future violence by the unemployed. These authors caution not to take these findings too literally. For example, employment may be a measure of exposure — employed subjects are less likely to be at home and thus have less interaction with the victim. They also note that the findings do not suggest that arrest should be dropped as a policy option.

In sum, these studies reveal that the deterrent effect of arrest is difficult to determine. Social bonds and a stake in conformity may be more effective restraints against crime than the threat of punishment. The experiments raise the possibility, however, that formal sanctions may "kick off" these social controls. Williams and Hawkins make this exact argument and outline three indirect "costs" of arrest:[47]

1. *Commitment costs*: Arrests may have an adverse effect on future opportunities (e.g., employment or education).

2. *Attachment costs*: Arrests can result in harm to or loss of personal relationships.

3. *Stigma*: Arrests can cause a loss of reputation.

Celerity

Celerity, or the swiftness of punishment, is the least studied aspect of deterrence theory. Psychological studies with animals suggest (and anyone who has successfully trained a dog understands) that swift punishments are more effective at reducing unwanted behavior than delayed punishment. The few available studies on offenders suggest, however, that immediate punishment does not decrease recidivism any more than delayed punishment.[48] Nagin and Pogarsky note that, unlike other animals, humans have the cognitive ability to connect an offense with punishment, regardless of whether or not that punishment is swift. They also point out that throughout criminal justice processing, offenders are reminded repeatedly of their offense.[49]

Summary of Deterrence Theory

Deterrence theory predicts that swift, certain, and severe punishment will reduce crime, both among the general public (general deterrence) and for those being punished (specific deterrence). Deterrence theory, because it is derived from classical school theorists, focuses on formal (arrest, prison) punishment rather than informal controls. As noted, the empirical evidence regarding these predictions is mixed (and in some cases downright confusing), but it seems fair to make two generalizations. First, if any ingredient in the punishment mix is potent, it appears to be certainty rather than swiftness or severity. Second, even where deterrent effects emerge, they tend to be modest. In other words, measures of deterrence sometimes predict offending, but not nearly as well as measures from other theories of crime. Although deterrence theory seems to makes sense, there are several possible explanations for the negative findings:

- Deterrence theory may rest on a faulty assumption; that is, people may not be as rational as they are portrayed in this theory (see the following rational choice theory).

- Almost all empirical tests focus on *marginal* increases in certainty and severity, rather that the absolute effect of deterrence.

- The capabilities of the criminal justice system are somewhat limited in a democratic society.

For example, a society in which secret police assassinate suspected offenders on the spot might have lower crime rates, but few people want to live in such a society.

Rational Choice Theory

Deterrence theory hinges in large part on the assumption that humans are rational beings, however, this assumption is tested only indirectly by looking at the effect of punishment on behavior. If people are rational and want to avoid pain and punishment, they should be deterred by formal sanctions. Rational choice theory explicitly examines the reasoning process followed by offenders. The main propositions in rational choice theory are that individuals will (1) weigh the costs or consequences of crime against the benefit of crime prior to engaging in criminal behavior and (2) choose criminal behavior when the rewards outweigh the costs.

Rational choice theorists allow for both formal (e.g., arrest, prison) and informal (e.g., shame, loss of job) sanctions. Furthermore, the benefits of crime can be tangible (e.g., money, property) or intangible (e.g., psychological thrill, respect of peers). In this sense, rational choice theory is much broader than deterrence theory; offenders consider multiple costs and rewards prior to making decisions about crime. Few rational choice theorists, however, portray criminals as *purely* rational.[50] Rather, the rationality of the decision process is constrained or "bounded" by such factors as time, cognitive ability, and moral values.

Cornish and Clarke's Rational Choice Theory

Derek Cornish and Ronald Clarke's rational choice theory distinguishes between two types of decision making.[51] Criminal involvement decisions involve whether to engage in crime in general, as opposed to satisfying needs and wants with noncriminal alternatives. Cornish and Clarke portray this as a multistage process that unfolds over a long period of time. Rationality (a pure cost-benefit analysis of whether to engage in crime) is constrained by a host of factors. The criminal event involves decision making about the how, where, and when of a particular crime. In other words, a person has decided that they are ready to engage in crime, but still considers a host of situational factors before

choosing to follow through with (or refrain from) criminal activity.

Cornish and Clarke argue that separate theoretical models are necessary for particular types of crime. The decision process leading to the use of illicit drugs, for example, is different from the decision process for burglary. Also, separate models are required to explain initial involvement, the criminal event, and the decision to persist in or desist from criminal activity.

A Rational Choice Model for Burglary

As an example, consider Cornish and Clarke's explanation of burglary in a middle-class neighborhood. As just noted, decisions about whether to engage in crime (criminal involvement) tend to be multistage and unfold over an extended period of time. The model presented here is a simplified version of Cornish and Clarke's explanation of criminal involvement for the crime of burglary. Note that both background factors and previous learning experience contain items that constrain a purely rational assessment of costs and benefits. For example, someone with a strong conscience, strong moral values, and a cautious temperament might choose a legitimate solution (e.g., work) to a need, even when a criminal solution would have a better payoff and carry little risk of detection or punishment. Indeed, such a person might never think to consider crime as an alternative.

- **Background factors:** Temperament, intelligence, cognitive style, broken home, parental crime, sex, class, education, neighborhood

    ↓

- **Previous learning experience:** Direct and observational experience with crime, contact with law enforcement agencies, conscience and moral code, self-perception

    ↓

- **Generalized needs:** Money, sex, friendship, status, excitement

    ↓

- **Evaluation of solutions:** Degree and effort, amount and immediacy of reward, likelihood and severity of punishment, moral costs

    ↓

- **Solutions:** Legitimate (work, gambling, marriage); illegitimate (burglary)

The criminal event model for burglary is a bit simpler and has few constraints on pure rational decision making. Again, this model pertains to individuals who have already decided to engage in burglary. In selecting both the area to engage in crime, and the particular house to burgle, offenders consider many situational factors that impact the rewards of the crime and the probability of detection.

- **Selection of area**
  - **Select:** Easily accessible, few police patrols, low security housing, larger gardens
  - **Reject:** Unfamiliar, distant, neighborhood watch, no public transportation
- **Selection of home**
  - **Burgled:** No one at home, especially affluent, detached home, patio doors, bushes and other cover present, corner site
  - **Not Burgled:** Nosey neighbors, burglar alarm, no rear access, visible from street, window locks, dog

Criticisms of Rational Choice Theory

Critics identify two related problems in rational choice theory. First, empirical tests find little evidence of pure rational decision making. If one was to ask, "Do individuals choose to begin engaging in crime after a thorough comparison of all costs and benefits associated with that crime to other non-criminal alternatives?" the answer appears to be no. For example, interviews with 3300 adult offenders, drug addicts, and high school dropouts from 1975–1979 found that the respondents were motivated by the reward aspect of rational choice theory (i.e., the benefits of the crime), but underestimated the cost or deterrent effect (i.e. the risk of punishment).[52] In other words, offenders are likely to be irrational regarding the threat of apprehension, which contradicts one of the premises of rational choice theory.

An interview with offenders imprisoned for property crimes revealed that the thought of punishment is rarely part of the crime selection process.[53] The offenders considered thoughts about the risk of punishment a distraction and focused instead on the benefits of the crime. Their experience with the criminal justice system also led them to discount the negative aspects of a prison sentence.[54] The author noted the discrepancy between what offenders said about planning a burglary in general, and the actual burglaries they committed:

> Most of our burglar informants could design a textbook burglary . . . [T]hey often described their past burglaries as though they were rationally conceived and executed. Yet, upon closer inspection, when their previous burglaries were reconstructed, textbook procedures frequently gave way to opportunity and situational factors.[55]

A similar study, using focus groups and interviews with a sample of "street robbers," concluded that:

> At first sight, it appeared that street robbers chose to commit an offense only after they weighed the relative advantages and disadvantages. However, after we examined to what extent impulsivity, moral ambiguity, and expressivity could make sense if considered as part of a rational choice process, we began to doubt whether the spontaneous and moral aspects of criminal behaviour can be understood if we assume that the crimes were committed as the result of rational and deliberate choice.[56]

Of course, most rational choice theories do not portray humans as purely rational. Cornish and Clarke include a host of background and learning experience factors in their criminal involvement model. Indeed, the impulsivity and moral ambiguity cited in the study just noted are concepts within their criminal involvement model. This brings one to the second major criticism of rational choice theory. The problem with including concepts like "impulsivity," "moral values," and "temperament" is that they are all borrowed from competing theories (e.g., social learning theory, psychological theory) of crime. Further, many of these things serve to *constrain* or *limit* a purely rational decision-making process. For example, a very impulsive person might not take the time to weigh the costs and benefits of their actions — their actions may be *irrational*. Similarly, someone with a strong moral code might never consider a criminal response to most circumstances, and therefore never weigh the risks and rewards of crime.

Rational choice theorists often portray themselves as the only theorists that allow for human choice and free will. Ronald Akers points out, however, that virtually all theories of crime allow for some rational choice, but emphasize the factors that limit or constrain that free will. For example, a social learning theorist would argue that delinquent peers and one's moral code (learned from parents and others) influence the decision to commit crimes.[57] In that sense, rational choice theories are not as different as some may think. Indeed, some view rational choice models not as independent theories, but rather as an attempt to integrate many theories into a single explanation of crime.[58]

Despite this criticism, rational choice theory maintains an important place in criminology because it focuses attention on situational factors that may influence specific criminal events. There is much evidence, for example, that criminals rationally plan to avoid detection by their selection of general areas and/or specific targets. For example, a study of professional burglars found that burglars often called ahead or rang the doorbell once they arrived to make sure that no one was home. If someone answered the door, they simply claimed that they were looking for a friend and had the wrong address. Further, the authors of the study discovered that burglars will avoid households with dogs or doors with deadbolt locks.[59] Understanding what makes a good target for crime leads to very concrete policy implications, which are described later in this chapter. First discussed, however, are routine activities and lifestyle approaches to crime, because they fit very well with rational choice theorists' focus on the criminal event.

 ## Routine Activities Theory and the Lifestyle Approach

Routine activities theory and the "lifestyle approach" share some similarities with deterrence and rational choice theory perspectives. Like deterrence and rational choice theories, both of these perspectives assume that offenders make rational assessments about crime targets. Yet, unlike rational choice theory, they shift attention away from offenders and toward the victims of crime.

Routine Activities Theory

Routine activities theory was originally developed by Lawrence Cohen and Marcus Felson to explain "direct contact predatory crimes where at least one offender comes into direct physical contact with at least one victim."[60] Marcus Felson has since extended the theory to include crimes such as illegal use and sale of drugs and white-collar crime.[61] The theory postulates that for any crime to occur, three elements must converge: (1) a motivated offender, (2) a suitable target, and (3) the absence of a capable guardian.

FIGURE 3-1 Routine Activities Theory

Although routine activities theory identifies three elements necessary for crime (see **FIGURE 3-1**), most of the discussion and empirical testing involves target suitability and guardianship — the availability of motivated offenders is typically taken for granted. Guardianship could include police, but according to Felson, the most significant guardians in society are "not usually someone who brandishes a gun or threatens an offender with quick punishment, but rather someone whose mere presence serves as a gentle reminder that someone is looking."[62] Guardians discourage offenders from committing the crime in the first place.

Felson identifies a number of factors that influence the suitability of a target[63]:

- *Value*: Sometimes value (money) is almost universal; other times it depends almost entirely on what is popular in the offender's world (e.g., specific CDs, sneakers, or jackets).
- *Inertia*: Some valuable property (e.g., large appliances) is simply too difficult to move; other property (cars, bicycles) provide their own getaway.
- *Visibility*: This might include valuables left in plain sight or living on a busy street.
- *Access*: Easy access, such as being within walking distance of a shopping mall (which attracts motivated offenders) or living on a street with exits on both sides as opposed to a cul-de-sac, contribute to suitability.

Cohen and Felson applied routine activities to explain why crime rates in most western countries increased substantially between the 1950s and the 1970s.[64] They argue that while traditional theories that focus on the motivation of offenders cannot explain this phenomenon, a routine activities approach holds promise. For example, during this time period, women became more likely to work outside of the home (and men no more likely to stay home). Thus, guardianship over homes during the daytime diminished. Advances in technology produced an enormous variety of lightweight, valuable items (e.g., stereos, televisions, VCRs) that increased the number of suitable targets. The advent of the interstate highway system and general improvement of roadways also made many targets more accessible.

Of course, routine activities theory is also used to explain current criminal behavior. This theory has been applied to explain a wide variety of crime problems, both within the same jurisdiction and across jurisdictions. One analysis looked at routine activities theory using an international crime data set drawn from several official sources.[65] This study discovered that routine activities theory applied more to property than to personal crime. Across countries, property crime was related to:

1. a per capita income between the low and high range (target attractiveness)
2. a level of hard-goods manufacturing between the low and moderately high range (target accessibility)
3. a high level of inequality (motivation)
4. a low level of urbanization (access)
5. a low-to-moderately high proportion of women in the work force (guardianship)

Many of the empirical tests of routine activities theory focus on victimization and overlap to some extent with the lifestyles approach.

The Lifestyle Approach

Closely related to routine activities theory is the lifestyle approach developed by Michael Hindelang, Michael Gottfredson, and James Garofalo.[66] This theory, grounded in victimization data, attempts to explain why certain groups of people (i.e., youths, males, the poor, singles, racial/ethnic minorities) have higher rates of victimization than others. The gist of the theory is that these groups, by virtue of their lifestyle, place themselves at greater risk of victimization. A *lifestyle* refers to the "patterned way in which people distribute their time and energies across a range of activities."[67] The lifestyle of a college student, for example, differs markedly from that of an elderly person in terms of companions, leisure activities, and how and where time is spent. Hindelang and his associates point out that lifestyles are not solely a matter of choice — they reflect role expectations and the constraints of one's position in society. A poor person living in the inner city, for example, cannot just decide to be a wealthy suburbanite.

Lifestyle theory includes several propositions that summarize the link between lifestyle and known correlates of victimization[68]:

- The more time that individuals spend in public places (especially at night), the more likely they are to be victimized.
- Following certain lifestyles makes individuals more likely to frequent public places.
- The interaction that individuals maintain tends to be with persons who share their lifestyles.
- The probability that individuals will be victims increases according to the extent to which victims and offenders belong to the same demographic categories.
- The proportion of time individuals spend in places where there is a large number of nonfamily members varies according to lifestyle.
- The chances that individuals will be victims of crime (particularly theft) increase in conjunction with the amount of time they spend among nonfamily members.
- Differences in lifestyles related to the ability of individuals to isolate themselves from those with offender characteristics.

The overlap between these lifestyle propositions and routine activities theory should be apparent. For example, time spent in public places at night (the first proposition) is a risk factor because there is less guardianship present in public places, especially at night, and a greater number of motivated offenders. Individuals who spend more time away from home have higher risks of victimization; due to their increased visibility and accessibility, they are more likely to become a target. In addition, their homes and property may be more at risk due to their absence (i.e., their decreased guardianship). For example, Cohen and Felson show that dispersion of activities away from the home is positively related to increased rates of homicide, rape, assault, burglary, and larceny.[69] The point here is that lifestyles predict victimization because they are often related to guardianship and target attractiveness.

In Chapter 2, the high rates of violent crime victimization among blacks was noted. A routine activity/lifestyle perspective can explain this finding. For example, blacks are more likely to live in segregated, public housing and spend their time in contact with motivated offenders. There may be an absence of capable guardians (e.g., neighbors who watch the area). Residents of public housing may tend to "mind their own business" and be reluctant to get involved because of fear of reprisal. Thus, a higher victimization rate for inner-city blacks is partly a function of an environment that increases the probability of crime.

LINK The lifestyles explanation of black victimization is similar to the social disorganization theory of offending outlined in Chapter 7. Ultimately, both victimization and offending are traced to characteristics of the neighborhoods where African-Americans disproportionately reside.

As this example makes clear, many aspects of lifestyle cannot easily be altered. A person cannot simply choose to move to a house in a nice area of the city. Are there aspects of a lifestyle that individuals might change to reduce their risk of victimization? An examination of data from three years of the U.S. National Crime Survey sought to answer this question.[70] The researchers found that persons with greater daytime and nighttime activity outside the home (greater target visibility or exposure to motivated offenders) and who had a reduction in the number of household members (reduced guardianship) had higher rates of both personal and property crime victimization. Persons who maintained high levels of nighttime activity outside the household were also more likely to remain victims across the time periods covered by the surveys. The most perplexing finding, however, was that persons who took extra precautions did not reduce their risk of victimization.

A similar study from Canada, based on survey results from the Canadian Urban Victimization Study,[71] examined the same research question: What makes people prone to victimization? The results suggested that getting older and getting married reduced victimization by reducing time spent in risky settings. For example, males who spent time in bars had an increased risk of victimization. In sum, risky settings were more likely to produce dangerous results.

In addition, the effect of personal lifestyle characteristics may depend on a person's neighborhood. A survey conducted in Seattle, Washington, revealed that lower levels of guardianship and high-target attractiveness strongly increased the risk of burglary for residents of more affluent areas.[72] However, these variables were unrelated to the risks of burglary among residents of more socially disorganized areas. This type of study demonstrates the importance of considering both individual and neighborhood characteristics in victimization studies.

The lifestyles of adolescents have also attracted some attention under this theory. With data from the National Youth Survey, a study investigated the relationship between routine activities and the risk of assault and robbery victimization among adolescents. Certain adolescent activities were related to the risk of violence. The most dangerous activities were delinquent behaviors. Delinquents were approximately two to three times more likely to be victimized by assault and robbery than nondelinquents. Engagement in conventional activities had little effect on risk once sociodemographic characteristics and delinquent involvement were considered.[73] Further analysis by the authors found a strong relationship between delinquent lifestyles and increased risk of both personal and property victimization.[74]

A routine activity/lifestyle approach has even been used to explain the victimization of inmates within prison. A study of inmates within three different prisons revealed that inmates who spent more time in structured, supervised activities (education, working) were less likely to be victims of a violent offense. This reflects the increased guardianship associated with such activities (participation in *unsupervised* recreation actually made violent victimization more likely). Unfortunately, time spent in supervised activities increased the likelihood of theft victimization, presumably because the inmates' property was left unguarded in their cells.[75]

Policy Implications: Situational Crime Prevention

Rational choice theory, routine activities theory, and the lifestyles approach share a focus on the situational factors (e.g., guardianship, target suitability) that impact whether victimization occurs. For this reason, they are sometimes grouped together under the title of opportunity theories (e.g., a focus on structure of opportunities for engaging in crime). The policy implications among these theories are therefore similar but vastly different from other theories of crime. Most crime prevention efforts, including rehabilitation and deterrence, focus on offenders because the theories from which they are derived focus on properties (e.g., personality, learning history) of offenders. The exception to this rule is incapacitation, where the opportunity for crime is removed simply by segregating the offender from society. Like incapacitation, the policy implication of opportunity theories is to reduce the opportunity for offending. Rather than target specific offenders, however, these theories focus attention on the *context* of crime.[76] In other words, opportunity theories lead one to ask, "Can the environment be changed in a manner that reduces the opportunity for crime?"

> **LINK** Theories discussed in the following chapters (see Chapters 4–7) tend to highlight deficits of offenders that cause them to engage in crime. In turn, crime prevention is typically equated with attempts to correct (through correctional treatment, or "rehabilitation") these deficits.

One of the first criminologists to focus on this question was C. Ray Jeffrey, who coined the phrase **crime prevention through environmental design (CPTED)**.[77] The basic premise of CPTED is that the way an environment is designed can promote or prevent crime. The term *environment* can mean something as broad as a community or as narrow as a convenience store. Around the same time (1972), an architect named Oscar Newman wrote *Defensible Space,* a book geared toward designing safe public housing (as opposed to high-rise projects). Newman's main idea was to create as much private space in housing developments as possible, so that people maintain more guardianship over themselves and their property.[78]

From these initial contributions, a large body of literature has emerged. Some scholars and policymakers continue to use CPTED to describe this work, although others prefer environmental criminology or situational crime prevention. Regardless of the terminology, the literature provides numerous methods or "principles" for crime prevention. Marcus Felson organizes these methods into three groups[79]:

1. **Natural strategies:** Security results from the design and layout of space.

2. **Organized strategies:** Security guards or police play the central role.

3. **Mechanical strategies:** Alarms, cameras, and other hardware are employed to control access and provide surveillance.

Felson believes that crime can most often be prevented by following nature as closely as possible. This means avoiding, so far as one can, the use of the criminal justice system, armed guards, violence, and threats. Instead, it is preferable to set up situations and environments in which acting legally feels like the comfortable thing to do. Natural crime prevention should occur as a consequence of everyday life. For example, Felson offers the following tips for preventing crime in college and university parking areas[80]:

- Arrange for nighttime students and workers to have parking near building doors, but not so close that they block the view of the parking area from the building.

- At low-use times, close off unneeded parking area or sections of large parking areas to concentrate people and cars for supervision.

- Require students and staff to sign up by name and have a sticker, even for nighttime or free areas.

- Eliminate nooks and corners in parking structures.

- Build parking structures as slopes so people on foot will have clear sight lines.

- Make seeing into parking structure stairwells easy.

- Orient buildings to face parking areas.

- Trim hedges and lower limbs of trees around parking areas and avoid thick foliage.

- Post signs and organize the flow of traffic so neither cars nor pedestrians will get lost.

Ronald Clarke has created a list of situational crime prevention techniques based on successful crime prevention programs; some of these techniques, along with examples, are illustrated in **TABLE 3-3**. Techniques such as those outlined by Clarke have been evaluated in many different contexts.

One of the earliest evaluations came from CPTED Demonstration Program directed by the Westinghouse National Issues Center. This was a 4-year (1974–1978) effort sponsored by the Law Enforcement Assistance Administration. One of the sites was Portland, Oregon, where the CPTED commercial demonstration program was designed

TABLE 3-3

Opportunity-Reducing Techniques of Situational Crime Prevention

Technique	Examples
Increase the perceived effort of crime	
Harden targets	Steering column locks
Control access to targets	Electronic access to garages
Deflect offenders from targets	Street closures, tavern locations
Control crime facilitators	Photos on credit cards, plastic beer glasses in taverns
Increase the perceived risks of crime	
Screen entrances and exits	Electronic merchandise tags, baggage screening
Formal surveillance	Red light and speed cameras, park attendants
Surveillance by employees	Park attendants, pay phone location
Natural surveillance	Street lighting, defensible space
Reduce anticipated rewards of crime	
Remove targets	Removable car radios, women's refuges
Identify property	Vehicle licensing, car parts marking
Reduce temptation	Rapid repair of vandalism, off-street parking
Deny benefits	PIN for car radios, graffiti cleaning

Source: Ronald Clarke, *Situational Crime Prevention: Successful Case Studies*, 2nd ed., (New York: Harrow and Heston, 1997).

to reduce crime in the Union Avenue Corridor (UAC). Due to socioeconomic changes, the UAC faced a rising crime rate and a rapidly deteriorating neighborhood. Businesspeople felt that crime was the single greatest obstacle to the successful operation of their businesses.

A number of tactics were implemented in the UAC to bring about changes in the physical and social environments, including the installation of high-intensity street lighting and creating a safe street for the people. Survey results suggested that the CPTED changes contributed to a reduction in the residents' fear of crime.[81] Furthermore, CPTED had a moderate degree of success in bringing about positive and lasting changes in the physical and social environments. It increased access control and surveillance (target hardening) in the area.[82] However, these commercial effects did not appear to carry over to residential neighborhood areas. A final study examined commercial burglary data from UAC to determine if CPTED applications were effective over time. The results indicated that commercial security surveys and street-lighting changes led to a significant reduction in commercial burglaries in the area. This effect had been maintained since the beginning of the project.[83]

For a number of reasons, situational crime prevention is more popular in other countries than in the United States. Indeed, throughout the 1980s and 1990s, situational crime prevention was the dominant strategy employed by the British government to reduce crime.[84] This focus led to a plethora of demonstration projects and evaluation research. For example, a 1997 study examined a program that sought to improve street lighting in an English neighborhood. Old street lights were replaced with 129 high-pressure sodium lights in one neighborhood, but left intact in a similar (control) neighborhood. Over the next year, household victimization decreased in the experimental, but not the control, neighborhood.[85] Other advantageous effects included an increase in the number of people on the street (especially women) after dark and a reduction in the fear of crime.

A more extensive program designed to reduce burglary also yielded favorable results.[86] The Safe Cities Program, in effect from 1985 to 1995, set up over 500 individual programs designed to prevent domestic burglary in British neighborhoods. Many of these programs involved situational crime prevention, such as improving household locks on doors and windows, providing gates for alleyways, and fencing back yards. When compared with similar areas where no improvements were made, the "improved" areas had substantially lower levels of burglary.

Despite such evidence, situational crime prevention is not without critics. The primary concern about such programs is the potential for **crime displacement**; that is, improving the environment in one area may simply shift crime to a different location. Far too often, the displacement effect of a crime control strategy is ignored. After all, most persons are satisfied when crime is moved out of

Burglar entering through a window.

? *What situational crime prevention techniques might reduce burglary?*

their area or neighborhood, no matter where it goes. Such a limited view ignores the fact that crime has social costs for everyone, regardless of where it exists. This criticism has been answered in recent years by research indicating "real" prevention. In the Safe Cities program, there was some evidence of displacement. Also, there was evidence of "crime switching," in which offenders switched from burglary to other forms of theft. In the areas where the most intense changes were made, how-

ever, there was actually a diffusion effect. The crime reductions occurred not only in the program areas, but also in surrounding areas.[87]

To be sure, situational crime prevention is not a panacea. Some crimes can be controlled through environmental design (e.g., vandalism, burglary) but they may have little or no effect on underlying problems. Further, many violent crimes (such as rape and murder) and instrumental crimes such as robbery may not be amenable to situational crime prevention. Nevertheless, based on the positive results thus far, it appears that momentum is building to increase this type of prevention program in the future.[88]

Conclusion

Theories from the classical school display the cyclical nature of criminological theory. To a great degree, Beccaria and Bentham were protest writers, attacking the arbitrary nature of punishment at the hands of the state. Their call for uniform sentencing was a direct assault on the unjust forms of punishment that existed then. They were critical of the exercise and abuse of power by the state. Conservative criminologists such as James Q. Wilson and Earnest van den Haag helped usher in the get-tough movement that brought the classical school back to the forefront. Their call for a return to determinate sentencing, incapacitation, and the death penalty were attempts to strengthen crime prevention policies. Thus, ideas that were once liberal are now conservative. It should be noted, however, that not all parts of the get-tough movement are consistent with the classical school. Indeed, Beccaria's 1764 essay *On Crimes and Punishment* argues for the abolishment of this penalty.

Politically, many neoclassical policies are very attractive because they give the impression of being tough on crime. However, the research on incapacitation and deterrence calls into question the effectiveness of such policies. In addition, their proposed benefits are not achieved without great increases in the prison population. The research also suggests that crime control policies should focus on increasing the certainty of arrest, conviction, and sentencing rather than on lengthening prison sentences — yet, the first response to a perceived new threat is typically the reverse. Most likely, this is due to the fact that altering the severity of punishment is much easier (simply pass a new law) than increasing the certainty of punishment.

The preventive potential of the classical approach is limited by its initial assumption about criminal behavior: that all criminals are rational. If the criminal justice system increases the certainty of apprehension and conviction and raises penalties, the rational criminal will go straight. If, however, the criminal is irrational (e.g., psychotic or high on drugs or alcohol), unimpressed by the threat of punishment, or lured by the promise of immense financial gain (e.g., drug sales, white-collar crime), deterrence will be ineffective.

The potential for crime prevention under this approach is also limited by its reliance on formal legal controls. There are other methods of control that fit the classical perspective and aid crime prevention. Informal social control theory emphasizes the prevention of crime through such ideas as self-control and social bonds.

Despite these limitations, the classical school has had a significant impact on criminological theory and the operations of the criminal justice system. Policies ranging from the rights of the accused to career criminal laws and capital punishment have their roots in classical theory. Their influence will continue to be felt. Recent evidence supporting situational crime prevention suggests that this recent branch of the classical school may have a promising future.

TABLE 3-4 summarizes the key theories of the neoclassical school.

TABLE 3-4

Summary of Neoclassical School Theories

Theory	Major Authors	Summary	Policy Implications
Deterrence	Cesare Beccaria Jeremy Bentham	Formal punishment that is swift, certain, and severe reduces crime.	Use the criminal justice system to increase the certainty, severity, and swiftness of punishment. For those who cannot be deterred, incapacitation (removing the opportunity to offend) is the only other option.
Rational Choice	Derek Cornish and Ronald Clarke	Offenders rationally choose whether and how to engage in crime.	
Routine Activities	Lawrence Cohen Marcus Felson	Crime occurs because of the convergence of motivated offender, suitable target, and lack of capable guardian.	Situational Crime Prevention
Lifestyle Approach	Michael Hindelang, Michael Gottfredson, and James Garafolo	Certain groups of people have higher rates of victimization because of their lifestyle.	

WRAP UP

Can Drunk Driving Be Deterred?

The evidence gleaned from tests of deterrence theory indicates that the certainty of punishment carries more weight with potential offenders than does the severity of sanctions. As with other crimes, there is evidence that highly publicized police "crackdowns" can reduce the occurrence of drunk driving. These effects, however, tend to be short lived. Certainly, the increased legal attention paid to drinking and driving over the past 30 years has increased the public's perceptions of the certainty and severity of punishment for this offense. Scholars continue to debate whether this increased attention has reduced drunk driving. Aside from legal penalties, some jurisdictions require repeat offenders to install an "ignition interlock" system that disables the car if the driver has been drinking alcohol. This is a form of situational crime prevention (removing the opportunity to offend).

Chapter Spotlight

- In the 1970s, rehabilitation was attacked as a goal of corrections. This amounted to an attack on the sociological and psychological theories that provide targets for rehabilitation programs. Conservative scholars argued for a return to classical school principles.

- Deterrence theorists assume that humans are rational and hedonistic. Therefore, formal punishments such as arrest and imprisonment should reduce crime by sending a message to both those being punished (specific deterrence) and the rest of society (general deterrence). The empirical evidence in favor of deterrence theory indicates that the certainty of punishment is more important than severity or swiftness.

- Rational choice theory is similar to deterrence theory, but takes into account a wider array of "costs" for violating the law. Rational choice theorists distinguish between criminal involvement (e.g., crime versus other activity) and criminal event decisions (e.g., when and how to commit crimes).

- Routine activities theory highlights the ingredients (motivated offender, lack of capable guardianship, suitable target) necessary for a criminal event. Similarly, the lifestyles approach highlights factors that influence victimization. The policy implication of these theories is situational crime prevention — the manipulation of the physical environment to reduce the opportunity for offending.

- Although not a theory of crime, incapacitation is a corrections policy advocated by some neoclassical theories. Incapacitation removes the opportunity to offend by isolating offenders from the rest of society.

Putting It All Together

1. Can criminal behavior be deterred? For what types of crime is deterrence likely to work?

2. Which part of deterrence theory (certainty, swiftness, severity) receives the most empirical support? Why do you think that is the case?

3. In rational choice theory, what is the difference between the criminal event and criminal involvement?

4. Does incapacitation work? Is it a feasible policy?

5. Is arrest the answer to the problem of domestic violence?

6. Using the data in this chapter, construct a debate concerning the death penalty as a deterrent to murder.

7. According to routine activities theory, what makes a target suitable? Give an example of how you might influence guardianship of your own property.

Key Terms

brutalization effect A concept used by researchers who find that executions actually increase some forms of homicide.

correctional boot camps Like their military counterparts, these programs emphasize physical training and military drill. Research suggests that most of these programs have little effect on criminal behavior.

crime displacement The idea that when crime is suppressed in one geographical area, it may simply shift to a new location.

crime prevention through environmental design (CPTED) A policy implication of routine activities theory. The way an environment is designed can promote or prevent crime.

criminal event In rational choice theory, decisions about how, when, and where of a particular crime.

criminal involvement In rational choice theory, decisions about whether to engage in crime in general, as opposed to satisfying needs and wants with noncriminal alternatives.

general deterrence Punishing criminals so that the general public will get the message that crime doesn't pay.

incapacitation The use of prison and the death penalty to prevent crime by removing offenders from society.

intensive supervision probation (ISP) Offenders are supervised in the community under strict conditions, including frequent drug testing, curfews, and contacts with a probation officer. These programs were designed to increase the punishing aspect of probation. Research suggests that ISP programs do not reduce criminal behavior any more than traditional probation.

just deserts A justification for punishment (e.g., prison) that emphasizes the pain caused and thus earned by the criminal. Punishment serves as a collective expression of society's disapproval for criminal acts.

Kansas City Preventative Patrol Study An experimental study of police patrols. The main conclusion from this finding was that increased police presence has little effect on crime. Later research suggests that more dramatic increases in police presence can suppress crime.

marginal deterrence The idea that incremental increases in the certainty or severity of punishment should produce decreases in criminal behavior.

retribution Similar to just deserts, retribution is a justification for punishment that suggests that criminals deserve punishment because they have violated the legal code from which everyone benefits.

specific deterrence Punishing criminals so that they will be less likely to commit crimes in the future.

Notes

1. Quoted in James O. Finckenauer, "Crime as a National Political Issue: 1963–1976 — From Law and Order to Domestic Tranquility," *Crime and Delinquency* 23 (1978): 23.
2. Quoted in Francis T. Cullen and Karen T. Gilbert, *Reaffirming Rehabilitation* (Cincinnati, OH: Anderson, 1982): 95-96.
3. Cullen and Gilbert, 1982, 89–149.
4. Grahm Newman, *The Punishment Response* (Philadelphia: Lippincott, 1985).
5. Ernest van den Haag and John P. Conrad, *The Death Penalty: A Debate* (New York: Plenum, 1983).
6. Marie L. Griffin, *The Use of Force by Detention Officers* (New York: LFB Scholarly Publishing, 2001): 38–40.
7. Stanley E. Grupp, *Theories of Punishment* (Bloomington: Indiana University Press, 1971).
8. David Young, "Let Us Content Ourselves with Praising the Work While Drawing a Veil Over Its Principles: Eighteenth Century Reactions to Beccaria's *On Crimes and Punishments*," *Justice Quarterly* 1 (1983): 155–170.
9. Earnest van den Haag, *Punishing Criminals* (New York: Basic Books, 1975): 15.
10. van den Haag, 60.
11. John K. Cochran, Mitchell B. Chamlin, and Mark Seth, "Deterrence or Brutalization? An Impact Assessment of Oklahoma's Return to Capital Punishment," *Criminology* 32 (1993): 107–133.
12. Ibid.
13. Thorsten Sellin, *The Penalty of Death* (Beverly Hills, CA: Sage, 1980).
14. Sam G. McFarland, "Is Capital Punishment a Short-Term

Deterrent to Homicide? A Study of the Effects of Four Recent American Executions," *Journal of Criminal Law and Criminology* 73 (1983): 1013–1032.

15. Ruth D. Peterson and William C. Bailey, "Felony Murder and Capital Punishment: An Examination of the Deterrence Question," *Criminology* 29 (1991): 367–395.

16. Isaac Ehrlich, "The Deterrent Effect of Capital Punishment: A Question of Life and Death," *American Economic Review* 65 (1975): 397–419.

17. William J. Bowers and Glen L. Pierce, "The Illusion of Deterrence in Isaac Ehrlich's Research on Capital Punishment," *Yale Law Journal* 85 (1975): 187–208.

18. John K. Cochran, Mitchell B. Chamlin, and M. Seth, "Deterrence or Brutalization? An Impact Assessment of Oklahoma's Return to Capital Punishment," *Criminology* 32 (1993): 107–133; William C. Bailey, "Deterrence, Brutalization, and the Death Penalty: Another Examination of Oklahoma's Return to Capital Punishment," *Criminology* 36 (1998): 711–733.

19. William J. Bowers and Glenn L. Pierce, "Deterrence or Brutalization: What Is the Effect of Executions?" *Crime and Delinquency* 26 (1980): 353–383.

20. John K. Cochran and Mitchell B. Chamlin, "Deterrence and Brutalization: The Dual Effects of Executions," *Justice Quarterly* 17 (2000): 685–706.

21. Theodore G. Chiricos and Gordon P. Waldo, "Punishment and Crime: An Examination of Some Empirical Evidence," *Social Problems* 18 (1970): 200–217.

22. Mitchell B. Chamlin, "A Longitudinal Analysis of the Arrest-Crime Relationship: A Further Examination of the Tipping Effect," *Justice Quarterly* 8 (1991): 187–199.

23. Charles R. Tittle and Alan R. Rowe. "Certainty of Arrest and Crime Rates: A Further Test of the Deterrence Hypothesis," *Social Forces* 52 (1973): 355–362.

24. Chamlin, 196.

25. George L. Kelling, Tony Pate, Duane Dieckman, and Charles Brown, *The Kansas City Preventative Patrol Experiment* (Washington, DC: The Police Foundation, 1973).

26. Richard C. Larson, "What Happened to Patrol Operations in Kansas City? A Review of the Kansas City Preventative Patrol Experiment," *Journal of Criminal Justice* 3 (1973): 267–297.

27. Lawrence W. Sherman, "General Deterrent Effects of Police Patrol in Crime 'Hot Spots': A Randomized, Controlled Trial," *Justice Quarterly* 12 (1995): 625–638.

28. Kirk R. Williams and Richard Hawkins, "Perceptual Research on General Deterrence: A Critical Review," *Law and Society Review* 20 (1986): 535–572.

29. Raymond Paternoster, "Assessments of Risk and Behavioral Experience: An Exploratory Study of Change," *Criminology* 23 (1985): 417–436.

30. Allen Beck and Bernard Shipley, *Recidivism of Prisoners Released in 1983,* (Washington, DC: Bureau of Justice Statistics, 1989).

31. Billie S. Erwin, "Turning Up the Heat on Probationers in Georgia," *Federal Probation* 50 (1986): 17–23.

32. Joan Petersilia and Susan Turner, "Evaluating Intensive Supervision Probation and Parole: Results of a Nationwide Experiment," *Research in Brief* (Washington, DC: National Institute of Justice, 1993); See also Joan Petersilia and Susan Turner, "An Evaluation of Intensive Probation in California," *Journal of Criminal Law and Criminology* 82 (1991): 610–658; Edward J. Latessa and Gennaro F. Vito, "The Effects of Intensive Supervision on Shock Probationers," *Journal of Criminal Justice* 16 (1988): 319–330.

33. Doris L. MacKenzie and James M. Shaw, "The Impact of Shock Incarceration on Technical Violations and New Criminal Activities," *Justice Quarterly* 10 (1993): 363–387.

34. Francis T. Cullen, John P. Wright, and Brandon K. Applegate, "Control in the Community: The Limits of Reform?" in Alan T. Harland, ed., *Choosing Correctional Options that Work: Defining the Demand and Evaluating the Supply* (Thousand Oaks, CA: Sage, 1996).

35. Cullen, Wright, and Applegate, 113.

36. Griffin, 41–44.

37. James O. Finckenauer, *Scared Straight and the Panacea Phenomenon* (Englewood Cliffs, NJ: Prentice Hall, 1982).

38. Lawrence W. Sherman, J.D. Schmidt, Dennis P. Rogan, P.R. Gartin, E.G. Cohen, D.J. Collins, and A.R. Bacich, "From Initial Deterrence to Long-Term Escalation: Short-Term Custody Arrest for Poverty Ghetto Domestic Violence," *Criminology* 29 (1991): 821–850.

39. Douglas A. Smith and Patrick R. Gartin, "Specifying Specific Deterrence: The Influence of Arrest on Future Criminal Activity," *American Sociological Review*, 53 (1989): 93–106.

40. Ronald L. Akers and Christine S. Sellers, *Criminological Theories: Introduction, Evaluation, and Application* (Los Angeles: Roxbury, 2003): 131–137.

41. Richard A. Berk and Lawrence W. Sherman, "Police Responses to Domestic Violence Incidents: An Analysis of an Experimental Design with Incomplete Randomization," *Journal of the American Statistical Association* 83 (1988): 70–76; Lawrence W. Sherman and Richard A. Berk, "The Specific Deterrent Effects of Arrest for Domestic Assault," *American Sociological Review* 39 (1983): 261–272.

42. Lawrence W. Sherman and Douglas A. Smith, "Crime, Punishment, and Stake in Conformity: Legal and Informal Control of Domestic Violence," *American Sociological Review* 57 (1992): 680–690.

43. Sherman, Schmidt, Rogan, Gartin, Cohen, Collins, and Bacich, 836.

44. Sherman and Smith, 685–688.

45. Anthony Pate and Edwin E. Hamilton, "Formal and Informal Deterrents to Domestic Violence," *American Sociological Review* 57 (1992): 691–697.

46. Richard A. Berk, Alec Campbell, Ruth Klap, and Bruce Western, "The Deterrent Effect of Arrest: A Bayesian Analysis of Four Field Experiments," *American Sociological Review* 57 (1992): 698–708.

47. Williams and Hawkins, 565–566.

48. Daniel S. Nagin and Greg Pogarsky, "Integrating Celerity, Impulsivity, and Extralegal Sanction Threats into a Model of General Deterrence: Theory and Evidence," *Criminology* 39 (2001): 865–892.

49. Nagin and Pogarsky, 867.

50. Akers and Sellers, 26–27.

51. Derek B. Cornish and Ronald V. Clarke, "Crime as Rational Choice," in *The Reasoning Criminal* (New York: Springer-Verlag, 1985).

52. Irving Piliavin, Craig Thornton, Rosemary Gartner, and Ross L. Matsueda, "Crime, Deterrence, and Rational Choice," *American Sociological Review* 51 (1986): 101–119.

53. Kenneth D. Tunnel, *Choosing Crime: The Criminal Calculus of Property Offenders* (Chicago: Nelson-Hall, 1992).

54. Ibid.

55. Tunnel, 1991, cited in Akers and Sellers, 28.

56. Willem De Haan and Jaco Vos, "A Crying Shame: The Over-Rationalized Conception of Man in the Rational Choice Perspective," *Theoretical Criminology* 7 (2003): 29–53.

57. Ronald L. Akers, "Rational Choice, Deterrence, and Social Learning in Criminology: The Path Not Taken," *Journal of Research in Crime and Delinquency* 27 (1990): 653–676.

58. Ibid.

59. Paul F. Cromwell, James N. Olson, and D'Aunn W. Avary, *Breaking and Entering: An Ethnographic Analysis of Burglary* (Newbury Park, CA: Sage, 1991).

60. Lawrence E. Cohen and Marcus Felson, "Social Change and Crime Rate Trends: A Routine Activity Approach," *American Sociological Review* 33 (1979): 588–608.

61. Marcus Felson, *Crime and Everyday Life*, 3rd edition (Thousand Oaks, CA: Sage, 2002).

62. Marcus Felson, *Crime and Everyday Life*, 2nd edition (Thousand Oaks, CA: Pine Forge, 1998): 53.

63. Ibid, 53–60.

64. Cohen and Felson, 591–593.

65. Richard R. Bennett, "Routine Activities: A Cross-National Assessment of a Criminological Perspective, *Social Forces* 70 (1991): 137–163.

66. Michael J. Hindelang, Michael R. Gottfredson, and James Garofalo, *Victims of Personal Crime: An Empirical Foundation for a Theory of Personal Victimization* (Cambridge, MA: Ballinger, 1978).

67. Vincent F. Sacco and Leslie W. Kennedy, *The Criminal Event: Perspectives in Time and Space* (Belmont, CA: Wadsworth, 2002): 63.

68. Hindelang, Gottredson, and Garofolo, 251–264.

69. Lawrence E. Cohen, and Marcus Felson, "Social Change and Crime Rate Trends: A Routine Activities Approach," *American Sociological Review* 44 (1979): 588–608.

70. Terrance D. Miethe, Robert F. Meier, and Douglas Sloane, "Lifestyle Changes and Risks of Criminal Victimization," *Journal of Quantitative Criminology* 6 (1990): 357–376.

71. Leslie W. Kennedy and David R. Ford, "Risky Lifestyles and Dangerous Results: Routine Activities and Exposure to Crime," *Sociology and Social Research* 73 (1990): 208–211.

72. Terance D. Miethe and David McDowall, "Contextual Effects in Models of Criminal Victimization," *Social Forces* 71 (1993): 731–760.

73. Janet L. Lauritsen, Robert J. Sampson, and John H. Laub, "The Link Between Offending and Victimization Among Adolescents," *Criminology* 29 (1991): 265–292.

74. Janet L. Lauritsen, Robert J. Sampson, and John H. Laub, "Conventional and Delinquent Activities: Implications for the Prevention of Violent Victimization Among Adolescents," *Violence and Victims* 7 (1992): 91–108.

75. John D. Wooldredge, "Inmate Lifestyles and Opportunities for Victimization," *Journal of Research in Crime and Delinquency* 35 (1998): 380–502.

76. David Weisburd, "Reorienting Crime Prevention Research and Policy: From the Causes of Criminality to the Context of Crime," *NIJ Research Report* (Washington, DC: National Institute of Justice, 1997).

77. C. Ray Jeffrey, *Crime Prevention Through Environmental Design* (Beverly Hills, CA: Sage, 1978).

78. Oscar Newman, *Defensible Space* (New York: Macmillan, 1972).

79. Felson, 1998, 150.

80. Felson, 1998, 163.

81. Allan Wallis, Daniel Ford, and Westinghouse Electric Corporation, *Crime Prevention Through Environmental Design: The Commercial Demonstration in Portland, Oregon.* (Washington, DC: U.S. National Institute of Justice, 1980).

82. James Kushmuk and Sherill Whitmore, *A Re-Evaluation of the CPTED Program in Portland, Oregon* (Washington, DC: National Institute of Justice, 1981).

83. David B. Griswold, "Crime Prevention and Commercial Burglary: A Time Series Analysis," *Journal of Criminal Justice* 12 (1983): 393–501.

84. Kate A. Painter and David P. Farrington, "Evaluation Situational Crime Prevention Using a Young People's Survey," *British Journal of Criminology* 31 (2001): 266–283.

85. Kate A. Painter and David P. Farrington, "The Crime Reducing Effect of Improved Street Lighting: The Dudley Project," in Ronald V. Clarke, ed., *Situational Crime Prevention: Successful Case Studies*, 2nd ed. (New York: Harrow and Heston, 1997), 209-226.

86. Paul Ekblom, Ho Law, and Mike Sutton, "Safer Cities and Domestic Burglary," *Home Office Research Study* 164 (London: Home Office, 1996).

87. Ekblom, Law, and Sutton, 35–40.

88. Paul Ekblom and Nick Tilley, "Going Equipped: Criminology, Situational Crime Prevention and the Resourceful Offender," *Journal of British Criminology* 40 (2000): 367–389.

OBJECTIVES

Learn the history of biological explanations of criminal behavior. This includes early biological theories and their policy implications, including eugenics.

Understand the methodologies used by scientists in their attempt to separate nature (genetics) from nurture (environment). This includes twin studies, adoption studies, and molecular genetics.

Grasp the known biological correlates of crime, which range from neurotransmitters to biological harms such as lead poisoning.

Understand biosocial theories of criminal behavior, and how policy implications differ between modern biosocial explanations and early biological theories.

Understand the basis of evolutionary theories of criminal behavior, and link this with a specific evolutionary theory.

Biology and Crime

Can Biological Risk Markers Identify Potential Criminals?

In his imaginative novel, *A Philosophical Investigation*, Philip Kerr describes a futuristic method of apprehending violent criminals before they commit crimes. The system, L.O.M.B.R.O.S.O. (named for the famed Italian criminologist), uses a screen for a biological trait among males (the absence of a Ventro Medical Nucleus [VMN]) that is predictive of violent behavior. In the novel, a Lombroso screen of over 4 million men finds that 0.003% were VMN negative. Of these, 30% were in prison or had some kind of criminal record. The program was instrumental in the apprehension of 10 murderers.

Is Kerr's fantastic notion a possibility? Is this where criminology is headed? Some believe that advances in molecular genetics, including the successful mapping of the entire human genome, might make this fantasy a reality in the near future.

Do you think that there is a genetic component to criminal behavior?

Assume that an instrument to screen humans for a biological trait related to criminality does evolve. What kinds of ethical dilemmas would such an instrument create?

Source: Philip Kerr, *A Philosophical Investigation* (New York: Plume, 1992).

Introduction

Most criminologists regard biological studies of crime with a mixture of indifference and ridicule. A 1990 survey, for example, found that only 20% of criminologists were receptive to the idea that genetic factors have an important influence on criminal behavior.[2] Certainly, this was not always the case. As noted in Chapter 1, many of the initial positive school theories were biological. How and when did biological theories fall from grace? What are the current biological theories of crime and are they empirically supported? Has the status of biological approaches to crime improved since 1990? This chapter addresses these questions and explores the biology of crime. The opening section examines those early pioneers of a scientific approach to crime. The remainder of the chapter outlines the current contributions of biology to the study of criminal behavior.

Early Biological Theories

The biological approach can be traced back to the early history of criminology. Because many early criminologists were physicians, it was natural for them to use the body to explain crime.[3] As a result, these scientists believed that the presence of certain physical traits made it more likely that an individual would become a criminal. They scientifically studied, objectively quantified, and accurately noted a wide array of constitutional (physical) attributes, including body build and bumps on the head. Early biological research also tended to point toward a single direct cause of criminality and to portray this cause as unchangeable. These early biological theories are summarized in **TABLE 4-1**. As will be noted, when a cause of crime is framed in this manner, the policy implications are rather narrow.

Phrenology was among the earliest schools of biological thought. Phrenologists believe that the exterior of the skull reflects the shape of the brain and the faculties of the mind; thus, "bumps" on the head could indicate certain criminal tendencies. Theorists (e.g., Lavater, Gall, Spurzheim, and Caldwell) compiled cases for scientific inquiry and categorization. They systematized popular stereotypes about physical features and crime (e.g., the beady-eyed criminal).[4] Others attempted to apply Darwin's theory of natural selection to criminal behavior.

TABLE 4-1

Summary of Early Biological Theories

Theorist	Theory	Core Elements
Cesare Lombroso	The "born criminal"	Lombroso used the concept of *atavism* — criminals as biological throwbacks on the evolutionary scale. The physical characteristics ("stigmata") identified these atavistic criminals. With a cranial capacity smaller than the "normal" man, low foreheads, and broad noses, the criminal was born with a strong tendency toward law breaking. He later modified this theory to recognize the influence of environmental forces. Subsequent research by Goring and Hooten did not support Lombroso's theory.
William H. Sheldon	Somatotype theory	This theory held that there was a strong link between body type and personality/behavior. Sheldon's study of delinquent boys found that they were likely to have the mesomorphic (muscular) body type. Subsequent research also documents this relationship. It remains unclear, though, *why* mesomorphy is related to delinquency.
Various, First Reported by Patricia Jacobs	XYY "supermale"	Since the Y chromosome dictates that the fetus will be biologically male, an extra Y chromosome was thought to make people "extra" male (more aggressive, violent). Initial studies on institutionalized men (and reports from the popular press) seemed to confirm this, but later studies did not. XYY males are no more likely to be violent than "normal" males, although they are moderately more likely to engage in criminal behavior. This may be due to other characteristics of the XYY anomaly, such as low intelligence.

Lombroso's "Born Criminal"

Cesare Lombroso, a 19th-century Italian physician, led the movement away from the classical school toward scientific positivism. His work with criminals helped to pave the way for the academic study of criminology. Lombroso's contributions extend beyond the biological school to highlight key features of the positivist approach, including the following[5]:

- A focus on the scientific study of the individual offender and conditions under which crime is committed
- The application of statistical methods to data collection and analysis, as well as the use of multiple-factor analysis
- The use of typological methods to classify and study criminals (e.g., female criminals, persistent criminals) and to examine criminological phenomena (e.g., the relationship between epilepsy and violent crime)

Consequently, Lombroso is "recognized as one of the pillars of criminological thought."[6] Influenced by Darwinian theory, Lombroso applied the concept of **atavism** to criminological theory. He concluded that criminals were biological throwbacks (atavists) on the evolutionary scale. He believed that modern criminals shared physical characteristics, or "stigmata," with primitive humans. With low foreheads, broad noses, and cranial capacities smaller than that of "normal" man, criminals were born with a strong tendency toward lawbreaking. While performing an autopsy, Lombroso experienced an epiphany[7]:

> At the sight of that skull, I seemed to see all of a sudden, lighted up as a vast plain under a flaming sky, the problem of the nature of the criminal — an atavistic being who reproduces in his person the ferocious instincts of primitive humanity and the inferior animals. These were explained anatomically by the enormous jaws, huge cheekbones, prominent superciliary arches, solitary lines in the palms, extreme size of the orbits, handle-shaped or sessile ears found in criminals, savages, and apes, insensibility to pain, extremely acute sight, tattooing, excessive idleness, love of orgies, and the irresistible craving for evil for its own sake, the desire not only to extinguish life in the victim, but to mutilate the corpse, tear its flesh, and drink its blood.

As his rather florid language attests, Lombroso believed the criminal to be an amoral person who had not evolved to the same social and biological level as other people.

Eventually, Lombroso acknowledged that social and environmental factors can contribute to are criminals because of some passion — of love or hate, politics, offended honor, or other intense emotion — that fueled their criminal rage.

Further Study of Physical "Deficiencies"

Researchers that followed Lombroso rejected his notion of an "atavistic" criminal but continued to argue that criminals were biologically inferior to law-abiding citizens. Charles Goring's influential book, *The English Convict: A Statistical Study*, recounted his study of 3000 English convicts, groups of college students, hospital patients, and soldiers. Among other things, Goring found no significant differences in various "stigmata" between the criminal and the noncriminal. The only significant

Cesare Lombroso, a 19th-century Italian physician, was among the first scientists to explore criminality. Although his theory of "atavism" has been discredited, his contributions (application of statistics and the scientific method) to the study of crime are still widely recognized.

? *How are modern biosocial theories different from Lombroso's theory of atavism?*

criminality. For example, he stated that environmental factors such as poverty, police corruption, high food prices, and emigration play an important role in crime causation. As he shifted his perspective from strict biological causation to a combination of nature and nurture, he came to identify types of criminals other than the atavist:

1. **Insane:** Those who are idiots, alcoholics, drug addicts, mentally retarded, and moral degenerates.

2. **Criminaloids:** Those who break the law of society but whose physical stigmatas and sense of moral degeneracy are less pronounced than the insane. These offenders are somehow pulled into a life of crime by environmental factors.

3. **Criminals by passion:** Those who are neither biological throwbacks nor criminaloids. They

Mark Hacking wipes tears from his face during his sentencing Monday, June 6, 2005, in Salt Lake City. Hacking was given six years to life for killing his pregnant wife Lori.

 Can a biological approach explain crimes such as this?

difference he discovered was that the criminal group was shorter and weighed less. Still, he concluded based on this finding that criminals were physically deficient. His most controversial finding, however, was that criminal behavior was related to "defective intelligence"; the convicts did not appear to researchers to be as intelligent as members of the noncriminal sample. Goring presumed that this factor was true of the entire criminal population.

In another study, American anthropologist Earnest Hooten examined more than 20,000 persons to determine whether physical traits play a role in crime causation. He concluded that criminals were physiologically inferior, characterized by low foreheads, pinched noses, compressed faces, and narrow jaws. Based on this evidence, Hooten suggested that he could predict specific forms of criminality. Murderers and robbers, for instance, were tall and thin; forgers, tall and heavy; and rapists, small.[8]

The research conducted by Lombroso, Goring, Hooten, and others has been roundly criticized on a number of grounds. For example, the comparison groups for some of these studies consisted of soldiers, fire fighters, or other types of individuals who were selected for the jobs based on physical stature. Should it be surprising that the average soldier or fire fighter is physically different from the average criminal? A more damaging criticism is that much of this research involved circular reasoning. Similarities between criminals and noncriminals, regardless of how extensive, were ignored. When even slight differences emerged, the researchers *assumed* that the difference meant that the comparison group was superior to the criminal group.

Sheldon's Somatotype Theory

A physician, William Sheldon, became the first researcher to carefully examine the relationship between body build and behavioral tendencies, temperament, life expectancy, and susceptibility to disease.[9] According to Sheldon, there are three basic human body types:

1. **Endomorphs:** fat, soft, and round; tend to be extroverts

2. **Ectomorphs:** thin and wiry; are easily worried, sensitive, and introverted

3. **Mesomorphs:** muscular; are gregarious, aggressive, assertive, and action-oriented

Sheldon noted that these are ideal types, meaning that no pure body type or <u>somatotype</u> actually exists. In other words, every person has some qualities from each category. For that reason, each individual had to be measured on a seven-point scale (with 343 possible combinations of body type).

In a study of 200 delinquents, Sheldon found that the majority were mesomorphic. Like Lombroso, he concluded that physical factors, when triggered by the environment, were related to criminal activity. A follow-up study conducted 30 years later found that 14 of the original 200 cases had adult felony convictions. Further, none of these individuals had any other psychiatric or medical problems that would account for their criminal behavior. These "primary criminals" had even more pronounced mesomorphic characteristics than the rest of the sample.[10]

The Gluecks, a husband-and-wife team at Harvard University, examined a sample of 500 white male delinquents and nondelinquents matched by IQ, age, and ethnicity. They also found that mesomorphs dominated the delinquent sample. Again, they concluded that body type is a factor in delinquent behavior but that other variables must also be considered.[11] Similar findings, using a similar research strategy, were obtained several decades later.[12] Thus it appears that body type is indeed related to officially recorded delinquency. As with other factors, the key question is why this relationship exists.

Jeffrey offers one explanation for the mesomorph's propensity for crime:[13]

> People who are muscular gain pleasure and rewards from large muscular activities, such as fishing, hunting, skiing, and football. The mesomorph is involved in "the Michelob weekend." In the same way people who are thin and dominated by nerve tissue are more sensitive to noise, light, and color, they are much more likely to find art or music more rewarding and pleasurable than duck hunting at 5 AM in freezing waters, or trying to cast a fly on the Yellowstone River in a 50-mph wind. The endomorph is one who likes good food and "no wine before its time."

In other words, criminal activity may be more appealing to the mesomorph. There are, however, other explanations for the relationship between a mesomorphic body and criminal behavior. For example, the mesomorphic body type may have an advantage in the rough-and-tumble activities of

Do muscles mean crime? According to Sheldon, individuals with a mesomorphic body type were more likely to engage in crime.

? *How have modern criminologists criticized this conclusion?*

The XYY "Supermale"

A final example of an early biological theory is actually quite recent, when compared to the work of Lombroso and Goring. Although the initial publication linking <u>XYY</u> males to crime appeared in 1965, the "supermale" phenomenon is included here because, like other early theories, it supposedly identifies a single, direct, and immutable cause of crime. This theory involves a particular chromosomal abnormality. Each human has 23 pairs of chromosomes; the last pair of chromosomes determines the biological sex of the person. For males, the normal chromosome pair is XY; the female structure is XX. Some individuals, however, have more unusual combinations. For example, some females have an XXX structure and some males have an XXY structure (also know as Klinefelter's syndrome).

The British scientist Patricia Jacobs found that the incidence of the XYY disorder (males with an extra Y chromosome) was 20 times higher among inmates in a Scottish prison than in the general Scottish population. She also reported that the double Y chromosome caused males to be unusually tall, aggressive, and violent.[15] On the basis of this and other early research, these "supermales" were believed to be prone to extremely violent, heinous crimes.

In the 1960s, a number of violent cases involving XYY offenders came to the attention of the world. Murder cases in Australia, France, Scotland, West Germany, and the United States featured XYY offenders. For example, the case of Richard Speck was a major influence in the study of the XYY male and crime. In 1966, Speck brutally murdered eight student nurses in Chicago. He had a lengthy criminal record and the physical stigmata associated with the chromosomal pattern (i.e., tall, lean, lanky, pimpled). Immediately, the XYY theory gained prominence; only later was it discovered that Speck did not actually have the extra Y chromosome.

In all, there have been more than 150 studies regarding violence and the XYY chromosome. An extensive summary of this research highlights the following findings[16]:

- XYY men tend to be taller than comparable XY men.
- XYY men convicted of crimes are more likely to be guilty of property offenses and less likely than convicted XY men to have committed violent offenses. Thus, even if XYY males were

street crime. Other persons may be more likely to "draft" a mesomorph for help in criminal activities. Also, the criminal justice system may view the mesomorphic criminal as a more serious threat to society. Keep in mind that many of these studies were based on institutional populations or official measures of crime. Perhaps the delinquent mesomorph is perceived as a threat and thus is more likely to be arrested and/or incarcerated. A recent reanalysis of the Gluecks' data supports this argument.[14] While mesomophic body types predicted *official* delinquency, it did not predict self-reported delinquency.

"born criminals," they were not more likely to commit violent crime.

- The families of XYY inmates tend to have less history of crime or mental illness than do the families of XY inmates.
- The prevalence of XYY men is higher in mental and penal institutions than in the general population.

In sum, it appears as though XYY males may be more likely to engage in criminal behavior, but not violent behavior. For example, an exhaustive Danish study of more than 4000 males found little or no evidence of violence. However, the XYY males did commit more nonviolent crimes than a matched control group of XY males.[17] Even here, many question whether this is a direct link, or whether crime amongst XYY males is caused by their lower intelligence. One thing is certain: Because the XYY chromosome structure is so rare (less than 0.1% of the male population has this pattern), it can only explain a tiny fraction of crime among males and none among females.

The Policy Implications and Legacy of Early Biological Research

Early biological research tended to share a similarity: a focus on a single factor (e.g., body type, defective intelligence, XYY chromosome) that was not amenable to change, and that directly caused crime. The policy implications of such theories are rather narrow. If the cause of crime cannot be changed, what can be done? One answer, of course, is to separate these individuals from society. For example, Earnest Hooten advocated large criminal reservations to separate "inferiors" from the rest of society[18]:

> Of course, I think that the habitual criminals who are hopeless constitutional inferiors should be permanently incarcerated and, on no account, should be allowed to breed. Nevertheless, they should be treated humanely, and, if they are to be kept alive should be allowed some opportunity for freedom and profitable occupation within their own severely restricted area.

This quote also illustrates a second option advocated by many early researchers — not allowing "defective" members of society to have children. Francis Galton coined the term eugenics (meaning well-born) to describe the process of improving the human race by not permitting persons of "bad stock" to reproduce.[19] The eugenics movement led

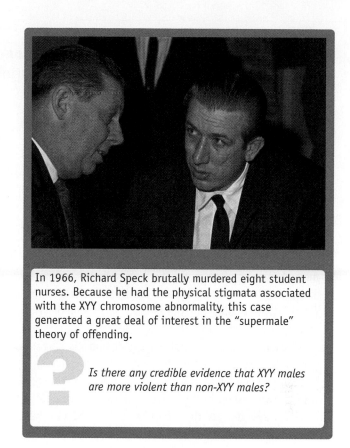

In 1966, Richard Speck brutally murdered eight student nurses. Because he had the physical stigmata associated with the XYY chromosome abnormality, this case generated a great deal of interest in the "supermale" theory of offending.

? *Is there any credible evidence that XYY males are more violent than non-XYY males?*

to (among other things) limitations on the immigration of southern and eastern Europeans into the United States in the early 1920s and to the institutionalization or forced sterilization of the poor, deviant, and disabled.[20]

The eugenics movement lost all of its momentum by the end of World War II. Nazi atrocities, including the mass executions of Jews, Gypsies, homosexuals, and other groups, was justified in part as an attempt to create a biologically superior Aryan race (e.g., having blue eyes and blond hair). Still, policies based on the initial XYY supermale findings were evident as late as the 1970s. For example, at the Boston Hospital for Women, a group of doctors started screening newborn male infants for the extra Y chromosome. In 1972, the California Center for the Study and Reduction of Violence set up a program to screen junior high school males for the XYY chromosome.[21] Such efforts could have severely stigmatized XYY males or at least have had a negative influence on their civil rights. More recently, some have argued that the legalization of abortion produced an "unintended eugenics movement" (see **Theory in Action: Freakonomics — Abortion as Unintended Eugenics**).

Freakonomics—Abortion as Unintended Eugenics

A 2005 book by economist Steven Levitt and coauthor Stephen Dubner generated a buzz among academics, commentators, and the general public that included a number 1 ranking on the *New York Times* best sellers list for nonfiction. *Freakonomics: A Rogue Economist Explores the Hidden Side of Everything* makes a number of interesting, and often controversial, arguments. For example, the authors suggest that parents have little influence over their children's personality and that swimming pools are more dangerous than guns. The authors' most controversial claim, however, is that the legalization of abortion is (in part) responsible for the large drop in violent crime experienced in the United States.

Based on past research by Levitt and his research associate, the gist of this argument is that because of the Supreme Court's 1973 decision in *Roe v. Wade*, many fetuses were killed in the United States that would otherwise have led to the birth of unwanted children. These "unwanted" children would have been more likely to commit crimes when grown. Therefore, their removal

from the population had an effect on the crime rate roughly 20 years later. In essence, the legalization of abortion created an (unintended) eugenics effect.

Although journalists and book reviewers have generally offered praise for the book, many scientists are very critical of the science behind the abortion–crime link. In particular, they note that crime rates actually increased during the period (the 1990s) that the first cohort (after *Roe*) reached their crime-prone years. Further, there is little evidence that the legalization of abortion halted unwanted pregnancies. Indeed, births of illegitimate children actually increased dramatically after the legalization of abortion. Some commentators even suggest that, because the crime drop was disproportionately among black males, the argument has racist undertones.

Sources: Steven D. Levitt and Stephen J. Dubner, *Freakonomics: A Rogue Economist Explores the Hidden Side of Everything* (New York: Harper Collins, 2005); Steve Sailer, "Did Legalizing Abortion Cut Crime?" Available at http://www.isteve.com/abortion.htm, accessed July 11, 2005.

These policy implications, combined with research that was often blatantly shoddy, led to a sharp decline in the popularity of a biological approach to crime. At the same time, sociologists (who often find biological explanations repugnant) came to dominate the field of criminology. From the 1950s until relatively recently, the study of biological influences in crime was almost taboo. Indeed, a 1992 conference sponsored by the National Institutes of Health (NIH) entitled "Genetic Factors and Crime" was cancelled due to public pressure (NIH withdrew funding). Because African-Americans are overrepresented in official crime statistics, opponents to the conference believed the proceedings were racist and intentionally excluded sociological explanations.[22]

A Modern Biological Approach to Crime

Despite a tarnished legacy, biological research on crime has made a "comeback" of sorts in recent years. Indeed, the cancelled conference on genetics

Sarah Jane Wiley in the former operating room at the old Virginia Colony for the Epileptic and Feebleminded in Lynchburg, Virginia. Wiley was one of thousands of people sterilized in the operating room as part of the eugenics movement.

 Is there a danger that modern biological research on criminality will spark a new eugenics movement?

and crime was actually rescheduled and took place in 1995. In this section, four modern areas of biological inquiry into crime are discussed: (1) behavioral genetics, (2) biological correlates of criminal behavior, (3) biosocial theories, and (4) evolutionary explanations of crime.

Behavioral Genetics

A major question posed by the biological school is, "Can criminality be inherited?" An affirmative answer would implicate some biological process in the creation of crime. This line of inquiry is typically referred to as **behavioral genetics**. Basically, there have been four approaches to examine the relationship between genetic factors and crime: (1) family studies, (2) study of twins, (3) adoption studies, and (4) molecular genetics. These strategies are summarized in TABLE 4-2.

Family Studies

The earliest studies looking into this question focused on degenerate families and feeblemindedness. For example, Dugdale traced the descendants of a woman he called Ada Jukes and found that most family members were criminals, prostitutes, or welfare recipients.[23] In a similar study, Goddard traced nearly 1000 descendants of Martin Kallikak from the time of the American Revolution and

identified "feeblemindedness" as his illegitimate line's dominant trait.[24]

The glaring problem with these studies is that environmental influences (e.g., poverty, area of residence) could easily explain why crime or feeblemindedness seemed to run in these families. Dugdale's own description of the "habitat of the Jukes" suggests as much[25]:

> They lived in log or stone houses similar to slave-hovels, all ages, sexes, relations and strangers "bunking" indiscriminately . . . To this day, the "Jukes" occupy the self-same shanties built nearly a century ago. . . . Sometimes I found an overcrowding so close it suggested that these dwellings were the country equivalents to city tenement houses.

Despite this obvious weakness, family studies were used by many to support a policy of eugenics. (See **Headline Crimes: Were the "Jukes" Really Bad or Just Badly Researched?** for a discussion of the recent discovery of documents that further damages the conclusions of Dugdale's original study.)

Modern studies continue to confirm that crime runs in families. Specifically, parental criminality is a relatively strong and consistent predictor of delinquency.[26] Although scholars continue to debate the meaning of this finding, most criminologists

TABLE 4-2			
Methods Used to Separate Nature from Nurture			
Method	**Research Design**	**Findings**	**Criticisms or Limitations**
Family Studies	Early studies traced family history; modern studies look at how parents' crime relates to their children's crime.	Parental crime consistently predicts the criminal behavior of their children.	Environment (nurture) could easily explain this finding. For example, criminal parents may be less likely to make a strong investment in parenting or socializing their children.
Twin Studies	Compare monozygotic (MZ) twins to dizygotic (DZ) twins. Because MZ twins are genetically identical and DZ twins are not, a genetic effect is assumed if concordance rates are higher for MZ twins.	MZ twins generally have higher concordance rates than DZ twins. This finding is more consistent early in childhood and in adulthood (but not during adolescence).	Because MZ twins look exactly alike, people (parents, teachers, etc.) may treat them more similarly than they do DZ twins. Also, MZ twins are more likely to share the same friends — including delinquent peers.
Adoption Studies	Compare the criminal record of adopted children with their biological parents (who only contributed genes) and adoptive parents (who provide the environment).	Children's criminal behavior appears to relate more to the biological parents' criminal records than to that of the adoptive parents.	Adoption agencies might match the environment of the adoptive parents to that of the biological parents. The adoptive parents' criminal records are not a comprehensive measure of environment.
Molecular Genetics	Isolate particular genes that may be related to a criminal disposition.	Some genes have been identified that may be related to a criminal disposition.	Any particular gene will have a minimal effect on human behavior. Most will slightly prod behavior in a particular direction.

favor an environmental explanation. For example, criminal parents may be less effective at socializing their children and may be role models for deviant behaviors. A 1993 study by criminologists Robert Sampson and John Laub found that poor parenting explained the relationship between parent and child criminal behavior. Criminal parents were less likely to supervise their children and more likely to use harsh and erratic punishment. According to Sampson and Laub, "A central characteristic of deviant and criminal life styles is the rejection of restrictions and duties — especially those that involve planning, patience, and investment in the future."[27]

> **LINK** In Chapter 7, several sociological theories that offer alternative explanations for the finding that crime "runs in families" are explored. For example, children might learn criminal behavior from their parents.

Twin Studies

Twin studies offer an alternative to simply tracing family histories or examining measures of parental crime. These studies typically compare identical (monozygotic) twins to same sex fraternal (dizygotic) twins. **Monozygotic (MZ) twins** are products of a single egg and sperm, and thus are exactly the same genetically. **Dizygotic (DZ) twins** are products of two eggs and two sperms, and thus are as genetically similar as any two siblings within a family. Researchers assume a genetic effect when MZ twins have more similar outcomes than DZ twins. These studies typically express findings in terms of a **concordance rate**. The outcome (crime) is concordant if *both* twins exhibit the behavior. When one is a criminal and the other is not, the pair is discordant. The effect of the environment is "controlled," because both types of twins share environments. In other words, one might expect that both types of twins would have some concordance, because they share similar environments (same parents, same household, same school, etc.). A genetic effect is assumed when the concordance rate for MZ twins is *higher* than that of DZ twins.

The most cited example of twin research is the Danish twin study — a study of more than 3500 pairs of twins born between 1881 and 1910 in Denmark.[28] Here, the concordance rate for conviction among identical twins was 52%; as opposed to 22% in the fraternal twin sample. In other words, if one twin is a criminal, the MZ twin is more than twice as likely to be involved in crime as the DZ twin. Similar but lower concordance rates were reported for female twins. In Ohio, a researcher had a sample of identical and fraternal twins respond to a self-report questionnaire concerning the delinquent behavior of each twin and the other twin's friends.[29] The author reported that the self-reported rates of delinquency were more similar among identical twins. He also found that the friends of

Monozygotic (MZ) twins are genetically identical.

? *Are observed concordance rates for the criminal behavior of MZ twins a product of shared genetics or environmental factors?*

the delinquent identical twins were prone to delinquency.

In essence, this research consistently documents a stronger concordance rate among identical twins than fraternal twins. Similar findings appear for males and females and for children (behavior problems) and adults. A recent review of 42 twin studies estimated (based on differences in concordance rates) that, on average, the genetic influence explained about 40% of the variation in antisocial behavior.[30] Still, there are several limitations of twin studies that might inflate concordance rates for MZ twins. In other words, the difference in concordance rates might be due to factors other than genetics. For example, because MZ twins look alike, they may be more likely to be treated the same by parents, teachers, and peers than DZ twins. Also, identical twins tend to spend more time with each other and tend to have the same friends.[31]

This is important for a couple of reasons. First, because association with delinquent friends is a strong predictor of delinquency, it may be some of the concordance among MZ twins is the result of their shared peer group. Secondly, if MZ twins spend more time together, one may simply imitate the other's antisocial behavior.[32] These processes were illustrated in a Danish study of MZ and DZ twins. After controlling for imitation and peer relations, the genetic effect was substantially reduced.[33] Thus,

even twin studies find it difficult to fully separate the influences of environment and heredity. The examination of twins reared apart may be an important research strategy for future understanding of crime.[34]

Adoption Studies

One other method of addressing the nature versus nurture debate is to use adoption as a natural experiment. In the adoption study approach, the behaviors of adoptees are compared with the outcomes of both their adoptive and biological parents. Similarities in outcome between adopted children and their *biological* parents are assumed to reflect a genetic effect. Similarities between the children and their *adoptive* parents are assumed to reflect their shared environment. The most widely read study involved over 4000 Danish boys and their biological and adoptive parents.[35] The results of this analysis are illustrated in **FIGURE 4-1**. As expected, boys whose adoptive and biological parents engaged in crime had the highest crime rate (24.5%).

The estimate of a genetic effect is obtained by moving from left to right on this table. The data indicate that regardless of whether the adoptive parents had a criminal record, the criminality of the boys was related to that of their biological parents. For example, the bottom half of the table contains only those boys whose adoptive parents had no criminal record. Within this category of boys, those who had criminal biological parents had a higher

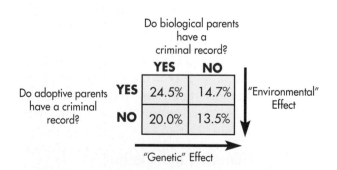

FIGURE 4-1 Results of the Danish Adoption Study

The numbers in the table refer to the percentage of adoptees within each category who had a criminal record.

Source: Data summarized from Sarnoff A. Mednick, William F. Gabrielli, and Barry Hutchings, "Genetic Influences in Criminal Convictions," *Science* 224 (1984): 891–894.

rate of criminal convictions (20%) than those who did not have criminal biological parents (13.5%).

The extent of the criminal career of the biological parents was also influential. Boys whose biological parents had three or more convictions were three times more likely than their counterparts with noncriminal biological parents to commit crimes. Thus, biological factors appeared to be more important than environmental ones. As was the case with twin studies, adoption studies tend to reach a similar conclusion — most uncover a moderate genetic effect. This finding, however, emerges only for property (and not violent) offending.[36]

The adoption research design has been questioned on a number of grounds. For example, critics correctly point out that the measure of adoptive parents criminality is not a comprehensive measure of environment. Second, adoption agencies sometimes seek to match the environmental characteristics of the biological parents' home to that of the adoptive parents' home. This process could create the illusion of a genetic effect.[37]

In sum, both adoption studies and twin research attempt to separate nurture from nature to establish a link between genetics and crime. There is a great deal of disagreement over where the weight of the evidence lies with this issue. A review of both of these methods calculated that genetics can explain roughly 40% of the variance in criminal behavior with the remainder being due to environmental influences. Such evidence suggests to leaders in the field of developmental psychology that, "Genetically informed research has revealed a moderate degree of heritability for aggression, delinquency, and antisocial behavior from childhood to adulthood."[38] Other reviewers note that adoption and twin research is often poorly designed and/or ambiguously reported.[39] Consistent with this point, a review of the literature reported that better-designed and more recently published studies provided *less* support for the gene-crime hypothesis.[40]

Molecular Genetics and the Human Genome Project

More recent (and "high-tech") attempts to establish the heredity of crime involve a search for specific genes. A deep understanding of this research requires a rather detailed knowledge of biology that is outside the scope of this book. Nevertheless, understanding the gist of this research requires only some basic terminology. Most people are familiar with deoxyribonucleic acid (DNA), which contains the chemical codes for all living organisms. DNA is made up of four chemicals, called *bases*, that bind together in different sequences. The specific order of bases within these sequences underlies all of the diversity in life. They dictate, for example, whether an organism is a human, a mosquito, or a grain of rice. A *gene* is a specific sequence of bases within a DNA molecule.[41] Genes, through the creation of different proteins, dictate the "instructions" for the development and functioning of a human being.

Technology now permits scientists to sift through DNA structure in order to isolate and study specific genes. One strategy for this new technology is called *gene-linkage analysis*. Here, a single gene is followed through a particular family that evidences a particular disease or disorder. A high-profile study illustrates this analysis. Geneticist Hans Brunner and his associates studied a Dutch family line with a history of rather bizarre and violent behavior among males (but not females).[42] For example, one of the males raped his own sister, another forced his sisters to undress at knifepoint, another stabbed a prison warden with a pitchfork, and another attempted to run over his work supervisor. Two of the men had a propensity for starting fires.

After a decade of laboratory research, Brunner and his associates isolated and identified a particular mutated gene that was in the males within this family. This gene was responsible for the production of monoamine oxidase A (MAOA). MAOA breaks down two neurotransmitters (serotonin and norepinephrine) so that they can be removed from the body. The mutation in the gene rendered the body unable to perform this important function. Serotonin levels, in particular, have been linked to violent behavior.

It is important to note that to date, this particular gene mutation has only been found in one Danish family. Thus, this type of mutation is unlikely to provide a general explanation for crime. In all likelihood, traits consistent with a criminal disposition are based on a wide variety of genes: "the nudge from any particular gene is not strong, and it could easily be countered by a favorable balance from another gene."[43] For example, several researchers have found a weak to moderate relationship between a dopamine receptor gene, and novelty-seeking behavior, as well as Attention

Deficit Disorder (ADD).[44] In turn, both ADD and novelty-seeking are related to criminal behavior.

Because no single gene is likely to have a strong effect on criminal behavior, the search for genes related to criminal behavior is likely to be slow and difficult. Results from the **Human Genome Project**, however, may aid in the search. Formally launched in 1990 and completed in 2003, the U.S. Human Genome Project (HGP) was a coordinated effort by the U.S. Department of Energy and the NIH to map the entire human genome. *Genome* is a term used to describe the total DNA in an organism.[45] The genome of humans (a copy of which is contained in almost all cells) consists of over 3 billion pairs of chemical bases. HGP plans to store this information in databases and develop tools to analyze the genetic codes. Ultimately, the data will be transferred to the private sector to stimulate bio-research.[46]

Overall then, there is some support from a variety of sources for the idea that a person's propensity for crime might be partially heritable. To be sure, this area of inquiry is extremely controversial, and many criminologists are still skeptical about whether research supports a genetic basis for crime. Even if there is a genetic link, biology-oriented

A lab technician examines a plate containing samples of purified DNA as it is prepared to be sequenced in the lab at MIT's Whitehead Institute in Cambridge, Massachusetts, as part of the Human Genome Project.

? *How will the Human Genome Project affect the study of genetics–crime link?*

criminologists readily admit that there is no "crime gene." Rather, they argue that "genetic factor is involved in the *predisposition* to antisocial behavior."[47] What, then, might be inherited that relates to predisposition for criminal behavior? Some of the possible suspects are highlighted in the discussion of biological correlates of crime.

Biological Correlates of Crime

Like the work of Lombroso and Sheldon, much of the current biological research focuses on physiological differences between criminals and noncriminals. Rather than skull features or body type, however, the modern approach focuses on a wide range of characteristics, including neurological (brain) functioning, the autonomic nervous system, hormones, and various "biological harms." Further, unlike early positivistic theories, modern-day scientists do not believe that biological differences can unequivocally identify criminals. Rather, the biology of criminals is likely to fall on a continuum with the biology of law-abiding citizens.[48] **TABLE 4-3** summarizes the biological correlates of crime.

Neurological Studies

Neurological factors may play a significant role in criminal behavior. In particular, researchers have focused on the **prefrontal cortex**, the part of the brain responsible for "executive functions." *Executive functions* include the ability to sustain attention, self-monitoring, abstract reasoning, and the inhibition of inappropriate or impulsive behavior. There are a number of avenues for studying the role of the brain in antisocial behavior. Technology now offers a number of direct measures of brain structure and activity, including positron-emission tomography (PET) scans, electroencephalogram (EEG), and magnetic resonance imaging (MRI).

PET scans detect which regions of the brain are active (and the extent of this activity). To utilize this technology, subjects are first injected with sugar that has a radioactive component. Next, they are asked to complete some cognitive task. Sugar provides "fuel" for the brain, so the most active regions of the brain will draw the radioactive-labeled sugar, which the PET scan then detects.[49] One PET scan study compared murderers to matched (on age and sex) noncriminal control groups. The murderers showed less brain activity in a specific part of the frontal lobe than the control groups.[50]

TABLE 4-3

Summary of Biological Correlates of Crime

Biological Factor	Specific Measures and Conclusions
Neurological Factors	
Direct measures of the brain	Measures of brain structure (MRI scans) and brain activity (PET scans) suggest that there are differences in the frontal lobe of the brain between certain types of criminals and noncriminal control groups.
Neurochemical measures	Neurotransmitters allow cells to communicate with each other. Low levels of serotonin have been linked with impulsive and aggressive behavior.
Indirect measures	IQ and other "neuropsychological" tests predict delinquency. Some biocriminologists assume that this reflects underlying neurological deficits.
Autonomic Nervous System	Some types of criminals have lower heart rates than noncriminal controls. Studies of skin conductance (sweat) yield mixed results.
Biological Harms	
Perinatal harms	Perinatal risks (maternal smoking and drinking during pregnancy) and delivery complications are associated with juvenile and adult crime. Some studies find that this effect is more pronounced in unstable families.
Exposure to lead	Lead is a highly toxic substance that produces biological damage, especially to children who are still developing. Exposure to lead (through lead paint and other sources) has been linked to delinquent behavior. In one study, lead exposure was among the strongest predictors of delinquency.
Nutrition and diet	Some research suggests that diet (particularly sugar intake) relates to antisocial behavior. In particular, some raised the prospect that hypoglycemia might cause violent, impulsive behavior. Recent research fails to support these findings.
Hormones	Higher levels of the male androgen testosterone have been linked to antisocial behavior. There is some evidence that premenstrual syndrome is related to female offending. This research, however, has been severely criticized.

Other types of brain scans (primarily MRI and EEG) also reveal differences between criminals and noncriminals. For example, in 2000, an MRI study compared individuals diagnosed with antisocial personality disorder (APD) to three separate control groups (a "normal" group, a group with other psychiatric disorders, and a group with substance-abuse problems). All of the subjects for the study were recruited from the general population. Through the use of powerful magnets, MRI scans provide a detailed three-dimensional picture of brain anatomy. In the study, the APD group had less "gray matter," in the prefrontal cortex than any of the control groups.[51]

Another route to studying the effect of brain processes on criminal behavior is to look at the chemicals within the brain. Leading biocriminologists offer this explanation for the link between neurochemical processes and human behavior[52]:

> Thoughts, behavior, and emotions are mediated by the transmissions of electrical impulses between neurons, the cells of the nervous system. Gaps that exist between neurons are called synapses, and communications between neurons requires the passage of electrical impulses across these synapses. Neurotransmitters such as dopamine, norepinephrine, and serotonin therefore form the basis for information processing and communication within the brain; and as a result they underlie all types of behavior, including sensation, perception, learning and memory, and — more controversially — antisocial behavior.

For example, one research review examined the literature on how an enzyme, monoamine oxidase (MAO), appears to affect brain functioning.[53] The review highlighted several studies that linked low MAO activity with high probabilities of criminality, psychopathy, childhood conduct disorders, sensation seeking, impulsivity, and drug abuse. Low MAO activity was more characteristic of males than females, lower in blacks than whites, and lowest during the second and third decades of life. The reviewer argued that these findings were encouraging indicators of the neurological underpinnings of criminal behavior.

Another neurotransmitter studied extensively is serotonin. Because serotonin helps conduct the electrical impulses in the brain, low levels of serotonin hinder communication between cells. The serotonin system is the target of a class of antidepressant drugs, including Prozac.[54] Although this is a simplification of the process, Prozac relieves depression generally by increasing the availability of serotonin. A number of research studies find that low levels of serotonin are related to impulsive, violent, or antisocial behavior. For example, a 1998 study found that low serotonin levels predicted both official and self-reported criminal behavior among a sample of New Zealand young adults.[55] The relationship held only for males, but appeared even after controlling for a host of physical and environmental variables. A 1999 study also lends support to the importance of serotonin. In this study, a small (10) sample of offenders was injected with a drug that increases the availability of serotonin. The researchers reported reductions in both aggression and impulsivity.[56]

As opposed to studying neurotransmitters and brain structure, some researchers use psychological tests as an indirect measure of neurological differences. Tests that focus on executive functions (cognition, attention, impulsivity) are assumed to reflect differences in brain functioning. Thus, neuropsychological tests are simply psychological tests that are assumed to reflect neurological differences.

There is a good deal of evidence that such tests are related to delinquency and crime. For example, one longitudinal study examined the relationship between neuropsychological measures and criminal behavior. The data were drawn from the Dunedin (New Zealand) Multidisciplinary Health and Development Study — a birth cohort of several hundred males, age 13 to 18. The study demonstrated that neuropsychological scores at age 13 predicted delinquency and criminal behavior in adulthood.[57] Some believe that IQ scores, which consistently predict delinquent behavior, are a broad measure of neurological health.[58] Of course, there are other interpretations of what IQ measures.

> **LINK** The relationship between IQ and crime is explored more fully in Chapter 5.

The Autonomic Nervous System

The autonomic nervous system (ANS) controls heart rate and gland secretions, among other things. Generally speaking, it controls how the body reacts to stimuli. The heart rate, for example, increases in the presence of stimuli that are stressful or exciting, such as when walking into a room to take an exam. A substantial body of research suggests that criminals may have a lower resting heart rate than noncriminals. A review of 14 studies on this topic revealed that regardless of how the heart rate (simple pulse to sophisticated equipment) or crime (self-reports, official records, psychiatric diagnosis) was measured, heart rates consistently predicted antisocial behavior.[59] Similar findings are obtained for children diagnosed with "conduct disorder."[60]

Skin conductance is another measure of how the body reacts to stimuli. In this type of research, electrodes attached to individuals' fingers measure how much a person sweats. The research in this area is much more mixed, with many studies finding no relationship between skin conductance and crime. Those studies that document a significant relationship find that criminals have lower levels of skin conductance than noncriminals.[61]

Why would heart rate and skin conductance relate to criminal behavior? Both of these measures (as well as some brain scan evidence) suggest that criminals may have low levels of arousal; that is, they do not respond as much to stimuli as the average person. There are two main interpretations of this finding.[62] First, if a person is in a constant state of underarousal, they may seek out activities (including crime) that are naturally arousing. An alternative explanation is that those with a criminal disposition have a higher level of fearlessness. Thus, when faced with situations that typically induce fear, their heart rate remains relatively low, and they do not sweat profusely. Obviously, such a characteristic would be beneficial for those who carry out criminal behavior.

Of course, neither of these propositions explains why some individuals engage in crime, while others find noncriminal solutions. For example, an underaroused individual might try bungee jumping or mountain climbing. Similarly, a fearless person might defuse bombs for the military or fight fires rather than engage in criminal behavior. A biological predisposition toward crime does not guarantee a person will become a criminal, but may increase the *risk* of criminal behavior.[63]

Biological Harms

Biological differences that relate to criminal behavior might be caused by a host of factors. The infamous violent Dutch family reviewed previously suggests that in some cases, genetics can play a role. Another line of research involves examining the effect various biological "harms," such as physical trauma, disease, or exposure to certain chemicals. Charles Whitman is perhaps the most celebrated case study relating brain tumors to violence. In 1966, Whitman killed 14 people from the Texas Tower at the University of Austin. Just prior to the shooting spree, he had murdered both his wife and his mother. After the incident, investigators discovered that Whitman had sought psychiatric help because he was experiencing irrational and violent thoughts (including a fantasy about shooting people from the tower).[64] Whitman kept journals and left behind numerous letters (some suggest this hypergraphia was an additional psychiatric symptom). In one of his final notes, he typed the following[65]:

> I don't quite understand what it is that compels me to type this letter. . . . I don't really understand myself these days . . . Lately I have been a victim of many unusual and irrational thoughts. These thoughts constantly recur, and it requires a tremendous mental effort to concentrate. I consulted Dr. Cochrum at the University Health Center and asked him to recommend someone that I could consult with about some psychiatric disorders I felt I had. . . . I talked to a doctor once for about two hours and tried to convey to him my fears that I felt overcome by overwhelming violent impulses . . . After my death I wish that an autopsy would be performed to see if there is any visible physical disorder. I have had tremendous headaches in the past and have consumed two large bottles of Excedrin in the past three months.

An autopsy did reveal a walnut-sized tumor, which was located in the hypothalamus region of the brain and pressing against the amygdala.[66] The amygdala is thought to be involved with emotion and memory formation. Of course, like the violent Danish family, the case of Charles Whitman is a dramatic example of how biological trauma might lead to criminal behavior. More commonly, researchers in this area focus on other biological harms, including perinatal risks and birth complications, exposure to a variety of environmental toxins, and diet and nutrition.

Perinatal Risk and Birth Complications A growing body of literature has examined the role that perinatal problems (perinatal meaning at or around the time of birth) play in the development of criminal behavior. Generally, these studies focus on high-risk maternal behavior (e.g., smoking, drinking alcohol, using illicit drugs) during pregnancy, trauma suffered by the fetus during delivery, and low-birth-weight infants.

There is a great deal of evidence that maternal behaviors during pregnancy can adversely affect the health of the fetus. For example, maternal consumption of alcohol in high doses during pregnancy can result in fetal alcohol syndrome (FAS). FAS is a well-documented condition defined by a host of characteristics, including central nervous system dysfunction, growth retardation, and organ anomalies.[67] There is some evidence that even lower doses of alcohol may relate to childhood problems and criminal behavior.[68] Evidence also exists that maternal smoking during pregnancy is related to criminal outcomes for children. A recent study found that maternal smoking predicted adult criminal outcomes (both property and violence offenses) in a sample of Danish males.[69] A 2000 study found a similar relationship for maternal use of marijuana during pregnancy.[70] By 10 years of age, the children of these mothers showed increased levels of inattention, hyperactivity, and delinquency.

Several studies have examined the impact of delivery complications on delinquency or criminal behavior. Researchers believe that complications (e.g., use of forceps to extract the fetus) cause injury to the fetus. One study, for example, examined the relationship between perinatal events and violent and property crime.[71] The researchers examined physical and criminal data from a birth cohort of Danish children. They reported that birth trauma–induced brain injury may have contributed to repeat violent offending. Specifically, they found that an index of delivery complications predicted adolescent and adult violent crime. A related line of inquiry considers the effect of low birth weight on childhood and adult outcomes.

Low birth weight can be caused by a host of factors including maternal smoking or drinking during pregnancy. A substantial body of evidence indicates that low-birth-weight children are more likely than children of normal birth weight to have mild learning disabilities, attention disorders, hyperactivity, behavioral problems, low intelligence, poor academic achievement, and a difficult temperament.[72] A recent study linked low birth weight with criminal behavior. Specifically, the interaction between low birth weight and disadvantaged environments (e.g., poverty, single-parent households, etc.) was related to the early onset to delinquency in a sample of inner-city black males.[73] In other words, those with *both* low birth weight and a disadvantaged environment were more likely to engage in delinquency early in life.

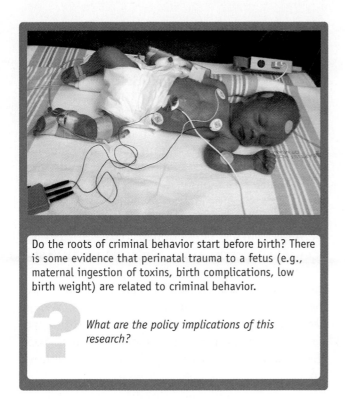

Do the roots of criminal behavior start before birth? There is some evidence that perinatal trauma to a fetus (e.g., maternal ingestion of toxins, birth complications, low birth weight) are related to criminal behavior.

? *What are the policy implications of this research?*

A major criticism of the studies involving perinatal problems is that the results might be explained by environmental influences. For example, mothers who drink and smoke during pregnancy may not be effective parents during the baby's childhood. To get around this problem, one research study looked at the effect of wartime famine on crime.[74] During World War II, the German army blockaded food supplies to western portions of the Netherlands. The researchers examined children whose mothers were pregnant during this period of severe nutritional deficiency. In this case, the potential injury to the fetus was clearly not caused by the mother. They found that, compared to children born in eastern Netherlands (no blockade), those born in western Netherlands were more likely to have APD as adults.

Exposure to Environmental Toxins — The Lead–Crime Link Researchers have examined how a variety of environmental toxins (e.g., mercury, lead, fluorocarbons) affect the human body. The toxin most commonly linked with criminal behavior is lead. Lead is a highly toxic substance. A large body of research links lead exposure or lead poisoning to a range of biological, neurological, and behavioral problems.[75] Lead exposure is especially damaging to children, because their brains and central ner-

vous system are still being formed. For them, even extremely low levels of exposure can result in cognitive difficulties, ADD, behavioral problems, impaired hearing, and kidney damage.[76] In severe cases, lead poisoning can even cause death. Although individuals can be exposed to lead from a number of sources, the two most likely suspects include gasoline and paint[77]:

1. Many houses built prior to the 1980s contain lead paint. Although lead paint that is in intact condition is not necessarily dangerous, lead paint that is allowed to deteriorate creates a hazard by contaminating household dust as well as bare soil around the house, where children may play.

2. During the last 60 years or so, the use of leaded gasoline, only recently banned in this country, contributed greatly to the number of cases of childhood lead poisoning in the United States. The lead, which was emitted by gasoline-powered vehicles, continues to present a hazard today because much of that lead remains in the soil where it was deposited over the years. This is especially true near well-traveled roads and highways.

Several recent studies, using a variety of methods, have linked lead exposure to criminal behavior. For example, one study linked estimates of air-based lead contamination with homicide levels across counties in the United States.[78] These results held, even after controlling for social correlates of crime (e.g., poverty, number of individuals in their crime-prone years). Another national study found that long-term trends in exposure to lead from gasoline correlated not only with violent crime trends, but also with trends in unwed pregnancies and IQ scores.[79]

At the individual level, a study of 900 African-American youths revealed that lead poisoning was one of the strongest predictors of male delinquency.[80] Recent results from the Cincinnati Lead Study (CLS) support this contention. The CLS is an ongoing research project designed to understand the effects of lead on the behavior of children. The sample for the study consists of 300 urban, inner-city youth. The examination of these individuals started even before they were born. A 2001 report from this project found that both prenatal and postnatal measures of lead levels predicted parent-reported and self-reported antisocial behavior during adolescence.[81]

The most common source of lead exposure is lead-based paint found in older houses.

? *Should the government require individuals who sell older houses to fix any known lead hazards?*

The dangers of lead exposure have led to government interventions. Notably, the U.S. Environmental Protection Agency began phasing out leaded gasoline in the 1970s. The Lead-Based Paint Hazard Reduction Act of 1992, known as Title X, targets lead-based paint in older households. According to this law, individuals selling a house built before 1978 must disclose any known lead hazards. Sellers and landlords must also provide a pamphlet on lead poisoning to the buyer or renter before the pre-1978 property is sold or rented. Some commentators suggest, however, that this law should be extended so that sellers are required to *fix* any known lead hazards.[82]

Diet and Nutrition The final biological harm to be considered is self-inflicted. If it is true that "you are what you eat," then perhaps there is a connection between nutrition and crime. Studies have examined the influence of a variety of dietary factors, including vitamin deficiencies and food allergies on behavior. Much of the research in this area focuses on the effects of sugar and junk food. One commentator noted that, "Sugar intake has been condemned as the cause of a large number of psychological problems, including alterations in mood, irritability, aggression, and violent behavior."[83]

Indeed, in a widely publicized case, former San Francisco Supervisor Dan White, who in 1978 shot to death Mayor George Moscone and Supervisor Harvey Milk, claimed that his violent behavior was the result of his addiction to junk foods. White's "Twinkie Defense" led to his conviction for manslaughter rather than first-degree murder. Soon after he completed his sentence, White committed suicide.

Of course, public perceptions about the evils of junk food do not necessarily mean there is a connection between sugar and crime. What does the empirical evidence suggest? One focus of research is **hypoglycemia** or low blood sugar. The brain has a chemical mechanism to control the level of blood sugar in the body. Some believe that excessive amounts of glucose (sugar) can cause hypoglycemia and in some cases, trigger violent, antisocial behavior (as in the "Twinkie" case).[84] The research on this issue, however, is far from settled. Critics point out, for example, that hypoglycemia is often misdiagnosed, and that research does not always show that high sugar intake causes this condition.

The interest in the relationship between hypoglycemia and violent behavior was initiated by a number of research papers that appeared to document correlations between hypoglycemia and habitual violent behavior. Critics point out, however, that this relationship can be interpreted in a number of ways. For instance, people who engage in violence are more prone to alcoholism. Because chronic alcoholics often "drink" their meals, their inadequate nutrition might produce hypoglycemia.[85]

Another series of studies investigated the results of changing the diet of incarcerated juveniles.[86] Among other things, changes included substituting molasses for sugar, fruit juice for Kool-Aid, and unsweetened cereal for presweetened cereal. Although the author of these research studies claimed dramatic reductions of institutional misconduct, there were substantial problems with the research design. These problems (e.g., guards knew of the experiment, one type of sugar was replaced with another) lower the confidence that the study conclusions are accurate. Despite their methodological problems, studies such as this led correctional facilities across several states to lower the sugar intake of inmates through changes in the food they offered.[87]

In a summary of the literature on sugar, hypoglycemia, and crime, one scholar concluded that no reliable evidence exists to suggest that a high-sugar diet causes hypoglycemia, that the condition is common among offenders, or that it causes violent, criminal, or antisocial behavior. She recommended that correctional administrators not take any drastic steps to modify the sugar intake of prisoners.[88]

Hormonal Influences

Most researchers studying hormonal influences on crime focus on the male sex androgen called testosterone. **Testosterone** is the hormone responsible for the fetus carrying a Y sex chromosome (this dictates that the fetus is male) and influences secondary sex characteristics (e.g., body hair, muscle distribution). Research consistently demonstrates a relationship between levels of testosterone and aggression. For example, a study of adolescent boys aged 15 to 17 found that testosterone levels predicted both verbal and physical aggression, as well as general "irritability."[89]

In another study, researchers examined a sample of 4462 American soldiers who served in Vietnam. The authors found a significant and moderately strong association between testosterone and adult deviance that was also related to the level of social integration and prior delinquency involvement. Men with lower levels of testosterone did not need a high level of social integration to keep them "in line." The conclusion was that the influence of testosterone on adult deviance is closely tied to social factors. As with other biological findings, these findings suggest that social factors should be considered in conjunction with biological variables.[90]

Scientists have also examined testosterone levels in prison inmates. A 1995 study found that inmates who were incarcerated for personal crimes of sex and violence had higher testosterone levels than inmates who had committed property crimes

of burglary, theft, and drugs.[91] Also, those with higher levels of testosterone were more likely to get involved in "overt, confrontational" misconduct while in prison. Although testosterone is present in females (at much lower levels), few studies examine whether testosterone predicts female criminal behavior. One exception is a study of female prison inmates. Similar to the relationship in males, the researchers discovered that higher levels of testosterone predicted aggressive behavior in prison.[92] Research of females, however, typically takes the study of hormones in a different direction.

The proposition that has received the most attention is that female menstrual cycles are related to criminal behavior. Prior to menstruation, hormonal changes such as reduced estrogen cause behavioral disturbances including anxiety, depression, irritability, aggressiveness, and mood swings for some women. Notably, during this period there is also a drop in serotonin levels. The diagnosis of premenstrual syndrome (PMS) is made when such behavioral disturbances cause substantial disruption in a woman's life.[93] PMS can range in severity from mild to incapacitating in both a physical and psychological sense.

The argument that PMS is related to criminal behavior has a long history. For example, a study published in 1945 found that 84% of women's crimes of violence were committed during the premenstrual and the early menstrual periods.[94] A few years later, a study of female inmates in New York reported that almost 80% of the women committed their crimes of violence during their menstrual cycles.[95] More recently, researchers reported that almost half of the 50 female prisoners they studied committed crimes of violence during the premenstrual period. They concluded that crimes are caused more by hormonal activity than by social or psychological factors.[96]

This body of research has been severely criticized. For example, one commentator noted that a PMS-crime link could be interpreted differently: The crime and the arrest could lead to changes in hormonal levels that *triggered* menstruation. Others argue that like the XYY supermale, the premenstrual syndrome thesis is "based upon stereotypical and unsupported views" of the sexes.[97] Diana Fishbein, a noted scholar in the area of biology and crime, however, contends that "there remains a general impression that a subgroup of women appear to be especially vulnerable to cyclical changes in hormone levels, causing them to be more prone to increased levels of anxiety and hostility during the premenstrual phase."[98]

Despite less-than-convincing scientific evidence, PMS has been successfully used as a criminal defense. Indeed, European courts recognized premenstrual defenses as early as the 1800s.[99] Two English cases in the early 1980s brought the PMS defense to the forefront. In both cases, female defendants in separate criminal actions successfully pleaded diminished responsibility or mitigating circumstances by establishing that they suffered from PMS. One of these defendants was found guilty of manslaughter rather than murder, despite admitting that she ran over her lover with her car after an argument.

Legal experts continue to debate the use of PMS as a criminal defense. Some experts have argued that PMS should not be asserted as a complete defense of criminal conduct, but should be used as a mitigating factor.[100] Even feminists are divided about the use of PMS as a defense or a mitigating factor during sentencing — such a defense may give some leniency to some women yet will also perpetuate stereotypes.

Certainly, more research must be conducted on this subject before any definitive statements can be made. Indeed, the medical profession continues to debate not only the symptoms of PMS, but also the validity of the syndrome itself.[101] Certainly, there is not enough empirical evidence to support the popular conclusion of a direct relationship between a woman's menstrual cycle and increased criminal activity.

Biosocial Theory

Early biological explanations of crime tended to focus on a single, direct cause of criminal behavior (e.g., body type, feeblemindedness) that affected crime independent of the environment. In other words, biology was destiny. In recent theories, biological effects are often portrayed as indirect and operate in conjunction with environmental influences. In this sense, there is no pure biological theory of crime. Instead, biosocial theories suggest that combinations of environmental and biological risk cause criminal behavior. These theories incorporate the biological correlates (e.g., neurological functioning) just discussed. A summary of the biosocial and evolutionary (see the following section) theories covered in the text is provided in TABLE 4-4.

Moffitt's Theory of Life-Course-Persistent Offending

The most widely recognized biosocial theory of crime is Terrie Moffitt's theory of life-course-persistent (LCP) offending. Moffitt contends that there are two types of criminal offenders. LCP-type offenders start their criminal careers early in

TABLE 4-4		
Biosocial and Evolutionary Theories of Crime		
Theorist	**Theory**	**Core Elements**
Biosocial Theory		
Terrie Moffitt	Life-course-persistent offending	Life-course-persistent offending (chronic offending that starts early in life) is caused by an interaction between neurological deficits and ineffective parenting.
Hans Eysenck	Personality-based theory	Personality traits, which are driven by underlying biology, cause crime. In particular, children with low arousal will be difficult to "condition" and socialize. In criminal families, however, low arousal might prevent children from learning patterns of criminal behavior.
Evolutionary Theory		
Various	Evolutionary theory of rape	Evolutionary processes allow males who are pushy and aggressive in the pursuit of sex to pass on their genes successfully.
Various	"Cads and dads" theory	Discusses two alternative strategies for reproductive success, the "cad" and "dad" strategies. Cads are essentially cheaters who pretend to want to make an investment in parenting, but really want to reproduce with as many females as possible.

childhood and show remarkable stability in anti-social behavior through their lives. In contrast, adolescent-limited (AL) offenders tend to confine their criminal behavior to adolescence. AL offending is explained largely by environmental (social learning) processes.[102]

To explain LCP offending, Moffitt focuses on the neuropsychological health of infants. In other words, she believes that biological and physiological processes within the nervous system influence psychological characteristics such as temperament, behavioral development, or cognitive abilities.[103] As noted, countless factors may influence the neuropsychological health of an infant. Examples include prenatal maternal drug or alcohol abuse, exposure to toxins such as lead, brain insult suffered due to pregnancy complications, or inherited individual differences in the nervous system.

According to Moffitt, even subtle neuropsychological deficits can produce an infant with a difficult temperament. These infants may be "clumsy and awkward, overactive, inattentive, irritable, impulsive, hard to keep on schedule, delayed in reaching developmental milestones, poor at verbal comprehension, deficient at expressing themselves, or slow at learning new things."[104] Such infants may be hard to socialize, even for the most competent parents. For a number of reasons, however, children with a difficult temperament are more likely to be raised in poor parenting environments.

For example, mothers who engage in behaviors that put an unborn child at risk may be less likely to have the characteristics associated with good parenting. Also, low birth weight or exposure to toxins may be the result of adverse social conditions. In sum, this theory holds that a combination of neurological deficits and family adversity leads to a series of failed parent-child encounters. This results in an unsocialized (and therefore antisocial) child.

Tests of Moffitt's biosocial hypothesis have received some support. The study of low birth weight discussed earlier is one example. The researchers found that those with both low birth weight and social disadvantage were most likely to engage in crime early in life. Results from Moffitt's New Zealand study indicated that boys with low neuropsychological test scores *and* adverse home environments had mean aggression scores that were four times higher than boys with just one of those characteristics.[105] Later analyses indicated that neuropsychological test scores were related to early onset delinquency and high-rate offending.[106] Despite this positive evidence, Moffitt's theory is relatively new. Although some parts of the theory have been tested extensively (with mixed results), the biological component of her dual hazard is still very much open to question.

Eysenck's Biosocial Theory

Hans Eysenck was among the first to propose a biosocial explanation of crime. The core of Eysenck's theory is that personality differences, which are biologically rooted, explain criminal behavior.[107] For example, he argues that extroverted people (personality) have central nervous systems (biology) that are less responsive to the environment. The research on heart rate discussed previously supports this position. Eysenck suggests that underarousal may explain crime in at least two different ways. First (as already discussed), it might lead people to seek out extra stimulation, including criminal behavior. Second, underaroused individuals may not feel the sting of punishment.

In this regard, Eysenck suggests that parents may have a harder time conditioning their children (through punishment) out of unwanted behaviors. This proposition leads to a rather novel prediction. In prosocial environments, he expects that children who are difficult to condition would be more likely to engage in crime. In poor environments (e.g., criminal parents), he believes that biological deficits (low conditionability) would actually protect children from negative influences. "Normal" children, who are more easily conditioned, risk becoming socialized to their parents' criminal habits.

Some components of Eysenck's biosocial theory have been empirically tested. In fact, much of this research has already been discussed. For example, research on heart rate and skin conductance offers some indirect support. Those with lower heart rates and lower skin conductance are more likely to engage in crime. Personality research also supports some of Eysencks' propositions. Unfortunately, few have directly tested his conditionability argument.

LINK The relationship between personality traits such as extroversion and criminal behavior is explored in Chapter 5.

A Biosocial Explanation of Female Delinquency

Although not a formal theory of crime, a group of researchers recently documented an interesting biosocial relationship that predicted female offending.

The starting point for this study was previous studies indicating that early onset of puberty (a biological process) among females was related to their criminal behavior. The researchers extended this line of inquiry by examining school settings among a sample of females.[108] In particular, early onset of puberty was related to offending for girls in a mixed-gender school settings, but not for those who attended all-female schools. The authors suggest that the females who start puberty early attracted the attention of older, crime-prone males. Female delinquency likely resulted from these associations.

Sociobiology and Evolutionary Explanations

Evolutionary explanations of crime are based in the Darwinian principles of natural selection and survival of the fittest. Although entire textbooks are devoted to this topic, the gist of evolution is rather simple. In essence, those individuals that are best adapted to their environment will survive to reproduce and therefore will pass on their genes to their offspring (thus, the most genetically "fit" survive).

E.O. Wilson first proposed the idea of "sociobiology" to apply the principles of evolution to explain modern human behaviors (e.g., parenting, aggression, altruism).[109] More recently, such explanations are referred to as evolutionary theory. In essence, these theories assume that if a particular trait or characteristic is present in a population, it is likely to have contributed somehow to the reproductive success of ancestors. Theorists typically take a particular trait and work backwards to craft an explanation as to how this may have increased reproductive success.

There is no single evolutionary theory of criminal behavior; rather, a number of different theories exist. These theories tend to be rather narrow in scope, explaining, for example, only property crime or rape. Some evolutionary theories, however, do attempt to explain a wider range of criminal behavior.

An Evolutionary Perspective on Rape and Sexual Assault

Since evolutionary theory emerged, several explanations have focused on the crime of rape and sexual assault. The basic proposition here is that sexual aggression has been "selected" within males because they can invest very little in conceived offspring. Because they are relatively free of parenting responsibility (i.e., the female provides for both the gestation and initial feeding), males benefit most from having multiple sex partners. Criminologists Lee Ellis and Anthony Walsh summarize this basic argument[110]:

> According to the evolutionary theory of rape, male reproductive advantage derived from having multiple sex partners has resulted in natural selection favoring genes promoting brain patterns for "pushiness" in pursuit of sexual intercourse. In some males, genes may carry pushiness to the point of actual force, especially after less violent tactics fail to yield results . . . over generations, pushy males will probably be more successful at passing on their genes, including any genes coding for readily learning pushy behavior.

One obvious prediction from this perspective is that males should predominate in the commission of rape (this is evident in crime statistics). Of course, mainstream theories could account for this finding just as easily by pointing to differences in how males and females are socialized or to the difference in physical strength between the sexes. A more novel prediction from this perspective is that if natural selection plays a role in rape among humans, the same phenomena should also appear in nonhuman species. Ellis and Walsh point out that forced copulation is perpetrated by the males of many animal species. Theories that tie rape to socialization and learning (uniquely human processes) would not predict this type of behavior in lower animal species.

Cads and Dads

A number of evolutionary theories highlight the competition of alternative behavioral strategies for passing on genes. Typically, one behavioral strategy is rare and the other prevalent. Similar to an ecosystem with predators and prey, the prevalence of these strategies will fluctuate with each other over time. "Cads" and "dads" describe two evolution-based strategies for reproduction. The "dad" strategy involves investing the time and energy to help nurture and raise offspring. Females are attracted to "dads" because by virtue of their biological role in reproduction, they must make a similar investment. Unfortunately for females, others give the illusion of a "dad," but in reality make a minimum investment in parenting. Instead, they minimize their involvement in any specific offspring. Depending upon the particular animal groups, researchers call such animals "cheaters," "satellites," "sneakers," or "cads."[111]

The main assumption behind this theory is that genetic predispositions underlie both of these strategies. In other words, a subpopulation of men has genetically evolved toward a strategy of minimal parental investment across as many females as possible. Some argue, however, that this behavior can also be learned. Because females are unlikely to find the cad strategy attractive, cads must be extremely deceptive (i.e., lie, cheat, etc.) and mask their true intentions.

This theory makes a number of predictions that are consistent with empirical evidence[112]:

- Criminality and psychopathy should be more prevalent among men than women.
- Criminals and psychopaths should be unusually promiscuous.
- Criminals and psychopaths should be more inclined to commit sexual assaults than males in general.
- The cad strategy should be more pronounced among males in the prime of their reproductive careers than in later life.

A Critique of Evolutionary Theory

Evolutionary theories have been criticized on a number of grounds. For example, many of these theories are difficult, if not impossible, to test. In essence, they are a "story" that is told about an already observed empirical finding. Thus, the hypotheses derived from these theories (e.g., men are more likely to rape than women) are often known empirical facts. It is relatively easy to conjure up a story about the evolutionary roots of a particular behavior. One biocriminologist, for example, suggests facetiously that the high prevalence of swimming pools in Phoenix, Arizona, is "adaptive," because the water cools men's sperm, making them more fertile.[113] Because of these difficulties, and because these theories are relatively new, there are very few empirical tests.

In instances where evolutionary theory is testable, evidence sometimes runs counter to predictions. For example, rape as a strategy to increase reproduction makes less sense in light of the empirical finding that females who are too young to reproduce are disproportionately more likely to be raped. Further, how would such a theory account for rapes involving oral or anal intercourse?[114]

Conclusion

Overall, the findings from research on biology and crime suggest that a host of biological factors may be involved in criminal behavior. Some of these factors are thought to be inherited, while others result from various biological harms. Current theorists argue that biological factors contribute to criminality under certain environmental circumstances. As unpalatable as it is to consider, humans may be partially driven toward crime by natural forces beyond their control. Keep in mind though, that many environmental factors (e.g., poverty, neighborhood of residence) thought to cause crime are no less positivistic.

There is no question that, after many years of neglect, biological criminology is enjoying a revival. Perhaps signaling this revival, James Q. Wilson and Richard Herrnstein incorporated biological factors into their general explanation of crime. In their widely read (and controversial) 1985 book *Crime and Human Nature,* the authors concluded that[115]:

> Criminals are more likely than noncriminals to have mesomorphic body types . . . to have fathers who were criminals even in the case of adopted sons who could not have known their fathers . . . to be of somewhat lower intelligence . . . to be impulsive or extroverted . . . and to have autonomic nervous systems that respond more slowly and less vigorously to stimuli.

In the 20 plus years following their book, some biologically oriented theories of crime have become more mainstream. Tests of Terrie Moffit's biosocial theory, for example, commonly appear in the top criminology journals. A recent empirical review of textbooks concluded that biological theories are now given much more, and more favorable, coverage.[116] One should be careful, though, not to overstate the popularity of the biological approach to crime. A quick scan of the citations in the notes for this chapter will show that most biological studies of crime still appear in journals devoted to the study of biology, psychology, or psychiatry. Indeed, many criminologists are still extremely skeptical of biological theories. Part of their concern involves ethical problems in applying biological perspectives to public policy decisions.

Early positivistic theories tended to frame biological causes of crime (and other undesirable qualities) as *direct* and *absolute*. The eugenics movement, bolstered by these arguments, aimed to sterilize dangerous and/or defective individuals to protect society. Critics of the biological approach suggest that one may be encountering the start of a "new eugenics."[117] Yet, much recent biological research points to a predisposition to criminal behavior that *may* emerge depending upon the environment. Thus, biology is not necessarily destiny. Further, many of the biological harms (lead poisoning, prenatal injury, maternal pregnancy behaviors) are very much amenable to change.

In that sense, some commentators suggest that biological explanations of crime are becoming part of a general movement to define criminality as a "public health problem."[118] For example, the provision of intensive prenatal health care to at-risk pregnant women might help prevent some forms (e.g., alcohol, cigarettes, illicit drugs) of trauma to the fetus.[119] Another common argument is that biological risk markers might identify children at risk for crime, so that environmental counterbalances (e.g., parenting, social bonds) could be strengthened.

Even here, there are serious ethical concerns. How exactly will people be screened for biological risk markers? Who will be screened? Will lower-class individuals automatically be the targets of policies? Certainly, stigmatizing those who *may* have a characteristic (e.g., low arousal) that *may* be conducive to criminality would be unethical. These issues are magnified when considering molecular genetics and the Human Genome Project. Gene-based criminology, it is feared, could justify the use of intrusive policies, raising the specter of totalitarianism. For example, gene therapy might be offered as a condition for probation, in lieu of prison. Even biocriminologists note that such concerns are valid[120]:

Perhaps a day will come when the strength of genetic dispositions can be predicted at birth, but it will not come soon. When, and if, it does come, let us hope that people have the wisdom to deal with that deeper knowledge of genetics and behavior.

Apart from policy implications, criminologists are generally critical of the methodologies used in biological research. In particular, much of this research is plagued by a pervasive methodological weakness — the <u>Lombrosian fallacy</u>; that is, the study of incarcerated persons is used to reach conclusions about the influence of biology on the general population.[121] This approach is flawed because the prison population does not automatically reflect the number and type of criminals in the general population. Social structure and criminal justice system processes may determine who goes to prison. Because minorities are overrepresented in the prison population, for example, there is the danger of misusing biology to provide unsound justifications for the control of minority popula-tions. In fact, one reason biological criminology originally fell into disrepute was that it was a "kind of people" approach — comparing white "normals" to criminals of color.

Finally, the biological approach ignores white-collar, organized, and political crime. Rather, it tends to focus on aggression or antisocial behavior in children, and so-called "street crime" in adults. Of course, many psychological perspectives, and even some sociological theories, suffer the same deficiency.

The lessons drawn from the biological school are thus limited to certain crimes and offenders. More focused research is necessary to determine exactly how biologicial factors influence criminal behavior before any policies are considered. Future study in this area will require interdisciplinary efforts among criminologists and physical and medical scientists.

WRAP UP

Can Biological Risk Markers Identify Potential Criminals?

Criminologists have used a number of research methodologies (e.g., twin studies, adoption studies, molecular genetics) in an attempt to separate nature from nurture. The evidence from such studies remains controversial. Many biologists and psychologists believe that these studies clearly demonstrate a genetic basis for criminal behavior. Sociologists remain skeptical of the evidence and conclusions from these studies.

The methodology most consistent with Kerr's novel is molecular genetics. Even here, it is unlikely that a specific gene will have such a strong relationship to violence or criminality of any sort. As research like the Human Genome Project advances, it is conceivable that a combination of biological "risk markers" might reliably predict offending. This raises a number of ethical dilemmas. What should be done with individuals who are biologically "at risk" for offending? Should fetuses be screened for biological risk markers? Even those who support a biological approach to the study of crime recognize that such research may create ethical problems.

Chapter Spotlight

- Early biological explanations of crime pointed toward a single, direct, immutable cause of crime. For example, Lombroso believed that some criminals were atavists, or evolutionary throwbacks. One policy implication derived from these theories was eugenics—the attempt to create a better stock of humans by controlling who is allowed to have children.

- Early biological research was often shoddy. Researchers often used institutional populations to draw conclusions about all criminals. Further, while researchers ignored physical similarities between criminals and noncriminals, differences (no matter how small) were assumed to reflect the superiority of noncriminals.

- The modern biological approach consists of a wide range of inquiry, including behavioral genetics (twin studies, molecular genetics),

neurological functioning, and biological harms (prenatal risk, exposure to lead).

- Biosocial theories of crime emphasize the interplay between biology and the environment. For example, Moffitt's developmental theory of offending focuses on the interaction between neurological deficits and inadequate parenting skills. In contrast to early biological theories, modern theorists argue that biology often has a subtle, indirect effect on criminal behavior. Further, some biological causes of crime (e.g., lead exposure, prenatal harms) are amenable to change.

- Evolutionary theory uses Darwin's concept of natural selection to explain criminal behavior. The underlying assumption is that behaviors in the population (including crimes such as rape) were "selected" because they increase the chance of passing on one's genes.

Putting It All Together

1. What are the common characteristics of early biological theories? Is this different from the modern biological perspective?

2. How is body type related to criminal behavior? What are the different explanations for this relationship?

3. How have scientists attempted to separate nature from nurture? Which factor do you feel is more responsible for crime: nature or nurture?

4. Identify and explain at least two biological correlates of criminal behavior.

5. What is a biosocial theory? Use a specific theory as an example in your answer.

6. What is eugenics? Do you feel that the biological approach to crime still leads to dangerous policy implications?

atavism Term used by Lombroso to describe people whom he believed were "evolutionary throwbacks" to a more primitive line of human beings.

behavioral genetics The scientific study of how genes and heredity affect particular behaviors.

concordance rate Focus of twin studies. The outcome (criminal behavior) is concordant if both twins exhibit the same behavior.

dizygotic (DZ) twins Fraternal twins who share the same amount of genetic similarity as non-twin siblings.

eugenics The goal of improving the human race through selective breeding. In the 20th century, eugenics led to limitations on the immigration of southern and eastern Europeans into the United States and the institutionalization or forced sterilization of the poor, deviant, and disabled.

fetal alcohol syndrome (FAS) A well-documented condition caused when pregnant women ingest high levels of alcohol. FAS is defined by a host of characteristics, including central nervous system dysfunction, growth retardation, and organ anomalies.

Human Genome Project (HGP) Begun formally in 1990 and completed in 2003, the HGP was a coordinated effort by the U.S. Department of Energy and the National Institutes of Health to map the entire human genome. *Genome* is the term used to describe an organism's complete set of DNA.

hypoglycemia Low blood sugar. Some studies suggest that hypoglycemia triggers violent behavior. Recent research casts some doubt on this proposition.

Lombrosian fallacy The use of incarcerated persons to reach conclusions about the influence of biology in the general population. This type of research is problematic because those who end up in prison might not reflect the true population of criminals.

monozygotic (MZ) twins Identical twins who are products of a single egg and sperm and thus are exactly the same genetically.

prefrontal cortex The part of the brain responsible for "executive functions" (i.e., abstract reasoning, the ability to sustain attention, self-monitoring, and the inhibition of impulsive behavior). Biological studies suggest that deficiencies in this region of the brain may lead to a criminal disposition.

serotonin A neurotransmitter that helps conduct the electrical impulses in the brain; low levels of serotonin hinder communication between cells. Research links low levels of serotonin with criminal behavior.

skin conductance A method for measuring how an individual's fingers sweat. Although research is mixed, some studies find that criminals have lower skin conductance than noncriminals.

somatotype The classification of human body types into three categories. Sheldon argued that body type related to a person's personality or disposition. Endomorphs are fat, soft, and round, and they tended to be extroverts. Ectomorphs are thin and wiry, and were easily worried, sensitive, and introverted. Mesomorphs are muscular, gregarious, aggressive, assertive, and action oriented. Some research suggests that the mesomorph is the dominant body type among delinquents.

testosterone The male sex hormone responsible for the fetus carrying a Y chromosome. Testosterone influences secondary sex characteristics (e.g., body hair, muscle mass). Research consistently demonstrates a relationship between levels of testosterone and aggression.

XYY A rare chromosome abnormality in which a male (typically XY) has an extra Y chromosome. Early research suggested these individuals were unusually aggressive ("supermales"). Later research indicates that they are no more violent than others, but perhaps slightly more crime prone.

1. CBS, "America's Deep, Dark Secret" (May 2, 2004), available at http://www.cbsnews.com/stories/2004/04/29/60minutes/main614728.shtml, accessed September 28, 2005.

2. Lee Ellis and Harry Hoffman, "Ideology: Views of Contemporary Criminologists on Causes and Theories of Crime," in Lee Ellis and Harry Hoffman, eds., *Crime in Biological, Social, and Moral Contexts* (New York: Praeger, 1990).

3. Gideon Fishman, "Positivism and Neo-Lombrosianism," in Israel Barak-Glantz and C. Ronald Huff, eds., *The Mad, the Bad, and the Different: Essays in Honor of Simon Dinitz* (Lexington, MA: Lexington, 1981): 17.

4. Saleem A. Shah and Loren H. Roth, "Biological and Psychophysical Factors in Criminality," in Daniel Glaser, ed., *Handbook of Criminology* (Chicago: Rand McNally, 1974).

5. Harry E. Allen, Paul C. Friday, Julian B. Roebuck, and Edward Sagarin, *Crime and Punishment: An Introduction to Criminology* (New York: The Free Press, 1981).

6. Randy Martin, Robert J. Mutchnick, and W. Timothy Austin, *Criminological Thought: Pioneers Past and Present* (New York: Macmillan, 1990): 21.

7. Cesare Lombroso and Gina Lombroso-Ferrero, *The Female Offender* (London: Fisher Urwin, 1895): xiv–xv.

8. Earnest Hooten, *Crime and the Man* (Cambridge, MA: Harvard University Press, 1939).

9. William Sheldon, *Varieties of Delinquent Youth* (New York: Harper, 1949); William Sheldon, *Atlas of Men* (New York: Harper, 1954).

10. Emil M. Hartl, Edward P. Monnelly, and Roland D. Elderkin, *Physique and Delinquent Behavior: A Thirty-Year Follow-up of William H. Sheldon's Varieties of Delinquent Youth* (New York: Academic Press, 1982).

11. Sheldon Glueck and Eleanor Glueck, *Unraveling Juvenile Delinquency* (New York: Commonwealth Fund, 1950).

12. Juan B. Cortes and Florence F. Gatti, *Delinquency and Crime* (New York: Seminar Press, 1972).

13. C. Ray Jeffrey, *Criminology: An Interdisciplinary Approach* (Englewood Cliffs, NJ: Prentice Hall, 1990): 178.

14. Robert J. Sampson and John H. Laub, *Crime in the Making: Pathways and Turning Points Through Life* (Cambridge, MA: Harvard University Press, 1993): 95.

15. Patricia Jacobs, "Aggressive Behavior, Mental Subnormality and the XYY Male," *Nature 208* (1965): 1351–1352.

16. Janet Katz and William J. Chambliss, "Biology and Crime," in Joseph F. Sheley, ed., *Criminology* (Belmont, CA: Wadsworth, 1991): 257–258.

17. Sarnoff Mednick and Jan Volavka, "Biology and Crime," in Norvell Morris and Michael Tonry, eds., *Crime and Justice: An Annual Review of Research,* Volume 2, (Chicago: University of Chicago Press, 1980): 93.

18. Hooten, 1939, 392.

19. David C. Rowe, *Biology and Crime* (Los Angeles: Roxbury, 2002).

20. Steven J. Gould, *The Mismeasure of Man* (New York: W.W. Norton and Co., 1996).

21. Katz and Chambliss, 1991, 257.

22. C. Ray Jeffrey, "Genetics, Crime and the Canceled Conference," *Criminologist* 18 (January/February 1993): 1–8.

23. Richard L. Dugdale, *The Jukes: A Study in Crime, Pauperism, Disease, and Heredity* (New York: Putnam, 1877).

24. Henry H. Goddard, *The Kallikak Family: A Study in the Heredity of Feeblemindedness* (New York: Macmillan, 1912).

25. Richard Dugdale, "The Jukes: A Study in Crime, Pauperism, and Heredity," in Joseph E. Jacoby, ed., *Classics of Criminology*, 2nd edition (Prospect Heights, IL: Waveland, 1994): 134.

26. Mark W. Lipsey and James H. Derzon, "Predictors of Violent or Serious Delinquency in Adolescence and Early Childhood: A Synthesis of Longitudinal Research," in Ralph Loeber and David Farrington, eds., *Serious and Violent Juvenile Offenders: Risk Factors and Successful Interventions* (Thousand Oaks, CA: Sage, 1998).

27. Sampson and Laub, 1993, 69.

28. Karl O. Christiansen, "Preliminary Study of Criminality Among Twins," in Sarnoff A. Mednick and Karl O. Christiansen, eds., *Biosocial Bases of Criminal Behavior* (New York: Gardner Press, 1977).

29. David. C. Rowe, "Sibling Interaction and Self-Reported Delinquent Behavior," *Criminology* 23 (1985): 223–240.

30. Soo Hyun Rhee and Irwin D. Waldman, "Genetic and Environmental Influences on Antisocial Behavior: A Meta-Analysis of Twin and Adoption Studies," *Psychological Bulletin* 128 (2002): 490–529.

31. Rowe, 2002, 21.

32. Gregory Carey, "Twin Imitation for Antisocial Behavior: Implications for Genetic and Family Environment Research," *Journal of Abnormal Psychology*, 101 (1992): 18–22.

33. Ibid.

34. Patricia A. Brennan, Sarnoff A. Mednick, and Jan Volavka, "Biomedical Factors in Crime," in James Q. Wilson and Joan Petersilia, eds., *Crime* (Lexington, MA: Lexington Books, 1995): 71.

35. Sarnoff A Mednick, William F. Gabrielli, and Barry Hutchings, "Genetic Influences in Criminal Convictions," *Science* 224 (1984): 891–894.

36. Brennan, Mednick, and Volavka, 1995, 75.

37. Rhee and Waldman, 2002, 496.

38. Kenneth A. Dodge and Gregory S. Pettit, "A Biopyschosocial Model of the Development of Chronic Conduct Problems in Adolescence," *Developmental Psychology* 39 (2003): 349–371.

39. Glen D. Walters and Thomas W. White, "Heredity and Crime: Bad Genes or Bad Research," *Criminology* 27 (1989): 455–486.

40. Glen D. Walters, "A Meta-Analysis of the Gene Crime Relationship," *Criminology* 30 (1992): 595–613.

41. Rowe, 2002, 89–91.

42. H. G. Brunner, M. R. Nelen, X. O. Breakefield, H. H. Ropers, and B. A. van Oost, "Abnormal Behavior Associated With a Point Mutation in the Structural Gene for Monoamine Oxidase A," *Science* 262 (1993): 578–580.

43. Rowe, 2002, 100.

44. Rowe, 2002, 101–102.

45. "Human Genome Project Information," available at

http://www.ornl.gov/sci/techresources/Human_Genome/project/about.shtml, accessed January 8, 2005.

46. Ibid.

47. Sarnoff A. Mednick and Jan Volavka, 1980, 101.

48. Rowe, 2002, 85.

49. Rowe, 2002, 81–82.

50. Adrian Raine, Monte S. Buchsbaum, Jill Stanley, Steven Lottenberg, Leonard Abel, and Jacqueline Stoddard, "Selective Reductions in Prefrontal Glucose Metabolism in Murderers," *Biological Psychiatry* 36 (1993): 365–373.

51. Adrian Raine, Todd Lencz, Susan Bihrle, Lori LaCasse, and Patrick Colletti, "Reduced Prefrontal Gray Matter Volume and Reduced Autonomic Activity in Antisocial Personality Disorder, *Archives of General Psychiatry* 57 (2000): 119–127.

52. Brennan, Mednick, and Volavka, 1995, 82.

53. Lee Ellis, "Monoamine Oxidase and Criminality: Identifying an Apparent Biological Marker for Antisocial Behavior," *Journal of Research on Crime and Delinquency* 28 (1991): 227–251.

54. Rowe, 2002, 75.

55. Terrie E. Moffitt, Gary L. Brammer, Avshalom Caspi, J. Paul Fawcett, Michael Raleigh, Arthur Yuwiler, and Phil Silva, "Whole Blood Serotonin Relates to Violence in an Epidemiological Study," *Biological Psychiatry* 43 (1998): 446–457.

56. Don Cherek and Scott Lane, "Effects of d,1-fenfluramine on Aggressive and Impulsive Responding in Adult Males with a History of Conduct Disorder," *Psychopharmacology* 146 (1999): 473–481.

57. Terrie E. Moffit, Donald R. Lynam, and Phil A. Silva, "Neuropsychological Tests Predicting Persistent Male Delinquency," *Criminology* 32 (1994): 277–300.

58. Terrie E. Moffitt, "The Neuropsychology of Juvenile Delinquency: A Critical Review," in Norval Morris and Michael Tonry, eds., *Crime and Justice: A Review of the Research,* Volume 12 (Chicago: University of Chicago Press, 1990).

59. Adrian Raine, *The Psychopathology of Crime: Criminal Behavior as a Clinical Disorder* (San Diego: Academic Press, 1993).

60. Keith McBurnett and Benjamin B. Lahey, "Biological Correlates of Conduct Disorder and Antisocial Behavior in Children and Adolescence," in Don C. Fowles, ed., *Progress in Experimental Personality and Psychopathology Research* (New York: Springer, 1994).

61. Adrian Raine, "Antisocial Behavior and Psychophysiology: A Biosocial Perspective and a Prefrontal Dysfunction Hypothesis," in *Handbook of Antisocial Behavior* (New York: John Wiley & Sons, 1997).

62. Adrian Raine, "The Role of Prefrontal Deficits, Low Autonomic Arousal, and Early Health Factors in the Development of Antisocial and Aggressive Behavior in Children," *Journal of Child Psychology and Psychiatry* 43 (2002): 417–434.

63. Brennan, Mednick, and Volavka, 1995, 81–82.

64. James A. Fox and Jack Levin, *Mass Murder: America's Growing Menace* (New York: Plenum, 1985): 16–17.

65. Clayton Stapleton, "It's Coming From the Tower," available at http://www.whatwasthen.com/uttower.html, accessed January 4, 2005.

66. Rhawn Joseph, "Charles Whitman: The Amygdala & Mass Murder," available at http://brainmind.com/Case5.html, accessed January 5, 2005.

67. Sandra J. Kelly, Nancy Day, and Ann P. Streissguth, "Effects of Prenatal Alcohol Exposure on Social Behavior in Humans and Other Species," *Neurotoxicology and Teratology* 22 (2000): 143–149.

68. Kelly, Day, and Streissguth, 2000, 144–145; Tresa M. Roebuck, Sarah N. Mattson, and Edward P. Riley, "Behavioral and Psychosocial Profiles of Alcohol-Exposed Children," *Alcoholism: Clinical and Experimental Research* 23 (1999): 1070–1076.

69. Patricia E. Brennan, Emily R. Grekin, and Sarnoff A. Mednick, "Maternal Smoking During Pregnancy and Adult Male Criminal Outcomes," *Archives of General Psychiatry* 56 (1999): 215–219.

70. Lidush Goldschmidt, Nancy L. Day, and Gale A. Richardson, "Effects of Prenatal Marijuana Exposure on Child Behavior Problems at Age 10," *Neurotoxicology and Teratology* 22 (2000): 325–336.

71. Elizabeth Kandel and Sarnoff Mednick, "Perinatal Complications Predict Violent Offending," *Criminology* 29 (1991): 519–530.

72. Patricia E. Brennan, Sarnoff A. Mednick, and Adrian Raine, "Biosocial Interactions and Violence: A Focus on Perinatal Factors," in Adrian Raine, Patricia Brennan, David Farrington, and Sarnoff Mednick, eds., *Biosocial Bases of Violence* (New York: Plenum Press, 1997).

73. Stephen G. Tibbetts and Alex R. Piquero, "The Influence of Gender, Low Birth Weight, and Disadvantaged Environment in Predicting Early Onset of Offending: A Test of Moffitt's Interactional Hypothesis," *Criminology* 37 (1999): 843–878.

74. Richard Neugebauer, Hans W. Hoek, and Ezra Susser, "Prenatal Exposure to Wartime Famine and Development of Antisocial Personality Disorder in Early Adulthood," *Journal of the American Medical Association* 282 (1999): 455–462.

75. U. S. Environmental Protection Agency, "Sources of Indoor Air Pollution — Lead (Pb)," available at www.epa.gov/iaq/lead.html, accessed January 8, 2005.

76. National Safety Council, "Lead Poisoning," available at http://www.nsc.org/library/facts/lead.htm, accessed January 5, 2005.

77. Ibid.

78. Paul B. Stretesky and Michael J. Lynch, "The Relationship Between Lead Exposure and Homicide," *Archives of Pediatric Adolescent Medicine* 155 (2001): 579–582.

79. Rick Nevin, "How Lead Exposure Relates to Temporal Changes in IQ, Violent Crime, and Unwed Pregnancy," *Environmental Research* 83 (2000): 1–22.

80. Deborah Denno, "Considering Lead Poisoning as a Criminal Defense," *Fordham Urban Law Journal* 20 (1993): 377–385.

81. Kim N. Dietrich, M. Douglas Ris, Paul A. Succop, Omer G. Berger, and Robert L. Bornschein, "Early Exposure to Lead and Juvenile Delinquency," *Neurotoxicology and Teratology* 23 (2001): 511–518.

82. "Lead Exposure Linked to Antisocial Behavior" (March 1, 2002), available at http://www.who.int/docstore/peh/ceh/articles/antisocial.htm, accessed January 5, 2005.

83. Robin B. Kanarek, "Nutrition and Violent Behavior," in Albert J. Reiss, Jr., Klaus A. Mixzik, and Jeffrey A. Roth, eds., *Understanding and Prevention Violence: Biobehavioral Influences,* Volume 2 (Washington DC: National Academy Press, 1994): 521.

84. D. H. Morris, "Sugar?" *Corrections Today* (July 1986): 116–120.

85. Kanarek, 524.

86. For a review, see Stephen J. Shoenthaler, "Nutritional Policies and Institutional Antisocial Behavior," *Nutrition Today* 20 (1985): 16–25.

87. Kanarek, 523.

88. Morris, 1987, 120.

89. Dan Olweus, Ake Mattsson, Daisy Schalling, and Hans Low, "Testosterone, Aggression, Physical and Personality Dimensions in Normal Adolescent Males," *Psychosomatic Medicine* 2 (1988): 253–269.

90. Alan Booth and D. Wayne Osgood, "The Influence of Testosterone on Deviance in Adulthood: Assessing and Explaining the Relationship," *Criminology* 31 (1993): 93–117.

91. James M. Dabbs, Timothy S. Carr, Robert L. Frady, and Jasmine K. Raid, "Testosterone, Crime, and Misbehavior Among 692 Male Prison Inmates," *Personality and Individual Differences* 18.5 (May 1995): 627–633.

92. James M. Dabbs, Jr., and Marian F. Hargrove, "Age, testosterone, and Behavior Among Female Prison Inmates," *Psychosomatic Medicine, 59* (1997): 477–480.

93. Sharon R. Thompson, "Premenstrual Syndrome," *Medline Plus Medical Encyclopedia*, available at http://www.nlm.nih.gov/medlineplus/ency/article/001505.htm, accessed September 24, 2005.

94. C. R. Cook, "Presidential Address: The Differential Psychology of the American Woman," *American Journal of Obstetrics and Gynecology* 49 (1945): 457–472.

95. L. Morton, H. Addison, R. Addison, L. Hunt, and J. Sullivan, "A Clinical Study of Premenstrual Tension," *American Journal of Obstetrics and Gynecology* 65 (1953): 1182–1191.

96. P. T. D'Orban and J. Dalton, "Violent Crime and the Menstrual Cycle, *Psychological Medicine* 10 (1980): 353–359.

97. Katz and Chambliss, 1991, 256.

98. Diana Fishbein, "The Psychobiology of Female Aggression," *Criminal Justice and Behavior* 19 (1993): 99–126, 113.

99. Connie Huang, "It's a Hormonal Thing: Premenstrual Syndrome and Postpartum Psychosis as Criminal Defense," *Southern California Review of Law and Women's Studies* 11 (2002): 345–367.

100. Elizabeth Holtzman, "Premenstrual Syndrome: The Indefensible Defense," *Harvard* Women's Law Journal 7 (1984): 1–3.

101. Huang, 2002, 349.

102. Terrie E. Moffitt, "Adolescent-Limited and Life-Course-Persistent Behavior: A Developmental Taxonomy," *Psychological Review* 100 (1993): 674–701.

103. Ibid.

104. Terrie E. Moffitt, "The Neuropsychology of Conduct Disorder." *Development and Psychopathology* 5 (1993): 135–151, 681.

105. Terrie E. Moffitt, "Juvenile Delinquency and Attention Deficit Disorder: Boys' Developmental Trajectories from Age 3 to Age 15," *Child Development* 61 (1990): 893–910.

106. Moffitt, Lynam, and Silva, 1994, 285–295.

107. Hans J. Eysenck, *Crime and Personality* (London: Paladin, 1977).

108. Avshalom Caspi, Donald Lynam, Terrie E. Moffitt, and Phil A. Silva, "Unraveling Girls' Delinquency: Biological Dispositional, and Contextual Contributions to Adolescent Misbehavior," *Developmental Psychology* 29 (1993): 19–30.

109. Edward O. Wilson, *The New Synthesis* (Cambridge: Harvard University Press, 1975).

110. Lee Ellis and Anthony Walsh, "Gene-Based Evolutionary Theories in Criminology," *Criminology* 35 (1997): 229–276.

111. Ellis and Walsh, 1997, 245.

112. Ellis and Walsh, 1997, 246–249.

113. Rowe, 64.

114. Francis T. Cullen and Robert Agnew, *Criminological Theory: Past to Present* (Los Angeles: Roxbury, 2003): 30, 48.

115. James Q. Wilson and Richard J. Herrnstein, *Crime and Human Nature* (New York: Simon & Schuster 1985): 66.

116. Richard A. Wright and J. Mitchell Miller, "Taboo Until Today? The Coverage of Biological Arguments in Criminology Textbooks, 1961 to 1970 and 1987 to 1996," *Journal of Criminal Justice* 26 (1998): 1–19.

117. John Horgan, "Eugenics Revisited," *Scientific American* 286 (1993): 125–131.

118. Nikolas Rose, "The Biology of Culpability: Pathological Identity and Crime Control in a Biological Culture," *Theoretical Criminology* 4 (2000): 5–34.

119. Brennan, Mednick, and Volavka, 1995, 88–89.

120. Rowe, 2002, 105.

121. Gennaro F. Vito, Deborah G. Wilson, and Edward J. Latessa, *Introduction to Criminal Justice Research Methods* (Springfield, IL: Charles C. Thomas, 1988).

OBJECTIVES

Understand the difference between psychiatric and psychological criminology.

Know the gist of psychoanalytic theory, including Freudian elements of personality and defense mechanisms. Know how psychoanalytic theory and psychoanalysis has been applied to delinquents and criminals.

Comprehend the principles of learning (operant conditioning, classical conditioning, and observational learning) and how they relate to theories of crime.

Understand the two areas of cognitive psychology, (cognitive structure and cognitive content) and how they have been applied to criminal behavior.

Distinguish between general personality research and research on a "criminal personality."

Grasp the debate on the relationship between IQ and criminal behavior.

Know the policy implications derived from theories of learning, personality, and cognition.

Psychology and Crime

"

Debi Newberry: You're a psychopath.

Martin Blank: No, psychopaths kill for no reason. I kill for money. . . . That didn't sound right.

— Minnie Driver (Debi) and John Cusack (Martin), *Grosse Pointe Blank*[1]

"

The BTK Killer

On February 25, 2005, Dennis L. Rader was arrested as a suspect in several killings in Wichita, Kansas, dating back to 1974. This long-term killer was known to police and the media as "BTK" based on his method of murder — bind, torture, kill. On June 28, 2005, Rader pled guilty to murdering 10 individuals between 1974 and 1991. Soon after the first murder, Rader taunted the police and media with mysterious messages, including poetry about or dedicated to the victims. After years of silence, he resurfaced in 2004, sending *The Wichita Eagle* a letter that included photographs of a 1986 murder victim, along with a photocopy of her driver's license.

In the plea hearing, Rader was emotionless but courteous as he recounted to the judge the details of each murder. He told of comforting a victim by giving her a glass of water before putting a bag over her head and strangling her. At times, he described his activities using almost academic language — discussing "phases" of a serial killer, such as "trolling" and "stalking." He admitted carrying a "hit kit" that included rope and tape. Rader described his victims as "targets" and the murders as "projects." He talked of "putting down" the victims as a veterinarian might discuss animals. As for the cause of his behavior, Rader said that the murders allowed him to fulfill sexual fantasies.

Dennis Rader was liked by some who knew him and despised by others. He was a husband and the father of two children. He was a Boy Scout leader and president of his church council. Some who knew Rader described him as arrogant, confrontational, and egotistical. Some residents of Park City, Kansas, where Rader was a city code compliance officer, described him as a control freak who enjoyed the power of his office. Some reported that he would film his neighbors in the hopes of catching them committing a minor misbehavior. He allegedly measured the grass of one woman he disliked in an attempt to catch her in violation of a city ordinance. Others described him as efficient, nice, and a friendly guy who was simply doing his job.

Convicted serial killer Dennis Rader walks into the El Dorado Correctional Facility in August 2005. Rader was convicted of killing 10 people over the course of 30 years.

How might a Freudian theorist explain Rader's letters to the police and media?

Does Dennis Rader show signs of being a psychopath? What characteristics of psychopathy appear to fit with Rader? What characteristics do not fit?

Sources: Matt Sedensky, "Suspect Pleads Guilty in BTK Murder Case," June 28, 2005, available at http://news.yahoo.com/news?tmpl=story&u=/ap/20050628/ap_on_re_us/btk_killings_28, accessed June 28, 2005; Marilyn Bardsley, Rachael Bell and David Lohr, "The BTK Story," available at http://www.crimelibrary.com/serial_killers/unsolved/btk, accessed June 28, 2005; Fred Man and Les Anderson, "Liked by Many, Loathed by Some," *The Wichita Eagle,* February 27, 2005, available at http://www.kansas.com/mld/kansas/news/special_packages/btk/11004728.htm, accessed June 28, 2005.

Introduction

Blockbuster movies and best-selling novels often star psychopathic killers. The killer is methodically tracked down by a psychologist or psychiatrist who has a keen understanding of the criminal mind. However, is there such a thing as a psychopath or criminal mind? How exactly does psychology contribute to the study of criminal behavior? This chapter introduces some of the basic psychological concepts developed to analyze and explain criminal behavior. Specifically, after a brief introduction to psychodynamic theory, four areas in psychology — behaviorism, cognition, personality, and IQ — are highlighted and examined as their contributions to the criminological theory and the effort to rehabilitate delinquents and criminals.

Like the biological approach, psychological theories focus on how characteristics of the individual lead to criminal behavior. Criminologists often contrast this individual approach with sociological theory. Sociological approaches tend to focus on how social structure causes crime. For example, they might suggest that neighborhood conditions (e.g., poverty, residential mobility) create high-crime rates in a certain geographical area. An important point to make is that there is room for both types of explanations. A psychological approach, for example, would question why some individuals succumb to the criminal pressures of the neighborhood, while others seem unaffected. A psychologist might highlight negative personality traits, low intelligence, or poor learning history. Of course, neither the psychological nor the sociological approach is *wrong* — ideally combining such approaches will give a more comprehensive portrait of criminal behavior.

Different psychologists use distinct approaches to explain criminal behavior. Bartol and Bartol distinguish between the psychological and psychiatric schools of criminology.[2] *Psychological criminology* is the science of behavior and the thought processes of the criminal. Both environmental and personality influences on criminal behavior are considered along with the mental processes that mediate that behavior. Psychological approaches to the study of crime also consider such factors as biology and heredity (see Chapter 4). This chapter covers the psychological concepts of personality traits, learning experience, and cognitive patterns.

Psychiatric criminology (forensic psychiatry) is dominated by the psychodynamic tradition. Here, criminal behavior is explained in terms of motives and drives. The prime determinant of human behavior lies within the person. After the first few years of life, the environment plays a minor role. Psychoanalytic theory is discussed next, followed by the central theories of psychological criminology in the remainder of the chapter.

Psychoanalytic Theory

Early theorists interested in the psychiatric aspects of crime focused on a variety of areas. For example, Henry Maudsley (1835–1918) studied the relationship between crime and insanity, especially "epileptic madness."[3] He believed that criminals suffered from "moral degeneracy" — a deficiency of moral sense. In writing of the criminal "who has such a strong interest in deceiving himself" and who is not thoroughly conscious of his crime, Maudsley anticipated the Freudian concept of the unconscious.[4]

As the father of psychoanalytic theory and psychoanalysis (a therapy derived from this theory), Sigmund Freud was perhaps the most influential psychological theorist at the beginning of the 20th century. Although psychoanalysis is still practiced, most acknowledge its limited application to criminal offenders. Nevertheless, psychoanalytic theory is discussed in some detail because many key concepts in this theory are utilized by current sociological and psychological theories of criminal offending.

Freud believed that one can understand human behavior best by examining early childhood experiences. These experiences, traumatic or not, can profoundly affect behavior without the individual being consciously aware of their impact. Freud developed psychoanalytic theory from the late 1800s through the early 1900s to explain both normal and abnormal behavior.[5] Although the full theory is extraordinarily complex and often vague (Freud himself changed his mind over time on a number of issues), the key concepts are fairly straightforward.

Freudian Elements of Personality

Freud's greatest contributions to psychology include his distinction between the conscious and the unconscious mind, and his concepts of id, superego, and ego. If you've ever seen a cartoon where the devil (id) appears on one shoulder and

Sigmund Freud. The 82-year-old Austrian-born psychoanalyst and neurologist is the father of psychoanalytic theory and psychoanalysis.

? How has Freud's theory influenced modern theories of crime?

models for the content of the superego. Even though it lies in the realm of the unconscious, the superego manifests itself in the restraints imposed by moral, ethical, and societal values. The <u>ego</u>, a conscious part of the personality, is a "psychological thermostat" that regulates the savage wishes and demands of the id and the social restrictions of the super ego. The ego delays certain behaviors until the time is suitable for their gratification and can entirely deny certain behaviors.

Freud was particularly concerned with anxiety. In psychoanalytic theory, anxiety stems from one of two sources. First, people feel anxious when a desire (whether conscious or not) is unmet. Second, people become anxious when an unconscious desire starts to become conscious.[7] Freud outlined a number of <u>defense mechanisms</u> that individuals employ (often unconsciously) to reduce or eliminate this anxiety. These mechanisms represent another major contribution of psychoanalytic theory to psychology and to the study of criminal behavior (see **TABLE 5-1**).

Based on the importance Freud placed on the unconscious mind, anxiety, and defense mechanisms, psychoanalysis (a treatment technique) is designed to bring to awareness inner conflicts and emotional problems. Basically, the therapist attempts to get the patient to replay those thoughts, feelings, and events from the past that are influencing present behaviors and to make unconscious desires

an angel (superego) appears on the other — and the character (ego) must choose a course of action, you can understand the gist of these basic elements of personality.

Lester and VanVoorhis note the Freud did not conceive of these concepts as actual parts within the brain. Rather, they are best conceived as wishes or desires.[6] The <u>id</u> is the unconscious, instinctual aspect of the personality. Id wishes often include the immediate gratification of basic drives (e.g., sex, aggression). The primary rule for the id is, "If it feels good, do it!" The <u>superego</u> is akin to a conscience — the keeper of prohibitions ("Stealing is wrong") and wishes about what a person wants to be ("I am going to be just like my father when I grow up"). Parents, schools, and other social institutions serve as

TABLE 5-1
Selected Freudian Defense Mechanisms

- *Denial:* The truth of some experience is denied. For example, a child's father abandons the family, but the family acts as though he just went on a vacation and will return soon.
- *Rationalization:* Finding a satisfactory reason for doing something inappropriate. For example, one indulges in fermented brews instead of studying and flunks a test the following day. The person reacts by saying, "That professor is a schmuck . . . this class sucks. . . . I think I'll switch majors."
- *Repression:* Desires or thoughts are forced back into the unconscious mind and their existence is denied. For example, memories of childhood abuse are forgotten.
- *Reaction formation:* An individual hides one instinct from awareness through the use of the opposite impulse. For example, love becomes a mask to hide hatred.
- *Projection:* Attributing one's desires or wishes to someone else. For example, a person is angry at someone and accuses them of being angry at that person.

conscious. This is sometimes facilitated through free association, where the patient verbalizes, uncensored, anything that comes to mind.

Freudian Explanations of Delinquency

The basic assumption behind Freudian theory is that human nature is inherently antisocial. Due to the influence of the id, infants start life with antisocial drives. As infants grow and develop, however, they confront social rules to which they are expected to abide. Thus, they must give up the primitive drives of instant gratification, unbridled sexuality, and unrestrained aggression. Children develop a superego from experience and from role models such as parents and siblings that guides them along the path of appropriate behavior. Ego development helps children negotiate id demands for instant gratification with superego demands against such behavior. Any problem or trauma that upsets the development of the ego or superego can increase the risk of delinquency and crime.

The Freudian perspective on the psychological roots of delinquency and criminality has been developed by theorists such as Redl and Wineman, Healy, and Aichorn. Redl and Wineman applied psychoanalytic theory to a group of delinquent children as part of a treatment program.[8] They dismissed the possibility that abnormally strong id wishes resulted in delinquent behavior. Instead, they focused on the ego and superego. For example, they describe a delinquent ego that effectively blocks any potential restraint from the conscience (superego) and permits the delinquent to rationalize criminal behavior. Inappropriate role models might create a delinquent superego, which is guided by a delinquent code of behavior, rather than appropriate values.

Yet another possibility is the overdeveloped superego. As noted earlier, the superego expresses displeasure (e.g., when its wishes are violated) in the form of anxiety. The result of this displeasure upon the personality is guilt. The more guilt the person accumulates, the more the person feels the need to be punished. It is only through punishment that the personality can truly be absolved of any guilt feelings. In this sense, some people may commit crimes because they want to be caught and punished.

As the concept of the overdeveloped superego indicates, Freudians often stress criminal acts as an indication of an underlying personality conflict. Aichorn, consistent with this Freudian principle, developed the concepts of "manifest" and "latent" delinquency. Aichorn wrote that manifest delinquency was the overt, expressed criminal behavior of stealing, robbing, and the like. Latent delinquency was the root cause of this behavior — the instinctual wishes lurking in the background, waiting for an opportunity to break through for satisfaction. According to Aichorn, the challenge of psychoanalysis is to "seek the provocation which made the latent delinquency manifest and also determine what caused the latent delinquency."[9]

Warren and Hindelang summarize several basic interpretations of Freudian psychology as it relates to crime.[10] Within the psychoanalytic tradition, criminal behavior is often viewed as a form of neurosis — guilt and anxiety stem from unconscious strivings. Criminals may therefore suffer from a compulsive need for punishment to alleviate guilt. Criminal activity is also considered a means for gratifying needs and desires not met by the family. Delinquency has roots in repressed memories of traumatic experiences and may be the result of displaced hostility towards those who caused trauma.

Policy Implications of Freudian Theory

The most obvious drawback of Freudian theory is that it is difficult, if not impossible, to test empirically. Concepts such as the id, ego, and superego cannot be directly observed or measured.[11] Moreover, motivations for delinquency are often hidden (unconscious), even to the offender. Psychoanalytic explanations of delinquency and crime therefore tend to be "after the fact" and untestable. As a rehabilitation technique, psychoanalysis is also wanting. Finckenauer notes that the effectiveness of psychoanalysis is limited to generally intelligent, articulate, adult neurotics. Conversely, the typical delinquent is less intelligent, inarticulate, and not neurotic.[12]

LINK In Chapter 1, it was noted that a good scientific theory must be testable; that is, one must be able to collect empirical information that can refute or support the theory. When a concept (e.g., id, superego) cannot be measured, the theory cannot be tested.

Not surprisingly then, recent studies of the rehabilitation literature confirm that insight-oriented therapies like psychoanalysis do not reduce criminal offending.[13] Finally, even if it were effective, psychoanalytic treatment lasts a long period of time (even a lifetime) and is expensive — traits unlikely to play well when the public foots the bill. Indeed, Redl and Wineman's treatment ended not because delinquents were deemed "cured," but because the funding ended. A complete treatment might have lasted several years.[14]

Despite these considerable drawbacks, psychoanalytic theory maintains an important place in the psychology of criminal behavior for a number of reasons. First, while most offenders are not neurotic adults, some crimes *are* tied to deep-seated (and perhaps unconscious) anxiety or hostility. Psychologist Palmer suggests that such unresolved issues may create a barrier to any rehabilitation effort.[15] The results of a 2004 study by Ted appear to support this position.[16] Here, researchers found that a well-supported cognitive-behavioral rehabilitation program did not have a positive effect on neurotic offenders.

Second, Lester and Van Voorhis argue that counselors (regardless of their theoretical background) who deal with offenders should be aware of the Freudian concepts of <u>transference</u> and <u>countertransference</u>.[17] Transference occurs when the client uses the counselor as a stand-in for someone in the client's past, such as a father or sibling. Countertransference occurs when the client "pushes the buttons" of the counselor so that the resulting anger and hostility interferes with treatment.

Finally, many Freudian concepts appear, albeit sometimes altered and often with different terminology, in other theories of crime. Thus, concepts within Freud's theory have been modified such that they can be scientifically tested. Freudian defense mechanisms, for example, occupy a central role in current cognitive and social learning theories of crime. Current theories also point to the importance of "morals" (e.g. superego) that are learned from role models and to the importance of "self-control" (ego strength).

Behavioral Psychology

The behavioral psychologist operates from a completely different perspective than a person trained in psychoanalysis. The focus is on specific behavior, and the orientation is very much on the here and now. A behaviorist-oriented rehabilitation program would not spend time on the childhood emotions of an adult offender.[18] The basic principle underlying behaviorism is that all behavior is learned. The father of behaviorism, John B. Watson, believed that the purpose of psychology is to understand, predict, and control human behavior.[19] B. F. Skinner, another dominant figure in behaviorism, felt that there is nothing emotionally or morally wrong with persons who commit crimes. Rather, they are simply responding to rewards and punishments within their environments.[20]

Principles of Learning

Psychologists have identified three types of learning — classical conditioning, operant conditioning, and observational (vicarious) learning. <u>Classical conditioning</u> was first identified by Ivan Pavlov, a Russian physician. Pavlov's work focused on the relationship between a stimulus and response. By pairing an unconditioned stimulus (meat) with a conditioned stimulus (a bell), he eventually reproduced a conditioned response (salivation) in dogs using only the bell.[21] John Watson later demonstrated this principle with a human subject, "little Albert" (see FIGURE 5-1). Initially, Watson used a loud noise, which produces the unconditioned response of fear in a child. Then, by pairing the loud noise with a white rat (the rat initially produced no fear), he was able to condition Albert to be afraid of the lab rat. Although this technology is still sometimes used to treat criminals (see the following sec-

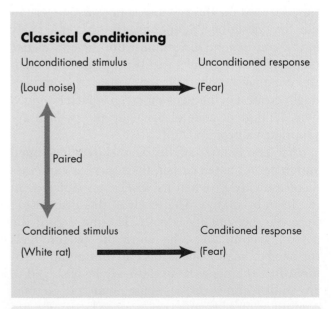

Classical Conditioning

Unconditioned stimulus → Unconditioned response

(Loud noise) → (Fear)

Paired

Conditioned stimulus → Conditioned response

(White rat) → (Fear)

FIGURE 5-1 The Classical Conditioning Process
Over time, the conditioned stimulus alone will produce the conditioned response.

tion on aversion therapy), few would argue that classical conditioning explains why people originally engage in crime. Typically, psychologists point to either operant or vicarious learning to explain the acquisition of criminal behavior.

In <u>operant conditioning</u>, some behavior (often called a target behavior) must first be displayed. A desired target behavior can then be reinforced, which increases the likelihood of this behavior in the future. An undesirable target behavior (e.g., lying, stealing) can be punished, which decreases the likelihood of this behavior in the future (see **TABLE 5-2**). <u>Positive reinforcement</u> increases the target behavior by rewarding the individual. This reward can be tangible (money, a treat) or intangible (praise, an approving look). Importantly, what is rewarding to each individual may be different. Many people confuse <u>negative reinforcement</u> with punishment. Negative reinforcement, however, *increases* the target behavior, while punishment has the opposite effect.

Negative reinforcement increases a target behavior by removing some unpleasant stimulus. For example, consider how small children often use behavior to manipulate others: Children are masters at using negative reinforcement to "train" parents. Suppose a child in a grocery store picks up a treat, but is told "no" by the parent. The child then proceeds to fall on the floor screaming, crying, and attracting the attention of other shoppers (in behavioral terms, the child has introduced a noxious stimuli). When the parent (out of embarrassment or perhaps frustration) relents, the child terminates the tantrum. The child has just used negative reinforcement (the removal of the tantrum and

Who is in charge here? Children are masters at training their parents. One common technique that kids use to obtain what they want is to throw a temper tantrum.

How would an effective parent respond?

parental embarrassment) to increase the odds that the next time, the parent will relent more quickly and easily. The child may even throw in some positive reinforcement ("You're the best daddy ever!") to further the cause.

Unlike reinforcement, <u>punishment</u> (a scolding, spanking) reduces the odds of the target behavior being repeated. Through experimentation with both animals and humans, behaviorists have developed a knowledge base about the most effective way to condition behavior. One golden rule is that the consistency of reinforcement and punishment matters more than the severity. Indeed, parental use of harsh but *inconsistent* punishment is a good predictor of delinquent behavior.[22] Additionally, reinforcement shapes behavior more efficiently than punishment — psychologists recommend that reinforcers outnumber punishers by a ratio of four to one.[23] Finally, both punishment and reinforcement should follow quickly after the target behavior.

There is an interesting connection between operant conditioning and deterrence theory (see Chapter 3). In essence, philosophers such as Beccaria and Bentham, writing during the 1800s, correctly predicted that swift and certain punishment would be most effective in controlling human behavior. Indeed, at least one commentator has suggested that deterrence could be absorbed into a broader theory of learning.[24] In that sense, punishment

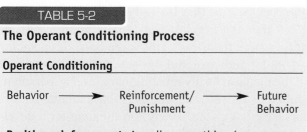

TABLE 5-2
The Operant Conditioning Process

Operant Conditioning

Behavior ⟶ Reinforcement/Punishment ⟶ Future Behavior

Positive reinforcement: Awarding something (e.g., money, food, praise) when a desired action is taken, in order to increase that behavior in the future.
Negative reinforcement: When target behavior is demonstrated, noxious stimuli (e.g., screaming, bad smell) is removed in order to increase the target behavior in the future.
Punishment: Introduction of noxious stimuli (e.g., scolding, spanking) to reduce or suppress a target behavior.

through the criminal justice system would represent another form of operant conditioning (among many) that shapes human behavior.

LINK In Chapter 3, the concept of specific deterrence — the idea that swift, certain, and severe punishment would teach offenders a lesson and reduce the odds that they will reoffend — was introduced. A behavioral psychologist would view criminal justice sanctions as a form of operant conditioning, one punishment (among many) in an offenders' life.

Theorists across the disciplines of psychology and sociology tie delinquency to the failure of parents to effectively condition their children (using operant conditioning) away from aggression, stealing, lying, and other antisocial behavior. Sociologists often refer to this as *direct parental control* (see Chapter 7). Research on children and adolescents has long supported the link between parental use of operant conditioning and delinquency.[25] Sheldon and Eleanor Glueck's study of 500 delinquent and 500 nondelinquent boys found that "harsh and erratic" punishment had a strong influence on delinquency.[26] Reviews of the literature find that other measures of parenting, including supervision and discipline, are among the stronger predictors of delinquency.[27] Reporters, commentators and the public often blame the parents of criminals in high-profile crimes (see **Headline Crime** for further discussion of this topic.)

Gerald Patterson and his associates at the Oregon Social Learning Center work extensively with delinquent children and their parents. Patterson's social interactional theory, derived from this work,

has parental efficacy (effectiveness) as its central concept.[28] Parents who monitor their children closely, recognize deviant behavior, and use consistent punishment and reinforcement, are more likely to rear nondelinquent children. Conversely, Patterson notes that parents of children who steal, "do not track, they do not interpret stealing . . . as 'deviant,' they do not punish, and they do not care."[29] Patterson recognizes, however, that parenting efficacy is dependent (to some extent) on family environment (see **FIGURE 5-2**). For example, single parents living on a marginal income might need to work two jobs and sacrifice some supervision over their children.

Patterson's theory and others that are similar are not without their critics. Judith Rich Harris' 1998 book entitled *The Nurture Assumption: Why Children Turn Out the Way They Do — Parents Matter Less Than You Think and Peers Matter More* was an argument against such theories.[30] This was a book designed for a popular audience and her research was acclaimed in the media as "truly revolutionary" and a "paradigm shifter."[31] Harris' main thesis is that parental behaviors have few effects (if any) on the long-term development of their children. What does Harris make of the substantial amount of research linking parenting behavior to delinquency? She explains this relationship by arguing that the children are influencing parenting behavior.[32] In other words, difficult children will produce (over time) the type of parenting characteristics (lax supervision, harsh/inconsistent punishment) highlighted in research.

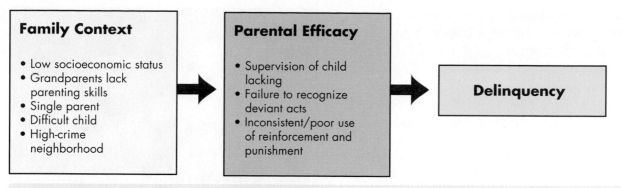

FIGURE 5-2 The First Stage of Patterson's Social Interactional Theory
Source: Adapted from Gerald Patterson, John Reid, and Thomas Dishion, *Antisocial Boys* (Eugene, OR: Castalia, 1992): 12.

One way to untangle the relationship between parenting skills and a child's behavior is to examine what happens when parenting practices change. If a change in parenting practices has no effect on the child, then Harris may be correct. If, however, changing parental behaviors reduces delinquency, Patterson's theory would be supported. Patterson and his associates have devised several methods for training parents. Those are discussed in greater detail later, but it is worth noting here that parent training programs are moderately successful at reducing delinquency.[33]

Although Harris dismisses the importance of parenting, she does believe the criminal behaviors are (in part) learned. Specifically, she argues that group socialization (childhood playgroups, adolescent peer groups) are an important source of childhood behaviors, including delinquency.

Modeling Theory

Research on peer effects usually focuses on <u>observational learning</u> — role modeling the behavior of others. Albert Bandura recognized that much of what is learned is not based on trial and error (operant condition). Rather, as humans, behaviors are acquired simply by observing others. Bandura argues that although everyone has the capacity for aggression, they must still acquire a behavioral repertoire (through observation) in order to act aggressively.[34] Bandura and his associates demonstrated this principle in the now-famous "Bobo doll" experiments.[35] The researchers randomly divided a sample of children into two groups, both of whom watched a videotape of a playroom. In the first group, the video included people punching and kicking an inflated doll that was weighted on the

bottom (the Bobo doll). The second group saw a similar video, but there was no violent behavior toward the doll. As one might expect, when the children were released into the playroom, only the group of kids who saw the Bobo doll kicked and punched in the video replicated this behavior.

Although this experiment is rather simple, the implications for explaining crime are immense. For example, children who observe their parents abusing each other, or adolescents who observe their friends engaging in delinquency, would be at risk for engaging in similar acts themselves. Of course, people do not randomly choose behaviors to model. Rather, people tend to imitate the behavior of those who are attractive and competent, especially if the role models are rewarded for the behavior.[36] Another important point is that people do not automatically use the behaviors that are acquired through observation.[37] Some are discarded without being used, while others are used extensively.

The effect of observational learning on criminal behaviors is difficult to determine. Researchers typically use indirect measures of learning. The most common measure is whether or not a person has delinquent peers — the assumption is that people imitate and role model the behavior of their peer group. Indeed, the relationship between delinquent peer associations and delinquency is among the strongest in criminology.[38] Parents have also played a central role in the study of observational learning. For example, it is possible that crime runsin families because children are modeling the behavior of adults. A study of 111 parolees from Buffalo, New York, found that children who observed their parents' violent confrontations were more likely to batter their partners during adulthood.[39] Childhood observations of parental violence predicted future violence better than childhood physical abuse.

Media and Crime

Psychologists have also focused on the effect of media (particularly television and movies) on aggression, violence, and some forms of criminal behavior. A host of studies have shown that television and movies are laden with violent content, and that Americans spend a great deal of time watching violent programs.[40] Violence in the media is often portrayed in a way that is conducive to role modeling. For example, perpetrators of violence are not punished, the target of violence shows little pain, and there are few long-term negative consequences for the violence.[41] There is no shortage of media-hyped examples of behaviors that seem to be direct imitations of television or movie characters. Examples of such anecdotal evidence include[42]:

- MTV cartoon characters Beavis and Butthead have been blamed for children starting fires.
- In a reenactment of a scene from the movie *Money Train*, two men armed with flammable liquid burned a clerk's booth inside of a Brooklyn subway.
- John Hinkley, Jr., who attempted to assassinate President Reagan, was imitating the main character in the movie *Taxi Driver*.
- A 15-year-old Seattle girl placed poison in a peanut butter sandwich that was intended for a playmate — she got the idea from the movie *Heathers*.

Not surprisingly, a 2001 survey indicated that roughly one half of Americans believe that movies, television, and video games substantially contribute to violence.[43] Is this anecdotal evidence and public opinion supported by scientific research? Researchers have studied this issue using a variety of methods, including survey research and laboratory and field experiments. Laboratory experiments, like the "Bobo doll" research by Bandura and his associates, typically demonstrate clear links between media violence and aggression.[44] Although results from survey research are less clear, the majority of studies do find a relationship. One recent study examined children from 707 families over 17 years.[45] The researchers found that the amount of time spent watching television during adolescence predicted self- or parent-reported aggression (including assault and robbery) during adulthood. This relation-

Some scholars believe that kids learn violence and other antisocial behavior from the mass media.

Do video games train kids for violent behavior in the real world?

ship was evident, even after controlling for a host of environmental influences (e.g., family income, childhood neglect, neighborhood violence). A 2002 review of this body of research found that regardless of the methodology, there is a moderate relationship between exposure to media violence and aggression or violence.[46]

Because studies of observational learning often use indirect measures, their conclusions are open to question. For example, one common interpretation of peer-delinquency relationship is that like-minded individuals hang out together. In other words, "birds of a feather flock together."[47] Similarly, critics of the media-violence link suggest that violence-prone individuals will seek out violent programming. If this logic is correct, then delinquent peers and television have no causal effect on a person's behavior. Common sense suggests there is some truth to this point; for example, one would not expect a hardcore delinquent to hang out with members of the chess club. These issues will be discussed in greater detail in the context of sociological learning theories (Chapter 7).

It is worth noting here that one way to test whether a relationship is causal is to put it into practice. With regard to delinquent-peer example, one might study what happens if a delinquent is denied access to his or her normal (delinquent) peer group. Regarding media effects, there is some evidence that reducing exposure to media violence reduces aggression among children. For example, Robinson and colleagues reported that one program designed to reduce television viewing significantly reduced aggression in a sample of third and fourth graders.[48]

Observational learning is a component in many theories of crime. Theorists in this area typically incorporate both operant and vicarious learning, as well as cognitive aspects into a single "social learning theory." Because sociologists and psychologists have both advanced similar social learning theories, they will be addressed in greater detail in Chapter 7.

Policy Implications of Behaviorism

Perhaps the most appealing aspect of behavioral theory is that it translates easily into treatments and interventions for delinquents and criminals. Further, unlike psychoanalysis, it does not require the presence of trained therapeutic personnel or years of therapy sessions. As a general principle, behaviorists argue that because criminal behavior is learned, it can be unlearned.[49] In addition, criminals can learn pro-social behaviors to replace criminal actions. One practical application of classical conditioning, for example, is **aversion therapy**. Aversion therapy is used to eliminate links between stimuli and troublesome behaviors. For example, alcoholics can be conditioned to experience alcohol as noxious rather than pleasant, or sex offenders can be conditioned so that deviant images are repulsive rather than stimulating.

Aversion therapy works by pairing a stimulus that elicits pleasure with a noxious stimulus (typically a light electric shock or a noxious odor). For example, a therapist might show a pedophile a sexual image of a child, while at the same time exposing them to a very noxious odor (rotting meat seems to be a favorite).[50] After repeating this procedure over time, the deviant sexual image produces revulsion and nausea rather than sexual stimulation. For ethical reasons (how does one procure a sexually deviant image?), and because the general public finds this process itself somewhat repulsive, aversion therapy is used sparingly.

The principles of both operant and vicarious learning, however, are present in virtually every successful rehabilitation program. One simple application of operant conditioning is a **token economy**. In a token economy, participants earn points (or tokens) if they behave in the appropriate manner and lose tokens for inappropriate behavior. Later, the participants can exchange the tokens for items that they desire (e.g., television privileges, weekend furloughs,

purchases from a store). In the same way that money motivates people in the outside world, tokens provide a way for institutions to establish a work-payment incentive system.[51] Token economies, when administered correctly, are efficient at reducing inmate misconduct and increasing desirable behaviors ranging from personal hygiene to academic achievement.[52] For this reason, they have become a mainstay of juvenile correction institutions. Of course, the main drawback to a token economy is its artificial nature. A juvenile released from a correctional institution quickly discovers that studying for school or keeping a neat room no longer elicits "tokens."

To avoid the artificial nature of token economies, many psychologists advocate working with parents and children within their home. Gerald Patterson, for example, trains parents to monitor the behavior of children and use reinforcements in the home.[53] To encourage adequate supervision and the consistent and correct use of reinforcement and punishment, he has parents chart out the frequency of problem behaviors (e.g., stealing, lying, staying out past curfew). Often, this is followed by a **contingency contract**, a formal contract signed by the parent and child that specifies behaviors that the child is to complete (chores) and avoid (stealing). In addition to the behaviors, the contract specifies how the child will be reinforced or punished based on their behaviors. Parent training programs have been moderately successful in reducing the delinquency of children.[54]

Note, however, that behavioral treatments are not a silver bullet for curing crime. In fact, behavioral programs that narrowly focus only on operant and/or classical conditioning (e.g., token economy, aversion therapy) have only limited impact on offender behavior.[55] Aversion therapy is portrayed in movies as almost magical (as in the movie *A Clockwork Orange*), but the reality is that conditioning is relatively easy to overcome. An alcoholic conditioned to experience alcohol as nauseating, for example, needs only to drink a few times (getting sick each time) before the conditioning wears off. Among the most effective treatments are those that combine behavioral principles with cognitive theory.[56]

Cognitive Psychology

Behavioral psychology is criticized by some for its portrayal of learning as a rather mechanical process. Cognitive psychologists believe that the human ability to engage in complex thought processes makes people different from other animals. Imagine, for example, walking down a crowded sidewalk on a busy city street. Someone walking in the opposite direction bumps a shoulder and almost knocks a person down. What thoughts go through that person's mind? They might think, "That #@!! is disrespecting me!" or perhaps, "Whoa, I should watch where I'm going." Cognitive theorists argue that those thoughts, more than the actual shoulder bump, will impact how a person responds.

Note that there is a great deal of overlap between cognitive psychology and behaviorism. For example, cognitions (like behaviors) can be learned. Once learned, a person's thoughts serve to prompt, reinforce, or punish behavior.[57] In other words, a person's mind can use operant conditioning to punish or reinforce behavior. With respect to crime, cognitive psychologists focus on two broad areas: the content of a person's thoughts (what is thought) and general thought structures (how a person thinks).[58]

Cognitive Structure

Cognitive structures refer to stable ways of thinking about one's self and the environment. Lawrence Kohlberg's theory of moral development fits well within this definition. Kohlberg argued that humans advance through predictable stages of moral reasoning, defined as how a person thinks about fairness, justice, and a right course of action. Kohlberg had subjects reason through various moral dilemmas and decide a course of action. He was less interested in *what* people decided than *how* they came to that decision. From this research, he developed six stages of moral reasoning (see TABLE 5-3). Subsequent research on Kohlberg's stages revealed that delinquents tend to have delays in moral development.[59] Moral education is now a component in many rehabilitation programs. Here, offenders work through moral dilemmas, and with the aid of a trained leader, learn to think about such issues in a more complex manner.[60]

Of course, moral reasoning is just one aspect of a person's cognitive structure. Criminologists often discuss cognitive structure as a series of skills acquired through prior learning and applied consistently to different situations. Examples of cognitive skills other than moral reasoning include self-control, the ability to empathize (take the perspective of others), the ability to formulate short-term

TABLE 5-3

Lawrence Kohlberg's Stages of Moral Development

Stage 1	The right course of action is determined by blindly obeying those with power and authority. Emphasis is on avoiding punishment. The interests of others are not considered.
Stage 2	The right course of action is to further one's own interests. The interests of others are important only as a way to satisfy self-interests.
Stage 3	Moral reasoning is motivated by loyalties to others and a desire to live up to other people's standards; to follow the Golden Rule.
Stage 4	Right is following the rules of society and maintaining important social institutions (e.g., family, community).
Stage 5	Moral decisions are made by weighing individuals' rights against legal principles and the common good.
Stage 6	Moral decisions are based on universal principles such as the concern for human dignity, a respect for life, and a desire for justice. These principles are considered across different contexts and are independent of the law.

Source: Lawrence Kohlberg, *Stages in the Development of Moral Thought and Action* (New York: Holt, Rinehart and Winston, 1969).

and long-term plans, the ability to anticipate the consequences of behavior, and the ability to recognize and control anger.[61] In the shoulder-bumping incident, someone who has high self-control, is empathetic, and anticipates consequences well would probably be unlikely to respond in a violent manner. Relating to criminal behavior, cognitive theorists in this area tend to focus on what a person *is not thinking about*, including the long-term consequences of his or her actions, how the victim might feel, and legal alternatives to the criminal act.[62]

Cognitive Content

The content of cognitions refers to what people think. Criminologists focus on rationalizations or denials (recall Freud's defense mechanisms) that support criminal behavior. Different theorists refer to such thoughts as criminal thinking errors, cognitive distortions, techniques of neutralization, or "stinking thinking."[63] All of these terms refer to illogical or irrational thoughts that can prompt or support behavior. For example, a criminal might rationalize a burglary by thinking, "They've got insurance; I'm not really hurting anyone." Almost without exception, research in this area finds that criminals or delinquents are more likely to express such thoughts than law-abiding citizens.

LINK The sociological learning theories identified in Chapter 7 include concepts that are similar to what a cognitive psychologist might call *cognitive content*. Within Edwin Sutherland's differential association theory, cognitions are called "definitions" (as in how one defines a situation) that can either support or run counter to the legal code.

The primary criticism of this research deals with time ordering and causation. Do these thoughts actually *cause* criminal behavior or are they simply after-the-fact excuses used to justify actions and deflect blame? To cognitive scholars, this is a relatively unimportant issue. Regardless of whether the thoughts happen before (a prompt) or after the criminal act (reinforcement), they serve to reduce the guilt of the offender. Recalling the discussion of negative reinforcement, the *thought* allows the burglar to terminate a noxious stimulus (guilt/anxiety), which increases the likelihood he or she will burgle again. Such rationalizations are especially common for sex offenders, where guilt associated with the act is strong. Pedophiles, for example, will report that children enjoy sexual contact with adults; they feel that sex is "good" for children and that children often initiate sex and know what they want.[64]

Policy Implications of Cognitive Psychology: Cognitive-Behavioral Programs

Like behaviorism, cognitive theory translates easily into practice. In fact, most cognitive-oriented rehabilitation programs incorporate principles of learning. The cognitive component of such cognitive-behavioral interventions includes the content of thought, the structure of thought, or both. Cognitive skills programs focus on cognitive structure and attempt to teach offenders skills such as moral reasoning, self-control, or anger management. The therapist teaches these skills using the principles of learning. Typically, a behavior is modeled by the therapist, and offenders are given several opportunities to practice the skill. Offenders are then reinforced when they employ these skills in role-playing sessions and (more importantly) outside of a specific session.[65]

Cognitive restructuring refers to attempts to change the content of an individual's thoughts. In essence, criminal-thinking errors (e.g., rationalizations, distortions) are identified and forcefully rejected by the therapist. Often times, this is done in a group setting where offenders are taught to identify and correct others' thinking errors. Cognitive-behavioral treatments have accumulated a track record of success for reducing the criminal behavior of children, adolescents, and adults.[66] For example, a 2002 review of evaluations from cognitive-behavioral programs concluded that "cognitive-behavioral programs can reduce recidivism rates by significant amounts. This was found to be true for the overall collection of cognitive-behavioral studies and also for the subcategories social skills development training and cognitive skills training."[67]

The same study found that strictly behavioral programs (e.g., token economy, contingency contracting) were not as effective. In that sense, treatments that have multiple targets for change and those that operate in the "real world" have proven more successful. Multisystemic therapy (MST) is a good example of this type of treatment. Devised by psychologist Scott Henggeler and his associates, MST is a cognitive-behavioral treatment that emphasizes "providing home-based and family-focused services that are intensive, time limited, pragmatic, and goal oriented."[68] MST has proven successful at reducing offending for a variety of populations, including inner-city juvenile offenders, adolescent sex offenders, and abusive parents (see **Theory in Action: Multisystemic Therapy** for a detailed description of this program through a case study.)

Personality and Crime

Personality theory provides further possible insights into the psychological aspects of crime. The primary assumption behind this perspective is that crime and delinquency are related to the presence of some personality trait. A personality trait is a characteristic of an individual that is stable over time and across different social circumstances. For example, an impulsive person is not likely to suddenly become a cautious person. Further, one would expect the person to be impulsive in a variety of domains — from driving a car to shopping for groceries. A personality is therefore the sum of personality traits that define a person. Psychologists typically link personality to criminal behavior in one of two ways. First, an offender may have specific traits within their personality that are conducive to crime. Second, some psychologists believe that certain criminal offenders, called

Multisystemic therapy has been hailed by many scholars as one of the best rehabilitation programs currently available. This praise stems from research findings that show MST reduces criminal behavior, even among very difficult populations. What makes MST unique is its comprehensive approach. While some cognitive-behavioral programs teach a set of skills or work with parents, MST targets many areas for change and uses many different techniques. Consider the case of "Homer," provided by MST creator Scott Henggeler and his associates:

> Homer is a 15-year-old Caucasian male with an extensive history of delinquent behavior, including assault and battery with intent to kill, simple assault and battery, malicious destruction of real property, trespassing, petty larceny, contempt of court, and resisting arrest. Homer had a reputation for fighting and bullying his peers and had been expelled in the 7th grade for assaulting a classmate and cursing his teachers. Homer was in a gang of juvenile delinquents who affectionately called themselves "Death Row." Aside from his criminal record and association with deviant peers, Homer had an extensive history of abusing inhalants, marijuana, and alcohol.
>
> At the time of referral, Homer had recently been released from a 45-day juvenile justice evaluation facility. He resides alone with his mother, who is employed full-time and has a history of alcohol abuse. Homer also has a 17-year-old sister with a history of crack cocaine dependence. She was recently released from a state-supported treatment facility and at the time of referral was living with her boyfriend and his family. A maternal uncle also lived in the community, though he refused to have contact with Homer due to his antisocial behavior.

The MST therapist (a graduate student) identified a number of targets for change, including:

- Homer's deviant peer group (he hung around with older, "streetwise" youth)

- Homer's refusal to go to school (he spent most days at home, getting high with friends)
- Homer's thinking biases (anyone who failed to comply with his requests was "dissing" him, and he felt justified in responding aggressively)
- Homer's mother failed to monitor or punish his behavior (Homer was allowed to stay out as long as he wanted and did pretty much as he pleased).

The therapists also identified a number of strengths:

- Homer's mother was still emotionally attached to her son and willing to learn new parenting skills.
- Homer was intelligent, could be quite personable, and excelled at sports.
- Both Homer and his mother wanted him to attend high school rather than continue in the 7th grade (Homer wanted to play high school football).

The therapist modified Homer's behavior by utilizing a number of behavioral techniques. For example, Homer's mother was trained to monitor Homer's whereabouts and punish his misbehavior (parent training). She produced a list of chores and responsibilities for Homer and consistently rewarded or punished him, depending upon whether he completed his chores (contingency contract). The therapist also worked with Homer and his mother to get him admitted into high school. Once admitted, his time was more structured; he had less access to delinquent peers and more access to prosocial peers. Further, playing football became a natural reward that helped shape Homer's behavior. Finally, as Homer's behavior improved, his uncle began to spend more time with him, serving as a good adult role model (observational learning).

Sources: Excerpt reprinted from Scott W. Henggeler, Phillippe B. Cunningham, Susan G. Pickrel, Sonja K. Schoenwald, and Michael J. Brondino, "Multisystemic Therapy: An Effective Violence Prevention Approach for Serious Juvenile Offenders." *Journal of Adolescence* 19 (1996): 55–56, with permission from Elsevier; Francis T. Cullen and Paul Gendreau, "Assessing Correctional Rehabilitation: Policy, Practice, and Prospects," in *Criminal Justice 2000* (Washington, DC: National Institute of Justice, 2001).

psychopaths, sociopaths, or antisocial personality disordered, have a criminal personality. In other words, they have a specific cluster of personality traits that drives them toward criminal behavior.

Personality Traits and Crime

In general, personality theorists attempt to define and outline basic traits that form the building blocks of human personality.[69] Typically, a number of related traits are combined to form "super factors" or broad dimensions of personality. For example, a common dimension of personality with which many are familiar is extroversion (i.e., outgoing, sociable) and introversion (i.e., reserved, private, cautious). A substantial number of general personality theories exist, each with their own traits and dimensions. One example is the five-factor model, which identifies five dimensions of personality (hence the name).[70] The dimensions include:

1. Neuroticism (emotional stability versus instability)

2. Extraversion (sociability)

3. Openness to experience (curiosity, interest in trying new things)

4. Agreeableness (antagonistic versus agreeable interpersonal strategy)

5. Conscientiousness (impulse control, ability to follow moral code, organizational ability)

Another example is Auke Tellegen's personality model.[71] Tellegen identifies three dimensions of personality: (1) positive emotionality, (2) negative emotionality, and (3) constraint. As outlined in TABLE 5-4, each of these dimensions is composed of several traits. An individual exhibiting high constraint, for example, would score high on *traditionalism* (desires conservative environment, endorses high moral standards), *harm avoidance* (avoids excitement or danger, prefers safe activities), and *control* (reflective, cautious, careful).

Personality researchers have constructed a number of personality inventories to measure the presence or extent of specific personality dimensions.[72] Generally, these are paper-and-pencil questionnaires asking a broad array of questions that tap into a variety of personality traits.

Early research linking personality and crime was plagued by methodology problems. For example, the Psychopathic Deviate (Pd) scale in the Minnesota Multiphasic Personality Inventory (MMPI)

TABLE 5-4
Personality Dimensions in the Multidimensional Personality Questionnaire

Constraint
- *Traditionalism:* desires a conservative social environment, endorses high moral standards
- *Harm avoidance:* avoids excitement and danger, prefers safe activities even if they are tedious
- *Control:* is reflective, cautious, careful, rational

Negative Emotionality
- *Aggression:* hurts others for advantage; will frighten and cause discomfort for others
- *Alienation:* feels mistreated, victimized, betrayed, and the target of false rumors
- *Stress reaction:* is nervous, vulnerable, sensitive, prone to worry

Positive Emotionality
- *Achievement:* works hard; enjoys demanding projects and working long hours
- *Social potency:* is forceful and decisive; fond of leadership roles
- *Well-being:* has a happy, cheerful disposition; feels good about self and sees a bright future
- *Social closeness:* is sociable, likes people and turns to others for comfort

Source: Avshalom Caspi, Terrie E. Moffitt, Phil A. Silva, Magda Stoughamer-Loeber, Robert F. Krueger, and Pamela S. Schmutte, "Are Some People Crime-Prone? Replications of the Personality-Crime Relationship Across Countries, Genders, Races, and Methods," *Criminology* 32 (1994): 163–195.

correlates well with criminal behavior. However, the scale was designed to identify dangerous individuals within psychiatric populations. Criminologists correctly criticized the use of these scales to predict criminal behavior, because the scales were constructed with questions that asked about failing on probation or engaging in crime.[73] It shouldn't surprise anyone that someone who reports failing on probation has engaged in crime.

Recent personality instruments do a better job of avoiding this pitfall. For example, a recent study used the Multidimensional Personality Questionnaire (MPQ), which measures Tellegen's model, to predict criminal behavior. In an impressive multinational study, researchers gave the MPQ to samples of youth in Pittsburgh, Pennsylvania, and Dunedin, New Zealand, to see what personality traits predicted self-reported, official (arrests), and parent / teacher-reported delinquency. Across samples, and regardless of how delinquency was measured, individuals with low constraint and high negative emotionality were more apt to engage in delinquency.[74]

LINK Gottfredson and Hirschi's general theory of crime is introduced in Chapter 7. The central concept in this theory, low self-control, is very similar to the personality trait of low constraint.

A 2001 review of personality-crime research considered evidence across four different models of personality (including both the Tellegen model and the five-factor model). The reviewers discovered that each model successfully identified traits that predicted antisocial behavior with moderate strength. Noting similarities across the personality models, the authors suggest a general personality profile of criminals[75]:

> Individuals who commit crimes tend to be hostile, self-centered, spiteful, jealous, and indifferent to others. They tend to lack ambition, motivation, and perseverance, have difficulty controlling their impulses, and hold nontraditional and unconventional values and beliefs.

Criminal Personality: The Psychopath

In contrast to personality theorists who focus on general traits common to everyone, some argue that there is a class of individuals who have a distinct criminal personality. The term *psychopath* is widely used (and often misused) by both professionals and the general public to describe this personality. Variations on the concept of psychopathy have existed within the professional field since the early 1800s. Indeed, in a 2004 article that addressed the history of criminology, Rafter concluded that "moral insanity" was among the first explanations of criminal behavior.[76] Isaac Ray, a 19th century psychiatrist, defined moral mania as a "cerebral disease" that could cause a person to commit horrible crimes without any motive or remorse.[77]

The term psychopathy was actually coined in 1845, and its meaning has changed over time (some people still prefer the term *sociopath*). The current conception of a psychopath is usually traced to Hervey Cleckly's book, *The Mask of Sanity*, originally published in 1941.[78] Cleckly, a psychiatrist who spent years working with criminal offenders, used case studies to outline key traits of a psychopathic personality. His laundry list of traits includes:

> Superficial charm, manipulative, above-average intelligence, absence of psychotic symptoms, absence of anxiety, lack of remorse, failure to learn from experience, egocentric, lack of emo-

Convicted murderer Keith Jesperson, right, shown here at a 1995 court appearance in Portland, Oregon. Jesperson, also called the "Happy Face Killer," is serving two life sentences in Oregon in connection with two murders in that state and has been sentenced to life in prison in Washington State for a third murder.

? *Although some serial killers are no doubt psychopaths, not all psychopaths are serial killers. What other types of criminals are likely to be psychopaths?*

tional depth, trivial sex life, unreliable, failure to follow a life plan, untruthful, suicide attempts rarely genuine, impulsive, antisocial behavior. . .

As the title of the book suggests, psychopaths are unlikely to come across as "crazy." They do not suffer from paranoid delusions, hallucinations, or breaks with reality (note "absence of psychotic symptoms" in the list). So, how does one identify a psychopath?

Currently, psychopathy is not listed in the latest *Diagnostic and Statistical Manual* (DSM-IV), the main tool used to diagnose mental disorders. Instead, the DSM outlines "antisocial personality disorder" (APD), a much broader concept — and one that probably includes the vast majority of prison inmates. Robert Hare, a Canadian psychologist, is a leader in the study of psychopathy. Hare refined Cleckley's original list of traits to create the Psychopathy Checklist (PCL).[79] Unlike other personality tests, the PCL is not a paper-and-pencil, multiple-choice instrument. Rather, a trained interviewer asks a number of questions in an effort to gauge whether a person exhibits certain traits, such as shallowness or superficial charm. The PCL

TABLE 5-5

Psychopathy Versus Antisocial Personality Disorder

DSM-IV Diagnostic Criteria for Antisocial Personality Disorder

A. There is a pervasive pattern of disregard for and violation of the rights of others occurring since age 15 years, as indicated by three (or more) of the following:

1. Failure to conform to social norms with respect to lawful behaviors as indicated by repeatedly performing acts that are grounds for arrest
2. Deceitfulness, as indicated by repeated lying, use of aliases, or conning others for personal profit or pleasure
3. Impulsivity or failure to plan ahead
4. Irritability and aggressiveness, as indicated by repeated physical fights or assaults
5. Reckless disregard for safety of self or others
6. Consistent irresponsibility, as indicated by repeated failure to sustain consistent work behavior or honor financial obligations
7. Lack of remorse, as indicated by being indifferent to or rationalizing having hurt, mistreated, or stolen from another

B. The individual is at least age 18 years.

C. There is evidence of conduct disorder with onset before age 15 years.

Hare's (1990) Psychopathy Checklist-Revised (PCL-R)

Emotional/Interpersonal Traits

Glibness/superficial charm

Grandiose sense of self-worth

Need for stimulation/prone to boredom

Conning/manipulative

Lack of remorse or guilt

Shallow affect

Callous/lack of empathy

Lack of realistic, long-term goals

Failure to accept responsibility for own actions

Pathological lying

Social Deviance

Many short-term marital relationships

Juvenile delinquency

Criminal versatility

Promiscuous sexual relations

Poor behavioral controls

Parasitic lifestyle

Early behavior problems

Impulsivity

Irresponsibility

Revocation of conditional release

Items scored on a scale of 0–2 by a trained interviewer
(0 = not applicable, 1 = uncertain, 2 = definitely present)

Sources: American Psychiatric Association, *Diagnostic and Statistical Manual of Mental Disorders,* 4th edition (Washington, DC: American Psychiatric Association, 1994); Robert D. Hare, *Without Conscience: The Disturbing World of Psychopaths Among Us* (New York: Guilford, 1999).

traits, along with the criteria for APD, are outlined in **TABLE 5-5** .

Hare and his associates have used the PCL to distinguish psychopathic prison inmates from nonpsychopathic inmates. Hare estimates that 15% to 25% of prisoners and perhaps 1% of the general population are psychopaths.[80] Researchers comparing nonpsychopathic prison inmates to psychopaths find some interesting differences in emotions, learning, speech patterns, and biological measures. One study, for example, revealed that psychopaths make

more logically inconsistent statements and other speaking errors than nonpsychopathic criminals.[81] As the examples in the **Theory in Action: Examples of Logical Inconsistencies in Speech Among Psychopaths** box illustrate, some of these logical inconsistencies can be downright funny. Less humorous is the finding that psychopaths do not seem to benefit from any form of rehabilitation. In fact, some effective treatment programs (for non-psychopaths) can actually increase their criminal behavior.[82] It is noteworthy that much of the biological research (see

Examples of Logical Inconsistencies in Speech Among Psychopaths

In his book, *Without Conscience: The Disturbing World of Psychopaths Among Us*, Robert Hare gives several examples of logically inconsistent speech patterns. Hare suggests that psychopaths may have trouble monitoring their own speech and keeping up with their own lies.

> When asked if he had ever committed a violent offense, a man serving time for theft answered, "No, but I once had to kill someone."

A woman with a staggering record of fraud, deceit, lies, and broken promises concluded a letter to the parole board with, "I've let a lot of people down . . . . One is only as good as her reputation and name. My word is as good as gold."

A man serving a term for armed robbery replied to the testimony of an eyewitness, "He's lying. I wasn't there. I should have blown his f@#!ing head off."

When Ted Bundy was asked what cocaine did to him, he replied, "Cocaine? I've never used it . . . I've never tried cocaine. I think I might have tried it once and got nothing out of it. Just snorted a little bit. And I just don't mess with it. It's too expensive. And I suppose if I was on the streets and had enough of it, I might get into it. But I'm strictly a marijuana man. All I do is . . . I love to smoke reefer. And Valiums. And of course alcohol."

Source: Robert D. Hare, *Without Conscience: The Disturbing World of Psychopaths Among Us* (New York: The Guilford Press, 1993): 125–126.

Chapter 4) focuses on either psychopathy or APD. Thus, psychopaths are more prone to lower heart rates, lower levels of skin conductance, and so forth.

The primary criticism of the concept of psychopathy centers on whether these individuals are qualitatively different from other offenders. Hare and others argue that the specific cluster of traits means that this is a specific type of offender. Others suggest that a psychopath may be nothing more than a chronic or serious criminal offender. In other words, each person may have a little "psychopath" — some simply have more than others. For this reason (and because of policy implications), future research on psychopathy will continue to generate controversy.

Policy Implications of Personality Theory

Personality explanations of delinquency and crime have become more accepted in criminology over the past decade. Much of this acceptance stems from the fact that personality traits (both general traits and psychopathy) consistently predict delinquency and crime. Despite this popularity, such theories are plagued by basic questions. How are personality traits formed? Where do they come from? Can traits be changed through rehabilitation

programs? By definition, personality tends to be stable over the life course. Oftentimes, personality traits are portrayed as almost impossible to change. A cognitive theorist, though, might argue that "traits" such as impulsivity or lack of empathy are simply cognitive skill deficits that can be remedied through training. In the research with the MPQ just described, the authors suggest that low constraint may stem from ineffective parenting, whereas negative emotionality may be a biological function — inherited and difficult to alter.

Hans Eysenck, one of the first theorists to outline a personality-based theory of crime, believes that basic dimensions of personality stem from differences in biology.[83] For example, he argues that arousal levels are related to the concept of extroversion, and "pyschotocism" is related to testosterone levels.[84] Similarly, Hare believes that at its core, psychopthy is a function of biology. He notes that, "the elements needed for the development of psychopathy — including a profound inability to experience empathy and the complete range of emotions, including fear — are provided in part by nature and possibly by some unknown biological influences of the developing fetus."[85]

There is a danger of viewing personality traits as something inborn and unchangeable. In particular, the concept of psychopathy can be used by psychologists eager to make money from the criminal justice system. Prosecutors can hire these folks to testify at trial. The psychologists (often after spending only a short time with the offender) testify that a defendant is indeed a psychopath. This testimony can lead (perhaps unfairly) to very harsh prison sentences.[86] Apart from the criminal justice system, the belief that crime stems from sources outside of one's control may lead people to ignore environmental conditions that foster crime.

Intelligence and Crime

Early positivists believed that feeblemindedness was a primary cause of crime. The emergence of psychological testing, including IQ tests, further heightened interest in this relationship. Currently, many people view IQ scores as a measure of general, native intelligence. Others view IQ as something other than intelligence and believe that environment affects scores. What exactly is IQ and how does it relate to criminal behavior?

A Brief History of Intelligence Testing

IQ tests allegedly measure mental differences from one person to another. Experimental psychologists were the first to design psychological tests to measure intelligence. For example, Hermann Ebbinghaus (1850–1909) believed that a large part of intelligence could be quantified by measuring one's ability to memorize. Alfred Binet (1857–1911) began his research on intelligence by measuring skull size, but quickly realized that this was insufficient.

Thus, in 1905, Binet and Theodore Simon developed a scale that would identify students who were performing poorly in school and in need of academic help. The scale was created by having children perform a hodgepodge of different tasks (e.g., counting coins, identifying which face was "prettier"). The tasks were labeled according to the age at which a child of normal intelligence should be able to complete them successfully. Children proceeded through increasingly difficult tasks until they were unable to complete a task. The age assigned to the last successfully completed task was considered their mental age. The concept of IQ, which stands for intelligence quotient, was born when a statistician later divided mental age by biological age, and multiplied the result by 100.[87] Note that average intelligence, where a person's bi-

ological and mental age are equal, is therefore always scored as 100.

Aware of how such a scale might be used by others (he once believed that intelligence was fixed at birth himself), Binet included several caveats with the publication of his scale that can be summarized[88]:

1. The scores are a practical device that do not support any theory of intellect. One cannot call what they measure intelligence.

2. The scale is a rough guide for identifying mildly retarded children. It is not a scale for ranking normal children.

3. Regardless of the causes of difficulty identified, emphasis should be placed on improvement through training. Low scores should not be used to mark children as incapable.

Unfortunately for Binet, his work was translated into English and made accessible to the United States at a time when the eugenics movement was in full swing. Eugenicists believed that intelligence was inherited and immutable. Therefore, great importance was placed on the ability to identify different types of feebleminded individuals so that they could be isolated and/or sterilized. Indeed, several slang terms come from the categories created by scientists. H.H. Goddard coined the term "moron" to describe the most important type of person — one that is mentally inferior, yet still able to function in society and therefore pass on genes.

In this light, Binet's testing procedures were modified and applied to various populations (e.g., World War I army soldiers, prisoners, immigrants) in an effort to identify mentally inferior people. Many of these early tests were obviously culturally biased and testing was often carried out in a shoddy manner. Stephen Jay Gould illustrates cultural bias with three questions from an early IQ test[89]:

1. Crisco is: patent medicine, disinfectant, toothpaste, food product

2. The number of Kaffir's legs is: 2, 4, 6, 8

3. Christy Mathewson is famous as a: writer, artist, baseball player, comedian

Most can probably get the Crisco question, but what about Christy Mathewson? Imagine a recent immigrant grappling with such a test. World War I army recruits who took this exam averaged a mental age of 13 years (just above "moron" status). Rather than question the exam or their testing procedure (both were flawed), the researchers took the results as valid. When the testers found that immigrants who had been in the country for at least five years performed better, they might have become suspicious that their tests were biased. However, their conclusion was that recent immigrants came from "poor breeding stock" and were therefore less intelligent.[90]

Lewis Terman, a Stanford University professor, devised the first standardized tests based on Binet's earlier scales. The resulting Stanford-Binet test was mass marketed to schools and became the gold standard for future IQ tests. The original Stanford-Binet test (and current IQ tests) no longer identified a mental age. Rather, the test was statistically manipulated so that the average score would be 100, regardless of the person's biological age. Most modern IQ tests are simply distant relatives of the Stanford-Binet test that follow the same format (tap into a variety of mental processes).[91]

How does one interpret modern IQ scores? Psychologists themselves disagree over the meaning of an IQ score. Although some interpret IQ as a measure of general intelligence that is mostly inherited and resistant to change, others argue that there are multiple forms of intelligence (learned, reflective, neural), some of which are very amenable to improvement.[92]

IQ and Crime

One of the earliest applications of mental testing was on criminals. Goddard, for instance, tested prisoners at various correctional institutions early in the 20th century and found that 70% were "feeble-minded."[93] This led him to conclude that criminality and feeblemindedness were interchangeable, and because one was tied in with the other, all such "affected" persons should be incarcerated and sterilized. However, by the 1920s, many people were critical of the IQ tests, noting their biases and flaws (both Terman and Goddard recanted many of their own claims). Edwin Sutherland, a prominent sociologist, argued that as testing procedures improved and as IQ tests became less culturally biased, the gap in IQ between criminals and noncriminals would disappear.[94] For many years after that, criminologists ignored research on IQ.

As it turns out, Sutherland was only half correct. Although the IQ-crime relationship did indeed shrink over time, recent research suggests that an 8- to 10-point gap between criminals and noncriminals still exists. The first thing to recognize is that this is not a very large difference. Many offenders have above-average IQ scores, while many law-abiding people have lower IQ scores. Still, what can one make of this difference? Several possibilities exist. It could be that smarter offenders commit less visible crimes and are less likely to be apprehended. The fact that IQ differences emerge even for self-reported delinquency (where detection of the crime is not an issue) casts this idea in doubt. It could also be that IQ tests are still biased, so that blacks, Hispanics, or those in poverty might perform worse. If this was the case, then IQ might simply be a proxy for race or class — factors that are related to offending. Yet, the IQ-crime link appears, even after statistically controlling for race and social class.

Criminologists Travis Hirschi and Michael Hindelang revived interest in the IQ-crime link by suggesting that a child's IQ was at least as significant an indicator of delinquency as social class or race (important factors in many sociological theories of crime).[95] However, they also argued that intelligence had only an indirect effect on delinquency. IQ relates to poor school performance and possibly school failure, which in turn can lead to delinquency.[96] More recently, Herrnstein and Murray renewed the argument that IQ measures a native, general intelligence. In their book, *The Bell Curve*, they claim that the effect of IQ on delinquency is direct: people who are mentally "dull" have difficulty understanding the rules of a complex society.[97] In other words, some people are not bright enough to learn right from wrong or legal actions from illegal behavior. They conclude that[98]:

> People of limited intelligence can lead moral lives in a society that is run on the basis of "Thou shalt not steal." They find it much harder to lead moral lives in a society that is run on the basis of "thou shalt not steal unless there is a really good reason to." The policy prescription is that the criminal justice system should be made *simpler* [emphasis in original].

Leaving aside the controversy about whether IQ measures general intelligence, one might question whether an 8- to 10-point difference in IQ warrants their sweeping conclusions. In a response to *The Bell Curve,* Francis Cullen and his associates point out that IQ is not a very strong predictor of criminal behavior. When ranked on a scale with other known predictors (e.g., attitudes, personality, delinquent peer associations) of crime, IQ ends up on the bottom of the list.[99]

Nevertheless, because the crime-IQ link is consistently documented, criminologists continue to study this relationship.[100] The bulk of research on this issue supports the indirect model outlined by Hirschi and Hindelang. For example, a 2004 study on a sample of 1727 American youth found that youths with lower IQ scores were more likely to encounter deviant peer pressure and to have lower school performance and lower levels of self-control. In turn, these factors (e.g., school performance, peer pressure) predicted delinquency. In other words, IQ was related to crime because it influenced these other factors. Of course, there are other interpretations of the IQ-crime relationship. In Chapter 4, it was noted that biologically oriented criminologists view IQ as a measure of neurological health.

Daryl Atkins walks into a Virginia court room in July, 2005. Atkins' case led the U.S. Supreme Court to bar execution of the mentally retarded.

? How does this legal issue relate to the discussion of IQ and crime presented in this chapter?

Policy Implications of the IQ-Crime Relationship

The policy implication of the IQ-crime relationship depends on one's view of IQ. Is IQ a measure of native intelligence or something else? It also depends on the interpretation of the IQ-crime relationship. Is IQ a direct cause of crime or does it influence other factors (school failure, peer associations) that cause criminal behavior? The policy implication in the direct-cause model has already been discussed. Early positivists believed that feeblemindedness was a direct and unchangeable cause of crime. These early criminologists advocated a policy of eugenics. Many believe that the policy implications outlined in *The Bell Curve* take a similar stance. Although the authors did not recommend sterilizing offenders, they portray crime as an almost unavoidable consequence of being "dull" and their policy implication is to make the world simpler.

The vast majority of criminologists believe that IQ plays a minor and indirect role in criminal offending. If the IQ-crime link is indirect, the policy implications would focus on those things related to both IQ and crime. For example, a program might focus on keeping learning-disabled youth in school. Another policy implication deals with newer (cognitive-behavioral) rehabilitation programs. Many of these programs require extensive reading and journaling. Some suggest using IQ tests to identify offenders who may have difficulty with a reading/writing intensive program.[101]

Summary of IQ and Crime

The meaning of IQ and its relationship to criminal behavior was neglected for many years in the field of criminology. Obviously, that situation has changed over the past 25 years. Modern studies consistently find that IQ is related to criminal behavior. Critics point out, however, that this relationship probably does not hold for many types of white-collar crime (e.g., insider trading). Also, they highlight the fact that IQ is a relatively weak predictor of criminal behavior. Most criminologists conclude that IQ matters because of its effect on other factors related to crime.

Conclusion

Psychology has made a number of important contributions to the study of crime. Each of the schools of thought has its own key concepts and theories concerning criminal behavior (see TABLE 5-6 for a summary). The validity of each theory must be considered in terms of its ability to account for criminality. Some of these theories (behavioral approaches, personality) are well supported by empirical evidence, while others (psychoanalytic theory) are not. The primary link between all of them, however, is their emphasis on the individual. Because of this emphasis, many psychological theories translate smoothly into treatment programs for offenders.

Psychologists Don Andrews and James Bonta are among the most strident supporters of a psychological approach to criminology. The authors contrast the psychology of criminal conduct with mainstream criminology. According to Andrews and Bonta, the psychology of criminal conduct "seeks a rational and empirical understanding of variation in the occurrence of criminal acts, in particular, a rational empirical understanding of individual differences in criminal activity."[101] They argue that psychological constructs from cognitive, behavioral, and personality theory have much stronger associations with crime than traditional sociological factors, and lament the "weak psychology" found in sociological theories. The authors argue that support of mainstream (sociology) theories of crime is based on faith and ideology rather than scientific evidence.

Andrews and Bonta make some valid points in their arguments. In their zeal for the psychological approach, however, they minimize the importance of sociological theories that are well supported in the literature. Many sociological theories do not focus on individual differences that predict offending; rather, they highlight macrolevel influences thought to influence crime rates across time or different geographical locations. Psychological theories largely ignore the "big picture," or macrolevel influences. A behavioral theorist, for example, would have a difficult time explaining why violent crime rates in the United States are higher than in other countries. Are American parents that ineffective? If they are, then why does it produce more violent crime, but not more property crime? And why does crime rise and fall within the United States from year to year? Certainly, a personality theorist would have a difficult time explaining why the violent crime rate suddenly dropped in the 1990s.

Many sociological theories address differences in criminal offending across groups and over time. Some sociological theories, however, do focus on individual traits.

TABLE 5-6

Summary of Psychological Theories

Theory	Key Theorists	Overview	Key Concepts
Psychodynamic Theory	Sigmund Freud	Criminal behavior can be understood by examining early childhood experiences when personality is formed. Often, behavior is caused by unconscious memories, wishes, and desires.	Id, ego, superego Defense mechanisms Psychoanalysis
Behaviorism	Ivan Pavlov Albert Bandura Gerald Patterson	Criminal behavior is learned through classical, operant, or vicarious (observational) learning. Crime can therefore be "unlearned."	Reinforcement Punishment Token economy Aversion therapy Cognitive-behavioral treatment
Personality	Auke Tellegen Hervy Cleckly Robert Hare	Personality traits or a criminal personality (psychopathy) are stable characteristics of individuals that cause crime.	Multidimensional Personality Questionnaire (MPQ) Psychopath Antisocial Personality Disorder (APD)
Intelligence	Alfred Binet H. H. Goddard Stephen Jay Gould	IQ scores predict criminal behavior, but this effect is most likely indirect.	Intelligence Quotient (IQ)

WRAP UP

The BTK Killer

Dennis Rader (the "BTK" killer) represents a fascinating case study. Certainly, the intense media scrutiny in this case has yielded a treasure trove of information about Rader's background. A useful exercise for mastering theories of crime is to try to fit the "known facts" of a particular case to a particular theory. Oftentimes, information appears to fit a number of different theories. Rader's notes to police appear to fit with the Freudian concept of an unconscious desire to get caught and punished (an overdeveloped superego). Rader also exhibits some characteristics of a psychopath — most notably his animated but emotionless description of his activities. Recognize, however, that much of the description of Rader does not fit the concept of psychopathy. For example, he maintained a family and job over a long period of time. This is inconsistent with the description of a psychopath as having "short-term marital relationships" and "poor behavioral controls." Although "case studies" such as this can be an important tool for learning the nuances of a theory, it is crucial to note that one particular case can neither prove nor disprove any theory of crime. Rather, researchers typically study large samples of individuals to assess the validity of a theory.

Chapter Spotlight

- Sigmund Freud is responsible for psychodynamic theory and psychoanalysis (a treatment derived from his theory). Freud deserves credit for devising a number of important concepts (e.g., ego, defense mechanisms) and distinguishing between the conscious and unconscious. Although psychoanalysis is typically not appropriate for criminal offenders, many of Freud's ideas have found their way into modern criminology.

- Psychologists have identified three types of human learning: operant conditioning, classical conditioning, and observational learning. Operant conditioning (e.g., parents socializing kids) and observational learning (e.g., television violence) are both implicated in theories of crime.

- Cognitive psychologists have highlighted the importance of cognitive content (e.g., antisocial attitudes) and cognitive structure (moral development) in the genesis of crime.

- Classical conditioning (aversion therapy), operant conditioning (parent training), and observational learning (modeling) have been used in attempts to rehabilitate offenders. Cognitive-behavioral programs have a track record of success in rehabilitating criminals.

- There is substantial evidence that certain personality traits are related to criminal behavior. A key issue in this research is how personality is formed.

- Psychopathy is among the oldest concepts in criminology. Here, the issue is whether or not a distinct, criminal personality (e.g., superficial, above average intelligence, pathological lying, egocentric) exists. In other words, are psychopaths qualitatively different from others, or do we all have a bit of psychopathy?

- There is a consistently documented link between IQ and criminal behavior. This relationship, however, is not very strong, and there is substantial debate about how to interpret the IQ–crime link.

Putting It All Together

1. Briefly describe the two general ways that psychologists have linked personality to criminal behavior.

2. How strong is the relationship between IQ-related and criminal behavior? Why are individuals with lower IQ scores more likely to engage in crime?

3. Discuss Freud's personality elements (id, ego, and superego). How might each of these elements produce criminal behavior?

4. What is a psychopath? How is this different from antisocial personality disorder? Is there a danger in using the term "psychopath?"

5. Describe the three types of learning outlined in this chapter. Give an example of each.

6. Discuss any two rehabilitation programs used by behaviorists. What type of learning (operant, classical, observational) do they use?

7. Make up a story using Gerald Patterson's social learning theory (see Figure 5-2). Explain how the person in your story becomes a criminal. Try to use as many elements in the theory as possible.

Key Terms

aversion therapy The use of classical conditioning to reverse an unwanted relationship between a stimulus (alcohol) and response (pleasure).

classical conditioning By pairing an unconditioned stimulus (e.g., meat) with a conditioned stimulus (a bell), over time a conditioned response (e.g., salivation) is reproduced using only the conditioned stimulus.

cognitive restructuring A rehabilitation technique for which criminal-thinking errors (cognitive distortions) are identified and contested.

cognitive skills programs Rehabilitation programs that attempt to build thinking skills, such as moral reasoning, empathy, and anger management.

contingency contract A tool to promote parental use of operant conditioning. Parents and children sign a contract that lays out expected behaviors, reinforcements, and consequences.

countertransference A term from psychoanalysis; when the client "pushes the buttons" of the counselor so that the resulting anger and hostility interferes with treatment.

defense mechanisms Psychological ploys that individuals use (often unconsciously) to reduce or eliminate anxieties.

delinquent ego Application of Freudian principles to describe an ego that effectively blocks any potential restraint from the conscience (superego) and permits the delinquent to rationalize criminal behavior.

delinquent superego Application of Freudian principles to describe a superego that is guided by a delinquent code of behavior, rather than appropriate values.

ego The conscious part of Freudian personality; the "psychological thermostat" that regulates the savage wishes and demands of the id and the social restrictions of the superego.

free association A technique used in psychoanalysis in which the patient verbalizes, uncensored, anything that comes to mind.

id The unconscious, instinctual aspect of the Freudian personality. Id wishes often include the immediate gratification of basic drives (e.g., sex, aggression).

negative reinforcement The removal of a noxious stimulus (e.g., bad smell) to increase a target behavior.

observational learning Learning behavior by observing and modeling the behavior of others.

operant conditioning The use of reinforcement and punishment to shape behavior.

overdeveloped superego Application of Freudian principles to describe a superego that causes a person to seek out punishment.

personality The sum of personality traits that define a person.

personality trait A characteristic of an individual that is stable over time and across different social circumstances.

positive reinforcement The use of rewards (e.g., praise, money, tokens) to increase a target behavior.

punishment The presentation of a noxious stimulus (e.g., spanking, scolding) to decrease a target behavior.

superego The conscience of the Freudian personality — the keeper of prohibitions ("Stealing is wrong") and wishes about what one wants to be ("I am going to be just like my father when I grow up").

token economy Application of operant conditioning to corrections. Individuals are reinforced and punished using "tokens" that can be exchanged for privileges.

transference A term from psychoanalysis to describe when the client uses the counselor as a "stand in" from the past.

1. *Grosse Pointe Blank,* DVD, directed by George Armitage (Hollywood Pictures, 1997).
2. Curt R. Bartol and Anne M. Bartol, *Criminal Behavior: A Psychosocial Approach,* 7th ed. (Englewood Cliffs, NJ: Prentice Hall, 2004): 14–16.
3. P. Scott, "Henry Maudsley," in H. Mannheim, ed., *Pioneers in Criminology* (Montclair, NJ: Patterson Smith, 1960): 208–231.
4. Scott, 1970, 216.
5. David Lester and Patricia Van Voorhis, "Psychoanalytic Therapy," in *Correctional Counseling and Rehabilitation* (Cincinnati, OH: Anderson, 2004).
6. Lester and Van Voorhis, 2004, 42.
7. Lester and Van Voorhis, 2004, 43.
8. Fritz Redl and David Wineman, *Children Who Hate* (Glencoe, IL: Free Press, 1951).
9. August Aichorn, "Wayward Youth," in *Classics of Criminology,* Joseph E. Jacoby, ed., (Prospect Heights, IL: Waveland, 1979): 124.
10. Margarite Q. Warren and Michael J. Hindelang, "Current Explanations of Offender Behavior," in *Psychology of Crime and Criminal Justice,* Hans Toch, ed. (Prospect Heights: Waveland, 1986): 172.
11. Ronald L. Akers and Christine S. Sellers, *Criminological Theories: Introduction, Evaluation, and Application* (Los Angeles: Roxbury, 2004).
12. James O. Finckenauer, *Juvenile Delinquency and Corrections: The Gap Between Theory and Practice* (Orlando, FL: Academic Press, 1984): 27.
13. Don A. Andrews, Ivan Zinger, Robert D. Hoge, James Bonta, Paul Gendreau, and Francis T. Cullen, "Does Correctional Treatment Work? A Clinically Relevant and Psychologically Informed Meta-Analysis," *Criminology* 28 (1990): 369–404.
14. Lester and Van Voorhis, 2004, 54.
15. Ted Palmer, "Issues in Growth-Centered Intervention with Serious Juvenile Offenders," *Legal Studies Forum* 18 (1994): 236–298.
16. Shelley Listwan, Kimberly Sperber, Lisa Spruance, and Patricia Van Voorhis, "Anxiety in Correctional Settings: It's Time for Another Look," *Federal Probation* 68 (2004): 43–50.
17. Lester and Van Voorhis, 2004, 56.
18. David Lester, Michael Braswell, and Patricia Van Voorhis, "Radical Behavioral Interventions," in *Correctional Counseling and Rehabilitation* (Cincinnati, OH: Anderson, 2004).
19. Curt R. Bartol and Anne M. Bartol, *Criminal Behavior: A Psychosocial Approach,* 7th ed. (Englewood Cliffs, NJ: Prentice Hall, 2004).
20. B. F. Skinner, *Science and Human Behavior* (New York: Macmillan, 1953).
21. Ivan Pavlov, *Conditioned Reflexes: An Investigation of the Physiological Activity of the Cerebral Cortex* (London, UK: Lawrence and Wishart, 1929).
22. Robert J. Sampson and John H. Laub, *Crime in the Making: Pathways and Turning Points Through Life* (Cambridge, MA: Harvard University Press, 1993).
23. Don Andrews and James Bonta, *The Psychology of Criminal Conduct,* 3rd edition (Cincinnati, OH: Anderson, 2003).
24. Ronald L. Akers, "Rational Choice, Deterrence, and Social Learning Theory: The Path Not Taken," *Journal of Criminal Law and Criminology* 81 (1990): 653–676.
25. William McCord and Joan McCord, *Origins of Crime: A New Evaluation of the Cambridge Sommerville Youth Study* (New York: Columbia University, 1959).
26. Sheldon Glueck and Eleanor Glueck, *Unraveling Juvenile Delinquency* (New York: Commonwealth Fund, 1950).
27. Ralph Loeber and Thomas Dishion, "Early Predictors of Male Delinquency: A Review," *Psychological Bulletin* 93 (1983): 68–98; Mark W. Lipsey and James H. Derzon, "Predictors of Violent or Serious Offending in Adolescence and Early Adulthood: A Synthesis of Longitudinal Research," in Rolf Loeber and David P. Farrington, eds., *Serious and Violent Juvenile Offenders: Risk Factors and Successful Treatments* (Thousand Oaks, CA: Sage, 1998).
28. Gerald Patterson, John Reid, and Thomas Dishion, *Antisocial Boys* (Eugene, OR: Castalia, 1992).
29. Gerald Patterson, "Children Who Steal," in Travis Hirschi and Michael R. Gottfredson, eds., *Understanding Crime* (Beverly Hills, CA: Sage, 1980).
30. Judith R. Harris, *The Nurture Assumption: Why Children Turn Out the Way They Do. Parents Matter Less Than You Think and Peers Matter More* (New York: The Free Press, 1998).
31. John P. Wright and Francis T. Cullen, "Parental Efficacy and Delinquent Behavior: Do Control and Support Matter?" *Criminology* 39 (2001): 677–706.
32. Judith R. Harris, "Where Is the Child's Environment? A Group Socialization Theory of Development," *Psychological Review* 102 (1995): 458–489.
33. John Reid, Gerald Patterson, and James Snyder, *Antisocial Behavior in Children and Adolescents: A Developmental Analysis and Model for Intervention* (Washington, DC: American Psychological Association, 2003).
34. Albert Bandura, *Aggression: A Social Learning Analysis* (Englewood Cliffs, NJ: Prentice Hall, 1973).
35. Albert Bandura, Dorthea Ross, and Sheila A. Ross, "Imitation of Film: Mediated Aggressive Models," *Journal of Abnormal and Social Psychology* 63 (1961): 3–11.
36. Albert Bandura, *Social Learning Theory* (Englewood Cliffs, NJ: Prentice Hall, 1977).
37. Ibid.
38. Mark Warr, *Companions in Crime: The Social Aspects of Criminal Conduct* (New York: Cambridge University Press, 2002).
39. Paul Mazerolle, Jeff Maahs, and Ronet Bachman, "Exposure to Violence in the Family: Unpackaging the Linkages to Intimate Partner Violence," in Greer Litton Fox and Michael L. Benson, eds., *Families, Crime, and Criminal Justice* (New York: JAI, 2000).
40. American Psychological Association, *Summary Report of the American Psychological Association Commission on Violence and Youth* (Washington, DC: American Psychological Association, 1993); UCLA Center for Communication Policy, *Television Violence Monitoring Project* (Los Angeles: UCLA Press, 1995).

41. Stacey L. Smith, Barbra J. Wilson, Dale Kunkel, Daniel Linz, W. James Potter, Carolyn M. Colvin, and Edward Donnerstein, *National Television Violence Study* (Thousand Oaks, CA: Sage, 1998).

42. Ray Surette, *Media, Crime, and Criminal Justice* (Belmont, CA: Wadsworth, 1998): 142.

43. Sourcebook of Criminal Justice Statistics, available at www.albany.edu/sourcebook/pdf/t239.pdf, accessed January 15, 2005.

44. Surette, 1998, 114.

45. Jeffrey G. Johnson, Patricia Cohen, Elizabeth M. Smailes, Stephanie Kasen, and Judith S. Brook, "Television Viewing and Aggressive Behavior During Adolescence and Adulthood," *Science* 295 (2002): 2468–2471.

46. Craig A. Anderson and Brad J. Bushman, "The Effects of Media Violence on Society," *Science* 295 (2002): 2377–2379.

47. Travis Hirschi, *Causes of Delinquency* (Berkley: University of California Press, 1969).

48. Thomas N. Robinson, Marta L. Wilde, Lisa C. Navracruz, Farish Haydel, and Ann Varady, "Effects of Reducing Children's Television and Video Game Use on Aggressive Behavior: A Randomized Controlled Trial," *Archives of Pediatrics & Adolescent Medicine* 155 (2001): 17–23.

49. Lester, Braswell, and Van Voorhis, 2004, 63.

50. Barry Maletzky, *Treating the Sexual Offender* (Newbury Park, CA: Sage, 1991).

51. S. B. Stolz, L. A. Wienckowski, and B. S. Brown, "Behavior Modification," in N. Johnston and L. D. Savitz, eds., *Justice and Corrections* (New York: Wiley, 1978).

52. R. Bippes, T. F. McLaughlin, and R. L. Williams, "A Classroom Token System in a Detention Center," *Techniques* 2 (1986): 126–132; W. B. Janzen and W. Love, "Involving Adolescents as Active Participants in Their Own Treatment Plans," *Psychological Reports* 41 (1977): 931–934.

53. Gerald Patterson, *Living With Children: New Methods for Parents and Teachers* (Champaign, IL: Research Press, 1976).

54. Alan Kazdin, "Parent Management Training: Evidence, Outcomes, and Issues," *Journal of the American Academy of Child and Adolescent Psychiatry* 36 (1997): 1349–1357.

55. Frank S. Pearson, Douglas S. Lipton, Charles M. Cleland, and Dorline S. Yee, "The Effects of Behavioral/Cognitive Programs on Recidivism," *Crime and Delinquency* 48 (2002): 476–496.

56. Pearson, Lipton, Cleland, and Yee, 2002, 489–490.

57. Patricia Van Voorhis and David Lester, "Cognitive Therapies," in *Correctional Counseling and Rehabilitation,* 5th ed. (Cincinnati, OH: Anderson, 2004).

58. Van Voorhis and Lester, 2004, 185.

59. John C. Gibbs, Granville B. Potter, and Arnold P. Goldstein, *The EQUIP Program: Teaching Youth to Think and Act Responsibly Through a Peer Helping Approach* (Champaign, IL: Research Press, 1995): 45–48.

60. Gibbs, Potter, and Goldstein, 1995, 43-65.

61. Robert R. Ross and Elizabeth A. Fabiano, *Reasoning and Rehabilitation: A Handbook for Teaching Cognitive Skills* (Ottawa, Ontario: Flix Desktop Services, 1989); Robert R. Ross and Elizabeth A. Fabiano, *Time to Think: A Cognitive Model for Delinquency Prevention* (Johnson City, TN: Institute of Social Sciences and Arts, 1985).

62. Van Voorhis and Lester, 2004, 192.

63. Samuel Yochelson and Stanton E. Samenow, *The Criminal Personality,* Volume 1 (New York: Jason Aronson, 1976); Gresham Sykes and David Matza, "Techniques of Neutralization: A Theory of Delinquency," *American Sociological Review* 22 (1958): 664–670.

64. Anthony Beech and Ruth Mann, "Recent Developments in the Assessment and Treatment of Sex Offenders," in James McGuire, ed., *Offender Rehabilitation and Treatment: Effective Programmes and Policies to Reduce Re-Offending* (West Sussex, England: John Wiley and Sons, 2002).

65. Van Voorhis and Lester, 2004, 192.

66. Andrews et al., 1990, 385–400; Pearson, Lipton, Cleland and Yee, 2002, 490.

67. Pearson, Lipton, Cleland, and Yee, 2002, 490–491.

68. Scott W. Henggeler, Phillippe B. Cunningham, Susan G. Pickrel, Sonja K. Schoenwald, and Michael J. Brondino, "Multisystemic Therapy: An Effective Violence Prevention Approach for Serious Juvenile Offenders." *Journal of Adolescence* 19 (1996): 55–56.

69. Joshua D. Miller and Donald Lynam, "Structural Models of Personality and Their Relation to Antisocial Behavior: A Meta-Analytic Review," *Criminology* 39 (2001): 765–798.

70. Robert R. McCrae and Paul T. Costa, *Personality in Adulthood* (New York: Guilford Press, 1990).

71. Auke Tellegen, "Structures of Mood and Personality and their Relevance to Assessing Anxiety with an Emphasis on Self-Report," in A. Hussain Tuma and Jack D. Maser, eds., *Anxiety and the Anxiety Disorders* (Hillsdale, NJ: Lawrence Earlbaum Associates, 1985).

72. Miller and Lynam, 2001, 768–771.

73. David J. Tenenbaum, "Personality and Criminality: A Summary and Implications of the Literature," *Journal of Criminal Justice* 5 (1977): 225–235.

74. Avshalom Caspi, Terrie E. Moffitt, Phil A. Silva, Magda Stoughamer-Loeber, Robert F. Krueger, and Pamela S. Schmutte, "Are Some People Crime-Prone? Replications of the Personality-Crime Relationship Across Countries, Genders, Races, and Methods," *Criminology* 32 (1994): 163–195.

75. Miller and Lynam, 2001, 780.

76. Nicole Rafter, "The Unrepentant Horse-Slasher: Moral Insanity and the Origins of Criminological Thought," *Criminology* 42 (2004): 979–1008.

77. Rafter, 2004, 994.

78. Hervey Cleckly, *The Mask of Sanity,* 5th edition (St. Louis, MO: Mosby, 1976).

79. Robert D. Hare, "Psychopathy: A Clinical Construct Whose Time Has Come," *Criminal Justice and Behavior* 23 (1996): 25–54.

80. Hare, 1996, 26.

81. Hare, 1996, 45–46.

82. Marnie R. Rice, Grant T. Harris, and Catherine A. Cormier, "An Evaluation of a Maximum Security Therapeutic Community for Psychopaths and Other Mentally Disordered Offenders," *Law and Human Behavior* 16 (1992): 399–412.

83. Hans J. Eysenck, *Crime and Personality* (London: Routledge Kegan Paul, 1977).

84. Hans J. Eysenck, "Personality and the Biosocial Model of Antisocial and Criminal Behavior," in Adrian Raine, Patricia A. Brennan, David P. Farrington, and Sarnoff A. Mednick, eds., *Biosocial Bases of Violence* (New York: Plenum, 1997).

85. Robert D. Hare, *Without Conscience: The Disturbing World of Psychopaths Among Us* (New York: The Guilford Press, 1999): 173.

86. Hare, 1996.

87. Stephen J. Gould, *The Mismeasure of Man* (New York: W. W. Norton, 1996).

88. Ibid.

89. Gould, 1996, 230.

90. Ibid.

91. Gould, 1996, 204–222.

92. David Perkins, *Outsmarting IQ: The Emerging Science of Learnable Intelligence* (New York: The Free Press, 1995).

93. H. H. Goddard, *Feeblemindedness: Its Causes and Consequences* (New York: Arno, 1972).

94. Edwin H. Sutherland, "Mental Deficiency and Crime," in Kimball Young, ed., *Social Attitudes* (New York: Holt, 1931).

95. Travis Hirschi and Michael J. Hindelang, "Intelligence and Delinquency," *American Sociological Review* 42 (1977): 571–587.

96. Ibid.

97. Richard J. Herrnstein and Charles Murray, *The Bell Curve: Intelligence and Class Structure in American Life* (New York: The Free Press, 1994).

98. Ibid, 544.

99. Francis T. Cullen, Paul Gendreau, G. Roger Jarjoura, and John P. Wright, "Crime and the Bell Curve: Lessons from Intelligent Criminology," *Crime and Delinquency* 43 (1997): 387–411.

100. David A. Ward and Charles R. Tittle, "IQ and Delinquency: A Test of Two Competing Explanations," *Journal of Quantitative Criminology* 10 (1994): 189–212; Jean M. McGloin, Travis C. Pratt, and Jeff Maahs, "Rethinking the IQ-Delinquency Relationship: A Longitudinal Analysis of Multiple Theoretical Models," *Justice Quarterly* 21 (2004): 603–635.

101. Cullen, Gendreau, Jarjoura, and Wright, 1997, 403–404.

102. D. A. Andrews and James Bonta, *The Psychology of Criminal Conduct* (Cincinnati, OH: Anderson, 1994): 1.

WWW.CRIMINOLOGY.JBPUB.COM

Interactivities

In the News

Key Term Explorer

Web Links

OBJECTIVES

Understand the meaning of a "structural" explanation of crime.

Recognize the contributions of Emile Durkheim and how his work connects to modern criminological theory.

Know the central themes captured by the Chicago School and social disorganization theory.

Understand the anomie/strain tradition, including the work of Robert K. Merton and subsequent revisions of his theory.

Grasp the different subcultural explanations of delinquency and connect them to broader theoretical traditions.

Connect the theories within this chapter to their respective policy implications.

Social Structure and Crime

Now Main Street's whitewashed windows and vacant stores
Seems like there ain't nobody wants to come down here no more
They're closing down the textile mill across the railroad tracks
Foreman says these jobs are going boys and they ain't coming back to your hometown

—Bruce Springsteen[1]

The Demolition of Cabrini-Green

The Cabrini-Green housing development, cited by many as a national symbol for public housing gone bad, is being demolished. The development started with the construction of the Frances Cabrini Rowhouses in 1942. Originally known as "Little Sicily," the development primarily housed Chicago's Italian-American community. By 1962, when the William-Green Homes were added to this composite public housing property, Cabrini-Green was one of the largest sites in the Chicago Housing Authority, with a mostly African-American residential population. In its heyday, the Cabrini-Green development was home to about 15,000 residents and 3500 public housing units. Over the years, physical deterioration, gang violence, and the proliferation of illicit drugs has plagued Cabrini-Green.

The demolition of the high-rise public housing projects is part of a larger movement to revitalize inner-city areas. The Urban Revitalization Demonstration Program was initiated in 1993 by the U.S. Department of Housing and Urban Development to "fundamentally reinvent" public housing by demolishing the most severely decayed housing projects and redeveloping them as mixed-use, mixed-income projects. A primary goal is to lessen the concentration of poverty within small geographical areas. In Chicago, the high-rise apartments are being replaced by a mix of affordable, market-rate, and public housing. While many applaud this plan, others are more critical. They fear that private owners are engaging in a land grab and that the promised affordable public housing will not materialize within these areas, leaving the poor worse off.

Is the demolition of inner-city high-rise housing projects a good idea? Will it reduce crime?

What problems might a "mixed" (subsidized with owned) housing area create?

Sources: Kate N. Grossman, "14 Cabrini High-Rises to Close; CHA Whittling Complex to 3 Buildings as Residents Fight to Stay," *Chicago Sun-Times*, January 10, 2005; Chicago Housing Authority, "Cabrini-Green Homes," available at http://www.thecha.org/housingdev/cabrini_green_homes.html, accessed July 28, 2005; David Peterson, "A Great Chicago Land Grab," available at http://www.zmag.org/ZMag/articles/apr97peterson.html, accessed July 28, 2005.

Introduction

Across the United States, many urban areas are undergoing drastic changes (see **You Are the Criminologist: The Demolition of Cabrini-Green**). Public housing projects, crime ridden and physically deteriorated, are being torn down in favor of townhouses and other forms of development. Why are public housing developments such as Cabrini-Green continually overrun by crime? Will such "urban renewal" projects change the characteristics of neighborhoods and reduce crime?

This chapter considers what role society may play in promoting or impeding criminal behavior, what social factors lead individuals to commit crime, and also what features of society relate to the crime rates of particular geographical areas (e.g., neighborhood, county).

In the early history of criminology, theories from psychology and biology dominated scientific inquiry into crime. Although these theories differed in terms of the exact cause of crime (e.g., atavism, feeblemindedness, moral insanity), they shared an important similarity: The cause of crime came from within individuals. Earlier chapters in this book considered the ways in which biological and psychological approaches to crime are still part of modern criminology. The dominance of these theories, however, was challenged in the early 1900s by a radically different perspective. During this time, the emerging discipline of sociology captured the imagination of many scientists interested in criminal behavior.

The major premise that drives the sociological approach is that criminality is rooted in and impelled by the very structure of society itself. In a way, the shift from individual to social responsibility for criminal behavior might have been expected.[2] Certainly, it makes sense given the social context of the early 1900s. During this period, the United States (especially American cities) experienced rapid social change, based largely on the shift from an agrarian society to an industrial society. Major urban areas developed quickly. For example, Chicago's population increased from 4100 residents in 1833 to 1 million in 1890 and to more than 2 million in 1910. Lilly and associates note that this rapid population growth created sanitation, housing, and other critical social problems.[3]

As did other citizens, criminologists in the 1920s and 1930s witnessed — indeed lived through and experienced — these changes that created bulging populations and teaming slum areas. It was only a short leap for them to believe that growing up in the city, particularly in the slums, made a difference in peoples' lives. In this context, crime could not be seen simply as an individual pathology, but made more sense when viewed as a social problem.

Interest in how the structure of society is related to crime eventually evolved into two distinct social structural traditions. The Chicago School tradition focuses on the structure of cities (and neighborhoods); the anomie tradition more broadly on the structure of America. Behind both types of theories, however, is the work of Emile Durkheim.

Emile Durkheim and Crime

Considered a pioneer in the field of sociology and the father of French sociology, Emile Durkheim (1858–1917) became world renowned for his emphasis on the relationship between social structure and social problems. He defined crime as behavior that shocks the sentiments and "healthy conscience" of any civilized society.[4] Nevertheless, as noted in Chapter 1, Durkheim regarded crime as a natural and inevitable part of any human society. To

Durkheim, the criminal is and will continue to be a functioning member of every society.

LINK As discussed in Chapter 1, Durkheim regarded crime as a "normal" part of any society.

Durkheim viewed crime as serving several functions in a society. First, criminals can act as an agent for change. Some individuals anticipate a change in social norms and pioneer the future morality. Socrates, for example, was considered a criminal under Athenian law, primarily because of the independence of his thinking. Second, crime calls attention to social ills, identifies those persons who violate social norms, and labels them as such. This labeling process actually serves as social cement that binds the "good people" in a society to one another and against the "bad people."

Durkheim also distinguished two types of criminals: altruistic and common. The **altruistic criminal** is somehow offended by the rules of society and wishes to change those rules for the better. This criminal is motivated by a sense of duty to improve society. Students who burned their draft cards in protest of the Vietnam War would fit this profile. The **common criminal** rejects all laws and discipline and purposely violates the law without concern for the rightness of the acts. With no social conscience, this person takes whatever action is necessary to serve his or her interests.

LINK Durkheim's concept of the "altruistic criminal" fits nicely with a conflict theory of crime (see Chapter 8). In particular, the conflict approach attempts to explain some forms of altruistic crime.

Durkheim's theories, hypotheses, and assumptions about human nature serve as the foundation for most current sociological theories of crime. Major themes within his research and writing include[5]:

- The view that humans by nature are selfish and greedy. He believed that humans have unlimited desires that must somehow be capped or controlled.

- A focus on the social integration of members of society. Durkheim emphasized that social ties to families, friends, and neighbors helped restrain human ambitions and strengthen the communication of norms and values.

- Durkheim referred to norms and values as a society's "collective conscience." He argued that strong norms and values were essential to a stable society.

Emile Durkheim, "the father of French sociology."

? *How did the writings and research of Durkheim influence both the social disorganization and the anomie perspective?*

- Durkheim coined the term <u>anomie</u> to describe a state of affairs for which the norms and values of society weaken and are no longer able to control behaviors.

Durkheim was leery of rapid social change, particularly the movement away from rural societies characterized by <u>mechanical solidarity</u> and toward industrial societies based on <u>organic solidarity</u>. Initially, all societies start in a "mechanical" form in which homogeneity reigns. There are few or no specialized functions within society; social groups are self-sufficient, and there is little division of labor or specialization of talents. In societies with mechanical solidarity, laws seek to enforce uniformity by repressing deviation from group norms. Because such a society is close knit, there are high levels of social integration, and group norms are strong.

As societies grow more complex, however, organic solidarity necessarily results. Members of modern industrial societies perform diverse functions and fill social demands for various talents.[6] Durkheim recognized that this division of labor might foster some interdependence (i.e., members must interact to trade goods and services). He believed, however, that industrial societies were more prone to low social integration and a weakening of norms. He was particularly suspicious of industrial prosperity[7]:

> Overweening ambition always exceeds the results obtained, great as they may be, because there is no warning to pause here. Nothing gives satisfaction and all this agitation is uninterruptedly maintained without appeasement.

In other words, when monetary wealth is the goal (instead of self-sufficiency), human tendencies toward insatiable desires are enhanced. As social integration decreases, norms lose their ability to guide behavior (anomie) and cap human desires. Durkheim applied this line of reasoning to explain suicide rates. In particular, he noted that suicide rates increased during periods of rapid social (especially economic) change, because the caps on human desires became less clear and forceful.

Various American criminologists pursued different aspects of Durkheim's writings. By borrowing selectively from Durkheim, these scholars created distinct theoretical traditions. The sociologists who created the Chicago School and social disorganization theory followed the idea that low social integration weakens social control. The anomie tradition is largely based on the idea that norms might weaken in a society that places an emphasis on industrial prosperity.

Social Disorganization and Social Ecology

<u>Social ecology</u> is the study of how human relationships are affected by a particular environment. Crime is one aspect of social ecology. A central premise of this tradition is that crime can be found in the social and physical structure of an environment; that is, the setting may promote crime. This approach was pioneered in several countries. In the United States, the city of Chicago became a hotbed for ecological studies of crime. The influx of immigrants and southern blacks into this city and the growth of organized crime during Prohibition made Chicago a case study in how neighborhoods de-

velop and change. Notably, Chicago was also home to the country's oldest sociology program, established in 1892. The theories and studies by sociologists in this program are now viewed as elements of the Chicago School of Crime. The central question to the Chicago School was why certain areas had higher crime rates than others. In studying ecological forces, these criminologists attempted to understand the role of environment in criminal activity.

Early Social Ecology: Concentric Zone Theory

Robert E. Park, a former Chicago news reporter, believed that the city could be used as a laboratory to study crime. Influenced by prominent sociologists W. I. Thomas, George H. Mead, Erving Goffman, and Georg Simmel, Park saw a connection between how animals live in natural settings and how humans live in urban settings.[8] Park considered the city a social organism within which neighborhoods survive, thrive, or fall apart. Using similar logic, Ernest W. Burgess (a colleague of Park's) argued that cities grew in a systematic way. Driven by economic forces and competition, cities grew outward in concentric rings, from the central business district.[9]

Burgess organized 1920s Chicago into a series of concentric zones according to residential, occupational, and class characteristics (see FIGURE 6-1).

The center zone, which contained industries and commercial activity, had access to transportation sources (e.g., waterway, trains). The nicer residential areas were farthest away from this central zone — away from the pollution, crowding, and poverty of the business district.[10] Burgess and his associates sought to understand how these urban zones changed over time and what effect this process had on rates of crime.

They identified the zone in transition as the major source of concern. As businesses expand into this area from the central zone and as zoning laws change to accommodate them, those residents who can afford to leave do so. With the stable wage earners gone, housing deteriorates and the zone becomes an undesirable place to live. Those who are left have no economic or political power. They are the poor, the unemployed, and the disenfranchised. In the context of Chicago during the early 1900s, the zone in transition hosted waves of new immigrants who were too poor to live elsewhere. Burgess and other Chicago School sociologists argued that these patterns of city growth produced *social disorganization* — or a weakening of the social ties that bind a community together (recall Durkheim's concept of social integration). They argued that social disorganization was the root cause of a host of social problems such as disease, infant death, and delinquency.

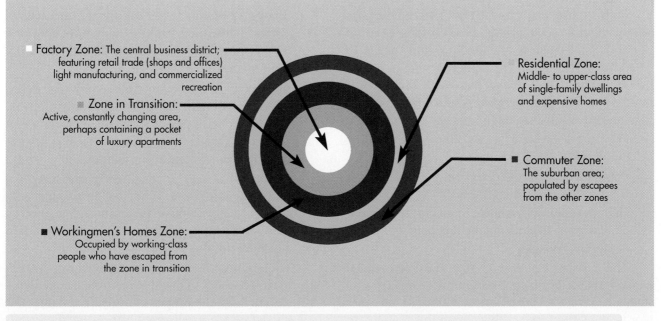

FIGURE 6-1 Concentric Zone Theory of Urban Development

Factory Zone: The central business district; featuring retail trade (shops and offices) light manufacturing, and commercialized recreation

Zone in Transition: Active, constantly changing area, perhaps containing a pocket of luxury apartments

Workingmen's Homes Zone: Occupied by working-class people who have escaped from the zone in transition

Residential Zone: Middle- to upper-class area of single-family dwellings and expensive homes

Commuter Zone: The suburban area; populated by escapees from the other zones

Social Disorganization Theory

Clifford Shaw and Henry McKay were not members of the sociology department; they worked at the Institute for Social Research in Chicago. They were well versed, however, in the theories flowing out of the University of Chicago. In particular, these researchers examined whether rates of delinquency would correspond with Burgess' concentric zones. Using court records, they methodically plotted the addresses of delinquents on a map of Chicago. Shaw and McKay repeated this methodology in several studies on delinquency in Chicago over a 30-year period. Their studies confirmed Burgess' belief that delinquency is highest in the zone in transition—the farther one moved from this zone, the lower the rate of delinquency.[11]

Perhaps more importantly, their findings suggest that the characteristics of the people living there mattered less than the particular geographical area. During the period they studied (1900–1930), the zone in transition was home to many different waves of immigrants (e.g., German, Irish, Polish, African-Americans). Regardless of what ethnic group occupied the zone in transition, their children had high rates of delinquency. This finding ran counter to the popular belief that the poor moral fiber of certain racial or ethnic groups made them criminals. Also, by locating high crime within the zone in transition, Shaw and McKay disproved another common belief: the notion that the "city" was itself criminogenic. Instead, they found that only certain parts of the city fostered delinquency and crime.

In this sense, Shaw and McKay's research efforts advanced an understanding of the ecological nature of crime. Nevertheless, the key question has yet to be addressed: How exactly does the zone in transition generate delinquency? Shaw and McKay outlined a number of ecological characteristics of the zone in transition that might answer this question.

- Physical decay (e.g., crumbling or abandoned buildings)
- Population heterogeneity (a mix of people from different ethnic groups)
- High population mobility (constant movement of residents in and out of the neighborhood)
- High poverty rates

The researchers argued that these ecological characteristics disrupted community organization (i.e., produced social disorganization).[12] In other words, they interfered with a community's ability to organize and reach common goals—including socializing and supervising children. For example, where population mobility is high, neighbors are less likely to know and trust each other. Therefore, they are less likely to intervene on behalf of one another. Social institutions (e.g., schools, community organizations) that help to shape youth are difficult to establish and maintain when community members hope to leave at the first available opportunity. Shaw and McKay also believed that once delinquency became entrenched, another process helped to keep crime rates stable. They argued that delinquent subcultures (gangs) developed and passed their norms and values across generations—a process they described as *cultural transmission*.

Social disorganization theory was a prominent explanation of crime from the 1950s through the 1960s. Interest in this theory declined in the 1970s, and it was relegated to the criminology "dust bin" for many years thereafter.[13] One reason for this decline was a general shift in emphasis from community-level studies to individual-level explanations. Another reason is that social disorganization was criticized on a number of grounds[14]:

- Social disorganization is a pejorative term implying inadequacy and inferiority. If something is disorganized, it must necessarily be dysfunctional. Because the Chicago School theorists were generally middle-class white males, critics argued that perhaps the communities were not disorganized, but organized around different principles.

- Shaw and McKay relied on official (arrest) statistics. Thus, their findings may have reflected police practices more than actual levels of delinquency.

- Shaw and McKay sometimes spoke of delinquency as an indicator of social disorganization. If delinquency is part of social disorganization, it would be circular (tautological) to also say social disorganization causes delinquency.

- Shaw and McKay never directly measured social disorganization. They assumed that ecological factors (poverty, mobility) caused a breakdown in social controls, but they could not measure this process.

Social disorganization has enjoyed a revival in the past 20 years. This resurgence started when scholars refined the propositions in the theory and clearly defined social disorganization as "the inabil-

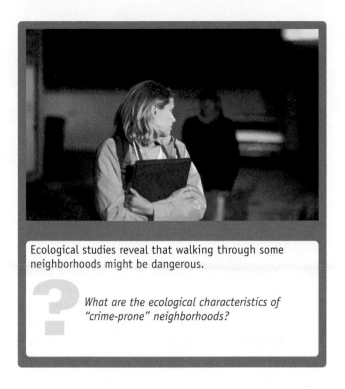

Ecological studies reveal that walking through some neighborhoods might be dangerous.

? *What are the ecological characteristics of "crime-prone" neighborhoods?*

ity of a community structure to realize the common values of its residents and to maintain effective social controls."[15] In essence, they left behind the cultural transmission part of Shaw and McKay's work and focused on informal social control. Informal social control means that neighbors assume responsibility for each other through actions such as questioning strangers, watching each other's property, and intervening in local disturbances.[16] The other crucial factor was that researchers developed ways to directly measure this process. In other words, they were able to connect ecological factors such as poverty and residential mobility with community measures of social control.

In this regard, Sampson and Grove's 1989 analysis of the British Crime Survey (BCS) was a turning point. Using BCS data, these researchers demonstrated that ecological characteristics of British neighborhoods (family disruption, poverty, residential mobility) influenced both informal social control (supervision of street-corner youth) and neighborhood cohesion (friendship networks, membership in community organizations). In turn, measures of social control and cohesion predicted crime victimization. Since that time, Sampson and his associates have replicated these findings in Chicago.[17] In the Project on Human Development in Chicago Neighborhoods, the researchers interviewed almost 9000 residents within 343 Chicago neighborhoods. FIGURE 6-2 outlines their research findings and is also a good summary of social disorganization theory.

This research once again found a relationship between ecological factors (residential mobility, concentrated disadvantage) and a neighborhood's level of cohesion and informal control. Because cohesion and control were strongly related, they combined these concepts under the title of collective efficacy. Sampson and his associates found that collective efficacy predicted neighborhood violence, even after controlling for the characteristics of individuals living in the neighborhood.[18] In other words, it is not simply a collection of "bad apples" that makes a neighborhood prone to crime. Since this early work, others continue to document similar effects in other urban centers and even in more rural settings.[19] There is a strong consensus among reviewers of the literature that certain neighborhoods are crime ridden because there is a lack of social cohesion and informal social control.[20]

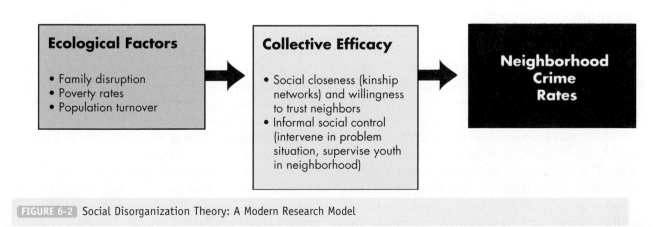

Ecological Factors

- Family disruption
- Poverty rates
- Population turnover

Collective Efficacy

- Social closeness (kinship networks) and willingness to trust neighbors
- Informal social control (intervene in problem situation, supervise youth in neighborhood)

Neighborhood Crime Rates

FIGURE 6-2 Social Disorganization Theory: A Modern Research Model

Race, Place, and Poverty: The Underclass

As noted in the discussion of Chicago during the early 1900s, waves of immigrants started out in the zone in transition. As they accumulated money, they were able to move out into residential zones and were replaced by newly arriving immigrants. However, evidence collected over the last 40 years indicates that inner-city residents are less able to accumulate wealth and move out to more desirable areas. Commentators have dubbed those left behind as the "underclass," the "truly disadvantaged," or the "unmeldables"[21]:

> The new underclass consists of the socioeconomic failures, some four generations deep now, of previous rural migrations to the city. Included, too, are the remnants of earlier immigrant groups. To these must be added the personally disorganized alcoholics, drug addicts, and the ambulatory mentally ill. The socially created and processed unmeldables consist of the ghetto blacks and Hispanics and, in some parts of the country, the native Americans.

This description raises the frightening possibility that entire groups of Americans are permanently blocked from the "ladder of success," trapped in criminogenic neighborhoods and a vicious cycle of poverty. As the description makes clear, the groups consist mostly of racial minorities. A key issue is why these groups were unable to make it out of the inner city.

William Julius Wilson has studied the development of the black underclass in the inner cities of America. Wilson contends that a concentration of disadvantage, in the form of poverty and joblessness, started in the 1970s and has continued to the present. During this time, several social forces collided in toxic fashion to foster its development: a legacy of racism, residential segregation, loss of manufacturing jobs in the inner city, and the failure of civil rights policies.[22] For many decades, manufacturing jobs allowed many European immigrants to earn a decent wage and escape the inner city. Over the past 30 years, this industry has largely left the inner city, and in many cases has left the United States altogether. The economy in the United States is now polarized. On one end are low-paying service jobs (e.g., working the counter at fast-food chain restaurants) that do not yield enough income to move up the social ladder. On the other end are high-wage jobs that demand a level of education and technical training that is largely beyond the reach of the underclass.[23]

Racial discrimination in housing also may have played a role in concentrating minorities in the inner city. Even where minority residents earned enough to escape their environment, housing discrimination limited their options. Furthermore, high-rise public housing ("projects") also served to condense and isolate minority populations.[24] Other researchers point to the role of the criminal justice system. The strategy of incapacitation (see Chapter 3) has had particularly strong effects on the underclass. The incarceration rate for young black males who reside in the inner city is almost 10% on any given day and 33% in their lifetime.[25] These rates climb even higher within specific neighborhoods. Thus, incapacitation may interfere with the social organization of these communities by fostering joblessness, reducing the marriageability of men, and reducing the supervision of youth.

Wilson and others suggest that now this geographically and culturally isolated underclass is permanently outside the mainstream of American society. What are the implications of this **concentrated disadvantage**? First, as noted earlier, because these locations inhibit informal social control, the underclass occupies criminogenic neighborhoods. Second, isolation from mainstream society and existence in concentrated high-crime areas might have influenced the "cognitive landscape" of youth. Children in these areas are more likely to witness violence, be exposed to poor role models, and have easy access to weapons (especially handguns).[26] In this sense, violence and crime (and the values that support them) become normalized.

This view of race, poverty, crime, and the underclass offers a rebuttal to those who view social isolation as a "bad choice."[27] For example, James Q. Wilson argues that moral poverty (as opposed to financial poverty) is the primary cause of crime.[28] Wilson suggests there is no real root cause of criminal behavior; rather, some criminals are simply bad people and others simply make bad choices. What Sampson, William Julius Wilson, and others make clear is that social structure and public policy shape the *context* of moral values. In other words, racial minorities and the poor are not inherently bad; instead, structural forces outside of a person's control shape available choices.

A 1995 photo of North Camden, New Jersey. In Camden, more than 3500 homes (10% of the residential properties) are abandoned, graffiti-covered, or targets of arsonists.

? *What is the relationship between the physical decay of buildings and crime rates?*

TABLE 6-1

Propositions on "Deviant Places"

- The greater the density of a neighborhood, the more contact there is between those most and those least predisposed to deviance.
- The greater the density of a neighborhood, the higher the level of moral cynicism. People in dense neighborhoods will serve as inferior role models for one another — the same people would appear to be more respectable in less-dense neighborhoods.
- When neighborhoods are dense and poor, homes will be crowded.
- Where homes are more crowded, people will tend to congregate outside the home, where there are greater temptations and opportunities to deviate.
- Where homes are more crowded, there will be lower levels of supervision over children.
- Poor, dense neighborhoods tend to be mixed-use neighborhoods, where homes, apartments, retail shops, and even light industry are jumbled together (the Chicago School's zone of transition).
- Poor, dense, mixed-use neighborhoods have high transience rates.
- Dense, poor, mixed-use, transient neighborhoods tend to be dilapidated. Dilapidation is a social stigma for residents.
- The larger the relative number of demoralized residents, the greater the number of available "victims."
- Stigmatized neighborhoods will suffer from more lenient law enforcement. More lenient law enforcement increases moral cynicism and increases the incidence of crime.

Source: Based on Rodney Stark, "Deviant Places: A Theory of the Ecology of Crime," *Criminology* 25 (1987): 893–909.

Stark's "Deviant Places" Theory

In his theory of deviant places, Rodney Stark combines social disorganization with routine activities approach.[29] Stark poses the question: How can neighborhoods remain the site of high crime rates despite a complete turnover in their population? His conclusion: There must be something unique about certain places that sustains crime. Stark examines five variables known to affect the crime rate in a community: (1) density, (2) poverty, (3) mixed use, (4) transience, and (5) dilapidation. These variables interact with four others: (1) moral cynicism among residents, (2) increased opportunities for crime and deviance, (3) increased motivation to deviate, and (4) diminished mechanisms of social control. **TABLE 6-1** outlines Stark' theory in greater detail.

LINK There is considerable overlap between routine activities theory (see Chapter 3) and social disorganization theory. In particular, both theories highlight characteristics of "dangerous places" that produce crime and victimization.

According to Stark, the nature of the neighborhood's ecology determines the crime rate. Even in low-income areas, the crime rate should be lower if the neighborhood is less densely populated, is more fully residential with less crowded and dilap-

idated housing, has a low concentration of demoralized residents, and has a low police tolerance of vice. Although Stark's full theory has not been tested, many of his ideas have been incorporated into tests of social disorganization and routine activities theories. In that regard, those tests support the central concepts of a theory of deviant places.

Hot Spots of Criminal Behavior

Another application of social ecology is the study of "hot spots" of criminal behavior. Recall that commentators prior to the Chicago School believed that the "city" was criminogenic. As the research on social disorganization makes clear, some neighborhoods are clearly more prone to crime than others. In other words, a focus on the "city" is much too broad. In the 1980s, policing researchers started to narrow the geographical area further, pointing to small high crime areas within particular neighborhoods.

The most well-known study was conducted by Lawrence Sherman and his associates in Minneapolis.[30] This study examined data on 323,979 calls to Minneapolis police citywide over a year and found that a few hot spots (as small as street intersections) accounted for *nearly all* calls to the police, especially for predatory crime (robbery, rape, and auto theft). As these findings suggest, certain locales are more susceptible to crime. Presumably, further examination of these areas might provide some tips on how to prevent offenses from occurring. If risks at these locations are stable, community problem-solving techniques may reduce crime and disorder substantially. If locations run high risks only temporarily, such strategies may not work. Sherman and his associates interpreted their data in light of routine activities theory (see Chapter 4). Others, however, have noted the similarity between hot-spots research and the social disorganization approach.

Spelman analyzed data on calls for service at high schools, housing projects, subway stations, and parks in Boston.[31] Similar to neighborhood crime rates, calls for service remain fairly constant over time. In a related study, he examined calls for service data from Austin, Texas, to determine if crime rates were higher on blocks with abandoned, residential buildings.[32] He found that blocks with unsecured buildings had 3.2 times as many drug calls, 1.8 times as many theft calls, and more than twice the number of violent crime calls.

Warner and Pierce explicitly used social disorganization theory to analyze assault, robbery, and burglary calls to the Boston police in 1980.[33] They found that neighborhood crime rates were related to such ecological variables as poverty, racial heterogeneity, family disruption, and structural density. As neighborhood controls become ineffective, crime increases and the police are more likely to receive calls for service.

Research on police calls for service, like neighborhood research, uses *places* as units of analysis in criminology. Indeed, Lawrence Sherman maintains that the concentration of crime in hot spots is more intense than it is among individual repeat offenders.[34] A similar argument could be made with respect to neighborhoods. Such places have characteristics that are like those considered in the criminal careers of persons: onset, continuance, specialization, and desistance. Sherman believes that such places should be stressed in criminology and can provide findings that can guide public policy. Clearly, a deviant

places theory demands further attention from criminologists as they attempt to provide information to guide public policy.

Policy Implications: Social Ecology and Social Disorganization

The policy implications of social disorganization theory and related concepts (the underclass, hot spots of crime) depend on where one jumps into the chain of events that leads to crime. The general argument is that broad ecological factors, such as poverty, residential mobility, and physical decay affect community cohesion and informal social control. Cohesion and control (or *collective efficacy*) increase crime. From a policy perspective, one might target the ecological factors, the cohesion and social process of a neighborhood, or both.

Shaw and McKay applied social disorganization theory by developing a large-scale delinquency prevention program called the **Chicago Area Projects (CAP)**. The first projects started in 1932, and they were carried out into the early 1960s. The projects targeted high-crime neighborhoods, and attempted, among other things, to[35]:

- Mobilize local informal social organization and social control among law-abiding citizens by creating "community committees" consisting of existing community groups, such as churches and labor unions, as well as residents who were city leaders.

- Overcome influence of delinquent peers and criminal adults by assigning "detached" (e.g., work with youth in non-organized, informal setting) local adults to neighborhood gangs, and through recreational programs designed to provide youth with associations with conventional peers and adults.

- Improve sanitation, traffic control, physical decay.

Although there was no rigorous evaluation of the CAP, long-term assessments suggest that the CAP met with mixed results. For example, there is some evidence that delinquency rates declined in neighborhoods with strong community committees. In other CAP neighborhoods, crime remained stable or increased. A 50-year follow-up study suggested that CAP had a marginal (but positive) influence on delinquency.[36] Unfortunately, this research was unable to tie differences in delinquency directly to the activities of CAP.[37]

Neighborhood watch programs seek to foster community organization, kinship, and informal social control.

? *Do these programs reduce crime rates where they are implemented?*

When asked to comment on the policy implications of social disorganization theory, most people will mention neighborhood watch programs. In this type of program, residents conduct neighborhood patrols and generally engage in the type of informal control implicated in social disorganization theory. Unfortunately, neighborhood watch programs tend to be successfully implemented in neighborhoods that are cohesive. In other words, they tend to take hold in the communities that need them the least.

The "Moving to Opportunity" program in Baltimore is a rather unique program with clear implications for ecological theory. In this program, randomly selected families are given the opportunity to move out of high-poverty neighborhoods into more stable, low-poverty neighborhoods. Over time, research indicates that delinquency among the youth of families who move declines and is substantially lower than the delinquency of children whose families are not selected for the program.[38] Although this program provides important evidence in favor of social disorganization theory, moving everyone out of poverty-stricken neighborhoods is probably not a realistic policy.

A related issue concerns urban renewal projects like the renovation of Chicago's public housing projects (see **You Are the Criminologist: The Demolition of Cabrini-Green** at the beginning of this chapter). These programs attract higher income residents into poverty-stricken neighborhoods. On the surface, it may appear that such a move could increase social cohesion and political clout and reduce crime rates. As more affluent people move in, however, property values and taxes increase. Neighborhood services do improve, but poor residents are pushed out into adjacent areas—creating a new community with even less social organization.[39]

There are also two policy considerations that relate to the criminal justice system. First, community policing involves the police taking an active role in working with neighborhood residents to identify and solve community problems.[40] This approach is very much in keeping with the spirit of social disorganization theory. As with CAP, community policing efforts have revolved around organizing community members and building community relationships. To date, the evidence regarding community policing is mixed. Such efforts may reduce the *fear* of crime in some locations, but there is little evidence at this time that they substantially reduce criminal behavior.[41] A second implication for the criminal justice system is that incarceration may have unintended consequences. As noted earlier, some research suggests that high levels of incarceration within a neighborhood might actually contribute to social disorganization and increase crime over the long run.

Criminologist Michael Tonry offers several policy recommendations based on this concern.[42] For example, he notes that the war on drugs has resulted in greater numbers of black offenders sentenced in numbers disproportionate to the presence in the community or among drug users. Tonry argues that such policies lead to destruction of minority communities and their impact should have been foreseeable. Sentencing laws should emphasize individualized punishments that stress the least restrictive alternative and provide judicial mitigation for special circumstances and treatment services. The effect of crime control policies on minority communities should be anticipated and controlled.

A recent federal initiative appears to blend many of the policy implications for social disorganization into a single **weed-and-seed strategy**. This strategy is outlined in the **Theory in Action: Weed and Seed** box. A recent evaluation of eight weed-and-seed sites yielded mixed findings. Some sites demonstrated reductions in serious crime, while others did not. Similar to neighborhood watch programs, sites that demonstrated success tended to be more cohesive and integrated, with a stable

Weed and Seed

Operation Weed and Seed is a program that is funded (in part) by grants from the federal government and directed primarily by local authorities. The program has grown from three grant sites in 1991 to over 300 in 2005. Weed-and seed-programs aim to prevent and reduce violent crime, drug abuse, and gang activity in targeted high-crime neighborhoods across the country. The "weeding out" involves targeting chronic violent offenders for incapacitation. The "seeding" consists of programs designed to bring human services to the area and promote economic and physical revitalization in neighborhoods. Community-oriented policing is advocated to gain information as to who needs "weeding" and aid residents in obtaining information about community revitalization and seeding resources.

A recent evaluation of eight weed-and-seed sites compared crime rates in the year prior to program implementation with crime rates in the two years following program implementation. The evaluation yielded mixed findings: although crime decreased in some sites,

it increased in others. Similarly, public perceptions of the program's effectiveness depended on the particular site. The more successful sites had the following characteristics:

- A stronger preexisting network of community-based organizations, less severe crime problems, and a more stable community population

- Early seeding programs, sustained weeding, and an active prosecutorial role

- More "intensity" — concentrating the funds on a small population or geographical area

- Active and constructive leadership by key individuals that led to greater coordination among agencies and programs

Sources: Terrence Dunworth and Gregory Mills, "National Evaluation of Weed and Seed," *Research in Brief* (Washington, DC: National Institute of Justice, 1999); Community Capacity Development Office, "Operation Weed and Seed," available at http://www.ojp.usdoj.gov/ccdo/nutshell.htm, accessed February 3, 2005.

---

community population, prior to program implementation.

The Strain/Anomie Theoretical Tradition

In a 1938 10-page article entitled "Social Structure and Anomie," Robert K. Merton started a rich theoretical tradition that still maintains an important place in criminology.[43] The Chicago School theorists built on Durkheim's notion of social integration and the need to control human appetites; Merton also borrowed heavily (and more explicitly) from Durkheim. In particular, he applied Durkheim's concepts of industrial prosperity and anomie to the context of the United States. The most prominent idea that Merton borrowed was that institutionalized norms can be weakened in societies that place an intense value on economic success.

Merton believed the United States was unique in its emphasis on the cultural goal of monetary

success. The "American dream" exhorted all to pursue material and financial wealth. Merton also believed that this cultural goal was almost universal — after all, part of the American dream is the idea that everyone has a fair and equal chance of becoming successful (anyone can go from "rags to riches" in America). What is wrong with setting such a lofty cultural goal? Merton argued, much like Durkheim, that too much emphasis on the pursuit of money can weaken norms that dictate the proper way to achieve this goal. Thus, people will pursue financial success even if it means violating norms or laws. Similarly, members of society will pay less attention to *how* wealth is achieved, in comparison to *whether* wealth is achieved. In this scenario, "The technically most feasible procedure, whether legitimate or not, is preferred to the institutionally prescribed conduct."[44] This is the very definition of anomie.

This problem is compounded by the fact that in reality, America is a stratified, or class-based society. In this sense, different classes have different ac-

Robert K. Merton, with a short journal article, launched the theoretical tradition of anomie, or "strain" theories.

? *What theories in this chapter can be traced back to the work of Merton?*

The intense pressure to succeed combined with a lack of conventional means to do so puts strain or pressure on many individuals. For this reason, Merton's theory is often called a strain theory. In sum, crime results when individuals are unable to achieve their goals through legitimate channels. Merton offers four possible adaptations to strain produced by the gap between the cultural goal of economic success and the reality of limited access to the proper means: innovation, ritualism, retreatism, and rebellion. Where there is no gap between the cultural goal of success and the means to achieve success, conformity is expected.

1. **Innovation.** The innovator buys into the culturally approved goals of society but pursues them through unacceptable means. This type of adaptation is most likely to lead to criminal behavior. For example, in the movie *Scarface*, the main character aspires to the same goals that most citizens strive for: a wife and family, fine cars, and a well-furnished home in an attractive neighborhood. However, he obtains these things through means deemed socially unacceptable: selling drugs. This adaptation strategy is more prevalent in the lower class where there are more obstacles in the way of achieving legitimate cultural goals. According to Merton, these obstacles account for the higher crime rate in the lower class.

2. **Ritualism.** This describes a person who, over time, abandons the goal of financial success. Despite this, they continue to embrace the accepted means. A ritualist seeks to play it safe. For example, Archie Bunker, from the 1970s TV show *All in the Family*, was a ritualist. Each night he came home from his job at the loading dock, hung up his coat and hat, sat down in his chair in front of the TV, and ordered his wife, Edith, to bring him a beer. He then would get up to eat his evening meal, watch some more TV, and go to bed. Every day, he performed the same weary ritual. Archie knew that the symbols of success in American culture (a nice car, a house in the suburbs, fancy clothes, and so on) were beyond his reach. His only "goal" was to make it through one more day and move on to the next. In modern times, a stereotypical ritualist might hold a dead-end service job, work for minimum wage, and barely make ends meet.

3. **Retreatism.** The retreatist is a social dropout. In Merton's words, retreatists include "psychotics,

cess to the means for success. An upper-class youth has access to high-quality education, business contacts, and other means for success. The lower-class youth, in particular, has little access to the legitimate, institutionalized means (education, contacts, good job) of achieving those goals.[45] For example, a common goal for middle-class Americans is to own a home. To achieve this goal, they will save their money for a down payment and then budget their income in order to make the mortgage payments each month. The means to realizing this cultural goal are finding legitimate employment and saving money. But what if there are no good jobs available and it is not possible to save enough money for a down payment? To quote the rock group The Violent Femmes, for some folks, "The American dream is only a dream."[46]

psychoneurotics, chronic autists, pariahs, outcasts, vagrants, vagabonds, tramps, chronic drunkards, and drug addicts."[47] Like the ritualist, this type of person will not resort to illegitimate means to achieve widely shared goals. Retreatists may be morally opposed to violating the norms of society or simply be powerless to violate such norms. Unlike the ritualist who keeps plodding along, these individuals simply withdraw from society.

4. **Rebellion.** The person who opposes both the culturally dominant goals and the means to achieve these goals is a rebel. The rebel seeks to establish a new social order and embraces a different cultural goal. For example, "hippies" might pursue the cultural goal of "peace" through their own prescribed means (free love, living in a commune). In criminological terms, the terrorist (see Chapter 11) and perhaps some street gangs (see the following subcultural theories) best exemplify this mode of adaptation.

Critique of Anomie Theory

Merton's theory is primarily utilitarian in nature: People engage in crime because they lack the legitimate means to achieve success. In that sense, his theory is geared to explain monetary crimes (robbery, burglary) as opposed to expressive (murder, rape) crimes. Further, because strain stems from a lack of legitimate means, Merton's theory explains crime only among the lower class (middle- and upper-class people generally have access to legitimate means). Because of these factors, strain theory has a rather narrow scope. In defense of Merton, strain theory was developed as a middle-range theory that would account for some, but not all, forms of deviant behavior.

The most damaging criticism of Merton's theory is that he fails to explain why people react to strain differently. In other words, why do people in almost identical social situations differ in their reaction to the feelings of helplessness? For example, why does one member of society (the ritualist) continue to pick up their lunch pail and trot off to work every day, while another (the innovator) deals drugs, and yet another (rebel) joins a street gang?

In addition to these criticisms, Merton's strain theory has never received much empirical support. One of the first tests of this theory compared ado-

Confessed Unabomber Ted Kaczynski being taken from Helena Federal Courthouse on April 19,1996.

? *Where might Kaczynksi fit in Merton's modes of adaptation?*

lescents' educational "aspirations" (How far in school would you like to get?) with their educational expectations (How far in school do you think you'll get?).[48] The strain theory would predict that youth with high aspirations but low expectations would be most likely to engage in crime. Instead, this study (and others that followed) found that delinquents tended to have low aspirations. Other measures of strain theory, including perceptions of blocked opportunities for success, and satisfaction with current monetary status, have suggested some support for the theory.[49] Even here, these relationships tend to be weak when compared to other predictors of crime.

Indeed, during the 1970s, many scholars started to question whether poverty and social class were even related to criminal behavior. For example, poverty and unemployment rates do not appear to fluctuate with crime rates over time in any meaningful, consistent manner (in some time periods, crime actually increases as poverty rates decline).[50] Further, self-report studies of criminal offending suggest that income levels are only weakly associated with delinquency.[51] One should note, however, that self-report surveys tend to measure less serious forms of delinquency and crime. The relationship between class and crime remains an unsettled issue in criminology.

LINK More recent theories of crime tend to argue that poverty is not directly related to offending (e.g., stealing to achieve the American dream). Instead, they argue that living in poverty strains the family and interferes with parents' ability to socialize their children. Gerald Patterson's theory of delinquency (see Chapter 5) is a good example of this recasting of the role of poverty.

The combination of weak empirical support and narrow scope led some scholars to call for an abandonment of strain theory as a valid explanation of crime.[52] Others, however, attempted to modify Merton's propositions in order to address criticisms and put forth an empirically supported model.

General Strain Theory

In 1992, Robert Agnew proposed a substantial overhaul of Merton's strain theory. Titled general strain theory (GST), this explanation of crime takes a much broader view of the sources of strain. Agnew suggests three sources of strain[53]:

1. The failure to achieve positively valued goals (e.g., economic success, good grades)

2. The removal of positively valued stimuli (e.g., death of parent, break up with boyfriend/girlfriend)

3. The presence of inescapeable negative stimuli (e.g., violent household, school troubles)

Strain in the context of GST is clearly available to all people, rich or poor. In that sense, Agnew addressed a major criticism of Merton's theory. Agnew also clearly explained how strain leads to crime. Specifically, he argues that strain produces negative emotional states, such as anger (violence) or depression (illicit drug use) that are conducive to many different types of delinquency and crime. The **Headline Crime: Bullied Boy Responds with Deadly Force** explores an extreme response to the strain of bullying. Finally, Agnew addresses why some individuals react to strain in a nondelinquent manner, while others react with criminal behavior. Individuals who lack the coping skills (intelligence, creativity, problem-solving ability) necessary to deal with strain in a constructive manner are more likely to have a delinquent response. Further, he outlines several factors (e.g., personality traits conducive to crime, delinquent peers) that may limit a person's response to strain.

Agnew's theory is much more complex and broader than Merton's modes of adaptation.

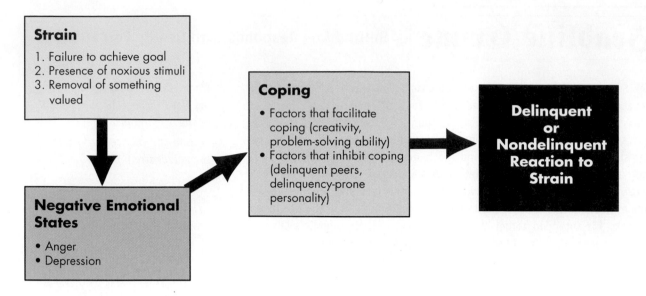

Strain

1. Failure to achieve goal
2. Presence of noxious stimuli
3. Removal of something valued

Negative Emotional States

• Anger
• Depression

Coping

• Factors that facilitate coping (creativity, problem-solving ability)
• Factors that inhibit coping (delinquent peers, delinquency-prone personality)

Delinquent or Nondelinquent Reaction to Strain

FIGURE 6-3 Summary of General Strain Theory

Source: Based on Robert Agnew, "Foundation for a General Strain Theory of Crime and Delinquency," *Criminology* 30 (1992): 47–86.

FIGURE 6-3 outlines the major concepts in his theory. The crucial issue is whether this reformulation has increased the support of strain theory. Although this is a relatively new theory, the core aspects of GST have received consistent empirical support. For example, Paternoster and Mazerolle studied a sample of over 1500 adolescents. The authors found that various measures of strain (negative life events, school/peer hassles, negative relations with adults) predicted delinquency. This relationship held even after controlling for measures from competing theories.[54] Numerous other studies have confirmed these initial findings.[55]

Nevertheless, some aspects (the exact role of coping skills and constraints on coping) of this complex theory remain in question.[56] Further, one might question whether GST is in keeping with the spirit of Merton's strain theory. Merton focused on social structure and broad cultural goals, while GST focuses more on the role of psychological stress.

Institutional Anomie Theory

Messner and Rosenfeld provide a different twist on Merton's theory of anomie.[57] Their theory of institutional anomie, proposed in 1993, took root from the recognition that Merton's writings were about more than just modes of adaptation. In particular, Messner argued that Merton actually offered a cul-

tural explanation for why the United States was more crime prone than other countries.[58] In keeping with Merton's (and indeed Durkheim's) notion of anomie, Messner and Rosenfeld suggest that the high level and distinctive pattern of crime in the United States are due to the cultural values in American society. They identify a cluster of values that constitute the American Dream[59]:

• **Achievement:** The American culture exhorts people to make something of themselves, to "be all they can be." Personal worth is evaluated on the outcome of these efforts. The failure to achieve is akin to the failure to make any meaningful contribution to society.

• **Individualism:** Americans are encouraged to make it on their own. Fellow members of society are thus competitors in the rat race.

• **Universalism:** Everyone is encouraged to social ascent and everyone is susceptible to evaluation based on the basis of individual achievement.

• **Materialism:** American culture values the accumulation of monetary rewards; money is literally the measure of success.

These core values of American culture place great pressure on Americans to achieve at any cost. The values are "highly conducive to the mentality that 'it's not how you play the game; it's whether you win or lose.'"[59] As with Merton's theory, Messner and Rosenfeld suggest that people are encouraged to use illegal ways to attain culturally approved goals (that is, U.S. culture promotes crime). Institutional anomie is different here in one important respect. Because there is no stopping point with regard to monetary success (how much is "enough" money?), the pressure to succeed is not dependent upon social class. In other words, the theory can account for why some wealthy people might engage in crime.

Institutional anomie theory really departs from Merton regarding social structure. Merton discusses social structure almost solely in terms of economic status. To Messner and Rosenfeld, social structure revolves around social institutions such as the economy, education, family, and polity (government). These institutions perform different roles in a society. For example, the government allows members of society to achieve collective goals (build a highway system) and the economy provides basic necessities (food, clothing, shelter). The family and the education system, among other things, allow members of society to socialize children.

The key concept in institutionalized anomie theory is an institutional balance of power. Because institutions often compete with each other (what is good for the economy might not necessarily be good for the family or education), any society can be measured on what institutions are valued over others. Messner and Rosenfeld suggest that in the United States, the economy towers over other institutions. The power of the economy weakens those institutions (family, education) that prevent crime. The authors provide a number of examples of how the economy dominates other institutions[61]:

- Noneconomic roles and values are devalued. For example, the homeowner is valued more than the homemaker. The excellent teacher does not receive the financial compensation relative to his or her business peers. The average childcare worker makes much less than the average bartender.

- Other institutions accommodate economic demands. For example, workers worry about finding time for their families, but never worry about finding time for their jobs. Few employers offer any form of paid parental leave, and few provide any childcare.

- Economic norms penetrate other institutions. For example, schools rely on grading systems similar to wages, and husbands and wives are now termed partners who manage the household division of labor.

In comparison to the United States, many European countries have strong safety nets (paid parental leave, long vacations, welfare payments) that balance the economy more equally against the family and the education system.

In sum, institutionalized anomie theory suggests that two forces shape crime in the United States: The cultural pressure to succeed financially and a social structure that weakens those institutions that socialize children (see FIGURE 6-4). This is a country- or society-level theory; institutionalized anomie predicts that countries that place exaggerated value on economic success and allow the economy to dominate other institutions will have high-crime rates. Although the theory is new and comparing countries is difficult, there is some support for institutionalized anomie theory.

One study examined property crime rates for all 50 states in 1980.[62] The researchers found that property crime rates were dependent on the capacity of noneconomic institutions (e.g., church membership, marriage, and voting behavior) to lessen the impact of poverty. Although consistent with institutional anomie theory, it was not a cross-national comparison. A more recent test found that

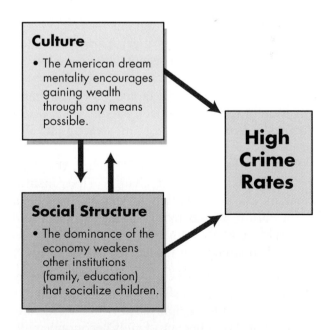

FIGURE 6-4 Summary of Institutional Anomie Theory

Source: Based on Steven F. Messner and Richard Rosenfeld, *Crime and the American Dream*, 2nd ed. (Belmont, CA: Wadsworth, 1997).

countries with stronger safety nets (e.g., the provision of pension, sickness benefits, unemployment compensation) to buffer the effects of the economy had lower rates of homicide.[63]

Policy Implications of Anomie and Strain Theories

The policy implications of anomie or strain theory depends on the specific theory in question. The implication of Merton's modes of adaptation is that reducing poverty and increasing opportunity for lower-class people would reduce strain and therefore crime. Notably, during this theory's peak in popularity, it had a great deal of influence on public and political debate over crime. The Delinquency Prevention and Control Act of 1961 and President Lyndon B. Johnson's "War on Poverty" sought to increase educational and economic opportunities for the lower classes. Specific delinquency prevention programs that focused on poverty, because of their association with subcultural explanations of crime, are highlighted later.

General strain theory and institutional anomie theory lead to rather different policy implications. General strain theory highlights the importance of psychological strain and its relation to negative emotional states such as anger. Those who cope with their emotions constructively are less prone to engage in delinquency. In that sense, cognitive-behavioral rehabilitation programs (see Chapter 5) that focus on skills such as anger management and conflict resolution are consistent with general strain theory. Of course, there are many other factors within this theory that one could target. Indeed, a major limitation of theories that lack parsimony is that it becomes difficult to figure out the exact policy implications.

Within institutional anomie theory, there are essentially two targets for change. First, institutional anomie suggests that altering the American dream culture would reduce crime. Messner and Rosenfeld suggest a number of policy implications designed to strengthen the institution of family[64]:

> Initiatives such as the provision of family leave, job sharing for husbands and wives, flexible work schedules, employer-provided child care, and a host of other "pro-family" economic policies should help alter the balance between the economic demands faced by parents and their obligations and opportunities to devote more time and energy to exclusive family concerns.

They acknowledge that transforming American culture is "fanciful," but contend that it is possible to push the culture in a less criminogenic direction. For example, goals other than the accumulation of wealth will need to be strengthened: "This implies greater recognition of and appreciation for . . . social roles such as 'spousing,' teaching, learning, and serving the community. . . ."[65]

Subcultural Explanations of Crime

Between the 1950s and early 1960s, several authors developed subcultural theories of delinquency. These theories branched off of the dominant explanations of crime during that period: the anomie and social disorganization perspectives. Subcultural theories share two common themes. First, they focus squarely on the lower class. Second, the theories attempt to explain the formation and activity of delinquent subcultures. A *subculture* is defined as a group, such as a street gang, that holds norms and values that are different from mainstream society.

Cohen: Status Frustration and Reaction Formation

In *Delinquent Boys*, Albert K. Cohen sought to explain why delinquent subcultures (gangs) developed and why they engaged in a particular kind of delinquency.[66] Cohen argued that most gang-related juvenile delinquency was nonutilitarian, malicious, and negativistic (e.g., vandalism, assaults). Even theft seemed to be based on factors other than the value of stolen goods (e.g., thrill, something to do). In this case, Merton's idea that "strain" produced innovation geared toward financial success made little sense. Still, Cohen argued that strain produced delinquency; he simply devised a different source of strain. In Cohen's theory, strain is caused by the failure of lower-class boys to achieve middle-class status. According to Cohen, most lower-class boys desire middle-class status and initially accept the goals and values (e.g., responsibility, delayed gratification, ambition, manners/courtesy, control over aggression, respect for property) of the middle class.

The turning point occurs when boys reach school age. Cohen noted that the school systems of the 1950s were "entrenched in middle-class values and social networks."[67] Lower-class boys, singled out by their dress, manners, and attitudes, failed to live up to this "**middle-class measuring rod**." Cohen suggested of the lower-class boy[68]:

> To the degree to which he values middle-class status, either because he values the good opinion of middle-class persons, or because he has to some degree internalized middle-class standards himself, he faces a problem of adjustment and is in the market for a "solution."

Like Merton, Cohen believed that different youth would react to this status frustration differently. A "college boy" will "buck up" and achieve middle-class status by working hard and achieving in school. Others will drop out and become "street-corner boys" (like Merton's retreatist). The delinquent solution involved the creation of a subculture that valued things in direct opposition to middle-class standards. Cohen borrowed the Freudian defense mechanism reaction formation to describe this process.

LINK Freud identified several defense mechanisms that are employed to reduce anxiety (see Chapter 5). With reaction formation, individuals hide one instinct (the desire to abide by middle-class morals) from awareness through the use of the opposite impulse (trash middle-class values).

In essence, because the boys cannot achieve middle-class status, they create a culture that rewards the opposite values. Thus, for example, physical aggression, toughness, and hedonism are stressed. Members of these delinquent groups do not consider the future consequences of their behavior, but instead focus on immediate gratification of their desires. Gang members are openly hostile to the agents of conformity. Moreover, they oppose other delinquent groups and use force to ensure loyalty and conformity to their own group. In short, it is a culture all their own and of their own making.

Cohen's theory leads to a rather unique prediction. If school experiences are the major source of strain, then dropping out of school might actually decrease delinquency. Although early research supported this position, more recent studies suggest that dropping out of school in itself has little influence on delinquency.[69]

Cloward and Ohlin: Differential Opportunity

Richard Cloward and Lloyd Ohlin's theory of differential opportunity followed closer to Merton. In keeping with Merton's notion of strain, they argued that much delinquency is primarily aimed at obtaining wealth through illegitimate means.[70] Most serious delinquents are predisposed toward "conspicuous consumption" (e.g., fast cars, fancy clothes, sex, drugs). Because their access to legitimate means is structurally blocked, delinquents will resort to illegitimate means (e.g., theft, drug sales, burglary) to achieve their material goals.[71]

Cloward and Ohlin's major departure from Merton's theory is the recognition that *illegitimate* means for success are not automatically available to all youth. Just as legitimate means (e.g. education, a good job) are unequally distributed in society, so too are illegitimate means. In some neighborhoods, illegitimate opportunities for success are readily available. For example, there may be a well-entrenched organization that distributes illicit drugs. Such an organization provides an illegitimate avenue to pursue financial success. In other areas, neighborhood conditions deteriorate to the point that even illegitimate organizations are unable to survive. In this sense, Cloward and Ohlin draw together Merton's work with the Chicago School theorists (neighborhood organization, cultural transmission of criminal values and skills).

Thus, differential opportunity speaks both to the availability of legitimate opportunities (blocked opportunity creates delinquency), and to the availability of illegitimate opportunities for success. Cloward and Ohlin argue that the presence or absence of illegitimate opportunity dictates the form taken by the delinquent subculture. If illegitimate opportunities are available, criminal gangs will engage in more utilitarian activities (organized crime, drug distribution) in pursuit of money and status. Even here, some retreatist gangs develop. Retreatist gangs consist of "double failures" — those individuals who could not achieve success through either legitimate or illegitimate means. To the extent that illegitimate means are unavailable, conflict gangs will organize around violence — and engage in activities that "protect turf." The three different delinquent subcultures identified by Cloward and Ohlin are summarized in **TABLE 6-2** .

Some qualitative data (ethnographic research) drawn from gang members appear to support differential opportunity theory. John Hagedorn's study of gang involvement in the illicit drug market is a good example. Hagedorn demonstrates how gang drug dealing is a response to the absence of legitimate employment opportunities.[72] His studies are based on interviews and observations conducted in

---

TABLE 6-2

Forms of Delinquent Subcultures

- **Criminal subculture:** follows the basic organized crime model. Areas where organized crime is firmly established provide a goal for delinquents. They rationally seek economic gain and view crime as a career.
- **Conflict subculture:** places high premium on violence. This subculture often occurs in neighborhoods populated with new immigrants, where the delinquent pursues opportunities lacking elsewhere.
- **Retreatist subculture:** emphasizes drug abuse or other forms of escape. This delinquent is a "double failure" who cannot achieve success in either the criminal or conflict subcultures.

Source: Richard A. Cloward and Lloyd E. Ohlin, *Delinquency and Opportunity: A Theory of Delinquent Gangs* (New York: The Free Press, 1960).

Milwaukee, Wisconsin, in 1987 and 1992. Drug organizations responded rationally to the demands of the market. When sales were made to low-income neighbors, they were done informally. New and more sophisticated structures were developed to handle sales to affluent whites and outsiders. There were differences in drug organizations across ethnic lines. Latinos maintained their gang membership but used kinship groups to expand operations. African-American adult gang members were more likely to freelance or use small businesses as covers. Most white adult gang members held down full-time jobs and sold cocaine on the side.

Over time, Hagedorn found that four types of adult gang members developed:

1. Those few who had gone "legit" or had matured out of the gang
2. "Homeboys" — a majority of both African-American and Latino adult gang members who alternately worked conventional jobs and took various roles in drug sales
3. "Dope fiends" — those addicted to cocaine and who were in business to maintain access to the drug
4. "New jacks" — those who saw the drug game as their career

Hagedorn argues that most gang members would accept legitimate employment. He believes that the key to their future lies in building social capital that comes from steady employment and a supportive relationship, without the constant threat of incarceration.[73] Employment, even a minimum-

level of involvement in the legitimate economy, could be an effective deterrent to gang involvement. In that light, jobs programs should focus on ways to encourage private and public investment in poor neighborhoods and advocate for more community control of social institutions.[74]

On the negative side, few people have directly tested whether the availability of *illegitimate* means directly influences the activities of gangs. Further, gang research often does not reveal typologies consistent with Cloward and Ohlin's framework. Rather, gangs tend to be diverse (e.g., drug use, drug sales, violence, property offenses) in their delinquency, rather than specialized in a particular vice.[75] Where evidence of specialization does exist, it does not match up with Cloward and Ohlin's typology.[76]

Miller: Focal Concerns of the Lower Class

Walter B. Miller outlines several focal concerns or values of the lower class that encourage deviance.[77] In essence, Miller's theory views the entire lower class as a unique subculture. He argues that members of the lower class, for example, place a high value on street smarts and toughness. In contrast, the middle class values delayed gratification and restraint of aggression. The focal concerns of the lower class are summarized in **TABLE 6-3**. Unlike Cohen, who viewed the values of gangs as a reaction to the middle class, Miller suggests that gang values are actually absorbed from the culture of the lower class.

Miller singles out the female-based household as another factor in producing gangs. He argues that in the lower classes, men do not fully participate in the rearing of children. Miller contends that young, lower-class males often go out on the streets to learn appropriate adult male behavior. In this context, the gang becomes the arena for demonstrating and exaggerating the core values (focal concerns) of the culture in an attempt to demonstrate manhood.

Qualitative data suggests that the focal concerns are an important influence in the development of gangs. For example, a former street gang leader interviewed by Weisfeld and Feldman stated that most members continued in crime because of adherence to the lower-class values of toughness, autonomy, and easy money.[78] The leader had become moderately successful as an independent

TABLE 6-3

Six Focal Concerns of Lower-Class Delinquents

1. Trouble: A preoccupation with getting into, or staying out of trouble — trouble can refer to violent situations or interactions with the police.

2. Toughness: The need to demonstrate that one can stand up to adversity and "take" whatever the street brings (e.g., run-ins with other gangs and the police).

3. Smartness: The high value placed on "street smarts"; one must know how to handle oneself on the street.

4. Excitement: The view that "life" is all about the thrill of engaging in conflict and ripping people off.

5. Fate: The belief that what happens in life is beyond one's control — whatever happens is meant to be.

6. Autonomy: The intolerance of challenges to one's personal sphere — the need to stand up to anything or anyone.

Source: Walter B. Miller, "Lower Class Culture as a Generating Milieu of Gang Delinquency," *Journal of Social Issues* 15 (1958): 5–19.

businessman. He noted that crime is a bad bargain in the long run. Many of his friends had died on the streets. However, the advantages of legitimate work and the costs of crime are not apparent to most urban youths. He suggests, though, a policy implication more consistent with the work of Merton or Cloward and Ohlin — improving employment opportunities for young people.

Miller's work has been heavily criticized on a number of grounds. The strongest critiques center on his failure to put the focal concerns of the lower class in any kind of context. In other words, he essentially blames the lower class for having particular values without recognizing the effects that concentrated poverty and pervasive joblessness may play in generating values such as fate and autonomy.[79] Also, research suggests that many middle-class youth hold values and attitudes similar to those identified by Miller.

The work of Elijah Anderson appears to address some of these criticisms. Anderson argues that many lower-class youth are guided by the "code of the streets."[80] This code is a set of informal rules that governs interpersonal public behavior. Anderson suggests that at the heart of this code is respect and fear of being disrespected. He locates the cause of such a code in the pervasiveness of racism, joblessness, alienation, and despair prevalent in some communities. Nevertheless, he points out that even in crime-prone areas, there are many decent families who have conventional, middle-class values.

A General Critique of Subcultural Explanations

In general, subcultural theories attempt to explain gang activity among lower-class boys. In other words, they have a very narrow scope. They cannot account for middle-class, upper-class (i.e., white-collar crime), or female offending. On the other hand, this perspective does provide a framework to study and examine gangs. The main theme is that gangs offer an opportunity to "be somebody" and achieve the status that has been denied by society.

Another general criticism is whether gangs are truly subcultures. The term subculture suggests that gangs are strong, cohesive units that have a distinct core of values that are subscribed to by all members. In contrast, some researchers portray many gangs as "near groups": less cohesive and structured than subcultural theories suggest.[81] Also, a substantial amount of research indicates that delinquents have rather conventional values but excuse or rationalize their criminal behavior.[82] A related criticism of these theories is that they do not allow for individual deviance — individuals are always adequately socialized.[83] In subcultural theories, they are simply socialized toward the wrong set of values.

Policy Implications of Subcultural Theories

As touched on previously, subcultural theories have had an influence on social policy during the past three decades. The notion that blocked opportunities spawned crime was embraced by the Kennedy and Johnson administrations in the 1960s. In a sense, President Johnson's "War on Crime" and "War on Poverty" were fought on the same battleground, against the same enemies. Lack of economic and educational opportunities were viewed as the catalyst, breeding anomie or social hopelessness, which in turn led some individuals to crime.

Differential opportunity theory (along with strain theory) was particularly influential in the formation of delinquency policies and programs during this period. The Delinquency Prevention and Control Act of 1961 and President Lyndon B. Johnson's War on Poverty sought to increase educational and economic opportunities for the lower classes. The most notable example was the **Mobilization for Youth Program (MFY)** that Cloward and Ohlin actively supported. MFY attempted to attack the root causes of crime in New York City's Lower East Side by securing social services and establishing political structures in lower-class neighborhoods. A focus on political structure differentiated this program from other community projects[84]:

> . . . the problem with employment was not simply that minorities lacked skills but that they were excluded from union apprenticeships; the problem of poor educational opportunities was a matter not simply of youths lacking books in the home but also of policies that assigned the newest and least talented teachers to schools in slum neighborhoods.

As it turns out, the focus on politics was MYF's undoing. The program became embroiled in political struggles with city officials, was investigated by the FBI (but exonerated of any wrongdoing), and ultimately disappeared. On the one hand, there is little available evidence that MYF reduced delinquency. On the other hand, it suggests the enormous difficulty of trying to achieve broad social change.[85]

Conclusion

This chapter outlines two broad theoretical traditions, the social disorganization and anomie/strain perspective, and discusses how each contains themes and ideas from the work of Durkheim. **FIGURE 6-5** demonstrates the relationships among these theories.

The key assumption shared by these theories is that aspects of the social structure can promote crime. These dominant social structural explanations of criminality remain vibrant in current research. In particular, research on social disorganization and revised anomie theories (general strain theory, institutional anomie) has blossomed in the past 15 years. **TABLE 6-4** outlines each of the theories covered in this chapter and describes their key concepts and policy implications.

Social disorganization theory, which evolved from the work of Chicago School theorists, highlights how ecological features of a neighborhood such as poverty and residential mobility can interfere with community cohesion and informal control. In turn, a lack of collective efficacy in a neighborhood allows crime to flourish. More recently, theorists note that over the past 25 years, such neighborhoods have become concentrated and isolated from mainstream society. An *effective* policy implication based on these insights remains elusive.

Nevertheless, this theory of place offers (perhaps) sociology's best explanation of the high rates of urban black delinquency and crime. In particular, Shaw and McKay found high delinquency rates in the zone in transition, regardless of what racial or ethnic group occupied this area. This is a powerful argument against those who view all crime as simply a personal and moral failure.

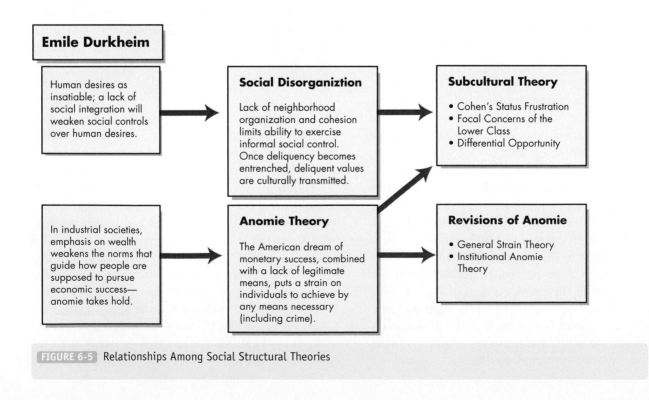

Emile Durkheim

Human desires as insatiable; a lack of social integration will weaken social controls over human desires.

Social Disorganiztion

Lack of neighborhood organization and cohesion limits ability to exercise informal social control. Once deliquency becomes entrenched, deliquent values are culturally transmitted.

Subcultural Theory

- Cohen's Status Frustration
- Focal Concerns of the Lower Class
- Differential Opportunity

In industrial societies, emphasis on wealth weakens the norms that guide how people are supposed to pursue economic success— anomie takes hold.

Anomie Theory

The American dream of monetary success, combined with a lack of legitimate means, puts a strain on individuals to achieve by any means necessary (including crime).

Revisions of Anomie

- General Strain Theory
- Institutional Anomie Theory

FIGURE 6-5 Relationships Among Social Structural Theories

TABLE 6-4

Summary of Social Structural Theories

Theory and Major Authors	Core Elements	Policy Implications
Anomie/Strain Tradition		
Robert Merton Anomie/Strain Theory	Most people recognize culturally approved goals and means to achieve them. Anomie develops when access to the approved means is blocked. Adaptation to anomie takes forms: ritualism, retreatism, innovation, rebellion, and conformity. Crime is primarily the result of innovation; the criminal uses illegal means to achieve the culturally approved goal of success.	Reduce poverty; provide legitimate opportunities for success to members of the lower class.
Robert Agnew General Strain Theory	Strain comes from three broad sources: (1) failure to achieve a goal, (2) presence of a noxious stimulus, and (3) the removal of positively valued stimuli. Strain produces negative emotional states (anger, depression) that, without adequate coping skills, are conducive to delinquency.	Because most people will encounter strain, focus on the ability to cope with strain (e.g., anger management, cognitive skills).
Steven Messner and Richard Rosenfeld Institutional Anomie Theory	Macro (country/society) level theory that predicts high crime rates based on culture and social structure. In cultures that place intense value on economic success, the norms guiding how a person attains wealth become weak. When the economy dominates and weakens those institutions responsible for socializing children (school, family), high crime rates result.	Push the culture of society away from a focus on money and toward the recognition that other roles are important. Increase the strength of socializing institutions — for example, employer-sponsored childcare.
Chicago School		
Clifford Shaw and Henry McKay Social Disorganization Theory	A macro (neighborhood) level theory. Crime rates are stable and high in areas with certain ecological features (high poverty, population mobility, physical decay). These features impede social organization and cohesion and prevent informal control of delinquency. Once crime is prevalent, delinquent norms and values are culturally transmitted to others and compete with normative values.	Target for change those ecological factors that relate to cohesion and control (or collective efficacy). Promote neighborhood cohesion and informal social control.
Subcultural Theories		
Albert Cohen Status Frustration	Delinquency is largely a lower-class phenomenon. The delinquent experiences status frustration and a loss of self-esteem. To combat this loss, the delinquent ridicules what is valued in society and develops a subculture that recognizes and rewards delinquent values.	Unclear. Perhaps prepare lower-class youth for school (Head Start programs).
Richard Cloward and Lloyd Ohlin Differential Opportunity Theory	As with Merton's theory, strain is primarily caused by a lack of legitimate opportunities for success (good job, education) among the lower class. Blocked economic aspirations lead to a poor self-image and this frustration leads to delinquency. The form that delinquency takes, however, depends upon whether access to *illegitimate* means for success (drug dealing, pimping) are also denied. Where illegitimate opportunities are present, criminal gangs will occur. In neighborhoods without a criminal structure, conflict gangs are more likely.	Provide legitimate opportunities for success to members of the lower class.
Walter Miller Focal Concerns of the Lower Class	Six focal concerns of the lower class foster delinquency: trouble, toughness, smartness, excitement, fate, and autonomy. The lower-class youth responds to these values and develops a subculture of delinquency. The predominance of female-based households contributes to this problem. Lower class adolescents often go out on the streets to learn appropriate adult male behavior.	Unclear. Theory suggests crime could be reduced by changing the values of the lower class or reducing the incidence of single (female-based) parent households.

The anomie tradition also points to the importance of the social structure. Many of these theories suggest that economic stratification generates crime. In particular, they imply that blocked economic opportunity causes some to search for illegitimate ways to achieve status or monetary success. Thus, unless these economic forces are dealt with directly, a certain level of crime will be built into a society.

Some scholars note that there is a relationship between these two perspectives. For example, factors that promote strain, such as poverty and lack of opportunity, are most prevalent in socially disorganized communities.[86] The subcultural theories of Cohen and Cloward and Ohlin also linked these two perspectives together. In these theories, strain causes the formation of delinquent subcultures, which are then maintained through a process of cultural transmission of values.

Of course, a focus on the lower class has drawn some criticism. With few exceptions (general strain theory, institutional anomie), these theories cannot explain white-collar crime or in many cases middle-class street crimes. Also, these theories tend to overpredict crime among the lower class. [87] In fact, the majority of people who reside in high-crime areas are actually law-abiding citizens. Despite such limitations, social structural theories remain the most viable explanations of group differences (neighborhood, country) in crime rates.

WRAP UP

The Demolition of Cabrini-Green

Projects such as the Urban Revitalization Demonstration Program aim to rejuvenate inner-city areas by demolishing older, high-rise public housing projects. In the case of Cabrini-Green, the old housing projects are being replaced by a mix of public and private housing. On the surface, such a plan appears to follow the policy prescription of social disorganization theory. In particular, mixed housing might produce more residential stability and give owners a stake in the well-being of the neighborhood. There is some cause for concern, however, because making some housing "market rate" will mean less available housing for the poor. What will become of those residents who are left out of the new project? There is also the potential for conflict between those who pay market rate and others who live in subsidized housing. Nobody knows for certain how urban renewal projects will shape social life in the effected neighborhoods. Whatever the outcome, social scientists will be watching this manipulation of neighborhood ecology with a great deal of interest.

Chapter Spotlight

- The major premise of social structural theories is that criminality is rooted in the very structure of society.

- Emile Durkheim's work serves as a foundation for the American theoretical traditions of social disorganization and anomie. Durkheim wrote about the importance of community ties and the need to control the insatiable desires of humans. He also believed that the pursuit of monetary wealth ("industrial prosperity") was criminogenic.

- The Chicago School of crime focused attention on ecological characteristics of the city. Early research by Shaw and McKay demonstrated that crime rates were consistently high in the "zone in transition." Eventually, social disorganization theory emerged as an explanation of why some neighborhoods are more crime-prone than others. Modern social disorganization theorists argue that ecological factors (e.g., residential mobility, concentrated poverty) inhibit a neighborhood's collective efficacy, which in turn increases crime.

- The policy implication of social disorganization theory is to increase collective efficacy among neighborhoods, or to change the ecological factors in a way (e.g., increase house ownership, repair or demolish dilapidated buildings) that would increase collective efficacy.

- Robert K. Merton argued that the disjuncture between culturally valued goals (the American Dream) and the availability of the institutionalized means for success (e.g., job, education) produced a strain. Individual reactions to strain might include rebellion, retreatism, ritualism, or innovation.

- Robert Agnew's general strain theory (GST) is a revision of Merton's theory that operates at the individual level. In GST, there are many causes of strain. Agnew argues that strain produces "negative emotional states," such as anger, that are conducive to crime. People react differently to strain based on their coping abilities.

- Institutional anomie theory updates Merton at the macro level. Messner and Rosenfeld argue that the American Dream culture causes Americans to pursue success through any (including criminal) means. Further, they believe that the economy dominates the institutions (e.g., family, education system) that are responsible for socializing children.

- The policy implications of the strain/anomie tradition depend upon the particular theory in question. Merton's theory suggests that increasing economic opportunity would reduce crime. GST points to factors such as anger management and constructive coping.

- Subcultural theories attempt to explain the formation and activities of street gangs. Cohen explains the content of street gang activity (e.g., malicious, negativistic) as a reaction to middle-class values. Cloward and Ohlin argue that the availability of both legitimate and illegitimate opportunities shape the formation of street gangs. Miller suggests that the lower class has a core set of values that differ from middle-class values — these "focal concerns" of the lower class are criminogenic.

Putting It All Together

1. Use Merton's anomie theory to explain the rise of a gangster such as Al Capone. In your own words, describe the societal pressures that might have been operating at that time and what means of adaptation that gangster might have used.

2. Some theorists claim that juvenile gangs are subcultures. What evidence would you cite to support such a claim? What is the evidence against such a claim?

3. What is "concentrated disadvantage?" How does disadvantage become concentrated and isolated?

4. Merton's theory of anomie assumes that "money is the root of all evil." Does society's emphasis on material success cause crime?

5. Prior to the Chicago School, many argued that "the city" and immigrants of poor stock caused crime. How did the work of Shaw and McKay refute these arguments?

6. What is the policy implication of social disorganization theory?

7. Describe one revision of Merton's anomie theory. How is the revised theory similar and different from Merton's original theory?

Key Terms

altruistic criminal Defined by Durkheim as a person somehow offended by the rules of society who wishes to change those rules for the better. This "criminal" is motivated by a sense of duty to improve society.

anomie Term coined by Durkheim to describe a state of affairs in which the norms and values of society weaken and are no longer able to control behaviors.

Chicago Area Projects (CAP) A large-scale delinquency prevention program developed by Shaw and McKay. The projects targeted high-crime neighborhoods and created "community committees" to promote community organization, assigned "detached" local adults to neighborhood gangs, and made efforts to improve sanitation, traffic control, and physical decay.

collective efficacy The combination of social cohesion and informal social control within a neighborhood.

common criminal Defined by Durkheim as a person who rejects all laws and discipline and purposely violates the law without concern for the rightness of the acts.

concentrated disadvantage The idea that poverty and unemployment have become concentrated within certain neighborhoods, leaving isolated pockets of "truly disadvantaged" citizens.

mechanical solidarity Term used by Durkheim to describe rural societies, which are homogeneous, cohesive, and self-sufficient.

middle-class measuring rod Term used by Cohen to describe a school system that favored middle-class dress, mannerisms, and etiquette. Cohen ar-

gued that lower-class boys were often unable to meet these standards, and therefore experienced strain, or "status frustration."

Mobilization for Youth Program (MFY) A program that Cloward and Ohlin actively supported. MFY attempted to attack the root causes of crime in New York City's Lower East Side by securing social services and establishing political structures in lower-class neighborhoods. The program became embroiled in political struggles with city officials, was investigated by the FBI (but exonerated of any wrongdoing), and ultimately disappeared.

organic solidarity Term used by Durkheim to describe industrial societies, which are more complex and based on exchanges of goods and services.

social ecology The study of how human relationships are affected by a particular environment (the Chicago School is based on social ecology).

weed-and-seed strategy A federal initiative designed to reduce violent crime, drug abuse, and gang activity in targeted high-crime neighborhoods across the country. The "weeding out" involves targeting chronic violent offenders for incapacitation. The "seeding" consists of programs designed to bring human services to the area and promote economic and physical revitalization to neighborhoods.

zone in transition In Burgess' concentric zone theory, this is the geographical area just outside the business district. Research by Shaw and McKay confirmed that the zone in transition had consistently high crime rates from 1900–1930.

Notes

1. Bruce Springsteen, "My Home Town," *Born in the U.S.A.* (Columbia Records, 1984).
2. J. Robert Lilly, Francis T. Cullen, and Richard A. Ball, *Criminological Theory: Context and Consequences*, 3rd ed. (Thousand Oaks, CA: Sage, 1995).
3. Lilly, Cullen, and Ball, 2002, 32.
4. John E. Conklin, *Criminology*, 8th ed. (New York: Macmillan, 2004).
5. Steven E. Barkan, *Criminology: A Sociological Understanding*, 2nd ed. (Upper Saddle River, NJ: Prentice Hall, 2001): 145–146.
6. Charles Chandler, Lee Sigelman, and Yung-Mei Tsai, "Division of Labor and Social Disorder: A Cross-National Test of a Durkheimian Interpretation," *International Journal of Comparative Sociology* 27 (1986): 161–171.
7. Emile Durkheim, *Suicide: A Study in Sociology* (New York: Macmillan, 1966, original manuscript published in 1897): 253.
8. Robert Park, *Human Communities* (Glencoe, IL: Free Press, 1952); Robert Park, *The Criminal Area* (New York: Humanities Press, 1966).
9. Ernest W. Burgess, "The Growth of the City: An Introduction to a Research Project," in Robert E. Park and Ernest W. Burgess, eds., *The City* (Chicago: University of Chicago Press, 1968, original work published in 1925).
10. Lilly, Cullen, and Ball, 2002, 33–34.
11. Clifford Shaw and Henry McKay, *Juvenile Delinquency and Urban Areas: A Study of Rates of Delinquency in Relation to Differential Characteristics of Local Communities in American Cities* (Chicago: University of Chicago Press, 1969).
12. Shaw and McKay, 1969, 383–388.
13. Robert J. Bursik Jr., "Social Disorganization and Theories of Crime and Delinquency: Problems and Prospects," *Criminology* 26 (1988): 519–546.
14. Bursik, 1988, 521–538.
15. Jeffrey D. Morenoff, Robert J. Sampson, and Stephen W. Raudenbush, "Neighborhood Inequality, Collective Efficacy, and the Spatial Dynamics of Urban Violence," *Criminology* 39 (2001): 517–560.
16. Eric Silver and Lisa L. Miller, "Sources of Informal Social Control in Chicago Neighborhoods," *Criminology* 42 (2004): 551–583.
17. Robert J. Sampson, Stephen Raudenbush, and Felton Earls, "Neighborhoods and Violent Crime: A Multilevel Study of Collective Efficacy," *Science* 277 (1997): 918–924; Robert J. Sampson, Jeffrey D. Morenoff, and Felton Earls, "Beyond Social Capital: Spatial Dynamics of Collective Efficacy for Children," *American Sociological Review* 64 (1999): 633–660; Jeffrey D. Morenoff, Robert J. Sampson, and Stephen W. Raudenbush, "Neighborhood Inequality, Collective Efficacy and the Spatial Dynamics of Urban Violence," *Criminology* 39 (2001): 517–559.
18. Sampson, Raudenbush, and Earls, 1999, 921–922.
19. Delbert S. Elliott, William J. Wilson, David Huizinga, Robert J. Sampson, Amanda Elliott, and Bruce Rankin, "The Effects of Neighborhood Disadvantage on Adolescent Development," *Journal of Research in Crime and Delinquency* 33 (1996): 389–426; D. Wayne Osgood and Jeff M. Chambers, "Social Disorganization Outside the Metropolis: An Analysis of Rural Youth Violence," *Criminology* 38 (2000): 81–116.
20. Ruth A. Triplett, Randy R. Gainly, and Ivan Y. Sun, "Institutional Strength, Social Control, and Neighborhood Crime," *Theoretical Criminology* 7 (2003): 439–467.
21. Simon Dinitz, "Nothing Fails Like a Little Success," *Criminology* 16 (1978): 225–238, 235–236.
22. William J. Wilson, The *Declining Significance of Race: Blacks and Changing American Institutions* (Chicago: University of Chicago Press, 1980); William J. Wilson, *The Truly Disadvantaged: The Inner City, the Underclass, and Public Policy* (Chicago: University of Chicago Press, 1987).
23. William J. Wilson, *When Work Disappears: The World of the Urban Poor* (New York: Alfred Knopf, 1996).
24. William J. Wilson and Robert J. Sampson, "Toward a Theory of Race, Crime, and Urban Inequality," in John Hagan and Ruth D. Peterson, eds., *Crime and Inequality* (Stanford, CA: Stanford University Press, 1995).
25. James P. Lynch and William J. Sabol, "Assessing the Effects of Mass Incarceration on Informal Social Control in Communities," *Criminology and Public Policy* 3 (2004): 267–294.
26. Wilson and Sampson, 1995. 40–45.
27. Francis T. Cullen and Robert Agnew, *Criminological Theory: Past to Present* (Los Angeles: Roxbury, 2003): 112.
28. James Q. Wilson, *Thinking About Crime* (New York: Vintage, 1975).
29. Rodney Stark, "Deviant Places: A Theory of the Ecology of Crime," *Criminology* 25 (1987): 893–909.
30. Lawrence W. Sherman, Patrick Gartin, and Michael E. Buerger, "Hot Spots of Predatory Crime: Routine Activities and the Criminology of Place," *Criminology* 27 (1989): 27–56.
31. William Spelman, "Criminal Careers of Public Places," in John Eck and David Weisburd, eds., *Crime and Place: Crime Prevention Studies,* volume 4 (Monsey, NY: Criminal Justice Press, 1995).
32. William Spelman, "Abandoned Buildings: Magnets for Crime?" *Journal of Criminal Justice* 21 (1993): 481–495.
33. Barbra D. Warner and Glenn L. Pierce, "Reexamining Social Disorganization Theory Using Calls to the Police as a Measure of Crime," *Criminology* 31 (1993): 493–517.
34. Lawrence W. Sherman, "Hot Spots of Crime and Criminal Careers of Places," in John.E. Eck and David Weisburd, eds., *Crime and Place, Crime Prevention Studies,* volume 4 (Monsey, NY: Criminal Justice Press, 1995).
35. Richard J. Lundman, *Prevention and Control of Delinquency,* 2nd ed. (New York: Oxford University Press, 1993).
36. Steven Schlossman, Richard Shavelson, Michael Sedlak, and Jan Cobb, *Delinquency Prevention in South Chicago: A Fifty-Year Assessment of the Chicago Area* (Santa Monica, CA: Rand, 1984).
37. Ronald L. Akers and Christine S. Sellers, *Criminological Theories: Introduction, Evaluation, and Application* (Los Angeles: Roxbury, 2004): 183–184.

38. Jens Ludwig, Greg J. Duncan, and Paul Hirschfield, *Urban Poverty and Juvenile Crime: Evidence from a Randomized Housing-Mobility Experiment* (Evanston, IL: Joint Center for Poverty Research, 1999).

39. Elijah Anderson, *Streetwise: Race, Class, and Change in an Urban Community* (Chicago: University of Chicago Press, 1990).

40. Dennis P. Rosenbaum, *The Challenge of Community Policing* (Thousand Oaks, CA: Sage, 1995).

41. Robert Trojanowicz, Victor E. Kappeler, and Larry K. Gaines, *Community Policing: A Contemporary Perspective*, 3rd ed. (Cincinnati, OH: Anderson, 2002).

42. Michael Tonry, *Malign Neglect: Race, Crime, and Punishment in America* (New York: Oxford University Press, 1995).

43. Robert K. Merton, "Social Structure and Anomie," *American Sociological Review* 3 (1938): 672–682.

44. Merton, 1938, 674.

45. Richard G. Mitchell, "Alienation and Deviance: Strain Theory Reconsidered," *Sociological Inquiry* 54 (1984): 330–345.

46. Violent Femmes, "America Is," *Add it Up* (Reprise Records, 1993).

47. Robert K. Merton, *Social Theory and Social Structure* (Glencoe, IL: Free Press, 1968): 236.

48. Travis Hirschi, *Causes of Delinquency* (Berkeley: University of California Press, 1969).

49. Velmer S. Burton Jr., Francis T. Cullen, T. David Evans, and R. Gregory Dunaway, "Reconsidering Strain Theory: Operationalization, Rival Theories, and Adult Criminality," *Journal of Quantitative Criminology* 3 (1994): a213–238; Velmer S. Burton Jr. and Francis T. Cullen, "The Empirical Status of Strain Theory," *Journal of Crime and Justice* 2 (1992): 1–30; Robert Agnew, Francis T. Cullen, Velmer S. Burton Jr., T. David Evans, and Gregory Dunaway, "A New Test of Classic Strain Theory," *Justice Quarterly* 4 (1996): 681–704.

50. Messner and Rosenfeld, 1997a, 93.

51. Charles R. Tittle, Wayne J. Villemez, and Douglas A. Smith, "The Myth of Social Class and Criminality: An Empirical Assessment of the Empirical Evidence," *American Sociological Review* 43 (1978): 643–656.

52. Ruth Kornhauser, *Social Sources of Delinquency: An Appraisal of Analytical Models* (Chicago: University of Chicago Press, 1978).

53. Robert Agnew, "Foundation for a General Strain Theory of Crime and Delinquency," *Criminology* 30 (1992): 47–86.

54. Raymond Paternoster and Paul Mazerolle, "General Strain Theory and Delinquency: A Replication and Extension," *Journal of Research on Crime and Delinquency* 31 (1994): 235–263.

55. John P. Hoffman and S. Susan Su, "A Latent Variable Analysis of Strain Theory," *Journal of Quantitative Criminology* 14 (1998): 83–110; Paul Mazerolle and Jeff Maahs, "General Strain and Delinquency: An Alternative Examination of Conditioning Influences," *Justice Quarterly* 17 (2000): 751–778; Robert Agnew, Timothy Brezina, John P. Wright, and Francis T. Cullen, "Strain, Personality Traits, and Delinquency: Extending General Strain Theory," *Criminology* 40 (2002): 43–72.

56. Robert Agnew, "Building on the Foundation of General Strain Theory: Specifying the Types of Strain Most Likely to Lead to Crime and Delinquency," *Journal of Research in Crime and Delinquency* 38 (2001): 319–361.

57. Steven F. Messner and Richard Rosenfeld, *Crime and the American Dream*, 2nd ed. (Belmont, CA: Wadsworth, 1997a).

58. Steven F. Messner, "Merton's 'Social Structure and Anomie': The Road Not Taken," *Deviant Behavior* 9 (1988): 33–53.

59. Messner and Rosenfeld, 1997a, 62–64.

60. Messner and Rosenfeld, 1997a, 63.

61. Messner and Rosenfeld, 1997a, 70–76.

62. Mitchell B. Chamlin and John K. Cochran, "Assessing Messner and Rosenfeld's Institutional Anomie Theory: A Partial Test," *Criminology* 33 (1995): 411–429.

63. Steven F. Messner and Richard Rosenfeld, "Political Restraint of the Market and Levels of Criminal Homicide: A Cross-National Application of Institutional Anomie Theory," *Social Forces* 75 (1997b): 1393–1416.

64. Messner and Rosenfeld, 1997a, 97.

65. Messner and Rosenfeld, 1997a, 104.

66. Albert Cohen, *Delinquent Boys: The Culture of the Gang* (New York: Free Press, 1955).

67. Robert Martin, Robert J. Mutchnick, and W. Timothy Austin, *Criminological Thought: Pioneers Past and Present* (New York: Macmillan, 1990).

68. Cohen, 1955, 119.

69. G. Roger Jarjoura, "Does Dropping Out of School Enhance Delinquent Involvement? Results from a Large-Scale National Probability Sample," *Criminology* 31 (1993): 149–171.

70. Richard A. Cloward and Lloyd E. Ohlin, *Delinquency and Opportunity: A Theory of Delinquent Gangs* (New York: Free Press, 1960).

71. Thomas J. Bernard, "Control Criticisms of Strain Theories: An Assessment of Theoretical and Empirical Adequacy," *Journal of Research in Crime and Delinquency* 21 (1984) 353–372.

72. John M. Hagedorn, "Homeboys, Dope Fiends, Legits, and New Jacks," *Criminology* 32 (1994a): 197–219; John M. Hagedorn, "Neighborhoods, Markets, and Gang Drug Organization," *Journal of Research in Crime and Delinquency* 31 (1994b): 264–294.

73. Hagedorn, 1994a, 214.

74. John M. Hagedorn, "Gangs, Neighborhoods, and Public Policy," *Social Problems*, 38 (1991): 529–542.

75. C. Ronald Huff, *Gangs in America* (Newbury Park, CA: Sage, 1990).

76. Mark Warr, "Organization and Instigation in Delinquent Groups," *Criminology* 34 (1996): 11–38.

77. Walter B. Miller, "Lower Class Culture as a Generating Milieu of Gang Delinquency," *Journal of Social Issues* 15 (1958): 5–19.

78. Glenn E. Weisfeld and Roger Feldman, "A Former Street Gang Leader Reinterviewed Eight Years Later," *Crime and Delinquency* 28 (1982): 567–581.

79. Wilson and Sampson, 1995, 38–40.

80. Elijah Anderson, *The Code of the Street: Decency, Violence, and the Moral Life of the Inner City* (New York: W. W. Norton, 1999).

81. Lewis Yablonski, "The Delinquent Gang as a Near Group," *Social Problems* 7 (1959): 108–109.

82. Gresham Sykes and David Matza, "Techniques of Neutralization: A Theory of Delinquency," *American Sociological Review* 22 (1958): 664–670.

83. Hirschi, 1969, 5–6.

84. Lilly, Cullen, and Ball, 2002, 68.

85. Ibid.

86. Wilson and Sampson, 1995, 50–52.

87. Hirschi, 1969, 6–7.

WWW.CRIMINOLOGY.JBPUB.COM

Interactivities
In the News
Key Term Explorer
Web Links

OBJECTIVES

Understand the nature of process theories of crime, including the important institutions within these theories and the role of socialization.

Explain the history and major concepts within the differential association/social learning perspective.

Identify what makes control theories different from other explanations of crime.

List the types of informal control and explain how they fit into the various control theories of criminal behavior.

Discuss the social context of labeling theory and the labeling process.

Summarize the policy implications derived from learning, control, and labeling theories of crime.

Social Process and Crime

> "
> The infectiousness of crime is like that of the plague.
>
> —Attributed to Napoleon Bonaparte[1]
> "

> "
> The question, "Why do we do it [crime]?" is simply not the question the theory is designed to answer. The question is, "Why don't we do it?" There is much evidence that we would if we dared.
>
> —Travis Hirschi[2]
> "

WWW.CRIMINOLOGY.JBPUB.COM

Interactivities
In the News
Key Term Explorer
Web Links

YOU ARE THE CRIMINOLOGIST

Jerry "the Tire Iron" Liederbach

Jerry Liederbach, a 22-year-old man, has just pleaded guilty to assault with a deadly weapon after beating another young man with a tire iron. The altercation started when Jerry cut off the driver of another vehicle. Jerry's case file reads like a textbook on criminology: At every turn, Jerry appears to fit the profile of a repeat offender.

Consider the following excerpts from Jerry's presentence investigation (PSI) report:

1. Jerry has an extensive history of delinquency and crime. He was first arrested for possession of drugs and resisting arrest at age 11. In total, he has been convicted of four crimes, including assault, burglary, and driving while intoxicated.

2. Jerry dropped out of high school after failing to complete 10th grade. According to school records, Jerry's IQ score (84) is well below average.

3. Jerry lives with his mother who is, according to relatives, an alchoholic with no stable employment and who spends considerable time on the street. Like Jerry, she has an extensive history of criminal behavior. Jerry's mother describes Jerry as a "street hood" who is "beyond redemption."

4. Jerry's parents divorced when he was 7 years old because his father repeatedly physically assaulted his mother. There is some evidence that Jerry was physically abused as a child.

5. According to Jerry's grandparents and neighbors, Jerry was a difficult child, very impulsive and easily angered.

6. Since his latest arrest, Jerry has maintained that his victim "was asking for trouble" and says that "It's not like I killed anybody." Jerry doesn't understand what the fuss is all about. His probation officer reports that Jerry has never owned up to any of his prior crimes.

7. Jerry's probation officer reports that Jerry hangs out with a group of drug-abusing troublemakers. Jerry has confirmed that most of his friends have been in trouble with the law.

8. Jerry has no history of stable employment. He has never been married, although he reports dating women from time to time. He claims to have lost all respect for his mother and hasn't had contact with his father in over a decade.

Which of the factors listed provide the best explanation for Jerry's criminal behavior? What process-oriented theories of crime best fit the facts in Jerry's PSI?

Assuming that Jerry is a candidate for a rehabilitation program, what are good targets for change? In other words, what specifically about Jerry or his social circumstances can be changed that will lower his risk for reoffending?

Introduction

This chapter covers theories of crime that focus on the interplay between the individual and society. These theories often point to the importance of family (parental supervision) and peers (delinquent role models). As with social-structural theories, process theories have developed within broad theoretical traditions. These theories are examined within three such traditions: informal social control, labeling, and differential association/social learning.

The aim of social process theory is to discover how social influences (e.g., family, religion, politics, industry) shape individuals over time. Social process theories assume that there is a vital interplay between the environment, the individual, and criminal behavior. Many of these theories emphasize the process of socialization. <u>Socialization</u> is the gradual process whereby a person learns the "proper" way to live, including the norms and values that guide human behavior. Because each of us belongs to society, the socialization process affects us all.

Two theoretical traditions within this chapter focus explicitly on socialization. <u>Informal social control</u> theories suggest that inadequate or incomplete socialization leads to criminal behavior. Often, these are referred to simply as *control theories*. The full name, however, distinguishes this tradition from theories of *formal* social control such as deterrence theory (see Chapter 4). <u>Social learning</u> theories focus on adequate socialization toward the incorrect norms and values. In other words, children are indeed socialized, but they are socialized to accept criminal norms and values.

Within each of these perspectives, social institutions (e.g., education, religion, family) are the primary source of socialization. These institutions provide information regarding proper behavior and social expectations. Although some theories touch on education or religion, the primary socializing institutions in both theoretical traditions are the family and the peer group.

Both the informal social control and social learning perspectives stem directly from the work of the Chicago School theorists and early versions of social disorganization theory. In the social disorganization theory, characteristics of neighborhoods (e.g., poverty, residential mobility) increase crime rates because they limit informal social control within the community. Also, once crime rates increase, delinquent gangs emerge and pass on values through a process of "cultural transmission."

> **LINK** The Chicago School approach and early social disorganization (see Chapter 6) emphasized the role of social institutions in maintaining control over communities and the "cultural transmission" of delinquent values. Process theories also focus on the importance of social institutions (the family, school) in controlling behavior (informal control theory) and the importance of delinquent or antisocial attitudes (differential association theory).

Different authors pursued these two aspects of social disorganization (a macro level structural theory) and applied them at the individual level. Thus, authors who focused on cultural transmission pursued theories of differential association and social learning. Those who focused on informal control attempted to explain in detail how institutions socialized individuals. **FIGURE 7-1** illustrates the relationship between the Chicago School and these theoretical traditions.

A great deal of overlap exists between some sociological-process theories and the psychology tradition of behaviorism. Sociologists have borrowed heavily from psychologists in order to explain how socialization unfolds over time. For example, sociological learning theories use operant conditioning and role modeling to explain criminal behavior.

> **LINK** Informal control theories and social learning theories in particular have borrowed heavily from psychologists (see Chapter 5). In particular, control theories emphasize parental use of operant conditioning and social learning theories emphasize observational learning.

The third type of process theory covered in this chapter is <u>labeling</u> theory. The labeling perspective focuses on how a person's self-concept may cause them to engage in crime. This tradition places emphasis on interactions between individuals and institutions of formal control (e.g., police, courts, prisons). In particular, labeling theorists suggest that contact with police and the courts may have a negative impact on a youth's self-image. Thus, formal interventions with kids may actually increase their criminal behavior.

Differential Association and Social Learning Theory

Social learning theorists argue that people become criminals much as they become anything else — through learning. In other words, the same techniques are involved in learning to change a tire, rob a bank, or hide criminal activity. Convicted serial killer Ted Bundy, for example, once explained how he diminished his vulnerability to detection when disposing of bodies. He would park on a curve so that he could see cars approaching from either direction. He learned this technique from a movie about a killer who had done the same thing. Asked how old he was when he saw this movie, Bundy replied he must have been 12 or 13. That movie did not turn Ted Bundy into a serial murderer; a whole variety of life experiences made him what he was. However, Bundy did *learn* this particular method.

Social learning theorists emphasize the influence of primary groups and significant others (admired individuals) on individual behavior. These are the key factors in the socialization process that help guide the individual into either criminal or law-abiding behavior.

Tarde's Law of Imitation

Nineteenth-century French criminologist Gabriel Tarde was unique for his time in rejecting the biological and physical theories of crime causation. Tarde launched an offensive against the idea of the born criminal (see Chapter 3). He argued that regional differences in crime rates were caused more

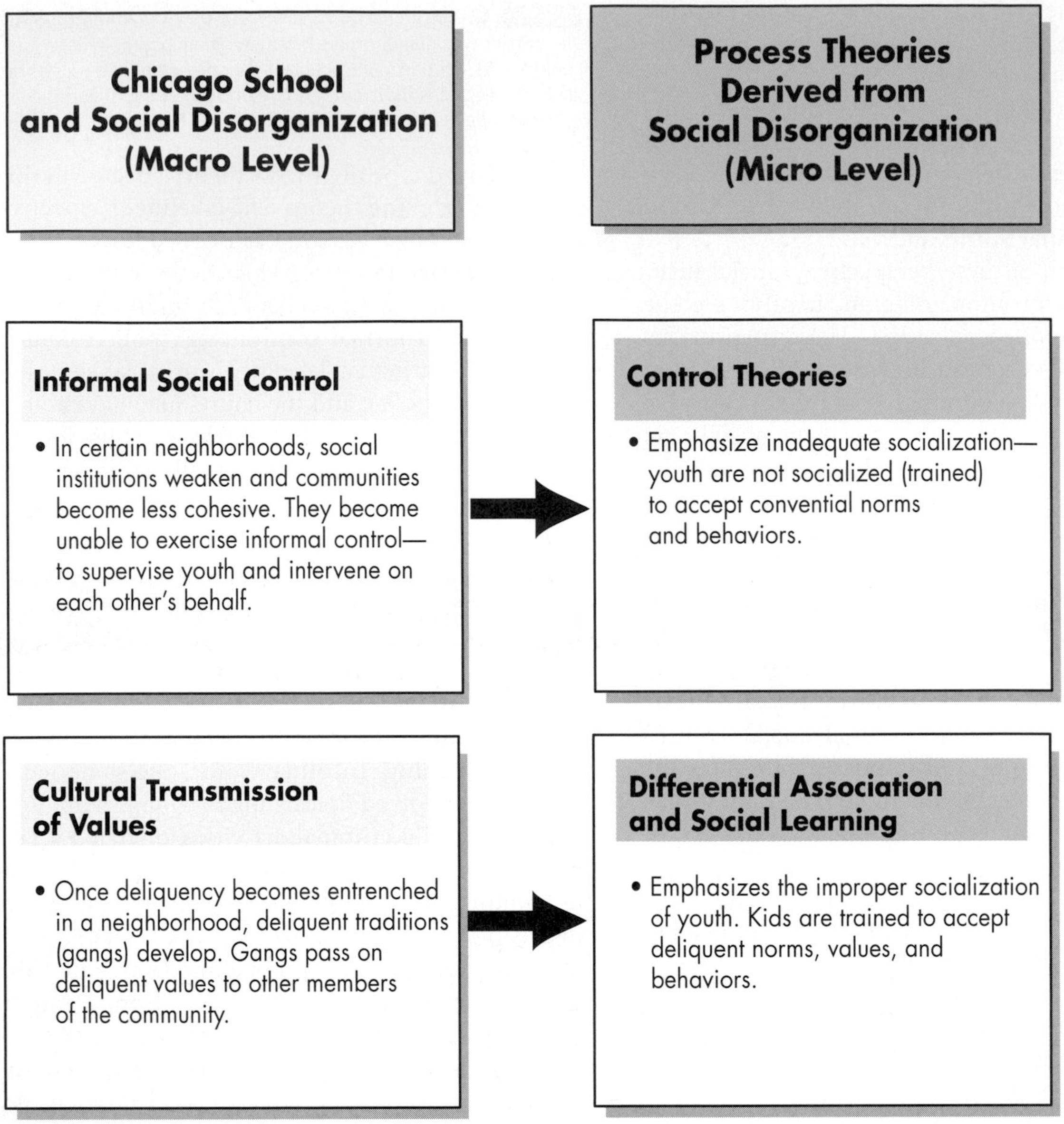

Chicago School and Social Disorganization (Macro Level)

Process Theories Derived from Social Disorganization (Micro Level)

Informal Social Control

- In certain neighborhoods, social institutions weaken and communities become less cohesive. They become unable to exercise informal control—to supervise youth and intervene on each other's behalf.

Control Theories

- Emphasize inadequate socialization—youth are not socialized (trained) to accept convential norms and behaviors.

Cultural Transmission of Values

- Once deliquency becomes entrenched in a neighborhood, deliquent traditions (gangs) develop. Gangs pass on deliquent values to other members of the community.

Differential Association and Social Learning

- Emphasizes the improper socialization of youth. Kids are trained to accept deliquent norms, values, and behaviors.

FIGURE 7-1 The Relationship Between Social Disorganization Theory and Individual Level Process Theories

by local variations in levels of poverty and alcoholism than biological factors.[3] Thus, slums, the underworld, and even prison conditioned the individual to a life of crime.[4]

Tarde also believed that criminality was a lifestyle (a "profession") learned through interaction with and imitation of others.[5] His **laws of imitation** attempt to explain criminality as a function of association with "criminal types."[6] In this sense, a criminal goes through a period of "apprenticeship," similar to a doctor, lawyer, or skilled worker. Tarde developed three laws of imitation to account for criminal behavior and imitation. The first law

states that people are more likely to imitate one another if they are in close contact. Thus, in active, densely packed towns or cities, imitation is most frequent.[7] The second law states that inferiors imitate superiors; crime originates in higher ranks and descends to the lowest ranks. The third law states that when two fashions come together, one can be substituted for the other. When this process of insertion occurs, there is a decline in the older method and an increase in the newer method.[8]

Another aspect of imitation was that certain forms of crime tended to originate in capital cities. For example, cutting corpses into pieces became a trend in Paris in 1876.[9] In recent times, large metropolitan cities (e.g., Los Angeles) have often been the sites of new crime fashions, such as drive-by shootings, "wilding" (i.e., random, racially motivated muggings), and carjacking (i.e., robbing persons in their cars at gunpoint). These crimes have then cropped up in other parts of the country. Internationally, terrorist tactics such as hijacking planes seem to follow a similar pattern.[10]

Sutherland's Theory of Differential Association

Edwin Sutherland moved Tarde's laws of imitation toward the general framework of the Chicago School of crime. Sutherland received his doctorate in sociology from the University of Chicago in 1913 and held a professorship there from 1930 to 1935.[11] In his 1939 *Principles of Criminology*, Sutherland outlined his **theory of differential association**. This theory speaks to the central Chicago School question: Why does crime remain stable in certain areas despite high population turnover? In keeping with the Chicago School, his theory elaborates on one Chicago School answer: the cultural transmission of delinquent values. It is important to note, however, that Sutherland did not buy into the full Chicago School explanation for crime. He argued, for example, that the lower class was not *disorganized*. Rather, all social classes were organized, and persons in a lower class are not by nature either inadequate or dysfunctional.[12]

Sutherland expressed his theory of differential association as a series of nine fundamental principles[13]:

1. **Criminal behavior is learned.** Negatively, this means that criminal behavior is not inherited, as such; also, the person who is not already trained in crime does not invent criminal behavior, just as a person does not make mechanical inventions unless he or she has had training in mechanics.

2. **Criminal behavior is learned in interaction with other persons in a process of communication.** This communication is verbal in many respects, but also includes the communication of gestures.

3. **The principal part of the learning of criminal behavior occurs within intimate personal groups.** Negatively, this means that the impersonal agencies of communication, such as movies and

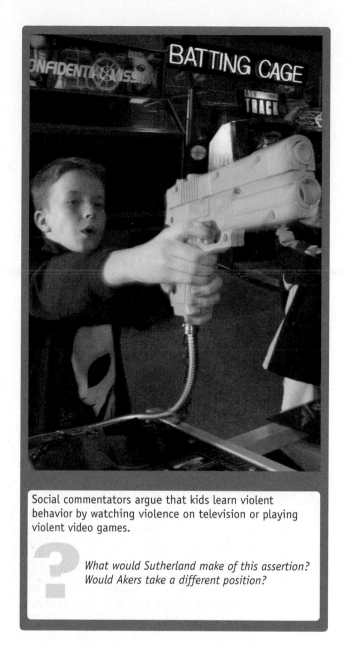

Social commentators argue that kids learn violent behavior by watching violence on television or playing violent video games.

? *What would Sutherland make of this assertion? Would Akers take a different position?*

newspapers, play a relatively unimportant part in the genesis of criminal behavior.

4. **Learning criminal behavior includes learning the techniques of committing the crime, which are sometimes very complicated, and learning the specific direction of motives, drives, rationalizations, and attitudes.**

5. **The specific direction of motives and drives is learned from definitions of the legal codes as favorable or unfavorable.** In some societies, an individual is surrounded by persons who invariably define the legal codes as rules to be observed, while in others he or she is surrounded by persons whose definitions are

favorable to the violation of the legal codes. In American society, these definitions are almost always mixed, with the consequence that there is cultural conflict in relation to legal codes.

6. **A person becomes delinquent because of an excess of definitions favorable to violations of law over definitions favorable of the law.** This is the principle of differential association. It refers to both criminal and anticriminal associations and has to do with counteracting forces. When persons become criminal, they do so because of contacts with criminal patterns and also because of isolation from anticriminal patterns.

7. **Differential association may vary in frequency, duration, priority, and intensity.** This means that associations with criminal behavior and also associations with anticriminal behavior vary in those respects. "Frequency" and "duration" as modalities of associations are obvious and need no explanation. "Priority" is assumed to be important in the sense that lawful behavior developed in early childhood may persist throughout life, and also that delinquent behavior developed in early childhood may persist throughout life. "Intensity" is not precisely defined but it has to do with such things as the prestige of the source of a criminal or anticriminal pattern and with emotional reactions related to the associations.

8. **The process of learning criminal behavior by association with criminal and anticriminal patterns involves all of the mechanisms that are involved in any other learning.** Negatively, this means that the learning of a criminal behavior is not restricted to the process of imitation. A person who is seduced, for instance, learns criminal behavior by association, but this process would not ordinarily be described as imitation.

9. **Although criminal behavior is an expression of general needs and values, it is not explained by those general needs and values, because noncriminal behavior is an expression of the same needs and values.** Thieves generally steal in order to secure money, but likewise honest laborers work in order to secure money. The attempts by many scholars to explain criminal behavior by general drives and values, such as the happiness principle, striving for social status, the money motive, or frustration, have been and will continue to be futile because they explain lawful behavior as completely as they explain criminal behavior. They are like breathing, which is a prerequisite for any behavior but which does not differentiate criminal from noncriminal behavior.

In short, Sutherland believed that people learn how to commit crimes mostly through primary group interactions; that is, through contact with others in intimate personal groups. Intimate personal groups might include one's family or set of friends. Sutherland was obviously skeptical of the idea that crime was learned through impersonal sources such as movies or television. This skepticism remains in updated versions of Sutherland's theory. In general, sociologists have been more doubtful that television and movies impact behavior than psychologists. Lessons learned within the socialization process include not only the techniques of committing crime, but also the motives, attitudes, and rationalizations that support it. These are described as *definitions* (i.e., how one defines a situation or behavior) that can either be consistent with or in opposition to the legal code. In particular, he noted that this process involved more than mere imitation (a reference, perhaps, to Tarde).

Sutherland's theory has been roundly criticized. The primary reason for this is the theory's vague concepts and phrasings, which make it difficult to test empirically. For example, what exactly is a definition and how might a person measure this concept? Also, to say that learning criminal behavior involves all of the mechanisms that are involved in any other learning does not really explain how behavior is learned. What exactly are the "mechanisms"?[14]

LINK As noted in Chapter 1, a scientific theory must be worded in such a manner that it can be tested empirically. Theories that are too vague are untestable.

Still, there is little question that Sutherland's contribution advanced the scientific development of criminology beyond biological determinism. Differential association gave a new direction and intellectual respectability to American criminology.[15] Despite its limitations, this theory became a dominant paradigm in criminology.[16] More importantly, this dominance led to efforts to restate differential association in a more clear and testable manner.

From Differential Association to Social Learning

The modification of differential association theory primarily involved borrowing principles of psychological behaviorism to explain the mechanics of learning. In the first revision, Ronald Akers and Robert Burgess created a differential reinforcement theory by adding the concept of operant conditioning (see Chapter 5).[17] Later, Akers added the concept of imitation and changed the title of the theory from differential reinforcement to social learning theory.[18] In addition to specifying the mechanisms of learning, these theorists also attempted to clarify the exact meaning of definitions. Akers' current social learning theory has four central concepts[19]:

1. *Differential associations*: In keeping with Sutherland, this is the notion that people are exposed throughout life to different sorts of people (role models) and different attitudes and values. Some of these people will model criminal behavior and communicate values or attitudes that are consistent with such behavior.

2. *Definitions*: Akers defines definitions as "one's own attitudes or meaning that one attaches to given behavior . . . that define the commission of an act as right or wrong, good or bad, desirable or undesirable, justified or unjustified."[20]

3. *Differential reinforcement*: The balance of anticipated or actual rewards or punishments that are consequences of behavior. These rewards can be social (praise, status) or more tangible (money, property). Reinforcement can also be internal (reinforcing or punishing oneself).

4. *Imitation*: This concept is the same as vicarious learning within psychology. Others serve as role models for behaviors. Individual characteristics of the models, and whether the models' behavior is rewarded, determine whether the model is imitated.

The concepts of differential association and definitions stem directly from Sutherland, and differential reinforcement and imitation are drawn from psychology. Like differential association theory, Akers emphasizes that not all sources of definitions or role models are equal. Some people, such as parents and close friends, will be more important than others.

FIGURE 7-2 provides a basic sequence that organizes these concepts. Akers suggests that differential associations (exposure to different people

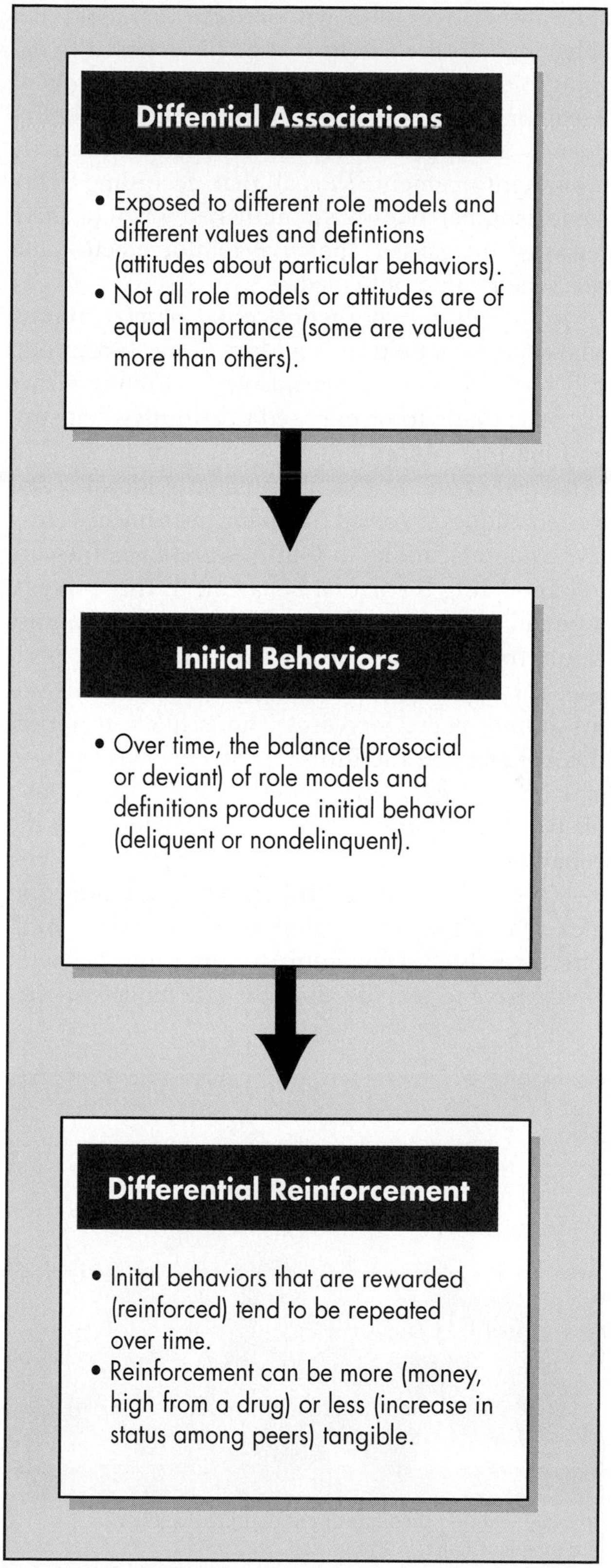

Diffential Associations

- Exposed to different role models and different values and defintions (attitudes about particular behaviors).
- Not all role models or attitudes are of equal importance (some are valued more than others).

Initial Behaviors

- Over time, the balance (prosocial or deviant) of role models and definitions produce initial behavior (deliquent or nondelinquent).

Differential Reinforcement

- Inital behaviors that are rewarded (reinforced) tend to be repeated over time.
- Reinforcement can be more (money, high from a drug) or less (increase in status among peers) tangible.

FIGURE 7-2 Akers' Social Learning Theory

Source: Based on Ronald L. Akers and Christine S. Sellers, *Criminological Theories: Introduction, Evaluation, and Application*, 4th ed. (Los Angeles: Roxbury, 2004): 85–89.

and values), over time, will produce an initial set of behaviors. To the extent that one is exposed to deviant role models and/or deviant values, delinquent behavior becomes more likely. Whether delinquency is repeated over time depends primarily upon reinforcement.[21] Recall that, according to behaviorism, behavior is strengthened when positive rewards are gained (positive reinforcement) and weakened when punished.

Consider a hypothetical child named Johnny whose parents are true "children of the 1960s" and still regularly smoke marijuana. As Johnny grows up, he is likely to be exposed to attitudes that support marijuana use ("It's no worse than alcohol" or "The real crime is that marijuana is illegal") and the techniques involved (smoking instruments, etc.). If the parents smoke in Johnny's presence, they are role modeling the actual behavior. In this context, it would be more likely that at some point, Johnny would try marijuana. To the extent that this experience is rewarding (Johnny likes the "buzz"; his status among peers increases), he is likely to repeat this behavior in the future. If he experiences punishment (he gets very paranoid and "freaks out"; his peers disapprove), he is less likely to repeat the behavior.

Of course, social learning theory is more complex than either the outline or Johnny story indicate. The full explanation for Johnny's behavior would have to include all of the role models and attitudes he was exposed to over time, including those that did not favor the use of marijuana. Further, future role models and attitudes would continue to have an impact. As noted in the discussion of psychological theories of learning, tests of social learning tend to be (necessarily) limited and indirect.

Differential association and social learning theory have been the subject of a great deal of empirical research. Typically, tests of social learning involve one or more of these measures:

- Attitudes that support crime (definitions)
- Exposure to delinquent peers/family members (differential associations)
- Rewards or punishment for delinquency (differential reinforcement)

Empirical tests consistently support these measures of the social learning theory. Akers and his associates studied a sample of more than 3000 male and female children in grades 7 through 12.[22] They found that measures of attitudes, associations, and reinforcement predicted both alcohol and drug use. Recent research continues to reveal strong relationships between measures of social learning and a wide range of outcomes, including smoking, computer crimes, gang-related delinquency, and other forms of criminal or delinquent activity.[23] For example, researchers surveyed 9th-grade students in an attempt to explain gang involvement and gang-related delinquency. The researchers found that social learning measures predicted whether or not a person was involved in a gang, and their involvement in both gang and nongang forms of delinquency.[24]

Many studies on social learning focus exclusively on either antisocial attitudes or delinquent peer associations. In Chapter 6, antisocial attitudes were discussed as a part of cognitive psychology. Constructs, such as criminal-thinking errors (attitudes that justify or rationalize criminal behavior), were identified. In sociology, the most widely known terminology to describe this same concept is Sykes and Matza's **techniques of neutralization**. In one of the first tests of differential association theory, Sykes and Matza documented common rationalizations for delinquency among a sample of delinquents.[25] The techniques of neutralization are outlined in TABLE 7-1 .

For example, delinquents denied injury, claiming they didn't really hurt anyone (The guy had insurance, didn't he?). Modern research continues to document relationships between techniques of

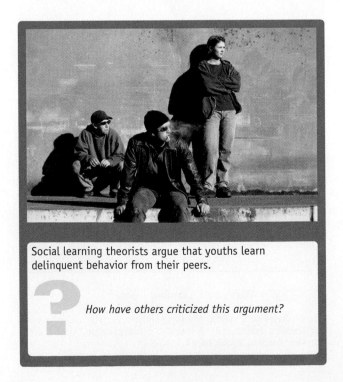

Social learning theorists argue that youths learn delinquent behavior from their peers.

?

How have others criticized this argument?

TABLE 7-1

Sykes and Matza's Techniques of Neutralization

1. **Denial of responsibility:** The offender argues that the act was caused by factors (e.g., a broken home, poverty, or peers) outside of his or her control. The youth thus claims to be a good person who was led astray.

2. **Denial of injury:** The offender insists no one was really hurt by the criminal act; that the injured party (e.g., wealthy person) can easily overcome the impact of the transgression (e.g., stolen property).

3. **Denial of victim:** The offender sees no real victim here. A social distance is placed between the offender and the victim. Beating up a rival gang member, "bashing the queers," and rolling street people are all examples of the victimization of devalued persons. The victims' status deprives them of their humanity.

4. **Condemnation of the condemners:** The offender rationalizes that "everybody is crooked" (e.g., public officials are "on the take" or "the cops beat innocent people"). By shifting the responsibility for their own delinquency to others, youths consider themselves undeserving of punishment.

5. **Appeal to higher loyalties:** The gang member often commits crimes "for the sake of the group." Loyalty becomes a license to commit crime and places gang members above the law.

Source: Based on Gresham Sykes and David Matza, "Techniques of Neutralization: A Theory of Delinquency," *American Sociological Review* 22 (1958): 664–670.

neutralization (or other antisocial attitudes) and different forms of criminal behavior. One study determined that older employees who stole and sabotaged production in their workplace engaged in both denial of injury and denial of the victim.[26] A case study of two hit men found that professional killers manage stigma through the neutralization process of "reframing." Basically, they reframed the victim as a "target" rather than a person. This allowed them to deny the victim, the injury, and responsibility.[27]

A common criticism of such findings is that such attitudes do not actually *cause* criminal behavior. Critics suggest that rationalization or justifications are utilized after the offense is committed and only when such behavior is called into question.[28] As noted in Chapter 6, even where this is true, it does not mean that rationalizations are unimportant. To the extent that these rationalizations neutralize guilt, they reinforce criminal behavior. There is evidence from the rehabilitation literature that suggests changing these attitudes reduces crime.

Association with delinquent peers is by far the most common measure of the social learning theory. Indeed, many people consider delinquent peers and social learning synonymous. Social learning emphasizes associations with those who engage in crime because they serve as role models and communicate deviant values and attitudes. Therefore, individuals who are surrounded by others who engage in crime should be more prone to crime themselves. In a review of this research, Mark Warr argues that: "Few, if any, empirical regularities in criminology have been documented as often or over as long a period as the association between delinquency and delinquent friends."[29] He suggests that no characteristic of an individual is a better prediction of crime and delinquency than delinquent peer associations.

In virtually every study where a measure of delinquent peers is included, the measure strongly predicts delinquency or crime.[30] Further, this is not simply a matter of whether a person has one delinquent friend. A 2002 study examined the connection between the proportion of a person's friends who were delinquent and delinquency.[31] Increases in this proportion corresponded with increases in delinquency. Youths who had *all* delinquent friends were twice as likely to engage in delinquency as youths with a mix of delinquent and nondelinquent friends. Of course, researchers have also examined the effect of having criminal parents or siblings. One study examined self-reported use of alcohol, cigarettes, marijuana, amphetamines, and depressants among 768 private high school students in a western U.S. metropolitan area. The study revealed that associations with drug-using friends had less impact than associations with drug-using parents or with pro-drug definitions received from parents or friends.[32]

Although few criminologists question the strength of these relationships, many have questioned their meaning. A common *nonsocial learning* interpretation is that "birds of a feather will flock together."[33] In other words, kids are not learning criminal behavior from their friends. Rather, delinquent youths attract one another as peers. Longitudinal research has provided some insight into this issue.

One study of data from five consecutive waves of the National Youth Survey (1976 to 1980 of 7600 youths, aged 11 to 21) found some evidence that like-minded delinquents attract each other. Those who engage in delinquency at an early point in time are more likely to have delinquent friends at a later time. Even so, peer relations (exposure to delinquent peers, time spent with peers, loyalty to peers) still had an impact on future delinquency.[34] Other longitudinal studies yield similar findings.[35] In short, it appears that birds of a feather do sometimes flock together. Apart from this process, however, peers appear to have a causal influence on future behavior. This has led Akers to counter the bird metaphor with his own animal metaphor—people who "lay down with dogs, wake up with fleas."[36] The relationship between delinquent peers and delinquency continues to generate debate and controversy within criminology.

Aside from attitudes (definitions) and peer associations, researchers have examined the role of reinforcement. For example, an analysis of survey data from 1600 high school students revealed that they engaged in substance abuse for the thrill of the experience. Illicit drug use was rewarding because it created a psychological high and provided excitement.[37] A focus on reinforcements suggests that society is moving in a circular fashion back to the classical school of criminology: When rewards outweigh punishments, certain types of behavior will result. As noted elsewhere, Akers believes that deterrence (formal punishment) could be easily absorbed into social learning theory.

LINK The principle of specific deterrence (Chapter 3) is that individuals who are caught and punished swiftly and severely through the criminal justice system should refrain from future criminal behavior. Learning theorists would consider this one of many consequences (differential reinforcements) of criminal behavior.

In sum, Akers' social learning theory, which was built on the framework of differential association theory, has accumulated a great deal of empirical support. To be sure, the theory is not without criticism. Scholars still question the exact role that delinquent peers and delinquent attitudes play in generating delinquency and crime. Nevertheless, the weight of empirical evidence appears to support the theory's central propositions.

Policy Implications: Social Learning Theory

As should be clear, there is a great deal of similarity between the differential association/social learning perspective in sociology and social learning theories within psychology. In that sense, the policy implications are also similar. To reduce crime, it would be necessary to (1) reduce access to delinquent peers, (2) confront and change antisocial attitudes, and (3) change the balance of reinforcement so that it supports prosocial behavior. The behavioral programs described in Chapter 5 (e.g., token economy, contingency contracting) are therefore consistent with social learning theory. Sutherland and Akers' concept of definitions is consistent with criminal-thinking errors. Cognitive restructuring programs, which target these attitudes for change, are therefore in line with social learning theory.

In fact, some of the earliest experiments in this type of rehabilitation were explicity designed to test principles of differential association. Psychologist D. A. Andrews used community volunteers (college students) to conduct group sessions with probationers and parolees.[38] In the typical group, several volunteers discussed various topics (e.g., the importance of rules, the limits of common rationalizations for offending) with several offenders. Andrews demonstrated that the community volunteers were able to reduce the antisocial attitudes (definitions) of the offenders. More importantly, this also led to reductions in offending.

Cognitive-behavioral programs also focus on a variety of social learning concepts as targets for change. Reviews of the rehabilitation literature consistently indicate that such programs are among the most promising means for reducing crime.[39] On the other hand, such programs typically include targets (personality, cognitive skills) that are not relevant to differential association.

Informal Social Control Theory

The central theme of social control theories is that inadequate socialization produces crime. Socialization produces control over individuals and these controls prevent people from engaging in crime. Social control theories also assume that crime is naturally appealing to many people. Standing other criminological theories on their heads, they ask, "Why aren't we all criminals?" Why is it that only certain individuals living in a crime-promoting environment become criminals and others do not?

Three Types of Informal Social Control

Many varieties of control theories exist. Every control theory, however, focuses on one or more of three general types of informal control[40]:

- *Indirect control* occurs when individuals have something valuable (a relationship, a good job) that ties them to conformity. In other words, a person has something positive that they do not wish to sacrifice by engaging in crime.

- *Direct controls* are exercised by those who have direct authority over others. For example, parents control their children by using punishments and rewards. In school, teachers exercise direct controls over their pupils.
- *Internal control* reflects the idea that individuals are able to exercise control over their delinquent impulses. Different researchers have used different terms (e.g., self-control, self-concept, conscience) to describe this concept.

Early Control Theory: Walter Reckless and "Containment"

A number of informal social control theories were put forth in the 1950s. Most of these theories have since been absorbed into modern control theories. One of the more comprehensive theories during this time was outlined by Walter Reckless. Reckless felt that criminological theory had not explained why many individuals who were exposed to criminal influences did not turn to crime. Noticing that some youngsters who lived in high-crime areas did not turn to delinquency, he concluded that they were somehow insulated.[41] Thus, his containment theory focuses on factors that insulate youth from crime. Reckless identified different types of <u>inner containment</u> and <u>outer containment</u>. A primary source of inner containment was self-concept. A favorable self-concept (a form of internal control) could lead an individual, even one faced with a crime-promoting environment, away from a life of crime. Outer containment included things such as parental and school supervision (direct control). Containment theory also included various "pushes and pulls" (poverty, delinquent subcultures, anger/frustration) toward delinquency.[42] These are the factors that containment had to counter. **TABLE 7-2** lists Reckless' ingredients of inner and outer containment.

Reckless believed that internal containments were stronger, more important, and more effective crime control elements than outer containments. Individuals lacking a high degree of inner containment, Reckless suggested, would be unlikely to be saved by external containment. For example, if unemployment or lack of educational opportunity pushes juveniles toward crime, the last line of defense is the self-concept. If it is strong, the juvenile can resist the lures of delinquency.

TABLE 7-2

Ingredients of Containment

Inner Containment

In addition to self-concept, Reckless outlined other forms of inner containment including:

- Self-control
- Ego strength
- Well-developed super ego (conscience)
- High frustration tolerance
- High resistance to diversions
- Ability to find substitute satisfactions
- Tension-reducing rationalizations
- These inner forces enable the individual to resist the lure of criminal behavior

Outer Containment

These elements represent the structural buffer in the person's immediate social world that is able to restrain the individual. They include:

- Presentation of a consistent moral front
- Institutional reinforcement of norms, goals, and expectations
- Existence of a reasonable set of social expectations
- Alternatives and safety valves
- Opportunity for acceptance

Source: Based on Walter Reckless, *The Crime Problem* (New York: Appleton Century Crofts, 1967).

Most research on containment theory therefore examined the role of self-concept. Reckless' research on self-concept indicated that "bad" boys had lower self-esteem than "good" boys.[43] Research conducted by Reckless' colleagues showed that the boys with a good self-concept avoided delinquency.[44] Follow-up research, however, failed to establish a firm link between self-concept and delinquency.[45] Part of the problem was that self-concept proved difficult to measure without referencing delinquency or misbehavior. More recent research provides little validity for Reckless' belief that high self-esteem insulates youth from delinquency. Not surprisingly then, an intervention project designed to improve the self-concept of pre-delinquent boys in Columbus, Ohio, junior high schools had no significant impact.[46]

Even though research on self-concept was not particularly fruitful, containment theory proved to be influential. Many aspects of inner and outer containment found their way into later control theories. Indeed, Reckless is cited as "one of the fathers of control theory laying the groundwork for the most sophisticated later versions of scholars like Travis Hirschi."[47]

Hirschi's Social Bond Theory

Travis Hirschi is perhaps the most well-known and influential social control theorist. Hirschi's 1969 book *Causes of Delinquency* represented a shift in how criminologists presented theories and how the field of criminology classified theories in general. In the book, Hirschi laid out his own theory of delinquency, provided measures of each concept, and presented data from a sample of high school students that supported his theory.[48] Hirschi also defined a "pure" informal control theory and compared it with other theories of crime. According to Hirschi, assumptions about human nature clearly differentiate control theories from other theories of crime. Most theories of crime seek to explain why individuals engage in crime. In doing so, they identify factors (e.g., strain, association with delinquent peers) that propel or push people toward deviance. Since a person must be "forced" into crime, Hirschi argued that these theories assume that humans are naturally "good."[49]

In contrast, control theories ask, "Why don't all people engage in crime?" After all, crime is often a quick and easy way to fulfill a desire. In that sense, the underlying assumption is that human nature leans toward deviance. Hirschi argued that because of this initial assumption, a control theory needed no "pushes" (as in containment theory) toward crime. Instead, they need only explain why some people refrain from crime. His explanation was that humans refrained from crime because they developed a social bond.

LINK Control theories and deterrence theory share the same assumption about human nature—that humans are naturally self-interested and hedonistic. The difference in these theories is the type of control considered most important. Deterrence theories emphasize formal controls (e.g., arrest, prison) while control theories emphasize informal controls.

Hirschi's theory identifies four elements of the **social bond** that tie an individual to society: attachment, commitment, involvement, and belief. A person that has an investment (commitment) in society is also tied to the norms of society. Conventional actions such as taking a job and developing a social reputation build prosocial ties and discourage criminal involvement. Seeking success, the conformist will not risk the chance of advancement by committing crimes. Similarly, to the extent that one cares for the opinions of others (attachment), they are less likely to engage in crime. Involvement in conventional activity is a time-consuming process.

The more heavily one is involved in conventional activities, the less time there is available to engage in deviant behavior. Finally, belief in the way society operates engenders sensitivity to the rights of others and respect for the laws. **FIGURE 7-3** summarizes the four elements of the social bond.

Although Hirschi included some forms of direct control (parental supervision), his theory focuses mostly on *indirect* control. Attachment (close relationships with others) and commitment (investment in society) are important because they represent something that might be lost if a person engages in delinquency. For example, a youth considering delinquency might wonder, "What would my parents think of me if they found out I did this?" Hirschi argued that direct controls were less important because most delinquency occurs when kids are outside of the supervision of authority figures. He also rejected internal control. He felt that concepts such as low self-control, conscience, and self-concept were too subjective and too difficult to measure.

Hirschi's own empirical test generally supported his theory. Among a sample of high school students, he found that measures of attachment (respect and desire to emulate parents) and commitment (average grades, aspirations to continue school) and belief (respect for law) predicted delinquency.[50] Subse-

Informal social control theorists believe that parents are the key to the proper socialization of children.

? *How are parents a source of direct, indirect, and internal control?*

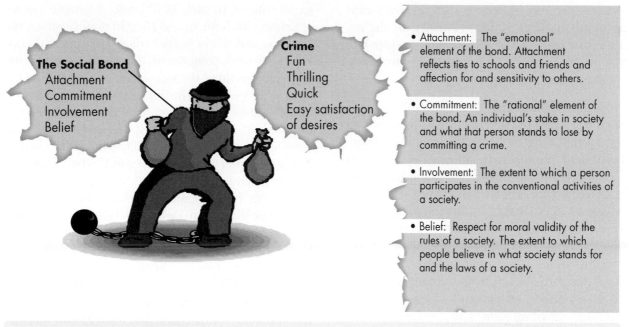

The Social Bond
Attachment
Commitment
Involvement
Belief

Crime
Fun
Thrilling
Quick
Easy satisfaction
of desires

• Attachment: The "emotional" element of the bond. Attachment reflects ties to schools and friends and affection for and sensitivity to others.

• Commitment: The "rational" element of the bond. An individual's stake in society and what that person stands to lose by committing a crime.

• Involvement: The extent to which a person participates in the conventional activities of a society.

• Belief: Respect for moral validity of the rules of a society. The extent to which people believe in what society stands for and the laws of a society.

FIGURE 7-3 Hirschi's Social Bond Theory

Source: Based on Ronald L. Akers and Christine S. Sellers, *Criminological Theories: Introduction, Evaluation, and Application*, 4th ed. (Los Angeles: Roxbury, 2004): 85–89.

quent investigations generally support the relationship between certain elements of the social bond and delinquency. Massey and Krohn found that commitment was the most important element of the bond.[51] They also discovered that the elements of the bond predicted less-serious delinquency much better than more serious forms of delinquency. Finally, they noted that control theory is more applicable in predicting female than male delinquency. More recent research continues to reveal a similar pattern.[52] For example, a relatively recent study examined the impact of social control variables on the behavior of 1974 5th graders in St. Louis. All of the elements of Hirschi's theory were tested, but only two elements (attachment and commitment) were related to conformity.[53] Overall, it appears as though some elements of the bond (particularly attachment and commitment) are moderately to weakly related to delinquency.

Research also indicates that a person's social bond might depend on personality characteristics. One such study examined survey data from 399 male and 300 female undergraduates enrolled in criminology and criminal justice courses at the University of Maryland.[54] Researchers tested the hypothesis that individuals who are more present oriented and self-centered invest less in social bonds,

and therefore are less deterred from committing crime by the possibility of damage to such bonds. They found that self-centered individuals were less likely to invest in personal capital: conventional attachments and commitments. There was some evidence that these individuals were less likely to be deterred from crime.

As this study illustrates, social bond theory may ignore the direction of influence on relationships. Hirschi theorized that weak social bonds cause delinquency. Critics suggest the reverse; that delinquency or a delinquent disposition may weaken a young person's social bond. Another criticism speaks to the relative importance of indirect versus direct controls. Research consistently demonstrates that direct parental controls (supervising, discipline) are better predictors of delinquency than indirect controls such as attachment to parents.[55] Finally, Hirschi predicted that attachments to others, regardless of whether they were criminal, insulated youth from delinquency. Hirschi described relationships among delinquents as "cold and brittle."[56] As already discussed, social learning theory makes the opposite prediction (association with delinquent peers should increase crime). Research on this issue consistently favors the social learning perspective. Studies of relationship quality suggest that relationships among delinquents are no different than relationships among nondelinquent youth.[57] Further, to the extent one attaches (forms strong relationships) to delinquent peers, they are more prone to delinquency themselves.[58]

Religion as a Source of Indirect Control

Although not a part of Hirschi's theory, many scholars suggest that religion can play a role in restraining delinquent impulses. In other words, faith or one's relationship with God is something that might be risked in order to engage in crime. Indeed, most studies do find an inverse relationship between religion and crime. A 2001 review of this research examined 60 studies of the connection between crime/delinquency and religion. The reviewers found that measures of religious behaviors (e.g., church attendance) and attitudes (e.g., belief in God, importance of religion) had a moderate effect on delinquent or criminal behavior.[59] A different review came to the same conclusion and also reported that better studies (methodologically sound) found stronger relationships than studies with weaker designs.[60]

Gottfredson and Hirschi's General Theory of Crime

Hirschi came almost full circle on his thinking about the causes of delinquency. As discussed, Hirschi's social bond theory focuses almost entirely on indirect social control. In their 1990 book, *A General Theory of Crime,* Gottfredson and Hirschi now suggest (like Reckless had many years earlier) that *internal* control is the vital component. The authors argue that **low self-control** is the sole cause of all criminal behavior, as well as behaviors that are analogous to crime.[61] In keeping with control theory perspective, Gottfredson and Hirschi assume that humans are born without self-control. The key question, then, is how does a person gain self-control? Their answer is proper parenting (a form of direct control). Borrowing heavily from Gerald Patterson (see Chapter 5), they argue that parents who supervise their children, recognize deviance, and punish deviant acts will build self-control in their children.[62]

As noted earlier, in his 1969 book, Hirschi argued that internal control was too subjective and too difficult to measure. How do these authors avoid this problem? Gottfredson and Hirschi take a rather novel approach to outlining what they call the nature of low self-control. The authors begin by describing the nature of crime; that is, they identify what different forms of crime have in common. They argue, for example, that crimes are generally easy to commit and usually require a victim to suffer some pain. A summary of their characterization of crime is provided in FIGURE 7-4 . They also point

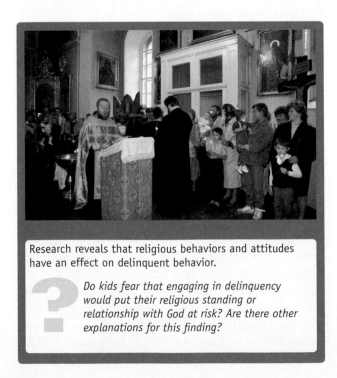

Research reveals that religious behaviors and attitudes have an effect on delinquent behavior.

? *Do kids fear that engaging in delinquency would put their religious standing or relationship with God at risk? Are there other explanations for this finding?*

The Nature of Crime	The Nature of Low Self-Control
Criminal acts...	**Criminals are therefore...**
• Are risky and thrilling	• Risk-takers
• Are easy/simple (they require little skill or planning)	• Physical (as opposed to mental); have low verbal ability
• Provide immediate gratification of desires	• Impulsive
• Provide few and meager long-term benefits	• Short-sighted
• Result in pain or discomfort to a victim	• Insensitive

FIGURE 7-4 A General Theory of Crime—The Nature of Crime and Low Self-Control

Source: Based on Michael Gottfredson and Travis Hirschi, *A General Theory of Crime* (Stanford, CA: Stanford Univeristy Press, 1990).

out that many acts (e.g., gambling, unprotected sex, adultery) that are not illegal share the same general "nature" as crime. They refer to such acts as *behaviors analogous to crime*. Gottfredson and Hirschi use the nature of crime to deduce the nature of low self-control. For example, if crime requires some pain and suffering to a victim, those with self-control should be insensitive to others. Through this process, they arrive at a definition of low self-control[63] :

> In sum, people who lack self-control will tend to be impulsive, insensitive, physical (as opposed to mental), risk-taking, short-sighted, and nonverbal, and they tend therefore to engage in crime and analogous acts.

Gottfredson and Hirschi argue that self-control is formed in early childhood. A person's level of self-control crystallizes around age 8 and remains stable thereafter. Given this argument and the description of low self-control, this theory is very similar to personality theories within psychology. Recall that the trait "low constraint," as outlined by a personality inventory, predicted delinquency and crime. Similarly, empirical studies consistently reveal that low self-control has a moderate to strong effect on both crime and analogous behaviors.

LINK   Gottfredson and Hirschi's characteristics of low self-control are very similar to the personality theory (see Chapter 5) of low constraint.

In a review of self-control research conducted from 1990 to 2000, criminologists Travis Pratt and Francis Cullen note that measures of low self-control[64]:

- Predict both "analogous behaviors" (fast driving, cigarette smoking) and crime
- Are among the strongest (compared to predictors from other theories) predictors of crime

- Predict delinquency, crime, and analogous behavior regardless of sample composition (male or female, adult or juvenile, offenders or general population)

In a fairly short period of time, the concept of low self-control has garnered a great deal of empirical support. Despite this empirical support, Gottfredson and Hirschi's theory has been criticized on a number of grounds. Foremost, it appears that low self-control, although important, is not the *sole* cause of criminal behavior. Studies continue to reveal that regardless of one's level of self-control, other things such as delinquent peers, antisocial attitudes, and neighborhood problems continue to matter.[65] Another issue deals with the genesis of self-control. Gottfredson and Hirschi claim that self-control comes completely from parenting. Recent research suggests that there are multiple sources of low self-control. For example, there is some evidence that Attention Deficit Hyperactivity Disorder is related to low self-control, regardless of parenting.[66]

Psychologists such as Andrews and Bonta question whether low self-control is a newly derived and distinct concept, or whether it is an "old wine in a new bottle."[67] They note, for example, that Gottfredson and Hirschi's definition of low self-control includes several of the most well-established (psychological) correlates of criminal behavior.[68]

A final criticism deals with the stability of low self-control. Gottfredson and Hirschi claim that low self-control is stable after early childhood. In doing so, they help to explain a common criminology finding; that criminal behavior tends to be stable over time. In other words, childhood misbehavior predicts juvenile delinquency; juvenile delinquency predicts adult crime, and so forth. Gottfredson and Hirschi can explain stability in crime because low self-control is also stable over time. The problem with this argument is that (despite some stability) most people desist from crime as they enter adulthood. If people commit crimes because they lack self-control, why do they stop committing crimes?

Despite these criticisms and limitations, it appears as though Gottfredson and Hirschi have identified and described an important concept (low self-control) that will continue to receive attention. The final control theory discussed in this chapter, however, reverts to Hirschi's "old" social bond theory as a starting point.

An Age-Graded Theory of Informal Social Control

The most recent development in control theory comes from two former students of Travis Hirschi — Robert Sampson and John Laub — who propose an extension of Hirschi's social bond theory. Hirschi's theory focuses on factors (school, parents) most relevant to youth. These factors, however, become less important as adolescents become young adults. Sampson and Laub's "age-graded" theory emphasizes both direct (parenting) and indirect (social bond) controls during childhood and adolescence.[69] Later in the life course, they emphasize **adult social bonds**. They argue that a quality marriage and/or a quality job help to explain why some people (even those who were crime-prone youth) desist from criminal behavior during adulthood.

Again, marriage and jobs are important to the extent that they produce informal control. They represent something that a person could lose by engaging in criminal behavior. This is why the *quality* of a job or relationship is important. A person considering crime would probably not be too upset about losing a low-paying job at a fast-food restaurant. That same person might think more carefully about disappointing a boss whose opinion they respect or losing a job that pays decent wages. Sampson and Laub found that marital attachment

Robert Sampson and John Laub argue that marriage is an adult bond that explains why some people desist from crime as they age.

? *How might marriage reduce criminal behavior?*

and job stability predicted desistence from crime among adults — even for those who had a history of juvenile delinquency.[70]

Even in the short term, it appears as though relationships and employment insulate people from crime. In a recent study, researchers interviewed newly convicted male offenders and examined their month-to-month activity prior to their incarceration. They found that crime patterns were correlated with social variables as expected. For example, during periods where the men were living with their wives, or employed, they were less likely to commit crimes.[71] The authors conclude that:

> Persons with a high rate of crime may be unlikely to graduate from school, unlikely to maintain meaningful employment, and unlikely to stay in a stable, meaningful relationship. Even so, they may sometimes go to school, sometimes work, and sometimes live with a wife, and at those times they are less likely to commit crimes.

What's Love Got to Do with It? Social Support and Altruism

Criminologist Francis Cullen offers a provocative critique of social control theory.[72] He does not dismiss control theories — indeed he notes that they have accumulated a great deal of empirical support. Instead, Cullen suggests that the control theory view of human nature (selfish and hedonistic) is too simplistic. In addition to instant gratification, humans also seek out and engage in altruistic and unselfish behavior. He points out that social support (parental love, nurturing, and caring) are "preconditions" for effective social control (effective parenting).[73] Further, "lack of love and nurturance is related to a host of emotional and cognitive deficiencies — deficiencies that are precursors for later conduct disorders."[74]

Cullen's thesis is that whether social support is delivered through government social programs, communities, social networks, families, interpersonal relations, or agents of the criminal justice system, it reduces criminal involvement. In that sense, evidence that "religiousness" or "quality marriages" reduces crime might not rest only on social control. Rather, they may provide nurturance and support, and therefore reduce crime.

A 2001 study using data from a national sample of adolescents demonstrates that *both* social support and social control have effects on delinquency. Parents who were more reliable (attended important events in the lives of children) and supportive (consistently used praise, affection, compliments, and encouraging hobbies) were less likely to have delinquent children. The measures of social support were related to social control (parental discipline) but predicted delinquency independent of parents' level of control.[75] At the macro level, research suggests that social altruism within cities reduces crime. Using a sample of more than 300 cities, researchers found that property and violent crime rates are higher in cities with lower United Way contributions.[76]

Over the past 30 years, social control and social learning perspectives have battled for supremacy in criminology. Cullen's theory of social support is a newcomer to this battle. Although there is some supportive evidence, it remains to be seen how much interest social support theory generates compared with the dominant theories of crime.

Policy Implications for Theories of Informal Social Control

The policy implications for theories of informal social control depend somewhat on the particular theory or form of control (e.g., internal, direct, indirect) in question. There are, however, some common themes. All of the control theories discussed in this chapter point to the importance of families. Parents can strongly contribute to conformity by providing supervision for, by building a quality relationship with, and by communicating with their children. Depending on the particular theory, effective parenting increases a child's attachment, generates self-control, or simply acts as a form of direct control. Hirschi remains skeptical that child-rearing programs could generate broad reductions in delinquency rates.[77] There is evidence, however, that parent training programs have had some success at reducing delinquency. The popularity of reality television programs such as *Supernanny* and *Nanny 911* suggest that many parents are indeed open to helpful parenting techniques.

J. David Hawkins and his associates emphasize both direct and indirect control (as well as some principles of learning) in the Seattle Social Developmental Project (SSDP). The SSDP project was designed to prevent childhood aggression and delinquency by focusing on both the family and the school. Within the program, teachers were trained in "proactive classroom management": the proper use of rewards and punishment to promote a good learning environment. Teachers were also trained in a number of techniques (interactive teaching, cooperative learning) designed to strengthen children's bonds with the school. Parents were offered (participation was voluntary) parent-skills training that focused on operant conditioning (recognize deviance, punish consistently). Parents were also encouraged to increase social support (spend time together, involve kids in family activities, develop children's school abilities).

This ongoing program started with children entering 1st grade — students were randomly assigned to the SSDP group or a control group. Comparisons between the control and SSDP group are now available for these youth when they were in the 5th grade and when they reached 18 years of age. By 5th grade, the SSDP kids were more committed and attached to school and slightly less likely to drink alcohol or engage in other misconduct.[78] At age 18, the SSDP youth maintained higher attachment and had higher academic achievement. Although the groups did not differ on many measures of delinquency, the SSDP youth were less likely to engage in violent forms of delinquency or heavy drinking.[79]

Sampson and Laub's adult bonds would require a much different approach. To be sure, few criminologists would recommend marriage as a policy to reduce criminal behavior. Employment — finding a quality job (i.e., stable, good pay, good relationship with employer) for those with prior criminal involvement — is more plausible.

Can't We All Just Get Along? Social Control, Social Learning, and Behaviorism

It is very easy to get confused about the difference between control theories and social learning theories. Moreover, it can be difficult to understand the difference between these perspectives and materials covered under the behaviorism heading of psychology. Within sociology, informal control and social learning theory both discuss aspects of learning. In control theories, the focus is on parental use of rewards and punishment to control the behavior of children. In social learning theory, the emphasis is on role models and attitudes that promote delinquency. In the discipline of psychology, there is no such distinction. Rather, psychologists speak only to different learning mechanisms (classical and operant conditioning, observational learning).

The distinction within sociology comes largely from a debate about the nature of humans. Control theories view humans as more evil and therefore in need of control; these theories emphasize how antisocial behavior is corrected through operant conditioning. Sociological learning theories view humans as more of a "blank slate" and are more likely to emphasize how deviant behavior is learned through observation and the communication of values and attitudes.

Not all criminologists agree that this distinction is crucial. Terrance Thornberry has put forth a theory that integrates social control and social learning measures into a single theory of crime. His Interactional Theory of Delinquency suggests that a lack of informal control allows youth to come into contact with delinquent peers.[80] Although his theory has attracted some attention, most criminologists prefer to keep control and learning as distinct theories.

Labeling Theory

Unlike social learning and social control theory, the labeling perspective does not feature a handful of well-known theories. Rather, a number of different scholars have contributed concepts and ideas within the same general framework. Although many of these contributions occurred from 1930 to 1950, the general perspective did not receive much attention in the United States until the 1960s. A number of scholars have noted that labeling theory perspective was a good fit to that social context.[81] In particular, this was a period of great social conflict where many questioned the motives and intentions of the government. Reaction to protests over civil rights and the war in Vietnam, the Watergate scandal, prison riots, and other events suggested to many that the government could not be trusted. The labeling perspective echoes this view. The gist of labeling theory is that government intervention in the lives of delinquents will make matters worse.

The Roots of the Labeling Perspective

The labeling perspective is built around three themes: (1) a view of crime and deviance as "relative," (2) a focus on how power and conflict shape society, and (3) the importance of self-concept. Before exploring the labeling process, here is a review of each of these themes.

The first theme is a general position that no act is inherently evil, bad, or criminal. Whether an act is considered deviant or criminal depends on a number of factors, including: (1) when and where the act is committed, (2) who commits the act and who is the victim, and (3) the consequences of the act.[82] Consider, for example, the use of mind-altering drugs. In some societies, such substances are legal, although in others they are considered illicit drugs. Within the same society, the status of an act can change. For example, many currently illicit drugs were once legal, and alcohol (for a brief time) was made illegal. Even behaviors such as the killing of another person are not always classified as homicide. During wartime, such behaviors are rewarded. Death from cancer caused by pollution is generally viewed as an environmental risk that is necessary for the economy.[83]

In short, the gist of this view is that no act is inherently evil or "bad." Whether these acts are considered deviant depends on the society in which they happen, the particular historical context, and the circumstances of the behavior. In the labeling theory, the crucial dimension is the *societal reaction* to the act, not the act itself. As Becker notes, ". . . deviance is not a quality of the act the person commits, but rather a consequence of the application by others of rules and sanctions to an 'offender.' The deviant is one to whom the label has successfully been applied; deviant behavior is behavior that people so label."[84]

The labeling perspective emphasizes the influence of powerful groups in society to both define and react to deviant behavior. Similar to conflict theory (see Chapter 8), labeling theorists argue that those in power (the middle and upper class) will define and enforce laws in a manner that benefits themselves to the detriment of the less powerful. Becker described those who define and enforce rules as __moral entrepreneurs__. "Rule creators" are interested in the criminalization of certain forms of behavior that they view as profoundly evil. They typically espouse a doctrine that sounds increasingly dogmatic or regressive. They also tend to leave the application of their desired policies to others.

Rule enforcers are professionals who enforce the law unflinchingly, whatever its content. They must justify their position and win the respect of those above them. They face the double dilemma of showing that the problem still exists but proving that it is being dealt with efficiently. Becker believes that rule enforcers, in response to the pressures of the job, will enforce the law selectively. Importantly, labeling the-

orists do not equate selectiveness with randomness. Rather, selective enforcement will be directed at those who lack power and status. Labeling theorists suggest that agents of the criminal justice system enforce the law in the interest of powerful groups in society. The law is selectively enforced so that it concentrates on certain segments of society. Few persons are caught, and those who are tend to be male, young, unemployed, lower-class, undereducated, minority residents of urban high-crime areas.[85]

A final piece in the labeling theory puzzle is derived from the general theory of __symbolic interactionism__. The thrust of this perspective is that people communicate through gestures, signs, words, and images that stand for, or represent, other things (symbols). In that sense, a single word (label) may contain a whole set of meanings. Labels such as "cool," "crack head," "psychotic," or "overachiever" conjure up a particular image. These exchanges of symbols, among other things, help people understand and define themselves. In other words, people interpret symbolic gestures from others and incorporate them into their self-image.

Charles Horton Cooley described this process as the "__looking-glass self__"; that is, one's own self-concept (how each one describes or thinks about themselves) are the product of other people's conceptions or symbolic labels.[86] In turn, the self-concept can dictate behavior. Individuals attempt (consciously or not) to live up to their image. Put another way, the labels that others use to describe a person can become a self-fulfilling prophesy.[87] Symbolic interactionists argued that this was not a one-way process. The people being labeled could respond back — and "negotiate" — their self-concept.

Putting the Pieces Together — The Labeling Process

By combining the three central themes, labeling theorists describe a general process whereby official intervention (e.g., arrest, trial) creates an unintended side effect. FIGURE 7-5 illustrates this general process. The starting point in the labeling process is the portrayal of childhood deviance as relative. Many children engage in various forms of deviance (there is no inherently evil act), including crimes such as shoplifting or vandalism. Such acts are typically portrayed in the labeling literature as unorganized and sporadic.[88]

Edwin Lemert termed these behaviors __primary deviance__. He suggested that if such acts go unno-

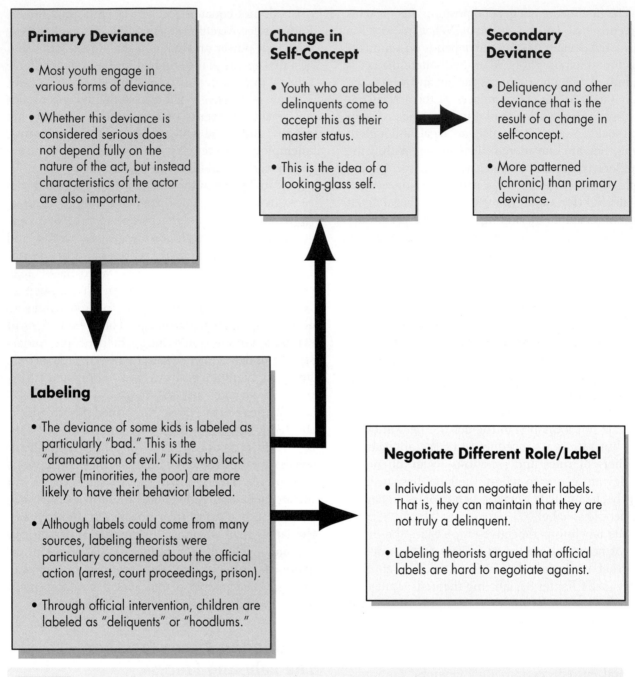

Primary Deviance

- Most youth engage in various forms of deviance.

- Whether this deviance is considered serious does not depend fully on the nature of the act, but instead characteristics of the actor are also important.

Change in Self-Concept

- Youth who are labeled delinquents come to accept this as their master status.

- This is the idea of a looking-glass self.

Secondary Deviance

- Deliquency and other deviance that is the result of a change in self-concept.

- More patterned (chronic) than primary deviance.

Labeling

- The deviance of some kids is labeled as particularly "bad." This is the "dramatization of evil." Kids who lack power (minorities, the poor) are more likely to have their behavior labeled.

- Although labels could come from many sources, labeling theorists were particulary concerned about the official action (arrest, court proceedings, prison).

- Through official intervention, children are labeled as "deliquents" or "hoodlums."

Negotiate Different Role/Label

- Individuals can negotiate their labels. That is, they can maintain that they are not truly a delinquent.

- Labeling theorists argued that official labels are hard to negotiate against.

FIGURE 7-5 Summary of the Labeling Theory Process

ticed, they have little impact. Most kids grow out of such behavior. Labeling theorists are therefore not concerned with the motivation behind the initial deviant acts.[89] Some acts, however, *will* be noticed. Frank Tannenbaum coined the phrase "<u>dramatization of evil</u>" to characterize the process whereby the primary deviance of certain people is singled out.[90] In other words, some individuals are tagged as delinquents or troublemakers. Once identified in this manner, others may see them in an entirely

new light. They may retrospectively interpret past actions in light of the new label (e.g., "I always knew he was a troublemaker").

Who is most likely to have their primary deviance singled out and how exactly are people labeled? The answer for most labeling theorists was that agents of the criminal justice system (e.g., police) start the process. In turn, society responds to delinquent activity by negatively defining and rejecting the offender. This response and rejection serve to identify to society the "evil in its midst."[91] Further, it was more important who the kid was (white or minority, wealthy or poor) than what he or she had done. In other words, people were tagged, not because of the particular act, but because of their status in society.

Drawing on the symbolic interactionism, labeling theorists point out negative consequences of this process. After the person is labeled, a change in self-identification may occur, so that an individual acts out the role of criminal. Thus, the label of "delinquent" becomes a self-fulfilling prophecy. Individuals organize their self-concept around deviance. They may even join with other "outsiders" in a delinquent subculture.[92] Lemert described delinquent behavior that results from this change in self-concept as <u>secondary deviance</u>. Others described it as *deviance amplification*. The criminal justice system, in effect, creates crime by trying to prevent it.

Recall that in symbolic interactionism, people could negotiate labels and their self-concept. Becker, for example, went to great pains to point out that not all labeled individuals will form a delinquent self-concept. For some, sanctioning might have the intended (deterrent) effect. Labeling theorists did argue, however, that the labels enforced by the agents of government would be difficult to negotiate. Once labeled as a delinquent, it is difficult to live down that definition.[93]

A Critique of Labeling Theory

Labeling theory has been severely criticized over the past 25 years. The most damaging criticism is that the central elements of the theory appear to have very little empirical support. Research appears to refute the following tenets of labeling theory:

- The characterization of primary deviance as relative, sporadic, and unimportant
- The idea that the nature of the person predicts official reaction more than the nature of the act
- The effect of official sanctions on future behavior (deviance amplification)

Labeling theorists cannot explain why some people engage in primary deviance, while others do not. Instead, they portray anything that happens before an official response as sporadic, unpatterned, and relatively unimportant. Studies of childhood and adolescent deviance indicate that this is not an accurate picture. Even young children demonstrate consistent, patterned, and chronic misbehavior.[94] Further, they are unlikely to simply "grow out" of

such behavior. The trend is that misbehavior, delinquency, or deviance continues over time, regardless of whether a child is officially labeled. Many critics also take issue with the complete relativity granted to deviant acts. This portrayal of deviance generates an underdog ideology that denies the heinous nature of certain crimes (some acts *are* bad), as well as the independence and responsibility of the actor.[95]

Another premise of labeling theory is that the social status of the offender rather than the particular offense dictates whether the person will be arrested and punished. To be sure, there is evidence of some racial bias in the criminal justice system. For example, despite procedural efforts to prevent it, death sentencing in the United States is plagued by racial bias. Studies of the capital sentencing process reveal that blacks who kill whites have the greatest probability of receiving the death penalty.[96] Some studies also find that race influences decisions to arrest or the severity of punishment (although others find that race doesn't matter). Even where racial bias is detected, though, it is a much weaker predictor of police or court decision making when compared with offense seriousness and prior record. In other words, the quality of the *act* is a more important determinant of whether or not the police make an arrest or whether a person is sentenced to prison.[97]

The central argument in labeling theory is that the stigmatizing effect of arrest or other formal action will increase (amplify) future criminal behavior. As noted with respect to deterrence theory (Chapter 3), arrest alone appears to have little effect on future behaviors. If anything, there is some evidence that arrest (in certain circumstances) decreases future crime. Aside from criminal justice actions, commentators have noted that "hitting bottom" can cause people to change their ways for the better.[98] For instance, admitting a problem (and accepting the label of "alcoholic" or "addict") is the first step in self-help groups like Alcoholics and Narcotics Anonymous.

LINK Deterrence (Chapter 3) and labeling theory make opposite predictions regarding the effect of criminal justice actions on future behavior. Deterrence theorists argue that formal intervention will reduce future offending, while labeling theorists argue that formal intervention will amplify criminal behavior.

The bulk of research indicates that the same factors (e.g., delinquent peers, poor bonds, personality traits, parenting behavior) that produce early (primary) deviance also predict later delinquency and crime regardless of whether a person has been officially labeled. The lack of empirical support for labeling theory does not mean that labels or official action *never* produce negative consequences (including more crime). It is clear, though, the label itself is much less important than other factors. As Cullen and Agnew note, "Labeling theory wishes to pretend that being raised in criminogenic conditions for 10, 15, or 20 years . . . pale in comparison to the effects, albeit over a more limited time, of being arrested and perhaps jailed."[99]

The most visible supporters of labeling theory (e.g., Becker, Schur, Lemert) later argued that labeling was never meant to be a "theory" of criminal behavior. Rather, they portrayed the perspective as a way to "sensitize" criminologists to issues regarding the effects of criminal justice actions.[100] In that respect, labeling theorists did call attention to issues that had been neglected in the study of crime.

Policy Implications of Labeling Theory

Labeling theory tells a story with an ironic twist. In trying to prevent crime, the criminal justice system actually produces or promotes more crime. As seen, however, this contention has not been empirically supported. Another irony is that despite a lack of empirical support, labeling was very popular for a brief period and influenced many policymakers. The policy implication of labeling theory is relatively easy to identify: Do not intervene in most matters of juvenile delinquency whenever possible. As Edwin Schur phrased it, engage in "radical non-intervention."[101]

Labeling theorists, for example, condemned the sanctioning by juvenile courts of status offenses — acts committed by juveniles that would be considered crimes if committed by adults (e.g., running away, truancy). Schur maintained that these are moral judgments that make a bad situation worse. A runaway (primary deviation), placed in a juvenile institution, can become a burglar (secondary deviation) because of the labeling process.[102] In 1974, Congress enacted the Juvenile Justice and Delinquency Prevention Act, which appeared to follow the policy prescription of labeling theory. The act called for the deinstitutionalization of status offenders and encouraged states to remove status offenses from the general category of delinquency. During this time, **diversion programs** be-

came very popular. These are programs designed to divert offenders away from the formal juvenile justice processing to programs run by other entities (social services).[103] Although interest in these programs lapsed in the 1980s, many are still around.

Extensions of Labeling Theory

Although interest in the labeling perspective has declined dramatically in the past 30 years, some scholars continue to test variations of labeling theory. Recent tests tend to portray labeling as having a much more minor role and to focus on the effect of informal labels. One study found that some parents are quicker to negatively label their children than others, regardless of their children's actual behavior. Further, these labels do predict (although weakly) the child's future delinquency.[104] Other theorists have attempted to find middle ground between deterrence theory and labeling theory.

Labeling theory suggests that official sanctions will magnify delinquency, while deterrence theory suggests the opposite. In his book *Crime, Shame, and Reintegration*, Australian criminologist John Braithwaite suggests that both perspectives may be partially correct. Braithwaite argues that effective punishment shames an offender, but does so in a reintegrative manner (e.g., hate the sin but love the sinner).[105] He points to cultures such as Japan, where ceremonies both shame offenders and recertify them as members of society after the shaming is complete. In contrast, punishment that stigmatizes creates societal outcasts, who are more prone to future criminal behavior.

Lawrence Sherman arrived at a similar conclusion from his observations of policing. Like Braithwaite, Sherman argues that sanctioning might produce different effects. He suggests that police sanctions can produce defiance (escalation in offending), deterrence (decrease in offending), or be irrelevant.[106] Both police behavior and social bonds determine an individual's response. Rude and/or discriminatory police action, for example, produces defiance rather than deterrence. As noted in the discussion of deterrence theory, sanction is more likely to deter offenders if they are socially bonded to society (e.g., have a good job).

These new twists on labeling theory (Braithwaite in particular) have supported the emerging concept of **restorative justice**. Restorative justice is envisioned by many as an alternative way to handle delinquent and criminal behavior.[107] The gist of

Restorative Justice

Consider the following scenario. A criminal smashes a window in a garage and steals $800 worth of possessions. The police apprehend the offender — he is charged with burglary and sentenced to six months in jail. A restorative justice advocate would ask, "What has been accomplished?" The victim has not been repaid the $800, and the offender will be released from jail, having never directly faced his victim. In addition, he probably never will have received treatment, counseling, or rehabilitation.

Restorative justice is a broad, ambitious philosophy regarding the best way to view and react to criminal offenses. Perhaps the easiest way to understand this philosophy is to compare it with the present criminal justice system. In the criminal justice system, crimes are considered offenses against the state, and the victim is only minimally involved in the sanctioning process. The offender is held accountable for their actions through some form of punishment (e.g., probation, prison, jail). In the restorative justice model, the victim is central to the process, and the focus of all proceedings is to repair the harm caused by the crime to the victim and community. Thus, accountability revolves around repairing harm and directly addressing the victim.

This philosophy stems from theory and research on the labeling and deterrence perspectives. In some ways, it is a compromise between the two theories. In restorative justice, perpetrators of crime are held accountable, but within a format that keeps them connected to the community. Offenders are also "shamed," in a personal and meaningful way, by community members and victims, as opposed to an impersonal criminal justice system. This follows empirical studies that suggest *informal* control is a more effective deterrent than formal control. Restorative justice programs include:

- Victim-offender mediation: The offender meets with the victim to discuss the offense and ways in which the harm can be repaired. The victim has the opportunity to ask questions of the offender and to describe how they have been affected by the incident. The mediation can also include family members of the offender.

- Restitution: Offenders literally pay back victims for the damage they caused.

- Sentencing circles: Members of the community, in concert with the victim, come up with a plan to restore the harm caused by an offense.

With regard to the opening scenario, restorative programming might include a face-to-face meeting between the owner of the garage and the offender, repayment of monetary damages, and a sentence agreed upon by the victim and members of the community.

Evaluations of restorative justice programs thus far are mixed. Programs such as victim-offender mediation generally increase both victim and offender satisfaction with the process. There is also some evidence that restorative justice programming can reduce criminal behavior. Despite this positive evidence, the restorative justice approach is not without criticism. Skeptics point out that restorative programming is limited, because it depends on voluntary participation from victims, offenders, and the community. In particular, for many offenses (e.g., rape), the victim may have no interest in restorative conferencing. Others worry that restorative programming might funnel money away from rehabilitation programs that have a better track record of success in reducing recidivism.

Despite this criticism, the popularity of the restorative justice approach has increased over the past two decades. As restorative programs spread, they will continue to generate empirical research. Ultimately this research has the potential to inform criminological theory. To the extent that mediation, shaming, and other restorative programs "work," they support the underlying theoretical concepts such as Braithwaite's reintegrative shaming.

Sources: Gordon Bazemore and Mark Umbreit, "Rethinking the Sanctioning Function of the Juvenile Court: Retributive or Restorative Responses to Juvenile Crime," *Crime and Delinquency* 41 (1995): 296–316; Edmund F. McGarrell, "Restorative Justice Conferencing as an Early Response to Young Offenders," *Juvenile Justice Bulletin* (Washington, DC: Office of Juvenile Justice and Delinquency Prevention, 2001); Jeff Latimer, Craig Dowden, and Danielle Muise, "The Effectiveness of Restorative Justice Practices: A Meta-Analysis," *Research and Statistics Division Methodological Series* (Ottawa: Department of Justice Canada, 2001).

this philosophy is that the goal of the criminal justice system should be to repair the harm created by the offense. The approach emphasizes victim-offender mediation, where crime victims have an opportunity to meet with offenders. The concept of restorative justice is featured in **Theory in Action: Restorative Justice**.

Conclusion

In this chapter, three general perspectives on delinquency and crime are examined. All three share the assumption that the deviant behavior is the result of individuals interacting with social institutions (family, criminal justice system, peer groups) over time. The three types of theories discussed in this chapter and summarized in **TABLE 7-3**. Social control theories and social learning theories both point to the importance of socialization. Control theories focus on inadequate socialization; that is, crime occurs because direct, indirect, or internal controls have not been properly established. Social learning theory suggests that delinquency results when individuals are socialized toward the wrong set of norms, attitudes, and behaviors. Each of these perspectives has generated a good deal of empirical support. Because they both focus on the role of learning, these perspectives have a great deal in common.

In some respects, labeling theory also focuses on socialization. Through interactions with the criminal justice system, individuals are socialized to accept their delinquent identity. The classic labeling explanation is not strongly supported by research. Revisions of this perspective (e.g., informal labeling, reintegrative shaming) may prove more promising. As noted, labeling theory had a clear policy impact on the juvenile justice system during the 1970s.

TABLE 7-3

Summary of Social Process Theories

Theory and Author(s)	Central Ideas	Policy Implications
Laws of Imitation: Gabriel Tarde	Criminals learn their behavior from other persons and imitate them. The law of imitation explains criminality as a function of association with criminal types. In imitation, the individual selects a role model and fashions behavior after that model. The three laws of imitation are fashion, custom, and insertion.	↑
Differential Association: Edwin Sutherland	Criminal behavior is learned through communication within intimate personal groups. A person becomes delinquent when exposure to law-breaking attitudes is greater than exposure to law-abiding attitudes. Learning criminal behavior includes both techniques of committing crime and rationalizations and attitudes.	Use the principles of learning to: • reduce access to delinquent peers • confront and change anti-social attitudes • change the balance of reinforcement so that it supports prosocial behavior
Social Learning Theory: Ronald Akers	Incorporates psychological learning principles (reinforcement and observational learning) into differential association theory. Delinquency is the result of exposure to delinquent role models or delinquent values/attitudes. Reinforcement determines whether delinquency is maintained.	↓
Containment Theory: Walter Reckless	Certain individuals who are exposed to criminal influences do not turn to crime or delinquency because they are insulated. The primary insulator is favorable self-concept.	Improve self-concept
Social Bond Theory: Travis Hirschi	Emphasizes indirect control. Individuals bonded to society are less likely to engage in delinquency. Elements of the social bond include attachment, commitment, involvement, and belief.	Increase attachment to school and parents. The Seattle Social Developmental Project is one example.
Low Self-Control Theory: Travis Hirschi and Michael Gottfredson	Emphasizes internal (self) control. Effective parenting (use of operant conditioning) produces self-control in children. Levels of self-control crystallize during early childhood and remain stable thereafter.	Train parents to effectively socialize their kids (consistent discipline)
Age-Graded Theory of Informal Social Control: Robert Sampson John Laub	At different stages in life, different forms of control are more or less important. Direct parental controls, attachment to parents, and commitment to schools are important during adolescence. During adulthood, attachment to a spouse and holding a quality job help form an adult social bond.	Similar to Hirschi's social bond theory for adolescence. In adulthood, job opportunities are important.
Labeling Theory: Frank Tannenbaum, Edwin Lemert Howard Becker	Suggests that formal intervention with delinquents actually leads to an escalation in delinquency. This happens because youth come to define themselves as "delinquents."	Radical nonintervention diversion programs
Reintegrative Shaming: John Braithewaite	The effect of formal punishment (e.g., arrest, court) on a person depends upon how they are punished. Punishment that is both "shaming" and reintegrative will reduce future crime. Punishment that is stigmatizing will increase future crime.	Restorative justice

WRAP UP

Jerry "the Tire Iron" Liederbach

Jerry "the Tire Iron" Liederbach is a purely fictional character. Nevertheless, the PSI excerpts presented in this scenario are not particularly outlandish. A review of any case file might produce similar findings. The facts in Jerry's file might fit any number of process theories, although particular facts seem to fit some theories better than others. Take, for example, Hirschi's social bond theory. Jerry appears to have a poor relationship with his mother, and his father is deceased. This suggests that Jerry's "attachment" is probably weak. Jerry is a school drop out and he lacks stable employment. In other words, his commitment (e.g., stake in society) is also poor. Finally, Jerry's attitudes toward his victim and toward crime generally indicate weak belief in the moral validity of the law. What would Hirschi make of Jerry's delinquent peers? Probably not much — Hirschi argues that while delinquents may attract each other, they do not cause each other to engage in crime. As you might imagine, Ronald Akers would have a different perspective on this issue. This is critical because theories have policy implications — they identify targets for change. Would separating Jerry from his "drug-abusing troublemaker" friends reduce his odds of reoffending? The answer depends upon which theorist you ask.

Chapter Spotlight

- Process theories focus on the interplay between the individual and society. They focus on how society (e.g., family, peers, religion) shapes individuals over time.

- The differential association/social learning tradition focuses on improper socialization. People learn values, attitudes, and behaviors that are consistent with violating the law. Edwin Sutherland believed that crime was learned through a process of communication within intimate personal groups. Ronald Akers extended this theory by specifying the learning mechanics (e.g., imitation, differential reinforcement) involved in this process.

- Research consistently reveals that delinquent peer associations and antisocial attitudes are among the strongest correlates of crime. Critics question whether these relationships are causal. For example, they point out that like-minded delinquents will attract each other as companions.

- Theories of informal social control suggest that crime results from inadequate socialization. Control theorists ask the question, "Why don't we all engage in criminal behavior?" Their answer, of course, is that we are controlled through our relationships with others in society.

- There are three basic forms of informal social control: direct control, indirect control, and internal control.

- Travis Hirschi's social bond theory and Sampson and Laub's age-graded theory both emphasize indirect control. To the extent that individuals have formed a societal bond, they will refrain from crime because they are unwilling to risk breaking this bond.

- Gottfredson and Hirschi's general theory of crime implicates both direct and internal control. In this theory, effective parenting (direct control) produces, over time, self-control (internal control).

- Informal control theories have garnered significant empirical support. In particular, measures of direct parental control (e.g., supervision, discipline) consistently predict delinquency. There is also some evidence that adult bonds reduce criminality, even among those with a history of offending.

- Labeling theorists argue that formal punishment might actually amplify future offending. Youths who are arrested and brought to court are stigmatized as "deviant." To the extent that they believe this, they may modify their behavior to fit the label.

- Many criminologists are critical of labeling theory. There is little empirical evidence to support the proposition that arrest or incarceration increases future crime. Further, by the time many youths are first arrested, they have already established a pattern of chronic antisocial behavior.

Putting It All Together

1. Compare any two social control theories of crime. What type of control (direct, indirect, internal) do they emphasize? Are the policy implications similar or different?

2. In "You Are the Criminologist: Jerry "the Tire Iron" Liederbach," there are host of factors that may have caused Jerry to engage in crime. Identify the theory (e.g., learning, informal control, labeling) that relates closest to each potential "cause."

3. Discuss the role of insulation in your own life as it applies to your own socialization process. How might this concept have contributed to your being a college student rather than a prisoner on death row?

4. What are the major criticisms of the labeling perspective?

5. Discuss the following statement: "It's not the quality of the act that accounts for the deviancy but rather the application of sanctions by those in power."

6. Discuss the assumption about human nature made by control theories and social learning theories. Which assumption do you think is more accurate?

Key Terms

adult social bonds An extension of Hirschi's social control theory from adolescence to adulthood. Adult social bonds include quality marriage and quality employment. They are a form of indirect control (something risked in order to engage in crime).

diversion programs Programs designed to divert juveniles away from official juvenile justice processing. A policy derived largely from labeling theory.

dramatization of evil Phrase coined by Frank Tannenbaum to characterize the process whereby the primary deviance of certain people is singled out and labeled as "bad."

informal social control The perspective that inadequate or incomplete socialization leads to criminal behavior.

inner containment A form of internal control (good self-concept) from Walter Reckless' containment theory.

labeling The perspective that a change in a person's self-concept, caused by criminal justice actions, may increase criminal behavior.

laws of imitation An early form of social learning theory. Gabriel Tarde identified three laws to explain how criminals learned to engage in crime.

looking-glass self The idea that self-concept is formed based on how other people respond to and react toward a person.

low self-control The key form of internal control in Gottfredson and Hirschi's "general theory of crime." The authors believe that effective parenting produces self-control in children.

moral entrepreneurs Describes individuals (in the context of labeling theory) who seek to pass laws that prohibit particular behaviors.

outer containment A form of indirect control (supervision) from Walter Reckless' containment theory.

primary deviance Term that describes deviant behavior that occurs prior to any official reaction. Labeling theorists portray primary deviance as sporadic and relatively unimportant.

restorative justice A general philosophy that the proper role of the criminal justice system is to repair the harm caused by an offense. Victim-offender mediation is a central program in this perspective.

Seattle Social Developmental Project (SSDP) A project that implements many of the policy implications from the social control theory in an attempt to prevent childhood aggression and delinquency. The project attempts to increase direct control over youth, as well as build attachment to parents and teachers and a commitment to education.

secondary deviance Deviance that is caused by the adoption of a delinquent self-concept. Without an official reaction to crime, secondary deviance would not be possible.

social bond From Hirschi's control theory. The social bond ties individuals to society, so that they are not free to engage in crime. Elements of the bond include attachment, commitment, involvement, and belief.

social learning The perspective that socialization toward the *wrong* norms and values produces criminal behavior.

socialization The gradual process whereby a person learns the "proper" way to live, including the norms and values that guide human behavior.

symbolic interactionism A general perspective within sociology that emphasizes communication through symbolic labels and gestures.

techniques of neutralization Common excuses for delinquency identified by Sykes and Matza. These excuses neutralize the guilt associated with criminal behavior. This represents one of the first attempts to measure Sutherland's concept of "definitions favorable to law violation."

theory of differential association Edwin Sutherland's influential learning theory. He proposed that crime is learned in intimate groups through communication.

Notes

1. Wikiquote, "Napoleon Bonaparte," available at http://en.wikiquote.org/wiki/Napoleon_Bonaparte, accessed November 3, 2005.
2. Travis Hirschi, *Causes of Delinquency* (Berkeley, CA: University of California Press, 1969): 34.
3. Piers Beirne, "Between Classicism and Positivism: Crime and Penalty in the Writing of Gabriel Tarde," *Criminology* 25 (1987): 785–819.
4. Robert Trojanowicz, *Juvenile Delinquency* (Englewood Cliffs, NJ: Prentice Hall, 1973).
5. Robert Martin, Robert J. Mutchnick, and W. Timothy Austin, *Criminological Thought: Pioneers Past and Present* (New York: Macmillan, 1990): 147.
6. Gwynn Nettler, *Explaining Crime* (New York: McGraw-Hill, 1984).
7. Mikkel Borch-Jacobsen, *The Freudian Subject* (Stanford, CA: Stanford University Press, 1988): 266.
8. Hermann Mannheim, *Pioneers in Criminology* (Montclair, NJ: Patterson-Smith, 1972).
9. Mannheim, 1972, 295.
10. Albert Bandura, "The Social Learning Perspective: Mechanisms of Aggression," in Hans Toch, ed. *Psychology of Crime and Criminal Justice* (Prospect Heights, IL: Waveland, 1979).
11. J. Robert Lilly, Francis T. Cullen, and Richard A. Ball, *Criminological Theory: Context and Consequences,* 3rd ed. (Thousand Oaks, CA: Sage, 2002): 38–39.
12. Edwin H. Sutherland and Donald R. Cressy, *Principles of Criminology,* 5th ed. (Chicago, J.B. Lippincott, 1955): 84–85.
13. Sutherland and Cressy, 1955, 77–79.
14. Francis T. Cullen and Robert Agnew, *Criminological Theory: Past to Present* (Los Angeles: Roxbury, 2003): 112.
15. Mark S. Gaylord and John F. Galliher, *The Criminology of Edwin Sutherland* (New Brunswick, NJ: Transaction Books, 1988).
16. John H. Laub, "The Lifecourse of Criminology in the United States: The American Society of Criminology 2003 Presidential Address," *Criminology* 42 (2004): 1–26.
17. Robert L. Burgess and Ronald L. Akers, "A Differential Association Reinforcement Theory of Criminal Behavior," *Social Problems* 14 (1966): 128–147.
18. Ronald L. Akers, *Deviant Behavior: A Social Learning Approach,* 3rd ed. (Belmont, CA: Wadsworth, 1985).
19. Ronald L. Akers and Christine S. Sellers, *Criminological Theories: Introduction, Evaluation, and Application,* 4th ed. (Los Angeles: Roxbury, 2004): 85–89.
20. Akers and Sellers, 2004, 85.
21. Akers and Sellers, 2004, 89–90.
22. Ronald L. Akers, Marvin D. Krohn, Lonn Lanza-Kaduce, and Marcia Radosevich, "Social Learning and Deviant Behavior: A Specific Test of a General Theory," *American Sociological Review* 44 (1979): 636–655.
23. William F. Skinner and Anne M. Fream, "A Social Learning Analysis of Computer Crime Among College Students," *Journal of Research in Crime and Delinquency* 34 (1997): 495–518; Jacqueline Monroe, "Getting a Puff: A Social Learning Test of Adolescent Smoking," *Journal of Child and Adolescent Substance Abuse* 13 (2004): 71–83; Fin Aage Esbensen and Elizabeth Piper Deschenes, "A Multisite Examination of Youth Gang Membership: Does Gender Matter?" *Criminology* 36 (1998): 799–827.
24. Thomas L. Winfree, Teresa Vigil-Backstrom, and G. Larry Mays, "Social Learning Theory, Self-Reported Delinquency, and Youth Gangs: A New Twist on a General Theory of Crime and Delinquency," *Youth and Society* 26 (1994): 147–177.
25. Gresham Sykes and David Matza, "Techniques of Neutralization: A Theory of Delinquency," *American Sociological Review* 22 (1958): 664–670.
26. Richard C. Hollinger, "Neutralizing in the Workplace: An Empirical Analysis of Property Theft and Production Deviance, *Deviant Behavior* 12 (1991): 169–202.

27. Ken Levi, "Becoming a Hit Man: Neutralization in a Very Deviant Career, *Urban Life* 10 (1981): 47–63.

28. John E. Hamlin, "The Misplaced Role of Rational Choice in Neutralization Theory," *Criminology* 26 (1988): 425–438.

29. Mark Warr, *Companions in Crime: The Social Aspects of Criminal Conduct* (Cambridge: Cambridge University Press, 2002): 40.

30. Ibid.

31. Dana L. Haynie, "Friendship Networks and Delinquency: The Relative Nature of Peer Delinquency," *Journal of Quantitative Criminology* 18 (2002): 99–134.

32. Richard E. Johnson, Anastasios C. Marcos, and Stephen J. Bahr, "The Role of Peers in the Complex Etiology of Adolescent Drug Use," *Criminology* 25 (1987): 323–340.

33. Ruth Kornhauser, *Social Sources of Delinquency: An Appraisal of Analytical Models* (Chicago: University of Chicago Press, 1978).

34. Mark Warr, "Age, Peers, and Delinquency," *Criminology* 31 (1993): 17–40.

35. Delbert S. Elliott and Scott Menard, "Delinquent Friends and Delinquent Behavior: Temporal and Development Patterns," in J. David Hawkins, ed., *Delinquency and Crime: Current Theories* (New York: Cambridge University Press).

36. Ronald L. Akers, "Social Learning and Social Structure: Reply to Sampson, Moorish, and Krohn," *Theoretical Criminology* 3 (1999): 477–493.

37. Peter B. Wood, John K. Cochran, and Betty Pfefferbaum, "Sensation-Seeking and Delinquent Substance Use: An Extension of Learning Theory," *Journal of Drug Issues* 25 (1995): 173–193.

38. D. A. Andrews, "Some Experimental Investigations of the Principles of Differential Association Through Deliberate Manipulations of the Structure of Service Systems," *American Sociological Review* 45 (1980): 448–462.

39. Frank S. Pearson, Douglas S. Lipton, Charles M. Cleland, and Dorline S. Yee, "The Effects of Behavioral/Cognitive Programs on Recidivism," *Crime and Delinquency* 48 (2002): 476–496.

40. Ivan F. Nye, *Family Relationships and Delinquent Behavior* (New York: Wiley, 1958).

41. Walter Reckless, "A New Theory of Delinquency and Crime," *Federal Probation* 25 (1961): 42–46.

42. Walter Reckless, *The Crime Problem* (New York: Appleton Century Crofts, 1967).

43. Walter Reckless, Simon Dinitz, and Barbara Kay, "The Self Component in Potential Delinquency and Potential Nondelinquency," *American Sociological Review* 25 (1957): 566–570; Walter Reckless, Simon Dinitz, and Ellen Murray, "Self Concept as an Insulator Against Delinquency," *American Sociological Review* 21 (1956): 744–756.

44. Simon Dinitz, Frank R. Scarpitti, and Walter C. Reckless, "Delinquency Vulnerability: A Cross Group and Longitudinal Analysis," *American Sociological Review* 27 (1962): 515–517.

45. J. D. Orcutt, "Self-Concept and Insulation Against Delinquency: Some Critical Notes," *Sociological Quarterly* 2 (1980): 381–390.

46. Walter Reckless and Simon Dinitz, *The Prevention of Juvenile Delinquency* (Columbus: The Ohio State University Press, 1972).

47. Martin, Mutchnick, and Austin, 1990, 185–186.

48. Travis Hirschi, *Causes of Delinquency* (Berkeley: University of California Press, 1969).

49. Hirschi, 1969, 1–14.

50. Ibid.

51. Marvin D. Krohn and James L. Massey, "Social Control and Delinquent Behavior: An Examination of the Elements of the Social Bond," *The Sociological Quarterly* 21 (1980): 529–543.

52. Robert Agnew, "Social Control Theory and Delinquency: A Longitudinal Test," *Criminology* 23 (1985): 47–61; Robert Agnew, "A Longitudinal Test of Social Control Theory and Delinquency," *Journal of Research in Crime and Delinquency* 28 (1991): 126–156.

53. Kimberly Kemph Leonard and Scott Decker, "The Theory of Social Control: Does it Apply to the Very Young?" *Journal of Criminal Justice* 22 (1994): 89–105.

54. Daniel S. Nagin and Raymond Paternoster, "Personal Capital and Social Control: The Deterrence Implications of a Theory of Individual Differences in Criminal Offending," *Criminology* 32 (1994): 581–606.

55. Sheldon Glueck and Eleanor Glueck, *Predicting Delinquency and Crime* (Cambridge, MA: Harvard University Press, 1959); Edward Wells and Joseph H. Rankin, "Direct Parental Controls and Delinquency," *Criminology* 26 (1988): 263–285.

56. Hirschi, 1969, 141.

57. Denise Kandel and Mark Davies, "Friendship Networks, Intimacy, and Illicit Drug Use in Young Adulthood: A Comparison of Two Competing Theories," *Criminology* 29 (1991): 441–469.

58. Josine Junger Tas, "An Empirical Test of Social Control Theory," *Journal of Quantitative Criminology* 8: 9–28; Kandel and Davies, 1991.

59. Colin Baier and Bradley R. Wright, "If You Love Me, Keep My Commandments: A Meta-analysis of the Effect of Religion on Crime," *Journal of Research in Crime and Delinquency* 38 (2001): 3–21.

60. Byron R. Johnson, De Li Spencere, David B. Larson, and Michael McCullough, "A Systematic Review of the Religiosity and Delinquency Literature," *Journal of Contemporary Criminal Justice* 16 (2000): 32–52.

61. Michael Gottfredson and Travis Hirschi, *A General Theory of Crime* (Palo Alto, CA: Stanford University Press, 1990).

62. Gottfredson and Hirschi, 1990, 97–100.

63. Gottfredson and Hirschi, 1990, 90.

64. Travis C. Pratt and Francis T. Cullen, "The Empirical Status of Gottfredson and Hirschi's General Theory of Crime: A Meta-analysis," *Criminology* 38 (2000): 931–964.

65. Pratt and Cullen, 2000, 948–949.

66. James D. Unnever, Francis T. Cullen, and Travis C. Pratt, "Parental Management, ADHD, and Delinquent Involvement: Reassessing Gottfredson and Hirschi's General Theory," *Justice Quarterly* 20 (2003): 471–500.

67. Pratt and Cullen, 2000, 951.

68. D. A. Andrews and James Bonta, *The Psychology of Criminal Conduct*, 2nd ed. (Cincinnati, OH: Anderson, 1998): 114.

69. Robert J. Sampson and John H. Laub, *Crime in the Making: Pathways and Turning Points Through Life* (Cambridge, MA: Harvard University Press, 1993).

70. Sampson and Laub, 1993, 145–156.

71. Julie D. Horney, D. Wayne Osgood, and Ineke Haen Marshall, "Criminal Careers in the Short-Term: Intra-Individual Variability in Crime and Its Relation to Local Life Circumstances." *American Sociological Review* 60 (1995): 655–673.

72. Francis T. Cullen, "Social Support as an Organizing Concept for Criminology: Presidential Address to the Academy of Criminal Justice Sciences." *Justice Quarterly* 11 (1994): 527–559.

73. Francis T. Cullen, John P. Wright, and Mitchell B. Chamlin, "Social Support and Social Reform: A Progressive Crime Control Agenda," *Crime and Delinquency* 45 (1999): 188–207.

74. Cullen, Wright, and Chamlin, 1999, 192–193.

75. John P. Wright and Francis T. Cullen, "Parental Efficacy and Delinquent Behavior: Do Control and Support Matter?" *Criminology* 39 (2001): 677–736.

76. Mitchell B. Chamlin and John K. Cochran, "Social Altruism and Crime," *Criminology* 35 (1997): 203–227.

77. Travis Hirschi, "Crime and Family Policy," in Ralph A. Weisheit and Robert G. Culbertson, eds., *Juvenile Delinquency: A Justice Perspective* (Prospect Heights, IL: Waveland Press, 1990).

78. J. David Hawkins, Richard F. Catalano, Diane M. Morrison, Julie O'Donnell, Robert D. Abbott, and L. Edward Day, "The Seattle Social Developmental Project: Effects of the First Four Years on Protection Factors and Problem Behaviors," in Joan McCord and Richard E. Tremblay, eds., *Interventions from Birth Through Adolescence* (New York: Guilford Press, 1992).

79. J. David Hawkins, Richard F. Catalano, Rick Kosterman, Robert Abbott, and Karl G. Hill, "Preventing Adolescent Health — Risk Behaviors by Strengthening Protection During Childhood," *Archives of Pediatric and Adolescent Medicine* 153 (1999): 226–234.

80. Terrance P. Thornberry, "Towards an Interactional Theory of Delinquency," *Criminology* 25 (1987): 863–891.

81. Lilly, Cullen, and Ball, 2002, 116–117.

82. Howard Becker, *The Outsiders: Studies in the Sociology of Deviancy* (New York: Free Press, 1963).

83. Stephen Phol, *Images of Deviance and Social Control: A Sociological History* (New York: McGraw-Hill, 1985).

84. Becker, 1963, 9.

85. Lilly, Cullen, and Ball, 2002, 116–117.

86. Charles Horton Cooley, *Human Nature and Social Order* (New York: Scribner, 1902).

87. Robert K. Merton, *Social Theory and Social Structure* (Glencoe, IL: Free Press, 1957).

88. Akers and Sellers, 2004, 139.
89. Edwin M. Lemert, *Human Deviance, Social Problems, and Social Control* (Englewood Cliffs, NJ: Prentice Hall, 1967).
90. Frank Tannenbaum, *Crime in the Community* (Boston: Ginn, 1938).
91. Clayton A. Hartjen, *Crime and Criminalization*, 2nd ed. (New York: Praeger, 1978).
92. Becker, 1963.
93. Ibid.
94. David P. Farrington, Ralph Loeber, and Wilmot B. Van Kammen "Long-Term Criminal Outcomes of Hyperactivity-Impulsivity-Attention Deficit and Conduct Problems in Childhood," in Lee N. Robins and Michael Rutter, eds., *Straight and Devious Pathways from Childhood to Adulthood* (New York: Cambridge University Press, 1990).
95. Edward Sagarin, *Deviants and Deviance* (New York: Praeger, 1975): 129–142.
96. Thomas J. Keil and Gennaro F. Vito, "Race and the Death Penalty in Kentucky Murder Trials: An Analysis of Post-Gregg Outcomes," *Justice Quarterly* 7 (1990): 189–207.
97. Travis C. Pratt, "Race and Sentencing: A Meta-Analysis of Conflicting Empirical Research Results," *Journal of Criminal Justice* 26 (1998): 513–523; Samuel Walker, Cassia Spohn, and Miriam DeLone, *The Color of Justice: Race, Ethnicity, and Crime in America* (Belmont, CA: Wadsworth, 2000).
98. Sagarin, 1975, 146–150.
99. Cullen and Agnew, 2001, 298.
100. See, for example, Howard Becker, *Outsiders: Studies in the Sociology of Deviance*, 2nd ed. (New York: Free Press, 1973).
101. Edwin M. Schur, *Radical Nonintervention: Rethinking the Delinquency Problem* (Englewood Hills, NJ: Prentice Hall, 1973).
102. Ibid.
103. Howard N. Snyder and Melissa Sickmund, "Juvenile Justice: A Century of Change," *Juvenile Justice Bulletin* (Washington, DC: U.S. Department of Justice, 1999).
104. Ross L. Matsueda, "Reflected Appraisals, Parental Labeling, and Delinquency: Specifying a Symbolic Interactionist Theory," *American Journal of Sociology* 97 (1992): 1577–1611.
105. John Braithwaite, *Crime, Shame, and Reintegration* (New York: Cambridge University Press, 1989).
106. Lawrence W. Sherman, "Defiance, Deterrence, and Irrelevance: A Theory of the Criminal Sanction," *Journal of Research in Crime and Delinquency* 30 (1993): 445–473.
107. Gordon Bazemore and Mark Umbreit, "Rethinking the Sanctioning Function of the Juvenile Court: Retributive or Restorative Responses to Juvenile Crime," *Crime and Delinquency* 41 (1995): 296–316.

CHAPTER

8

OBJECTIVES

Understand the difference between a consensus and conflict view of society, and the core themes of critical theories.

Recognize how conflict among different interest groups shapes the content of the law and the operation of the criminal justice system.

Understand the evidence regarding the relationship between race, class, and criminal justice outcomes.

Know how radical criminologists explain the law, criminal justice system, and criminal behavior.

Recognize extensions of radical theory, including peacemaking criminology and left realism.

Appreciate how gender may shape both criminal justice processing and theories of crime.

Link specific critical theories with their policy implications.

Social Conflict and Crime

"Is a person who kills another in a bar brawl a greater threat to society than a business executive who refuses to cut into his profits to make his plant a safe place to work? By any measure of death and suffering the latter is by far a greater danger than the former."

—Jeffrey Reiman[1]

YOU ARE THE CRIMINOLOGIST

What Is a "Serious" Crime?

Consider the following two scenarios:

A. Stephanie Pratt, after being introduced to illicit drugs by her boyfriend, developed a serious addiction to crack cocaine. In a matter of months, she lost her job as a factory worker and went from living in a nice apartment to living on the street. In order to procure money for her drug habit, Stephanie robbed a local gas station, armed with a pistol. During the robbery, the gas station clerk tried to grab the pistol. The gun fired and the gas station clerk was seriously wounded.

B. The Jeffco Seatbelt Company produces seatbelts for automobile manufacturers. In the late 1990s, Jeffco designed a new seatbelt, the "Restrainer," for several SUV models. Late into the production process, engineers at Jeffco discovered that the restrainer model has a critical flaw. Under certain extreme conditions, the new seatbelt design fails and crash-test dummies are thrown through the windshield of the SUV. The engineers notify the top executives at the company who must make a decision about whether to immediately recall this product from auto manufacturers (none of the SUVs have yet reached the public). The executives calculate that if they remain silent, their seatbelt will result in approximately 1000 serious injuries per year, with over half resulting in death. They conclude that even after settling lawsuits from those injured and paying government fines, Jeffco will make more money with the flawed design. The executives take no action and shred all of the engineering documents.

When the two scenarios are compared, who is the more "serious" criminal?

How do you think that the individuals in each scenario should be punished for their acts? Is this different from how they might be punished in the "real world" of criminal justice?

Does the cover-up in the second scenario qualify as murder?

Assuming that scenario B qualifies as a criminal act, who made the most "rational" decision (Stephanie or the executives) to engage in crime?

Introduction

Are the crimes of wealthy individuals and corporate leaders treated with kid gloves compared with typical street crimes? If so, why does this situation exist? The theories in this chapter raise just such questions. Critical approaches to criminology question why certain acts are illegal while others are not (even though they may cause as much or more harm). Furthermore, they note that the criminal justice system only targets certain laws and certain individuals for full enforcement. In seeking to understand the content of the law and the operation of the criminal justice system, critical approaches are quite different from the mainstream theories covered in previous chapters.

In the early 1960s, American criminology was dominated by anomie or strain theories of delinquency and crime. Criminologists such as Cloward and Ohlin argued that broad social reforms, including the reduction of poverty, were necessary to reduce crime. Support for their Mobilization for Youth program and the general "war on poverty" indicated that many agreed with their position. By the 1970s, however, the social context had changed dramatically. The political vision of a "great society" wilted under the reality of the Vietnam War, the Watergate scandal, prison riots, the shootings at Kent State University, and civil rights demonstrations. Criminologists saw that crimes of the powerful (e.g., Watergate, FBI violations of civil rights, crimes against blacks) were ignored, while violations of victimless crimes (e.g., marijuana use, vagrancy) were pursued vigorously. Arguments for increasing support for the poor gave way to the belief that an economic and political system that created these class differences was corrupt beyond saving.[2]

LINK Chapter 6 outlined several anomie (or strain) theories of crime that pointed to the importance of poverty in the genesis of crime.

Labeling theory emerged from this context as a popular explanation of crime. Labeling theorists stated that crime was a social construction and that government intervention only made delinquency worse. Theories that emerged during the 1970s, however, were "much more explicit about the connection between the criminal justice system and the underlying economic order, sometimes condemning the state itself."[3] Different commentators have referred to these theories as *critical criminology* or the *new criminology*. As will soon be noted, these general titles capture a very diverse body of theories including conflict theory, Marxist/radical theory, and feminist criminology.

Despite this diversity, it is possible to identify a number of broad themes that tie these theories together[4]:

1. Inequality and power as central concepts: Power can be based on social class, race, gender, or other factors. The powerful will use their power to control the law and the operation of the criminal justice system.

2. Crime as a political concept: The law is not an objective, agreed-upon list of behaviors that cause the most social damage. Many acts by the powerful that cause damage are not considered criminal.

3. The criminal justice system as serving the interests of those in power: The criminal justice system targets those who lack power and ignores the crimes of those who have power.

4. The solution to crime as the creation of a more equitable society: Criminologists should work to foster social justice by supporting humane policies aimed at preventing harm.

In sum, the focus of critical criminology is much different than mainstream criminology. Until now, the discussed theories sought to explain why people engage in crime or why some groups are more prone to crime than others. The theories in this chapter focus more on the content of the law (What is illegal?) and the actions of the criminal justice system (What laws are enforced?). As will be discovered, some of these theories attempt to explain some forms of criminal behavior. Still, at their core, these theories make predictions about how law is both formed and enforced.

At the heart of critical theory is the belief that the law reflects the outcome of a struggle over power. Prior to this time, the popular view was that the law and its enforcement reflected societal consensus. In the **consensus model**, the law reflects common agreement over the fundamental values held by society; that is, it reflects the interests of the vast majority and the "shared popular viewpoint" in society.[5] Certain acts are prohibited because society generally agrees that this is necessary. Norms against certain behaviors begin as folkways and mores and are eventually codified into law. Law is a mechanism to resolve conflicting interests and maintain order. Here, the state is a value-neutral entity. Lawmakers resolve conflicts peacefully, the police enforce the law, and the courts arbitrate. Any biases that arise are temporary and unintended.[6]

In the **conflict model**, the law is the result of a battle between people or groups that have different levels of power. Control over the state (including the law and the criminal justice system) is the principal prize in the perpetual conflict of society.[7] In that regard, conflict theorists see bias in the criminal justice system as conscious and intentional. Those in power use the legal system to maintain power and privilege; the law and criminal justice system reflect the interests of those who won the power struggle. Further, crime can directly result from the conflict between competing groups in society.

A host of theories assume that conflict is a natural part of social life. Early conflict theories tended to be pluralistic; that is, they portrayed conflict as a result of clashes among many groups. The pluralistic perspective is discussed in this chapter under **conflict theory**. In the 1970s, theories focused on one central conflict: the battle between the very wealthy and the rest of the population. This perspective can be considered Marxist or **radical theory**.

Conflict Theory

George Vold produced the first criminology textbook that prominently featured the conflict perspective. Vold argued that content and enforcement of the law was the result of the values and interests of those in power: "Those who produce legislative majorities win control over the police power and dominate the policies that decide who is likely to be involved in violation of the law."[8] In the 1960s, a number of theorists, including William Chambliss, Richard Quinney, and Austin Turk heightened interest in how conflict shapes law.

Conflict Theory and the Law

As with labeling theorists, conflict theorists argued that mainstream criminology focused too much attention on why people break the law, while ignoring the reasons that certain acts are illegal. As Chambliss put it, "Instead of asking, 'Why do some people commit crimes and others do not?' we ask 'Why are some acts defined as criminal while others are not?'"[9] Their answer was that those with power and influence defined the laws in a way that promoted their interests.

> **LINK** A great deal of overlap exists between labeling theory (discussed in Chapter 7) and conflict theories. In particular, both theories argue that the law will be enforced against those in society who lack power.

Within conflict theory, power is derived from a variety of sources. Power can come from membership in a more powerful group based on gender, social class, or race. In the United States, those who are white, male, and wealthy have more power than those who are poor, from a minority group, or female. Power is also equated with "resources," which might include money, organization, or access to the media. There are multiple sources of power and many different groups.[10] The competition among these groups creates a society defined by a continual state of struggle and conflict.[11] Still, many conflict theorists acknowledge that there is a high degree of consensus for some crimes — particularly violent acts such as murder, rape, and robbery. Even here, it is crucial to recognize that there is disagreement over how particular physical acts are defined. If a corporation causes someone's death by selling them an unsafe product or by polluting the air, is this "murder?"[12] The **Headline Crime: The Case Against DuPont's Teflon** box explores this issue in the context of legal action against the makers of the nonstick coating Teflon.

A substantial body of empirical evidence supports the conflict view of law. To be sure, research on public support for laws indicates a great deal of agreement among different segments of society for many crimes. There is also consensus on which crimes are more (violent crime) or less (property crime, drug offenses) serious.[13] Despite this agreement, a substantial amount of conflict also exists. Disagreements are apparent in laws regarding things like public order offenses (e.g., public drunkenness) and the regulation of consensual sex (e.g., prostitution).[14] Even where there is agreement on the law,

there is conflict regarding how individuals who violate the law should be punished.[15]

Few people would dispute the fact that political interest groups shape the criminal law in the United States. The power of interest groups is apparent in a diverse range of issues, including abortion, gun control, pollution laws, and the death penalty. Groups such as the National Rifle Association, the American Association of Retired People, and the National Right to Life pay individuals to lobby members of Congress to push for laws consistent with their values and interests. On a larger scale, conflicts arising from social movements (e.g., the civil rights movement), broad segments of society (e.g., the "religious right"), and political parties (e.g., Republicans versus Democrats) also influence the development of law.[16]

Conflict Theory and the Criminal Justice System

Those with power not only define the law to serve their interests, but also have an impact on the operation of the criminal justice system; that is, they have power over what laws are (or are not) enforced. Within the conflict framework, Austin Turk sought to understand crime through society's au-

Demonstrators gather on the Colorado State Capitol grounds to protest against the National Rifle Association's annual meeting, which took place after shootings at nearby Columbine High School.

 What kind of interest groups would support gun control laws? How do pro-gun control and anti-gun control interest groups derive their power?

The Environmental Protection Agency (EPA) made headlines when it brought legal action against DuPont, the manufacturer of the popular stick-resistant coating called Teflon. The case involves Dupont's failure to notify the EPA of the toxic hazards posed by the chemical (prefluoro-octanoic acid or PFOA) used to make Teflon. Dupont has been producing Teflon at the Washington Works Facility in a small West Virginia town for over 50 years. In the late 1990s, the cattle in a farm near the DuPont facility started to die. The farm owners sued DuPont, claiming the cattle deaths were due to a creek that was contaminated by a DuPont landfill. Later, a class action suit was filed on behalf of 60,000 area residents based on allegations that their drinking water was contaminated with PFOA. This lawsuit yielded a treasure trove of internal DuPont documents, memos, and e-mails that found their way to the EPA.

Among other things, the internal DuPont documents indicate that:

- In 1981, DuPont discovered that one of its employees passed PFOA on to her fetus and two other workers had babies born with birth defects in the eyes and nostrils, similar to those found in lab rats exposed to PFOA. DuPont subsequently moved all female workers from the production area.
- In the early 1980s, DuPont tested wells near the plant and found that they were contaminated with PFOA. The company failed to notify either the community or the EPA.
- By 1991 DuPont had information that the chemical was in water supplies at a level that exceeded the company's exposure guidelines. By DuPont's own guidelines, they could not claim that the level of chemical exposure would have no effect on members of the community.

In accordance with the Toxic Substance Control Act (passed in the 1970s), DuPont was required to notify the EPA of information that indicated substantial public risk. The case against DuPont continues to unfold as scientists try to get a grip on the effects of PFOA on the environment and humans. Researchers have long known that PFOA causes cancer, birth defects, and other physical problems in lab animals. Additional research reveals that the vast majority of humans have absorbed some PFOA in their bodies. There is also some evidence that exposure to PFOA increases cancer rates in humans. Scientists and environmentalists are particularly troubled by the chemical, because it does not break down in the environment; time will not heal contamination. In essence, they believe that DuPont's failure to notify the government gave the chemical a 20-year window to spread without any effort to study the effects. DuPont officials indicate that although they share the concerns about PFOA levels in humans, they did nothing wrong. Further, they claim that this chemical affects humans differently from animals. Nevertheless, the company recently settled the class action suit for over $100 million, a sum that could increase depending on any health problems of those exposed to PFOA. Additionally, the EPA could fine DuPont up to $313 million — over 10 times larger than the maximum fine ever assessed by the agency. To put these numbers in perspective, however, DuPont nets an estimated $200 million per year from sales of Teflon. Since the early 1980s then, DuPont has profited substantially from this product.

Is DuPont's failure to notify the EPA of the hazardous effects of PFOA a serious crime? If so, is the monetary punishment sufficient?

What resources does DuPont have, as opposed to the average citizen, to fight these allegations?

How does this article relate to conflict and/or Marxist theory?

Sources: Legal News Watch, "DuPont Under Fire for Teflon Chemical PFOA," available at http://www.legalnewswatch.com/news_398.html, accessed August 10, 2005; Environmental Working Group, "EPA Finds DuPont Guilty of Withholding Teflon Blood and Water Pollution Studies: Company Faces Fines of Up to $313 Million," available at www.ewg.org/issues/pfcs/tsca8e_teflon/index.php, accessed August 9, 2005.

thority relationships. He suggested that criminologists should focus primarily on the process of *criminalization* or the assignment of criminal status to an individual.[17] In other words, whose behavior is targeted for enforcement? Like labeling theorists, he believes that criminalization may depend less on the particular behavior of people and more on their relationship with authority figures.

TABLE 8-1

Factors Influencing Conflict Between Authority Figures and Law Violators

Factor	Relationship to the Likelihood of Conflict
Organization	Conflict is more likely when those engaging in crime are organized (gangs and syndicate criminals will likely be more resistant to authority).
Sophistication	The probability of conflict increases where the law violator is less sophisticated (a street thug as opposed to a white-collar criminal).
Relative power of enforcers and resisters	Criminalization is more likely when enforcers (police, prosecutors) have substantially more power than resisters. However, some resisters who have little power may be passed over as not being worth the trouble.
The correspondence of cultural and social norms	Cultural norms are "what is expected" (the letter of the law), whereas social norms refer to "what is actually being done" (how laws are actually enforced). When there is congruence between these sets of norms, criminalization is more likely.

Source: Austin T. Turk, *Criminality and Legal Order* (Chicago: Rand McNally, 1969).

Turk devised a number of concepts intended to explain criminalization. **TABLE 8-1** outlines some of his more important ideas. For instance, consider Turk's concepts of organization and sophistication. Criminalization is most likely for an organized but unsophisticated norm resister (e.g., delinquent gang member) than for an organized and sophisticated person (e.g., Mafia member). Turk's theory has recently found some support in research analyzing police-citizen encounters.[18] A 2005 study of data from police observations found that organization and sophistication of the police and suspects significantly predicted overt conflict (use of force).[19]

William Chambliss and Robert Seidman authored another influential conflict-oriented text. The starting point for their analysis was the assumption that as society becomes more complex, dispute resolution will move away from "reconciliation" and toward "rule enforcement."[20] A complex society will therefore depend heavily on sanctioning (police action) to keep order among parties in conflict. In the United States, Chambliss pointed to the dominance of middle-class values. Thus, the middle class could impose their own standards and view of proper behavior upon others in society. Further, the bureaucratic nature of the legal system meant that enforcement of the law would be biased against lower-class people. Bureaucratic agencies tend to maximize the rewards and minimize strains against the organization. As a result, police are expected to avoid enforcing crimes committed by the powerful (which might cause trouble) and focus on crimes of the poor. Those who lack power are less able to successfully resist enforcement.[21]

Research on Race and Criminal Justice Processing

Conflict theory suggests that enforcement of laws will be biased against those who lack power. One way to test this proposition is to see whether the less-powerful groups in society (e.g., racial minorities, the poor) receive harsher treatment from the criminal justice system. In other words, are black offenders more likely to be arrested, prosecuted, and imprisoned than white offenders? A simple inspection of arrest and prison statistics appears to support the conflict perspective. Minorities (especially African-Americans) are overrepresented at every stage of the criminal justice system — from arrest to imprisonment. In 2003, white Americans were incarcerated at a rate of 465 per 100,000. African-Americans had an incarceration rate of roughly 3400 per 100,000, and Hispanics 1200 per 100,000.[22] On the other hand, males are incarcerated at a dramatically higher rate than females — a finding that contradicts conflict theory, because men have more power.

The fact that a particular group is overrepresented in the criminal justice system does not, however, definitively support or refute conflict theory. Many consensus theories predict that minorities or members of the lower class are more likely to be involved in serious forms of criminal behavior. Social disorganization theory (see Chapter 6), for example, predicts that because minorities often live in poverty-stricken, disorganized neighborhoods, they are more likely to engage in crime. Conflict theory, on the other hand, would suggest that differences in arrest and imprisonment are not simply due to differences in criminal behavior. The key issue is whether **extra-legal factors** (e.g., race, class, and gender) have a substantial impact on decision making, regardless of **legal factors** (e.g., offense seriousness and prior record).

At the least, it appears as though legal factors, particularly offense seriousness and prior record, are the strongest predictors of decisions made by the police, prosecutors, and judges.[23] This finding should not come as a shock to anyone. Common sense dictates that someone with prior felony convictions who is caught in the act of armed robbery has a greater risk of arrest and imprisonment than someone with no prior record who gets caught shoplifting. Still, an important issue is whether race, class, or other factors still matter. The vast majority of research in this area focuses on race. This research asks (sticking with the example): "If neither has a prior record, are black and white shoplifters treated equally?"

Answering this type of question requires a multivariate analysis, which statistically controls for (holds constant) legal factors in order to examine factors such as race or class. That is the only way to find out whether the size of the black prison population is due to legitimate factors (e.g., more serious offenses, more severe prior record) or to discrimination.

The research examining race and the criminal justice system is extremely complex and often contradictory. Typically, a study examines official decision making within a jurisdiction, at a particular stage (e.g., arrest decisions, court decisions) of the criminal justice system. The most difficult decision makers to evaluate are the police. Police decisions typically occur out on the streets, and there are no records of individuals who are let go without formal action. To overcome this problem, a number of researchers have directly observed the behaviors of police.

Reiss's 1966 observational study found that race in itself did not influence police decisions to arrest. Black suspects were more likely to be arrested because they were suspected of more serious crimes, were more hostile toward police, and were more likely to have complainants that demanded official action.[24] It is important to remember that hostility toward police does not arise in a vacuum; minority communities are subject to a stronger police presence than other areas. Later studies reached very similar conclusions. A few observational studies, however, have found some evidence of racial bias.[25] An important limitation of this type of research is that police might act differently (and be less biased) simply because they are being observed.

Over the past 20 years, <u>racial profiling</u> (racially biased law enforcement) has become an extremely controversial issue. Many minorities believe that they are pulled over for traffic stops simply because of the color of their skin (i.e., "driving while black"). A great deal of evidence exists that African-Americans are more likely to be stopped, to have their cars searched, and to be ticketed, than would be expected given their numbers in the population.[26] Still, it is difficult to determine the cause of this difference. For example, it could reflect the fact that minorities are more likely to live in high-crime areas that are heavily patrolled by police. This issue promises to be an important research topic in the coming years.

Once a person is arrested, tracking decision making becomes much easier because a paper trail exists. Scholars have examined whether race impacts bail decisions, prosecution decisions (whether to charge or release a suspect), and sentencing decisions (both sentence length and whether or not a person gets prison time). Once again, there are no simple answers. Instead, different studies yield different results. As a starting point, consider Alfred Blumstein's research comparing arrest rates to incarceration rates at a national level. If there were no bias in the criminal justice system, the percentage of blacks arrested should be roughly equal to the percentage of blacks incarcerated. In two separate studies, Blumstein found that a large portion (76% and 80%) of the racial disparity in incarceration rates were due to disparities in arrest rates.[27] Still, incarceration rates were slightly higher for blacks than would be expected given their arrest rates. Further, as the seriousness of the offense decreased, arrest disparities were less important in explaining disparities in black incarceration.

This finding suggests that, as discretion in the criminal justice system increases, blacks find themselves at a disadvantage. In a replication of this study in a single jurisdiction (Pennsylvania), researchers concluded that race differences in arrests accounted for even less (70%) of the race differences in imprisonment.[28] In other words, 30% of the racial differences in incarceration were not due to racial differences in offending. For drug crimes, where discretion is higher, racial differences in offending accounted for only 20% of racial differences in incarceration.[29]

Another approach is to track offenders within a jurisdiction. Joan Petersilia conducted a detailed study of the California criminal justice system based on Offender-Based Transaction Statistics (OBTS).

African-Americans have much higher arrest and incarceration rates than white Americans.

? *How would the conflict perspective account for this fact? What does the empirical evidence indicate?*

more likely to go to prison than white offenders, once legal factors (e.g., prior adult or juvenile history, use of a weapon) were controlled, race differences disappeared. In other words, knowledge of race, independent of legal factors, did not help predict who goes to prison versus who gets probation.[33]

Studies such as this led William Wilbanks to conclude that it was a myth that the criminal justice system is discriminatory. Wilbanks argues that, although some persons in the system may make decisions on the basis of race, there is no *systematic* racial bias in the criminal justice system.[34] Once other factors (e.g., prior record, offense seriousness) are held constant, the effect of race is minimal. Wilbank's position, however, is by no means the final word on this subject. This body of research does not capture, for example, differences in police patrolling.[35] In other words, police presence helps to determine who accumulates a prior record. In that sense, statistically controlling for prior record might mask racial bias in policing.

A final body of empirical research examines the relationship between the presence of a "threatening" social group and measure of punitiveness within a certain geographical area. The <u>racial threat hypothesis</u> — that as minority populations increase relative to the white population, punitive measures will increase — has received some support in the literature.[36] Scholars have documented correlations between the percentage of black citizens and a diverse number of outcome measures, including lynching, the size of police forces, arrest rates, and sentencing practices.[37] For example, McGarrell tested a conflict model of incarceration rates in the United States for 1971, 1980, and 1988. He compared the effects of both social and structural variables and the crime rate. He determined that two variables (percentage of black population and the violent crime rate) were strong and consistent predictors of the incarceration rate.[38] Critics of such research correctly point out, however, that a measure such as "percentage of black citizens" is at best only an indirect measure of "social threat."[39] The research evidence on race criminal justice processing demonstrates, if nothing else, the necessity of considering this problem over time in different jurisdictions, using different research methods.

As should be clear from the preceding, the research on race and the criminal justice system is complex and oftentimes contradictory. On the broad question of whether the system is biased, there is

She found that minority suspects were more likely than whites to be released after arrest. Yet, following a felony conviction, minority offenders were more likely than whites to receive a long prison sentence. These differences held even after controlling for prior record, offense seriousness, previous violence, and probation or parole status.[30]

Additional information from the Rand prisoner survey in California, Texas, and Michigan revealed that minorities *are not* overrepresented in the arrest population compared with the number of crimes that they actually commit, nor are they more likely to be arrested.[31] A similar analysis of court data from Georgia between 1976 and 1982 found that sentencing was equitable.[32] No racial group of offenders was treated more harshly or leniently than others. An analysis of more than 11,000 California offenders convicted of assault, robbery, burglary, theft, forgery, or drug crimes revealed a similar pattern. Although black and Latino offenders were no easy answer. Looking within certain categories of crime or punishment, however, sometimes yields a clear (and disturbing) picture.

Race and the War on Drugs

Conflict theory appears to be particularly relevant to a discussion about the law, race, and the criminal justice system in the context of illicit drugs. The history of legislation against drug use in the United States is in many ways a story of linking particular drugs with a "dangerous" (and powerless) class of citizens. In an effort to portray these drugs as particularly bad, opium was linked to Chinese immigrants and marijuana to Mexicans.[40] In essence, the "drug of choice" of the less-powerful group is criminalized — laws against the particular drug are then enthusiastically enforced.

David Cole summarizes the conflict argument regarding the latest example — crack cocaine[41]:

> Politicians impose the most serious criminal sanctions on conduct in which they and their constituents are least likely to engage. Thus, a predominantly white congress has mandated prison sentences for the possession and distribution of crack cocaine 100 times more severe than the penalties for powder cocaine. African-Americans comprise more than 90% of those found guilty of crack cocaine crimes. By contrast, when white youth began smoking marijuana in large numbers in the 1960s and 1970s, state legislatures responded by reducing penalties. . . .

There is little doubt that police targeted the sale and distribution of crack cocaine throughout the 1980s and 1990s. Not surprisingly, a shift in focus from powder cocaine and other drugs toward crack increased racial disparities in drug arrests. In the 1970s, African-Americans accounted for roughly 20% of drug arrests. By the early 1990s, they made up 40% of all drug arrests.[42] Minorities are about four times as likely to be arrested for drugs as white individuals, even though the vast majority of drug users are white. The primary enemy in the war on drugs appears to have been young black males.[43] Society must recognize that crime and illicit drug use do disproportionately affect minority communities. Criminologist Michael Tonry has argued, though, that the effect of the war on drugs on the black community was a foreseeable tragedy[44]:

> What was clear both then and now is that a program built around education, drug abuse

When crack cocaine spread rapidly though urban areas in the 1980s, legislators across the country responded with harsh penalties for possessing or selling this drug.

? *What impact did this legislative decision have on racial minorities? Could this impact have been prevented?*

treatment, and social programs designed to address the structural, social, and economic conditions that lead to crime and drug abuse would have a much less destructive impact on disadvantaged young blacks than would a program whose primary tactics were the arrest, prosecution, and lengthy incarceration of street-level sellers who are disproportionately black and Hispanic.

Capital Sentencing and Race

Historically, race has also played a role in the imposition of the death penalty in the United States. In *Furman v. Georgia*,[45] a number of the Supreme Court justices raised serious questions about discrimination and arbitrariness in the application of the death penalty. For example, Justice Douglas noted[46]:

> It would seem incontestable that the death penalty inflicted on one defendant is "unusual" if it discriminates against him by reason of his race, religion, wealth, social position, or class, or if it is imposed under a procedure that gives room for the play of such prejudices.

In other words, the death penalty was cruel and unusual because it was applied in a discriminatory manner. Although this decision is the subject of several different interpretations, it prohibited the arbitrary infliction of the death penalty.[47]

At that time, a massive body of research indicated that racial bias clouded the capital-sentencing process. In particular, it clearly demonstrated that blacks were far more likely to receive a death sentence than were whites.[48] Also, it was determined that whites were more likely to have their death sentences commuted to a lesser sentence.[49] Other studies found that capital sentencing was not only based on the race of the killer but also was determined by the race of the victim. For example, one study found that Philadelphia blacks charged with murdering whites were more likely to receive a death sentence than any other offender-victim race combination.[50] This pattern was also present in rape cases — blacks convicted of raping whites were 18 times more likely to attract a death sentence.[51]

This research evidence served as the backdrop for the *Furman* decision — yet, *Furman* did not outlaw the death penalty. Rather, it questioned the results of the unbridled discretion typically at work in the capital-sentencing process. In 1976, the Supreme Court (*Gregg v. Georgia*) approved a new Georgia system. The Supreme Court ruled that Georgia's "guided discretion" statute provided adequate protection against the arbitrary and capricious application of the death penalty. In other words, the Supreme Court concluded that the Georgia process provided adequate protection against racial bias and other arbitrary, extra-legal influences.

The Georgia law had several significant features. First, it required a bifurcated trial. In the first phase of the trial, the jury addressed the issue of guilt or innocence. In the second or sentencing phase, the penalty was decided. Second, the law delimited specific aggravating (and later, mitigating) circumstances that juries would consider during the sentencing phase of the trial. The court would later give broad latitude to the defense regarding what could be introduced in mitigation. Third, the Georgia law required an automatic appeal of all death sentences to the state supreme court. The Court believed that these processes provided sufficient protection for rights of the accused.

Research on capital sentencing conducted following *Gregg* indicates that race is still a dominant factor in the decision to execute. For example, studies of the capital-sentencing process in Florida revealed that blacks who kill whites have the greatest probability of receiving the death penalty.[52] Other studies found evidence of this specific pat-

Thomas Miller-El gained a stay of execution from the U.S. Supreme Court in 2002. He was granted a new trial because of alleged racial discrimination in his first trial.

How prevalent is racial discrimination in the legal system generally, and specifically in death penalty cases?

tern of discrimination in different states, including Arkansas, Georgia, Illinois, Kentucky, Louisiana, Mississippi, New Jersey, North Carolina, Ohio, Oklahoma, South Carolina, Texas, and Virginia.[53] This pattern of racial discrimination was not a function of other factors. For example, cases in which blacks killed whites were not more aggravated or particularly heinous homicides.[54]

This research evidence was the focus of an evaluation synthesis conducted by the U.S. General Accounting Office (GAO).[55] This analysis was required under The Anti-Drug Abuse Act of 1988. Specifically, this legislation called for a study of capital-sentencing procedures to determine if the race of either the victim or the defendant influenced the capital-sentencing process. The GAO uncovered 53 studies of capital sentencing. They excluded those that did not contain empirical data or were duplicative. As a result, 28 studies were judged methodologically sound. Based on their review, the GAO concluded that[56]:

- In 82% of the studies, race of the victim was found to influence the likelihood of being charged with capital murder or receiving the death penalty (especially those who murdered whites).
- The influence of the victim's race was found at all stages of the criminal justice system process. This evidence was stronger at the earlier stages of this process (e.g., prosecutorial decision to seek the death penalty or to proceed to trial rather than plea bargain) than in the later stages.
- Legally relevant variables (e.g., aggravating circumstances, prior record, culpability level, heinousness of the crime, and number of victims) were influential but did not fully explain the reasons for racial disparity in capital sentencing.

The GAO concluded that this evidence represented a strong race-of-victim influence over capital sentencing. It appears that the capital-sentencing process is significantly influenced by race. Blacks who killed whites are more likely to be charged with a capital offense and to receive a death sentence. They are singled out by the capital-sentencing process.

Conflict Theory as an Explanation of Criminal Behavior

As noted earlier, the conflict explanation of the law and criminal justice system suggests that those who have power will make and enforce laws that are in their interests. Several sociologists have used this as a starting point to explain criminal behavior. Criminal conduct may originate when a less-powerful group adheres to their group norms while simultaneously violating those of another group. Basically, behavior that is valued in one group is denounced (and criminalized) by another. All the while, individuals believe they are acting appropriately.

This theme is apparent in the study of 1313 gangs conducted by Frederic Thrasher.[57] He reported the existence of a gang culture whose norms clashed with those of society. One dominant activity was orgiastic behavior: drinking, gambling, smoking, and sex. The values of the gang created an esprit de corps that carried over to all their activities.

LINK This theme is consistent with the subcultural theories discussed in Chapter 6. Critics, of course, question whether such group norms (e.g., value placed on drinking alcohol or partying) are all that different from the norms of society.

Similarly, Sutherland's culture conflict theory stated that the different values present in segments of society could lead an individual to criminal behavior.[58] This basic principle was further developed by Thorsten Sellin. Sellin was primarily concerned with the culture conflict faced by immigrants, not the conflict between specific socioeconomic classes. He proposed that culture conflict was the result of the difference in norms between ethnic groups.[59]

In complex societies like the United States, people from diverse ethnic, cultural, religious, and social backgrounds are living in close proximity to each other, yet they may not accept the values or divergent lifestyles of their neighbors. Moreover, in most social situations, each group has right and wrong ways of behaving. People are socially conditioned by these "conduct norms,"[60] but different groups have different norms. Culture conflict results when these groups meet.

Sellin defined **primary conflict** as that which may arise between two different cultures — again, between an established culture and recent immigrants. Because immigrants bring divergent religious beliefs, norms, and values from their homeland, culture conflict is inevitable. Moreover, what was considered appropriate conduct in the old country may be a crime in the new culture. To illustrate, Sellin cites the Sicilian father in New Jersey who murdered the youth who seduced his daughter. The father expressed surprise at his arrest because he was merely defending his family's honor in the traditional Sicilian fashion. Here, customary behavior in Sicilian society clashed with American definitions of legal behavior.

Another recent example of primary conflict is the use of "Khat" among East African (e.g., Somalia, Ethiopia, Yemen) immigrants. Khat is a stimulant that is legal and culturally accepted in East Africa and the Arabian Peninsula, but illegal in the United States. Khat has created conflict between East African immigrant communities and law enforcement.[61]

More recently, the practice of circumcising females (which can include the removal of the clitoris), still common in some cultures, has been denounced under American law.[62] In such situations, the norms of the dominant culture become the deciding factor in characterizing the incident as crime.

Secondary conflict occurs within a single culture that has different subcultures, each with their own conduct norms. Here, Sellin anticipates the development of subcultural theories in criminology (see Chapter 6). Norm conflict can develop within a single culture when the norms of one subculture come into conflict with another. Sellin considered conduct norms to be universal and common to all forms of society. His theory was criticized, however, for being too narrow in its focus on norms, not people. As history shows, migrant groups are seldom accepted, and this rejection often leads to anomie and resentment. However, as succeeding generations of immigrants are socialized by the dominant culture, family ties as well as old-world cultural norms weaken. In short, Sellin overlooked the fact that heterogeneity must develop in modern complex societies.

George Vold turned the attention of conflict theory toward a class of crimes that were obviously political[63]:

- Crimes resulting from political protest movements (e.g., disorderly conduct arrests from clashing with police)
- Crimes that arise from strife between management and labor unions (e.g., the use of illegal tactics to "break" unions, employee sabotage of factory equipment)
- Crimes that result from attempts to change or upset the caste system that enforces racial segregation (e.g., lynching)

In such situations, Vold argues, "criminality is the normal, natural response of normal, natural human beings struggling in understandably normal and natural situations for the maintenance of the way of life to which they stand committed."[64] In this case, conflict directly produces criminal behavior. Further, criminality depends on which side ultimately wins the conflict. Take, for example, the "Jim Crow laws" enforced by whites. These laws were passed by 19th-century legislatures of the southern states to segregate blacks and maintain a racial caste system. Blacks who violated these laws were seen as criminal; their churches were bombed and their leaders lynched. Ultimately, after the spread of civil rights, the white supremacists who enforced these laws were seen as criminals. In a similar vein, individuals who are a direct threat to a government regime are often branded as dissidents or terrorists and jailed. As power shifts, such criminals may become leaders of a new government.

A Critique of Conflict Theory

Within a certain realm of behaviors, conflict theory appears to have some support, both as a theory of criminal behavior and as a theory of law. There is little disagreement that conflict is a central feature of democratic societies, nor is there argument against the idea that political groups attempt to shape the law in their favor. Conflict can (as in the case of labor strife or abortion protests) directly lead to criminal behavior. Early conflict theorists such as George Vold recognized that conflict theory should not be stretched to account for behaviors or laws that were outside of its scope. Chambliss, for example, points out that in many circumstances, there is no conflict whatsoever. There is wide public consensus that crimes such as murder, assault, and rape should be prohibited by law.[65]

In that sense, conflict theory does not explain the core of the legal code, much of which seems to be agreed on and to benefit society as a whole. Further, the vast amount of delinquent and criminal behavior is not political in nature, nor does it tend to pit one group against another. Rather, victimization studies clearly demonstrate that most crime occurs within the same groups. Minorities generally victimize other minorities; poor people generally victimize other poor people, and so forth. In this regard, conflict theory has been criticized for explaining too little. On the other hand, some criticized the pluralistic model for not going far enough. In the 1970s, many conflict theorists shifted their attention toward one main source of conflict — the distribution of wealth.

Radical Criminology

Over time, many conflict theorists came to believe that conflict results not from a struggle among many groups but from a larger struggle between the very wealthy and the rest of society. Radical (or Marxist) criminologists use Karl Marx's theories of social structure to explain both (1) the nature and extent of crime in society, and (2) the content and enforcement of the criminal law. Although Marx did not address the issue of crime directly, his ideas do spotlight the linkage between capitalism and criminality.

Karl Marx and Crime

Marxist criminology focuses on the conflict among three socioeconomic classes[66]:

Karl Marx wrote extensively about the evils of capitalism. Although he wrote little about crime, his ideas are an integral part of modern radical theories.

? *How do radical theories use Marx's work to explain the content of the criminal law?*

1. the capitalists, who own the means of production and exploit the surplus labor of others
2. the bourgeoisie, who hold salaried and management (i.e., middle-class) positions
3. the proletariat, who comprise the working class

Marxists view the enactment and enforcement of laws as an outgrowth of the conflicts engendered by unequal distribution of wealth, power, and control within a capitalist society. In short, the law enforces the ideology of the capitalist ruling class.

Marx's critique of capitalism is relevant to the study of crime in several ways. Marx saw crime as largely a function of class conflict. The capitalist class owned the means of production — the use and distribution of tools, technical knowledge, and human labor. In addition, it profited from the creation of surplus value — the value of commodities workers produce above what they are paid in wages.[67]

According to Marx, the capitalist economic system is supported by the superstructure of social institutions (e.g., law, education, and politics) that "lend legitimacy to both the class structure and the dominant set of economic relationships underpinning" the structure.[68] They were the foundation of the legal and political structures of the state. In this context, crime became an expression of the individual's struggle against unjust social conditions. Criminals were part of the lumpenproletariat — the dispossessed, unorganized workers' underclass. They did not contribute to the production of goods and services; instead, they made their livelihood from others who did work.[69] Criminal life was a natural reaction by those who were cut off from the fruits of capitalism and brutalized by under- or unemployment. Crime was a product of poverty and the conditions of inequality bred by capitalism. Because crime was the result of an unjust economic system, the only way to prevent crime was to change that system.

Engels and the Social Revolution

Friedrich Engels, Marx's friend, sponsor, and collaborator, directly addressed the issue of crime. To Engels, crime was a form of revolt — too primitive (criminals lacked class consciousness) and unorganized to succeed — waged against the dreadful oppression of the capitalist industrial system. Society was the original offender. It created crime by depriving unfortunates of a place at the "feast of life." Social revolution was the ultimate solution to crime[70]:

> To protect itself against crime, against direct acts of violence, society requires an extensive, complicated system of administrative and judicial bodies, which require an immense labor force. In communist society, we eliminate the contradiction between the individual man and all others, we counterpoise social peace to social war, we put the ax to the root of crime. Crimes against property cease to their own accord where everyone receives what he needs to satisfy his natural and spiritual urges, where social gradations and distinctions cease to exist.

Bonger and Egoistic Capitalism

One of the first Marxist criminologists was Wilhelm Adrian Bonger. He expanded the definition of criminal behavior by viewing crime as an "immoral" act against a prevailing social structure. Bonger stated that unless the act injures the ruling class as well as the subject class, it was unlikely to be punished.[71]

Bonger believed that **altruism** was a defining characteristic of primitive societies: Production was for mutual consumption, not exchange; social solidarity was high. The problem with a capitalist society was that it transformed the basic nature of humankind. Capitalistic societies are characterized by **egoism**: Capitalists produce for themselves and attempt to build a surplus to create a profit. They are not interested in the needs of others. In this manner, capitalism builds social irresponsibility and creates a climate of motivation for crime.

Bonger also considered what he called rich men's crimes: fraudulent bankruptcies, adulteration of food, stock market manipulators, land speculation, and the like. This type of criminal forced the masses to pay more than required for the necessities of life: "What an ordinary criminal does in a small way, they do on a gigantic scale; while the former injures a single person, or only a few, the latter brings misfortune to great numbers."[72]

According to Bonger, the solution was to create a socialist society. Socialism, he claimed, would cure many ills and allow the spirit of altruism to come forward and flourish. He noted, however, that crimes would still be committed by persons with medical or psychiatric problems. Bonger's writings — especially his focus on the crimes of the wealthy, and his suggestion that capitalism corrodes empathy for fellow citizens — are still reflected in modern radical theories.

Rusche and Kirchheimer and Penal Systems

Another early Marxist analysis of crime was offered by George Rusche and Otto Kirchheimer.[73] They examined how a prison system operated in a capitalist state. Until the rise of capitalism, they noted, punishments for criminal behavior were largely determined by one's ability or inability to pay a fine. Thus, they argued, it was only natural that punishments would become more severe as economic conditions worsened. For example, over 72,000 thieves were hanged in England during the reign of Henry VIII. However, when the potential of inmate labor power became apparent, convicts were transported to distant lands to provide more markets for the British Empire instead of being executed. Rusche and Kirchheimer regarded economic conditions as the central issue in penal policy[74]:

The penal system of any given society is not an isolated phenomenon subject only to its own special laws. It is an integral part of the whole social system, and shares its aspirations and its defects. The crime rate can be influenced only if society can offer its members a certain measure of security and to guarantee a reasonable standard of living.

Thus, crime was an outgrowth of unemployment and poor social conditions. Rusche and Kirchheimer argued that imprisonment served as a solution to economic problems once Western society moved from feudalism to capitalism. They concluded that the complex legal systems found in capitalist societies provide only an illusion of security. They do not deal with the root problems of social inequality.

Rusche and Kirchheimer theorized that imprisonment served an important role in capitalistic societies—the regulation of the labor force.[75] In essence, their argument implies that imprisonment should increase when surplus labor (typically measured as using the unemployment rate) is high and decrease when there is a labor shortage. The research findings on this hypothesis are inconsistent. A multivariate analysis of time-series data on imprisonment in the United States from 1948 to 1981 found evidence of an effect of unemployment on prison admissions.[76] However, a historical analysis of the New York State prison system offered little support to Rusche and Kirchheimer's claim that imprisonment is a consequence of the desire to exploit and train captive manufacturing labor.[77] A longitudinal study that investigated the effect of unemployment rates on rates of pretrial jail incarceration in Florida and found no relationship between these variables at either the felony or misdemeanor levels.[78] This finding suggests that Rusche and Kirchheimer overstated this relationship. Pretrial incarceration was not used to control labor surpluses.

The Marxist influence has extended to modern criminology. Radical criminologists argue that the power of the capitalist state depends entirely on its ability to use the criminal justice system to maintain social order. The economic elite define and enforce the law to favor specific interests. The law reflects the unequal distribution of wealth in society and enforces the will of the ruling class. Moreover, they point out, the state is very selective about whom it punishes.

TABLE 8-2

Richard Quinney's Typology of Crime

Type of Crime	Description
Crimes of Domination	
Crimes of control	Felonies and misdemeanors by law enforcement agents against persons accused of crimes (e.g., violations of the civil liberties of citizens).
Crimes of government	Actions by elected and appointed officials of the capitalist state to maintain political control over others (e.g. Watergate, Iran-Contra, warfare, political assassination).
Crimes of economic domination	Corporate crimes (e.g. price fixing, pollution, hazardous work conditions, marketing of unsafe products) that protect and further the accumulation of capital. Organized crime also seeks to perpetuate the capitalist system because it invests some of its profits from illegal goods and services in legitimate businesses.
Social injuries	Denial of basic human rights (e.g. sexism, racism, economic exploitation) that are not typically defined as crime.
Crimes of Accommodation	
Predatory crimes	Crimes such as burglary, robbery, drug dealing that are produced out of a need to survive. These are reproductions of the capitalist system.
Personal crimes	Violent crimes (e.g. murder, rape, robbery) usually directed against members of the same class and pursued by those who have already been brutalized by the capitalist system.
Crimes of resistance	Crimes that are an expression of political consciousness (e.g., the sabotage of factory equipment) directed at the capitalist class.

Source: Richard Quinney, *Class, State, and Crime*, 2nd ed. (New York: Longman, 1980): 56–66.

Richard Quinney: Class, Crime, and the State

Richard Quinney remains one of the most influential radical criminologists in the United States. Quinney's ideas have evolved substantially over time — from conflict theory in the 1960s to radical theory throughout the 1970s and 1980s, and finally to his most recent statements on peacemaking criminology. In his 1977 *Class, State and Crime*, Quinney portrays the criminal justice system as the last supporting prop for a slowly decaying capitalist social order.[79] It controls a population that can no longer be restrained by employment or social services. Of particular interest is Quinney's definition of criminal behavior (see **TABLE 8-2**).

Quinney ties together the work of Marx, Engels, Bonger, and others to characterize most forms of criminal behavior as the result of capitalism. Quinney describes several types of crime committed by capitalists in order to maintain their control over society. Consistent with the radical theory, Quinney argues that law enforcement exists primarily to control members of the lower class. "Crimes of control" result when police violate the civil rights of others (such as police brutality). "Crimes of economic domination" include most forms of white-collar crime (e.g., price fixing, pollution). The capitalist elite also engage in socially injurious behavior, such as the denial of basic human rights (e.g., sexism, racism, economic exploitation) that are not defined as criminal. They are not defined as criminal because the capitalists control the definition of criminal behavior and are unlikely to pass laws against their interests.

Apart from crimes committed by capitalists, Quinney portrays crimes among the lower class as acts of *survival*. Because they are economically exploited, members of the lower class rob, steal, and burgle in order to meet basic needs. Ironically, by exploiting other members of their class, these predatory offenders reproduce the capitalist system. Quinney argues that acts of violence (murder, rape, assault) are a reaction to the brutality of the capitalist system. Ultimately, Quinney advocates the development of a socialist society to halt the abuses of the capitalist state.

Radical Explanations of the Law and the Criminal Justice System

Quinney's work clearly suggests that criminal law and the criminal justice system are used solely as tools to control the lower classes. Considered **instrumental Marxism**, this type of theory argues that the law and criminal justice system are always instruments to be used by the capitalist class.[80] The purpose of radical analyses within this perspective is to demonstrate the true purpose of the criminal law and the justice system. A major weakness of instrumental Marxist analyses is that there is a substantial body of law that appears to run against the interests of the capitalist class. Why, for example, would economic elites allow laws against pollution, price fixing, or false advertising?

Structural Marxism grants the government (at least in the short run) a degree of political autonomy. In other words, some laws may indeed run counter to the desires of the capitalist class. Further, capitalists are not portrayed as a single, homogenous group. Rather, some laws may serve the interests of particular fractions of the capitalist elite, but not others.[81] In the long run, both perspectives argue that the content of the legal code and enforcement of the laws will benefit the economic elites. What is the evidence to support this position?

Jeffrey Reiman's *The Rich Get Richer and the Poor Get Prison* is a classic treatise on this issue. Reiman argues that dangerous actions perpetrated by the wealthy are often not even defined as criminal.[82] For example, studies estimate that over 12,000 Americans die from unnecessary surgeries each year. Countless more die from pollution, hazardous work conditions, and unsafe products. Even where these actions are defined as criminal, they are framed as actions that require regulatory oversight, rather than criminal prosecution. To the extent that white-collar criminals convicted of acts such as insider trading, embezzlement, and fraud are even sanctioned, their penalties pale in comparison to the typical sanctions for street crimes.[83]

Reiman argues that at virtually every stage of the criminal justice system, the wealthy and middle-class members of society are weeded out, leaving U.S. prisons to fill with predominantly poor individuals. Moreover, crimes that are likely to be committed by wealthy individuals (e.g., insider trading, embezzlement, violations of occupational safety standards, bribery, consumer fraud) are viewed as less serious and are less likely to be enforced. Reiman highlights the savings and loan scandal in the 1980s, and more recent corporate crime sagas (e.g., Enron, Arthur Andersen, Adelphia, Tyco, WorldCom). Where prison sentences were handed out for these crimes, they were very light compared with the typical sentence for a comparable street crime.

For example, the savings and loan scandal cost American taxpayers over $480 billion, but led to only a handful of convictions. Of those convicted, most ended up serving between one and four

Sam Waksal leaves federal court after being sentenced in 2003 for insider trading. Waksal was sentenced to seven years and three months in prison for the scandal that ensnared his family and Martha Stewart. Despite such high-profile cases, prosecution for insider trading and other white-collar crimes appears to be the exception rather than the rule.

How do radical theorist account for this fact?

years in prison.[84] This sort of filtering process helps to create the public image of an offender as young, black, inner-city resident. Ironically, because many white-collar crimes are rational and involve cost-benefit calculations, harsh punishments have greater potential to produce a deterrent effect. This concept is explored further in the **Theory in Action** box.

Where wealthy and poor individuals engage in similar conduct, the police are more likely to target the crimes of the poor. Consider again the sentencing disparity between those caught using powdered cocaine (preferred by the wealthy) and those caught using crack cocaine. Reiman highlights research that indicates that (1) the police are more likely to take formal action where the suspect is poor, (2) the wealthy are less likely to be formally charged for an offense, and (3) even when charged, the wealthy are often able to avoid punitive sanctioning.[85]

Historical Support for Marxist Criminology

Another source of support for radical criminology comes from historical analyses of the law and systems of formal control. William Chambliss uses such

Corporate Crime — A Civil or Criminal Response?

Studies that examine the deterrent effect of formal punishment on street crime consistently yield disappointing results. It appears that only the certainty of punishment has any substantial effect on offending. Even here, the evidence is marginal. Critics of a deterrence approach often point to the theory's underlying assumption about human nature as its primary flaw. The theory assumes that offenders are rational and calculating. Interviews with offenders, however, reveal that considerations of the costs of crime are minimal. Most offenders do not think at all about the consequences of their actions, simply believing that they will not get caught.

In contrast, a hallmark of a bureaucratic institution (such as a corporation) is rational, cost-benefit analyses of most decisions. Indeed, civil and criminal actions against corporate offenders often rest on internal documents that show a deliberate, rational calculation of the costs (typically a fine) and benefits (profit) of criminal activity. Might increasing the certainty and severity of punishment put a damper on corporate crime? In the current criminal justice landscape, this is a difficult question to answer.

The prevailing thought regarding corporate crime is that civil damages (monetary damages awarded from private lawsuits) are a more effective deterrent than criminal action. This view is summarized by Richard Parker, a professor at George Mason University Law School: "Since a corporation has no mind, it can commit no crime." Parker claims "there is no legitimate function to corporate criminal liability that cannot be served equally as well, if not better, by civil enforcement."

Other experts, like Columbia University law professor John Coffee, agree that in theory civil penalties could effectively combat corporate crime. In practice, however, they don't work as well as the criminal law: "When it comes to allocating blame, assessing responsibility, and shaming wrongdoers, the criminal law works much better than the civil law." He argues that because corporations are sanctioned almost exclusively by civil penalties, their wrongdoing appears less blameworthy than the conduct of ordinary street criminals.

Do you believe that increasing the severity of penalties (e.g., long prison terms) for corporate leaders would curb corporate crime?

What interest groups would support such action? Who would oppose stiffer penalties?

Source: Citizen Works, "Corporate Crime," available at http://www.citizenworks.org/issues/democracy/demo-issuepapers-corp-crime.php, accessed April 2, 2005.

---

a historical analysis to support his theory. For example, he argues that the English vagrancy law of 1349 was enacted solely to provide a pool of cheap labor and combat the collapse of the feudal system[86]:

> The law was clearly and consciously designed to serve the interests of the ruling class at the expense of the working class. The vagrancy laws were designed to alleviate a condition defined by the lawmakers as undesirable.

The vagrancy law was later amended to protect the transportation of goods and to control recidivism by branding the letter *V* on the forehead of repeat offenders.[87] In this way, enforcement of the vagrancy law was adapted to meet changing social conditions. Although his study has been severely criticized, it remains a classic work in criminology.[88]

Another example of how history has been used to support Marxist theory is Anthony Platt's study of the origins and development of the juvenile court system in the United States.[89] To Platt, this system was formed to control immigrant youths and instill discipline. It was dominated by wealthy upper-class matrons who promulgated the values of the white, Anglo-Saxon, capitalist class[90]:

> The child saving movement was heavily influenced by middle-class women who extended their housewifely roles into public service and economic resources to advance the cause of child welfare. The child savers defended the importance of the home, of family life, and parental supervision. These institutions traditionally gave purpose to a woman's life.

Platt charges that, under the guise of the child-saving movement, delinquency was invented to control the behavior of lower-class youths. The combination of a capitalist society (which creates a surplus labor pool) and the child labor laws (which prevent children from working) created a dangerous class that necessitated control. Platt argues that the juvenile courts were created largely to serve this purpose.

A Radical Critique of "Traditional" Criminologists

Even the discipline of criminology itself has not escaped blame. Critics contend that mainstream criminology concentrates on the behavior of the offender, accepts the legal definitions of crime, and largely ignores the proposition that crime is created by political authority. Thus, criminologists serve as agents of the state who provide information that the government uses to manipulate and control those who threaten the system.[91]

Radical criminologists point out, for example, that most mainstream theories of crime are actually theories of street crime that largely ignore crimes of the affluent.[92] Consider, for example, Gottfredson and Hirschi's theory of low self-control. Most persons in a position of power have demonstrated enough self-control to accumulate the credentials (e.g., employment education) to rise to a position of power. Robert Merton's modes of adaptation virtually require offenders to be poor (only the poor lack legitimate means for achieving success). Criminologists also lend legitimacy to the image of criminals as urban, poor, and nonwhite by relying on the FBI Uniform Crime Report (UCR) data. The UCR does not track corporate or government crime.[93] Further, despite recent attempts to remedy this situation, the UCR does not provide reliable information on other forms of white-collar crime.[94] Radical scholars urge mainstream criminologists to question this preoccupation with street crime, and to scrutinize the political and social institutions that support the crimes of the powerful.

A Critique of Radical Criminology

Radical criminology has been criticized on several grounds. First, there is the question of whether radical criminologists offer much that is new.[95] For example, like Durkheim, radical criminologists assert that crime is normal and that diversity should be tolerated. Like labeling theorists, they emphasize rule making, not rule breaking. In fact, some scholars argue that the only thing the radicals managed to do was to politicize traditional criminological theories.[96]

Second, some claim that radical criminologists have been unable to clearly define the ruling class.[97] Are the capitalists all powerful? Can they really decide exactly how the law is made and enforced? In some ways, radical criminologists portray crime policy as a conspiracy theory. Critics are also leery of radical theory's dependence on historical analysis, which is far more difficult to test (it is essentially someone's *interpretation* of historical events) and falsify than quantitative analysis.[98]

Third, Criminologist Jackson Toby argues that the radicals provide an idealized view of the deviant as a rebel. This underdog mentality appears to excuse all lower-class criminality. He notes that crimes of the elite, however, do not legitimate other crimes. Toby also asserts that the radicals must acknowledge that imperfect justice is the product of an imperfect world: "What the radical criminologists refuse to recognize is that the political process in a reasonably open society is responsive (not perfectly) to public opinion."[99]

Finally, radical criminologists must now contend with the failure of communism in the Soviet Union and Eastern Europe. Certainly, these states were not model Marxist societies; they were more bureaucratic and party dominated than Marx would have liked. However, they did represent an attempt to put Marxian theory into practice and their demise supports the view that Marx's utopian vision of society is difficult, if not impossible, to carry out. Even more damaging is the fact that some capitalist countries (e.g., England, Japan) have relatively low crime rates. If capitalism is the sole cause of criminal behavior, how is this possible?

Does the failure of communism and the low crime rates of some capitalist countries mean that the radicals were wrong? Perhaps, but their work has forced criminologists to broaden their perspective. Criminal law can be used as a weapon to oppress the public, and it can be overextended in damaging and self-defeating ways. Radical theorists also deserve credit for highlighting the difference in sanctioning between crimes of the powerful and crimes of the poor. As discussed briefly earlier (and will be seen more clearly in Chapter 15), crimes of the powerful are far more destructive than street crime. Radical theorists also act as a conscience for the discipline of criminology. They remind criminologists not to allow their discipline to be co-opted by the status quo.

Extensions of Radical Criminology

Thomas and O'Maolchatha have outlined several new trends that are attributable to the radical perspective. Acknowledging that radical criminology is often viewed as polarizing, personalized, and narrow, they remind one that[100]:

> Critical criminology is not a utopian perspective but an invitation to struggle; it is a call to recast definitions of social offense more broadly than do traditional criminologists, who rarely challenge unnecessary forms of social domination.

British ("Left") Realism

Radical criminologists have always been concerned with praxis — "action that is guided by theory and that has social change as its goal,"[101] yet they also have been criticized for relying on socialist revolution and the state to solve social problems. The British realists offer practical solutions to street crime in an attempt to reduce this dependence. They argue that street crime is a serious problem for the working class and not a "proto-revolutionary" activity by the oppressed masses.[102] Working-class people are victimized not only by the powerful classes in society but also by the poor.

However, the British realists are critical of the policies developed by the government to deal with street crime. They question conservative crime policies that emphasize deterrence, military-style policing, and increasing use of prisons. As an alternative solution, left realists suggest the use of minimal policing and police accountably to local communities.[103] Specifically, minimal policing calls for maximum public initiation of police action, minimum coercion by the police, minimal police intervention, and maximum public access to the police.[104]

Elliott Currie: The United States as a - "Market Society"

The gist of radical theory is that capitalism causes crime. Elliott Currie suggests the following update: *Some forms* of capitalism encourage crime. Currie uses the concept of a *market society* to explain the difference.[105] A *market economy* is based on the principles of capitalism — and capitalism is an important aspect of the global economy. Many societies (e.g., Japan, Great Britain) with capitalist economies nevertheless have relatively low crime rates. Currie refers to the economic and social arrangements in these countries as compassionate capitalism. In other words, the government curbs the free market by ensuring that economic inequality does not be-

come too severe and provides strong safety nets for those who are not involved in the economy. In contrast, a <u>market society</u> involves[106]:

> [T]he spread of civilization in which the pursuit of personal economic gain becomes increasingly the dominant organizing principle of social life; a social formation in which market principles, instead of being confined to some parts of the *economy*, and appropriately buffered and restrained by other social institutions and norms, come to suffuse the whole social fabric — and to undercut and overwhelm other principles, that have historically sustained individuals, families, and communities. [emphasis in original]

In other words, a market society is a completely Darwinian society with a sink-or-swim mentality. There are few cushions against disabilities or misfortunes in the labor market. This central idea is very similar to Messner and Rosenfeld's institutional anomie theory. In both cases, that adherence to a hard-core form of capitalism produces America's high rates of violent crime. As a critical criminologist, however, Currie takes this central idea in a more radical direction.[107] He identifies seven mechanisms that link a market society to high rates of violence. The mechanisms are outlined in **TABLE 8-3**.

LINK Institutional anomie (see Chapter 6) shares a great deal of overlap with Currie's idea of a market society.

In particular, Currie points out that a market society tolerates high levels of inequality and poverty. The idea of having a strong safety net (e.g., job training and relocation, child care, universal health care) runs counter to the everyone-for-themselves mentality of a market society. Even the regulation of handguns is very limited, when compared with other advanced countries. These characteristics interfere with the childhood development (poverty), informal control (job relocations, lack of child care), and other buffers against high levels of crime. Thus, while Marxist radicals support a revolution to overthrow capitalism, Currie suggests that a softer, gentler capitalist society (allowing a little socialism to creep in) might suffice.

Criminology as Peacemaking

Another new direction in radical thought involves using criminology to promote a peaceful society. This approach draws on many religious traditions (e.g., Buddhism, Quakerism, Judaism) that see crime

TABLE 8-3

How a Market Society Breeds Violent Crime

Premise	Explanation
1. A market society breeds violent crime by destroying livelihood.	In a market society, labor is always a cost to be reduced, rather than a social institution valued in its own right. Benefits and wages are cut, and the number of working poor is high. A lack of stable or rewarding work breeds alienation and undercuts the idea of having a stake in society.
2. A market society has an inherent tendency toward extremes of inequality and material deprivation.	Income inequality in the United States is more dramatic than in other advanced countries. Poor children are more prevalent in the United States and they are poorer than in other industrialized countries. Children living in poverty (especially extreme poverty) are more likely to be physically abused and neglected and less likely to develop intellectually.
3. A market society weakens public support.	A market society is opposed to the provision of public support that may inhibit violent crime. For example, while other countries provide nearly universal child care to working parents, the United States "allows" parents to take unpaid leave without getting fired for certain family emergencies.
4. A market society erodes informal social support.	Employers' desire for a flexible workforce means that workers continuously move locations, uprooting them from their communities and families. This interferes with social organization and removes a source of social support.
5. A market society promotes a culture that exalts brutal individual competition and consumption.	A culture of materialism (or "hypermaterialism") emphasizes money, rather than other values, such as a job well done. In such a culture, throwing people out of a job is not considered bad, but rather good business practice.
6. A market society deregulates the technology of violence.	The virtual absence of national-level gun control distinguishes the United States from virtually every other advanced nation.
7. A market society weakens alternative political values and institutions.	The prevailing ideology (or myth) is that inequality and deprivation are simply the nature of things. Labor unions or political parties that address the needs of the poor or disenfranchised are weak or nonexistent.

Source: Elliott Currie, "Market, Crime and Community: Toward a Mid-Range Theory of Post-Industrial Violence," *Theoretical Criminology* 1 (1997): 147–172.

as a form of suffering from both the criminal's and the victim's perspective[108]:

> Crime is suffering passed on from one person to another; one kind of suffering becomes another; we have to suffer with the criminal to put an end to the suffering the criminal inflicts upon others. As long as we persist in trying to make the criminal suffer for us, the problem will get worse.

One concrete example of a course of action is mediation. Mediation transforms criminal disputes into civil matters by bringing victims and offenders to the bargaining table. It attempts to offer forms of reconciliation that are constructive for both parties.[109] This approach also calls for the development of a "nonviolent criminology of compassion and service."[110] This, Quinney suggests, runs counter to the interests of the criminal justice system, which he says is driven by violence[111]:

> It is a system that assumes that violence can be overcome by violence, evil by evil. Criminal justice at home and warfare abroad are of the same principle of violence. This principle sadly

dominates much of our criminology. Fortunately, more and more criminologists are realizing that this principle is fundamentally incompatible with a faith that seeks to express itself in compassion, forgiveness, and love.

The warlike image of the criminal justice system, so this argument goes, contributes to the crime problem. Criminologists must seek to make peace by confronting such issues as homelessness, sexual assault, and the use of prisons.[112] The primary criticism of this perspective is that it rejects any effort to scientifically study crime or crime control. Rather, it is simply a call to love thy neighbor. In that sense, peacemaking criminology no longer portends to be a theory of criminal behavior.[113]

Feminist Criminology

Historically, females were largely ignored in criminology. Most empirical tests used data on males to explain male offending; theories of crime explained why boys or men engaged in crime.[114] Until the last 40 years, only a handful of scholars directly addressed female criminality. Even here, the portrayal of female offenders was often blatantly sexist. In essence, because female offenders deviated from their "natural temperament" (e.g., warm, passive, caring), they were viewed as biologically or psychologically defective.[115] Over the past few decades, this situation has changed substantially. A major turning point was the women's movement and the fight for gender equality. Among other things, this movement created a wave of female criminologists by paving the way for women to enter graduate school.[116]

As **TABLE 8-4** illustrates, the feminist perspective takes different forms.[117] Liberal feminists, who emphasize equal opportunity and the importance of sex-role socialization, had the most influence in the early days of the feminist movement.[118] Critical (e.g., socialist and radical) feminists emphasize the structural inequality in power between men and women. This approach links male and female crime to *patriarchy*—a cultural arrangement where males exert dominance over females through financial and physical power. In a patriarchal society, male behaviors are defined as "normal," and male control of females is viewed as legitimate.[119]

In a now-classic article, Kathleen Daly and Meda Chesney-Lind outlined two central problems for a male-dominated criminology.[120] The **generalizability problem** suggests that (in part, because most criminology theorists are male) mainstream criminological theories may not be applicable to female offending. The **gender-ratio problem** speaks to the empirical observation that males account for the vast majority of delinquent and criminal offending. The key task before researchers is to identify factors that account for this gender difference.

The Gender Ratio

There is little doubt that males are more prone to crime than females. Uniform Crime Report data indicate that males account for the vast majority of arrests for both property (70%) and violent (80%) crime. The National Crime Victimization Survey reveals a similar pattern: Males account for roughly 85% of violent offenders.[121] Self-report studies that measure serious forms of delinquency tell a similar story. The central issue for theorists is explaining male overrepresentation in criminal behavior. It is hard to overstate the importance of this issue. If, as many believe, the gender gap is due to environmental influence such as different parenting practices, the policy implications are enormous. Sticking with the example of parenting — if parents "parented" their boys as they do girls, male offending would be expected to decline dramatically. Ironically though, the first investigations into the gender ratio did not seek to explain its existence. Rather, they argued that the gender ratio was shrinking.

In 1975, two controversial works appeared. Freda Adler's *Sisters in Crime* and Rita Simon's *Women and Crime* argued that the women's movement provided greater opportunities for females in both legitimate and illegitimate enterprises.[122] The as-

TABLE 8-4	

Three Feminist Perspectives on Crime

Perspective	Description
Liberal Feminism	Highlights problems arising from gender discrimination and stereotypical views concerning the traditional roles of women in society. It emphasizes the use of affirmative action and equal opportunity as major weapons of change. This perspective has been criticized as limited because it ignores class and race differences among women. It has also been characterized as less threatening because it does not strongly question "white, male, and/or capitalist privilege" and typically uses the traditional scientific, quantitative (positivist) methodology to study crime.
Socialist Feminism	Views gender discrimination as a function of capitalist society, which fosters both social class divisions and patriarchy. The criminality of males and females varies in frequency and type because of the social relations of production (class) and reproduction (family). Patriarchal capitalism creates two groups — the powerful (males and capitalists) and the powerless (females and the working class). The opportunity to commit crime is limited by position in the social structure.
Radical Feminism	Views the origins of patriarchy and subordination of women in male aggression and the control of female sexuality. For example, radical feminists have redefined rape as a crime of violence and male power, control, and domination, rather than as a sexual one.

Source: Sally S. Simpson, "Feminist Theory, Crime, and Justice," *Criminology* 27 (1989): 605–632.

sumption was that feminism would thus lead to a growth in the female crime rate. According to this "liberation hypothesis," female offenders were now capable of committing the same offenses as men, and female criminality would approach that of males in both nature and volume.

Both Adler's and Simon's studies were criticized by feminists because they[123]:

> [P]roposed ideas about women's criminality that were troubling to feminists because they were largely an outgrowth of the unexamined assumption that the emancipation of women resided solely in achieving legal and social equality with men in the public sphere. Although the books reached different conclusions, they touched a raw nerve by linking women's crime to the women's movement and to the goal of equality with men in the public sphere.

Indeed, analysis of crime statistics reveals that women have not radically changed their patterns of crime. Women are still much less likely to commit violent crimes although their rate of involvement in property crime (e.g., petty theft and fraud) has increased. Overall, their involvement in crime remains far less than that of males.[124] This pattern is not limited to street crime. Women convicted of white-collar crimes tend to be clerical workers, not managers or administrators, as with their male counterparts.[125] Female white-collar offenders are also more likely to act alone and to profit less from their offenses than the males.

Over the past 20 years, several scholars have devised empirical tests to examine and explain the gender gap. Typically, these studies use variables from mainstream theories of crime (e.g., social learning and social control) to account for the difference in offending across genders. The assumption in this research is that male and female offending is caused by the same factors, but that males are exposed to more risk factors than females. These investigations have yielded mixed results. Typically, researchers find that they can account for some, but not all, of the gender gap. Generally, social learning variables (e.g., delinquent peers, antisocial attitudes), school performance, and sex-role attitudes (e.g., traditional gender beliefs, masculinity) do the best job of explaining gender differences in offending.[126]

The Generalizability Issue

Virtually all theories of crime, until recently, were created by men to account for male offending. An

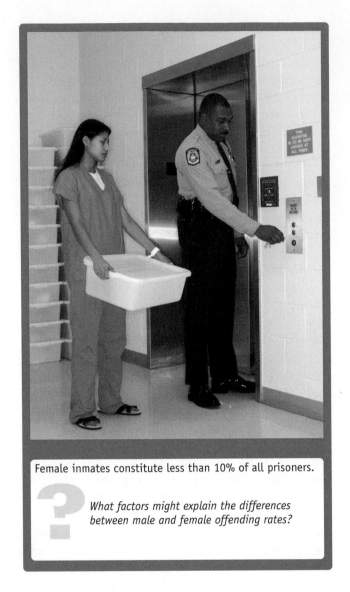

Female inmates constitute less than 10% of all prisoners.

What factors might explain the differences between male and female offending rates?

important question is whether such "male" theories can also explain female offending. The general finding is that variables derived from mainstream theories of crime also explain female offending.[127] Hirschi's social bond theory (see Chapter 7) actually explains female offending better than male offending. More commonly, authors find little difference in how well theories predict offending across gender. Paul Mazerolle's recent analysis of general strain theory (see Chapter 6) is a good example. Mazerolle found that, for the most part, measures of strain (e.g., negative life events, peer hassles) explain both male and female offending.[128]

The fact that mainstream theories can explain female offending does not necessarily mean that they offer a *complete* explanation. Feminist scholars point out that the male perspective may overlook factors that are unique to females. Research

TABLE 8-5

A Typology of Female Offenders

Type of Offender	Description
Street women	Street women have experienced high levels of abuse, which is their primary reason for living on the street. This type of woman is likely to be arrested for prostitution, theft, or drug-related offenses.
Harmed-and-harming women	This type of offender, abused and/or neglected as children, are labeled as "problem children." They are more likely to be addicted to alcohol or drugs, have psychological problems, and engage in violent behavior.
Battered women	Battered women are currently in a relationship with an abusive partner. Often they are in court for harming the person who is battering them.
Drug-connected women	This type of offenders distributes drugs in conjunction with her family or her boyfriend, husband, or family.
"Other" women	"Other" women are those who do not fit in other categories. They are more likely to be in court for crimes of greed, such as embezzlement or fraud, which are not committed to meet basic needs.

Source: Kathleen Daly, *Gender, Crime, and Punishment* (New Haven, CT: Yale University Press, 1994).

reveals that victimization in general, and in particular sexual victimization, is implicated in much female offending.[129] Studies on incarcerated girls reveal that between 40% and 73% were sexually abused.[130] Importantly, abuse can lead to girls (and boys) running away from home. Prostitution, theft, and other crimes result from the attempt to survive in this environment.

Criminologist Kathleen Daly used presentence investigation reports and other court records to examine what factors led females to engage in crime.[131] **TABLE 8-5** presents Daly's typology of female offending. *Street women*, for example, are those who have experienced high levels of abuse and are arrested primarily for prostitution, theft, and drug-related offenses. *Battered women* were typically arrested for harming (and in some cases killing) their abusers.

Taking a different path, Heimer and De Coster use the feminist perspective to "gender" differential association theory. The authors believe that definitions favorable to law violation have different sources for males and females. Among males, proviolence

attitudes are learned when parents fail to correct their violent acts (e.g., "boys will be boys"). Females, because of their greater concern for interpersonal relationships, are more likely to learn violent attitudes when there is a breakdown of relationships in the family.[132]

LINK Social learning theory, discussed in Chapter 7, focuses on how individuals learn criminal attitudes and behaviors from others.

Feminist explanations of female offending, such as Daly's typology and Heimer and De Coster's revision of differential association, represent an exciting new area in criminology. After much neglect, it appears as though the female perspective and feminist theory are gaining a voice within criminology. This relatively new area of criminology will continue to generate important insight into the gender gap, the issue of generaliziblity, and female (as well as male) offending in general.

Gender and the Criminal Justice System

What predictions would a feminist criminologist make on the relationship between gender and the law? A patriarchic society is by definition male dominated. Following the logic of other critical theories, those who lack power should have their behavior criminalized and should be singled out by the criminal justice system for punishment. Also, crimes against the less powerful should be given less priority. Disparities in the treatment of women in the criminal justice system have been studied by both conflict and radical theorists. Are persons treated equally under the law or is gender a key indicator of how a case will be handled?

As with race and class, research on this area examines whether gender has an impact on criminal justice decision making independent of other factors. The general pattern found in this research is that if there is a gender effect, it benefits females.[133] As with race, significant gender effects tend to be small and appear at different stages of processing. In fact, Daly notes that gender decisions favoring women are found more often than race decisions favoring whites.[134]

The finding that females are treated leniently within the criminal justice system was long ago tabbed the **chivalry hypothesis**. Because police, prosecutors, and judges are predominately male, they may have a chivalrous attitude toward women and be more inclined to treat them with leniency. Evidence suggesting the differential processing of women in the criminal justice system is mixed, however. Visher found that police make arrest decisions about women based on the image the woman projects, not the type of offense (violent versus property). The officers were more likely to be chivalrous toward older, white females and to arrest their young, hostile, black counterparts.[135] A study of plea bargaining in Washington, D.C., showed that women were less able to bargain and were more willing to plead guilty than men. In other words, they were not rewarded for pleading guilty with a lesser sentence.[136]

Even where females receive more lenient treatment, feminists are more inclined to regard this as

paternalism. A paternalistic response, unlike a chivalrous response, could lead to leniency, but also to a punitive response if it serves to keep women in a submissive role.[137] Bishop and Frazier's examination of Florida delinquency processing suggests a degree of paternalism. For more serious offenses, boys were treated more harshly, and for most status offenses, there were no differences across gender. For contempt-of-court cases, which resulted largely from repeated attempts to run away from home, girls were more likely to be incarcerated than boys.[138]

Like conflict theorists, feminists have also highlighted certain crimes that were not enforced because women lacked power and status. Male violence against women, particularly nonstranger rape and battering of intimates, was traditionally not sanctioned or penalized by the state.[139] Only through sustained campaigning and activism have feminists managed to alter this situation. Terms such as *date rape* and *marital rape,* unheard of only a short time ago, are now part of the common vocabulary. Further, intimate violence has been reframed as a crime of violence rather than a personal problem between intimates.

Conclusion

Critical theories highlight the manner in which laws are made and enforced. Conflict, Marxist, and feminist theories of criminology often challenge the basis and legitimacy of the criminal justice system and law enforcement. Collectively, they have changed the manner in which crime is studied, considered, and analyzed. They remind society that crime is not an objective behavior, but rather a politically constructed label. In this sense, they have significantly broadened both the definition and the scope of criminology. Critical theories also challenge criminologists to explain crimes often neglected in the mainstream literature. Feminist theories call attention to female criminality and the male-female offending gap, and radical theories call attention to white-collar, government, and corporate crime. Critical analysis of the operations and nature of the criminal justice system must be continued if criminology is to have a beneficial impact on society.

WRAP UP

What Is a "Serious" Crime?

The scenarios provided here are intended to contrast a "street" crime with a "suite" crime. In the context of this chapter, the central issues are the content of the legal code and the operation of the criminal justice system. Conflict and radical theorists argue that those with power shape both the content of the law (e.g., the particular acts that are considered illegal) and the operation of the criminal justice system (e.g., whether and to what extent laws are enforced). Thus, those with power (the Jeffco executives) would be unlikely to either have their actions defined as criminal, or be prosecuted for their actions. Indeed, many might regard their decision as "good business" practice. Which scenario describes the most "serious" crime? If a person defines seriousness as the level of harm that results from an act, there is little doubt that the actions of the Jeffco executives are more serious. Their decision to remain silent will result in 500 auto deaths per year. Stephanie's actions resulted in injury to one victim. In the "real" criminal justice system, Stephanie has much greater odds of getting caught, prosecuted, and punished harshly for her criminal act than the Jeffco executives.

Chapter Spotlight

- Although critical (e.g., conflict, radical, feminist) theories of crime include a diverse body of theories, they share some commonality. In particular, they view crime as a political concept, where those in power shape both the content of the law and the operation of the criminal justice system.

- Conflict theory is based on a pluralistic view of power. There are many interest groups that shape the law. Conflict is primarily used to explain the law and actions of criminal justice agents, but can also explain some forms of criminal behavior (e.g., an abortion clinic bombing).

- Radical theory stems from the work of Karl Marx. Radical theorists emphasize the conflict between the wealthy elite and the working class. They point out that many harmful acts perpetrated by the wealthy are not defined as criminal. To the extent that such acts are defined as criminal, they are not strongly enforced. Those prosecuted for "white-collar crimes" rarely receive long prison sentences.

- A central empirical issue in radical theories is whether criminal justice decisions (e.g., the decision to arrest or prosecute) are related to race and class. This body of evidence is extensive, complex, and often contradictory. There is some evidence of racial disparities in criminal justice decision making. Racial disparity is most clear in the areas of illicit drug use and capital sentencing.

- Modern extensions of radical theory include Currie's concept of a "market society," as well as peacemaking criminology and left realism.

- Feminist scholars point out that most criminological theories were written by males and about male criminality. They question whether such theories apply to females. Further, they point out that mainstream theory cannot adequately explain why males are more likely to engage in crime than females.

- As with race and class, researchers have studied whether gender has an effect on criminal justice processing. There is some evidence that females are treated more leniently by the system. For some acts, (e.g., contempt of court cases arising from repeated runaways), however, the reverse holds true.

Putting It All Together

1. Is the criminal justice system racist? What factors would you have to take into consideration to research this question?

2. Does American society operate under a consensus or conflict model?

3. Describe the gender ratio and generaliziblity problems.

4. What does Currie mean by a market society? How does a market society breed violence?

5. Think of a current scandal involving wealthy individuals or corporations engaging in crime. How might radical theorists explain this?

Key Terms

altruism According to Bonger, altruism was a characteristic of primitive societies. In these societies, social solidarity was high, and individuals were more selfless and looked after each other's needs.

bourgeoisie Within the Marxist theory, those who hold salaried and management positions.

capitalists Within the Marxist theory, they are the owners of the means of production.

chivalry hypothesis The idea that females are treated leniently by the criminal justice system because police, prosecutors, and judges are predominately male and have a gracious attitude toward women.

conflict model The belief that the law is the result of a battle between people or groups that have different levels of power. Control over the state (including the law and the criminal justice system) is the principal prize in the perpetual conflict of society.

conflict theory Theories that emphasize a pluralistic perspective — multiple groups within a society wield different levels of power.

consensus model The belief that the law reflects common agreement over the fundamental values held by society.

egoism A lack of consideration for others. According to Bonger, capitalism encourages selfishness, greed, and insensitivity to others.

extra-legal factors Characteristics such as race, class, and gender that can impact criminal justice decision making.

gender-ratio problem A key issue for criminologists is to explain the empirical observation that males account for the vast majority of delinquent and criminal offending.

generalizability problem Because most criminology theorists are male, mainstream criminological theories may not be applicable (they may not generalize) to female offending.

instrumental Marxism This type of theory argues that the law and criminal justice system are always instruments to be used by the capitalist class.

legal factors Factors such as offense seriousness and prior record that play a role in criminal justice decision making.

lumpenproletariat Within Marxist theory, the dispossessed, unorganized workers.

market society A country (such as the United States) where the capitalist economy dominates all other spheres of life. This is a sink-or-swim society that does not provide a strong safety net for citizens.

primary conflict A concept from Thorsten Sellin's culture-conflict theory. Primary conflict may arise between an established culture and a less-powerful culture. For example, recent immigrants may conduct themselves based on codes from the old country that may be criminal in the dominant culture.

proletariat Within Marxist theory, the working class.

racial profiling Racially biased law enforcement; targeting individuals for law enforcement based primarily on their race.

racial threat hypothesis The idea that as minority populations increase relative to the white population, they will be viewed as a threat and punitive measures will increase.

radical theory Theoretical perspective that emphasizes conflict between the wealthy elite and the rest of society.

secondary conflict Concept from Thorsten Sellin's culture-conflict theory. Secondary conflict occurs within a single culture that has different subcultures, each with their own conduct norms.

structural Marxism This type of Marxist analysis grants the government (at least in the short run) a degree of political autonomy. Some laws may run counter to the desires of the capitalists.

superstructure The system of social institutions (e.g., law, education, and politics) that lend legitimacy to capitalist arrangements.

Notes

1. Jeffrey Reiman, *The Rich Get Richer and the Poor Get Prison: Ideology, Class, and Criminal Justice,* 7th ed. (Boston: Allyn and Bacon, 2004).
2. J. Robert Lilly, Francis T. Cullen, and Richard A. Ball, *Criminological Theory: Context and Consequences,* 3rd ed. (Thousand Oaks, CA: Sage, 2002): 132–133.
3. Lilly, Cullen, and Ball, 2002, 132.
4. Francis T. Cullen and Robert Agnew, *Criminological Theory: Past to Present* (Los Angeles: Roxbury, 2003): 334–335.
5. William J. Chambliss, "The Law of Vagrancy," in William J. Chambliss, ed., *Criminal Law in Action* (New York: John Wiley, 1984).
6. William J. Chambliss and Robert T. Seidman, *Law, Order, and Power* (Reading, MA: Addison-Wesley, 1982): 33–38.
7. Ibid.
8. George B. Vold, *Theoretical Criminology* (New York: Oxford University Press, 1958): 208–209.
9. William J. Chambliss, *Criminal Law in Action* (Santa Barbra, CA: Hamilton, 1975): i–ii.
10. Frank P. Williams III and Marilyn D. McShane, *Criminological Theory,* 4th ed. (Upper Saddle River, NJ: Prentice Hall, 2004): 167–168.
11. George Ritzer, *Sociological Theory,* 3rd ed. (New York: McGraw Hill, 1992): 263–270.
12. Marc C. Kennedy, "Beyond Incrimination: Some Neglected Facets of the Theory of Punishment," *Catalyst* 5 (1970): 1–37.
13. Ronald L. Akers and Christine S. Sellers, *Criminological Theories: Introduction, Evaluation, and Application,* 4th ed. (Los Angeles: Roxbury, 2004): 200–201.
14. Marvin E. Wolfgang, Robert M. Figlio, Paul E. Tracy, and Simon Singer, *The National Survey of Crime Severity* (Washington, DC: Bureau of Justice Statistics, 1985).
15. Francis T. Cullen, Bonnie S. Fisher, and Brandon K. Applegate, "Public Opinion About Crime and Punishment," *Crime and Justice: A Review of the Research* 27 (2000): 1–79.
16. Akers and Sellers, 2004, 197–198.
17. Austin T. Turk, *Criminality and Legal Order* (Chicago: Rand McNally, 1969).
18. Richard G. Greenleaf and Lonn Lanza Kaduce, "Sophistication, Organization, and Authority Subject Conflict: Rediscovering and Unraveling Turks' Theory of Norm Resistance," *Criminology* 33 (1995): 565–586.
19. Robert R. Weidner and William Terrell, "A Test of Turk's Theory of Norm Resistance Using Observational Data on Police-Suspect Encounters," *Journal of Research in Crime and Delinquency* 42 (2005): 84–109.
20. Chambliss and Seidman, 1982, 31.
21. Chambliss and Seidman, 1982, 269.
22. *Sourcebook of Criminal Justice Statistics,* available at www.albany.edu/sourcebook/pdf/1627, accessed April 3, 2005.
23. Akers and Sellers, 2004, 203–206.
24. Donald Black, "The Social Organization of Arrest," in Richard J. Lundman, ed., *Police Behavior: A Sociological Perspective* (New York: Oxford University Press, 1980).
25. Samuel Walker, Cassia Spohn, and Miriam DeLone, *The Color of Justice: Race, Ethnicity, and Crime in America* (Belmont, CA: Wadsworth, 2000).
26. Robin Shepard Engel, Jennifer M. Calnon, and Thomas J. Bernard, "Theory and Racial Profiling: Shortcomings and Future Directions in Research," *Justice Quarterly* 19 (2002): 249–273.
27. Alfred Blumstein, "On the Racial Disproportionality of the United States' Prison Populations," *Journal of Criminal Law and Criminology* 73 (1982): 1259–1281; Alfred Blumstein, "Racial Disproportionality of U.S. Prison Populations Revisited," *University of Colorado Law Review* 64 (1993): 1259–1281.
28. Roy L. Austin and Mark D. Allen, "Racial Disparity in Arrest Rates and an Explanation of Racial Disparity in Commitment to Pennsylvania's Prisons," *Journal of Research in Crime and Delinquency* 37 (2000): 200–220.
29. Ibid.
30. Joan Petersilia, *Racial Disparities in the Criminal Justice System* (Santa Monica, CA: Rand Corporation, 1983).
31. Petersilia, 1983, xxiii.
32. Martha A. Myers and Susette M. Talarico, *Disparity and Discrimination in Sentencing: The Case of Georgia* (Athens, GA: National Institute of Justice, 1985).
33. Stephen Klein, Joan Petersilia, and Susan Turner, "Race and Imprisonment Decisions in California," *Science* 247 (1990): 812–816.
34. William Wilbanks, *The Myth of a Racist Criminal Justice System* (Belmont, CA: Wadsworth, 1987).

35. Institute for the Study of Labor and Economic Crisis, *The Iron Fist and the Velvet Glove* (San Francisco: Synthesis Publications, 1975).

36. Hubert M. Blalock Jr., *Toward a Theory of Minority-Group Relations* (New York: John Wiley and Sons, 1967).

37. David Eitle, Steward J. D'Alessio, and Lisa Stolzenberg, "Racial Threat and Social Control: A Test of the Political, Economic, and Threat of Black Crime Hypothesis," *Social Forces* 81 (2002): 557–576.

38. Edmund F. McGarrell, "Institutional Theory and the Stability of a Conflict Model of the Incarceration Rate," *Justice Quarterly* 10 (1993): 7–28.

39. David Jacobs and Ronald Helms, "Collective Outbursts, Politics, and Punitive Resources: Toward a Political Sociology of Spending on Social Control," *Social Problems* 77 (1999): 1497–1523.

40. Howard Abadinsky, *Drugs: An Introduction* (Belmont, CA: Wadsworth, 2001): 19–42.

41. David Cole, *No Equal Justice: Race and Class in the American Criminal Justice System* (New York: The New Press, 1999): 8.

42. Michael Tonry, *Malign Neglect: Race, Crime, and Punishment in America* (New York: Oxford University Press, 1995): 104–112.

43. Ibid.

44. Tonry, 1995, 123.

45. *Furman v. Georgia* 408 U.S. 238 (1972).

46. *Furman*, 1972, 242.

47. Samuel Gross and Robert Mauro, *Death and Discrimination* (Boston: Northeastern University Press, 1989).

48. H. C. Brearley, "The Negro and Homicides," *Social Forces* 9 (1930): 247–253; Elmer H. Johnson, "Selective Forces in Capital Punishment," *Social Forces* 36 (1957): 165–169.

49. Marvin E. Wolfgang, Arlene Kelly, and Hans C. Nolde, "Comparison of Executed and Commuted Among Admissions to Death Row," *Journal of Criminal Law and Criminology* 53 (1962): 301–311.

50. Franklin E., Zimring, Joel Eigen, and Sheila O'Malley, "Punishing Homicides in Philadelphia: Perspectives on the Death Penalty," *University of Chicago Law Review* 43 (1976): 227–252.

51. Marvin E. Wolfgang and Marc Riedel, "Race, Judicial Discretion, and the Death Penalty," *The Annals of the American Academy of Political and Social Science* 407 (1973): 119–133.

52. Stephen D. Arkin, "Discrimination and Arbitrariness in Capital Punishment: An Analysis of Post-Furman Murder Cases in Dade County, Florida, 1973–1976," *Stanford Law Review* 33 (1980): 75–101; Michael L. Radelet and Glenn L. Pierce, "Choosing Those Who Will Die: Race and the Death Penalty in Florida," *Florida Law Review* 43 (1991): 1–34.

53. See, for example, Sheldon Ekland-Olson, "Structured Discretion, Racial Bias, and the Death Penalty: The First Decade After *Furman* in Texas," *Social Science Quarterly* 69 (1988): 853–873; M. Dwayne Smith, "Patterns of Discrimination in Assessments of the Death Penalty: The Case of Louisiana," *Journal of Criminal Justice* 15 (1987): 279–286.

54. Thomas Keil and Genaro F. Vito, "Race, Homicide Severity, and Application of the Death Penalty: A Consideration of the Barnett Scale," *Criminology* 27 (1989): 511–531.

55. U.S. General Accounting Office, *Death Penalty Sentencing: Research Indicates a Pattern of Racial Disparities* (Washington, DC: Author, 1990).

56. U.S. General Accounting Office, 1990, 5–6.

57. Frederic M. Thrasher, *The Gang: A Study of 1,313 Gangs in Chicago* (Chicago: University of Chicago Press, 1927).

58. Edwin H. Sutherland, "Crime and the Conflict Process," *Journal of Juvenile Research* 13 (1929): 38–48.

59. Thorsten Sellin, *Culture Conflict and Crime* (New York: Social Science Research Council, 1938).

60. Ysabel Rennie, *The Search for Criminal Man* (Lexington, MA: Lexington Books, 1978): 132.

61. T. Trent Gagaz, "Meet the Khat-heads," *Newsweek* 140 (September, 2002): 35.

62. Gregory A. Kelson, "Female Circumcision in the Modern Age: Should Female Circumcision Now Be Considered Grounds for Asylum in the United States?" *Buffalo Human Rights Law Review* 4 (1998): 185–209.

63. George Vold, *Theoretical Criminology* (New York: Oxford University Press, 1958).

64. Vold, 1958, 219.

65. William J. Chambliss, *Crime and the Legal Process* (New York: McGraw Hill, 1969): 10.

66. Michael J. Lynch and W. Byron Groves, *A Primer in Radical Criminology,* 2nd ed. (New York: Harrow and Heston, 1989): 11.

67. Lynch and Groves, 1989, 10.

68. Lynch and Groves, 1989, 13.

69. Ian Taylor, Paul Walton, and Jock Young, *The New Criminology: For a Social Theory of Deviance* (New York: Harper and Row, 1973).

70. Friedrich Engels, "Crime in Communist Society," in David F. Greenberg, ed., *Crime and Capitalism* (Palo Alto, CA: Mayfield, 1981): 51.

71. Rennie, 1978, 112.

72. Wilhelm A. Bonger, *Criminality and Economic Conditions* (Bloomington: Indiana University Press, 1969): 141.

73. George Rusche and Otto Kirchheimer, "Punishment and Social Structure," in W. J. Chambliss, ed., *Criminal Law in Action* (New York: John Wiley, 1975).

74. Rusche and Kirchheimer, 1975, 364.

75. Franklin E. Zimring and Gordon Hawkins, *The Scale of Imprisonment* (Chicago: University of Chicago Press, 1991).

76. James Inverarity and Daniel McCarthy, "Punishment and Social Structure Revisited: Unemployment and Imprisonment in the U. S., 1948–1984," *Sociological Quarterly* 29 (1988): 263–279.

77. Gil Gardner, "The Emergence of the New York State Prison System: A Critique of the Rusche-Kirchheimer Model," *Crime and Social Justice* 29 (1987): 88–109.

78. Stewart J. D'Alessio and Lisa Stolzenberg, "Unemployment and the Incarceration of Pretrial Defendants," *American Sociological Review* 60 (1995): 350–359.

79. Richard Quinney, *Class, State, and Crime* (New York: David McKay, 1977).

80. Akers and Sellers, 2004, 219–220.
81. Akers and Sellers, 2004, 220.
82. Reiman, 2004, 75-94.
83. Ibid.
84. Reiman, 2004, 140-143.
85. Reiman, 2004, 103–140.
86. Chambliss, 1984, 35.
87. Ibid.
88. For criticism, see Jeffrey S. Adler, "A Historical Analysis of the Law of Vagrancy," *Criminology* 27 (1989): 209–230.
89. Anthony Platt, *The Child Savers: The Invention of Delinquency* (Chicago: University of Chicago Press, 1969).
90. Platt, 1969, 83.
91. Richard Quinney, *Critique of Legal Order* (Boston: Little, Brown, 1974): 27.
92. David M. Gordon, "Class and the Economics of Crime," in David F. Greenberg, ed., *Crime and Capitalism* (Palo Alto, CA: Mayfield, 1981): 90.
93. Cynthia Barnett, "The Measurement of White-Collar Crime Using Uniform Crime Reporting (UCR) Data," *NIBRS Publication Series* (Washington, D.C., U.S. Department of Justice, 2000):1.
94. Ibid.
95. Richard F. Sparks, "A Critique of Marxist Criminology," in Norval Morris and Michael Tonry, eds., *Crime and Justice,* volume 2 (Chicago: University of Chicago, 1980): 173–175.
96. Robert F. Meier, "The New Criminology: Continuity in Criminological Theory," *Journal of Criminal Law and Criminology* 67 (1976): 461–469.
97. Sparks, 1980, 190.
98. Carl Klockars, "The Contemporary Crises of Marxist Criminology," *Criminology* 16 (1979): 477–515.
99. Jackson Toby, "The New Criminology Is the Old Sentimentality," *Criminology* 16 (1979): 516–526.
100. Jim Thomas and Aogán O'Maolchatha, "Reassessing the Critical Metaphor: An Optimistic Revisionist View," *Justice Quarterly* 6 (1989): 143–172.
101. Greenberg, 1981, 484.
102. John Lea and Jock Young, *What Is to Be Done About Law and Order* (London, Penguin, 1984).
103. Richard Kinsey, John Lea and Jock Young, *Losing the Fight Against Crime* (London: Blackwell, 1986).
104. Walter DeKeseredy, "The Left Realist Approach to Law and Order," *Justice Quarterly* 5 (1988): 635–640.
105. Elliott Currie, "Market, Crime and Community: Toward a Mid-Range Theory of Post-Industrial Violence," *Theoretical Criminology* 1 (1997): 147–172.
106. Currie, 1997, 151–152.
107. Cullen and Agnew, 2003, 338.
108. Harold E. Pepinsky, "Peacemaking in Criminology and Criminal Justice," in Harold E. Pepinsky and Richard Quinney, eds., *Criminology as Peacekeeping* (Bloomington: Indiana University Press, 1991): 304.
109. Peter J. Cordella, "Reconciliation and the Mutualist Model of Community," in Harold E. Pepinsky and Richard Quinney, eds., *Criminology as Peacekeeping* (Bloomington: Indiana University Press, 1991); Russ Immarigeon, "Beyond the Fear of Crime: Reconciliation as the Basis for Criminal Justice Policy," in Harold E. Pepinsky and Richard Quinney, eds., *Criminology as Peacekeeping* (Bloomington: Indiana University Press, 1991).
110. Richard Quinney, "The Way of Peace: On Crime, Suffering, and Service," in Harold E. Pepinsky and Richard Quinney, eds., *Criminology as Peacekeeping* (Bloomington: Indiana University Press, 1991): 4.
111. Quinney, 1991, 12.
112. John R. Fuller, *Criminal Justice: A Peacemaking Perspective* (Boston: Allyn and Bacon, 1998).

113. Cullen and Agnew, 2003, 387.

114. Joanne Belknap, *The Invisible Woman: Gender, Crime, and Justice* (Belmont, CA: Wadsworth, 1996).

115. See, for example, Dorie Klein, "The Etiology of Female Offending: A Review of the Literature," *Issues in Criminology* 8 (1973): 3–30.

116. Cullen and Agnew, 2003, 397–398.

117. Sally S. Simpson, "Feminist Theory, Crime, and Justice," *Criminology* 27 (1989): 605–632.

118. Cullen and Agnew, 2003, 398.

119. Ibid.

120. Kathleen Daly and Meda Chesney-Lind, "Feminism and Criminology," *Justice Quarterly* 5 (1988): 497–533.

121. Lawrence A Greenfeld, and Tracy L. Snell, *Women Offenders* (Washington, DC: U.S. Department of Justice, Bureau of Justice Statistics, 1999).

122. Moyer, 1985, 198–200.

123. Daly and Chesney-Lind, 1988, 510.

124. Darrell Steffensmeier and Emile Allan, "The Nature of Female Offending: Patterns and Explanation," in Ruth T. Zaplin, ed., *Female Offenders: Critical Perspectives and Effective Interventions* (Gaithersburg, MD: Aspen, 1998).

125. Kathleen Daly, "Gender and Varieties of White-Collar Crime," *Criminology* 27 (1989): 769–794.

126. Gary F. Jenson, "Gender Variation in Delinquency: Self Image, Beliefs, and Peers as Mediating Mechanisms." Paper presented at the annual meeting of the American Society of Criminology, San Francisco, 2000.

127. Steffensmeier and Allan, 1998, 15–16.

128. Paul Mazerolle, "Gender, General Strain, and Delinquency: An Empirical Examination," *Justice Quarterly* 15 (1998): 65–91.

129. Meda Chesney-Lind and Karlene Faith, "What About Feminism? Engendering Theory-Making in Criminology," in Raymond Paternoster and Ronet Bachman, eds., *Explaining Crime and Criminals* (Los Angeles: Roxbury, 2001).

130. Joanne Belknap and Kristi Holsinger, "An Overview of Delinquent Girls: How Theory and Practice Have Failed and the Need for Innovative Changes," in Ruth T. Zaplin, ed., *Female Offenders: Critical Perspectives and Effective Interventions* (Gaithersburg, MD: Aspen, 1998): 34–35.

131. Kathleen Daly, *Gender, Crime, and Punishment* (New Haven, CT: Yale University Press, 1994).

132. Karen Heimer and Stacey De Coster, "The Gendering of Violent Delinquency," *Criminology* 37 (1999): 277–318.

133. Akers and Sellers, 2004, 247–251.

134. Kathleen Daly, "Neither Conflict nor Labeling nor Paternalism Will Suffice: Intersections of Race, Ethnicity, Gender, and Family in Criminal Court Decisions," *Crime and Delinquency* 35 (1989): 136–168.

135. Christy Visher, "Gender, Police Arrest Decisions, and Notions of Chivalry," *Criminology* 21 (1983): 5–28.

136. Josefina Figueira-McDonough, "Gender Differences in Informal Processing: A Look at Charge Bargaining and Sentence Reduction in Washington, D.C." *Journal of Research in Crime and Delinquency* 22 (1985): 101–133.

137. Akers and Sellers, 2004, 237.

138. Donna M. Bishop and Charles E. Frazier, "Gender Bias in Juvenile Justice Processing: Implications of the JJDP Act," *Journal of Criminal Law and Criminology* 82 (1992): 1162–1186.

139. Cullen and Agnew, 2003, 400.

WWW.CRIMINOLOGY.JBPUB.COM

Interactivities
In the News
Key Term Explorer
Web Links

OBJECTIVES

Identify the elements of crime over the life course.

Discuss how Sutherland's *The Professional Thief* sponsored career criminal research.

Summarize the findings of criminal cohort research.

Explain how career criminal programs (for both adults and juveniles) have been implemented and discuss their effectiveness.

Describe the rationale for California's "three-strikes" law and the arguments against it.

Crime and Criminal Careers

> " In designing selective policies and defining dangerous offenders, the goal should be to distinguish the guiltiest offenders based upon past activity and to punish them for their blameworthy conduct rather than to predict which offenders will be most active in the future on the basis of any characteristics which aid in prediction, and incapacitate those predicted to be offenders for as long as they appear dangerous.
>
> —Mark H. Moore, Susan R. Estrich, Daniel McGillis, and William Spelman [1] "

YOU ARE THE CRIMINOLOGIST

Which Offender Should Be Incarcerated Under California's Three-Strikes Law?

From the following descriptions, determine which of the following offenders should be incarcerated under California's three-strikes legislation.

James Valdez: Valdez has a criminal history that includes 5 felony convictions, 11 misdemeanors, and 5 parole violations. He was convicted of the forcible rape of two minor girls in 1977. He forced one of the victims to commit oral sex before raping her and threatened to kill both of the girls if they told anyone. His most recent conviction is also for rape. He assaulted his wife's best friend, took her to a deserted area, beat and raped her, and threatened to throw her over a cliff. In violation of his parole, he never registered as a sex offender, saying he "just forgot to."

Leon Andrews: Andrews has a history of arrests for misdemeanor thefts and felony burglaries dating back to 1982. In 1990, he was convicted of the transportation of marijuana and was sentenced to federal prison. He escaped in 1991, was arrested for a state parole violation, and sent to state prison. He was paroled in 1993. In his present offense, he stole five videotapes worth $84.70 from a Wal-Mart store and was apprehended by security guards.

Herbert King: As a juvenile in the 1960s, King served prison time for robbery and kidnapping. In the late 1970s, he was arrested for murder but acquitted. Two weeks later, he killed a man in a bar and was convicted. While in prison, he became a member of the Aryan Brotherhood prison gang. Shortly after his parole in 1986, he raped his mother and threatened to kill her. Convicted of this offense, he threatened the sentencing judge saying that he would "track him down." He was paroled again in 1996. His parole was revoked in 24 hours when he again threatened the judge and failed a drug test. His most recent offense is also a parole violation for possessing two deadly weapons (a machete and a sledge hammer).

Charles Ellis: Ellis was convicted of theft in 1984. In 1988, he was sentenced to 1 year in jail and 3 years probation plus a $300 fine for a felony grand theft auto conviction. After he completed the term of probation, the sentencing judge reduced the crime to a misdemeanor, permitted Ellis to withdraw his guilty plea, and dismissed the case. In 1990, he was convicted of petty theft and sentenced to 60 days in jail and 3 years probation. In 1992, Ellis was convicted of battery and sentenced to 30 days in jail plus 2 years probation. This crime was followed by a theft conviction 1 month later. In January 1993, Ellis was convicted of burglary and sentenced to 60 days in jail and 1 year of probation. In February 1993, he was convicted of possessing drug paraphernalia and sentenced to 6 months in jail and 3 years probation. In October and November of 1993, Ellis committed three burglaries and one robbery at an apartment complex over a 5-week period. During the burglaries, he confronted and threatened the apartment residents with a knife. He was sentenced to 9 years and 8 months in prison. He was paroled in 1999. His last offense occurred 10 months later when he stole a set of golf clubs from a department store. He was convicted of one count of felony grand theft of personal property in excess of $400.

Introduction

One of the persistent features of the history of criminology is the issue of career criminals and what to do about them. Throughout the 20th century, this group has been labeled in different ways. The label "career criminal" often begins with juveniles. Delinquents have been classified as "defective," "wayward," "delinquent youths," "<u>chronic offenders</u>," and "superpredators."[2] Adult criminals have been termed "habitual," "predatory," "dangerous," and "persistent."[3] Policy prescriptions are concerned with their identification, apprehension, and

ultimately incapacitation to protect society and lower the crime rate. As a result, habitual offender or career criminal laws are common in the United States. One example of such laws is the "three-strikes" laws. Under such laws, repeat offenders draw a life sentence after their third felony conviction. The hope is that their lengthy incarceration will protect the public from their future crimes. In order for such laws to be effective, it is necessary to know: (1) when criminal careers begin and end, (2) how much crime habitual offenders commit, and (3) to what extent violence is a feature of career criminality.

The idea of career criminality is based on the assumption that such criminals are committed to a life of crime; in other words, they have a worldview built around criminal activity. They define themselves as criminals and tend to associate with other criminals. Their careers accelerate or progress as they become more skilled and engage in different types of offenses. In addition, career criminals view crime as a profession like law or medicine in that it involves the acquisition of specialized knowledge and skill.[4]

Criminologists have examined the activities of a large group of offenders in an attempt to determine the characteristics and motives of career criminals. These studies considered two types of data: (1) crimes reported by officials and (2) those admitted by offenders during self-report studies. These studies provided the basis for criminal justice policies aimed at controlling the repeat offender.

However, the effectiveness of these policies is questionable. What can society do about career criminals? How do they operate? These questions surround the theories and research findings on repeat offenders. Life-course criminology is the theoretical foundation for the examination of criminal careers.

Crime Over the Life Course

Life-course criminology is concerned with three major issues: (1) the development of criminal behavior, (2) risk factors at different ages, and (3) the effects of life events on the development of a criminal career.[5] John H. Laub identifies four principles that frame the life-course criminology paradigm[6]:

1. The life course of individuals is embedded in and shaped by the historical times and places they experience over their lifetime.

2. The developmental impact of a succession of life transitions or events is contingent on when they occur in a person's life.

3. Lives are lived interdependently and social and historical influences are expressed through this network of shared relationships.

4. Individuals construct their own life course through the choices and actions they take within the opportunities and constraints of history and social circumstances.

Thus, life-course theories consider the events that take place in the offender's life and how they relate

to the development of a criminal career and affect the likelihood of continued criminal behavior (TABLE 9-1).

Age is the centerpiece of career criminal research. One of the few accepted facts of criminology is that crime peaks in the late adolescent years and declines through adulthood.[7] A study by the National Academy of Sciences lists four dimensions in the development of a criminal career[8]:

1. *Participation*: The distinction between those who engage in crime and those who do not

2. *Frequency*: The rate of criminal activity among active offenders

3. *Seriousness*: The gravity of the offense committed

4. *Career length*: The length of time that the offender is active

However, just how criminal careers develop over time is the subject of analysis and discussion. For

A drug deal in progress.

? *According to research findings, how does drug abuse figure into the development of a criminal career?*

TABLE 9-1

Crime Over the Life Course — Key Concepts

Duration: The length of a criminal career.

Age at onset: The age at the beginning of a criminal career.

Desistance: The end point of a criminal career. It involves either a decrease in the frequency of offending, a reduction in specialization, or a reduction in the seriousness of offending.

Frequency (also known as lambda— λ): An individual's rate of criminal activity; the number of offenses that the individual commits over a certain period of time. Determining what accounts for the variation in frequency of offending (age, race, sex, education, marriage, employment, drug use, etc.) is the heart of criminal career research because it provides an explanation and perhaps policy recommendations to stop criminal careers. Related to frequency are the concepts of:

- **Trajectories:** A sequence of linked states within a conceptually defined realm of behavior. The important elements of trajectories include entrance, success, and timing.
- **Transitions:** These represent turning points in the life course. For example, a delinquent may desist because he or she gets a good job and thus has a firmer bond to conventional society. Teenagers who have children are making a precocious transition: a change that leads to negative educational, financial, and health consequences. They are also related to the concept of social capital: the investment in social relationships with law-abiding people that help an individual to accomplish his or her goals through legitimate means.
- **Activation:** The continuity, frequency, and diversity of criminal activities. It consists of:
  - **Acceleration:** increased frequency
  - **Stability:** consistency in offending over the life course (the tendency for juvenile offenders to become adult offenders)
- **Diversification:** The offender engages in different types of criminal activities.
- **Hazard rate:** The rate at which persons in a cohort experience an event (i.e., arrest) compared to those who have not. For example, if 100 males age 20 are sampled and 10 of them were arrested at age 18, this rate would be 10% (10 per 100).

Seriousness of offending: Do habitual offenders engage in more serious crimes as they extend their criminal careers (aggravation) or do their offenses become less serious as they near the end of their criminal careers? If so, why?

Cumulative continuity: The way in which behavior at one point in life influences opportunities later in life.

Cumulative disadvantage: Piling up negative experiences makes it difficult for a person to succeed in life.

Self-selection: The tendency of individuals to select experiences that are consistent with internal traits or dispositions that are established early in life.

Sources: Michael L. Benson, *Crime and the Life Course* (Los Angeles: Roxbury, 2002): 10–14, 72, 122; George B. Vold, Thomas J. Bernard, and Jeffrey B. Snipes, *Theoretical Criminology* (New York: Oxford University Press, 2002): 291–292, 296–297.

---

example, Michael Gottfredson and Travis Hirschi argue that most offenders do not follow a "career" in the traditional sense. Instead, they have a short-term, hedonistic orientation and tend to pursue immediate pleasure without regard to future consequences. In addition, offenders often are socially disabled and have problems managing the ordinary tasks of life — getting an education, working, supporting a family — staying "straight." Furthermore, Gottfredson and Hirschi believe that the decline in crime with age characterizes even the most active offenders. They conclude that the word *career* is an imperfect metaphor for what appears to be chronic criminal behavior.[9]

William Rhodes's analysis of 1710 offenders released from federal prisons in 1978 supports the traditional view of the relationship between age and crime. His study revealed that recidivism declined with age for crimes such as larceny, burglary, and robbery/assault. He reported that as offenders age, they are less likely to commit crime. In addition, as they age, offenders who persist in committing crimes do so at a decreasing rate.[10] Similarly, Rudy Haapanen studied the criminal careers of about 1300 males committed to the California Youth Authority in the 1960s. Both social forces (e.g., unemployment) and race affected when and how long these individuals committed crimes, yet, the rate of adult arrest clearly declined with age.[11]

On the other hand, some researchers argue that, although the individual frequency of offending stays constant with age, participation in offending does not.[12] In other words, the rate of particular crimes is constant but the people who participate in the crimes change. In addition, career criminals present a distinct crime pattern that features continued lawbreaking after middle age.[13]

This controversy was addressed by the Robert Sampson and John Laub study of the research cohort originally constructed by Sheldon and Eleanor Glueck. The cohort consisted of 500 delinquents and nondelinquents. Their analysis determined that there were marked personality differences between the two. Delinquents were assertive, fearless, aggressive, extroverted, unconventional, and unbound by social conventions.[14] Sampson and Laub followed these groups over time years later. In their book *Crime in the Making: Pathways and Turning Points through the Life Course*, Sampson and Laub argue that the social bonds in adulthood (e.g., work, family, and community—social control theory) account for differences in criminality over the life span. Several social variables have been found to account for the persistence of criminal behavior into adulthood. For example, delinquents are four times more likely to abuse alcohol, seven times more likely to have a history of unstable employment, and three to five times more likely to be divorced or receive welfare as adults.[15]

LINK Social control theory was presented in Chapter 7.

Similarly, job stability is related to both alcohol abuse and criminality. Men aged 17–25 who had low job stability were at least four times more likely to have severe alcohol problems later in life. They were also five times more likely to engage in crime as those with high job stability. Because this pattern holds true for both delinquents and nondelinquents, job stability could mediate the effect of a juvenile record. Teamed with marital attachment and education, job stability could halt an adult criminal career. Such firm attachments to others and to jobs give people something to lose. Therefore, life events in adulthood are just as important as a juvenile record in explaining the pattern of an adult criminal career.[16]

Why do persistent offenders stop? Desistence, or how criminal careers stop, is an important life-course concept. Sampson and Laub conducted a long-term follow-up of the Glueck study groups. They confirmed the accepted fact that even active, career criminals, regardless of the type of crime they engage in, "age out" of crime.[17] Aging causes criminals to reflect on their life experiences and to question their choices. Persistent thieves often become more rational with age and realize how they had made stupid choices that were costing them the benefits of a more conventional life.[18] They had no legitimate career and no home or family; their life was in shambles.

Fatherhood can also put the breaks on a criminal career. Even among active criminals, fatherhood can heighten the deterrent affect of a prison sentence and act to reverse a criminal career. Ac-

A worker sorts inventory in a warehouse.

? *How does work contribute to the desistence of a criminal career?*

cording to one study, fathers wish to maintain their connection to their children.[19] Sampson and Laub also found that men who desisted from crime had strong routines and ties to their family and to the community.[20]

Another turning point is employment. Research demonstrates that work has an impact on desistence in a criminal career but it often varies by the age of the offender. Older offenders often stop their criminal career for meaningful work.[21] Marriage and families cut down on the amount of time an offender can spend on the street with criminal peers; working to support them is also a more productive use of time.[22]

By considering the impact of life choices and events, life-course criminology lends structure and meaning to the analysis of criminal careers.

Case Studies of Criminal Careers

Case studies are descriptive life histories of particular individuals; in the field of criminology, case studies focus on offenders who engage in particular types of crime. The aim of these studies is to gain in-depth knowledge of the motives and methods of criminals engaged in certain crimes. Case studies can lead to the development of theories to explain criminal behavior and thus they have the ability to inform policies and programs that are aimed at crime prevention and rehabilitation. Examples of this style of career criminal research follow.

The Professional Thief

Many of the previously presented assumptions about criminal careers originated in Edwin Sutherland's classic work, *The Professional Thief*.[23] This study followed the career of one professional criminal and served as the basis for Sutherland's theory of differential association.

LINK Sutherland's theory of differential association was presented in Chapter 7.

Sutherland distinguished between the career criminal and the occasional offender and developed the idea that crime can be viewed as a profession. According to Sutherland, professional thieves use their wits and talking ability rather than force to commit crimes; they also develop techniques acquired through education from other professional thieves. Status in the profession is based on their technical skill, financial standing, connections (to other thieves and power brokers), power, dress, and manners. According to Sutherland, *thief* is an honorary title bestowed on persons who have proven their skill.

Moreover, Sutherland believed professional thieves have a set of norms that govern their behavior. They work together without serious disagreement because of their shared values and strong group loyalties develop. They view the law as a common enemy. Thieves are not expected to cooperate with authorities; to them, "squealing" is a heinous offense. Crime becomes organized in the sense that unity and reciprocity are common among members. When the group recognizes the individual as a professional, status is secured. The group will select and tutor certain individuals, but only those who are successful are recognized as professional thieves. In this manner, the designation of professional thief is a status that is bestowed by a group and is not based solely on the self-conception of that person.

The Professional Fence

Several criminological studies have followed Sutherland's lead and used the case study approach to examine career criminals who chose to specialize in a particular kind of crime. Carl Klockars examined the secret world of a professional fence, Vincent Swaggi (a pseudonym).[24] Klockars found that in order to attain the status of a professional fence, one must be a dealer (both a buyer and a seller) in stolen property, regularly and profitably for a considerable period. The fence must also have a reputation as a successful dealer among both thieves and law enforcement officials. In short, Klockars discovered that fencing is an acquired status based on skills and knowledge that are not readily available to just anyone — a finding that echoes Sutherland's research.

According to Klockars, the successful fence is a businessperson and must know how to operate a business that has the additional feature of being illegal. The fence must learn how and what to buy, how to sell it, and how to deal with the traditional business issues of capital, supply, demand, and distribution. Swaggi said that people are less likely to buy a good from him unless they believe that it is stolen and that they are getting a bargain. To become successful, then, the fence must have knowledge of the product, avoid getting caught, and have the convincing appearance of a law-abiding business.

The final step in becoming a professional fence is "going public"; becoming known to the police, thieves, and others as a fence. It is a tricky process. The fence must display toughness toward the police and demonstrate to thieves the willingness to accept the threat of arrest and conviction. Going public is a right of passage into illegitimate society. Simultaneously, it estranges the fence from law-abiding individuals who would not accept him or her in society, yet who continue to seek bargains from the inventory.

Klockars' study is another example of how criminologists use information from one individual to study crime. Although the validity of such studies is suspect, they provide valuable information on subjects that are otherwise unknowable.

Another study conducted in the early 1990s considered the role of the nonprofessional fence in initiating and sustaining property crime.[25] Using interviews with 30 burglars, 6 thieves, and 19 customers who bought stolen property, plus information from 190 police arrest reports, Cromwell, Olson, and Avary reached several conclusions about the professional fence. Burglars, shoplifters, and other thieves sold a substantial proportion of their stolen property to these receivers. According to their study, fences preferred not to do business with juveniles, inexperienced thieves, or drug addicts. They considered these groups too risky. Therefore, those groups had to go elsewhere to market their stolen goods and only professional criminals could make use of the professional fence.

Fraud Masters and Stoopers

The values of the professional thief also fit the world of the credit card thief. Jerome E. Jackson did field research and conducted interviews with fraud masters — individuals who conducted fraud as their personal business.[26] These masters of fraud operated like professional businesspeople while taking advantage of their access to the illegal opportunities to commit crime. Credit card thieves often traveled to different cities and states for the sole purpose of engaging in their craft and tended to avoid their hometowns (where they were more likely to be recognized). They were career criminals — on average, specialists with more than a dozen years of experience. They siphoned the funds of victims either quickly or over a prolonged period of time, victimizing friends, acquaintances, or strangers.

Similarly, John Rosecrance used the Sutherland framework to describe the styles and activities of "stoopers," persons who retrieve discarded winning racetrack tickets. Based on interviews with 13 stoopers from California and Louisiana, Rosecrance reported that they followed the classic description of the professional thief with motives, rationalizations, and specialized skill to conduct their crimes.[27]

Sutherland's career criminal model clearly has held its validity over time. The question of motives and values of career criminals is a crucial aspect of their decision to commit crimes.

A woman enters her credit card information to make a purchase over the Internet.

? *How do credit card thieves typically operate?*

A Career Criminal Typology

A Typology of Criminal Behavior

Marshall B. Clinard, Richard Quinney, and John Wildeman have developed a typology to explain a range of criminal behaviors. A typology is a framework and theoretical construct. Here, it provides a means to describe and compare different forms of criminal behavior. These five basic dimensions reflect several strains within criminological theory[28]:

1. **Legal aspects of selected offenses:** Crime is a definition of human conduct created by authorized agents in a politically organized society. Laws are created to protect the interests of the ruling class.

2. **Criminal career of the offender:** The career of the offender includes the social role, self-concept, progression in criminal activity, and identification with crime.

3. **Group support of criminal behavior:** Group support of criminal behavior is dependant upon the offender's support for the norms of the group.

4. **Correspondence between criminal and legitimate behavior:** The behavior of the offender is viewed in relation to the norms. The norms are under the control of the segments of society that have the power to formulate and administer criminal law with regard to what they perceive to be the norms of the general public.

5. **Societal reaction and legal processing:** Social reactions are affected by the visibility of the offense and the degree to which the criminal behavior corresponds to the interests of the power structure of society. Types of criminal behavior vary in the ways that they are processed through the system. Patterns of detection, arrest, prosecution, conviction, sentencing, and punishment or treatment exist for each type of crime.

The authors also use this typology to examine nine types of criminal behavior:

violent personal, occasional property, public order, conventional, political, occupational, corporate, organized, and professional. **TABLE 9-2** summarizes Clinard, Quinney, and Wildeman's view of the criminal careers of offenders. Again, this typology provides another framework with which to compare the findings of various career criminality studies.

Cohort Research

Note that research on criminal careers examines crime that persists over many years; the list of crucial questions in the study of career criminals includes:

1. How frequently are crimes committed?
2. How serious are they?
3. How long does a career last?
4. How does a criminal career end?

One goal of this research is to determine the most effective time to intervene in a criminal career, for

TABLE 9-2

Criminal Careers of Offenders by the Type of Crime Committed

Type of Crime	Offenders' View of Their Criminal Career
Violent personal	Offenders do not see themselves as criminals. Crime is not a part of their career.
Occasional property	Offenders do not identify with crime or see themselves as criminals. They are able to rationalize their criminal behavior.
Public order	Most offenders do not regard their behavior as criminal or have a clearly defined criminal career. Their ambiguous self-concept is produced by continued contact with legal agents.
Conventional	Offenders begin their careers early in life, often in gangs. Crimes are committed for economic gain. Offenders have a vacillating self-concept and partial commitment to a criminal subculture.
Political	Offenders usually do not believe themselves as criminals and do not identify with crime. They are defined as criminal because they are perceived as threatening to the status quo (as in crimes against the government). They are criminal when they violate the laws that regulate the government itself (crime by government).
Occupational	Offenders occasionally violate the law, accompanied by appropriate rationalizations. Violation tends to be a part of their work. Offenders accept the conventional values in society and have little or no criminal self-conception.
Corporate	Offenders and their corporations have high social status in society. Offenses are an integral part of corporate business operations. Violations are rationalized as being basic to the business enterprise.
Organized	Crime is pursued as a livelihood. There is a progression in crime and an increasing isolation from the larger society. A criminal self-concept develops.
Professional	Offenders have highly developed criminal careers. They engage in specialized offenses, all of which are directed toward economic gain. They enjoy high status in the world of crime and are committed to other professional criminals.

Source: Based on Marshall B. Clinard, Richard Quinney, and John Wildeman, *Criminal Behavior Systems: A Typology* (Cincinnati, OH: Anderson, 1994): 18–20.

either crime control or rehabilitative purposes.[29] In other words, what does this research tell about bringing a criminal career to an end — for both the protection of the public and the salvation of the criminal?

One method of studying career criminality is through a cohort study. A **cohort** is a group of individuals who share the same experience in time. In this case, birth cohorts are often used because they permit the study of individuals over an extended period of time. Through the cohort, life patterns can be examined and criminal careers reconstructed. Two of the most influential birth cohort studies in criminology were conducted in Philadelphia.

The Philadelphia Birth Cohort Studies

The 1945 Birth Cohort research on criminal careers has been substantially advanced by the work of Marvin Wolfgang and his colleagues at the Center for Studies in Criminology and Criminal Law at the University of Pennsylvania. They studied a cohort of 9945 males who were born in the city of Philadelphia in 1945 and who lived there between the ages of 10 to 18. This study uncovered a small group of 627 chronic offenders who were responsible for the majority of crimes committed by the entire cohort. Their total offense rates are presented in **TABLE 9-3**.

The study revealed a number of facts about chronic offenders. First, criminal careers were related to the age at which they first committed a crime. According to this study, the earlier an individual committed his or her first offense, the greater the number of offenses committed by age 17. Second, race and family income had an impact. Over two-thirds of the chronic offenders were black, yet, according to the study, family income had more of an impact than race. For example, nonwhites with low socioeconomic status were three times more likely to be chronic offenders than whites of the same status.[30] Third, chronic offending was related to intelligence and educational performance. The study showed that chronic offenders also had lower

mean IQ scores, below-average school achievement, and a higher incidence of retardation.

The second phase of the research conducted on the 1945 cohort focused on their rate of adult offending. Wolfgang interviewed 567 of the original subjects at the time of their 25th birthday. Overall, the chance of an urban male in this study being arrested by age 30 was 50%. Race was related to adult criminality, with blacks four times more likely to have an arrest record before and after age 18 than whites. The crime rate of all the nonwhite males in the cohort was three times higher than their white counterparts. The rate among nonwhites was eleven times higher for homicide and robbery, ten times higher for rape, and four times higher for assault. According to the study, the probability that a nonwhite male will commit a violent crime was three times higher than the chances for a white male.

Wolfgang looked at two groups of chronic offenders: those who committed their fifth offense before age 19 and those who had five offenses by age 30. The rate of offending increased as the offenders grew older. The first group (early chronics) accounted for 18% of the offenses committed by this subsample; the second group (late chronics) accounted for 30%. Late chronics were likely to commit personal offenses involving injury to the victim.

Another follow-up study traced the adult criminal careers of a random subsample of the 1945 cohort described. Police records were collected ($N = 975$); 567 of the cohort subjects who were interviewed at age 26. The police records revealed that 47% of the sample had an officially recorded arrest by age 30. Nonwhite and lower socioeconomic status groups were more likely to be offenders. By age 30, 70% of the nonwhites and 60% of the lower socioeconomic status subjects had been arrested, compared to 38% of the whites and 36% of the higher socioeconomic status subjects. Unlike whites, the criminal careers of nonwhites were more persistent through both juvenile and adult years. Persistent offenders had more serious adult offenses and were more likely to come from socially disadvantaged groups.[31]

Chronic juvenile offenders were most likely to commit adult offenses; juvenile delinquency status was the best predictor of adult criminality. The interview data revealed that offenders committed crimes in a spontaneous, unplanned fashion. In particular, gang members move from crime to crime without pattern. Again, chronic offenders accounted for the bulk of crime: 74% of all arrests and 82% of the index crimes.

TABLE 9-3

Offense Rates of Chronic Offenders in the 1945 and 1958 Philadelphia Birth Cohorts (Percentage of the Entire Cohort)

Year	Cases	Offense	Murder	Rape	Robbery	Assault
1945	6.3	52	71	73	82	69
1958	7.5	61	61	75	73	65

The 1958 Birth Cohort

The primary aim of the 1958 Philadelphia birth cohort study was to replicate the earlier study.[32] It tracked all 13,160 males and 14,000 females born in Philadelphia in 1958 who resided there until their 17th birthday. The study makes comparisons with the first cohort possible while considering new variables, such as gender.

One difference between the two cohorts concerns race. In the second cohort, the rate of chronic offending increased for whites (from 10% to 15%) and slightly decreased for nonwhites (29% to 27%). In addition, the difference in the rate of violent crime between the races was narrower in the second cohort (6 times higher versus 15 times higher). The 1958 cohort had a higher rate of offending per 1000 subjects: 1059 versus 1027. However, the members of the second cohort committed almost twice as many index offenses and three times as many violent crimes as the 1945 cohort. The 1958 cohort had an offense rate that was five times higher for robbery, three times higher for homicide, twice as high for assault, and 1.7 times higher for rape. Injury offenses were much more prevalent and harmful in the 1958 cohort. The offenses committed by the 1958 cohort were more serious than those committed by the first cohort.

Like the 1945 cohort, the 1958 cohort contained a group of chronic offenders. Chronic offenders in the 1958 cohort were a larger group and committed a higher percentage of the total number of offenses. Although the percentages for the chronic offenders in the 1958 cohort dropped, they still accounted for the majority of serious violent crime committed by the group.

According to the study, the high number of crimes committed by chronic offenders was related to race and socioeconomic status. Among whites, chronics committed 50% of the offenses; among nonwhites, they accounted for 65%. Chronics of high socioeconomic status committed 51% of the offenses for their group. Chronic offenders of low socioeconomic status committed 65% of the offenses for their group, while chronics of low socioeconomic status were plagued by the same set of social problems as those in the first cohort: they moved more often, had lower achievement scores, had less schooling, and were more likely to have disciplinary problems at school.

Elisabeth S. Piper considered the relationship between chronicity and violent recidivism in the 1958 cohort.[33] Among violent delinquents, there were a greater proportion of chronic offenders than among nonviolent delinquents. Chronic offenders were also more likely to repeat a violent offense. She found that violent recidivists also committed a large proportion of nonviolent index offenses.

Kimberly L. Kempf focused on the adult criminal careers of the members of the 1958 cohort. Over 29% of all delinquents and over 6% of nondelinquents committed offenses as adults. The delinquents, particularly the chronic offenders, dominated all categories of adult offending. Kempf found that the adult offenders were most likely to be males from low socioeconomic status areas with a prior delinquent record. Fifty-five percent of the delinquents with at least five police contacts became adult offenders.[34]

Kempf also analyzed the data to learn whether these chronic offenders specialized in certain types of crime. The findings revealed a "minimal level" of specialization with "general, random, or 'cafeteria style' offending" as the common pattern. Their status as career criminals had more to do with the volume than the pattern of their criminal activity.[35] The adult criminality of the 1958 cohort was found to be significantly related to the number of juvenile offenses they had committed, low socioeconomic status, beginning their juvenile career at a young age, continuing it through their adolescence, and being active in crime at age 17.[36]

Conclusions of the Birth Cohort Studies

A comparison of the findings from both birth cohorts led to the following conclusions. Evidently, delinquency was prevalent among nonwhites and subjects with low socioeconomic status. Delinquency was also related to residential instability, poor school achievement, and failure to graduate from high school.[37] The offenders in the 1958 cohort committed a greater number of crimes and their crimes were more serious. A core of chronic offenders was responsible for the bulk of the crimes committed. These chronics "started their violent harm early in life and will apparently continue to do so."[38]

In reaction to these findings, experts have suggested that the juvenile courts adopt a policy of close (intensive) supervision for perhaps first-time and certainly second-time index offenders. After a third index offense, incapacitation should become "the rule rather than the exception. Juveniles can and should receive severe penalties in juvenile court when their most current offense and prior record warrant such action."[39] Policies should be established to better identify the chronic offender. An enhanced system of record keeping should ease identification.

The Racine Birth Cohort Studies

Lyle Shannon and his colleagues conducted a longitudinal study that examined the criminal careers of 6127 persons born in Racine, Wisconsin, in 1942, 1949, and 1959.[40] The study examined the development of criminal careers within the three birth cohorts. Data on reported police contacts were collected through 1974. As in the Philadelphia studies, the goal was to identify those individuals who were more likely to engage in delinquency, who stopped committing crimes, and who continued their criminal careers into adulthood. However, the findings were different from those in the Philadelphia study.

Shannon reported that the rates for serious felonies more than doubled from 1942 to 1955 for the age group 6–17 and the rate more than tripled for the 18–20 age group. Crime rates were highest in the inner-city areas where unemployment and underemployment were commonplace. In addition, offenders with a juvenile record were more likely to commit crime as adults, yet it was impossible to predict which juveniles would become adult offenders.

The Cambridge (United Kingdom) Study of Delinquent Development

The Cambridge Study of Delinquent Development followed 410 London working-class males from age 8 to 32, recording data starting in 1961. Data were obtained from: (1) tests and interviews conducted at ages 8, 10, and 14 years; (2) interviews conducted at ages 16, 18, 21, 25, and 32; (3) parental interviews; (4) questionnaires completed by the subjects' teachers; and (5) statistics compiled by the Criminal Record Office in London. These data were analyzed to identify predictors of participation (prevalence) in officially recorded offending between ages 10 and 20 years; early onset (between ages 10 and 13) versus later onset (ages 14 to 20) of offending; and persistence versus desistance of offending in adulthood (ages 21 to 32).

In this study, David P. Farrington found that the peak age for offending (the annual prevalence of convictions) was 17 (9.2 males per 100 convicted).[41] The best childhood predictors (at age 10) of prevalence were childhood antisocial behavior, convicted parents, impulsivity and daring, low

intelligence and attainment, low income and poor housing, and poor childrearing practices (including separation from parents). The number of offenses committed per year peaked at age 17 (16.8 per 100 males). The peak age of onset was 14 (4.6 first convictions per 100 males) with a secondary peak at 17; age 23.3 years was the "age of desistance" or the age at which the last offense was typically committed. Farrington also determined that violent offenders committed their crimes frequently. Therefore, he concluded that measures designed to reduce future violence might as well be targeted on frequent as well as currently violent offenders.

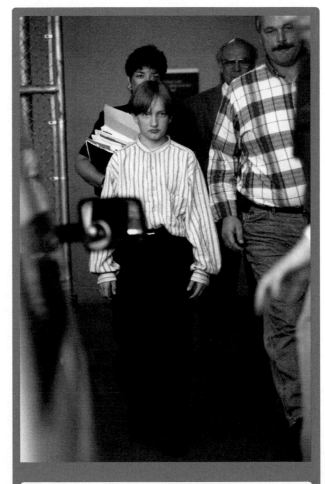

Ray DeFord, 12, after his sentencing on arson charges. Although initially hailed as a hero for warning his neighbors about the fire, he eventually admitted to setting the fire that killed eight Mexican immigrants.

 Reviewing the findings of Farrington's delinquent development study, do you think it is likely that DeFord will continue to offend? What could derail his criminality?

In particular, the early onset of offending was predicted by low paternal involvement with the boy in leisure activities. The same factor led to persistence in crime between ages 21 and 32 together with a low degree of commitment to school and low verbal IQ at ages 8–9.[42] A long-term follow-up study of the cohort found that nearly all subjects had been sent to prison. Most of the subjects thought imprisonment had no effect on them, although some believed it had made them less likely to reoffend. Generally, chronic offenders led more dysfunctional lives in adulthood than other offenders. The most important childhood risk factors for chronic offending were troublesomeness, daring, and having a delinquent sibling or a convicted parent. On the basis of such features, the authors of this study believed that most of the chronic offenders might have been predicted at age 10 and that treatment could have been identified.[43] Another study of the life course of these offenders revealed that several social variables (work history, relations with spouses) distinguished between chronic and other types of offenders.[44] The results of the Cambridge study emphasize the need to consider the different stages and elements of a criminal career as separate entities. It also seems that the most promising methods of preventing offending appear to be behavioral parent training and preschool intellectual enrichment programs.[45]

In sum, all the cohort studies discussed here reveal that a small group of chronic offenders is responsible for the bulk of crime committed. However, it is difficult, if not impossible, to accurately identify who these individuals are and to do something about them *before* crimes are committed. A truly proactive approach is impossible because society cannot take action against citizens until they actually commit a crime. From a rehabilitative standpoint, a number of social variables (such as education and employment) appear to be correlated to chronic offending that could serve as the basis for prevention programs. Focusing on how many prior convictions offenders have or their age provides little direction for supervision and improvement.

The Violent Juvenile Offender

The findings from the cohort birth studies have resulted in changes in the juvenile justice system, particularly with respect to those juveniles who commit serious, violent offenses — particularly trying juveniles as adults and thus subjecting them to adult criminal penalties. Critics charge that the juvenile justice system is now too lenient with those who commit serious crimes, allowing them to "get away with murder."[46] Several studies have tested this idea. For example, Donna Hamparian and her colleagues studied the criminal careers of 1138 youths born in Columbus, Ohio, between 1956 and 1960.[47] The purpose of the study was to learn about the criminal careers of chronically violent juveniles. In her study, only 2% of all the juveniles had committed a violent offense, and those offenders did not progress from less serious (e.g., status offenses) to more serious criminality.

However, within this small subsample, 60% of the violent juveniles were arrested at least once as a young adult (before age 20) for a felony offense. These youths also tended to be arrested more often (at least five times), to have spent time in a juvenile correctional facility, and to have committed serious crimes earlier and more frequently.[48] In fact, their study showed these chronic juvenile offenders accounted for two-thirds of the crimes committed by the entire cohort and two out of every five arrests made for violent index crimes. These violent offenders did not specialize, however, and few were repeat violent offenders.[49] In terms of personal characteristics, the chronic juveniles were predominantly black and male; females were not likely to be arrested for a violent offense. Blacks were more likely to have their first arrest earlier than whites and were more likely to be repeat offenders. When they did commit a violent offense, the entire cohort was unlikely to use a weapon.

As adults, nearly three out of five of these offenders were arrested at least once for an adult index offense. This was particularly true for males with a violent juvenile index offense who were first arrested at age 12 and eventually incarcerated as youths. Over a 5- to 9-year period, these 721 offenders were arrested a total of 2958 times.[50] Four out of 10 adult offenders were arrested at least once for a violent index offense and half of these offenders were sentenced to prison. Eventually, over 80% of these prisoners were released but half of them were reincarcerated. These findings show that there was a clear link between juvenile and adult crime. Juveniles who committed serious crimes went on to commit more crimes as adults, but lenient treatment had nothing to do with it. These juveniles were treated in the same fashion as adult offenders.

Hamparian and her colleagues recommended that chronic violent offenders should be dealt with severely, not just with punishment, but also with a graduated series of programs. These programs should range from incarceration to work readiness projects that provide sheltered employment such as a community conservation corps for young adults. The researchers stressed the importance of not waiting for chronic juvenile offenders to become adult criminals.

In 1984, the federal government concluded that it was necessary to focus on the serious juvenile offender. In particular, programs that had the potential to decrease the probability that serious juvenile offenders would spend their "adult lives in prison" were encouraged.[51] As a result, the <u>Violent Juvenile Offender (VJO) Program</u> was established. It places chronically violent juvenile offenders in an intervention program that features four elements[52]:

1. Reintegration (treating the offender in the community rather than in the artificial environment of an institution)
2. Case management (pertaining to the individual needs and problems of the offender)
3. Social learning processes (promoting prosocial values)
4. A phased reentry from secure facilities to intensive supervision in the community (using community facilities to begin with and then placing restrictions on the juveniles' behavior in the community)

This program is now in operation in Detroit, Michigan; Memphis, Tennessee; Newark, New Jersey; and Boston, Massachusetts; the experimental and control groups have permitted a test of its effectiveness.

One study found that the average juvenile in a VJO program had been involved in more than 10 crimes that resulted in more than five formal juvenile court adjudications per offender. Violence predominated: Almost 60% of the youths were charged with and 40% adjudicated for three or more violent crimes.[53] Self-reports showed an even more intense involvement in violent crime. These youths averaged approximately one violent, one property, and one drug offense per week. These youths did not specialize in violent crime alone, however, and did not progress from a less serious offense to violent crime. They tended to commit violent acts early in their delinquent careers.

The life experiences of these youths contained several elements that encouraged delinquency. Their families were typically single-parent households headed by the mother. Because more than 70% of the mothers were unemployed, they and the juve-

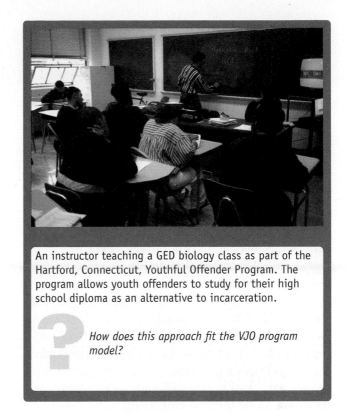

An instructor teaching a GED biology class as part of the Hartford, Connecticut, Youthful Offender Program. The program allows youth offenders to study for their high school diploma as an alternative to incarceration.

? *How does this approach fit the VJO program model?*

niles lived in poverty. Family life was marked by violence, particularly a history of wife battering. There also was a high rate of criminal justice system involvement among family members, particularly among fathers and siblings. Over a quarter of the youths were not enrolled in school at the time of the most recent offense. Eighteen percent of the juveniles were employed during this period.

Although a high degree of gang involvement was not noted in this study, friends of these youths were also engaging regularly in delinquent behavior. Over 22% of the youths admitted to substance abuse problems (either drugs or alcohol). They also believed that drugs and alcohol contributed to their violent behavior.[54]

Research Findings from the National Youth Survey

Delbert S. Elliot studied serious violent offending in data from the National Youth Survey (NYS), a national probability sample of 1725 youths who were aged 10–17 in 1976. His group has been continuously interviewed. In the eighth wave of data (1993), the respondents were aged 27–33. The data set contains both self-report and official record data for respondents and official record data for parents or primary caretakers. Elliot focused on serious violent offending and his findings also illuminate the concept of a violent juvenile offender. In 50% of these events, a weapon was used; in about two-thirds of these, a gun or knife was used and some medical treatment was required.

At the peak age of 17, 36% of African-American males and 25% of white males report one or more serious violent offense. For females, nearly one black female in five and one white female in ten report involvement in serious violent offending. With regards to gender, Elliot reported three significant differences in the age curve: (1) the peak age in prevalence is earlier for females, (2) the decline (maturation effect) is steeper for females, and (3) the gender differential becomes greater over time.[55]

According to results from Elliot's study, serious violent offending begins between the ages of 12 and 20 and the risk of initiation is close to zero after age 20. By age 18, nearly 40% of black males have become involved compared with 30% of white males. However, when socioeconomic status is taken into account, the difference between races was insignificant. Over 60% of all males who would ever be involved in serious violent offending were actively involved by age 17. Elliot noted that the rates of serious violent offending in this study were three to four times greater than those studies based on official records alone.

Unlike previous studies on this subject, Elliot reported that the activity of serious violent offenders followed a progression. The typical sequence was from assault to robbery to rape. The overall pattern suggested a clear escalation in the seriousness of criminal behavior over time in a criminal career. Similar to the chronic group from the birth cohort studies, the serious violent offenders were less than 5% of the NYS sample but they accounted for 83% of the index offenses and half of all offenses reported. Compared with males, far fewer females were serious violent offenders, but those who continued their careers into adulthood did so at almost the same rate as males (18% to 22%, respectively).[56]

In terms of continuing their offending as adults, the study showed that nearly twice as many blacks as whites continued their violent careers into their twenties; blacks had longer violent criminal careers than whites. What can explain this racial difference? Elliot suggests that whites are more likely than blacks to be living with their parents (in more conventional and supportive environments). He notes that blacks may be more likely than whites to be involved in the illicit economy, particularly the drug distribution networks in their neighborhoods.

However, it is also possible that the finding that blacks are more likely to continue adult offending is due to the nature of these data. Official data typically concentrate on street-level crime, and minorities may be more likely to be arrested by the police and sentenced by the courts.

LINK The accuracy of official crime statistics is questioned in Chapter 2 and the problems of racial bias and prejudicial treatment of minorities in the criminal justice system are presented in Chapter 8.

Policy Implications

Compared to other studies, Elliot's study on serious violent offenders had several different conclusions: Their prevalence is much higher; the onset of violent offending occurred much earlier; the demographic correlates were much weaker; evidence for escalation in seriousness, frequency, and variety of offenses over the career was much stronger; evidence for the sequencing of serious forms of violent behavior was stronger; and the continuity of serious violent offending from the juvenile to the adult years was similar for males and for females.

In addition, Elliot's study noted that blacks were more likely to continue their violent offending into their adult years. Elliot concludes that it is possible that, once African-Americans begin their career of violence, theft, and substance use, these offenders who are often from disadvantaged families and neighborhoods are trapped. They have fewer opportunities for conventional adult roles (via education and employment), and they are more deeply embedded in and dependent on the gangs and the illicit economies that flourish in their neighborhoods. However, if they were able to make the transition to a conventional lifestyle of work and family, they dropped their involvement in violent crime. Therefore, policies and programs should target youths for work and conventional adult roles of work and family.[57]

LINK The bonds that prevent crime and hold a person to conventional roles of family and employment are discussed in Chapter 7. An analysis of race and crime is presented in Chapter 8.

Jeffrey A. Fagan reported on the development of VJO programs in the four cities of Boston, Detroit, Memphis, and Newark. He tracked the experiences of 227 males who had been adjudicated for an index felony (e.g., homicide, rape, robbery, assault). The program was based on an intervention model derived from an integration of the strain, control, and learning theories, stressing early childhood socialization factors. In other words, the model attempted to use criminological theories to keep offenders out of trouble and convert them to conventional values.[58]

Fagan determined that the recidivism rate of youths in the Boston program were substantially lower than those of the control group. Thus, the findings indicate that the program was effective in reducing recidivism in this high-risk group. The results from the study of the VJO programs indicate that it is possible to meld the goals of both crime control and rehabilitation. Fagan concluded that juvenile corrections should reallocate resources to emphasize institutional treatment, reintegration, and community reentry. The VJO program should focus on the reintegration of these serious offenders. Fagan and Martin Forst recommend that theory and program design for these VJO programs be integrated so that treatment programs with social skills and behaviors are offered to provide violent youths aid with their reintegration to society.[59]

Serious Habitual Offender/ Drug-Involved Program

Another program that targets chronic juveniles is the **Serious Habitual Offender/Drug-Involved (SHODI) Program**, which provides a structured, coordinated focus on serious, habitual juvenile crime and seeks to improve the law enforcement system's response to drug-related, juvenile crimes.[60] In 1983, the Office of Juvenile Justice and Delinquency Prevention developed this program via a demonstration project involving police departments. The National Council of Juvenile and Family Court Judges established guidelines for the SHODI Program. Acknowledging the seriousness of the problem posed by these offenders, the judges caution that SHODI juveniles must be properly and carefully identified. At that point, the system can take the appropriate response and hold juveniles accountable for their crimes. Juvenile records should be made available to adult courts so that habitual juvenile offenders do not appear to be first offenders. Records should also be shared across law enforcement and social agencies to provide a full picture of the nature of the juvenile's criminal involvement and home life.

However, treatment and rehabilitation should not be abandoned. Substance abuse programs for these juveniles should be readily provided and other appropriate community resources should be developed as well. The judges emphasize that SHODIs are only a small part of the juvenile justice system and should not become the court's sole focus. In fact, research results clearly indicate that serious juvenile offenders can be identified, removed from the community, effectively treated, and returned.[61] Treatment programs for chronic juvenile offenders in both Orange County, California, and Philadelphia, Pennsylvania, report positive results in changing the behavior of these juveniles.[62]

Career Patterns in Crime

Other studies of career criminality are based on the examination of the official criminal records of offender groups. One study in 1979 examined the criminal careers of a nationwide sample of 10,397 prison inmates. Only inmates who were at least 40 years of age at the time of their last prison admission were selected for study. Their criminal careers were then reconstructed using the model in FIGURE 9-1. Three time periods were examined: adolescence (ages 7–17), young adulthood (ages 18–39), and middle age (age 40 and older). In addition, four criminal types were suggested.

1. Type 1 offenders had the longest criminal career, extending across all three time periods.
2. Type 2 offenders abstained from criminality during young adulthood only.
3. Type 3 offenders skipped the adolescent period but were consistently criminal in later years.
4. Type 4 offenders committed crimes in middle age only.

As expected, these offenders had different types of criminal histories. The Type 4 offenders were most likely to be serving time for a violent crime. Typically, the Type 4 offender was an older (at least middle-aged) individual who was in prison due to the severity of the crime committed (e.g., murder: 64.7%). Type 3 offenders also tended to be incarcerated for a violent crime (e.g., robbery: 46.7%). Type 1 offenders who were criminals across all three time periods were incarcerated because of the gravity of their offenses (e.g., burglary: 32.9%) and the longevity of their careers. The typical Type 1 offenders had spent approximately one-quarter of their lives in confinement.

As determined in other studies, the majority (92%) of the inmates who had been incarcerated as adolescents continued their criminal careers as adults. Consequently, only 10 Type 2 inmates were discovered in the study. Offenders who begin their

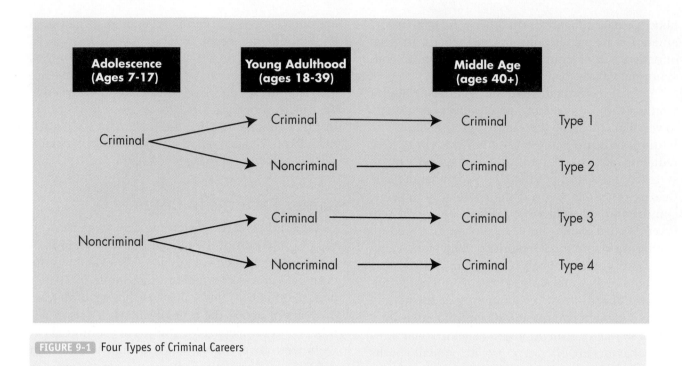

FIGURE 9-1 Four Types of Criminal Careers

careers as juveniles tend to continue, not desist from crime.

These offenders also had social problems that are associated with criminality. For example, Types 1 and 3 accounted for the majority of heroin users. Over two-thirds of all the offenders had participated in an alcohol treatment abuse program. Over 23% of the inmates were unemployed at the time of their present prison offense. Almost 42% of the inmates had less than a 9th-grade education. Given this history of substance abuse coupled with low education and high unemployment, the need for rehabilitation programs for these offenders is evident.

Violent crime was evident across the sample. Middle-aged inmates were accountable for almost 7500 deaths — one human life for every three middle-aged inmates. About 40% of the inmates serving time for property (or other nonviolent) crimes had prior records for violent crime. Therefore, according to this study, offenders do not seem to specialize and criminal careers often do lead to violence.[63]

The Federal Armed Career Criminal Study

In 1984, Congress passed the Armed Career Criminal Act. This law gave the Bureau of Alcohol, Tobacco and Firearms (ATF) the authority to target career criminals. The act calls for a mandatory 15-year sentence for anyone possessing a firearm who has three or more previous convictions for a violent felony or serious drug offense or both. The ATF studied 471 offenders sentenced under this law. These offenders had a total of 3088 prior felony convictions between them for an average of 6.55 per inmate.

Interviews with 100 such inmates revealed that:

- The average career criminal had spent 66% of his adult life in prison.
- 69% were admitted illegal drug users.
- In an average week, they committed three crimes.

Thirty-four percent of these inmates felt that a strong mandatory sentence has no deterrent value.

The career criminals interviewed in this study clearly stated their views on the mandatory-sentence gun law[64]:

If a guy makes a living with a gun, he is going to do what he has to do and believes he is not going to be caught. Criminals will shoot at officers to avoid facing the 15 years; it's a life sentence anyway.

Yes, if I got out today I'd have a gun today. If a government agent showed up at my doorstep, I'd kill her. I'm not going down again. This law is creating a monster — it's creating a lot of people who will kill agents because you've made them hardened criminals — what does he have to lose? A guy facing mandatory sentences will resort to violence.

Yes, if a cop pulls up on me after this, we will hold court right there. I won't do 15 years again for carrying or having a gun.

These blunt quotes from interviews indicate that cracking down on career criminals may have unintended and undesirable side effects. These quotes also raise questions about the effectiveness of deterrence. These particular criminals had above-average educational levels. Despite their background and their understanding of the law, they chose to continue their criminal careers and were not deterred by the presence of enhanced punishment.

The Rand Corporation Habitual Offender Research

Research conducted by the Rand Corporation attempted to estimate the actual rate at which crimes are committed by habitual offenders. It featured the use of a self-report study of incarcerated offenders; a survey that asked offenders to reconstruct their criminal careers, including the offenses that they "got away with" (crimes that the offenders admittedly committed but for which they were never apprehended). Thus, it sought to uncover the actual number of crimes committed by habitual offenders during their criminal career, not just the crimes in their official record.

In the first Rand career criminal study, 49 male armed robbers from a California prison were surveyed. These inmates had also served at least one prior prison term. They accepted responsibility for a total of over 10,500 crimes during their careers — an average of 20 crimes per year on the street. The study found that the rate of crimes committed during a career declined with age. Although the inmates noted that they were unconcerned about the possibility of punishment, they did recognize that they were spending substantial portions of their lives behind bars. Inmates who served longer sentences were not less likely to be reincarcerated. To break the cycle of recidivism, these inmates said that they needed job training in prison and employment upon release. Inmates with substance abuse problems had the highest crime rates overall, indicating that drug treatment programs should be provided in prison.[65]

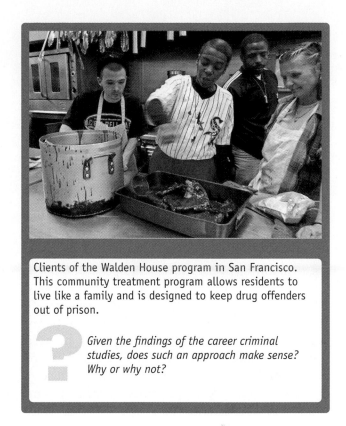

Clients of the Walden House program in San Francisco. This community treatment program allows residents to live like a family and is designed to keep drug offenders out of prison.

? *Given the findings of the career criminal studies, does such an approach make sense? Why or why not?*

In the second Rand career criminal study, 624 male inmates from five California prisons were surveyed. The researchers constructed scales to consider the number of crimes committed and the frequency with which they were committed, considered together with the length of a criminal career. In terms of specialization, the study uncovered few specialists (52) who commit one type of crime at a high rate. However, among the criminals themselves, there was a classification system. Inmates who described themselves as "straights" committed crimes at a significantly lower rate than others. The "boosters" or "robbers" admitted to a wide range of crimes, while the "violent persons" and "gang members" usually reported only violent crimes. Within each group, the highest rate of crime coincided with their self-description.

This study showed that, as a whole, these offenders were unconcerned about the probability of punishment. They admittedly used the money from their crimes to live high and enjoy drugs and alcohol. They believed that skill and practice would enable them to evade capture and enjoy the fruits of crime. The inmates predicted that they would not go straight after prison and were unlikely to get caught. Their responses fit the "psychological definition of habitual offenders."[66]

Drugs and alcohol played a significant role in their criminal behavior. During the 3-year period before their present incarceration, 42% of the study sample admitted to the use of heavy drugs (e.g., heroin). Drug abusers committed more, different, and higher rates of crime than nonusers. Drug abusers also had higher rates of both violent and property crimes.

The third Rand career criminal study surveyed over 2200 prisoners from three states: California, Michigan, and Texas. In this analysis, Jan M. Chaiken and Marcia R. Chaiken constructed a profile of the most criminally active offender: the violent predator. In their study, violent predators were prolific offenders, committing over 135 robberies per year.67

Violent predators tend to be young — less than 23 years old when they enter prison. They typically begin committing violent crimes before age 16 and commit property crimes by age 18. They are more socially unstable, usually unmarried and unemployed, and their unemployment tends to encourage more crime. They use and sell hard drugs and commonly abuse more than one drug: The study showed the use of "heroin with barbiturates, barbiturates with amphetamines, barbiturates with alcohol, amphetamines with alcohol, or multiple combinations of these."68 This type of multiple-drug abuse is highly correlated with violent crime.

Although the research documented the existence of violent predators, it concluded that they are not easily identified by their criminal records alone. Their intentions and motives cannot be perceived by just their formal record of offenses. They are good candidates for incapacitation but other policies should be considered. It is obvious that they could benefit from well-designed and implemented work and drug treatment programs.

James Q. Wilson and Allan F. Abrahamse examined the economic (estimated) gains from crime and from work for state prison inmates in California, Michigan, and Texas from the third Rand Inmate Survey. Their goal was to help explain how repeat offenders view their behavior in terms of economic gain: In short, does crime pay? The inmate surveys revealed that "mid-rate" (average) burglars estimated that they earned $2368 per year, tax-free, for their average 9 burglaries, 10 thefts, and 85 drug sales, plus other offenses each year. After taxes, their legitimate work earnings were $7931 per year ($5.78/hour). "High-rate" burglars faced a much greater risk of being caught and incarcerated. Their criminal records revealed that they were free on the street only 60% of the time. When on the street, they would commit 322 crimes per year, for an estimated take of $5710 per year, tax-free. Legitimate work netted them $5540 per year after taxes. Wilson and Abrahamse concluded that a person who chooses burglary/theft as an occupation will not do better than a person working at $5.78/hour.

If it is so unprofitable, why did these offenders commit their crimes? Wilson and Abrahamse reported that the inmates believed that crime paid very well. Clearly, they did not make rational decisions about offending. Would someone be willing to become a high-rate robber if they knew that, on average, they would spend more than half of any given year in jail or prison, in exchange for an annual, "tax-free" salary of $14,286?

However, for the study the inmates did offer several reasons why they engaged in crime. The first reason was the absence of legitimate work opportunities. On average, inmates held approximately two different jobs while on the street. These inmates were not so much excluded from the job market as casual and relatively unsuccessful participants in it. Second, their drug/alcohol problems rendered them unfit or uninterested in regular 9-to-5 jobs. Third, the inmates may have been disposed to overvalue the benefits from crime and to undervalue its costs. Repeat offenders are "inordinately impulsive or present-oriented." The benefits of crime are immediate but the costs of crime are often delayed considerably. To them, even small sums of money were attractive when serious penalty was not to be paid until 5 or 6 months in the future. They felt that crime could lead to "high living," "owning expensive things," and "being my own man." Over the long term, they believed that the benefits of crime would be much higher than they in fact were. Wilson and Abrahamse concluded that if the costs of committing a series of crimes were presented all at once, there would probably be far fewer career criminals.69

However, Pierre Tremblay and Carlo Morselli reanalyzed the same financial data and reached a different conclusion. They noted that nearly half of the sample of offenders had illegal earnings of $2780 or more per year. These "relatively successful" offenders could stand as a positive example to others and encourage them to pursue a life of crime.70

Challenges to the Rand Studies

The Rand Corporation studies document the nature of career criminality within incarcerated populations. The findings lend support to the policy of selective incapacitation. However, other studies challenge the Rand findings. Julie Horney and Ineke H. Marshall have displayed the difficulty of measuring individual rates of crime through self-report studies. They interviewed 403 Nebraska inmates and used calendars to record when crimes had been committed versus when an individual was incarcerated. There was evidence of exaggeration and time confusion on the part of the inmates concerning their criminal records. Based on this study, the researchers concluded that the Rand studies may have inflated the rate of crimes committed by career criminals.[71]

Similarly, Alfred C. Miranne and Michael R. Geerken used the Rand interview instrument to study the crime rate of 200 male inmates from New Orleans, Louisiana. They found that the total rate of offending was comparable to that of the Rand study. However, the upper 10% of their sample reported that they committed over 160 offenses per year.[72] Also, their burglary rate was several times higher than that reported in the Rand study — yet, when the upper 10% of criminals were compared,

the New Orleans sample had a lower rate of offending than the Rand samples. Based on the comparison of these studies, it would appear that it is necessary to conduct studies in different locations to decide the rate of career criminality.

In addition, career criminal studies often fail to examine the societal impact that career criminals have on their victims. In one cohort of 500 adult criminals, offenders totaled over 29,000 arrests, including 58 homicides, 201 rapes, 55 kidnappings, 405 armed robberies, and 1101 aggravated assaults. These activities led to 2801 felony convictions and 1739 prison sentences. Given this level of activity, the authors estimated that these habitual offenders generated over $415 million in victim costs, required over almost $137 million in criminal justice systems costs to process them, and over $14 million in lost earnings. In sum, the crimes of this group of career criminals cost society over $550 million in victimization costs.[73] **TABLE 9-4** summarizes the findings of career criminal research.

TABLE 9-4

Key Findings of Career Criminal Research

The research on the career criminal shows that:
- The prevalence of offending peaks in the late teenage years (15–19).
- The peak age of onset of offending is between 8 and 14.
- The peak age of desistance from offending is between 20 and 29.
- The most active juvenile offenders are most likely to become adult criminals.
- The main risk factors for early onset of offending before age 20 are:
  - *Individual factors*: low intelligence, low school achievement, hyperactivity-impulsiveness and risk taking, aggression and bullying
  - *Family factors*: poor parental supervision, harsh and/or inconsistent discipline, child physical abuse, low involvement of parents with children, parental conflict, broken families, criminal parents, and delinquent siblings
  - *Socioeconomic factors*: low family income and large family size
  - *Peer factors*: delinquent peers, peer rejection, and low popularity
  - *School factors*: a high delinquency rate
  - *Neighborhood factors*: a high-crime neighborhood
- The main life events that encourage desistance after age 20 are:
  - Getting married
  - Getting a satisfying job
  - Moving to a better area
  - Joining the military
- Males have higher rates of crime than females.
- Career criminal research focuses exclusively on patterns of street crime and delinquency and ignores white-collar crime.
- Offenders who abuse drugs and alcohol commit more crimes during their career.
- Offenders tend to commit a variety of crimes during their career, not specialize in a certain type.
- Rates of offending tend to decline with age.

A small proportion of offenders are responsible for most crime, yet these chronic offenders are not easily identified.

Sources: David P. Farrington, "Developmental and Life Course Criminology: Key Theoretical and Empirical Issues — The 2002 Sutherland Award Address," *Criminology* 41 (2003): 223–225; Joan Petersilia, "Criminal Career Research: A Review of Recent Evidence," in Norval Morris and Michael Tonry, eds., *Crime and Justice*, volume 2, (Chicago: University of Chicago Press, 1980): 368–370.

In an effort to win public support for his election in 2005, former Conservative leader Michael Howard proposed a get-tough, "war on crime" approach to British policies. He also pledged to aggressively attack drug abuse, increase discipline in schools, and control abuses in the asylum system in a manner that would make Britain the envy of other countries both within and outside of the European Union.

Focusing on crime proposals, Mr. Howard vowed to "take the gloves off" and use the zero tolerance approach to crime across Britain that was popularized by New York City Mayor Rudolph Giuliani. He also pledged to make certain that the rights of victims were upheld over those of criminals. Rather than ignore the repeated crimes of released inmates, Howard promised to

ensure that dangerous and career criminals would be sent to prison, even if more cell space was required. He lamented the absence of a strong police presence on the streets of London and promised to recruit 5000 more police officers per year. He insisted that policies enacted by a Conservative government would tackle crime in a strong, disciplined fashion designed to ease the worries of the British people.

What crime policies does this politician advocate? Are they supported by the career criminal research findings presented in this chapter?

Source: "Howard Pledges Less Talk, More Action," *The Conservative Party*, May 10, 2004, available at http://www.conservatives.com/popups/print.cfm?obj_id=116342&type=print, accessed October 11, 2004.

The Criminal Careers of Women

Criminology has traditionally focused on male criminals and their offenses. Part of this neglect was due to the belief that females are more likely to be moral and their offenses less serious. Another aspect of the chivalry hypothesis is that women are protected in a male-dominated world in order to bear children or work in "pink ghetto" jobs (e.g., teaching, nursing). It was also believed that females feared social disapproval more than males and thus they committed fewer and less-serious crimes.[74] When they do offend, their crimes are limited by their social status and position. Therefore, women have tended to specialize in minor property crimes (shoplifting) or sex crimes (prostitution). Recent trends, however, indicate that this view of female criminality needs to change.

The Crime Patterns of Females

Several studies have compared the criminal patterns of males and females. Michael J. Hindelang examined Uniform Crime Reports and victimization data from the National Crime Survey between 1972 and 1976. Both data sets revealed that males had a higher degree of involvement in rape, robbery, assault, larceny, burglary, and motor vehicle

theft. The victims of crimes perpetrated by women were less likely to report the offense to the police than the victims of men.[75] Other researchers studied male and female arrests over a 13-year period (1971–1984) in the state of New York. They found that race, regional differences, and the seriousness of the crime affected the distribution over time.[76] These factors were just as important as gender. For example, race may play a more primary role. John H. Laub and Michael J. McDermott used victimization data to examine the rates of juvenile offenses committed by black and white females. They reported that black females had higher rates of violent crime.[77]

Beginning in the 1960s, Darryl Steffensmeier and Emilie Allan examined female and male arrests for four decades and learned that females were most likely to be arrested for minor property crimes. Women were also involved with prostitution, substance abuse (especially alcohol and marijuana), petty thefts, and "hustles" (e.g., shoplifting, theft of services, credit card forgery, drug dealing). When females are associated with more serious or lucrative types of crime, they tend to serve as accomplices to males.[78]

However, studies in 2002 revealed that women are just as likely as men to engage in crime as a career. In his assessment of 500 career criminals,

Rochdale, United Kingdom: One of Rochdale's most prolific criminals who stole dozens of high-value cars in a seven-month crime spree is starting a seven-year prison sentence.

Ryan Grogan, age 28, was charged with 75 offenses, including 53 burglaries in which cars were taken from homes in Bamford, Littleborough, and Milnrow. Between February and September 2004, Grogan used his skills as a former window fitter to break into homes to steal the keys to vehicles. At the height of his crime spree, police believe he was committing at least two burglaries a week. Since his arrest, the number of such offenses has fallen 60%.

The crime wave finally ended after he was caught on video trying to use a credit card he had stolen during one of the burglaries. Police then spotted him driving a recently stolen car. With this key information, officers were able to arrest Grogan and link eight further offenses to him. When he was arrested, he had keys for another car stolen in the same burglary. Later, he took detectives on a tour of Rochdale lasting two days to point out the dozens of houses into which he had burgled.

The detective inspector of Rochdale's Volume Crime Unit said Grogan had an 18-page criminal record stretching back to when he was just 10 years old and described him as a "professional thief." He told how Grogan would stalk homes with high-valued cars and break in to take the car keys before stealing the vehicles. Grogan would then park the cars a few miles away before returning days later to check if the coast was clear; he would then sell the vehicle. Grogan told officers that he made about $90,000 from his crimes. Police said that the true value of the cars was over $1.3 million.

Reacting to the sentence, the detective inspector said: "We had been looking for Grogan for some time, we knew he was a threat to the borough of Rochdale and that his arrest would have an effect on crime figures. We were aware of his activities and suspected him of many offenses. Many of my officers worked around the clock on Grogan and gathered strong evidence relating to several burglaries. Eventually, he realized the game was up and he had no other option but to help police with their inquiries. These kind of offenses have tremendous effects on victims and so we are delighted to bring such an offender to justice."

Based on the career criminal research findings covered in this chapter, how does Grogan fit the profile of a career criminal? What sentence do you think he would have received if he committed his offenses in California instead of the United Kingdom?

Source: "Career Criminal in £750,000 Spree." *Rochdale Observer,* February 4, 2005, available at http://www.rochdaleobserver.co.uk/news/s/45/45758_career_criminal_in_75000_spree.html, accessed October 4, 2005.

Matt DeLisi found a group of chronic female offenders who were more likely than their male counterparts to engage in forgery, fraud, and prostitution. They were also younger, less mobile, and had shorter criminal careers than males, but their presence in the cohort indicated that females are also habitual offenders.[79]

Females in the 1958 Philadelphia Birth Cohort

The 1958 Philadelphia birth cohort analyses also addressed the issue of gender and noted the delinquency pattern for females was very different from that of the males. Only about 14% of the 1972 women studied had at least one police contact before age 18. The delinquency rate for males was about two and a half times higher than that for females. Females were primarily one-time delinquents (60% of their cohort). Thus, the female offenders were more likely to commit one crime and then desist (or one and a half times more likely than the males). Only 7% of the females were chronic offenders. Males were three times more likely to be chronic offenders. However, when race and socioeconomic status were considered, females displayed a similar offense pattern as those of the males studied. Low socioeconomic status and nonwhite females were about twice as likely to be delinquent and one and a half times as likely to be recidivists than other females.[80]

According to the 1958 Philadelphia Birth Cohort, males committed a greater number of serious crimes than females. The female rate of offending was much lower for every type of crime (personal or property). Only half as many violent offenses committed by females caused grave harm to victims (e.g., death or hospitalization). For theft, males had a higher median dollar loss per offense ($40) than females ($25). However, again, this offense pattern varies by race. Nonwhite females in the cohort committed more crimes than white females. Nonwhite females committed about three and a half times more serious felonies and about five and a half times more violent crimes than white females.[81]

Female Chronic Offenders

The pattern of crime among female chronic offenders was also unlike that of males. Only 1% of the females were chronic offenders and they were responsible for 27% of the total number of crimes. Female chronics accounted for 26% of the serious felonies committed by females whereas male chronic offenders committed 68% of the total serious felonies. The relationship between race and socio-economic status among the chronic offenders was similar for males and females. Nonwhites and low socioeconomic status offenders were most likely to be chronic delinquents for both males and females. However, the size and impact of the female chronic delinquents was much smaller than that of males.[82] These percentages are listed by type of crime in FIGURE 9-2 . Note in this figure that female chronics committed the same percentage of homicides as their male counterparts. For all other types of crime, however, their rate was far less than that of males.

Crime as a Career for Females

Reanalyses of the 1958 cohort data focused on differences between male and female careers. Women were older when they began their criminal careers and the minor delinquent females ended their careers sooner than their male counterparts. This study failed to confirm the existence of a female chronic career offender comparable to that found among males in the Philadelphia cohort.[83] Although there were time differences in the onset of careers between the two sexes, males and females did not dif-

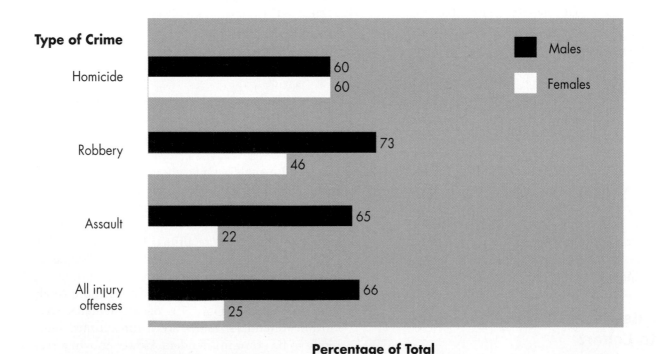

FIGURE 9-2 Male and Female Chronic Offenders, 1958 Philadelphia Birth Cohort

fer in their crime specialization patterns. Both males and females who began their criminal careers early persisted as criminals into adulthood and had more diverse patterns of offending than those who began later in life. Thus, male and female career criminals, while they differ in the types of offenses they commit, are similar in their pattern and persistence of offending over time.[84]

Females in Criminality Studies

Stephen Lab and William Doerner compared female delinquency patterns to that of the males in the three Racine, Wisconsin, birth cohorts. These cohorts consisted of all males and females born in Racine in 1942, 1949, and 1955 who stayed in that city through their adolescence. They reported that over time, female delinquency rose for status, victimless, and minor property offenses. However, in terms of major property and personal offenses, the female rates did not match that of their male counterparts.[85]

Another study tracked the criminal careers of 159 females committed to the California Youth Authority in the 1960s who primarily committed status offenses as juveniles. The researchers discovered that the overwhelming majority of the females (96%) had adult arrests and that 47% had three or more arrests. Almost half the females had committed offenses of high severity. Because of their adult activities, 85% of the sample was convicted and 60% were incarcerated (15% in state prison).[86]

These studies of female criminality reveal a consistent pattern. Although the total amount and rate of offenses may be increasing, the pattern of involvement in crime by females has not essentially changed. Female offenders still tend to be primarily involved in minor property and sex offenses. When they are involved in more serious crimes, the nature of their crimes is still different and less serious than that of males — yet it is important to consider the criminal career of women with respect to other variables, such as race. For example, the crime rate for "underclass" (low education and low socioeconomic status) black females was unlike that of other race and gender groups.[87] They were more likely to engage in violent behavior fueled by drug abuse. It is possible that race and social class differences between women make a difference in the nature and extent of their criminal careers and patterns of offending. Whether the career criminal is male or female, race and social class combine to drive serious offending rates and crimes.

Research conducted by Robert Tillman reveals why it is so difficult to deal with chronic offenders in an effective and just manner. He traced the adult arrest histories of all persons born in 1956 who were arrested in California between 1974 and 1985. He found that arrest was not an uncommon experience for young adults in California. Twenty-four percent of the cohort was arrested during this period. One in 10 members was arrested for an index felony and this rate was highest for black males (40% arrest rate for index crimes).

As in the Philadelphia birth cohorts, Tillman uncovered a group of chronic offenders. Offenders who were arrested three or more times accounted for 67% of the total number of arrests and were responsible for over half (53%) of all index arrests. What is particularly surprising is the size of this group. Tillman estimated that each year California's criminal justice system must absorb 29,000 new chronic offenders.[88]

Repeat Offender Programs

Police programs have been developed to supplement career criminal prosecution programs.[89] Repeat offender projects (ROP, pronounced "rope") selectively focus police resources on career criminals. These programs take a proactive approach by having the police target offenders or certain types of crime and try to catch them red-handed rather than wait for a citizen's call.[90] Typically, ROP squads focus their efforts on the offenders who are most active. Working in close conjunction with prosecutors, these programs attempt to apprehend career criminals and effectively incapacitate them. Early ROP initiatives were developed in Washington, D.C. and Phoenix, Arizona.

Research suggests that these programs have been productive. In Washington, D.C., Susan E. Martin and Lawrence W. Sherman conducted an experiment to evaluate the performance of ROP. They focused on the ROP squad of the Washington, D.C., Metropolitan Police Department; the study compared the number and seriousness of arrests made by ROP officers and comparison officers, outcomes of arrests, and arrestees' criminal histories before and during ROP Time 1 (April–September 1981) and Time 2 (April–September 1983). A sample of 40 officers (Group 1) who had street assignments before ROP and were in the ROP unit during

Time 2 was compared with a sample of 169 officers (Group 2) who had the same assignment during Time 1 and Time 2.

They found that ROP increased the likelihood of arrest, the seriousness of the criminal histories of its arrestees, the probability of felony prosecution, and the length of sentence.[91] However, they also noted that ROP reduced the arrest productivity of police officers (a difference resulting more from an organizational effect than from initial differences among officers) and was expensive to implement. The success of ROP was also dependent on street information provided by other officers. In addition, they found that the performance of this unit was a reflection of the charismatic leadership of a particular captain.

In an experimental evaluation of the Phoenix, Arizona ROP, offenders were randomly assigned as experimentals (offenders targeted by ROP) and controls (not targeted). There was no significant increase in conviction rate for the experimental cases, but there were significant increases in the likelihood of commitment to prison and in the length of term imposed. ROP generated similar results. The rate of conviction and incarceration for ROP cases was higher than the control group. Once convicted, ROP offenders were more likely to be sentenced to prison for longer periods. On average, convicted ROP offenders received an additional 9.4 months. Close cooperation with prosecutors in case preparation was cited as an essential factor in the program.[92]

"Three-Strikes" Laws

The latest attempt to sentence career criminals is aimed at offenders with three convictions. Only two states (Maine and New Hampshire) do not have some form of a habitual offender law. Sixteen states (California, Colorado, Connecticut, Florida, Georgia, Indiana, Kansas, Louisiana, Maryland, New Jersey, New Mexico, North Carolina, Tennessee, Virginia, Washington, and Wisconsin) have three-strikes laws that typically call for a term of life imprisonment without possibility of parole for persons convicted for a third time of certain specified violent or serious felonies. The remainder of the states have sentencing enhancement of different types and lengths depending on the number of career felony convictions.[93]

In California, the three-strikes idea became law following the notorious case of Richard Allen Davis, an unrepentant repeat offender who abducted 12-

year-old Polly Klaas from a slumber party and murdered her. Davis had been paroled after serving half of his 16-year sentence for kidnapping. The case became a hot political issue. As a result, the three-strikes law proposal was placed on the 1994 California ballot with strong support from petitions. It passed with over 71% of the votes cast.[94] The aim of the law was to reduce serious crime while incapacitating and also deterring others from becoming repeat offenders.[95] If an offender commits any of 500 listed felonies when they already have one "strike" (conviction), the new sentence is automatically doubled. If the offender has two strikes, a new felony conviction carries a prison sentence of 25 years to life.[96] The California law differs from

An activist stages a demonstration to protest the incarceration of thousands of inmates under California's three-strikes law.

Should such laws focus solely on persons convicted of violent offenses?

other states in that this sentence enhancement can be invoked when the offender has only one prior conviction for a serious crime. In addition, the crime that triggers the enhancement need not be violent. As a result, by year end 2002, over 42,000 offenders had been incarcerated under this California law — four times as many inmates as all of the other three-strike states combined (10,624 prisoners).[97] One estimate is that nearly two-thirds of these California offenders have been imprisoned for nonviolent offenses.[98]

Impact of the California Three Strikes

Research on the impact of the California law reveals that it has not achieved its goals. It has failed to lower the crime rate, even in those counties that have enacted it the most.[99] One potential drawback of the law, prison overcrowding, failed to materialize. A study of the law's effect on the prison population found that it did not aggravate the growth of the state prison population and will not increase the percent of violent offenders or the number of elderly offenders incarcerated.[100]

However, another proposal (Proposition 66) that aimed to limit the use of the three-strikes law was on the ballot in the fall of 2004. The proposal tried to limit the career criminal law to be used only in violent crime cases. California Governor Arnold Schwarzenegger opposed Proposition 66 and it was defeated.[101] The proposed limitation would have focused the impact of three-strikes law to violent crime and avoided negative consequences, namely targeting property offenders and increasing the prison population. The failure to pass Proposition 66 clearly demonstrates that "punitive laws often remain on the books well past their usefulness either as public policy or political props."[102]

Policies Other than Incapacitation

As discussed in Chapter 3, the policy of incapacitation is difficult, if not impossible, to implement fully and effectively. Career criminal research not only documents the extent of criminality in the population, but also points out that crime is inextricably linked to other social problems. Punishment and incapacitation are not the only policies called for to interrupt, or effectively prevent, a destructive career in crime.

Programs and policies that address the risk factors and age-graded periods revealed by life-course criminology research can be effective interventions. Family-based interventions such as training programs to provide parental management skills and programs to improve the health of newborns and children are promising. Investing in school programs to improve education and employment can increase social ties to the community and social capital.[103] Drug treatment of offenders should also be emphasized to speed and enhance offender desistance.[104]

There are other methods to limit the deleterious impact of career criminal laws. For example, states that enact or already have adopted career criminal legislation should prepare prison-impact statements that consider the influence of these laws on the size and make-up of the existing prison population. These laws could also include sunset provisions that cause them to expire after a certain number of years and be reconsidered by the legislature. In short, punitive approaches alone are not enough to change the course of career criminality, truly protect the public, and limit the use of a scarce resource — prison space.

WRAP UP

Which Offender Should Be Incarcerated Under California's Three-Strikes Law?

In terms of the nature of their present offense and prior criminal histories (Valdez and King have committed much more violent offenses than Ellis and Andrews), all four California offenders would be eligible for incarceration under the three-strikes law. This example illustrates how the law is implemented and fails to focus only on the most dangerous or culpable violent offenders and also targets property offenders.

Chapter Spotlight

- The idea of career criminality is based on the assumption that such criminals are committed to a life of crime; in other words, they have a worldview built around criminal activity. They define themselves as criminals and tend to associate with other criminals. Their careers accelerate or progress as they become more skilled and engage in different types of offenses. In addition, career criminals view crime as a profession like law or medicine in that it involves the acquisition of specialized knowledge and skill.

- Many of the assumptions about criminal careers originated in Edwin Sutherland's classic work, *The Professional Thief*. This study followed the career of one professional criminal and served as the basis for Sutherland's theory of differential association.

- Life-course criminology is concerned with three major issues: (1) the development of criminal behavior, (2) risk factors at different ages, and (3) the effects of life events on the development of a criminal career.

- In the field of criminology, case studies focus on offenders who engage in particular types of crime. The aim of these studies is to gain in-depth knowledge of the motives and methods of criminals engaged in certain crimes. Case studies can lead to the development of theories to explain criminal behavior and thus they have the ability to inform policies and programs that are aimed at crime prevention and rehabilitation.

- A typology is a framework and theoretical construct that provides a means to describe and compare different forms of criminal behavior.

- Birth cohorts are often used in criminology research because they permit the study of individuals over an extended period of time. Through the cohort, life patterns can be examined and criminal careers reconstructed. Two of the most influential birth cohort studies in criminology were conducted in Philadelphia.

- Criminology has traditionally focused on male criminals and their offenses. The chivalry hypothesis suggested that women tend to be more moral or fear social disapproval more than men and therefore committed fewer and less-serious crimes. Recent studies, however, indicate that these views need to change.

- Policies aimed at coping with chronic offenders include repeat offender projects, three-strikes laws, family-based interventions, investing in school programs to improve education and employment, and drug treatment programs.

Putting It All Together

1. What do professional criminals have in common with their law-abiding counterparts? How do they differ?

2. What findings do the various cohort studies have in common? How do they differ? What policies do these factors suggest?

3. Do the criminal careers of men and women differ? How? What does this mean to the criminal justice system?

4. What is a SHODI program? The VJO program? Are such programs a good idea?

5. What is a typology? How does it help us explain criminal behavior?

Key Terms

chronic offenders Persons who habitually engage in crime; in both Philadelphia Birth Cohorts (all persons born in 1945 and then 1958), the small group of offenders who were responsible for the bulk of serious crimes committed by the entire array.

cohort A group of individuals who share the same experience in time. Birth cohorts are often tracked to determine the groups that have the highest rates of offending.

Repeat Offender Projects (ROP) Projects that selectively focus police resources on career criminals and take a proactive approach. Police target offenders and try to catch them in the act.

Serious Habitual Offender/Drug-Involved (SHODI) Program Program that targets serious, habitual juvenile crime and enhances the system response to drug-related, juvenile crimes. It emphasizes a system-wide effort to coordinate records and services to apprehend and treat the habitual juvenile offender.

typology A framework and theoretical construct that is used to describe and compare different forms of criminal behavior.

Violent Juvenile Offender (VJO) Program Program that places chronically violent juvenile offenders in an intervention program designed to halt their criminal career.

Notes

1. Mark H. Moore, Susan R. Estrich, Daniel McGillis, and William Spelman, *Dangerous Offenders: The Elusive Target of Justice* (Cambridge, MA: Harvard University Press, 1984): 57.
2. John H. Laub, "The Life Course of Criminology in the United States: The American Society of Criminology 2003 Presidential Address," *Criminology* 42 (2004): 9.
3. John P. Conrad, "The Puzzle of Dangerousness," in Israel Barak-Glantz and C. Ronald Huff, eds., *The Mad, the Bad, and the Different: Essays in Honor of Simon Dinitz* (Lexington, MA: Lexington, 1981): 101–110.
4. Peter Letkemann, *Crime as Work* (Englewood Cliffs, NJ: Prentice Hall, 1973).
5. David P. Farrington, "Developmental and Life Course Criminology: Key Theoretical and Empirical Issues — The 2002 Sutherland Award Address," *Criminology* 41 (2003): 221.
6. Laub, 2004, 4–5.
7. Alex Piquero and Paul Mazerolle, "Introduction," in Alex Piquero and Paul Mazerolle, ed., *Life-Course Criminology: Contemporary and Classic Readings* (Belmont, CA: Wadsworth/Thomson, 2001): x.
8. Piquero and Mazerolle, 2001, xi; Alfred Blumstein, Jacqueline Cohen, Jeffrey A. Roth, and Christy Visher, *Criminal Careers and Career Criminals* (Washington, DC: National Academy Press, 1986).
9. Michael Gottfredson and Travis Hirschi, "Science, Public Policy, and the Career Criminal," *Criminology* 26 (1988): 37–55.
10. William Rhodes, "The Criminal Career: Estimates of the Duration and Frequency of Crime Commission," *Journal of Quantitative Criminology* 5 (1989): 3–32.
11. Rudy Haapanen, *Selective Incapacitation and the Serious Offender: A Longitudinal Study of Career Criminal Patterns* (New York: Springer-Verlag, 1990).
12. Alfred Blumstein, Jacqueline Cohen, and David P. Farrington, "Career Criminal Research: Its Value for Criminology," *Criminology* 26 (1988): 1–35.
13. Don C. Gibbons, "Age Patterns in Criminal Involvement," *International Journal of Offender Therapy and Comparative Criminology* 31 (1987): 237–260.
14. Sheldon and Eleanor T. Glueck, *Unraveling Juvenile Delinquency* (Cambridge, MA: Harvard University Press, 1950); Sheldon and Eleanor T Glueck, *Delinquents and Nondelinquents in Perspective* (Cambridge, MA: Harvard University Press, 1968).
15. Robert J. Sampson and John H. Laub, *Crime in the Making: Pathways and Turning Points through Life* (Cambridge, MA: Harvard University Press, 1995).
16. Robert J. Sampson and John H. Laub, "Crime and Deviance Over the Life Course: The Salience of Adult Social Bonds," *American Sociological Review* 55 (1990): 609–627.
17. Robert J. Sampson and John H. Laub, "Life-Course Desisters? Trajectories of Crime Among Delinquent Boys Followed to Age 70," *Criminology* 41 (2003): 585.
18. Neal Shover, *Great Pretenders: Pursuits and Careers of Persistent Thieves* (Boulder, CO: Westview Press, 1996): 131–132.
19. Kathryn Edin, Timothy J. Nelson, and Rechelle Paranal, *Fatherhood and Incarceration as Turning Points in the Criminal Careers of Unskilled Men* (Evanston, IL: Northwestern University, 2001).
20. John H. Laub and Robert J. Sampson, *Shared Beginnings, Divergent Lives: Delinquent Boys to Age 70* (Cambridge, MA: Harvard University Press, 2003).
21. Christopher Uggen, "Work as a Turning Point in the Life Course of Criminals: A Duration Model of Age, Employment, and Recidivism," *American Sociological Review* 65 (2000): 529–546; Jenny Williams and Robin C. Sickles, "An Analysis of the Crime as Work Model: Evidence from the 1958 Philadelphia Birth Cohort Study," *Journal of Human Resources* 47 (2002): 479–509.
22. Mark Warr, "Life-Course Transitions and Desistance from Crime," *Criminology* 36 (1998): 183–216.
23. Edwin H. Sutherland, *The Professional Thief* (Chicago: University of Chicago Press, 1937).

24. Carl B. Klockars, *The Professional Fence* (New York: Free Press, 1976).

25. Paul F. Cromwell, James N. Olson, and D'Aunn W. Avary, "Who Buys Stolen Property? A New Look at Criminal Receiving," *Journal of Crime and Justice* 16 (1993): 75–95.

26. Jerome E. Jackson, "Fraud Masters: Studying an Illusory, Non-violent, Gang Specializing in Credit Card Crimes," *Gang Journal* 1 (1993): 17–36.

27. John Rosecrance, "The Stooper: A Professional Thief in the Sutherland Manner," *Criminology* 24 (1986): 29–40.

28. Marshall B. Clinard, Richard Quinney, and John Wildeman, *Criminal Behavior Systems: A Typology* (Cincinnati, OH: Anderson, 1994): 14–15.

29. Joan Petersilia, "Criminal Career Research: A Review of Recent Evidence," in Norval Morris and Michael Tonry, eds., *Crime and Justice,* volume 2 (Chicago: University of Chicago Press, 1980): 322.

30. Marvin E. Wolfgang, Robert M. Figlio, and Thorsten Sellin, *Delinquency in a Birth Cohort* (Chicago: University of Chicago Press, 1972): 91.

31. Paul Mazerolle, Robert Brame, Ray Paternoster, Alex Piquero, and Charles Dean, "Onset Age, Persistence, and Offense Versatility: Comparisons Across Gender," *Criminology* 38 (2000): 1143–1172.

32. Paul E. Tracy, Marvin E. Wolfgang, and Robert M. Figlio, *Delinquency Careers in Two Birth Cohorts* (New York: Plenum Press, 1990).

33. Elisabeth S. Piper, "Violent Recidivism and Chronicity in the 1958 Philadelphia Cohort," *Journal of Quantitative Criminology* 1 (1985): 319–344.

34. Kimberly L. Kempf, "Career Criminals in the 1958 Philadelphia Birth Cohort: A Follow-up of the Early Adult Years," *Criminal Justice Review* 15 (1990): 159.

35. Kimberly L. Kempf, "Crime Severity and Career Criminal Progression," *Journal of Criminal Law and Criminology* 79 (1988): 524–540.

36. Paul E. Tracy and Kimberly L. Kempf, *Continuity and Discontinuity in Criminal Careers* (New York: Plenum Press, 1996); Alex Piquero, Raymond Paternoster, Paul Mazerolle, Robert Brame, and Charles W. Dean, "Onset Age and Offense Specialization," *Journal of Research in Crime and Delinquency* 36 (1999): 275–299.

37. Tracy, Wolfgang, and Figlio, 1990, 292.

38. Ibid., 294.

39. Ibid., 295, 297.

40. Lyle W. Shannon, *Criminal Career Continuity: Its Social Context* (New York: Human Sciences Press, 1988).

41. David P. Farrington, "Criminal Career Research in the United Kingdom," *British Journal of Criminology* 32 (1992): 521–536.

42. David P. Farrington and J. David Hawkins, "Predicting Participation, Early Onset and Later Persistence in Officially Recorded Offending," *Criminal Behaviour and Mental Health* 1 (1991): 1–33.

43. David P. Farrington, and Donald J. West, "Criminal, Penal and Life Histories of Chronic Offenders: Risk and Protective Factors and Early Identification," *Criminal Behaviour and Mental Health* 3 (1993): 492–523.

44. Daniel S. Nagin, David P. Farrington, and Terri E. Moffitt, "Life-Course Trajectories of Different Types of Offenders," *Criminology* 33 (1995): 101–139.

45. David P. Farrington, "Implications of Criminal Career Research for the Prevention of Offending," *Journal of Adolescence* 13 (1990): 93–103.

46. Albert S. Regnery, "Getting Away with Murder," *Policy Review* (Fall 1985): 34–39.

47. Donna M. Hamparian, James M. Davis, John M. Jacobson, and Robert E. McGraw, *The Young Criminal Years of the Violent Few* (Washington, DC: U.S. Department of Justice, 1985); Donna M. Hamparian, Richard Schuster, Simon Dinitz, and John P. Conrad, *The Violent Few: A Study of Violent Juvenile Offenders* (Lexington, MA: Heath, 1978).

48. Hamparian, Davis, Jacobson, and McGraw, 1985, 4.

49. Ibid., 17.

50. Ibid., 16.

51. National Advisory Committee for Juvenile Justice and Delinquency Prevention, *Serious Juvenile Crime: A Redirected Federal Effort* (Washington, DC: Office of Juvenile Justice and Delinquency Prevention, 1984): 10.

52. Jeffrey A. Fagan, "Social and Legal Policy Dimensions of Violent Juvenile Crime," *Criminal Justice and Behavior* 17 (1990a): 93–133.

53. Eliot Hartstone and Karen V. Hansen, "The Violent Juvenile Offender: An Empirical Portrait," in Robert A. Mathias, Paul DeMuro, and Richard S. Allinson, eds., *Violent Juvenile Offenders: An Anthology* (San Francisco: National Council on Crime and Delinquency, 1984): 83–102.

54. Ibid.

55. Delbert S. Elliott, "Serious Violent Offenders: Onset, Developmental Course, and Termination — The American Society of Criminology 1993 Presidential Address," *Criminology* 32 (1994): 1–21.

56. Ibid.

57. Ibid.

58. Jeffrey A. Fagan, "Treatment and Reintegration of Violent Juvenile Offenders: Experimental Results," *Justice Quarterly* 7 (1990b): 233–263.

59. Jeffery Fagan and Martin Forst, "Risks, Fixers, and Zeal: Implementing Experimental Treatments for Violent Juvenile Offenders," *Prison Journal* 76 (1996): 22–59.

60. Robert O. Heck, Wolfgang Pindur, and Donna K. Wells, "The Juvenile Serious Habitual Offender/Drug Involved Program: A Means to Implement Recommendations of the National Council of Juvenile and Family Court Judges," *Juvenile and Family Court Journal* 36 (1985): 28.

61. James C. Howell, "Diffusing Research into Practice Using the Comprehensive Strategy for Serious, Violent, and Chronic Juvenile Offenders," *Youth, Violence and Juvenile Justice* 1 (2003): 219–245.

62. Michael Schumacher and Gwen A. Kurz, *The 8% Solution: Preventing Serious Repeat Juvenile Crime* (Thousand Oaks, CA: Sage, 2000); Peter R. Jones, Phillip W. Harris, Jamie Fader, and Lori Grubstein, "Identifying Chronic Juvenile Offenders," *Justice Quarterly* 18 (2001): 479–508.

63. Patrick A. Langan and Laurence A. Greenfeld, *Career Patterns in Crime* (Washington, DC: Bureau of Justice Statistics, 1983).

64. Bureau of Alcohol, Tobacco & Firearms, *Protecting Amer-*

ica: The Effectiveness of Federal Armed Career Criminal Statutes (Washington, DC: Department of the Treasury, 1991): 14.

65. Joan Petersilia, Peter Greenwood, and Marvin Lavin, *Criminal Careers of Habitual Felons* (Santa Monica, CA: Rand Corporation, 1977).

66. Mark A. Peterson, Harriet B. Braiker, and S. M. Polich, *Who Commits Crimes: A Survey of Prison Inmates* (Cambridge, MA: Oelgeschlager, Gunn, and Hain, 1981): 121.

67. Jan M. Chaiken and Marcia R. Chaiken, *Varieties of Criminal Behavior: Summary and Policy Implications* (Santa Monica, CA: Rand Corporation, 1982): 13.

68. Ibid., 17.

69. James Q. Wilson and Allan F. Abrahamse, "Does Crime Pay?" *Justice Quarterly* 9 (1992): 361–377.

70. Pierre Tremblay and Carlo Morselli, "Patterns in Criminal Achievement: Wilson and Abrahamse Revisited," *Criminology* 38 (2000): 633–659.

71. Julie Horney and Ineke H. Marshall, "Measuring Lambda through Self-Reports," *Criminology* 29 (1991): 485.

72. Alfred C. Miranne and Michael R. Geerken. "The New Orleans Inmate Survey: A Test of Greenwood's Predictive Scale. *Criminology* 29 (1991): 506.

73. Matt DeLisi and Jewel M. Gatling, "Who Pays for a Life of Crime? An Empirical Assessment of the Assorted Victimization Costs Posed by Career Criminals," *Criminal Justice Studies* 16 (2003): 283–293.

74. Harry E. Barnes and Negley K. Teeters, *New Horizons in Criminology* (Englewood Cliffs, NJ: Prentice Hall, 1959): 61–62.

75. Michael J. Hindelang, "Sex Differences in Criminal Activity," *Social Problems* 27 (1979): 143–156.

76. Margaret Farnworth, M. Joan McDermott, and Sherwood E. Zimmerman, "Aggregation Effects on Male-to-Female Arrest Rate Ratios in New York State, 1972 to 1984," *Journal of Quantitative Criminology* 4 (1988): 121–135.

77. John H. Laub and Michael J. McDermott, "An Analysis of Serious Crime by Young Black Women," *Criminology* 23 (1985): 81–98.

78. Darryl Steffensmeier and Emilie Allan, "Gender, Age, and Crime," in James F. Sheley, ed., *Criminology: A Contemporary Handbook* (Belmont, CA: Wadsworth, 1991): 70.

79. Matt DeLisi, "Not Just a Boy's Club: An Empirical Assessment of Female Career Criminals," *Women and Criminal Justice* 13 (2002): 27–45.

80. Kempf, "Career Criminals in the 1958 Philadelphia Birth Cohort" 1990, 161–162.

81. Tracy and Kempf, *Continuity and Discontinuity,* 1990, 161–162.

82. Tracy, Wolfgang, and Figlio, 1990, 101–103.

83. Amy V. D'Unger, Kenneth C. Land, and Patricia L. McCall, "Sex Differences in Age Patterns of Delinquent/Criminal Careers: Results from Poisson Latent Class Analyses of the Philadelphia Cohort Study," *Journal of Quantitative Criminology* 18 (2002): 349–375.

84. Paul Mazerolle, Robert Brome, Ray Paternoster, Alex Piquero, and Charles Dean, "Onset Age, Persistence, and Offending Versatility: Comparisons Across Gender," *Criminology* 38 (2000): 1043–1072.

85. Stephen P. Lab and William G. Doerner, "Changing Female Delinquency in Three Birth Cohorts," *Journal of Crime and Justice* 10 (1987): 101–116.

86. Margarite Q. Warren and Jill L. Rosenbaum, "Criminal Careers of Female Offenders," *Criminal Justice and Behavior* 13 (1986): 393–418.

87. Sally S. Simpson, "Caste, Class, and Violent Crime: Explaining Differences in Female Offending," *Criminology* 29 (1991):105–135.

88. Robert Tillman, "The Size of the 'Criminal Population': The Prevalence and Incidence of Adult Arrest," *Criminology* 25 (1987): 576.

89. Susan E. Martin, "Policing Career Criminals — An Examination of an Innovative Crime Control Program," *Journal of Criminal Law and Criminology* 77 (1986): 1159–1182.

90. Susan E. Martin and Laurence W. Sherman, "Selective Apprehension: A Police Strategy for Repeat Offenders," *Criminology* 24 (1986): 155–156.

91. Ibid., 170.

92. Allan F. Abrahamse, Patricia A. Ebener, Peter W. Greenwood, N. Fitzgerald, and T. E. Kosin, "An Experimental Evaluation of the Phoenix Repeat Offender Program," *Justice Quarterly* 8 (1991): 141–168.

93. For example, Truth in Sentencing (TIS) laws require convicted violent offenders to serve at least 85% of their sentence before being considered for parole (or release). Bureau of Justice Statistics, *State Court Organization, 1998* (Washington, DC: U.S. Department of Justice, 1999): 4–9; James Austin and John Irwin, *It's About Time: America's Imprisonment Binge* (Belmont, CA: Wadsworth, 2001): 184–214; David K. Shichor and Dale K. Sechrest, eds., *Three Strikes and You're Out: Vengeance as Public Policy* (Thousand Oaks, CA: Sage, 1996); Elsa Chen, *Impacts of Three Strikes and Truth in Sentencing on the Volume and Composition of Correctional Populations* (Washington, DC: National Institute of Justice, 2000): 1.

94. Chen, 2000, 4.

95. Peter W. Greenwood, Susan S. Everingham, Elsa Chen, Allan F. Abrahamse, Nancy Merritt, and James Chiesa, *Three Strikes Revisited: An Early Assessment of Implementation and Effects* (Santa Barbara, CA: Rand Corporation, 1998): i.

96. Chen, 2000, 13.

97. Data Analysis Unit, *Second and Third Strikers in the Institution Population* (Sacramento, CA: Department of Corrections, 2003); Vincent Schiraldi, Jason Colburn, and Eric Locke, *Three Strikes and You're Out: An Examination of The Impact of 3 Strike Laws 10 Years After Their Enactment* (Washington, DC: The Justice Policy Institute, 2004): 5.

98. Schiraldi, Colburn, and Locke, 2004, 4.

99. Ibid., 7–8.

100. Kathleen Auerhahn, "Selective Incapacitation, Three Strikes, and the Problem of Aging Prison Populations: Using Simulation Modeling to See the Future," *Criminology and Public Policy* 1 (2002): 353–388.

101. ABC News, "Voters Reject Three Strikes Proposition," available at http://abclocal.go.com/kgo/news/politics/

print_10030ap_politics_three_strikes.html, accessed October 9, 2004.

102. Schiraldi, Colburn, and Locke, 2004, 12.

103. Piquero and Mazerolle, 2001, xvi. Richard E. Tremblay, Frank Vitaro, Lucie Bertrand, Marc LeBlanc, Helene Beauchesne, Helene Boileau, and Lucille David, "Parent and Child Training to Prevent Early Onset of Delinquency: The Montreal Longitudinal-Experiment Study," in Alex Piquero and Paul Mazerolle, ed., *Life-Course Criminology: Contemporary and Classic Readings* (Belmont, CA: Wadsworth/Thomson, 2001): 355–373; David Olds, Charles R. Henderson Jr., Robert Cole, John Eck-

enrode, Harriet Kitzman, Dennis Luckey, Lisa Pettit, Kimberly Sidora, Pamela Morris, and Jane Powers, "Long-Term Effects of Nurse Home Visitation on Children's Criminal and Antisocial Behavior: 15-Year Follow-Up of a Randomized Control Trial," in Alex Piquero and Paul Mazerolle, ed., *Life-Course Criminology: Contemporary and Classic Readings* (Belmont, CA: Wadsworth/Thomson, 2001): 374–391.

104. Marc Mauer, "Analyzing and Responding to the Driving Forces of Prison Population Growth," *Criminology and Public Policy* 1 (2002): 390–391.

WWW.CRIMINOLOGY.JBPUB.COM

Interactivities
In the News
Key Term Explorer
Web Links

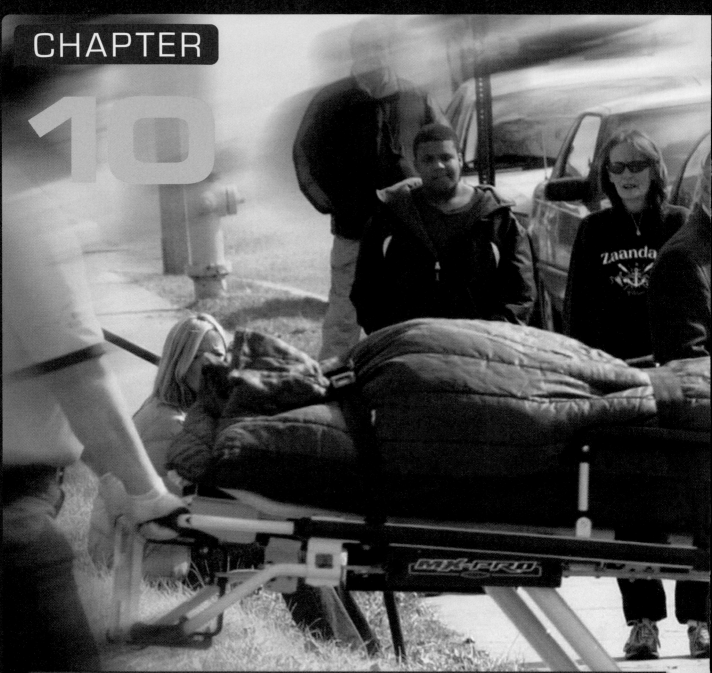

CHAPTER

10

OBJECTIVES

Define violent crime, including the various forms of homicide, rape, robbery, and assault.

Know the current rates and trends for violent crimes in the United States.

Be aware of homicide levels and trends in the United States, grasp the nature of homicide, and understand explanations for differences in homicide rates between the United States and other industrialized countries.

Know the prevalence rates for various forms of rape, the proposed motivations for rape, and explanations of rape and sexual assault.

Grasp the level and trends of robbery rates in the United States, know what distinguishes robbery from other forms of violence, and understand explanations of robbery.

Understand the nature and prevalence of assault in the United States.

Understand why some criminologists propose general explanations for violence and know the range of theories proposed to explain violence.

Be familiar with explanations for the recent decline in violent crime.

Crimes of Violence

> *Nothing left to do, but buy some shells for my glock*
> *Why? so I can rob every known dope spot*
> *I got 19 dollars and 50 cents up in my pocket with what?*
> *With this automatic rocket*
> *Gotta have it to pop it, unlock it, and take me up a hostage*
>
> — Snoop Dogg[1]

YOU ARE THE CRIMINOLOGIST

The Use of Rape as Terrorism During Wartime

Consider the news reports regarding the war in Bosnia-Herzegovina (1992–1995) and the ongoing war in the Darfur region of Sudan. Like other war situations, these conflicts resulted in mass rapes of civilian women. In the war in Bosnia, Amnesty International estimated that somewhere between 20,000 and 50,000 Serbian and Croatian women (mostly Muslims) were systematically raped by Serbian forces. There is clear evidence from the testimony of survivors that rape was being used as a way to achieve ethnic cleansing, either by impregnating women or terrorizing them and their families into leaving the region. In February of 2001, the international war crimes tribunal sentenced three Bosnian Serbs to a combined sentence of 60 years in jail. The tribunal also elevated systematic rape from being a "violation of the customs of war" to one of the most heinous war crimes of all — a crime against humanity. The verdict was read aloud by the presiding judge, Florence Mumba of Zambia, and included the following:

> You abused and ravaged Muslim women because of their ethnicity and from among their number you picked whomsoever you fancied. You have shown the most glaring disrespect for the women's dignity and their fundamental human rights on a scale that far surpasses even what one might call the average seriousness of rapes during wartime.

This ruling appears to have had little effect in the Sudanese region of Darfur. Here, a government-armed militia, referred to by many as the Janjaweed ("armed men on horses"), has been systematically killing and driving out black Sudanese from the region. As with the Bosnian war, rape also has been used to terrorize a population. An Amnesty International report conveys the following statement from a victim:

> I was sleeping when the attack on Disa started. I was taken away by the attackers, they were all in uniforms. They took dozens of other girls and made us walk for three hours. During the day we were beaten and they were telling us: "You, the black women, we will exterminate you, you have no god." At night we were raped several times.

Many of the rapes were designed to humiliate the women and their families. For example, women were raped out in the open and in front of their families. Because being a victim of rape is a cultural taboo in Sudan, this is particularly tragic. Some rape survivors have reportedly remained at the border between Chad and Sudan or to have sought sanctuary in the refugee camps in Darfur, far from the eyes of their relatives and close community.

What is the motivation for rape in the circumstance of the wars in Bosnia and the Sudan?

Is rape a sexual offense or a violent offense?

What are the similarities and differences between rapes discussed here and those perpetrated outside of war?

Sources: Alexandra Stiglmayer (ed.), *Mass Rape: The War Against Women in Bosnia-Herzegovina* (Lincoln: University of Nebraska Press, 1994); Amnesty International, "Darfur: Rape as a Weapon of War: Sexual Violence and its Consequences," available at http://web.amnesty.org/library/index/engafr540762004, accessed February 25, 2006.

Introduction

More than any other type of crime, violent crime has the greatest impact on the public's perception of crime in general: People fear violent crime. Although people are much more likely to be victims of burglary, larceny, and car theft, what affects people's behavior and attitudes toward crime is their fear of homicide, rape, robbery, and assault. Fear of violence leads people to stay in at night, refuse to open their doors to strangers or help strangers in need, and travel in groups when walking the streets.

There is little doubt that the public's fear of violent crime is related to the media. Newspapers, television (both the news and dramas), movies, and other media outlets portray violence (especially violence perpetrated by strangers) as a "typical" rather than rare form of crime.[2] This is not to say that Americans' fear of violence is irrational. Although rare, violent crimes can have a life-altering effect on victims and/or their families.

Why do some people behave violently? Why are some societies or communities more violent than others? Criminologists, sociologists, psychologists, and many others have attempted to address such questions throughout history. Most agree that no single explanation exists for violent crime. This chapter explores the nature and extent of the most common types of violent crime — homicide, rape, robbery, and assault. Other forms of violent crime are discussed in Chapter 11.

Violent Crime Trends in the United States

Although people may have valid reasons for their fears, violent crime — like crime in general — has been on the decline throughout the early part of the 21st century. Uniform Crime Report (UCR) data reveals that in 2004, over 1.3 million serious violent crimes (homicide, robbery, rape, aggravated assault) were known to police. The violent crime index, calculated from this figure, is 466 violent crimes per 100,000 citizens.[3] The 2004 figures indicate that the United States continues to experience a reduction in violent crime that began in 1991, when the UCR violent crime index peaked at 758 crimes per 100,000 citizens. Preliminary UCR data suggest that violent crime continued to decline in the first half of 2005.[4] Data from the National Crime Victimization Survey (NCVS) also reveal a substantial decline in violent offending over the past decade.[5]

The examination of violent crime rates and trends raises many questions. For example, why has violent crime declined across the nation? What explains this multiyear trend? Despite the recent decline in overall violent crime rates, Americans remain more likely to murder each other than citizens of other industrialized countries. Why then, in contrast to other countries, does the United States experience stubbornly high levels of homicide? This chapter explores these questions (and others related to the causes of violence) through the examination of homicide, assault, rape, and robbery.

Homicide

Homicide is the unlawful taking of life by another human. As the word unlawful makes clear, not all acts of taking another's life are illegal. Most societies allow some agents of the state — police officers and soldiers, for example — to kill in certain situations. Also, some homicides are considered justifiable. A *justifiable homicide,* such as a homicide committed in self-defense, occurs when the death of the other person is unavoidable or is in some fashion warranted. There is no malice or negligence involved and the law acknowledges that any other prudent and socially aware person would have acted the same under similar circumstances.

As TABLE 10-1 indicates, there are a number of ways to classify homicides. Murder is a homicide that includes the element of malice aforethought. *Malice aforethought* is the manifestation of a deliberate intention to take the life of a fellow human. *First-degree murder* is committed with premeditation and deliberation. *Premeditation* means that the act of fatal violence was consciously considered beforehand; *deliberation* means that the killing was planned and not a spontaneous or impulsive act. In *second-degree murder,* there is also malice aforethought, but not premeditation and deliberation. Murder can also include the killing of another person in the process of committing another felony.[6] Murder is typically considered the most serious offense in the United States. This is reflected in the fact that in most death-penalty states, murder is the only crime for which an offender can receive the death penalty. Further, murder is one of the few criminal offenses for which there is no statute of limitations; killers may be brought to justice any time after their crime has been committed.

Manslaughter is the unlawful taking of a human life without malice. *Voluntary manslaughter* is the killing of another person in some circumstance where emotions cloud the offender's judgment. In *involuntary manslaughter,* the death is neither deliberate nor premeditated; rather, it is the result of some type of negligent behavior.

TABLE 10-1

Examples of Different Forms of Homicide

Types of Homicide	Examples
First-degree murder	Husband kills wife for the insurance money after months of planning
Second-degree murder	Husband impulsively kills wife during an argument over the monthly bills
Voluntary manslaughter	Husband kills wife after walking in on her with another man
Involuntary manslaughter	Husband is driving under the influence and crashes his car; his wife dies

Murder Levels and Trends

According to the past 20 years of Uniform Crime Report data, the murder and non-negligent manslaughter rate peaked in 1993 at 9.5 per 100,000. It slowly dropped until leveling off in 2000. The 2004 murder rate of 5.5 per 100,000 represents a total of 16,503 murders and non-negligent manslaughters.[7] FIGURE 10-1 displays the homicide trend since 1900 based on the National Vital Statistics System. The Vital Statistics are based on death certificate records, and yield slightly different estimates of the homicide rate than the UCR. This figure illustrates that a person would have to go back to the 1960s to find a time when homicide rates were lower than current levels.

Despite this decline, however, the homicide rate of the United States is still substantially higher than most other industrialized nations. Although differences in how crimes are classified, defined, and reported typically make cross-national crime comparisons dicey business, homicide statistics are among the most reliable. A 2002 World Health Organization report compared the homicide rates among individuals aged 10–29 across 75 countries. For this subset of homicide cases, the 1998 U.S. murder rate was 11 (per 100,000 citizens). Most other industrialized countries, such as the United Kingdom (0.9), France (0.6), Canada (1.7), and Japan (0.4) had murder rates less than one-tenth of the U.S. rate. Countries with comparable homicide rates include Mexico (15), Kazakhstan (11.5), and Cuba (9.6). Explanations for this finding are explored later.

Within the United States, homicides are not equally distributed across the country. Historically, the Southern region has had higher homicide rates than other parts of the country. In 2004, for example, the Southern region had a higher (6.6) homicide rate than the Northeast (4.2) or Midwest (4.7). Murders were more likely to occur in urban than rural areas, but there is also wide variation among large metropolitan areas. Consider the differences in 2004 murder rates (per 100,000) in Chicago (16), New York City (7), Boston (10), Detroit (42), and Houston (13).[8]

FIGURE 10-1 U.S. Homicide Trend

*Figures include the deaths resulting from the 9/11 terrorist attacks.

Source: United States Department of Justice, Bureau of Justice Statistics, "Homicide Rate Trends," available at http:www.ojp.usdoj.gov/bjs/glance/tables/hmrttab.htm, accessed February 20, 2006.

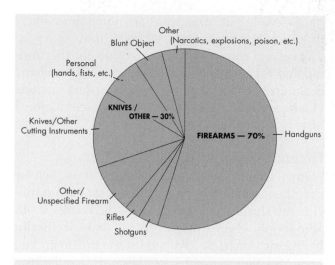

Weapons in Homicide

UCR data indicate that 70% of homicides involve handguns, shotguns, rifles, and other firearms (see **FIGURE 10-2**). Partly in response to highly publicized mass murders and drug-related murder cases, high-powered assault weapons are often singled out as especially lethal instruments in homicides. Handguns alone, however, account for roughly half of all homicides committed in the United States and almost 80% of the homicides caused by firearms.[9]

Circumstances Leading to Homicide

How does the typical homicide unfold? Marvin Wolfgang's classic 1958 study classified one-quarter of homicides as "victim precipitated." Wolfgang defined homicides as victim precipitated when the victim was the first to use physical force.[10] Later research using alternative definitions suggests that the rate of victim precipitation in homicides might be much higher.[11] For those homicides where the circumstances are known to the police (65% of murders), the UCR also sheds some light on the context of homicides. The most common (44%) pathway to homicide by far is an argument. This lends some credence to the role of victim precipitation. Just over 20% of homicides are classified as **felony murder**. In other words, these homicides were committed while the offender engaged in a separate felony offense (e.g., rape, robbery, arson). Other circumstances include bar brawls (2%) and juvenile gang killings (6%).[12]

Offender and Victim Characteristics

Of those arrested for murder, nearly nine out of ten are males.[13] Males also represent roughly four out of five homicide victims, a pattern that has remained relatively constant since 1964. Males are responsible for over 85% of male homicide victims (females kill 14% of the male victims) and 90% of the female victims.[14]

Homicide is a young person's crime. While only 10% of homicide offenders and victims are under the age of 18, over one-third are young adults (18–34).[15] The same can be said of homicide victims: Most victims of homicide are between 25 and 34 years old. Regarding race, African-Americans are overrepresented as both homicide victims and offenders. Blacks account for roughly half of all homicide arrests and represent half of all homicide victims. In cases where the perpetrator was known, almost 95% of black victims were killed by black perpetrators. In cases of white victims, the perpetrators were also white in almost 85% of the cases. Thus, homicide is overwhelmingly an intraracial crime.[16]

Finally, most homicides involve offenders and victims who are known to each other. For homicides where investigators can determine the relationship between the victim and offender (66% of

Police investigate the scene of a homicide.

? *How does a "typical" homicide unfold? What are the demographic profiles of homicide perpetrators and victims?*

cases) about three-quarter of victims knew their perpetrator. Among these nonstranger homicides, 30% were perpetrated by family members and the remainder by acquaintances.

Intimate Partner Homicide

A type of homicide for which the offender and victim are clearly known to each other is known as *intimate partner homicide*. Intimate partner homicide (homicides in which the perpetrator and victims are current or former intimate partners) make up a substantial portion of homicides. This is especially true for female victims: When victims are female, they are significantly more likely than males to be victims of this type of homicide. In 2004, for example, 33% of female victims were killed by their husband or boyfriend; only 3% of male victims were killed by a wife or girlfriend.[17]

There is a correlation between intimate partner homicide and intimate partner abuse: Intimate partner homicide is often preceded by physical, emotional, or sexual abuse. This link is important for both female victims and offenders. Studies have found that women tend to kill during domestic disputes. This is typically after a long history of physical and psychological abuse at the hands of their male intimate partner, after the male "victim" initiated the attack, and more often than men, women claim self-defense.[18] Men who kill often have a long history of abuse toward their female intimate partners. Men are also significantly more likely to kill their female partners or expartners and then commit suicide.[19]

In response to research linking intimate partner abuse to intimate partner homicide, some states have made attempts to develop risk assessment tools to enable criminal justice personnel to intervene in cases most likely to escalate into intimate partner homicide. For example, the risk of escalation increases where the perpetrators have a criminal history, the couples have had prior separations or a separation was imminent, and the victim and offender are married at the time of the incident (as opposed to cohabiting).[20] Regardless, this type of homicide continues to be a serious criminal problem.

Explaining America's Homicide Rate

Cross-national victimization surveys of crime reveal that American violent crime rates are on par with other industrialized nations.[21] The exception (as noted previously) to this finding concerns homicide rates. Simply put, Americans are much more likely to kill each other than members of most other industrialized countries. What accounts for this finding and for cross-national differences in homicide generally? Three common explanations include (1) the availability of firearms, (2) a violent national history, and (3) economic inequality.

Firearm Availability

Many criminologists and commentators believe that there is a rather simple reason for high homicide rates in the United States — the readily available supply of firearms in general, and specifically, handguns. American civilians own over 200 million firearms; over a quarter of these are handguns.[22] Household handgun ownership rates in the United States (roughly 30%) are much higher than in most other industrialized countries (1% to 14%). Indeed, American handgun possession rates exceed those of any nation for which data are available.[23] The gist of the gun-murder argument is that, because of the availability of firearms, violent incidents (an argument/brawl or robbery) are more likely to become lethal. For example, a bar brawl in which participants suffer only minor injuries could turn deadly if a gun is introduced. Some evidence supports this view. Although the non-gun homicide rate for the United States in only 2.5 times higher than the average rate of other industrialized nations, the *gun-related* homicide is more than 7.5 times higher. A 2001 study, using data from 36 nations, concluded that firearm availability was a strong predictor of homicide rates. If this hypothesis is correct, what is the policy implication? The typical response is a call for more stringent gun control.

The Gun Control Debate Gun control is among the most hotly debated public policy issues in America. Gun control advocates argue that reducing the availability of firearms (especially handguns) and keeping them out of the hands of criminals will reduce homicides and other forms of violence. Others believe that gun control laws will either have no impact on violence or that gun control actually increases violence because criminals will feel freer to victimize unarmed citizens. Where does the weight of research evidence lie? Unfortunately, this is an area in which there is no clear pattern of empirical evidence.

Different forms of gun control legislation operate at the local, state, and federal level. One strategy is to regulate those who sell firearms. The Federal Gun Control Act requires firearms dealers to be licensed, to carefully document each sale or purchase, and to refrain from selling guns to those prohibited (e.g., minors, felons) from owning firearms. The "Brady Bill" (named after Press Secretary James Brady, who was shot in the attempted assassination of President Ronald Reagan) passed in 1993 and mandated a five-day waiting period before a licensed dealer could sell a handgun to a nonlicensed person. In 1998, this law was amended and now requires a background check (which can be instant) to see whether the buyer is prohibited from owning firearms. A 2000 study compared states that implemented the Brady Law with states that already had similar legislation. No evidence was found that the Brady Law reduced homicides.[24]

Criminologist James Jacobs suggests several reasons why laws aimed at restricting licensed arms retailers in American are ineffective[25]:

- Criminals tend not to directly buy guns through licensed dealers; they may use a third party (relative, friend) with a clean record to buy guns indirectly.
- The secondary market (e.g., gun shows, classified ads) is completely unregulated.
- Firearms can be purchased illegally "on the street."
- Those ineligible to buy a gun may steal guns during burglaries or borrow a gun from a friend or relative.

Some cities have gone so far as to ban handguns within their jurisdiction. For example, Washington, DC, banned the possession and sale of handguns in 1975. There was some evidence that the handgun ban led to a reduction of suicides and homicides. Specifically, while gun-caused homicides and suicides decreased, nongun suicides and homicides remained steady.[26] Critics correctly note, however, that similar patterns emerged during this time in cities without a handgun ban. Handgun bans by two Illinois cities (Morton Grove and Evanston) in the early 1980s appear to have had no effect on gun-related crimes.[27] A 2001 review of 49 studies that assessed the impact of gun-control laws found that 7 studies indicated a significant reduction in crime, 12 found mixed support for gun control, and the remaining 30 found no impact.[28]

The debate over gun control shows no sign of being resolved. In fact, over the past two decades, many states have enacted conceal-and-carry or shall-issue legislation. *Conceal-and-carry legislation* directs local authorities to grant citizens who meet

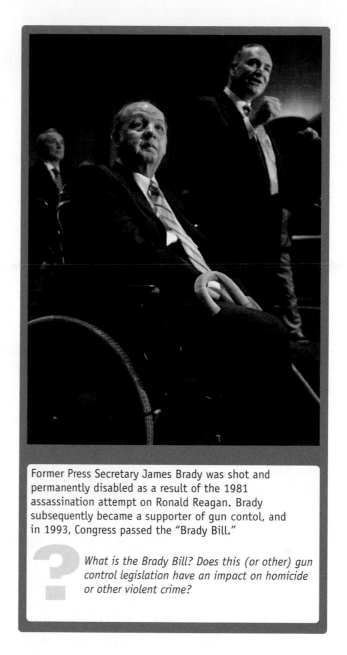

Former Press Secretary James Brady was shot and permanently disabled as a result of the 1981 assassination attempt on Ronald Reagan. Brady subsequently became a supporter of gun contol, and in 1993, Congress passed the "Brady Bill."

? *What is the Brady Bill? Does this (or other) gun control legislation have an impact on homicide or other violent crime?*

certain criteria (e.g., nonfelon, no history of mental disorders) a permit to carry a concealed firearm. Economist John Lott lends support to such legislation with his provocative book that bluntly argues "more guns" mean "less crime."[29] The conceal-and-carry debate and the argument that armed citizens deter crime is explored in the **Theory in Action — Do More Guns Mean Less Crime?**

Economic Inequality

Apart from firearms possession, the United States is distinct from other industrialized countries in terms of social structure. Specifically, the country has a high level of economic inequality and a low level of social support (e.g., no national health or child care,

Does More Guns Mean Less Crime?

With the title of his book, *More Guns, Less Crime: Understanding Crime and Gun Control Laws,* economist John Lott, Jr. gets his main (and controversial) point across. Conventional wisdom among criminologists (and many Americans) is that the United States' homicide rate is due in part to the widespread availability of firearms. Lott and others turn this argument on its head by arguing that less gun control (and more guns) will actually decrease crime. The gist of their argument is that the criminal element will be more leery of a well-armed citizenry. From a rational choice perspective, arming citizens increases the expected cost of crime. Further, when offenders do choose to victimize, armed citizens will be able to protect themselves and fend off criminal attacks.

Much of Lott's work focuses specifically on so-called shall-issue or right-to-carry (RTC) laws, which are designed to make it easier for citizens to carry concealed weapons in public places. In the absence of such laws, states generally have may-issue regulations, where county-level authorities have the discretion to issue permits, based on broad criteria, such as the applicant having "good moral character." In contrast, shall-issue regulations direct local authorities to issue permits unless the applicant fails to meet some objective criteria

(e.g., no history of mental disorder or alcohol/drug abuse, no felony conviction, successful completion of a gun safety course). RTC laws have been adopted by 22 states and are currently under consideration in others.

While Lott clearly believes that such laws reduce crime, critics contend that RTC laws will have little effect on crime. For example, skeptics note that very few people (even in RTC states) apply for permits. Moreover, many who apply for permits already had been carrying weapons (illegally) for protection. What does the empirical evidence indicate? Over two dozen studies have been conducted on this topic; most compare states that adopted RTC laws with those that did not and assess the impact of this legislation on violent crime over time. Unfortunately, different researchers reached very different conclusions: Some find that RTC laws reduce violent crime, some find slight increases in violence for RTC states, and others find the laws have no impact. The divergence in findings is partly a function of the complex statistical models used in this research — altering statistical assumptions or changing the time period of study substantially changes the findings. A 2003 study moved beyond simple measures of whether a state has a RTC law and focused instead on the usage of these laws. The au-

---

low support for the unemployed). Both Messner and Rosenfeld's institutional anomie theory and the work of Elliott Currie suggest that the failure to provide a buffer (or safety net) for the less advantaged members of society ultimately breeds violence.

> **LINK** Institutional anomie theory is discussed in Chapter 6, while Currie's work is described in Chapter 8.

Two relatively recent cross-national studies appear to support the link between inequality and homicide. In Messner and Rosenfeld's own test of their institutional anomie theory, a "decommodification index" (a measure of the strength of the safety net in any society) predicted homicide rates. A 2003 study that examined 46 nations found that those countries with *both* high levels of economic inequality and low levels of social support (such as the United States) experienced higher levels of homi-

cide. Although these tests suggest that inequality and low social support breed violence, it is unclear why American homicide rates (as opposed to all violent crime) would be uniquely affected by these factors.

American History

Yet another theme in the literature is that American homicide rates are tied specifically to a sociocultural tradition of violence. Is there an American "cultural predisposition" toward violence? For example, what Americans view as a take-charge attitude appears to people from other cultures as a violence-before-reason mentality. Historians note that the founding of this country resulted from a brutal war with England. They also point to the bloody legacy of slavery, the use of violence (Civil War) to end slavery, and the near genocide committed against Native Americans. The vigilantism of the "wild west" thors found that the number of permits issued under the law had no effect on violent crime. Despite being hailed by criminologist John Donohue III as "the final bullet in the body of the more guns less crime hypothesis," this study will undoubtedly encourage more (not less) research and controversy regarding RTC laws.

Apart from whether a concealed weapon serves as a general deterrent is this question: Can a victim successfully fend off an attack by brandishing or using a weapon? That is, once a criminal event has started, does possession of a handgun help the victim? Throughout his book, Lott provides compelling case examples of *defensive gun use* (*DGU*) such as the following:

> As more than 30 diners sat in Sam's St. John's Seafood [in Jacksonville, Florida] about 7:20 pm, a masked man entered the eatery and ordered everyone to the floor, said co-owner Sam Bajalia. The man grabbed waitress Amy Norton from where she and another waitress were huddled on the floor and tried to get her to open the cash register. At that point, [Oscar] Moore stood up and shot him. Another diner pulled out a .22-caliber derringer and fired at the man as he ran out of the restaurant . . . "I'm glad they were here because if that girl couldn't open the register, and he didn't get [any] money, he might have started shooting," Bajalia said.

Empirical evidence reveals that there are between 300,000 and 1.2 million cases of DGU in a given year.

Research reveals that DGU is effective at thwarting robbers, burglars, and assault situations, although there is some evidence that it also increases the victims' odds of suffering injury or death. Others caution that the benefit of DGU might be outweighed by the harm caused by the presence of handguns. For example, there is evidence that the "house gun" kept for one's own defense is more likely to kill someone in the household or to be used in a domestic quarrel as to defend against an attack. DGU remains a hotly debated topic in criminology and there is little doubt this topic will generate more research.

What are the gun control laws in your state?

Has RTC legislation been recently passed or is it under consideration?

How does the RTC debate relate to neoclassical theories of crime?

Sources: John R. Lott, Jr., *More Guns, Less Crime: Understanding Crime and Gun Control Laws* (Chicago: University of Chicago Press, 2000); Jeffrey Fagan, "Guns, Science, and Social Policy," *Criminology and Public Policy* 3 (2003): 359–362; Tomislav V. Kovandzic and Thomas B. Marvell, "Right-to-Carry Concealed Handguns and Violent Crime: Crime Control Through Gun Decontrol?" *Criminology and Public Policy* 3 (2003): 363–396; John Donohue III, "The Final Bullet in the Body of the More Guns, Less Crime Hypothesis," *Criminology and Public Policy* 3 (2003): 397–410; William Wells, "The Nature and Circumstances of Defensive Gun Use: A Content Analysis of Interpersonal Conflict Situations Involving Criminal Offenders," *Justice Quarterly* 19 (2002): 127–157; Gary Kleck, *Targeting Guns: Firearms and Their Control* (New York: Aldine de Gruyter, 1997).

and the violent reaction to labor unions also reflect a history of American violence. Does this violent heritage account for modern American homicide? This is a difficult question to answer empirically. It is worth noting, however, that many other nations (e.g., Germany, Scotland, Japan) with a cultural history of violence have low homicide rates today.[30]

Explaining Homicide Rates in the South

As noted previously, the homicide rates of southern states are higher than in other regions of the United States. The common explanations for violence in the South are similar to those discussed with respect to U.S. homicide rates (versus other countries). In other words, the factors that distinguish the United States from other countries also distinguish the South from other regions of the country. In particular, scholars have advanced a southern subculture of violence explanation; that is, members of the South adhere to a set of norms (e.g., independence, exaggerated sense of honor, frontier mentality) that are conducive to violence.[31] Others note that both firearm availability and economic inequality are higher in the South than in other regions of the country.

Rape and Sexual Assault

Rape has been recognized as a crime since the earliest written legal codes. Historically, though, legal definitions were very limited and narrow in scope. For example, in English common law, rape included only forced sexual intercourse perpetrated by a man against a woman who was not his wife.[32]

Today, rape laws are more global and do not reference marriage; rape can occur among strangers, dating partners, marital partners, heterosexuals, people of the same sex, young and old, and with either men or women as victims. Moreover, rape may involve anal, oral, vaginal-penile intercourse, or even assault using a foreign object.

Some debate remains about whether the definition of rape should require the use of force. Although many legal jurisdictions continue to rely on force as evidence of rape, researchers, practitioners, and some rape statutes include <u>coercive rape</u> in their definitions. Here, *rape* is defined as unlawful sexual intercourse by force or without legal or factual consent.[33] Another legal debate surrounds what has been termed *initial consent rape*. Here, the victim initially agrees to a sexual encounter. After sex is initiated, the victim requests that the encounter end, but the partner does not comply with the request. Courts in some jurisdictions define this scenario as rape, but others consider initial consent binding; once consensual sex has started, rape is not legally possible.[34] <u>Sexual assault</u> is more broad and inclusive than rape and can be defined as any forced or coerced sexual intimacy (unwanted touching with no consent).[35]

Rape Incidence, Prevalence, and Trends

Statistics on rape vary greatly. It is estimated that rape is among the most underreported crimes. Victims are unwilling to report sexual assaults for many different reasons: They do not want anyone to find out; they do not define what happened to them as rape (particularly in date or marital rape situations); they blame themselves; they do not want their friend, boyfriend, or husband to get in trouble; they fear how criminal justice personnel will treat them; they think nothing can be done; or they just want to forget and get on with their life. Because of this lack of reporting, it is likely that both official records (victims do not report to police) and victimization surveys (victims may still have many reasons for not disclosing) underestimate rape. Moreover, the way rape is defined impacts the estimates. For example, some studies only include completed rapes, while others include attempted. Finally, certain types of rape are disproportionately reported (stranger rapes where victims are seen as "typical" victims) and this can bias explanations of rape.

With those caveats in mind, what is known about the prevalence and incidence of rape in the United States? According to UCR data, almost 95,000 rapes were reported to the police in 2004; this translates into a rate of 63 rapes per 100,000 women in the United States.[36] Like other violent crimes, rape has been on the decline. In fact, among victimizations measured by the NCVS, rape (-81%) and attempted rape (-70%) declined more since 1993 than any other offense. Despite this decline, the NCVS data indicate that about 210,000 rapes and sexual assaults against individuals aged 12 or older occurred in 2004.[37]

The lifetime prevalence rates suggest that rape is all too common. The National Violence Against Women (NVAW) survey interviewed a national, random sample of 8000 women and 8000 men. This survey indicated that 18% of women and 3% of men (or 1 in every 6 women and 1 in every 33 men) experienced a completed or attempted rape in their lives (including childhood).[38] A recent victimization study of college women revealed that about 1 in 36 college women experience a completed or attempted rape during an academic year. The study authors calculate that during the course of a college career, rape victimization (completed and attempted) among women at higher education institutions might be as high as 20% to 25%.[39]

Although rape and sexual assault are often portrayed as crimes occurring between strangers (e.g., the stranger jumping out of an alley on a dark street), victimization surveys reveal that they are much more likely to be perpetrated by nonstrangers. In the survey of college women just described, about 90% of the offenders were known to the victim.[40] Acquaintances included boyfriends (or exboyfriends), classmates, coworkers, and friends. More generally, NCVS data reveal that victims of rape and sexual assault report that in nearly three out of four incidents, the offender was not a stranger.[41] Finally, in 90% of sexual victimizations involving child victims, the child knows the offender.[42] Two forms of acquaintance rape — date rape and marital rape — have captured the attention of scholars and mainstream America over the past 25 years.

Date Rape

Perhaps one of the most underreported types of rape is *date rape* — rape that takes place in the context of a legitimate dating arrangement. Date rape can occur on a first date or among people in a long-term committed relationship. This type of rape was largely unrecognized until the 1980s. Today, criminologists know that a substantial portion of rapes occur in the context of dating. For example, a recent study found that 12% to 15% of female students in South Dakota high schools had been forced to engage in sex while on a date.[43] Unfortunately, less is known about those who commit date rape than other forms of rape. Still, there is some evidence of similarities between date and stranger rape. For example, studies of date rapists and stranger rapists have found that both report stereotypical views of women and narrow definitions of masculinity.[44]

Date-Rape Drugs

A phenomenon that has generated a great deal of media attention recently is the use of so-called *date-rape drugs,* such as GHB, Rohypnol, and Ketamine.[45] These drugs are sometimes used to assist someone perpetrating a sexual assault upon a victim. The drugs typically render the victim physically helpless, thus unable to refuse the unwanted sexual assault, and in many cases, unable to remember the attack itself. Date-rape drugs can come in various forms. GHB, for example, may come in a liquid form, powder, or pill. Rohypnol comes in a pill form, while Ketamine comes in the form of a white powder. The suddenness of the effects is drastic, but will vary based on the amount of the drug taken and the physiology of the victim. Of course, as is often the case, if alcohol is ingested by the victim, the effect will be more immediate. **TABLE 10-2** identifies the symptoms associated with common date-rape drugs.

How can one protect oneself from a date rape involving date-rape drugs? The National Women's Health Information Center offers the following advice[46]:

- Don't accept drinks from other people except trusted friends.
- Open containers yourself.
- Keep your drink with you at all times, even when you go to the bathroom.
- Don't share drinks.
- Don't drink from punch bowls or other large, common, open containers. They may already have drugs in them.
- Don't drink anything that tastes or smells strange. Sometimes GHB tastes salty.
- Have a nondrinking friend with you to make sure nothing happens.

Marital Rape

Marital rape has only recently been legally recognized. English common law had a marital exemption to rape; forced sex was not classified as rape if the offender and victim were married. The chief justice of England, Sir Mathew Hale, writing in

---

TABLE 10-2

Symptoms Associated with Selected Date-Rape Drugs

GHB	Rohypnol	Ketamine
Relaxation	Inability to recall	Hallucinations
Drowsiness	Lower blood pressure	Loss of time
Dizziness	Sleepiness	Loss of identity
Nausea	Muscle relaxation	Distorted perceptions
Unconsciousness	Drunk feeling	of time and sounds
Seizures	Nausea	Feelings of loss of control
Breathing problems	Problem talking	Loss of motor functions
Inability to recall	Motor impairment	Breathing problems
Tremors	Mental confusion	Convulsions
Sweating	Visual problems	Vomiting
Vomiting	Dizziness	Out-of-body experiences
Slow heart rate	Confusion	Memory problems
Dream-like feelings	Stomach problems	Dream-like feelings
Coma		Numbness
Death		Loss of coordination
		Violent behavior
		Slurred speech

Source: The National Women's Health Information Center, "Date Rape Drugs," available at http://www.4woman.gov/faq/rohypnol.htm, accessed February 15, 2006.

Bars frequented by young adults may offer opportunities for perpetrators of sexual assault to slip date-rape drugs into the drinks of unsuspecting females.

? *What protective steps can women take to reduce their exposure to date-rape drugs?*

1736, stated, "But the husband cannot be guilty of rape committed by himself upon his lawful wife, for by their mutual matrimonial consent and contract the wife hath given up herself in this kind onto her husband, which she cannot retract."[47] In other words, the marriage contract guaranteed husbands unlimited sexual access to their wives. As recent as the 1980s, most American states followed the Lord Hale doctrine and refused to recognize marital rape. By 1993, however, marital rape became a crime in at least one section of the sexual offense statutes in all 50 states.[48] Still, states criminalize a narrower range of offenses if committed within marriage, subject the marital-rape perpetrator to less-serious sanctions, and sometimes create special procedural hurdles for marital-rape prosecutions.[49]

Like date rape, it is estimated that marital rape is greatly underreported. Depending upon how rape is defined, research has revealed prevalence rates from 8% to 23%.[50] The National Violence Against Women survey revealed that 7.7% of women reported being raped by an intimate partner at some point in their lives. This includes, however, former partners, as well as cohabitating and noncohabitating (but not married) partners. Diana Russell's survey of a random sample of San Francisco women remains the classic study on the prevalence of mar-

ital rape. Russell found that 14% of the women had experienced at least one attempted or completed marital rape — 10% experience rape within a pattern of physical abuse, while 4% experienced only a sexual attack. Respondents in this research reported twice as many marital rapes as stranger rapes.[51] A central finding in much of this research is that a strong relationship exists between battering and marital rape. Research indicates that 30% to 50% of battered women experience marital rape.[52]

This is not to say that marital rape occurs only in the context of battering. For example, one typology distinguishes among battering rapes, nonbattering rapes, and obsessive rapes.[53] *Battering rapes* occur in the context of intimate partner abuse (meaning that they occur in addition to physical and emotional abuse). *Nonbattering rapes* occur in relationships where there is little to no violence, yet rape occurs often as a result of sexual conflicts. Finally, *obsessive rapes* involve various sexual obsessions, largely perpetrated by men who consume large amounts of pornography. Diana Russell identified the following typology of marital rapists[54]:

1. Husbands who prefer raping their wives to having consensual sex with them
2. Husbands who are able to enjoy both consensual sex and rape with their wives and are ambivalent to which it is
3. Husbands who prefer consensual sex with their wives but are willing to rape when their sexual advances are rejected
4. Husbands who would like to rape their wives, but do not
5. Husbands who do not want to rape their wives

Victims of Rape

Although it should be noted that rape victims are from all classes, races, genders, and age groups, research has uncovered some patterns. Foremost, rape and sexual assault victims are disproportionately young. Estimates indicate that over 15% of sexual assault victims are under 12 years of age.[55] Among those over 12 years of age, women younger than 25 years are disproportionately rape victims. Evidence also suggests that race is related to sexual victimization. Black females are slightly more likely to be victims of rape or sexual assault and there is evidence that Native Americans are more likely to be victimized than women of other races.[56]

Effects of Victimization

Those who experience rape and sexual assault experience a range of physical and psychological harm. NCVS data reveals that about 25% of rape victims are physically injured during the attack (other than the direct injuries resulting from the rape).[57] Injuries ranged from black eyes and bruises to broken bones and other severe bodily harm. In addition to injuries, many rape victims incur other medical problems such as sexually transmitted disease and pregnancy. Because of their long-term nature, the psychological effects of rape often are more severe than the physical harm. Immediate emotional reactions include shame, intense fear, anxiety, stress, and fatigue. Victims may develop a host of serious psychological problems, including eating disorders, suicidal feelings, depression, and obsessive-compulsive disorders (especially washing rituals).[58] The cluster of emotional and psychological responses to rape and sexual assault is clinically recognized as *rape trauma syndrome (RTS)*.[59]

Those people close to the sexual-assault victim (e.g., spouses, partners, peers, siblings) are often affected by the sexual assault and are sometimes considered secondary victims. Husbands or partners of rape victims, for example, must help the victim cope and recover. While the spouse or partner may play a positive role in the recovery process, some may become withdrawn or partially blame the victim.[60]

Explaining Rape and Sexual Assault

A central controversy surrounding the explanation of rape is the motivation of the offender. Historically, most social scientists viewed rape as a sexually motivated crime. In other words, rape allows males to fulfill sexual desires that cannot be met legitimately. More recently, many scholars have argued that rape is actually an act of *violence* in which sex is used as a weapon. In this case, rape is analogous to acts such as assault or battering. Feminist scholars discuss rape within the larger political/historical context of men's oppression of women. Susan Brownmiller argues that rape is "nothing more or less than a conscious process of intimidation by which *all* men keep *all* women in a state of fear."[61] Men rape, Brownmiller contends, to keep women in their place and to validate their masculinity.[62] It is likely that there is some merit to each of these arguments; there may be multiple motives for rape or sexual assault.[63]

Psychological Typologies of Rapists

One way to approach the study of rape is to explicitly consider different motivations by constructing typologies. Researchers (typically psychologists) develop typologies for a number of reasons. Typologies are a useful starting point for research on the causes of rape; they may help police identify potential offenders (based on circumstances of crime) and can suggest useful forms of treatment for offenders.[64] One study, for example, explored the characteristics of over 100 rapists and identified four types of rapists[65]:

1. **Power reassurance rapist:** Socially and sexually inadequate, he rapes for sex, although sex for him is distorted. He rapes close to where he lives and works and is often employed in menial jobs. He is interested in pornography and rapes periodically.

2. **Anger retaliation rapist:** He has an overarching desire to hurt women and uses rape as a weapon. Socially competent, he works in an action-oriented occupation and is often married, but his wife is typically safe from his assaults. He is sexually permissive with a quick and violent temper. Often, he commits blitz attacks close to his home and injures his victims with his hands, fists, or other type of weapon.

Most people think of rape as perpetrated by a stranger on a dark street. Although this is the stereotype, women are much more likely to be raped by someone they know than a stranger.

? *What different types of acquaintance rape have researchers considered?*

3. **Power assertive rapist**: He feels a sense of superiority simply because he is male. Women are there for his use, abuse, and disposal. He is usually unhappy with his marriage, dresses in a flashy manner, and frequents singles bars, where he finds his victims.

4. **Sadistic rapist**: The most dangerous of rapists, his goal is to hurt, demean, and cause as much physical and psychological pain as possible. Many of these rapists are sociopaths and their aggression is evident even in their everyday life. Considered to be a good "family man," he is seen by others as an asset to the community. However, there is a dark and sadistic side to his personality: He has made the very vital connection between personal violence and sexual gratification. This rapist tends to become more violent over time, and if not checked, may even begin to murder his victims.

Typologies such as this make clear that not all rapists are alike. Such typologies also suggest a cautious approach in advising women how to react in a rape situation. For example, whereas the power reassurance rapist may bolt from the victim if she resists, the sadistic rapist may become all the more excited. Even when the behavioral characteristics or the verbal clues suggest a particular type of rapist, the individual rapist may not possess all the qualities. Therefore, a simplistic response — fight or comply — may be exactly the wrong advice depending upon the type of rapist.

An Evolutionary Perspective on Rape

As explored in Chapter 4, evolutionary explanations of crime are based in the Darwinian principles of natural selection and survival of the fittest. Those individuals that are best adapted to their environment will survive to reproduce and therefore will pass on their genes to their offspring. In the controversial book, *A Natural History of Rape* published in 2000, Randy Thornhill and Craig Palmer outline an evolutionary theory of rape. According to the authors, rape is an "adaptive strategy" that developed in human males in order to allow them to sire more offspring. Rather than *natural* selection, these authors point to the role of *sexual* selection:

> The males of most species — including humans — are usually more eager to mate than the females, and this enables females to choose among males who are competing with one another for access to them. But getting chosen is

not the only way to gain sexual access to females. In rape, the male circumvents the female's choice.[66]

One way to gain access to females is to possess certain traits (e.g., physical attractiveness) that females prefer. Another route is to win various forms of male-male competition or to otherwise attain influential status among peers. A final strategy, used instead of (or in combination with) the first two, is to use sexual coercion (rape, intimidation, harassment).[67]

The strength of this type of explanation is that it points to consistency in the use of sexual coercion among humans and other species (e.g., insect and bird behavior) that would not be expected if human socialization or cultural values were the only cause of rape. Yet, the evolutionary perspective has been criticized on a number of grounds. In particular, the evolutionary hypothesis that rape occurs predominantly among women of child-bearing age runs counter to the evidence of high rape rates among preadolescents.[68]

A Feminist Explanation of Rape and Sexual Assault

Feminist scholars emphasize the patriarchal nature of society; that is, males have historically dominated almost all important political and economic activities — women are exploited and treated as subordinates. Within feminist theory, sexual gratification is not the primary motivation for sexual assault. Rather, rape is simply another tool used to maintain control and dominance over women. Accordingly, some feminists refer to rape as a pseudosexual act. Ultimately then, rape is the consequence of deep-seated social tradition of male dominance and female exploitation.[69] In this paradigm, men who rape are not psychologically abnormal; rather, they are responding to the values, attitudes, and norms of their specific culture.

There is some support for hypotheses derived from feminist theories of rape and sexual assault. For example, one hypothesis is that societies that are less patriarchal should have lower rapes than societies where males and females are equals. Anthropologist Peggy Reeves Sanday directly tested this hypothesis by comparing rape-prone tribal societies with tribes in which rape was rare. She discovered that women had more power in those societies in which rape was uncommon.[70] Comparing individual states (within the United States), researchers also discovered a relationship between gender inequality and rape. States with higher scores on a "gender equality index" (e.g., higher levels of social, economic, political gender equality) had lower rape rates.[71] The evidence in this realm, however, is complex. Some studies find, as inequality between sexes diminishes, that rape actually *increases*. Feminists account for this finding by noting that where male power and dominance decreases in political and economic spheres, males will seek (at least in the short term) to reestablish dominance through sexual coercion.[72]

A central question facing feminist theories is *how* sociocultural tradition influences male behavior. Here, feminist theories point to the role of (1) cultural values/attitudes and (2) socialization practices. In a patriarchal society, one should expect attitudes and values that support or justify rape. Researchers have documented many prejudicial attitudes, stereotypes, or rape myths that justify or condone rape and sexual assault. Myths or stereotypes prevalent in American culture include thinking that:[73]

- Women secretly desire to be raped
- Women who dress or act seductively are asking to be raped
- When a woman says "no" to a sexual advance, she actually means "yes"

Members of a patriarchal society would also be likely to socialize youth toward particular sex roles. A masculine sex role encourages boys to be aggressive and forceful, and to avoid being empathetic and relationship oriented.

A Social Learning Perspective on Rape

Social learning–oriented explanations of crime were covered in both Chapter 5 (psychological behaviorism) and Chapter 7 (Sutherland's differential association theory and Aker's social learning theory). A behavioral approach to studying sexual assault starts with the assumption that sexual aggression (like other behaviors) is learned. Behaviorists highlight how the balance of role models, attitudes and values (cognitions), and reinforcement/punishment shape a person's behavior. Like feminist scholars, social learning theorists point to the importance of attitudes that excuse or justify rape. For a behaviorist, such *cognitive distortions* or *criminal thinking errors* act as negative reinforcement, by eliminating noxious stimuli (e.g., guilt, shame, anxiety) associated with rape.[74]

Socialization (through learning process) toward a sex role is also important in social learning theory. For example, behavioral theorists suggest that *hostile masculinity,* a male orientation toward females that is controlling and adversarial, is a central feature of sexual assault perpetrators.[75] Apart from what individuals learn, cognitive and behavioral theorists also point to what *is not* learned. With regard to rape and sexual assault, there is some evidence that perpetrators lack the cognitive and social skills (e.g., empathy, conversation skills) that allow them to express sexuality in a normative fashion.[76]

There is considerable overlap among social learning and feminist theories of rape. Both emphasize the importance of sex-role socialization and attitudes that justify rape (rape myths or cognitive distortions). One difference between these perspectives is that the motivation for rape is more ambiguous in social learning theory; sexual aggression may be a means to dominate females (as in the feminist perspective) but may also result from a true desire to engage in sex.[77] Both feminist theory and social learning theory also suggest that pornography encourages sexual assault (although there are differences as to why).

Pornography and Rape   Within the feminist theory, pornography in general (because it is degrading to women) is viewed as both a reflection of patriarchy and a cause of rape and sexual assault. The gist of the argument is that pornography makes the inequality of woman — the domination of woman and their submission — sexy.[78] Additionally, social learning theorists view *violent* pornography, or depictions that reinforce rape myths (e.g., women secretly want to be raped), as particularly troublesome. This type of pornography reinforces cognitive distortions, desensitizes men to the pain and humiliation of sexual aggression, and provides role modeling for sexual violence.[79] Although there is some evidence that pornography (especially violent pornography) increases aggression in laboratory experiments, the evidence of real-world effects is more ambiguous.[80] The link between pornography and rape remains a controversial area of inquiry in criminology.

Integrating Perspectives on Rape and Sexual Assault

As the review of evolutionary, cognitive-behavioral, and feminist perspectives makes clear, the empirical evidence regarding the motivation for and explanation of rape remains unsettled. Mary Koss, a highly regarded researcher on sexual assault and rape, offers this blunt summary regarding the motives for rape:

> Clearly, a man is not engaging in a sex act when he screams "You know you like this bitch" while penetrating a woman and forcefully restraining her. The force behind the criminal act of rape is a mixture of sexual motives and motives to control, dominate, or punish that vary in degree from case to case. My example would be low in sexual motives. Some date rapes might provide scenarios for rapes in which sexual motives appear more prominently.[81]

In other words, the motivation for rape might range along a continuum between pure sexual motives on one end and domination/control as a motive on the other end. Wartime rape (discussed in **You Are the Criminologist**) would fall toward the domination and control end of the spectrum, whereas some forms of date rape may fall on the sexual motives end of the continuum. The typologies reviewed previously attempt to make sense of different motives for rape and sexual assault by classifying offenders based on motivation (and other characteristics). Another approach is to integrate the various theories into a single explanation of rape. For example, some evolutionary perspectives also incorporate environmental and social factors to create a more comprehensive theory.[82] Criminologists Larry Baron and Murray Straus have developed an integrated model of sexual violence that incorporates gender inequality, social disorganization, and cultural legitimization of violence to explain rape rates at the state level.[83] Other theorists incorporate developmental experiences (e.g., learning), personality, and broad cultural views of sex roles.[84]

Rape and Correctional Intervention

Treatment programs for rapists are as varied as the theories that attempt to explain rape and sexual assault. Some treatment modalities focus on the sexual aspect of offending. For example, a common behavioral treatment is aversion therapy. Here, the therapist pairs deviant thoughts, fantasies (e.g., a rape fantasy), or other stimuli with a noxious stimulus (e.g., foul odor). Over time, the deviant fantasy is associated with nausea rather than sexual pleasure. Other forms of treatment are more direct. With so-called "chemical castration," offenders take drugs such as Depro-Provera or Leupron that result in a complete lack of sexual drive. Behavioral and chemical strategies have both been criticized for treating the "symptom" rather than the underlying problem.[85]

Over the past 20 years, cognitive-behavioral programs have come to be the dominant treatment modality for sex offenders (as with other types of offenders). Cognitive-behavioral programs focus on eliminating cognitive distortions — justifications or rationalizations that allow offenders to sexually assault without experiencing guilt and anxiety. They also teach cognitive skills such as self-control, problem solving, and anger management.[86] Research on the effectiveness of treatment tends to focus broadly on *sex offenders,* (e.g., pedophiles, exhibitionists, and others are included) rather than specifically on rapists. Review of the literature suggests that overall, treatment of sex offenders can be successful and that chemical castration and cognitive behavioral programs are the most successful forms of treatment.[87]

The Criminal Justice Response to Rape

It is often said that rape victims are victimized twice — once by the actual rapists and again by the criminal justice system if they decide to report their rape. There is often a stark difference between what is "good" for the victim and the goals and organizational nature of the criminal justice system. The primary goal of police and prosecutors is to prove beyond a reasonable doubt that a crime occurred. The successful prosecution of a case hinges upon physical evidence and corroborating witnesses. In most rape and sexual assault cases, the sole witness is the victim.

The hospital is the key institution for rape investigation, because this is often the first place that victims go after a sexual assault. The hospital is responsible for a medical examination and the collection of physical evidence. Physicians and hospital staff have been called the "reluctant partner" in systems that work with rape victims. Rape victims are often not viewed as "real" patients (especially if there is no physical injury) and doctors are reluctant to perform rape exams (they are long and intrusive) and to testify in court.[88] Even where physical evidence confirms sexual relations, it often cannot speak to whether the sex was consensual.

The primary role of police officers is to "build a good case."[89] Police officers, attempting to get a thorough and clear statement, often come across as "interrogating" the victim. Accordingly, victims often feel as though the police do not believe their story.[90] Prosecutors generally strive to secure a conviction that results in punishment appropriate to the level of harm caused by the crime. Prosecutors represent the state rather than the victim and generally prefer plea bargaining (a sure conviction) to trial. Research suggests that prosecutors are more likely to either dismiss or plea bargain rape cases than other types of criminal cases.[91] There is also evidence that prosecutors try to find discrepancies in a victim's statements, determine if the victim had ulterior motives for alleging rape, and see if the victim fits the criteria for a "typical" victim when deciding whether to charge a rape case.[92] Prosecutors may also be more leery about accepting the victim's testimony as the truth and may require the victim to take a polygraph test.[93] Prosecutors justify these actions by noting that coercion is difficult to prove, which makes it hard to secure convictions for rape and sexual assault cases.[94]

For the rare case that goes to trial, the victims must face defense attorneys who are bound by an ethical code to vigorously advocate (e.g., do whatever is necessary) for their clients. Prior to the 1980s, defense attorneys were allowed to bring up the victims past sexual behavior, her chastity (or lack thereof), or any motive she might have to falsely claim that a consensual encounter was rape. Rape shield laws now prohibit defense attorneys from bringing up the promiscuity or character of the victims. However, the defense can generally skirt these laws by indirectly attacking the victim's character.[95]

Aside from rape shield laws, can the justice process be made more victim friendly to victims of sexual assault? In a recent book that examines organizations, networks, and people who work with rape victims, Patricia Martin suggests that a rape crisis center (RCC) should serve as the primary interface between victims and other agencies (e.g., police, prosecutors, and hospitals). Within these other agencies, rape victims are only a small part of what workers confront. In contrast, RCCs, because their sole focus is victim support, may be the missing link that can bring all of these organizations into a network that is most favorable for the victim.[96]

Robbery

The UCR defines <u>robbery</u> as taking or attempting to take anything of value from the care, custody, or control of a person or persons by force or threat of force or violence and/or by putting the victim in fear.[97] The two key elements in the legal definition of robbery are (1) the taking of another person's property and (2) the possibility of force. Because violence is either threatened or used to take a person's possessions, robbery is typically classified as a violent (rather than property) crime.

The UCR tracks robberies for both commercial (e.g., gas station, bank) and personal victimization, while the NCVS covers only personal robberies. Both sources indicate that robbery rates have been decreasing since the early 1990s. The NCVS estimates that roughly 500,000 robberies occurred in 2004. This is the lowest robbery rate (200 per 100,000 citizens) recorded since the inception of this victimization survey in 1973.[98] As expected (some do not report robberies to the police), the UCR data report lower estimates of robbery. Just over 400,000 robbery offenses were recorded by police nationwide in 2004 or a rate of 137 per 100,000. Despite the decline in robbery rates, robbery is still a prevalent crime in this country. Robberies represent roughly 30% of all serious violent crimes recorded by police; they are much more common than rape (7%) or homicide (1%).[99]

Characteristics of Robbery and Robbers

Several characteristics of robbery distinguish this offense from other forms of violent crime. In contrast to rape and homicide, the majority of robberies (56%) are perpetrated by a stranger. Robberies are also more likely than other forms of violence to involve multiple offenders. Finally, robbery is more apt to be an interracial crime. NCVS data reveal, for example, that white robbery victims perceived the offender as black in roughly one-third of all single-offender robberies. In many respects, however, robberies are similar to other violent offenses. Robbers tend to be disproportionately young, African-American, and male. About 90% of persons arrested for robbery are male and over 50% are black.

TABLE 10-3 illustrates UCR data regarding common locations of robberies and the average financial loss from robberies across these locations. The most common place (43%) for a robbery to occur is on a street; other common locations include restaurants/stores (15%) and residences (14%). The average financial loss is greater for businesses than for individuals. Within businesses, some targets are clearly more lucrative than others. While bank

TABLE 10-3

Location and Average Loss for Robbery

Location	Percent of Robbery Total	Average Financial Loss (in $)
Street or highway	43	923
Restaurants/supermarkets/stores	15	1,529
Gas/service station	3	1,749
Convenience store	6	653
Residence	14	1,488
Bank	2	4,221
Miscellaneous	17	1,682

Source: Federal Bureau of Investigation, *Crime in the United States: Uniform Crime Report 2004* (Washington, DC: Federal Bureau of Investigation, 2005): 32, 34.

robberies netted an average of $4,221, the average loss from convenience stores was $653.[100] The breakdown of robberies by location also reveals an interesting trend. Over the past several years, street robberies and robberies of gas stations and convenience stores have declined. In contrast, bank robberies actually increased 25% between 2000 and 2004.[101] The **Headline Crime** feature explores one of the largest successful bank robberies in history, the February 2006 Securitas Depot Robbery in England.

The UCR reveals that robbers use firearms in 41% of robberies, strong-arm tactics (e.g., hands, fists, feet) in 41%, and knives and cutting instruments in 9% of the cases. Other weapons were used in the remaining 9% of robberies.[102]

Explaining Robbery

The primary motivation for robbery (e.g., the value of money and/or property) is obvious to even the causal observer. Still, there are differences among robbers. John Conklin's classic typology of robbers (see TABLE 10-4) highlights such differences. For example, *professional robbers* carefully plan for the "big score" and treat robbery as their main livelihood. *Addict robbers* and *alcoholic robbers* rob in order to sustain their substance use. Here, money from robbery is a means to purchase illicit drugs or alcohol. Recent research suggests that while money is a factor, there may be other motives for robbery.

For example, criminologist Jack Katz argues that the "take" from a typical robbery is too small to be the sole motivation for the crime. He points out that other forms of crime (e.g., drug sales) are much more lucrative. Instead of (or in conjunction with) monetary motivation, Katz suggests that robbery

helps individuals maintain a street reputation of "bad ass." Robbery proves the participants willingness to use violence even in the face of legal and physical threat:[103] A recent study of armed robbers lends some support to both Conklin's typology and the Katz critique of money as the primary motivation for robbery. Unlike most studies, where incarcerated robbers are interviewed, this study was based on interviews with 86 *active* (nonincarcerated) armed robbers operating in St. Louis, Missouri.[104] Akin to

Teller 405
9/30/2005 4:03:44 PM

The video surveillance footage from a bank robbery gives only one indication of the security measures employed by banks. Banks have some of the most elaborate and technologically sophisticated security systems in existence.

Why (despite this fact) have bank robberies increased in recent years, while other forms of robbery have decreased?

Headline Crime

The Securitas Depot Robbery

The largest cash robbery in British crime history sounds like something straight out of a Hollywood film. Colin Dixon, manager of the Securitas Cash Management Ltd Depot in Kent, England, was driving home from work on February 21, 2006, when he was pulled over by what appeared to be an unmarked police car (there were blue lights behind the car's front grill). A man in police-style clothing took Dixon to the fake police car, where he was handcuffed by others in the vehicle. He was then transferred to a white van and driven to a farm in an unknown location. During this same timeframe, the manager's wife and eight-year-old son were being held hostage at their home. Again, the robbers pretended to be police officers. This time, they told Dixon's wife that the manager had been involved in a traffic accident. Dixon's wife and son were then driven to the farm at which the manager was being held. Dixon and his family were threatened at gunpoint and told to cooperate in the robbery.

Early in the morning of February 22, the robbers took the manager and his family, at gunpoint, to the cash depot and forced him to let one of the gang members onto the premises. The robber then forced a depot employee at gunpoint to open a gate, allowing the other robbers to enter in several vehicles. At least six men, wearing masks or balaclavas and armed with handguns, tied up Dixon, his family, and 14 depot employees. The robbers then loaded over £53 million (U.S. $92.5 million) into a 7.5-ton motor truck

and drove away. An hour later, an employee managed to activate an alarm to notify police.

In the weeks following the robbery, the police have pursued several fruitful leads. They have recovered many of the vehicles involved in the raid, including the van used to transport Dixon and his family (which contained over £1 million, guns, and masks) and the motor truck used to haul away the cash. As of March 16, 2006, the police have made several arrests related to the robbery. John Fowler, a car dealer and owner of the farm suspected to have been used in the robbery, along with two others, have been charged with conspiracy to rob and kidnapping. On March 7, police arrested two employees of a firm that contracted with Securitas, confirming suspicions that this was, in part, an "inside job." Through various raids the police have recovered almost £20 million of the stolen money.

The Securitas depot robbery comes on the heels of the 2004 robbery of the Northern Bank (Belfast, Ireland). The Northern Bank robbers used tactics similar to those of the Securitas robbers to steal £26.4 million. Specifically, a group of men disguised as police officers simultaneously broke into the homes of two Northern Bank (Ireland) officials and took the officials and their families hostage. While the families were held at gunpoint, the hostage-takers gave bank officials precise orders on what they had to do the following day. The officials reported to work the next day as if nothing were wrong and at the end of the day

(after other employees went home), the bank officials let members of the gang into the bank. Unlike the Securitas robbery, police have had little luck tracking down either the Belfast robbers or the stolen money.

The Belfast and Securitas robberies also bear an eerie resemblance to another 2006 robbery. Here, robbers held Jack Stanfield's family hostage in order to force Jack (the bank's security systems expert) into stealing $10,000 from each of the bank's 10,000 wealthiest customers. This robbery takes place in the 2006 movie *Firewall*. Unlike the real robberies (but true to Hollywood film-making), the bank employee (played by Harrison Ford) ends up foiling the robbery and saving the day.

Is there commonality between these high-profile robberies and more common forms of robbery? Where would the Securitas robbery fit in Conklin's typology?

Why do you suppose that bank robberies are increasing, whereas other forms of robbery are on the decline?

Sources: BBC News, "Securitas Robbery: How it Happened," available at http://news.bbc.co.uk/1/hi/england/kent/4754786.stm, accessed March 27, 2006; BBC News, "Securitas Robbery: The Investigation," available at http://news.bbc.co.uk/1/hi/england/kent/4742972.stm, accessed March 13, 2006; BBC News, "Timeline: Northern Belfast Robbery," available at http://news.bbc.co.uk/2/hi/uk_news/northern_ireland/4117219.stm; accessed March 1, 2006; Rachael Bell, "Belfast's Northern Bank Robbery," available at http://www.crimelibrary.com/gangsters_outlaws/outlaws/major_heists/index.html, accessed February 12, 2006; Wikipedia, "Securitas Depot Robbery," available at http://en.wikipedia.org/wiki/Securitas_depot_robbery, accessed March 16, 2006.

TABLE 10-4

A Typology of Robbers

Type of Robber	Defining Characteristics
Professional robber	For this type of robber, crime is considered a profession; a source of livelihood (they are unlikely to hold any steady, legitimate job). Professional robbers are more likely to work in groups, to carefully plan their crimes, and to go after a few "big scores" (e.g., bank, stores) each year.
Opportunistic robber	Opportunistic robbers tend to steal relatively small amounts of money from vulnerable targets (e.g., cabbies, drunks, those walking alone at night). They tend to be young and belong to a racial minority. Their crimes reflect little planning, organization, or sophistication.
Addict robber	This type of offender robs to get money in order to support a drug habit. Addict robbers are less likely to plan their crimes than the professional robber, but are more cautious than the opportunistic robber.
Alcoholic robber	Alcoholic robbers often commit robberies while they are drunk and disoriented. Their primary motive is to secure more alcohol. Their robberies are almost never planned, and they are unlikely to use a weapon.

Source: John Conklin, *Robbery and the Criminal Justice System* (New York: Lippincott, 1972).

Conklin's portrayal of some robbers as alcoholics, opportunists, or addicts, the robbers suggested that robbery netted "fast cash" that fueled participation in "street culture," which includes gambling, hard-drug use, and heavy drinking. One robber made the following comments:

> I [have] a gambling problem and I . . . lose so much so I [have] to do something to [get the cash to] win my money back. So I go out and rob somebody. That be the main reason I rob someone. I like to mix and I like to get high. You can't get high broke. You really can't get high just standing there, you got to move. And in order to move, you got to have some money.[105]

The interview with active robbers, however, revealed other motivations for robbery. Some robbers reported enjoying a psychological thrill; others report using robbery as a way to intimidate or get revenge against others.[106] This motivation may explain why a substantial number of robberies are among acquaintances. There is evidence that among acquaintance robberies, the primary motive may be revenge rather than monetary reward.[107]

Robbery and Rationality

A good deal of evidence shows that robbers (even those who are opportunistic) are rational in their approach to robbery. For example, robbers will point to the advantages of robbery as opposed to other forms of crime. Robberies take less time than alternatives such as burglary or drug sales, and successful robberies typically yield cash rather than property. For this reason, robbers avoid many of the middlemen (pawn shops, fences, drug dealers) associated with other offenses.[108] Robbers display rational behavior by preying on "vulnerable" victims. Among the most vulnerable targets are those who are also involved in crime. For example, drug dealers or men who seek prostitutes are both likely to carry cash and are unlikely to report the robbery to the police.

If robbers are at least somewhat rational in their actions, then robbery should be a crime that is amenable to situational crime prevention. Discussed in Chapter 3, situational crime prevention is the idea that the environment can be altered in a way that would make crime less likely. There is evidence that target-hardening techniques (adding surveillance cameras, having two clerks on duty) can make convenience stores and gas stations less susceptible to robbery.[109] For individuals, the policy implication is clear: Avoid being viewed as a vulnerable target. Examples include traveling in a group (rather than alone), avoiding the display of cash in public places, and refraining from criminal activity (such as the solicitation of prostitutes).

Assault

The UCR (and most jurisdictions) divided assault into two categories. **Aggravated assault** involves the "unlawful attack by one person upon another for the purpose of inflicting severe or aggravated bodily injury."[110] Aggravated assaults usually involve a weapon or other means likely to produce death or serious bodily harm. Simple assaults do not involve a weapon and do not result in serious injury to the victim.

The UCR includes only aggravated assault among its Part I offenses, while the NCVS measures both aggravated and simple assaults. Only an estimated 40%-60% of assaults are ever reported to police. Victims of assault decide not to report the crime to police for many reasons. Often the assault involves family members who are reluctant to bring in outsiders to solve a family problem. Some victims fear reprisals if they report the offense to the authorities. Others view the attack as not serious enough to report or simply a private matter between the assailant and the victim.[111] Because of substantial underreporting, the NCVS data yield a more reliable accounting of the number of assault victims each year. In 2004, the NCVS estimates that there were roughly 1.1 million aggravated assaults and over 3.5 million simple assaults. Combined, aggravated and simple assaults account for roughly 85% of all violent crime detected by the NCVS.[112]

The patterning and characteristics of assault are similar to that of homicide. For example, those arrested for assault (or identified by victims) are overwhelmingly male, and tend to be young. Indeed, some criminologists suggest that the only substantial difference between the two crimes is that for assaults, the victim survives. For this reason, there are few if any stand-alone explanations of assault. The exception to this general rule concerns assaults that occur in the home. Explanations for intimate partner abuse and child abuse are discussed in Chapter 11.

General Explanations for Violent Crime

To this point in the chapter, each type of violent crime (e.g., homicide, rape, robbery) has been treated as a separate entity that appears to require a separate explanation. Yet, a global finding in criminology is that offenders tend to be *versatile*; they are apt to engage in a variety of crime, including rape, robbery, assault, and homicide.[113] Trends among the various violent crimes appear to support this position. For example, all categories of violent crime have dropped over the past decade — a finding that a crime-specific analysis would not anticipate. It makes sense therefore to explore some general explanations for violence.

Neighborhood-Level Explanation of Violence

As the discussion of homicide in this chapter made clear, violent crime is neither equally likely in all societies nor randomly spread throughout a specific country. For example, violent crimes such as assault, robbery, homicide, and rape are more likely to occur in large cities than in rural areas. Violence is also patterned within cities — occurring predominately in areas characterized by extreme poverty, physical decay, and residential mobility. Social disorganization offers an empirically supported explanation for this finding. Briefly, neighborhood institutions and processes (e.g., informal control) that usually prevent crime are weak or absent in these communities. Although social disorganization is typically discussed in the context of crime generally, empirical tests suggest that social disorganization helps to explain violent crime, including rape and homicide.[114]

Another theme in some versions of social disorganization theory is that persistently high neighborhood crime rates are due in part to the "cultural transmission" of deviant values. Once crime becomes entrenched in a particular location, violence becomes a natural part of the cognitive landscape.[115] Violence becomes a way of life — a means to solve personal and life problems. The most widely recognized theory in this area is Wolfgang and Ferracuti's **subculture of violence** theory.[116] As discussed in Chapter 7, a *subculture* is a segment of society that holds norms and values that are distinct from the norms and values of mainstream society. Wolfgang and Ferracuti were careful to point out that members of subcultures shared many of the dominant cultural values in society. Nevertheless, in some subcultures, norms and values evolve that support and legitimize the use of violence. For example, the expected (normative) response to disrespect becomes violence as opposed to some other alternative; violence is not condemned and perpetrators of violence do not feel guilt for their actions. Violent subcultures are also characterized by a high level of gun ownership, stories or songs that glorify violence (as in the Snoop Dogg lyrics at the opening of this chapter), and rituals (e.g., gang initiations) that stress macho behavior.[117]

There is some empirical support for the existence of violence-legitimizing norms among residents of impoverished inner-city areas. It is important to recognize, however, that such norms do not arise out of a vacuum. Rather they are tied to the cultural isolation, extreme poverty, and violence that exist in such neighborhoods.[118] Further, some scholars believe that the recent decline in violent crime is tied in part to a rejection of the cultural values that legitimize violence (see Explaining the Crime Drop in Violent Crime in the following section).

Individual-Level Explanations of Violence

Individual-level theories seek to explain why some people commit violent crimes when other people refrain from violence. Most individual-level theories of crime attempt to account for a wide range of behavior (including both property and violent crime). Indeed, readers are encouraged to explore what theories (Chapters 3–8) appear most applicable to violence.

Social Learning Theory

Social learning theorists propose that all behavior (including violence) is learned. Primary learning mechanisms include operant conditioning (e.g., parental discipline) and vicarious learning. Within psychology, social learning theory was proposed by Albert Bandura to explain the acquisition and use of aggression.[119] Recall that Bandura and his associates demonstrated (e.g., the "Bobo doll" experiment) that children can learn violent behavior simply by watching a movie.[120] Although there is some evidence that exposure to violence in mass media may increase violent crime, this remains a hotly debated topic.[121] Regardless, most scholars would agree that real role models are more important than "virtual" role models.

Within sociology, Edwin Sutherland suggested that crime is learned in intimate personal (e.g., family, peers) groups. Strong evidence exists that peer groups play a role in the genesis of crime, including violence. Moreover, researchers consistently document a strong correlation between experiencing or witnessing violence in the family as a child and later violent behavior. For example, a study published in 2002 found a relationship between family violence directed against the mother and the emergence of violence in early childhood of the children.[122] Exposure to family violence as a child has also been linked to later adult violence. This phenomenon is generally referred to as the *intergenerational transmission of violence*.

This is not to say, however, that social learning theory provides the only family-based explanation of violence. Feelings of isolation and rejection can also play a part in future violent behavior. For example, Mays and Manaster analyzed episodes of school shootings perpetrated by students. Specifically, they focused on the home life of one school shooter, Barry Loukaitis, who voiced concerns about being bullied and rejected at home and suffered a general feeling of being unwanted and unloved.[123] In this case, the authors portrayed the family violence in a manner more consistent with general strain theory.

LINK The intergenerational transmission of violence is discussed in Chapter 11.

Biological Explanations

Is there a biological basis for violence? Adoption and twin studies of the heredity-crime relationship typically rely on general measures of crime (e.g., conviction for an offence) rather than violence. In fact, some studies find a genetic relationship for property, but not violent offending. The research by Hans Brunner (see Chapter 4) on a Dutch family with a history of violence suggests that genes may account for at least some forms of violence.[124] Some biological correlates of crime also appear to specifically predict violence. For example, evidence suggests that testosterone levels are related to violent crime.

Gender and Violence

The relationship between gender and violent crime is perhaps the most obvious (and overlooked) empirical finding in the violence literature. Although it is true that males are more likely to engage in most forms of crime than females, gender differences are most apparent for violent crimes. For ex-

Assault is the most common form of criminal violence.

? *Why are some individuals more prone to violence than others? Why are some neighborhoods more violent than others?*

ample, as noted previously, males make up over 90% of those arrested for robbery, rape, homicide, and assault. Where females are involved in violent crime, it often differs qualitatively from male-perpetrated violence. For example, a study by Kirkpatrick and Humphrey found that women who kill usually murder males they know, often because they perceived themselves to be in life-threatening situations.[125]

What accounts for gender differences in violence? Sociological theories focus predominantly on sex-role socialization. The masculine sex role includes many factors, including competitiveness, aggressiveness, and a lack of emotionality. Generally then, masculinity is conducive to violence. Some theorists suggest that economic success is a key attribute of the masculine sex role. Therefore, males who cannot measure up economically will seek to demonstrate their masculinity through other roles (including violence).[126] Of course, there are other explanations for the gender-violence relationships. Biologists, for example, might point to physical (e.g., size, strength) or physiological (e.g., testosterone levels) differences. This remains a critical and unsettled area of research within criminology.

Explaining the Drop in Violent Crime

Criminologists, journalists, and other commentators have no shortage of explanations for increases in violent crime — but can they explain a crime drop? Most forms of crime have been on the decline in the United States for over a decade. The most dramatic reductions, however, have been among violent crime. The drop in violent crime over the past decade calls into question the accuracy (or completeness) of many common explanations for crime increases. For example, take a popular explanation for violence — the media. Have movies, video games, or television become *less violent* over the past decade? Are children less likely to be exposed to violent media? The answer to both of these questions is an obvious "no."

Many legislators have been quick to point to criminal justice policies as the answer to the crime drop. In New York City, people point to innovative and aggressive police tactics. Others point more generally to the increases in prison populations and argue that the country is finally seeing the fruits of the get-tough movement. Yet, an honest look at the evidence betrays such a simple explanation. For example, crime did decline in New York City during the shift in policing policy — but it also declined in cities that embraced community-oriented policing and in areas that made no changes in their policing philosophy. Similarly, not all states took part in the incarceration boom of the 1980s and 1990s, but crime declined all across the United States.

In the book, *The Crime Drop in America*, some of the most widely recognized criminologists in the country contributed research that sought to explain the change in crime rates. Readers of this book will find research regarding many of the "usual suspects," including economic conditions, changes in demographics (fewer crime-prone youth, more elderly Americans), increases in prison population, and police tactics (community-oriented and zero-tolerance policing). Among the most interesting explanations are two chapters that deal with the role of illicit drugs.

Bruce Johnson and his associates provide research on the relationship between illicit drugs and inner-city violence in New York City.[127] Although the city of New York is used as a case study, they also tie the relationship between drugs and violence to the broader context of the United States. The authors conclude that the use of three drugs (marijuana, cocaine, and heroin) has gone in cycles. They refer to the 1960s as the "heroin injection era," the 1980s as the "cocaine/crack era," and the 1990s as the "marijuana/blunt era" (*blunt* refers to marijuana rolled into cigar leaves). They suggest that increases in violent crime corresponded with the popularity of heroin in the late 1960s and with cocaine (crack) in the mid- to late 1980s. The preferred drug by those born in the 1970s has been marijuana; a drug not generally associated with violent crime.

Taking a different approach, Al Blumstein points out that much of the *increase* in violence during the 1980s was confined to a small segment of America — black youth residing in inner-city areas. He suggests that two primary factors, the increased availability of handguns and the crack cocaine epidemic, explain this surge in violence. In essence, a good deal of the violence created in the 1980s was caused by clashes over control of a new drug market. As the crack epidemic subsided (and control over the illicit distribution of crack stabilized), so too did the violence.[128]

Anthropologist Richard Curtis offers an alternative explanation (echoed by others) for the recent decline in violence.[129] Curtis views the crime drop as one outcome of an improbable and unexpected change in the culture of inner-city America. His ethnographic research suggests that the generation growing up in the height of inner-city decay (e.g., the crack epidemic, economic despair, dysfunctional/multiproblem families, crumbling social institutions) witnessed the havoc wreaked upon their older siblings, parents, and peers and took a different path:

> But by the mid-1990s . . . many youths began to withdraw from social life, afraid of lingering in public spaces for fear of violence. The impact of drug misuse by parents and/or older siblings on family life was also deeply felt by many young residents, often narrowing the parameters of their own drug use, and they made a conscious attempt to avoid similar fates.[130]

Conclusion

This chapter explored the prevalence, trends, and nature of four types of violent crime: homicide, robbery, rape, and assault. Many commonalities exist across these different forms of violence. Foremost, data from both the UCR and the NCVS reveal substantial declines for all four types of violent crime over the past 10 to 15 years. Another theme that emerges is that for most violent crime (robbery is the exception), the majority of perpetrators are known to the offender. This runs counter to the common image of the offender as a stranger lurking in the shadows. Despite the recent declines, violent crime is still an all-too-common feature of life in the United States. Victims of such violence may experience immediate physical harm and/or long-term emotional trauma. For this reason, Americans fear violent crime more than any other type of criminal behavior.

Ultimately, criminological research on violent crime seeks to uncover the causes of violence and develop effective public policy. The chapter reviewed many theories of violent crime and each theory holds some promise for policy. For example, research on robbery reveals a rational component, which suggests that situational crime prevention may be an effective policy. There are also implications for the operation of the criminal justice system. Rape shield laws and the use of rape crisis centers have helped to make the criminal justice system more victim friendly for rape survivors. Despite advances in knowledge, much is still to be learned about the roots of violent crime. Only by gaining a greater knowledge about the dynamics of violent behavior can law officials help to develop and implement policies, not only for the detection, apprehension, and treatment of offenders but also for the protection of citizens.

WRAP UP

The Use of Rape as Terrorism During Wartime

Unfortunately, history is replete with examples of mass rapes committed during wartime. The wars in Bosnia and Sudan both appear to involve *ethnic cleansing* or the attempt by one ethnic group to kill or expel another ethnic or religious group from a specific area. Survivors of rape from both wars emphasize that rape was used to humiliate and terrorize women, as well as their families and communities. In that sense, one might consider this type of wartime rape a qualitatively distinct form of rape that requires its own explanation. On the other hand, one might also consider *terroristic rape*, an extreme form of the "control/domination" motivation for rape discussed in this chapter. Here rape is analogous to assault or murder; a violent crime where sex is used as a weapon. As noted, the motivation for rape remains a controversial issue in criminology. While some suggest that rape is always a violent and nonsexual (or pseudosexual) crime, others suggest that the motivation for rape may vary. For some rapes, domination and control (or terrorism) might be the sole purpose, but for other forms of rape, sexual motivation may play a role.

Chapter Spotlight

- The rate of serious violent crime (robbery, rape, homicide, aggravated assault) has declined since 1991. U.S. rates of violent crime are generally now similar to that of other industrialized nations, with the exception of homicide. American homicide rates are much higher than most other industrialized countries.

- Three explanations for the United States' high homicide rates were reviewed: firearm availability, economic inequality/low social support, and the country's history of violence.

- Homicide perpetrators and victims are disproportionately young, male, and African-American. Homicide is largely an intraracial crime.

- In general, rapes are committed by sole offenders who had a previous relationship with the victim. Two forms of acquaintance rape include date rape and intimate partner rape.

- A great deal of debate surrounds the issue of motivation for rapes. In some cases, it appears that rape is a pseudosexual act of violence akin to assault or homicide. Some maintain that there is a sexual component to rape.

- Explanations of rape take many forms: typologies of rapists, feminist explanations, social learning explanations, and evolutionary theories. The dominant treatment modality for sex offenders is cognitive-behavioral therapy, although so-called chemical castration may also be effective.

- Robbery includes two legal elements: taking another's property and the use of force. Unlike other violent crimes, robbery tends to be perpetrated by strangers and is often an interracial crime. Explanations for robbery typically focus on money and property as motivation; there is evidence that robbers act rationally. Some scholars suggest that there are additional motives for robbery such as maintaining a street reputation and revenge.

- Much evidence exists in criminology to suggest that offenders are versatile, that they may engage in various forms of violent crime. General explanations of violent crime at the neighborhood level include social disorganization theory and the subculture of violence. Most individual-level theories of offending attempt to explain violence as part of a general explanation for crime.

- Recently, the central task facing criminologists has been to explain the recent decline in violent crime. Scholars point to a number of factors that might help explain the crime drop, including the subsiding of the crack epidemic and a change in the values and attitudes of children who grew up witnessing the violence of the 1980s and 1990s.

Putting It All Together

1. How different is the United States' homicide rate from that of other industrialized countries? What might account for this difference?

2. What have different scholars proposed as the primary motivation for rape? Describe a rape scenario that appears to fit each of these motivations.

3. Describe one macro-level and one individual-level theory that may explain violent crime.

4. What has been the violent crime trend in the United States over the past decade? What might account for this trend?

5. Debate the potential effects of gun control legislation on violent crime. Why do some believe that right-to-carry legislation will reduce violent crime? Is there evidence for this position?

Key Terms

aggravated assault The unlawful attack by one person on another for the purpose of inflicting severe or aggravated bodily injury. Aggravated assaults usually involve a weapon or other means likely to produce death or serious bodily harm.

coercive rape Unlawful sexual intercourse by force or without legal or factual consent. This is a more inclusive definition of rape; it does not require force.

felony murder A homicide committed during the course of another felony offense. For example, an offender burglarizes a house and kills one of the occupants of the house during the crime.

homicide The unlawful taking of life by another human. Types of homicide include first- and second-degree murder and voluntary and involuntary manslaughter.

murder The unlawful, premeditated taking of another human's life.

rape Unlawful sexual intercourse, against another's will, by using force or the threat of force.

rape myths Cultural beliefs or stereotypes that justify or condone rape and sexual assault. Rape myths include thinking that women secretly desire to be raped and that women who dress or act seductively are asking to be raped.

robbery Taking or attempting to take anything of value from the care, custody, or control of a person by force or threat of force or violence.

sexual assault Any forced or coerced sexual intimacy (unwanted touching with no consent).

subculture of violence Wolfgang and Ferracuti's theory that some segments of society hold values that legitimatize or justify violence. Violent subcultures are characterized by a high level of gun ownership, stories or songs that glorify violence, and rituals that stress macho behavior.

violent crime index The Uniform Crime Report creates this measure of serious violent crime based on four crimes: homicide, robbery, aggravated assault, and rape.

Notes

1. Snoop Dogg, "20 Dollars 2 My Name," *Da Game Is to Be Sold, Not to Be Told* (Priority Records, 1998).
2. Ray Surette, *Media, Crime, and Criminal Justice: Images and Realities* (Belmont, CA: Wadsworth, 1998).
3. Federal Bureau of Investigation, *Crime in the United States: Uniform Crime Report 2004* (Washington, DC: Federal Bureau of Investigation, 2005).
4. Federal Bureau of Investigation, *Uniform Crime Reports: 2005 Preliminary Semiannual Report,* available at http://www.fbi.gov/ucr/2005prelim/2005openpage.htm, accessed January 30, 2006.
5. Callie Rennison, *Criminal Victimization 2001, Changes 2000–2001 with Trends 1993–2001* (Washington, DC: National Institute of Justice, 2002), Shannon M. Catalano, Criminal

Victimization, 2004 (Washington, DC: National Institute of Justice, 2005).

6. Thomas Gardner, *Criminal Law* (St. Paul, MN: West Publishing Co., 1989).

7. Federal Bureau of Investigation, 2005, 15.

8. Ibid, 136–182.

9. Ibid, 19.

10. Marvin Wolfgang, *Patterns in Criminal Homicide* (Philadelphia: University of Pennsylvania Press, 1958).

11. Richard B. Felson and Henry J. Steadman, "Situational Factors in Disputes Leading to Criminal Violence," *Criminology* 21 (1983): 59–74.

12. Federal Bureau of Investigation, 2005, 23.

13. Ibid.

14. Ronald Holmes and Stephen Holmes, *Murder in America* (Thousand Oaks, CA: Sage, 2001).

15. James Allen Fox and Jack Levin, *The Will to Kill: Making Sense of Senseless Murder* (Boston: Allyn and Bacon, 2001).

16. Federal Bureau of Investigation, 2005, 18.

17. Ibid.

18. Angela Browne, *Battered Women Who Kill* (New York: Free Press, 1987); Jacquelyn C. Campbell, "Prediction of Homicide of and by Battered Women." In Jacquelyn C. Campbell, ed., *Assessing Dangerousness: Violence by Sexual Offenders, Battered, and Child Abusers* (Thousand Oaks: Sage, 1995); Ann Goetting, "Female Victims of Homicide: A Portrait of Their Killers and the Circumstances of Their Deaths," *Violence and Victims* 3 (1991): 303–324; Nancy C. Jurik and Russ Winn, "Gender and Homicide: A Comparison of Men and Women Who Kill," *Violence and Victims* 5 (1990): 227–242.

19. Jacquelyn Campbell, "If I Can't Have You, No One Can: Power and Control in Homicide of Female Partners," in J.Radford and D.E.H. Russell, eds., *Femicide* (New York: Twayne Publishers, 1992); Goetting, 1991; Judith M. McFarlane, Jacquelyn Campbell, Susan Wilt, Carolyn J.U.Y. Sachs, and Xio Xu, "Stalking and Intimate Partner Femicide," *Homicide Studies* 3 (1999): 300–316.; Emma Morton, Carol W. Runyan, Kathryn E. Moracco, and John Butts, "Partner Homicide-Suicide Involving Female Homicide Victims: A Population Based Study in North Carolina, 1988–1992," *Violence and Victims* 13 (1998): 91–106.

20. Margaret L. Abrams, Joanne Belknap, and Heather C. Melton, *When Domestic Violence Kills: The Formation and Findings of the Denver Metro Domestic Violence Fatality Review Committee* (Denver, CO: Project Safeguard, 2000).

21. Franlin E. Zimring and Gordon Hawkins, *Crime Is Not the Problem: Lethal Violence in America* (New York: Oxford University Press, 1997).

22. Gary Kleck, *Targeting Guns: Firearms and Their Control* (New York: Aldine de Gruyter, 1997): 94.

23. Anthony W. Hoskin, "Armed Americans: The Impact of Firearm Availability on National Homicide Rates," *Justice Quarterly* 18 (2001): 569–592.

24. Jens Ludwig and Philip Cook, "Homicide and Suicide Rates Associated with the Implementation of the Brady Violence Prevention Act," *Journal of the American Medical Association* 284 (2000): 585–591.

25. James B. Jacobs, "Crime Control via Federal Dealer Regulation," *Criminology and Public Policy* 2 (2002): 183–186.

26. Colin Loftin, David McDowall, Brian Wiersema, and Talbert J. Cottey, "Effects of Restrictive Licensing of Handguns on Homicide and Suicide in the District of Columbia," *New England Journal of Medicine* 325 (1991): 1085–1101.

27. Kleck, 1997.

28. Gary Kleck and Tomislav Kovandzic, "The Impact of Gun Laws and Gun Levels on Crime Rates," paper presented at the 1998 annual meeting of the American Society of Criminology, Atlanta, GA.

29. John R. Lott, Jr., *More Guns, Less Crime: Understanding Crime and Gun Control Laws* (Chicago: University of Chicago Press, 2000).

30. Steven E. Barkan, *Criminology: A Sociological Understanding,* 3rd ed. (Upper Saddle River, NJ: Prentice Hall, 2006): 274.

31. Raymond D. Gastil, "Homicide and a Regional Subculture of Violence," *American Sociological Review* 36 (1971): 412–427.

32. Jill Elaine Hasday, "Contest and Consent: A Legal History of Marital Rape," *California Law Review* 88 (2000): 1373–1505.

33. George E. Rush, *Dictionary of Criminal Justice* 6th Ed. (Guilford, CT: Dushkin/McGraw-Hill, 2004).

34. Brett M. Kyker, "'Initial Consent' Rape: Inherent and Statutory Problems," *Cleveland State Law Review* 53 (2005): 161–186; Dana Vetterhoffer, "Comment: No Means No: Weakening Sexism in Rape Law by Legitimizing Post-Penetration Rape," *St. Louis Law Journal* 49 (2005): 1229–1260.

35. Joanne Belknap, *The Invisible Woman: Gender, Crime and Justice* (Belmont, CA: Wadsworth, 2001).

36. Federal Bureau of Investigation, 2005, 27.

37. Catalano, 2005.

38. Patricia Tjaden and Nancy Thoennes, "Prevalence, Incidence, and Consequences of Violence Against Women," *Research in Brief* (Washington, DC: U.S. Department of Justice, 1998).

39. Bonnie S. Fisher, Francis T. Cullen, and Michael G. Turner, "The Sexual Victimization of College Women," *Research in Brief* (Washington, DC: National Institute of Justice, 2000).

40. Ibid.

41. Catalano, 2005, 10.

42. Lawrence Greenfeld, *Sex Offenses and Offenders: An Analysis of Data on Rape and Sexual Assault* (Washington D.C: U.S. Department of Justice, 1997).

43. David B. Schubot, "Date Rape Prevalence Among Female High School Students in a Rural Midwestern State During 1993, 1995, and 1997," *Journal of Interpersonal Violence* 16 (2001): 291–296.

44. Linda J. Skinner and Kenneth K. Berry, "The Perpetrators of Date Rape: Assessment and Treatment Issues," in Thomas L. Jackson, ed., *Acquaintance Rape: Assessment, Treatment, and Prevention* (Sarasota, FL: Professional Resource Press, 1996).

45. The National Women's Health Information Center, "Date Rape Drugs," available at http://www.4woman.gov/faq/ro-hypnol.htm, accessed February 15, 2006.

46. Ibid.
47. Diana E.H. Russell, *Rape in Marriage* (Bloomington: Indiana University Press, 1990): 17.
48. Jennifer A. Bennice and Patricia A. Resick, "Marital Rape: History, Research, and Practice," *Trauma, Violence, and Abuse* 4 (2003): 228–246.
49. Hasday, 2000, 1375.
50. Bennice and Resick, 2003, 235.
51. Ibid, 234.
52. Ibid.
53. David Finkelhor and Kersti Yllo, *License to Rape: Sexual Abuse of Wives* (New York: Free Press, 1985).
54. Russell, 1990.
55. Patrick A. Langan and Caroline W. Harlow, *Child Rape Victims, 1992* (Washington DC: U.S. Department of Justice, 1994).
56. Tjaden and Thoennes, 1998.
57. Thomas Simon, James Mercy and Craig Perkins, *Injuries from Violent Crime, 1992–98* (Washington DC: U.S. Department of Justice, 2001).
58. Karen J. Terry, *Sexual Offenses and Offenders: Theory, Practice, and Policy* (Belmont, CA: Wadsworth, 2006): 41.
59. Ann W. Burgess and Lynda L. Holstrom, "Rape Trauma Syndrome," *American Journal of Psychiatry* 131 (1974): 981–986.
60. Terry, 2006, 114.
61. Susan Brownmiller, *Against Our Will: Men, Women and Rape* (New York: Simon & Schuster, 1975): 15.
62. Ibid.
63. Ronald Holmes and Stephen Holmes, *Sex Crimes* (Thousand Oaks, CA: Sage, 2002).
64. David Lester and Gail Hurst, "Treating Sexual Offenders," in *Correctional Counseling and Rehabilitation* (Cincinnati, OH: Anderson, 2004): 245.
65. Raymond Knight and Robert Prentky, "The Developmental Antecedents and Adult Adaptations of Rapist Subtypes," *Criminal Justice and Behavior* 14 (1987): 403–425.
66. Randy Thornhill and Craig T. Palmer, *Rape: A Natural History of Rape* (Cambridge, MA: MIT Press, 2000): 53.
67. Ibid, 53–54.
68. Mary P. Koss, "Evolutionary Models of Why Men Rape: Acknowledging the Complexities," *Trauma, Violence, and Abuse* 1 (2000): 185.
69. Terry, 2006, 119–120.
70. Peggy Reeves Sanday, "The Socio-Cultural Context of Rape: A Cross-Cultural Study," *Journal of Social Issues* 37 (1981): 5–27.
71. Larry Baron and Murray A. Straus, *Four Theories of Rape in American Society: A State Level Analysis* (New Haven, CT: Yale University Press, 1989): 93–94, 180–181.
72. Rachel Bridges Whaley, "The Paradoxical Relationship Between Gender Inequality and Rape: Toward a Refined Theory," *Gender and Society* 15 (2001): 531–555.
73. Martha R. Burt, "Cultural Myths and Supports for Rape," *Journal of Personality and Social Psychology* 38 (1980): 217–230.
74. Anthony Beech and Ruth Mann, "Recent Developments in the Assessment and Treatment of Sexual Offenders," in James McGuire, ed., *Offender Rehabilitation and Treatment: Effective Programmes and Policies to Reduce Re-Offending* (West Sussex, England: John Wiley and Sons, 2002): 263–264.
75. Ibid, 261.
76. Lester and Hurst, 2004, 249.
77. Lee Ellis, *Theories of Rape: Inquiries into the Causes of Sexual Aggression* (New York: Hemisphere Publishing, 1989): 13.
78. Catharine A. MacKinnon, "Pornography as Sex Discrimination," in Ronald R. Berger, ed., *Rape and Society* (Boulder, CO: Westview Press, 1995).
79. Ellis, 1989, 13.
80. Julie A. Allison and Lawrence S. Wrightsman, *Rape: The Misunderstood Crime* (Newbury Park, CA: Sage, 1993): 37–40.
81. Koss, 2000, 182–190.
82. Koss, 2000, 188.
83. Baron and Straus, 1989, 173–195.
84. Beech and Mann, 2002, 261.
85. Lester and Hurst, 2003, 246–247.
86. Pamela Yates, "Treatment of Adult Sexual Offenders: A Therapeutic Cognitive-Behavioral Model of Intervention," *Journal of Child Asexual Abuse* 12 (2003): 195–232.
87. Gordon Hall, "Sexual Offender Recidivism Revisited: A Meta-Analysis of Recent Treatment Studies," *Journal of Consulting and Clinical Psychology* 63 (1995): 802–809.
88. Patricia Yancey Martin, *Rape Work: Victims, Gender, and Emotions in Organizational and Community Context* (New York: Routledge, 2005): 52.
89. Martin, 2005, 73–93.
90. Terry, 2006, 123.
91. Lisa Frohman, "Discrediting Victims' Allegations of Sexual Assault: Prosecutorial Accounts of Case Rejection," *Social Problems* 38 (1991): 213–226.
92. Cassia Spohn and David Holleran, "Prosecuting Sexual Assault: A Comparison of Charging Decisions in Sexual Assault Cases Involving Strangers, Acquaintances, and Intimate Partners," *Justice Quarterly* 18 (2001): 651–688.
93. Martin, 2005, 55–58.
94. Lisa Frohmann, "Discrediting Victims' Allegations of Sexual Assault: Prosecutorial Accounts of Case Rejections," in P. Searles and R. J. Berger, eds., *Rape and Society* (Boulder, CO: Westview, 1995).
95. Terry, 2006, 128–129.
96. John Hamlin, "Review of Patricia Yancey Martin's *Rape Work: Victims, Gender, and Emotions in Organizational and Community Context, Social Forces* (Forthcoming).
97. Federal Bureau of Investigation, 2005, 31.
98. Catalano, 2005, 5.
99. Federal Bureau of Investigation, 2005, 11.
100. Ibid, 32-35.
101. Ibid, 33.
102. Ibid, 34.
103. Bruce A. Jacobs and Richard Wright, "Stick-Up, Street Culture, and Offender Motivation," *Criminology* 37 (1999): 149–174.
104. Ibid, 155.

105. Richard Wright and Scott Decker, *Armed Robbers in Action: Stickups and Street Culture* (Boston: Northeastern University Press, 1997).

106. Richard Felson, Eric Baumer, and Steven Messner, "Acquaintance Robbery," *Journal of Research in Crime and Delinquency* 37 (2000): 284–305.

107. Jacobs and Wright, 1999, 160–162.

108. John Eck, "Preventing Crime at Places," in *Preventing Crime: What Works, What Doesn't, and What's Promising,* available at http://www.ncjrs.gov/works/, accessed February 23, 2006.

109. Federal Bureau of Investigation, 2005, 37.

110. Sourcebook of Criminal Justice Statistics Online, available at http://www.albany.edu/sourcebook/pdf/t3332003.pdf, accessed March 16, 2006.

111. Catalano, 2005, 2.

112. Michael R. Gottfredson and Travis Hirschi, *A General Theory of Crime* (Stanford, CA: Stanford University Press, 1990): 91–94.

113. Baron and Strauss, 1989, 125–146; Robert J. Sampson, Stephen Raudenbush, and Felton Earls, "Neighborhoods and Violent Crime: A Multilevel Study of Collective Efficacy," *Science* 277 (1997): 918–924.

114. William J. Wilson and Robert J. Sampson, "Toward a Theory of Race, Crime, and Urban Inequality," in John Hagan and Ruth D. Peterson, eds., *Crime and Inequality* (Stanford, CA: Stanford University Press, 1995).

115. Marvin Wolfgang and Franco Ferracuti, *The Subculture of Violence: Towards an Integrated Theory in Criminology* (Beverly Hills, CA: Sage, 1982).

116. Frank Schmalleger, *Criminology Today: An Integrative Introduction,* 3rd ed. (Upper Saddle River, NJ: Prentice Hall, 2002): 214.

117. Wilson and Sampson, 1995; Liqun Cao, Anthony Adams, and Vickie Jensen, "A Test of the Black Subculture of Violence Thesis," *Criminology* 35 (1997): 367–379.

118. Albert Bandura, *Aggression: A Social Learning Analysis* (Englewood Cliffs, NJ: Prentice Hall, 1973).

119. Albert Bandura, Dorthea Ross, and Sheila A. Ross, "Imitation of Film: Mediated Aggressive Models," *Journal of Abnormal and Social Psychology* 63 (1961): 3–11.

120. Surette, 1998, 114–154.

121. Ellen R. Devoe and E. Smith, "Impact of Domestic Violence on Urban Preschool Children: Battered Mothers' Perspectives," *Journal of Interpersonal Violence* 17 (2002): 1075–1101.

122. M. Mays and G. Manaster, "Youth and Violence: Reflections," *Journal of Individual Psychology* 56 (2000): 226–232.

123. H. G. Brunner, M. R. Nelen, X. O. Breakefield, H. H. Ropers, and B. A. van Oost, "Abnormal Behavior Associated with a Point Mutation in the Structural Gene for Monoamine Oxidase A," *Science* 262 (1993): 578–580.

124. G. Collins. "A Study Assesses Traits of Women Who Kill," *The New York Times* (July 7, 1986): C18.

125. Barkan, 2006, 276–277.

126. Bruce Johnson, Andrew Golub, and Eloise Dunlap, "The Rise and Decline of Hard Drugs, Drug Markets, and Violence in Inner-City New York," in Alfred Blumstein and Joel Wallman, eds., *The Crime Drop in America* (New York: Cambridge University Press, 2000).

127. Alfred Blumstein, "Disaggregating the Violence Trends," in Alfred Blumstein and Joel Wallman, eds., *The Crime Drop in America* (New York: Cambridge University Press, 2000).

128. Richard Curtis, "The Improbable Transformation of Inner-City Neighborhoods: Crime, Violence, Youth and Drugs in the 1990s." *National Institute of Justice Journal* (October 1998): 16–17.

129. Ibid, 16.

WWW.CRIMINOLOGY.JBPUB.COM

Interactivities
In the News
Key Term Explorer
Web Links

OBJECTIVES

Explain why some forms of violent crime are considered "emerging."

Define the various forms of emerging violent crimes, including intimate partner abuse, stalking, child abuse, pedophilia, hate crimes, terrorism, and multicide.

Explain the theory of intergenerational transmission of violence and describe how it explains intimate partner abuse.

Describe the criminal justice response to the various forms of emerging violent crimes.

List the categories of hate crimes and understand the specific motivations behind the different types.

Emerging Forms of Violence

> *The methods, gains, and motives of serial murder are unique to each type of killer. If investigators are able to attain some understanding of the psychology of the serial killer and his propensity for violence, if they realize that the serial murderer feels that he is all-powerful and all-knowing, and that it is his birthright to feel this way, they may have a better understanding of the psychopathic serial killer.*
>
> — Ronald M. Holmes and Stephen T. Holmes[1]

Crime Scene Investigation

On July 22, 2005, a skull was found in a vacant lot by some construction workers excavating the lot for a new business to be built at the site. The workers called the police who then called the coroner's office. After arriving at the scene, the coroner made the decision to contact the medical examiner's office and the state forensic anthropologist for help.

The site was once an adult entertainment building that featured live entertainment and, it was rumored, prostitutes. The business closed down almost eight years ago. During careful examination of the site, a skull, several vertebrae, a finger, and several hand bones were located. The excavator indicated that more than three containers of trash had already been hauled from the site to a local dump. The state anthropologist stated that she could tell the person had her hands bound with duct tape and that one finger was "enveloped" by the decaying bones of the spine. Also, evidence showed a trauma to the back of the head. The coroner's office ruled the case a homicide, and the report from the medical examiner indicated that the cause of death was blunt force trauma.

In the last 12 years, two other young women were killed in the same fashion. Their bodies were also discovered within a three-block radius.

What would be one avenue for investigation of this particular homicide case? What would you consider important considering the victimology of the victim(s)?

Introduction

The forms of violence covered in this chapter have a considerable history, although they have usually occurred on the periphery of public awareness. Recently, however, the media have drawn attention to these crimes. These forms of violence are not necessarily new: They are emerging only in the sense of our increasing awareness of them.

This chapter focuses on these "emerging" forms of violence as well as the types of personalities involved, such as the founding members of certain hate groups, terrorist groups, and some infamous serial and mass murderers. Although these crimes have been prevalent for many years, the consciousness of the American people regarding these crimes has been raised to a new level in recent years, due to both increased enforcement and heightened media awareness.

These forms of violence — domestic violence, hate crimes, terrorism, and multicides — do not share a common thread of motivation and are not easily profiled. They are, however, all crimes of violence that are increasingly in need of social control.

Domestic Violence

The manifest purpose of the family is to provide a physically and emotionally safe place for all its members; unfortunately, not all families do so. Each year, thousands of children, spouses, and intimate partners are abused. Public awareness of **domestic violence** is a fairly recent phenomenon; this crime has increasingly become defined as a social and criminal problem in need of formal social control. Unfortunately, it is also one of the most difficult crimes to control because so much of it occurs outside of the public eye. It has been said that intimate partner abuse and child abuse (along with sexual assault) may be among the least reported crimes.[2] Reasons for the low report rates include fear of reprisal, not wanting the abuser to get in trouble, not defining the behavior as abusive, not wanting others to find out, and feeling as though nothing can be done — among many other reasons. This section discusses some of the issues surrounding family violence. Included are discussions of intimate partner abuse, stalking (the majority of stalking cases involve persons who were or are intimately involved), and child abuse.

Intimate Partner Abuse

Finding a term to accurately describe the violence that occurs between intimates is a difficult task. Historically, the label domestic violence has been used to describe family violence that included spousal abuse, child abuse, elder abuse, and sibling abuse. Often, however, the term *domestic violence* is assumed to be synonymous with spousal abuse. Critics have argued that domestic violence ignores the gendered nature of the problem (the majority of the victims are women and the offenders are men), ignores violence that occurs between couples who are not living together, and ignores other types of abuse that are not necessarily violent. "Spousal abuse" ignores violence among dating couples and same-sex partner violence. Thus, the most inclusive term used today and the term used in this chapter is **intimate partner abuse**.

Intimate partner abuse can take on a number of forms, including physical battering, sexual battering, psychological battering, and destruction of property and pets.[3] It includes being slapped, punched, hit with a fist, kicked, thrown, hit with objects, cut, choked, bitten, stabbed, shot, physical intimidation, sexually assaultive acts, verbal abuse, threats, or any other aggressive act towards an intimate or former intimate.[4] It involves current or former heterosexual or homosexual intimate partners. The gendered nature of intimate partner violence is debated and often depends on the methods of studies used and the questions used to identify abuse. A considerable amount of recent research indicates, however, that the majority of the victims of intimate partner abuse are women and their abusers are men.[5]

Estimates of intimate partner abuse vary greatly, especially influenced by whether one is drawing on official or self-reported data and on how intimate partner abuse is defined. The National Violence Against Women survey, which involved interviewing 8000 women and 8000 men about their experiences with victimization, found that 22% of women and 7% of men reported ever experiencing intimate partner abuse as victims.[6] Using official records, the Bureau of Justice Statistics found that on average, from 1992 to 1996, there were more than 960,000 violent victimizations of women by an intimate partner.[7] Like crime in general, intimate partner abuse rates declined throughout the 1990s and into the 21st century. It is not clear, however, whether the rates really declined or whether reporting of intimate partner abuse declined.

Significant controversy exists regarding racial, ethnic, and class differences among offenders and victims of intimate partner abuse. Some argue that people of color and people of a lower socioeconomic status are more likely to experience intimate partner abuse,[8] whereas others have found evidence suggesting this is not the case.[9] It is clear, however, that African-Americans and lower-class people are overrepresented in official statistics. Many argue that this could be due to racial and class bias on the part of law enforcement and the criminal justice system as well as access to better resources (i.e., middle- and upper-class people do not need to use the police because they have the means to access therapists, civil lawyers, etc.). One of the few studies examining intimate partner abuse in the Asian-American community, using a method that allowed the respondents to define the behavior as abusive, found that 61% of a sample of 1053 women of Japanese descent living in the Los Angeles area had experienced some form of abuse by their male intimate partners. Intimate partner violence appears to cut across all racial, ethnic, and class lines.[10]

TABLE 11-1 provides data on intimate partner abuse in America and **TABLE 11-2** outline patterns in intimate partner abuse.

Many theories exist to explain intimate partner abuse. The major sociological theory regarding this problem is the theory of **intergenerational transmission of violence**. Proponents of this theory argue that individuals who either observed violence as children or experienced violence themselves are more likely to engage in intimate partner abuse as adults or be victims of intimate partner abuse themselves as adults than those who did not.[11] Studies have found a correlation between observing and/or experiencing violence as a child and later offending or victimization as an adult.

Others argue that social stress plays a role in intimate partner violence.[12] Proponents of these theories argue that stress caused by lack of access to money, housing, education, and employment leads people to commit intimate partner abuse, and thus, proponents assume that violence occurs mainly in low-income families.[13] More recent studies, however, report that violence cuts across all classes, although middle- and upper-class violence is more likely to be hidden.

TABLE 11-1

Intimate Partner Abuse in America

- Of all victims of intimate partner abuse, 95% are women.
- Women are more likely to be assaulted, injured, or raped by their male partners than by any other type of assailant.
- Each year, 3 to 4 million women are battered by their husbands or partners.
- Wife-battering results in more injuries that require medical treatment than rape, auto accidents, and muggings combined.
- Roughly 30% of female homicide victims are killed by their husbands or boyfriends; 6% of male homicide victims are killed by their wives or girlfriends.
- Violence occurs in at least two-thirds of all marriages.
- Women are the victims of violent crime committed by family members at a rate of three times that of men.
- After a woman is victimized by intimate partner abuse, her risk of being victimized again is high. Approximately 32% of women are victimized again within 6 months.

Source: Data were gathered by the Spouse Abuse Center, January 2, 2005, Louisville, KY.

Feminist theories focus on male domination as the key explanation for intimate partner abuse perpetrated by men against their female partners and ex-partners. Feminists argue that men's use of violence against women arises from men's power over women in the family and in society.[14] In patriarchal societies, historically, men have been socialized to be aggressive and even encouraged to use violence to keep women in line.[15] Evidence does suggest that intimate partner abuse is more prevalent in patriarchal societies.[16] A central component of patriarchy is the predominance of violence by both men and male-dominated organizations. Physical violence by men, then, is a manifestation of patriarchy. Some argue that intimate partner abuse against women results naturally from patriarchy: Males act violent to maintain dominance and control over women.[17] Critics of feminist theory argue that it cannot explain why some women are violent toward men or violence that occurs in same-sex relationships.

The Criminal Justice Response

The criminalization of intimate partner abuse is a relatively recent phenomenon. Historically, laws around the world have been in place that condoned intimate partner abuse by a husband against his wife. In 1140, the first systematization of church law specified that "women were 'subject to their

men' and need to be corrected through castigation or punishment."[18] The Napoleonic Civil Code of the 19th century gave absolute power in the family to the head male member and recognized violence as grounds for divorce for the woman only if the violence was found by a court to constitute attempted murder.[19] The term "rule of thumb" comes from British Common Law, which legally allowed men to beat their wives with sticks as long as they were no bigger than the thickness of their thumb, citing that anything bigger would be too uncivilized.[20] In the United States, although the Puritans implemented a policy in the 17th century against wife beating, in non-Puritan society during this time, wife beating was only punished informally. Thus, historically, intimate partner abuse was rarely addressed by the criminal justice system in any formal or meaningful way.

In the first three-quarters of the 20th century, the traditional criminal justice response to cases of intimate partner abuse was dominated by the belief that intimate partner abuse was a personal matter, and for that reason, the formal system should not respond. The traditional police response to cases of intimate partner abuse was dominated by the "overriding goal to extricate [themselves] from the dangerous and unpleasant duty with as little cost as possible and to re-involve [themselves] with 'real'

TABLE 11-2

Patterns in Intimate Partner Abuse

Controlling behaviors: Batterers exhibit extreme controlling behaviors, including controlling the finances, the dress, and the time of their victims.

Fear and intimidation: Batterers often display acts that are intent on causing fear or intimidation, including displaying or discharging weapons.

Manipulation: Batterers often use extreme manipulation. They may engage in acts of coercion to get the victim to do as they want.

Excessive rule making: Batterers often engage in excessive rule making for the victim. For example, they may give their victims curfews or not allow them to do certain things.

Isolation: Batterers isolate their victims in many different ways. It may include physically isolating them by living in an isolated area — for example, living in a rural or secluded area with no public transportation. It may also involve isolating the victim from their friends or family by "turning them against them" or not allowing the victim to visit friends or family.

Source: Denise Kindschi Gosselin, *Heavy Hands: An Introduction to the Crimes of Family Violence* (New Jersey: Prentice Hall, 2002).

Rally to promote awareness of domestic violence.

? *Why do you think this crime has been underreported and ignored?*

police work."[21] The typical response of both police and court personnel was to do nothing or to respond with minimal action. In the 1960s and 1970s, in response to pressure from feminists and battered women's advocates to lawsuits against criminal justice personnel alleging inadequate responses to intimate partner abuse, and to new research concerning police response, many police chiefs, politicians, and sociologists began to review and debate the existing police and court practices regarding intimate partner abuse. Today, mandatory and presumptive arrest policies are the norm across the nation; if there is probable cause, the police are mandated to arrest somebody in an intimate partner abuse situation. Although many have cheered this policy, there continues to be room for improvement in the criminal justice response to intimate partner abuse.

Stalking

The emergence of <u>stalking</u> as a social problem occurred only recently. The 1989 murder of actress Rebecca Shaeffer by a stalker was one of the first high-profile stalking cases that the media covered and helped to bring the issue of stalking to the public's attention.

The majority of stalking incidents involve individuals who are or were intimates or acquainted,[22] with a high correlation existing between stalking and intimate partner abuse.[23] In general, stalking refers to the willful, repeated, and malicious following, harassing, or threatening of another person.[24] Legal definitions differ from state to state, however, as do the estimates of stalking incidents. Conservative estimates place stalking incidents at about 200,000 nationally in the United States in recent years.[25] More recent studies suggest that stalking may affect roughly 1.4 million victims annually in the United States — 1 million women and 400,000 men.[26]

Research has identified several different categories of stalking. Michael Zona and his colleagues found three types of stalkers: erotomanic, love obsessional, and simple obsessional. Erotomanic stalkers hold the delusional belief that they are passionately loved by their stalking victims. They most often stalk people whom they do not know except through the media, entertainment, and/or politics. Stalkers in the love obsessional group may also hold the delusion that their victims love them, but the erotomania is only one part of their delusion. They are also delusional about other issues in their lives. They stalk people who they do not know. In contrast, simple obsessional stalkers have a prior relationship with their victims, and many start stalking when their relationship ends or when they perceive some sort of mistreatment on the part of the stalking victim.[27] Roberts and Dziegielewski (1996) distinguished the nuisance stalker from the domestic stalker, the erotomanic stalker, and the delusional stalker. They define the nuisance stalker as someone who continually targets and harasses the victim. Holmes distinguished between six types of stalkers:

1. The celebrity stalker — similar to the erotomanic or delusional stalker
2. The lust stalker — a sexual stalker who stalks strangers who possess certain characteristics because of a depraved sense of sexual lust
3. The hit stalker — a stalker who is hired by someone to kill someone else
4. The love-scorned stalker — stalkers who want and think that they have a relationship with a known victim
5. The domestic stalker — stalkers who are currently or were previously intimately involved with the victim
6. The political stalker — stalkers who stalk political personalities for the sake of expressing their political ideology[28]

The relationships between stalkers and their victims can be characterized in one of three ways: intimates or former intimates, acquaintances, or strangers. Victims are most often the current or former spouses or intimate partners of their stalkers.[29] Some researchers estimate that as many as 80% of all stalking cases involve a prior or current intimate relationship.[30] Moreover, studies show a high correlation between stalking and verbal and physical abuse in intimate relationships.[31] One study found that 80% of the victims of stalking reported having been physically assaulted by the partner who later stalked them and 31% reported having been sexually assaulted by their partners.[32] In addition, it is estimated that between 29% and 54% of all female murder victims are battered women — in 90% of these cases it is believed that stalking preceded the murder.[33]

Recently, it has been suggested that domestic stalkers, those currently or formerly intimately involved with their victims, differ significantly from other types of stalkers. First, two pre-existing characteristics are used to identify domestic stalkers: (1) a current or former relationship exists between the stalker and the victim and (2) the stalker and the victim share a common history and background. Second, some studies identify differences between how stalking behaviors are "acted out," depending on whether the stalker is a current or former intimate partner. For example, two studies found that domestic/intimate partner stalkers are more likely to threaten their victims.[34] Another study reported that domestic stalkers are more likely than other types of stalkers to be violent toward their victims.[35] One study found that stalkers are likely to be violent in 25% to 35% of stalking cases — the majority of these involving current or former intimates.[36] Additionally, this study found that domestic stalking often culminated in a violent attack directed at the victim.

Another study found that stalking is usually precipitated by a single event in domestic stalking cases, such as the relationship ending or a perception on the stalker's part of some type of mistreatment by the victim. Moreover, researchers recognize that the most dangerous time for many battered women is when the relationship is ending and the parties are separating (i.e., "separation assault"). Coleman (1997) noted that stalking victims are particularly vulnerable when their partners try to win them back and/or control their behaviors. The

U.S. Department of Justice (1998) found that victims of domestic stalking reported in 43% of the cases that the stalking began as the parties were separating and the relationship was ending, whereas in 36% of the cases, the stalking occurred both during the relationship and as it was ending, and in only 21% of the cases, the stalking occurred only during the relationship. Thus, the evidence suggests that ending the relationship may serve as the precipitating event in many domestic stalking cases. Finally, one study found that domestic stalkers were more likely than other types to make person-to-person harassing contact.[37]

Stalking includes a variety of different behaviors. Using factor analysis, Coleman (1997) identified two categories or types of stalking behaviors. She identified *violent behavior stalkers* as those who broke into or attempted to break into the victim's home or car; violated restraining orders; threatened, attempted to, or did physically harm the victim; physically harmed or threatened to harm themselves; stole/read mail; and damaged property of a new partner. Coleman's *harassing behavior stalkers* were typified by those who called the victim at home, work, or school; followed or watched the victim; made hang-up calls; came unwanted to the home, work, or school of the victim; sent unwanted gifts, letters, or photos; left unwanted messages on the answering machine; or made threats against or harmed the victim's new partner. Meloy (1996) identified the following stalking behaviors in his review of existing studies: the sending of aggressive letters, unwanted following, property damage, annoying phone calls, assaults, and gift giving. Finally, Burgess and her colleagues identified the following forms of stalking behavior: written and verbal communications; unsolicited and unrecognized claims of romantic involvement on the part of the victims; surveillance, harassment; loitering; and following that produces both intense fear and psychological distress to the victim. Thus, researchers have identified a variety of behaviors that constitute stalking.

<u>Cyberstalking</u> is the most recently identified form of stalking. Emma Oglivie defines cyberstalking as analogous to traditional stalking.[38] With the advent of technology, cyberstalking has taken three primary forms. The first is *e-mail stalking*, which essentially entails using e-mail to initiate behavior that the law defines as stalking. It also involves a direct communication with another through e-mail. The second form is *Internet stalking*. In this format,

the manner of communication is global through the general format of the Internet. The third form is *computer stalking*, which involves computer control that may employ viruses. With cyberstalking, the investigation is hampered by the anonymity of the perpetrators. J. A. Hitchcock reports that there are many hiding places for stalkers on the Internet, and tracing the suspects is very difficult for law enforcement personnel.[39]

Motivations for stalking vary. One study cited control, obsession, jealousy, revenge, and anger as possible motives for stalking.[40] Studies that have focused on stalking in the context of intimate partner abuse have found that the need to control the victim or the desire to reestablish a relationship may motivate domestic stalkers.[41] Using data that specifically asked stalking victims their perceptions of their stalkers' motivations, the U.S. Department of Justice (1998) reported that 21% of the victims said that the stalkers wanted to control them. Twenty percent said that the stalker wanted to keep them in the relationship. Sixteen percent said that the stalker wanted to scare them. Twelve percent were not sure. Seven percent said that the stalker was mentally ill or abusing drugs/alcohol. Five percent said that the stalker liked or wanted attention, and 1% said that the stalker wanted to catch the victims doing something. These data suggest that stalkers have many different reasons for engaging in stalking.

Research examining the link between intimate partner abuse and stalking has found that stalking is highly correlated with both psychological and physical abuse.[42] Studies that have examined this link focused on the relationship between abuse and stalking, when stalking begins in an intimate partner abuse relationship, and the effects and consequences of stalking on the victim. In a study examining intimate partner abuse victims' experiences with stalking, Mechanic and colleagues (2000) found that stalking appears to be more correlated with psychological abuse than physical abuse — the emotional abuse variables in the study predicted stalking better than the physical abuse variables did. Regarding the relationship between the abuser and the victim, Mechanic and her colleagues (2000) found that stalking in the relationship escalated among women who left their partners. In another study examining stalking victimization among a population of men and women who experienced intimate partner abuse, Logan and colleagues (2000) concluded that stalking is a continuation of intimate partner abuse after the relationship has ended. Finally, regarding the effects of stalking, Mechanic and her colleagues (2000) found that women who are severely stalked compared with those who are infrequently stalked are more likely to suffer from depression and post-traumatic stress disorder (PTSD). Davis and his colleagues (2000) found that experiences with stalking in the context of intimate partner abuse were related to increased levels of fear, anger, distress, and PTSD.

Dawnette Knight reacts to her three-year prison sentence for stalking the movie actress Catherine Zeta-Jones.

? *How would you classify a stalker of celebrities?*

The Criminal Justice Response

The criminal justice system has only recently begun responding to stalking as a problem in its own right. In 1990, the California legislature responded to a series of homicides by stalkers by establishing the nation's first antistalking law and criminalizing "the repeated harassment or following of another person in conjunction with a threat."[43] Today, all states and the District of Columbia have antistalking statutes on their books. Regardless of the stalking laws, the majority of stalking in the context of intimate partner abuse cases is addressed through domestic violence laws. In other words, the criminal justice response to this type of stalking has been to treat it like intimate partner abuse. Specifically, stalking in the context of intimate partner abuse is charged as domestic violence. For example, a study conducted by Tjaden and Thoennes (2000) found that in a review of domestic violence police reports, 1 in 6 showed evidence of stalking, but only 1 of the 1785 reported cases carried the charge of stalking. The rest of the cases were solely charged as domestic violence.

Child Abuse

The abuse of children has an enormous impact on society. Many theorists argue that child abuse plays a large role in the intergenerational transmission of violence — the idea that violence is learned and passed on from generation to generation. <u>Child abuse</u> includes the following:

1. Nonaccidental physical injury
2. Sexual abuse or exploitation
3. Emotional or psychological injury
4. Neglect or maltreatment to a person under the age of 18 years (or the age specified by the law of the state)

Many children will experience a variety of these behaviors during one incident.

The full extent of child abuse in this country is unknown, and it has proven difficult to arrive at a reliable figure. Many victims of child abuse are too young to communicate. Older children may be embarrassed or too afraid to report it. Even when adults know about abusive situations, they may be reluctant to report the abuse because they may not want to get involved in a "family matter." Undoubtedly, much child abuse goes unreported to the police, social workers, researchers, or other professionals in the field. A survey conducted in 1995 indicated that 1.8 million adolescents ages 12 to 17 years had been sexually assaulted, 3.9 million had been severely physically assaulted, and another 2.1 million had experienced some form of physical punishment.[44] Girls were more likely to report sexual assaults, whereas boys were more likely to report physical assaults. Child protective service agencies received roughly 2.97 million maltreatment reports in 1999.[45] Of these reports, 28% were substantiated. Eighty-seven percent of the victims were maltreated by one or both of the parents. In contrast, according to official statistics, child abuse is most likely to be committed by acquaintances (who do not take care of the children — 63% of the child abuse cases reported to the police); parents and other caretakers are responsible for nearly one in five (19%) of all violent crimes committed against juveniles, whereas strangers are only responsible for 10% of all these crimes.[46] The difference between these statistics may be due to differences in reporting — parental abuse may be much less likely to be reported to the police.

Although child abuse is known to affect children of all races and classes, some studies have found that African-American children are at a higher risk than white, Asian, or Hispanic children to suffer abuse.[47] As with crime in general, official statistics indicate that child abuse rates declined throughout the 1990s and into the 21st century.

The negative consequences of child abuse are considerable, especially for children who are abused by a parent. Abused children are at greater risk of aggressive behavior themselves, PTSD, conduct disorders, anxiety, depression, and suicide. From a criminal justice perspective, perhaps most important is the relationship between being victimized as a child and later offending: Children who are abused are much more likely than children who are not abused to become delinquent or criminal later in their lives.

Like intimate partner abuse, various theories explain why some people abuse children. Although child abuse is extremely complex with neither a single cause nor solution, the following are often seen as contributing to child abuse in the family:

1. The perpetrator experienced or observed violence themselves (either child abuse or intimate partner abuse of one of their parents). Evidence supports the idea of the intergenerational transmission of violence. This is important for both child abuse and intimate partner abuse. Although there is a correlation, many people who experience or observe violence do not become violent themselves.
2. The presence of unrelated adults in the home. There appears to be some connection between stepparents and child abuse. It has been argued that stepparents have less emotional attachment to their stepchildren and thus may be more likely to resort to abuse to solve problems or express their frustration.
3. The family is isolated and alienated. It has been found that families who are isolated or alien-

ated from others (i.e., their extended families, friends, and neighbors) may be at greater risk for engaging in child abuse. It has been argued that when parents are isolated, they do not have a support system to help them deal with stress and thus may be more likely to resort to abuse.

The Criminal Justice Response

Until fairly early in the 20th century, children were regarded as the property of their parents both by law and the parents. This meant that parents could legally mete out many forms of punishment as they saw fit, short of death or gross physical injury. The reporting of child abuse cases in the United States dates back to the late 19th century and the case of Mary Ellen Wilson. Neighbors in her apartment building reported to a nurse that she was being abused. After investigation, the nurse discovered that Mary Ellen was being repeatedly beaten and was extremely malnourished. Although the police became aware of the case, they claimed that the law allowed the parents to raise the girl as they saw fit and did not take the child away. Legend has it that the Society for the Prevention of Cruelty to Animals got involved, but in reality, the case was brought before a judge, and it was decided that the child needed protection; ultimately, she was taken away from her parents and placed in an orphanage.[48]

After this time, increased attention was paid to the lives and treatment of children. Child labor laws were enacted, and in 1899, the first juvenile court was founded in Cook County, Illinois. One premise of the juvenile court system is that the courts operate in "parens patriae" (in place of the parent). Recognizing their responsibility to protect children, juvenile courts have acted in cases related not only to delinquency, but also to physical and later sexual abuse.

In 1974, Congress passed the Child Abuse Prevention and Treatment Act. This act provides federal funding at the state level for prevention and response to child abuse. With this act, many states strengthened their response to child abuse and established child abuse statutes in which parents may be prosecuted for abusing their children. Many parents have been prosecuted and children taken out of the home; however, the typical response is to try and do everything possible to avoid taking the child away (i.e., enter the family into treatment and monitor the family). Regardless of the legal response to child abuse, it is clear that much child abuse

never comes to the attention of the criminal justice system and is, unfortunately, never dealt with.

Pedophilia

Pedophilia is an unnatural desire for sexual relations with children.[49] Like other crimes discussed in this chapter, pedophilia is not a new crime. What is new is the attention that it is getting in the public arena.

Characteristics of Pedophiles

Pedophiles are age and sex specific. In other words, the pedophile will normally prefer children of a certain sex and within a certain age cohort. Usually, pedophiles are interested in children under the age of 15 or 16 years. Some researchers and practitioners further distinguish between the pedophile and the hebephile. The latter desires an erotic relationship with a child between puberty and approximately age 15 years, whereas the pedophile is interested only in children who have not yet reached puberty.

Child molesters fall into several categories. Burgess and her colleagues described the fixated pedophile as one who never moves beyond the attraction he or she felt for children when he or she was a child.[50] The regressed pedophile often turns to children in response to stressful life events (e.g., domestic problems, job pressures). Although most pedophiles do not physically harm children, the mysoped makes the ritual connection between fatal sexual violence and personal gratification.[51] This sadistic pedophile abducts children for the purpose of torturing and eventually killing them to achieve sexual gratification.

Pedophiles come from a variety of backgrounds. Some are well educated, whereas others are illiterate. Many were not close to their fathers, and many came from homes where alcohol was a problem for at least one parent (usually the father). Pedophiles often have weak verbal skills, and almost 9 of 10 felt particularly close to their mothers.[52]

The small size of the child provides the pedophile with an opportunity to exert power and authority. At the same time, the sex of the child has little to do with the adult sexual orientation of the molester. For example, a pedophile may be very interested in sex with boys ages 9 or 10 years old, but at the same time be married and consider himself heterosexual.[53]

Most pedophiles derive sexual gratification from child pornography. They photograph the child victim and expose the child to "kiddie porn" because they believe that doing so will lower inhibitions and "validate" the sex act with the child. The pedophile and the child pornographer are threats to children worldwide. For example, of the estimated 35 million children now surfing the Internet, one in five has received an online sexual solicitation in the last year.[54]

Treatment of Pedophiles

The prognosis for rehabilitating pedophiles is not encouraging. Many argue that pedophilias are more difficult to treat than other sex offenders. Many states have initiated sex offender registries that include not only pedophiles but also other sex offenders, including rapists and voyeurs. The registries were developed to serve multiple purposes (e.g., inform the community and act as a deterrent), but the verdict is out on the effect that these registries have on recidivism. In addition to the publication of sex offenders on the Internet, other techniques being used include physiological assessment of the sexual arousal of the pedophile. This measurement of erectile excitation determines whether the pedophile is dangerous to society or a candidate for treatment.[55]

Law Enforcement Approach to Pedophilia

To cope with this serious problem, research efforts are focusing on ways to predict pedophiliac behavior. Unless the nation places a higher priority on lessening the danger of the pedophile to children, however, the problem will continue.[56] Indeed, trafficking in minors is enormously lucrative and shows no signs of abating. The best hope for fighting this problem is through an interdisciplinary task force approach that draws on law enforcement and social service agencies. Vigorous investigation by the various elements of the criminal justice system appears to be one key to the reduction of this most shameful and despicable crime.[57]

Hate Crimes

A <u>hate crime</u> is one in which a person intentionally selects a victim because of the race, color, religion, national origin, ethnicity, gender, or sexual orienta-

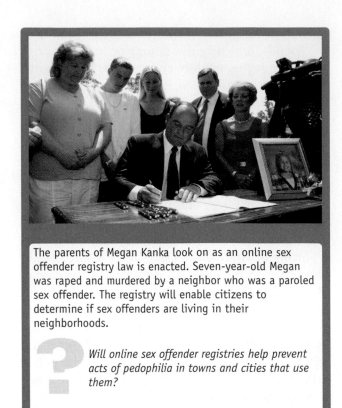

The parents of Megan Kanka look on as an online sex offender registry law is enacted. Seven-year-old Megan was raped and murdered by a neighbor who was a paroled sex offender. The registry will enable citizens to determine if sex offenders are living in their neighborhoods.

? *Will online sex offender registries help prevent acts of pedophilia in towns and cities that use them?*

tion.[58] The term *hate crime* is meant to distinguish criminal behavior that is motivated by prejudice from behavior that is motivated by greed, jealousy, anger, politics, and the like. The United States passed The National Hate Crime Law in 1993 to protect its citizens from hate crimes. The Uniform Crime Report stated that there were 7489 hate crime incidents in 2003. Slightly more than half were related to racial bias, 18% to religious bias, and almost 17% to sexual orientation. Thirteen percent were based on ethnicity/national orientation and less than 1% to disability bias.[59] These numbers indicate how significant a social problem hate crimes are.

Hate groups differ from one another in terms of their membership, ideology, and activities, but they do share one feature: They direct violence against an "undesirable" group of people.[60] Members of hate groups often believe that they are "chosen people" and are doing the work of God in their perpetration of violence.

Levin and McDevitt identify the following types of hate crimes that reflect varying motives for perpetrating the crime.

1. *Thrill-seeking hate crimes.* Perpetrators seek out victims for a sadistic thrill. There is not necessarily a precipitating event for this kind of

crime; for the perpetrators, inflicting pain and suffering on those they "hate" is the reward.

2. *Reactive hate crimes.* Perpetrators use a precipitating event to serve as a catalyst to express their anger. They justify their acts by arguing that they were protecting their community from "outsiders." Unlike thrill-seeking hate crimes, this type almost always takes place in the perpetrators' neighborhood, school, or workplace.

3. *Mission hate crimes.* This is considered the rarest type of hate crime. Perpetrators believe that their mission is to rid the world of evil by attacking members of a despised group. The perpetrator of this type of hate crime is often psychotic.[61]

Ku Klux Klan

The <u>Ku Klux Klan (KKK)</u> was founded on Thanksgiving eve in 1865 by six Confederate soldiers meeting in a small cabin in Tennessee. Eventually the group adopted the familiar disguise of white robes and hoods and launched its campaign of hate across the South. From 1865 until 1903, at least 1985 African-Americans were hanged or burned alive by the Klan or other southern lynch mobs, and countless others were beaten, raped, harassed, and intimidated. In response, the U.S. Congress passed the Ku Klux Klan Act in 1871, which established severe penalties for these criminal acts and forced the Klan to operate in a more clandestine fashion.

The Klan's history can be divided into three phases. The first phase commenced at the end of the Civil War. When newly freed blacks began to prosper under Reconstruction, resentful whites responded with a campaign of terror to restore the pre-Civil War social and economic order. Barred from voting and exploited economically by landowners, blacks were soon reduced to a status equivalent to slavery. Worse still, vengeful whites funneled their anger toward the victorious North against blacks.

The second phase began in 1915 in Stone Mountain, Georgia, when William Simmons launched a campaign of hate directed at Catholics and Jews. Blacks became a lesser, but not an ignored, target of violence. Klansman also directed violence at the "ne'er-do-wells, and the allegedly immoral of the very same background as the Klansmen: white, Anglo-Saxon Protestant."[62]

The third phase commenced shortly after World War II. Centering on civil rights and desegregation

Ku Klux Klan members give the "white power" salute at a rally in Cleveland, Ohio.

? *What are the origins of the Klan? Should members of this group be permitted to express their views in public?*

issues, Klan activities in the 1950s and 1960s were especially brutal. For example, in 1957, the Klan allegedly abducted a black man, Judge Aaron, castrated him, and poured turpentine into his wounds. In the early 1960s, the Klan was suspected of murdering three young civil rights workers, James Chaney, Andrew Goodman, and Michael Schwerner, in Mississippi. In July 1965, another black man, Lieutenant Colonel Lemuel Penn, was killed by shots fired from a passing car. That same year a white civil rights worker, Viola Liuzzo, was murdered. In 1966, NAACP official Vernon Dahmer died of burns after a firebomb was thrown inside his home.[63]

Klan activities are not confined to the deep South: Maryland, Tennessee, North and South Carolina, New York, and Ohio have all experienced Klan violence. The incidence of violence and the total membership of the various Klan groups are not known. Although KKK activities appear to be declining, this by no means signifies an end to KKK activities. In the 1980s, leaders were arrested, prosecuted, and incarcerated for their illegal activities. Membership in the Klan has declined since the late 1970s (**TABLE 11-3**). Unfortunately, other violent hate groups have emerged.

Identity Churches

Predicated on a perverse ideology of "white supremacy," the <u>Identity Church</u> movement and its

TABLE 11-3

Klan Membership, 1973–2005

Year	Number of Members
1973	5000
1975	6500
1978	6000–8000
1979	8000–10,500
1981	9700–11,500
1982	8000–10,000
1984	6000–6500
1998	4500–5500
2005	5000

Source: Southern Poverty Law Center, January 2, 2005

various offshoots direct their hatred and violence principally at Jews. Members of the various Identity Churches believe that they are the "chosen people" and are therefore naturally superior to all other races. In effect, nonwhites are placed into a category that includes animals. The Jews especially are condemned because Identity Church followers see them as responsible for America's economic problems and thus ultimately in control of the white man's destiny.

Dr. Wesley Swift was an early leader in the Identity Church movement.[64] In the late 1950s, this

White supremacist Richard Butler, leader of the Aryan Nations.

? *What are the aims of the white supremacist movement?*

one-time member of the KKK founded the Christian Defense League and established his own church, the Anglo-Saxon Christian Congregation, in Los Angeles. After Swift died in 1970, the mantle of leadership was passed to Richard Butler, the leader of the Idaho-based hate group nominally called the <u>Aryan Nations</u>.[65] The Aryan Nations is headquartered in Hayden Lake, Idaho, and draws on the precepts of Butler's Church of Jesus Christ Christian.[66] Its philosophy is blatantly bigoted and violent, and it focuses its violence on Jews and blacks.

The Posse Comitatus has been active since 1969. Latin for "power of the county," this organization holds that the federal government has no rightful control over the lowest unit of political power, the county. Often, members of the Posse Comitatus refuse to observe the laws of the state or federal government, including a refusal to pay taxes. These members are inclined to enforce local laws by carrying guns and rifles as part of their "law enforcement responsibilities." Acts of violence associated with the Posse Comitatus have been reported in various states, primarily in the Midwest and West. In 1983, Gordon Kahl and several members of the Posse Comitatus killed two U.S. marshalls. Kahl himself was shot by state and federal agents in Arkansas several months later.[67]

The Covenant, the Sword, and the Arm of the Lord (CSA) was a paramilitary group based in Missouri and Arkansas that believed that the country was drifting inexorably toward a complete economic failure. By training its followers in military preparedness, the CSA sought to ensure them of their "rightful" place in the new order to come. Seminars were offered in many parts of the country in urban warfare, riflery and pistolry, military tactics, and riot training.[68] The CSA was disbanded in the mid-1980s, however, after an attack on a courthouse in Missouri and the murder of an Arkansas state trooper.[69]

The Christian-Patriot Defense League centered in Louisville, Illinois, is an ultraconservative survivalist group immersed in military training. Preaching a message against communism and the wave of immigrants into this country, members of this Identity Church subgroup maintain a constant state of military preparedness for the inevitable war. This group claims that the Anti-Christ, whom they believe to be a communist, is coming. Thus, its mission is to alert patriots of the impending catastrophe and to be prepared to deal with it.

The Order, sometimes called "The Silent Brotherhood," is an underground arm of the Aryan Nations. Since the early 1980s, this group has unleashed a campaign of violence with a major goal of overthrowing the U.S. government, often referred to as the "Zionist Occupation Government." According to The Order, Jews are responsible for all of America's social and economic ills and thus must be eliminated. In their literature, they encourage the assassination of public officials, including police, judges, bankers, business leaders, and journalists who are sympathetic to Jews.[70] In a number of instances, group members have done just that. For example, David Tate, a former member of The Order, was found guilty in the slaying of a Missouri state trooper and was sentenced to life in prison. Richard Scutari, a one-time member of The Order, was given a 60-year sentence for his part in the robbery of a Brink's armored car in 1984. In 1986, Eldon Cutler was convicted of paying an undercover FBI agent $2,000 to decapitate a government official who had information on The Order.

The Committee of the States first came to the attention of authorities in 1985. Founded in 1984, it loosely held the same beliefs as the Posse Comitatus: The power belongs to the base political unit, the county; the courts are operating under martial law in opposition to the ideals of the Founding Fathers, and government laws are inferior to the group. Members of the committee have committed acts of violence, especially against Jews and nonwhites.[71]

Skinheads

Originally a British subculture group that emerged in the 1960s, <u>skinheads</u> espoused the values of the struggling working class and expressed their dislike of government and big business. Since those early days, the skinhead movement has been reborn in a number of ways, most notably as a racist and extremely political organization (neo-Nazi skinheads). It is important to note that not all people who identify themselves as skinheads engage in hate crimes or perpetrate violent acts; however, those who do, including several notorious gangs in the United States, pose a considerable threat to the groups they target.

Since the late 1970s, skinhead groups have appeared in many large American cities and have become a concern for law enforcement officials and the FBI. The FBI divides skinheads into two categories: criminally motivated and hate motivated.[72] Skinheads who espouse neo-Nazi beliefs will attack anyone not adhering to a white supremacist philosophy, including other whites, Jews, blacks, and other minorities. Their ultimate goal is to eradicate the target minorities from the face of the earth to ensure white power and white supremacy. Since the terrorist attacks on September 11, 2001, it has been estimated that recruitment in right wing groups such as the skinheads has increased dramatically.[73]

Responding to Hate Crimes

Throughout the 1990s, numerous states strengthened their hate crime legislation. Laws in most states fall into one of three categories: substantive crimes, sentence enhancements, and reporting statutes.[74] Substantive hate crime statutes are based on the Anti-Defamation League's Model Hate Crime Law in which a separate "intimidation" offense is added to the criminal statutes. Sentence enhancements either upgrade an existing offense or increase the penalty for offenses that are found to be motivated by prejudice.[75] Finally, reporting statutes require states to collect data on hate crimes in order to generate statistics on the problem. Justifications for creating specialized responses to crime motivated by hate and prejudice include the following: the crime can be expected to have special effects on the victim; hate crimes have deleterious effects on communities; and the expression of bias in this type of

A group of skinheads participating in a march in Germany.

? *What are the motives of this group?*

crime is separable from the crime itself (i.e., the fact that bias is the motivator will have an effect independent of the impact of the crime itself).[76]

Terrorism

After the bombings of the Alfred P. Murrah Federal Building in Oklahoma City, the U.S.S. Cole, and the U.S. Embassies in Kenya and Tanzania and the attacks on the World Trade Center and the Pentagon in 2001, terrorist activities have become increasingly familiar to American citizens. Because of the complexity of the problem, defining terrorism is a difficult task. Throughout history, debates have raged over specific groups and whether they qualified as "terrorists" — those defined as terrorists by one group may be considered heroes by another. Definitions may be too broad (i.e., not differentiate between street crime and terrorism) or too narrow (e.g., not include terrorism that is perpetrated by the state). For the purposes of this chapter, terrorism is defined as "the premeditated, deliberate, systematic murder, mayhem, and threatening of the innocent to create fear and intimidation in order to gain a political or tactical advantage, usually to influence an audience."[77]

Types of Terrorists

Many different types of terrorists exist, which is one reason why defining the term is so difficult; terrorists vary by behaviors, goals, ideologies, and motivations. The most common types of terrorists include the following:

- *Revolutionary.* Their ultimate goal is to replace the existing government with one they support; they use violence to frighten those in power as a means to achieve that goal.
- *Political.* Violence is directed at people or groups who oppose the terrorists' political ideology or toward people or groups the terrorists see as outsiders. Examples include the Ku Klux Klan and the Aryan Nations.
- *Nationalist.* They promote the interests of a minority group (usually ethnic or religious) that has been persecuted under majority rule.
- *Cause based.* Violence is used by groups who espouse a particular cause. Examples include Osama Bin Laden and Al-Qaeda, antiabortion groups, the Animal Liberation Front, and Earth First! (a radical environmental protection group).

- *State sponsored.* When a governmental regime uses terror to force its citizens into obedience, oppresses certain groups, and does not allow political dissent. The United States identifies the follow states as engaging in state-sponsored terrorism: Iraq, Iran, Libya, Cuba, North Korea, Syria, and Sudan.

Others differentiate between domestic and international terrorism; enforcement and agitational; and instrumental, demonstrative, prophylactic, and incidental.[78]

Incidence of Terrorism

Acts of terrorism have increased dramatically since the mid-1960s. There have been over 7000 acts of terrorism worldwide since then, with some 40% occurring in the United States and Canada.[79] According to the FBI, there were 651 significant international terrorist attacks in 2004, the majority of which occurred in the Near East or south Asia. The most common methods were armed attack (46%), bombing (29%), kidnapping (16%), assault (4%), suicide bomb (3%), other (2%), and arson (1%). U.S. interests were the primary target in only 10% of the terrorist incidents.[80]

Terrorism has increased for reasons other than political issues. As Wayne Kerstetter stated, increased access to modern transportation has made it much easier for terrorists to go from one country to another and even across continents in just a few hours.[81] Air transportation not only increases mobility, but also serves as another opportunity for terrorism. Modern communication technology also works to terrorists' advantage. The media, particularly television, gives terrorists an immediate audience so that they can make the entire world aware of their demands.

Characteristics of Terrorism

For terrorism to be effective, it must generate a high level of fear within the intended audience.[82] In addition, terrorists must be willing to wield some form of formidable power for a particular purpose for which they are willing to die. Finally, the terrorist act must be "cost effective" and, as a form of nonverbal communication, must get across the group's ideological point.

Daniel Goleman found that many terrorists share common social and behavioral experiences.[83] Many had suffered from some type of life-threatening experience in their youth, such as disease or war.

The burning of the Two Elks Mountain Restaurant in Vail, Colorado. An environmental group took responsibility for this act, indicating that it was protesting the growth of the resort town.

? *How should such an act of terrorism be classified?*

This exposure may have blunted their sense of vulnerability and led them to deny the risk of death. Others have developed a sense of anomie because of their social and personal conditions. They emotionally and psychologically attach themselves to an ideology that parallels their own needs and offers them a potential solution. This ideology often polarizes the world into good and bad. This same ideology justifies the use of violence: "there are no innocents" (see **TABLE 11-4**). Kerstetter suggested two additional traits common to terrorists: (1) They are mainly young, unmarried males, and (2) they make calculated moves to bring attention to the perceived injustices.[84]

LINK Anomie theory is covered in Chapter 6.

In psychological terms, Anthony Cooper postulates that the typical terrorist is either a criminal or a psychopath or both, but not a psychotic.[85] Other observers of terrorism disagree, however. Some suggest that often the terrorist was a younger child in a family with older brothers, growing up with an abiding hatred of the father. Moreover, the terrorist has lost contact with reality and has delusions of both grandeur and persecution. Further-more, the terrorist suffers from depression and despair over a perceived lack of self-worth.[86]

According to Strentz, the leader of a leftist terrorist group, either male or female, is likely 25 to 40 years old, has some college education, belongs to the middle class, is urban and sophisticated, speaks several languages, and is a dedicated and professional political activist. Foreign terrorists, he adds, tend to be male and slightly older.[87]

There may be yet another side to terrorists' personalities: a cultural one. Luigi Bonanati suggested that terrorism is one of only a few strategies open to persons outside of a major power such as the United States to focus world attention on their plight.[88] This becomes especially important to a terrorist organization that wishes to become better known. Witness the bombing of the World Trade Center in New York City. In that attack, six people died, more than 1000 were injured, and more than 55,000 workers were displaced.[89] More than a score of terrorist organizations who claimed responsibility for the explosion had their names electronically transmitted around the world. More recently, of course, were the attacks on the United States on September 11, 2001. With thousands killed at the hands of very few terrorists, new names and groups emerged to become a part of the American lexicon. Osama Bin Laden became a household name; the Taliban and Al-Qaeda were groups that were unknown to most Americans before 9-11. Now all

---

TABLE 11-4

Nettler's Six Characteristics Shared by Terrorists

1. **No rules:** Terrorists differ from soldiers and police officers in that they consciously violate all conventions.
2. **No innocents:** Terrorists fight the "unjust system," which includes all people within that system who do not side with them.
3. **Economy:** Terrorists frighten tens of thousands or even millions of people by a single act.
4. **Publicity:** Terrorists seek publicity, which in turn encourages more terrorism. Well-publicized violence advertises the terrorist cause.
5. **Individual therapy:** Terrorists find their acts to be enjoyable or therapeutic. Fighting for a "just cause" gives purpose to a life that is otherwise meaningless.
6. **Varied objectives:** Terrorists seek to acquire or exercise power, although different members of the group may have different ideas about what the power should be used for.

Source: Gwynn Nettler, *Killing One Another* (Cincinnati: Anderson, 1982): 228–237.

three are known to most Americans and linked to murder, suffering, and terrorism.

Osama Bin Laden had been known to the intelligence community in the United States since at least 1980. The 17th of 52 children born to wealthy parents, Osama graduated from King Abdul Aziz University with a degree in civil engineering in 1979. After his limited involvement in the Iranian Revolution and the Soviet invasion of Afghanistan, he became involved in the raising of money, rebuilding roads, and compensating the families of dead soldiers. Operating within a limited role until the invasion of Kuwait in 1990, he became more visibly involved with his fortune only to be rejected by the royal family of Saudi Arabia; they rejected his citizenship in 1994 and confiscated some of his funds. He later relocated to Afghanistan and became involved with the Taliban and Al-Qaeda.

Based on a presumed link voiced by President George W. Bush to the 9-11 attacks, he has been hunted by armed forces of the United States and other allies as a terrorist and threat to the safety of millions of people. He has linked himself to Al-Qaeda by adopting the mission to expel all "nonbelievers" from the Middle East. The group encourages all Muslims to fight the battle of terrorism against all who fail to live according to their extremist interpretation of Islamic ideals. As Bin Laden has said on many occasions, there is no distinction made between those who wear the uniform of an "infidel" and those who do not. This coincides with the terrorist's belief that there are no innocents.

The Response to Terrorism

Despite the world's responses to terrorism — which include SWAT teams, hostage negotiation squads, a perceived hardening of the judiciary system's attitude toward terrorism, and increased security at airports, train stations, and public facilities — terrorism will continue to be a part of the world scene.

No intelligence organization and no one country, whatever its resources, can combat terrorism alone. The chief of the Security Specialties Division of the Federal Law Enforcement Training Center in Glynco, Georgia, calls for cooperation among all major powers to fight terrorism around the world. The United States, despite being the target of more than 100 acts of terrorism, has been rather successful in this battle. Partially because of the courses offered across the country to law enforcement per-

Osama Bin Laden, flanked by his top aide Ayman al-Zawarhi, broadcasts his praise for the September 11 attacks on the United States, vowing that America "will never dream of security" until "the infidel's armies leave the land of Muhammad."

 How would Al-Qaeda be classified under the definitions of terrorism provided in this chapter?

sonnel and the awareness of the threat posed by terrorists, law enforcement in America is serious about the problem.[90]

One important strategy employed by the United States is the Anti-Terrorism Assistance Program within the U.S. Department of State. Since 1983, more than 70 countries and 11,000 international government officials have participated in this program. The Anti-Terrorism Assistance Program focuses on three objectives:

1. Enhancing the antiterrorism skills of participating countries

2. Strengthening the bilateral ties of the United States with friendly countries

3. Fostering an increased respect for human rights by sharing modern, humane, and effective antiterrorism techniques with international civil authorities

Perhaps through these and other similar efforts, inroads will be made against the real and present danger of domestic and international terrorism.[91]

Since 9-11, the United States government has taken an aggressive posture to fight terrorism. One controversial measure has been the USA Patriot Act, which enhances the U.S. government's powers in fighting terrorism. The act includes funding for counterterrorist activity and enhanced technical support, broadens the government's ability to collect electronic evidence, provides guidelines for detaining terrorists, and gives the FBI greater power to perform "warantless" seizures when national security is in jeopardy — among other things. Proponents argue that it will strengthen our response to terrorism by giving the government the tools it needs. They maintain that the greater powers given to the government are necessary and worth the small infringement on American citizens' rights. Opponents argue that this act goes against our core civil and individual rights. They are most concerned with the government's power to monitor the lives of average American citizens, and for this reason, debate and controversy still exist over the act. Time will tell whether its impact on the United States' fight against terrorism has been positive.

The Department of Homeland Security was created by the Homeland Security Act of 2002 to protect the nation from terrorist attack. The department is charged with coordinating the efforts of law enforcement agencies, especially at the federal level, to combat terrorism.[92]

▌ Multicide

Mass Murder

<u>Mass murder</u> is the killing of a number of people at one time and in one place.[93] Unfortunately, many examples of mass murderers exist. Perhaps the most infamous is James Oliver Huberty, who killed 21 customers and wounded 19 others at a McDonald's restaurant in San Ysidro, California, in July 1984. In 1965, Charles Whitman fatally shot 15 people and wounded 14 others from the top of a tower on the campus of the University of Texas in Austin. Ronald Gene Simmons killed 14 family members and two co-workers near Russellville, Arkansas, in December 1987. On August 20, 1986, former postal worker Patrick Sherill walked into his old post office in Edmond, Oklahoma, and shot 21 people, killing 14.

Characteristics of Mass Murderers

Mass murderers tend to kill in the area where they reside.[94] Park Dietz has noted that mass murderers tend to be males, problem drinkers, depressive personalities, and collectors of firearms, hand grenades, and silencers.[95] Some mass murderers have a survivalist mentality and an expectation of approaching global catastrophe. To prepare for this event, they may plan a suitable retreat. These traits, however, are not common to all mass murderers. Like members of any other group, mass murderers differ in personality traits, social core variables, anticipated gains, and motivations.

Typology of Mass Murderers

Park Dietz has developed a typology of mass murderers that describes three basic types:[96]

1. *Family annihilator.* Usually the senior male in the household, he sometimes has a drinking problem and is often depressed. He will murder each member in the household and sometimes even the family pets. The event ends when he takes his own life (homicide–suicide scenario) or "forces" the police to kill him.

2. *Pseudocommando.* Preoccupied with firearms, he may keep a stash of handguns, rifles, and grenades at home or in secret hiding places. He deliberates for quite a while before committing his crime. Again, he is usually killed by the police at the scene.

3. *Set-and-run killer.* Unlike the other two types, the set-and-run killer has no intention of dying and will leave himself some avenue for escape. He may set a bomb in a building or an automobile and then either watch the explosion from a distance or immediately leave the scene. He may have only one victim in mind, with no concern for the others who die incidentally. His motivation is also varied: revenge, anger, money, or ideology.

Recently, incidents of workplace violence have brought to the public's attention a new type of mass murderer: the disgruntled citizen.[97] This offender enters a present or former workplace and may seek out specific victims to eliminate or may kill indiscriminately. Joseph Wesbecker is an example of this type of mass murderer; after being placed on disability, Wesbecker returned to his office and killed seven coworkers and wounded 13 others.[98] Workplace violence can be an act of violence perpetuated by an employee, a former employee, a customer, or a stranger.[99]

Serial Murder

The term <u>serial murder</u> refers to the killing of a number of people, usually three or more, over the course of more than a month.[100] This type of multicide has captured the attention of the American public since the early 1970s, following the convictions of notorious serial killers such as Ted Bundy, Randy Craft, John Wayne Gacy, David Berkowitz, and Arthur Shawcross.

Ted Bundy was executed in 1989 in Florida for three murders, and he is suspected of killing more than three dozen other victims in as many as 10 states. Randy Craft, the "Score Card Killer," was sentenced to death in 1989 for killing 16 victims in California between 1972 and 1983. He is also believed to have been involved in the death of more than 60 victims in California, Oregon, and Michigan.[101]

John Wayne Gacy, the "Killer Clown," was convicted of 33 murders of young men in Illinois. Although he consistently maintained his innocence, more than 20 bodies were dug up from the crawl space under his home. David "Son of Sam" Berkowitz was convicted in the killing of six young women in New York City. Berkowitz may also have been a member of a Satanic cult, the same one that Charles Manson once belonged to.[102] In 1991, Arthur Shawcross was convicted in the murder of 10 women. When asked what the police should do with him, Shawcross remarked that he should be put in jail for the rest of his life because if he ever got out he would kill again.[103]

During the 1980s and 1990s in the Portland and Seattle area, one serial killer continued to find victims while the case remained unsolved. It was not until 2002 that Gary L. Ridgeway — the "Green River Killer" — was finally apprehended. In November 2003, Ridgeway admitted to killing 48 women in the greater Seattle area. Most of the women were prostitutes who ranged in age from 15 to 38 years. Ridgeway admitted to these killings and offered some explanations for his crimes: He hated prostitutes because of the crime and disease they spread and was therefore helping police by murdering them. He admitted to creating cemeteries (which he called "clusters") and would drive by these clusters and think about the women he killed and placed there.

Dennis Rader, the notorious "BTK Killer," terrorized the residents of Wichita, Kansas, during the 1970s and was finally apprehended in early 2005. He pled guilty to 10 murders spanning almost 30 years. Rader has said that he was possessed by a "demon" from an early age and could not contain himself.

LINK Chapter 5 includes more information on Dennis Rader.

Some serial killers travel long distances in their search for victims, as well as to confuse law enforcement; others do all their killing in their home area or nearby area. One important element of serial murder is the killer's motivation.[104] Some are motivated to kill by their own internal psychological demands; others kill because they are motivated by voices or visions. Most serial murderers also anticipate psychological gain (e.g., pleasure and hedonistic achievement); others seek material gain (e.g., money, inheritance, the ownership of a business). The latter seems particularly true of female serial killers.

Attempts have been made by practitioners and academics alike to understand serial murderers.[105] Apparently, the "typical" serial killer does not exist. Some are intelligent and well educated, but many are not. For example, Bundy was a law school student, although other serial killers could barely read or write their names. In short, serial killers fit no single profile. The one characteristic they do often share is the ability to blend into society and appear to be normal citizens — this is precisely what makes them so dangerous.

The case of Aileen Wuornos increased interest in female serial killers. Wuornos was convicted of killing six of her clients while serving as a prostitute. She was executed in Florida on October 9, 2002. Her life and case was the subject of the film *Monster*.[106] Although most researchers agree that the majority of serial killers are male, some estimates suggest that as many as 10% to 15% of all serial killers are female. Keeney and Heide found some important genders differences in their study of female serial killers.[107] For example, women were more likely to use relatively passive forms of violence (e.g., smothering or poisoning), were more likely to "lure" their victims to their death, were more likely to be diagnosed with a broad range of mental disorders, and were older than their male counterparts.

A Typology of Serial Murderers

Holmes and DeBurger offer a typology of serial killers that contains four basic types[108]:

1. *The visionary.* This killer is propelled to kill because he hears a voice or sees a vision that commands the murderous acts. The apparition may take the form of God or a devil, a demon, or an angel. Serial killer Joseph Kallinger was commanded by a floating head named Charlie to kill everyone in the world.[109] The visionary serial killer is truly psychotic, suffering a severe break with reality. He or she is ordinarily geographically stable. The crime reflects the disoriented personality — the crime scene is chaotic with a great deal of physical evidence.

2. *The missionary.* This killer takes it upon himself or herself to rid the community or the world of an undesirable type of person. Although not psychotic or compelled by outside influences such as voices or visions, the missionary has a "job" to do. For example, one serialist killed those whom he had judged to be prostitutes (although none of the three female victims were indeed prostitutes) because it was his job to rid his community of "bad" women and sexually transmitted diseases.

3. *The hedonist.* This killer has made the vital connection between fatal violence and personal/sexual gratification. He or she may commit acts of necrophilia, mutilate bodies, and collect personal souvenirs. Jerry Brudos, the convicted killer of at least four young women in Oregon, kept an ankle of one victim, one breast of another, and both breasts of a third, and he sent electrical shocks through the dead body of his fourth victim.[110]

4. *The power/control seeker.* This killer achieves gratification from the complete possession of the victim. The power/control killer has eroticized possession of the victim as an object in the same fashion as the hedonistic killer has eroticized aggression.

Conclusion

This chapter discusses violent crimes that, although not new, have received greater attention in the public arena. For many of these crimes, our awareness and our attempts at intervention, prevention, and response are in their infancy. More and continued attention must be paid to understanding the characteristics, motivations, and rationalizations of those who commit violent personal crimes. As our understanding of these forms of violence grows, we will be better equipped to develop appropriate law enforcement and criminal justice responses. Until then, we can expect to see more of these and other "emerging" forms of violence.

WRAP UP

Crime Scene Investigation

The first step would be to attempt to further identify the victim by checking past employment records at the former club to determine whether one of the women who worked there fit the general description and if she had disappeared. The circumstances of her death would be important. How does her case compare with the others mentioned? Did the victim match the physical characteristics of the other homicide victims in terms of their physical attributes and other factors? Were the same tactics used to subdue the victim?

Chapter Spotlight

- The forms of violence covered in this chapter are emerging only in the sense of our increasing awareness of them. Although these crimes have been prevalent for many years, the consciousness of the American people regarding these crimes has been raised to a new level within the last few years, due to both increased enforcement and heightened media awareness.

- Intimate partner abuse can take on a number of forms, including physical battering, sexual battering, psychological battering, and destruction of property and pets. It involves current or former heterosexual or homosexual intimate partners. The major sociological theory regarding the problem of intimate partner abuse is intergenerational transmission of violence.

- Stalking consists of the willful, repeated, and malicious following, harassing, or threatening of another person. The majority of stalking incidents involve individuals who are or were intimates or acquainted, with a high correlation existing between stalking and intimate partner abuse.

- Child abuse includes nonaccidental physical injury, sexual abuse or exploitation, emotional or psychological injury, and neglect or maltreatment to a person under the age of 18 years. The full extent of child abuse in this country is unknown, and it has proven difficult to arrive at a reliable figure. In 1974, Congress passed the Child Abuse Prevention and Treatment Act, which provides federal funding at the state level for prevention and response to child abuse.

- A hate crime is one in which a person intentionally selects a victim because of race, color, religion, national origin, ethnicity, gender, or sexual orientation. Significant hate groups acting in this country include the Ku Klux Klan, Identity Churches, and the skinheads. Throughout the 1990s, many states strengthened their hate crime legislation.

- Defining terrorism as a crime is a difficult task, in part because many different types of terrorists exist; terrorists vary by behaviors, goals, ideologies, and motivations. The most common types of terrorists include revolutionary, political, nationalist, cause based, and state sponsored.

- Multicide includes both mass murder and serial murder. Because it is so difficult to typify this kind of killer, law enforcement faces serious hurdles in preventing these crimes.

Putting It All Together

1. Discuss the major differences between mass murder and serial murder.

2. How have the target groups for hate crimes changed over the years? Why has this hap-

pened? What do you see as future targets for the hate crime groups?

3. Explain the relationship between intimate partner abuse, stalking, and child abuse. What role does the intergenerational transmission of violence play in the commission of these crimes?

4. Select a nationally known serial killer. According to the typology of serial killers presented in this chapter, what type — visionary, missionary, hedonist, or power/control seeker — is he or she? Why?

Key Terms

Aryan Nations Organization founded on the notion of white supremacy that preaches violent anti-Jewish and antiminority messages. The Aryan Nations' stated goal is the "establishment of a White Aryan homeland on the North American continent."

child abuse Physical, emotional, or sexual abuse or maltreatment of a child.

cyberstalking A specialized form of stalking that occurs when the perpetrator uses a computer and the Internet to follow and harass their victim.

domestic violence Term used to describe abuse or violence that occurs in the context of the home or family. It includes spouses, co-habiting partners, former intimates, children, and parents.

hate crime Crime in which a person intentionally selects a victim because of the race, color, religion, national origin, ethnicity, gender, or sexual orientation.

Identity Church Organization of churches that believes in the supremacy of the white race and preaches a message of hate, particularly toward Jews.

intergenerational transmission of violence The process by which children who observe or experience violence themselves become violent or abusive later in life.

intimate partner abuse Abuse that occurs between current or former, heterosexual or homosexual intimates. Includes physical, sexual, and emotional abuse and violence.

Ku Klux Klan (KKK) Fraternal organizations that promote the "white rights movement" and anti-Semitism. Known for terrorizing minority groups, especially blacks and Jews.

mass murder The killing of a number of people, usually three or more, in one place at one time.

pedophilia The unnatural desire for sexual relations with children.

serial murder The killing of a number of people, usually three or more, at different times.

skinheads Originally, a group of rebellious working-class youths from England. The movement spread to the United States where youths have adopted a message of group hatred directed typically at minorities.

stalking The act of willfully, maliciously, and repeatedly following or harassing another person and making threats with the intent of placing that person in imminent fear of death or serious bodily injury.

terrorism The instilling of fear through violence or threats of violence. Terrorist groups worldwide often seek to achieve political goals and objectives.

Notes

1. Ronald M. Holmes and Stephen T. Holmes, *Profiling Violent Crimes: An Investigative Tool* (Thousand Oaks, CA: Sage Publications, 1996): 91.
2. Richard B. Felson, Steven F. Messner, Anthony W. Hoskin, and Glenn Deane, "Reasons for Reporting and Not Reporting Domestic Violence to the Police," *Criminology* 40 (2002): 617–648.
3. Rosemarie Tong, *Women, Sex, and the Law* (Totowa, NJ: Rowman and Allanheld, 1984).
4. Angela Browne, "Violence in Marriage: Until Death Do Us Part?" in Albert P. Cardarelli, ed., *Violence Between Intimate Partners: Patterns, Causes, and Effects* (Boston: Allyn and Bacon, 1997): 48–69.
5. Joanne Belknap, *The Invisible Woman: Gender Crime, and*

Justice (Belmont, CA: Wadsworth, 2001); Russell P. Dobash, R.E. Dobash, Margo Wilson, and Martin Daly, "The Myth of Sexual Symmetry in Martial Violence," *Social Problems* 39 (1992): 71–91; Heather C. Melon and Joanne Belknap, "He Hits, She Hits: Assessing Gender Differences and Similarities in Officially Reported Intimate Partner Violence," *Criminal Justice and Behavior* 30 (2003): 328–348.

6. Patricia Tjaden and Nancy Thoennes, "Prevalence and Consequences of Male-to-Female and Female-to-Male Intimate Partner Violence as Measured by the National Violence Against Women Survey," *Violence Against Women* 6 (1998): 142–161.

7. U.S. Department of Justice, *Bureau of Justice Statistics Factbook: Violence by Intimates* (Washington, D.C.: U.S. Department of Justice, 1998).

8. Richard Gelles, "Constraints Against Family Violence: How Well Do They Work," *American Behavioral Scientist* 36 (1993): 575–585; Angela M. Moore, "Intimate Violence: Does Socioeconomic Status Matter?" in Albert P. Cardarelli, ed., *Violence Between Intimates: Patterns, Causes, and Effects* (Boston: Allyn and Bacon, 1997): 90–103.

9. Gill Hague and Ellen Malos, *Domestic Violence: Action for Change* (Gretton, England: New Clarion Press, 1998); Suman Kakar, *Domestic Abuse: Public Policy/Criminal Justice Approaches Toward Child, Spousal, and Elderly Abuse* (San Francisco: Austin and Winfield Publishers, 1998); Susan L. Miller and Charles F. Wellford, "Patterns and Correlates of Interpersonal Violence," in Albert P. Cardarelli, ed., *Violence Between Intimates: Patterns, Causes, and Effects* (Boston: Allyn and Bacon, 1997).

10. Ibid.

11. Ibid.; Aysan Sev'er, "Recent or Imminent Separation and Intimate Violence Against Women," *Violence Against Women* 3 (1997): 566–589; Harvey Wallace, *Family Violence: Legal, Medical, and Social Perspectives* (Boston: Allyn and Bacon, 1996).

12. Hague and Malos, 1998.

13. Ibid.

14. Hague and Malos, 1998; Kakar, 1998; Sev'er, 1997; Damian O'Neill, "A Post-Structural Review of the Theoretical Literature Surrounding Wife Abuse," *Violence Against Women* 4 (1998): 457–490; Kersti Yllo, "Through A Feminist Lens: Gender, Power, and Violence," in Richard J. Gelles and Donileen Loeske, eds., *Current Controversies on Family Violence* (Newbury Park, CA: Sage, 1993): 47–62.

15. R.E. Dobash and Russell Dobash, *Violence Against Wives: A Case Against the Patriarchy* (New York: Free Press, 1979).

16. Kakar, 1998.

17. Dobash and Dobash, 1979; Kakar, 1998; O'Neill, 1998, 457–490.

18. Donald Dutton, *The Domestic Assault of Women: Psychological and Criminal Justice Perspectives* (Vancouver: University of British Columbia Press, 1995): 19.

19. Ibid.

20. Stephen Brown, "Police Response to Wife Beating: Neglect of a Crime of Violence," *Journal of Criminal Justice* 12 (1984): 277–288; Elizabeth Pleck, "Criminal Approaches to Family Violence, 1640–1980," in Lloyd Ohlin and Michael Tonry, eds., *Family Violence* , Volume 11 (Chicago: The University of Chicago Press, 1989).

21. Eve Buzawa, *Domestic Violence: The Criminal Justice Response* (London: Sage Publications, 1990): 27.

22. Frances Coleman, "Stalking Behaviors and the Cycle of Domestic Violence," *Journal of Interpersonal Violence* 12 (1997): 420–432; National Institute of Justice, *Domestic Violence, Stalking and Antistalking Legislation: An Annual Report of Congress Under the Violence Against Women Act* (Washington, D.C., U.S. Department of Justice, 1996); Albert Roberts and Sophia Dziegielewski, "Assessment Typology and Intervention with the Survivors of Stalking," *Aggression and Violent Behavior* 1 (1996): 359–368; Patricia Tjaden, *The Crime of Stalking: How Big Is the Problem?* (Washington, D.C.: U.S. Department of Justice, National Institute of Justice, 1997); U.S. Department of Justice Violence Against Women Grants Office, *Stalking and Domestic Violence: The Third Annual Report to Congress Under the Violence Against Women Act* (Washington, D.C.: U.S. Department of Justice, 1998).

23. Coleman, 1997, 420–432; Keith Davis, April Ace, and Michelle Andra, "Stalking Perpetrators and Psychological Maltreatment of Partners: Anger-Jealously, Attachment Insecurity, Need for Control, and Break-up Context," *Violence and Victims* 15 (2000): 473–487; T.K. Logan, Carl Leukefeld, and Bob Walker, "Stalking as a Variant of Intimate Violence: Implications from a Young Adult Sample," *Violence and Victims* 15 (2000): 91–111; Judith M. McFarlane, Jacquelyn C. Campbell, Susan Wilt, Carolyn J.U.Y. Sachs, and Xiao Xu, "Stalking and Intimate Partner Femincide," *Homicide Studies* 3 (1999): 300–316; Mindy B. Mechanic, Terri L. Weaver, and Patricia A. Resick, "Intimate Partner Violence and Stalking Behaviors: Exploration of Patterns and Correlates in a Sample of Acutely Battered Women," *Violence and Victims* 15 (2000): 55–72; Mindy B. Mechanic, Mary H. Uhlmansiek, Terri L. Weaver, and Patricia A. Resick, "The Impact of Severe Stalking Experienced by Acutely Battered Women: An Examination of Violence, Psychological Symptoms and Strategic Responses," *Violence and Victims* 15 (2000): 443–458; Patricia Tjaden and Nancy Thoennes, "The Role of Stalking in Domestic Violence Crime Reports Generated by the Colorado Springs Police Department," *Violence and Victims* 15 (2000): 427–441; Jacquelyn White, Robin M. Kowalski, Amy Lyndon, and Sherri Valentine, "An Integrative Contextual Developmental Model of Male Stalking," *Violence and Victims* 15 (2000): 373–388.

24. Coleman,1997, 420–432; J.R. Meloy and Shayna Gothard, "Demographic and Clinical Comparison of Obsessional Followers and Offenders with Mental Disorders," *American Journal of Psychiatry* 152 (1995): 258–263; J.R. Meloy, "Stalking (Obsessional Following): A Review of Some Preliminary Studies," *Aggression and Violence Behavior* 1 (1996): 147–162; Patricia Tjaden and Nancy Thoennes, *Stalking in America: Findings from the National Violence Against Women Survey* (Washington, D.C.: U.S. Department of Justice, 1998).

25. Albert Roberts and Sophia Dziegielewski, "Assessment Typology and Intervention with the Survivors of Stalking," *Aggression and Violent Behavior* 1 (1996): 359–368; James A. Wright, Allen G. Burgess, Ann W. Burgess, Anna T. Laszlo, Gregg O. McCrary, and John E. Douglas, "A Typology of Interpersonal Stalking," *Journal of Interpersonal Violence* 11 (1996): 487–502.

26. Tjaden and Thoennes, 1998.

27. Michael Zona, Kaushal Sharma, and John Lane, "A Comparative Study of Erotomanic and Obsessional Subjects in a Forensic Sample," *Journal of Forensic Sciences* 38 (1993): 894–903.

28. R.M. Holmes, "Stalking in America: Types and Methods of Criminal Stalkers," *Journal of Contemporary Criminal Justice* 9 (1993): 17–27.

29. Ann Burgess, Timothy Baker, Deborah Greening, Carol R. Hartman, Allen Burgess, John E. Douglas, and Richard Halloran, "Stalking Behaviors Within Domestic Violence," *Journal of Family Violence* 12 (1997): 389–403; Coleman, 1997, 420–432; Roberts and Dziegielewski, 1996, 359–368; Tjaden and Thoennes, 1998.

30. Coleman, 1997, 420–432; Roberts and Dziegielewski, 1996, 359–368.

31. Ibid.; Keith Davis, April Ace, and Michelle Andra, "Stalking Perpetrators and Psychological Maltreatment of Partners: Anger-Jealously, Attachment Insecurity, Need for Control, and Break-up Context," *Violence and Victims* 15 (2000): 473–487; Logan, Leukefeld, and Walker, 2000; McFarlane, et al., 1999; Mechanic, Weaver, and Resick, 2000, 55–72; Mechanic, et al., 2000; Tjaden and Thoennes, 2000; White, et al., 2000.

32. Tjaden and Thoennes, 1998.

33. R.A. Guy, "The Nature and Constitutionality of Stalking Laws," *Vanderbilt Law Review* 46 (1993): 991–1029; U.S. Department of Justice Violence Against Women Grants Office, 1998.

34. Meloy and Gothard, 1995, 258–263; Zona, Sharma, and Lane,1993, 894–903.

35. U.S. Department of Justice Violence Against Women Grants Office, 1998.

36. Wright, et al., 1996, 487–502.

37. Zona, Sharma, and Lane, 1993, 894–903.

38. Emma Oglivie, "Cyberstalking," *Crime and Justice International* 17 (2001): 26–28, 29.

39. J.A. Hitchcock, "Cyberstalking and Law Enforcement," *The Police Chief* 70 (2003): 16–26.

40. National Institute of Justice, 1996.

41. Roberts and Dziegielewski, 1996, 359–368.

42. Davis, Ace, and Andra, 2000, 473–487; Mechanic, Weaver, and Resick, 2000, 55–72.

43. Guy, 1993, 992.

44. D.G. Kilpatrick, B.E. Saunders, and D.W. Smith, *Youth Victimization: Prevalence and Implications* (Washington, DC: National Institute of Justice, 2003).

45. U.S. Department of Health and Human Services, *Child Maltreatment 1999: Reports from the States to the National Child Abuse and Neglect Data System* (Washington, DC: U.S. Government Printing Office, 2001).

46. David Finkelhol and Richard Ormrod, *Child Abuse Reported to the Police* (Washington, DC: Office of Juvenile Justice and Delinquency Prevention, 2001).

47. Kilpatrick, Saunders, and Smith, 2003; U.S. Department of Health and Human Services, 2001.

48. Richard Gelles and Claire Pedrick Cornell, *Intimate Violence in Families* (Newbury Park, CA: Sage, 1990).

49. Clayton Thomas, *Taber's Encyclopedic Medical Dictionary* (Philadelphia: F.A. David, 1985).

50. Ann Burgess, Nicholas Holstrom, Lynda Lytlesgroi, and Nicholas Groth, *Sexual Assault of Children and Adolescents* (Lexington, MA: D.C. Heath, 1978).

51. Ronald Holmes, *The Sex Offender and the Criminal Justice System* (Springfield, IL: Charles C. Thomas, 1983).

52. D. Tingle, G. Bernard, L. Robbins, and G. Newman, "Childhood and Adolescent Characteristics of Pedophiles and Rapists," *International Journal of Law Psychiatry* 9 (1986): 103–116.

53. D. Finkelhor and S. Araji, "Explanations of Pedophilia: A Four-Factor Model," *Journal of Sex Research* 22 (1986): 145–161.

54. Kelly Kyrik, "Trolling for Predators," *Police Magazine,* available at www.policemag.com/t_cipick.cfm?rank=91870, accessed December 12, 2005.

55. Kurt Freund, Robin Watson, and Douglas Rienzo, "Heterosexuality, Homosexuality, and Erotic Age Preference," *Journal of Sex Research* 26 (1989): 107–117.

56. S. Araji and D. Finkelhor, "Explanations of Pedophilia: Review of Empirical Research," *Bulletin of the American Academy of Psychiatry and Law* 13 (1): 17–36.

57. Ronald Holmes and Stephen Holmes, *Sex Crimes* (Thousand Oaks, CA: Sage, 2002).

58. George E. Rush, *The Dictionary of Criminal Justice* (Columbus, OH: McGraw-Hill/Dushkin, 2004).

59. Federal Bureau of Investigation, *Crime in the United States, 2003* (Washington, DC: U.S. Department of Justice, 2004).

60. Bob Stewart, Michael Lieberman, William R. Celester, et al., "Hate Crimes: Understanding and Addressing the Problem," *The Police Chief* 61 (1994): 14–18.

61. Jack Levin and Jack McDevitt, *Hate Crimes: The Rising Tide of Bigotry and Bloodshed* (New York: Plenum Press, 1993).

62. Neil Weiner, Margaret Zahn, and Rita Sagi, *Violence: Patterns, Causes, Public Policy* (New York: Harcourt Brace Jovanovich, 1990).

63. Anti-Defamation League, *The Committee of the States* (New York: Anti-Defamation League of the B'nai B'rith, 1987).

64. Jonathon White, *Terrorism: An Introduction* (Pacific Grove, CA: Brooks/Cole, 1991).

65. Ibid., 40–41.

66. Ibid., 23.

67. Ibid., 28, 111.

68. Ibid., 44–45.

69. Ibid., 40–44.

70. Ibid., 23, 185.

71. Ibid., 40–45.

72. Walter Bouman, "Best Practices of a Hate/Bias Crime Investigation," *FBI Law Enforcement Bulletin* 72 (2003): 21–25.

73. Wendy L. Hicks, "Skinheads: A Three Nation Comparison," *Journal of Gang Research* 11 (2004): 51–74.

74. James B. Jacobs and Kimberly A. Potter, "Hate Crimes: A Clinical Perspective," in Michael Tonry, ed., *Crime and Justice: A Review of Research* , Volume 22 (Chicago: The University of Chicago Press, 1997): 1–50.

75. Ibid.

76. James Garofalo and Susan E. Martin, "The Law Enforcement Response to Bias-Motivated Crimes," in Robert J. Kelly, ed., *Bias Crime: American Law Enforcement and Legal Responses* (Chicago: Office of International Criminal Justice, 1991): 64–80.

77. James M. Poland, *Understanding Terrorism: Groups, Strategies, and Responses* (Upper Saddle River, NJ: Prentice Hall, 2005): 10.

78. Ibid.

79. Wayne Kerstetter, "Terrorism," in Stanford H. Kadish, ed., *Encyclopedia of Crime and Justice* (New York: Free Press, 1993).

80. National Counterterrorism Center, "A Chronology of Significant International Terrorism for 2004", available at www.tkb.org/documents/Downloads/NCTC_Report.pdf, accessed January 3, 2006.

81. Kerstetter, 1993, 1530–1531.

82. Anthony Cooper, "Terroristic Fads and Fashions," in B. Danto, B. Bruhns, and A.H. Kutscher, eds., *The Human Side of Homicide* (New York: Columbia University Press, 1982).

83. Daniel Goleman, "The Roots of Terrorism Are Found in Brutality of Shattered Childhood," *The New York Times* (September 4, 1986): C1, C8.

84. Kerstetter, 1993.

85. Cooper, 1982.

86. J. E. Brody, "Researchers Trace Key Factors in Profiles of Assassins on the American Scene," *The New York Times* (April 15, 1981): C1; L. Freedman, "Presidential Assassins Strike Out More at the Symbols than the Man," *The Boston Globe* (April 5, 1991): A3.

87. T. Strentz, "A Terrorist Psychological Profile: Past and Present," *FBI Law Enforcement Bulletin* 57 (1988): 13–19.

88. Luigi Bonanati, "Terrorism and International Political Analysis," *Terrorism* 3 (1977): 47–67.

89. B. Kandel and B. Frankel, "Cuomo: Back in Business," *USA Today* (March 5, 1993): A8.

90. David Schwartz, "The Terrorist Threat," *The Police Chief* 63 (1991): 36–37.

91. R. Putney, "Enhancing Anti-Terrorism Skills," *The Police Chief* 63 (1991): 40–42.

92. U.S. Department of Homeland Security, "DHS Organization — The DHS Strategic Plan — Securing Our Homeland," available at www.dhs.gov/dhspublic/interapp/editorial/editorial_0413.xml, accessed December 24, 2005.

93. Ronald Holmes and James DeBurger, "Profiles in Terror: The Serial Murderer," *Federal Probation* 44 (1985): 29–34.

94. Ibid.

95. Park Dietz, "Mass, Serial and Sensational Homicide,"

Bulletin of the New England Medical Society 62 (1986): 477–491.

96. Ibid.

97. Ronald Holmes and Stephen Holmes, *Profiling Violent Crimes: An Investigative Tool* (Thousand Oaks, CA: Sage, 2002).

98. L. Scanlon and A. Wolfson, "Disturbed Worker Kills 7 and Wounds 13 in a Rampage with AK-47 at Louisville Plant." *The [Louisville] Courier Journal* (September 15, 1989): A1, 11.

99. Vaughan Bowie, "Defining Violence at Work: A New Typology," in Martin Gill, Bonnie Fisher, and Vaughan Bowie, eds., *Violence at Work: Causes, Patterns, and Prevention* (Uffculme, United Kingdom: Willan Publishing, 2002): 1–20.

100. Eric Hickey, *Serial Murderers and Their Victims* (Pacific Grove, CA: Brooks/Cole, 1981).

101. J. Hicks, "Score Card Killer?" *The [Louisville] Courier Journal* (March 9, 1987): A1, A16.

102. Terry McGarry, *The Ultimate Terror* (New York: Doubleday, 1987).

103. Jack Olson, *The Misbegotten Son* (New York: Delacourte, 1990).

104. Holmes and Deburger, 1985.

105. Tammy Castle and Christopher Hensley, "Serial Killers with Military Experience: Applying Learning Theory to Serial Murder," *International Journal of Offender Therapy and Comparative Criminology* 46 (2002): 453–465; L. Schlesinger and L. Miller, *Learning to Kill: Contract, Serial and Terroristic Homicide* (Springfield, IL: Charles C. Thomas, 2003); Stephen Singer and Christopher Hensley, "Applying Learning Theory to Childhood and Adolescent Firesetting: Can It Lead to Serial Murder?" *International Journal of Offender Therapy and Comparative Criminology* 48 (2004): 461–476; Terry Whitman and Donald Akutagawa, "Riddles in Serial Murder: A Synthesis," *Aggression and Violent Behavior* 9 (2004): 693–703.

106. American Civil Liberties Union and the American Friends Service Committee, *The Forgotten Population: A Look at Death Row in the United States Through the Experiences of Women* (New York: American Civil Liberties Union, 2004): 208.

107. Belea T. Keeney and Kathleen M. Heide, "Gender Differences in Serial Murderers: A Preliminary Analysis," *Journal of Interpersonal Violence* 9 (1994): 383–398.

108. Holmes and DeBurger, 1985.

109. Flora Schreiber, *The Shoemaker* (New York: Signet Books, 1984).

110. Andy Stack, *The Lust Killer* (New York: Signet Books, 1983).

WWW.CRIMINOLOGY.JBPUB.COM

Interactivities
In the News
Key Term Explorer
Web Links

CHAPTER

12

OBJECTIVES

Discuss the nature and extent of property crime.

Critically explore the types of burglars, their motivations, and how they go about selecting a target.

Understand the characteristics of the victims of various property crimes.

Examine the various types of forgery.

Understand the impact of identity theft and credit card fraud.

Evaluate statistics about property crime rates and victimization rates.

Summarize trends in property crime rates in the United States.

Explain the various motivations for arson.

Identify the various types of shoplifters.

Distinguish among the various forms of property crimes: burglary, arson, larceny-theft, and motor vehicle theft.

Explain the common forms of identity theft and what to do if victimized.

Property Crimes

> Offenders typically decided to commit a residential burglary in response to a perceived need. In most cases, this need was financial, calling for the immediate acquisition of money. However, it sometimes involved what was interpreted as an attack on the status, identity, or self-esteem of the offenders. Whatever its character, the need almost invariably was regarded by the offenders as pressing, that is, something that had to be dealt with immediately.
>
> — Richard T. Wright and Scott Decker[1]

Curbing Identity Theft

Identity theft is emerging as a significant problem: Many people are falling victim to this form of criminal behavior. Identity theft is the deliberate assumption of another person's identity, usually to gain access to their credit, to gain monetary rewards, or to place the person in a situation of criminal suspicion. Many forms of identity theft exist, including the stealing of credit cards and PIN numbers. Phishing, a form of identity theft, involves a fraudster who spams the Internet with email claiming to be from a reputable financial institution or e-commerce site. The email message urges the recipient to click on a link to update their personal profile or carry out some other financial transaction. The link takes the victim to a fake Web site designed to look like the legitimate Web site. However, any personal or financial information entered is routed directly to the scammer. In this manner, the fraudster gains viable information about someone and is able to illegally reap financial rewards.

You are invited to be a consultant with local, state and federal agencies to combat identity theft in your locale. Because of your expertise in human behavior, the criminal mind, white-collar crime, and computers, your information and knowledge is often sought.

Who would you recommend to be on the task force to investigate Internet fraud in your community? What kind of professional backgrounds would you consider to be integral to the mission of the task force?

What would be your first line of activity? How are you going to commence your work?

One of the members of the task force offers a recommendation to initiate a "sting operation." What would be the benefits and liabilities of such an activity?

Introduction

Crimes against property account for over three-quarters of all crime in the United States.[2] The major property crimes examined in this chapter include larceny-theft, burglary, arson, and motor vehicle theft. These crimes are identified by the Federal Bureau of Investigation in their Crime Index and are considered index crimes (other index crimes include violent offenses such as homicide, rape, robbery, and aggravated assault). This chapter also examines forgery, credit card fraud, and confidence games, as well as the nature and extent of property crimes and provides a critical assessment of the impact these crimes have on the public and law enforcement. The data on property crimes available to criminologists (or any crimes for that matter) come from three main sources: (1) Official data from the FBI in the Uniform Crime Report (UCR); (2) Data gathered from victims of crime in the National Crime Victimization Survey (NCVS); (3) and offender-based research.

LINK Chapter 2 discusses the usefulness of the Uniform Crime Reports and the National Crime Victimization Survey in terms of shaping one's understanding of the incidence of crime in the United States.

Property Crime Trends

According to the UCR, property crime (i.e., burglary, larceny-theft, motor vehicle theft) rates have decreased 23.4% since 1995 (**TABLE 12-1**). The NCVS also revealed a decrease, indicating that property crime (i.e., household burglary, motor vehicle theft, and theft) had declined 49.5% for roughly the same period (**TABLE 12-2**). It is important to note that the

TABLE 12-1

Estimated Rate of Property Crimes Known to the Police (per 100,000 inhabitants)

Year	Property Crime	Burglary	Larceny-Theft	Motor Vehicle Theft
1980	5,353.3	1,684.1	3,167.0	502.2
1985	4,666.4	1,291.7	2,911.2	463.5
1990	5,073.1	1,232.2	3,185.1	655.8
1995	4,590.5	987.0	3,043.2	560.3
2000	3,618.3	728.8	2,477.3	412.2
2004	3,517.1	729.9	2,365.9	421.3

Sources: U.S. Department of Justice, Office of Justice Programs, Bureau of Justice Statistics, *Sourcebook of Criminal Justice Statistics, 2003,* January 2006, available at http://www.albany.edu/sourcebook, accessed January 12, 2006; U.S. Department of Justice, Federal Bureau of Investigation, *Crime in the United States, 2004,* Washington, DC: Government Printing Office.

TABLE 12-2
Property Crime Victimization Rates (1973 to 2004)

Property crime rates

Adjusted victimization rate per 1000 households.

*The National Crime Victimization Survey was redesigned in 1993. Therefore, rates after that time are shaded.

Source: U.S. Department of Justice, Bureau of Justice Statistics, available at http://www.ojp.usdoj.gov/bjs, accessed January 10, 2006.

UCR and NCVS measure the extent of property crime differently.

Examination of the UCR data indicates that property crimes are more prevalent in the South, where an estimated 41.3% percent of all property crimes are committed. The West accounted for an estimated 25.4% of the country's property crimes, followed by the Midwest (20.9%) and the Northeast (12.5%). Research indicates that areas of the country where there is more residential mobility and a greater ethnic diversity have higher rates of property crime.[3] In terms of cost, the U.S. Department of Justice reports that property crimes (excluding arson) accounted for an estimated loss of $16.1 billion in 2004. This was a decrease of 5.0% from the previous year. The department also stated that law enforcement agencies cleared 16.5% of the property crimes in 2004. Crimes are cleared by the police when (a) an arrest is made or (b) when elements beyond the control of law enforcement prevent the formal arrest and charging of an offender.[4]

Again, according to the U.S. Department of Justice, the vast majority of those arrested for property crimes are adults (72.5%). Males are more likely to be arrested for property crimes (68.1%) than females. In terms of race, in 2004 the majority of property crime offenders were white (69.0%); blacks accounted for 28.5% and other races made up the remaining 2.5%.[5]

A closer examination of the characteristics of households that are victimized by property crimes reveals some important differences.[6] Poor, minority households in suburban areas are more likely to be victimized than white households. Hispanic households led property crime victimization (204 per 1000), followed by black households (191 per 1000), and white households (157 per 1000). Households with lower incomes are disproportionately affected by property crimes, with the highest rates reported in households with annual incomes under $7500 (197.1 per 1000) and households with incomes from $7500 to $14,999 (181.5 per 1000). Comparatively, households with incomes of $50,000 to $74,999 (167.0 per 1000) and $75,000 and over (176.5 per 1000) are less likely to be victimized, but still at rates that are close to the average. Furthermore, when property crime victimization is examined by region, it is noted that households in the West (204.0 per 1000) are much more likely to be victimized than those in the Midwest (168.8), the South (158.3), and especially the Northeast (107.1). Those households that are situated in more densely populated urban areas are more likely to be victimized (214.7 per 1000) than those in suburban (143.2) and rural areas (134.4).

Research supports the existence of a *neighborhood effect*, whereby offenders are more likely to see soft targets within their own neighborhoods and communities.[7] In particular, habitual offenders in lower income neighborhoods seek out homes they know even if it is someone with whom they are friendly. Furthermore, there is a greater chance of an offender being identified as a stranger in a neighborhood they are not likely to have visited in the past. Lastly, lower victimization rates are apparent in higher income neighborhoods because they are more likely to have security measures in place to combat the possibility of property crimes.

Home ownership is another factor in victimization. Data indicate that those who rent their homes are more likely to be victims of property crimes (201.4 per 1000) than those who own their homes (142.8).[8] Home owners may take more precautions to ensure that their property is safe and may also live in areas where neighbors are likely to look out for one another. People who rent their homes or apartments may move more frequently, thereby diminishing their ability to establish strong bonds with neighbors. Research highlights that neighbors could in fact be a key to preventing certain types of property crime.[9] Furthermore, apartment complexes have many people coming and going from them and create a greater potential for property crimes. Also, individuals may be living in areas that are not as well protected in terms of security measures to protect their properties. For example, many apartment complexes have open parking areas, which make stealing items from cars — or stealing the cars themselves — much easier. Conversely, houses are more likely to have a driveway and/or garage, thereby making it difficult for a would-be motor vehicle thief.

Burglary

A number of movies over the past decade (e.g., *The Italian Job, Ocean's Eleven*) have highlighted complex burglary schemes involving a number of people who use their various skills to pull off the "perfect" crime. Although films tend to glamorize the offense and present the burglaries as meticulously planned, a great deal of empirical evidence suggests that burglaries are more about easy or "soft" targets and opportunity than elaborate schemes.

Burglary is traditionally defined as the unlawful entry into a building or dwelling (the *actus reus*) with the purpose or intent of committing a crime (*mens rea*); this distinction is crucial because it means that an individual can be arrested for burglary even if there was no actual felony committed. The problem lies in whether an individual has the intent to commit a felony upon unlawful entry. This is highly subjective and is often left to the discretion of the police. What complicates matters even further is the need to obtain an actual account of such an incident if nothing was actually taken from the dwelling or business. Furthermore, most states have a special provision in the criminal code for motor vehicle burglaries. Burglary differs from robbery in that there is no interaction between the victim and offender in the burglary transaction, and there is no violence against the person during the burglary event. Some states (e.g., Michigan and Rhode Island) use **breaking and entering** to mean the same as burglary. <u>Trespassing</u>, legally defined in most states as knowingly entering a structure or dwelling and remaining there unlawfully, differs from burglary in that there is no intent to commit a crime. Official data sources make a distinction between residential burglaries and nonresidential (business) burglaries. Data from the NCVS reflect only residential burglaries, because it takes its sample from households only. According to the NCVS, in 2004, 53% of the burglaries that took place were reported to the police.[10] People may fail to report the burglary to the police because the objects were recovered, the offender was unsuccessful, and the victim believed there was a lack of proof; some victims indicated that they felt as though the police do not want to be bothered.[11] The UCR, on the other hand, accounts for both residential and nonresidential burglaries reported to the police and therefore is a better overall indicator of the extent of this crime.

Burglary Trends

In 2004, there were an estimated 2.1 million burglary offenses committed in the United States.[12] Arrest trends from 1995 to 2004 indicate that there was a decrease (20.4%) in burglary arrests overall, with the most significant decrease in juvenile arrests (down 35.2%). As for the victims of burglary, the NCVS provides the most thorough data on the extent and nature of victimization. Since 1993, the Bureau of Justice Statistics reports that the burglary victimization rate has decreased by 49.1%. Rates in 1993 were at 58.2 per 1000 households and by 2004 the rate had dropped to 29.6 per 1000 households.[13]

Nature and Extent of Burglary

Data indicate that residential properties are more likely to be the targets of burglaries than nonresidential properties. A majority of these properties are targeted during the daytime hours from 6 A.M. to 6 P.M. According to the UCR (2004), approximately 61.4% of burglaries involved forcible entry. Burglars are known to use various tools to gain entry to target homes, including crowbars, hammers, bolt cutters, and other tools.

Burglary, like the majority of crimes, is committed mostly by males. According to the 2004 Uniform Crime Reports, males accounted for 85.7% of all burglary arrestees. Of the males, juveniles constituted 28.6% of those arrested; of the 14.3%

of total females arrested for burglary, 22.7% were juveniles. In terms of race, of those arrested for burglary in 2004, 70.9% were white and 27.2% were black. The average dollar loss per burglary offense was $1642. In 2004, nonresidential burglaries had a higher average loss ($1000 more) than residential burglaries.[14] Businesses are seen as being more profitable targets for some offenders while others prefer to burglarize homes they know to be easy or soft targets. The victims of burglary are not only harmed by the monetary loss, but also often face psychological damage. Many people who have experienced a burglary in their homes struggle with feelings of violation.[15]

According to the 2004 NCVS, there is a relationship between household income and victimization rates. The survey found households with annual incomes less than $25,000 were burglarized at rates higher than those with higher annual incomes. Burglary victimization rates were highest in the South (34.0 per 1000), followed by the Midwest (32.8), the West (27.8), and the Northeast (18.6). Rates of burglary victimization are typically higher in urban areas (41.9 burglaries per 1000) than in rural (27.8) and suburban (23.2) areas of the country.[16] Rented households are more likely to be victimized by burglary than households that are owned. Burglars can easily identify soft targets within rental properties and can carry out their activities in a more secretive fashion because they are better able to blend into the crowd. Furthermore, the mobility of residents within rental property areas creates more suitable targets. Victimization reports indicate that dwellings occupied for less than six months are victimized more often than homes occupied for five years or more.[17]

Research on Burglars and Burglary

Amateur burglars are typically unskilled and haphazard in their approach, and seek out targets that are close to where they live so as not to appear as a stranger. Furthermore, amateurs are more likely to seek a quick turnaround in terms of acquiring goods and selling to get cash. They will tend to offend when the need arises, which can be often depending upon the lifestyle they are leading.

Professional burglars are fairly competent and skilled in their abilities to assess a potential target and successfully carry out the act. They gain a certain amount of profit from their activities and are better at eluding law enforcement than amateurs.

Professional burglars have a certain reputation within the criminal subculture that allows them to obtain information quickly on potential targets. It must be stated that burglars are not necessarily loners in their illegal activities. Residential burglars in particular are known to work in groups, gaining information, assessing the attractiveness of a target, and carrying out the offense. A "good" burglar is an individual who can get along well with others within a group's context; this is crucial given the way in which many of these offenses are carried out.[18]

Current research has focused attention on women's involvement in burglary. Research reveals that women tend to fall into two categories: accomplices and partners. Female accomplices tend to play subservient roles in the burglary event and are more likely to be the lookout or driver. Female partners in the burglary event participate as "equals" and the tasks are usually divided equally among the male and female offenders. Males and females in the research conducted by Scott Decker and associates were often introduced to the burglary scene by older friends, family members, or street associates.[19]

There is also indication from research findings that men and women are both motivated to commit burglaries for financial gain and to help finance a party-type lifestyle filled with drugs and other activities. Females, however, did note that some of their financial gain went to support their children, while males utilized the financial gain to pursue sexual conquests. There was variation in the way in which males and females selected targets. Males were more likely to have a job (e.g., cable television installer, construction worker, or gardener) that provided information on potential targets. Females, on the other hand, were unable to access information on such a scale and relied on information from their male counterparts in the social network of burglars.[20]

Offender-based research on burglars indicates that the burglary transaction is usually done quickly and haphazardly with little planning involved. Furthermore, burglars who continue their offending often do so because of the low risk of being caught and the possibility of a monetary benefit. This monetary benefit assists in providing support for many offenders' drug habits. Although monetary gain may be the central motivation for many burglars, the decision-making process of the burglar is often influenced by a number of environmental factors. Burglars engage in what is known as *target selection*: assessing whether a residence is suitable to burglarize. According to Cromwell and associates, burglars weigh the following factors when assessing a target[21]:

1. <u>Occupancy cues</u>: *Occupancy cues* indicate whether a home is vacant. These cues include lights on in the house, cars parked in the driveway, and people coming in and out of the residence.

2. <u>Surveillability cues</u>: *Surveillability cues* include ecological factors such as the amount of lighting or shrubbery around a home. Offenders tend to seek out properties that have poor lighting and are isolated from other homes on the street.

3. <u>Accessibility cues</u>: *Accessibility cues* reflect the ease with which a burglar might enter the dwelling itself. Burglars look for homes with an open window or door and tend to avoid homes that may have an alarm system, a dog that could bark upon entry, or complex locks.[22]

Successfully entering a home, of course, is only part of the crime. The offender must then decide whether to take the stolen goods and keep them or, as is usually the case, sell the stolen property and convert them into cash. In many urban areas where burglaries occur, an **underground economy** often exists and thrives.[23] This system allows burglars to transform goods acquired in a burglary into cash and then trade them for drugs. The *professional fence* — the specialist who buys and sells stolen goods — is a main player in the underground economy.[24] Fences may participate in a wider operation, known as a *stolen property system,* in which burglars, thieves, and fences work together to ensure that their criminal activities are profitable for all parties.[25] It is important to note that individuals who knowingly come to possess stolen goods could be held accountable if caught by the police. It is unlawful to possess stolen property. The crime of *receiving stolen property* has a slightly different definition in each state, but is similar to the one used in the Maine Criminal Code: An individual is guilty of the offense when he or she "receives, retains or disposes of the property of another knowing it has been stolen, or believing it has been stolen."[26] This can be problematic for prosecutors because it must be proven that the person with the property knew it was illegally obtained.

LINK Chapter 9 explores the career criminal, including the professional thief and the fence, in more detail.

Response to Burglary

Burglaries have considerably low clearance rates. According to the FBI, law enforcement agencies in 2004 cleared only 12.9% of the nation's burglary offenses.[27] Law enforcement officials face significant hurdles when attempting to investigate burglaries, including the lack of physical evidence, the victim's inability to identify what was taken, and the amount of time needed to investigate the crime. Especially problematic to police is the fact that other burglaries may have been carried out by the same offender who leads a criminal career lifestyle, and it takes time to investigate a series of burglaries, connect the leads, balance the caseloads before them, and relate evidence.

Because the police cannot patrol every street, burglary prevention relies on community education (i.e., teaching people how to make their homes and businesses less attractive targets for would-be burglars). Neighborhood Watch programs have also been created to reduce the incidence of property crimes. These groups of neighbors and business owners actively patrol their towns and report suspicious activity to the local law enforcement agency.

Arson

Arson is traditionally defined as "any willful or malicious burning or attempting to burn, with or without intent to defraud, a dwelling house, public building, motor vehicle or aircraft, personal property, etc."[28] The UCR categorizes the types of structures that are damaged by arson as structural, mobile, and other. Arson accounts for hundreds of millions of dollars in property damage each year. The crime of arson is a more intense form of property crime given the fact that it can cause so much damage (TABLE 12-3). Often this damage is uncontrollable, because once the fire is set the offender does not always realize the amount of potential damage that can be done if the fire spreads to other dwellings or buildings. The destructive nature of the crime can cause serious social trauma and family disruption as well as the loss of property. Arsonists are treated more harshly by the criminal justice system, having longer sentences imposed upon them when compared to other property crime offenders.[29]

According to the UCR, in 2004 the burning of structures such as homes, apartments, business

TABLE 12-3
Intentionally Set Fires

- An estimated 36,500 intentionally set structure fires occurred in 2004, a slight decrease of 2.7%.
- Intentionally set fires in structures resulted in 320 civilian deaths, an increase of 4.9% from the previous year.
- Intentionally set structure fires also resulted in $714,000,000 in property loss, an increase of 3.2% from the previous year.
- 36,000 intentionally set vehicle fires occurred, an increase of 18.0%, and caused $165,000,000 in property damage, an increase of 25.0%.

Source: M. Karter. *Fire Loss in the United States During 2004: Full Report* (Quincy, MA: National Fire Protection Association, 2005).

properties, storage facilities, and schools accounted for 44.5% of all arsons. The report also notes a decrease of 6.4% in arsons from 2003 to 2004; this reflects a downward trend in the number of arsons that began in the late 1970s.[30]

Nature and Extent of Arson

Arson is another crime committed mostly by males. In 2004, the UCR noted that males accounted for 83.5% of arson arrests. Of those arrested, over 50% were juveniles. Juveniles are more likely to target community or public buildings (e.g., churches, jails, or schools), a finding that reflects the expressive

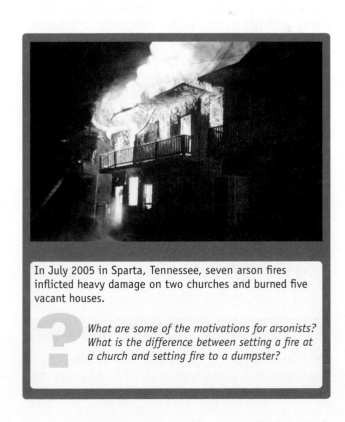

In July 2005 in Sparta, Tennessee, seven arson fires inflicted heavy damage on two churches and burned five vacant houses.

? *What are some of the motivations for arsonists? What is the difference between setting a fire at a church and setting fire to a dumpster?*

nature of this crime: Young offenders may use arson as a way to convey frustration. **TABLE 12-4** lists common motiviations for arson. The majority of individuals arrested for arson (67.6%) are under the age of 25; whites make up 77.0% of all persons arrested for arson.[31]

Research on Arson and Arsonists

Along with arson, there are other actions taken by individuals — especially juveniles — that although not legally defined as arson could possibly lead to the act of arson; these include fireplay and firesetting. A major focus in recent years has been on juvenile arson, and there is evidence that suggests that juvenile firesetting is a precursor to future incidents of arson.[32] These behaviors differ in the levels of intent and malice behind them. For juveniles, fireplay includes experimenting with fire out of curiosity and fascination; typically, the damage done is minimal. Deliberate firesetting, on the other hand, has a higher level of intent in terms of its damage. The significance here is that firesetting has the potential to do much more damage and be a threat to public safety.[33] Adults may also engage in deliberate firesetting — behavior that is roughly synonymous with arson, given the intent.

Hired torch is the term often used to describe the professional arsonist who is paid to set a fire for financial gain.[34] Hired torches are usually males between the ages of 30 and 50 with above-average intelligence and an impulsive or erratic lifestyle. They tend to be employed and have a criminal past with some arrests and convictions for a variety of offenses. Hired torches are motivated by economic incentive (often receiving a cut of the insurance check as part of the transaction) and can be loosely affiliated with other arsonists or other criminal enterprises.[35]

Pyromania is a relatively rare mental disorder. Afflicted individuals have an obsession with fires and firesetting, although not for material gain or with conscious motivation for their actions.[36] Pyromania was officially recognized in 1980 by the American Psychological Association as a disorder of impulse control.[37]

Larceny-Theft

The crime of larceny-theft entails a number of different actions taken on the part of an offender. The definition includes the unlawful taking, carrying,

TABLE 12-4
Common Motivations for Arson

- Financial reward
- To cover up another crime (e.g., about 1% of murders are carried out using fire as a method)[38]
- Political purposes
- Mixed motives (e.g., depression, as a cry for help, under the influence of alcohol)
- Mental disorder
- Revenge
- To get attention
- Sexual satisfaction or excitement

Source: H. Prins, G. Tennet, and K. Trick, "Motives for Arson (Fire Raising)," *Medicine, Science and the Law* 25: 275–278.

and leading or riding away of property from the possession of another; attempts to commit these acts are also included. The Uniform Crime Report includes shoplifting, pocket-picking, purse-snatching, thefts from motor vehicles, theft of motor vehicle parts and accessories, and bicycle thefts where there is no force, violence, or fraud involved. Larceny-theft can take two forms: grand larceny and petit (or petty) larceny. Grand larceny involves the theft of property worth over a certain amount of money, usually $300. Petit larceny involves the theft of property worth less than $300. The former is usually considered as felony and the latter a misdemeanor. Motor vehicle theft is considered an entirely different offense category (discussed later in this chapter).

The most common form of larceny is also the most difficult to study: the act of shoplifting. Shoplifting takes place every day in retail stores all over the world; however, a national survey of retailers indicated they only prosecute about 24% of shoplifters who are apprehended.[39] This is due in part to the fact that retailers are unlikely to call attention to their establishment and because they are able to get their merchandise back; they feel as though it is not worth the time and money to call the police and begin the arrest process.

Larceny-Theft Trends

In 2004, the UCR noted that larceny-theft accounted for over 67% of all property crimes known to the police. Trend data from 1995 and 2000 indicate a decline in the frequency of larceny-theft with an estimated 6,947,685 larceny-thefts occurring in 2004.[40] The NCVS also indicates a decrease in theft from 1995 to 2000.[41] (The NCVS accounts for those

Shoplifting is one of the most prevalent crimes and it costs retailers millions of dollars each year.

? *In your opinion, are males or females more likely to shoplift and why? What does the research tell us? Do you think you would be able to tell if someone was a shoplifter simply based on his or her age, race, or gender?*

under 25 years of age. More males were arrested for larceny-theft in 2004 and accounted for 61.7% of the arrestees. It is crucial to note that women make up 38.3% of those arrested.[43] This is noteworthy because there is no other offense for which the number of women arrested is even close to this mark (women made up 17.1% of those arrested for motor vehicle theft, 16.5% of those arrested for arson, and 14.3% of those arrested for burglary in 2004).[44] The numbers can be explained in part by women's heavy involvement in shoplifting.

Research on Larceny-Theft: A Focus on Shoplifting

Obvious among the motives of larceny-theft is financial gain. Juveniles may engage in theft as a means to acquire things they do not have or in a group setting to prove something to their peers. Adults have been known to steal to support drug habits, for financial gain, and because they enjoy the thrill of it. Self-report studies on shoplifting, police arrest records of shoplifters, and observation of shoplifters by researchers and security personnel are inconclusive when it comes to identifying a specific profile of a shoplifter based on race, gender, or even age.[45]

Research indicates that some shoplifting is the result of <u>kleptomania</u>, a psychological condition that compels those afflicted to steal, even when they have the money to pay for the item(s).[46]

Types of shoplifters include impulse, occasional, episodic, amateur, and semiprofessional.[47] *Impulse shoplifters* include kleptomaniacs who shoplift because of an uncontrollable urge to do so; they usually give little thought to what may happen if they are caught. *Occasional shoplifters* may be heavily influenced by peers and engage in the behavior out of boredom. *Episodic shoplifters* do so to satisfy specific needs, and they may also do so in a ritualistic fashion. These particular shoplifters may wrestle with serious psychological problems as the following account of an episodic shoplifter reveals:

> A pattern of stealing laxatives was present for about seven years. The person steals a bottle of laxative, drinks the entire bottle in a short time and suffers severe diarrhea for several hours. The episodes were triggered by contact with the person's mother.[48]

Those categorized as being *amateur shoplifters* shoplift when they are unwilling to pay for an item and see an opportunity arise. *Semiprofessional*

individuals who were victimized by theft, but accounts for it differently than the FBI. For one, the NCVS does not account for businesses that may have been victimized by shoplifters, thereby making the extent of the offense even more difficult to assess.)

The UCR noted that arrests for larceny-theft were up 1% in 2004 from the year before; arrests for juveniles declined while arrests for adults increased. In comparison with data for 1995, arrests for larceny-theft declined by 23.1%.[42]

Nature and Extent of Larceny-Theft

Larceny-theft is a heavily underreported crime. Therefore, the data presented must be understood as only part of the extent of this offense. Thefts from motor vehicles account for a majority of the offenses in the category of larceny-theft, followed by shoplifting. The cost of larceny-theft offenses was an estimated $5.1 billion in 2004. Of those arrested for larceny-theft offenses, a majority (53.8%) were *shoplifters* are those who steal in order to resell the goods for money.[49] Furthermore, it is crucial to understand the motivations that underlie some of these offenders. This understanding allows for better strategies to combat this underresearched phenomenon and can prove useful in the development of prevention strategies for store personnel and law enforcement. Cromwell and associates in their study of 320 shoplifters identify the following motivations for shoplifting[50]:

- The individual wanted the item but did not want to pay for it.
- The individual was pressured by his/her peers.
- Individuals in some instances steal for a living.
- The individual wanted the item but could not afford it.
- "I don't know why. It was an impulse thing."
- "I was under the influence of drugs or alcohol."
- "I enjoy the thrill/rush/danger involved."
- "I was under a lot of stress."
- "I can't help myself. It's compulsive."

Response to Shoplifting

Many people feel that the law enforcement response to shoplifting should be more aggressive; shoplifters are rarely caught and, if they are, they are not necessarily likely to be prosecuted or given an appropriate sanction. A study by Robert Kraut noted that shoplifters in the study felt they were less likely to be caught and, less likely to experience severe consequences if caught than nonshoplifters.[51] In another study, an experiment was devised to simulate a shoplifting incident. Only slightly more than one in four clerks observed the pilfering. Indeed, research shows that only about 10% of actual shoplifting cases are observed by store personnel. To compound the problem, store customers are usually unwilling to report cases.[52]

To reduce shoplifting, the retail industry has launched training programs, conducted awareness seminars, and pursued other strategies. For example, retail personnel are instructed in the basic characteristics of shoplifters and their typical methods of stealing. Some retailers have begun arranging sale items in a conspicuous place where surveillance is possible. Some stores attach tags to merchandise that trip a sound alarm as they leave designated areas. In addition, many sales clerks are instructed to require everyone to present a sales receipt before exchanging goods for cash.

From a mental health perspective, there is some movement toward recognizing that many shoplifters can benefit from counseling and treatment. Gail Caputo examined a sample of adults who were arrested for shoplifting and found that most were poor and uneducated and that they stole to improve their style of life.[53] The offenders benefited from their exposure to the program and, although the rate of recidivism was not reported, the author reported that the plan had been adopted by other mental health agencies.

Motor Vehicle Theft

<u>Motor vehicle theft</u> is defined as the theft or attempted theft of a motor vehicle (e.g., automobiles, trucks, buses, motorcycles, snowmobiles). What is excluded from this particular definition by the FBI is the taking of a motor vehicle for temporary use by persons having lawful access. In 2004, 1,237,114 motor vehicles were reported stolen — a decrease of 23,357 vehicles from 2003; **TABLE 12-5** lists the top ten most stolen vehicles in 2004. Overall in the United States, motor vehicle theft was down by 1.9%.[54] Victimization rates for motor vehicle theft also decreased for the same period, from 9.0 per 1000 in 2003 households to 8.8 per 1000 households in 2004.[55] Data suggest that ecological factors play a role in motor vehicle theft. More specifically, 40% to 50% of motor vehicle theft occurs close to one's place of residence.[56]

Research on Motor Vehicle Theft

Although a great many vehicles now have antitheft devices, research on auto thieves indicates that, for the most part, they are fairly competent at disarming security measures in cars.[57]

Dennis Challinger and Zachary Fleming have researched the motivations behind motor vehicle theft, including:[58]

1. Profit motives — including thefts for resale, chopping, stripping, and/or fraud; for juveniles, they may be part of a larger adult theft ring

2. Transportation motives — temporary acquisition for short-term or extended use, including use in the commission of other crimes

3. Recreation motives — temporary appropriation of automobiles for thrill and status seeking by young persons, also known as *joyriding*. One juvenile summarized his joyriding exploits this

TABLE 12-5
The Top Ten Most Stolen Vehicles in the United States for 2004
1. 1995 Honda Civic
2. 1989 Toyota Camry
3. 1991 Honda Accord
4. 1994 Dodge Caravan
5. 1994 Chevrolet full-size C/K 1500 Pickup
6. 1997 Ford F150 Pickup Series
7. 2003 Dodge Ram Pickup
8. 1990 Acura Integra
9. 1988 Toyota Pickup
10. 1991 Nissan Sentra

Source: National Insurance Crime Bureau, available at www.nicb.org/public/newsroom/hotwheels/index.cfm, accessed January 13, 2006.

People who steal cars may not be overly concerned about getting caught.

? *What are the motives for auto theft?*

way[59]: "It's not your car. You can do whatever you want, beat it up, go as fast as you want, bake the tires, do jumps."

This last statement offers some insight into the rationale for this behavior. Furthermore, research reveals that young offenders are not especially concerned about being caught and if they are caught, they are willing to pay the price even if it means incarceration. This fact is illustrated by the words of one 15-year-old in the study: "I think it's pretty much worth it. I've only spent two and a half months in jail and I have gotten away with hundreds [of auto thefts]."[60]

Forgery

Codified as a crime in 18th-century England, <u>forgery</u> is the production of a false or altered document or other item with the intent to defraud another individual. Forged items include paintings, passports, alien work forms, tracings, old baseball cards, checks, prescriptions, and transcripts. Forged artwork has had a particularly dramatic impact, causing insurance rates for paintings to skyrocket.

Common Types of Forgery

Passport Forgeries
A significant number of illegal aliens live and work in the United States, which accounts for a small amount of the country's total work force. Because of the economic opportunities in this country, there is a huge market for forged passports; a forged passport may cost the recipient more than a $1000. Customs agents confiscate thousands of counterfeit, forged, or illegal immigration documents each year at border stops throughout the United States. Needless to say, as long as there is a demand, there will always be a supply.

Medical Prescriptions
A medical prescription may be forged by changing either the drug name or the number of pills that the physician has prescribed. This can be done simply by adding a "0" to the number. As noted by the Office of National Drug Control Policy's Pulse Check, a major concern revolves around the drug OxyContin.[61] Sellers of this drug are known to either make their own prescription forms or steal prescription pads to write out their own prescription for the drug. By going from one druggist to another, this forger will be limited only by the number of pages left on the pad.

Checks

Most checks are written without the intent to defraud. Many have written a check in the hopes of "beating it to the bank." Some individuals, however, deliberately write checks in order to realize a financial benefit.

Check forgers are usually of higher-than-average intelligence and begin their criminal activity in their late twenties or early thirties.[62]

Edwin Lemert divided check forgers into two groups: naive and systematic.[63] *Naive* check forgers are the amateurs — often first-time offenders whose illegal behavior may have been precipitated by alcohol consumption (which may be a persistent problem) or a domestic argument. Frequently, their crimes are committed in an attempt to resolve a financial "crisis," so decisive intervention, sometimes in the form of counseling, may be an effective remedy. *Systematic* check forgers are the professionals. Although relatively few people make their living by passing bad checks (so-called *paper hangers*), those who do cost society many millions of dollars each year. In addition, professional criminals make money off businesses by using company account numbers. Often, they obtain these numbers by sorting through dumpsters looking for discarded bank account statements.

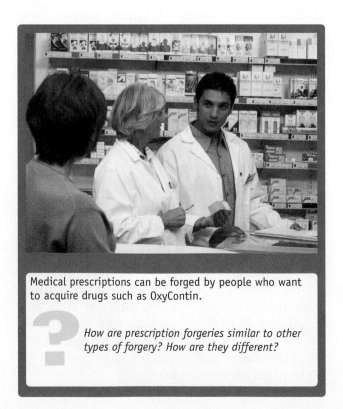

Medical prescriptions can be forged by people who want to acquire drugs such as OxyContin.

? *How are prescription forgeries similar to other types of forgery? How are they different?*

Check-cashing rings operating in many large cities also steal many millions of dollars each year. These rings steal payroll checks from companies and employ outsiders to cash the checks by posing as employees of the company. Sophisticated means are often utilized. For example, the ring may employ a check-writing machine to make letterhead checks and emboss the amount of the check.

Joseph Sheley reported that, in 1972, one out of four persons arrested for forging checks was a women.[64] He found increasing numbers of women shoppers who were writing *"cold"* or stolen checks to cover purchases.[65] This is a noteworthy trend because historically criminologists assumed that the "average" check forger was a white male who held a white-collar job and played no role in the criminal subculture. Criminologists may have to change their stereotype of the check forger and be willing to accept a different perspective on this type of criminal.

Combating Forgery

Determining exactly how much money is lost each year through forgeries is difficult. In 1985, there were 87,600 arrests for forgery. The naive check forger seldom goes to prison, and the admission rate for check forgers in correctional institutions other than jails is low — only 2%. The average stay is 26 months if sent to a minimum-security institution and 53 months if sent to a maximum-security institution. Still, the prognosis for successful rehabilitation of forgers is not encouraging. According to the Bureau of Justice Statistics, 74% of forgers were rearrested after they were released from prison; 59% were reconvicted; and 56% were reincarcerated.[66] These statistics hardly serve as a cause for optimism.

Perhaps other strategies and policies might bring this problem under control. For instance, to protect themselves, some businesses now require that check writers submit to a thumbprint test. The print is entered into a data file, and the check is cashed by the merchant only if the print matches the one on file.[67]

Another way to deter forgery is to authenticate signatures with computers. Digitizing signatures enables comparisons at the cash counter. Using data reduction techniques a coded description of a signature can be created, which can subsequently be used as the basis for authentication. This technique has proven effective in detecting falsified signatures.

Credit Card Fraud

As "plastic money" becomes a more integral part of society, the number of credit card frauds is bound to increase. In the early 1980s, credit card fraud resulted in losses of $30 million. By the end of the decade, losses amounted to $1 billion — a figure that is expected to double in the next few years.[68] The latest trends of credit card fraud include counterfeiting cards and altering stolen cards (**TABLE 12-6**).

Characteristics of Credit Card Fraud

Several factors explain the enormous rise in credit card fraud. First, more and more credit cards are being used. Second, it is easy to commit this crime. Third, not only does credit card fraud usually go undetected long after the criminal has completed the crime, but also law enforcement efforts are lax and state and federal laws are inadequate.

Because the victim is liable for only $50 of fraudulent charges, the public tends to believe that banks cover the losses. However, the real victim is the consumer, who will in some fashion compensate the credit card companies for the enormous amount of money lost each year.

Although is it easy to obtain a credit card in today's world, it is almost as easy to obtain someone else's. There are several ways. Thieves may acquire credit cards during the course of a robbery or burglary; pickpockets and purse snatchers often procure several cards when they commit their crimes; and prostitutes may go through their customers' belongings while the customer is otherwise engaged. In addition, sales personnel in department or grocery stores and gas stations are well positioned to obtain credit card numbers to make fraudulent purchases. The sad reality is that two-thirds of illegal purchases are made before the cardholder suspects that the card has been used fraudulently.[69] Indeed, the fraud may begin even before the card has been mailed to a cardholder; An employee of a credit card manufacturing facility might send a duplicate card to an accomplice, who then charges goods against the card before the original card reaches the intended customer.

Counterfeiting or altering cards is yet another method of procuring credit cards. The crude, home-made cards produced by amateur counterfeiters are fairly easy to recognize. However, professionals are quite adept at generating high-quality counterfeit cards; they may use photo offset equipment, silk screens, color copiers, and image transfers to produce the cards.

Combating Credit Card Fraud

Because of the huge amount of money that credit card fraud costs the business world (and perhaps in part because the personal liability is relatively small), companies know the importance of credit card fraud prevention. Thus seminars and workshops are conducted nationwide to combat the problem. The National Crime Prevention Institute (NCPI) of the University of Louisville, for example, offers advice to companies wishing to lower their risk. The NCPI recommends that businesses maintain current files on all credit card cancellations. Banking industry officials suggest that all credit cards be imprinted with a hologram, which make the cards much harder to counterfeit. They recommend that if the retailers do not see the hologram on the credit card, they should assume that it is a counterfeit and reject it.[70] Unless proactive measures are taken, credit card fraud will continue to be a major problem.

Identity Theft

Over the past decade, identity theft has become a serious problem in the United States. As technology has advanced, so too has the ability of savvy thieves to acquire someone's social security number and make life difficult for that victim. Law enforcement and criminologists face significant hurdles in coping with this crime. For law enforcement, the problem is centered on the investigation process. Police agencies are not well staffed and have few

TABLE 12-6
Forms of Credit Card Fraud

- Knowingly receiving stolen credit cards
- Using of the credit card without the cardholder's consent
- Using a revoked or canceled credit card
- Knowingly using a counterfeit or altered credit card
- Illegally using a credit card number
- Using an expired credit card
- Using an illegally held credit card to negotiate a check
- Receiving or possessing an illegally obtained credit card with intent to defraud
- Delivering or selling of an illegally obtained credit card

Source: Gardner, T. *Criminal Law: Principles and Cases* (St. Paul, MN: West, 1989): 417–418.

resources to combat such complex crimes; current efforts tend to be centered on typical street crime. Furthermore, the police who are assigned to such cases may feel overwhelmed by the intense investigation that has to take place. For those who research identity theft, the problem is the paucity of information in the field about identity thieves — who they are, how they operate, and how they get involved in such schemes. This section briefly examines the crime of identity theft in its known forms and provides recommendations on how victims can deal with it.

Techniques Used by Identity Thieves

Identity theft can be broadly defined as the unlawful acquisition and use of a person's personal identifying information. This can include a person's name, address, social security number, date of birth, mother's maiden name, or driver's license information. Identity thieves use a number of techniques to acquire information; some techniques are as simple as stealing wallets and purses or dumpster diving. **Dumpster diving** is the process whereby people sort through trash looking for personal information found on bills from credit cards, bank statements, medical records, or employment records.[71] More complex techniques include **skimming**, the process whereby offenders use computers to read and store the information encoded on the magnetic strip of an ATM or credit card. The information can be re-encoded onto any other card with a magnetic strip, changing the blank card into a machine-readable ATM or credit card identical to that of the victim.[72] The following is a list of common techniques used by identity thieves[73]:

- The imposter opens a new credit card account using the victim's name, date of birth, and social security number. The offender subsequently uses the entire credit line and, because there is no payment made, the delinquent account is recorded on the victim's credit report.
- The imposter calls the victim's credit card issuer and, pretending to be the victim, changes the mailing address on the account. The offender runs up the charges and, because the bills are not being mailed, the victim does not immediately realize a problem exists.
- The imposter establishes a cell phone account in the victim's name.
- The imposter opens a bank account in the victim's name and begins writing bad checks on the account.

- The imposter e-mails a request posing as the victim's Internet service provider (ISP), stating that the account information needs to be updated and/or that the credit card used to register is invalid or expired and that the information needs to be reentered to keep the account active.

The FBI does not keep accurate accounts of identity theft. The agency that provides the most accurate information on this crime is the Federal Trade Commission (FTC), which was charged to do so by the Identity Theft and Assumption Deterrence Act (1998). In 2000, 31,117 cases of identity theft were reported to the FTC; this rose to 86,198 in 2001 and then 161,819 in 2002.[74] As awareness of the crime increases, reports of victimization are likely to increase.

What Victims Can Do

The FTC advises victims of identity theft to take the following steps[75]:

- Place a *fraud alert* on your credit reports and review your credit reports. Fraud alerts can help prevent an identity thief from opening any more accounts in your name. Contact the toll-free fraud number of any of the three consumer reporting companies (Equifax, Experian, and TransUnion) to place a fraud alert on your credit report. You only need to contact one of the three companies to place an alert. The company you call is required to contact the other two, which will place an alert on their versions of your report as well.
- Close the accounts that you know (or believe) have been tampered with or opened fraudulently.
- File a report with your local police or the police in the community where the identity theft took place.
- File a complaint with the FTC. By sharing your identity theft complaint with the FTC, you will provide important information that can help law enforcement officials across the nation track down identity thieves and stop them.

Confidence Games

Confidence (or "con") *games* involve obtaining money or property by means of some trick, device, or swindling operation in which the swindler takes advantage of the confidence placed in him or her by the victim. *Swindlers,* or *con artists,* tend to target young people, women, and service personnel in inner cities, schools, and mass transit systems. Even people at home, however, are not immune to con games. Almost everyone is familiar with the help-wanted ads that offer the chance to make "big money in stuffing envelopes in their own home in their spare time." Often, these offers sound too good to be true — and they are. The catch is that to make money stuffing envelopes, the targets must secure their own customers; the ads make it sound like the ad agency will secure more customers than the target can handle.

Con games typically involve some type of get-rich-quick scheme. Con artists operate on the assumption that "there is a sucker born every minute" and there is a little bit of larceny in everyone. An essential element in many con games is the victim's willingness to take advantage of a third party. Thus, victims play a key role in their own victimization. The con artist should be considered a professional thief — a person committed to a life of crime. Con artists often see the conning as a legitimate enterprise. Starting later in life than other criminals, con artists are not affected by unemployment or economic downturns. Moreover, the older the offenders become, the more their skills improve. Some con artists, after retiring from a life of crime, start their own consulting businesses and advise banks and businesses how to cut down on con games.

There are two types of con games. The **short con** is a scheme to take as much of the victim's money as possible at one time (e.g., the pigeon drop or dropped wallet or purse). Many carnivals feature rigged games that are virtually impossible to win. Another short con preys on the grief of victims. The con artist reads newspaper death announce-ments each day. A week or two later, he goes door to door, from one mourning family to the next, to "deliver" (cash on delivery, of course) a Bible with the survivor's name embossed in gold on the front cover. His story is that the deceased had purchased this Bible only a day or two before passing away. What family member would not want to have this "very last gift" of the deceased?

The **long con** extends over a period of time and the take is typically much larger than in the short con. In a bankruptcy swindle, the con artist establishes a business, orders some sort of inventory, and quickly sells it off. He then declares bankruptcy before paying the bills, thus realizing large profits.

Confidence games take a variety of forms, including the following:

1. *Bank examiner scan:* Posing as an investigator, the con artist approaches someone who has a savings or checking account in a bank that has a "dishonest teller." The mark is asked to withdraw all of the money and give it to the "bank examiner." The mark is told he or she will be rewarded for helping in the investigation. Of course, after the mark is relieved of the money, the "bank examiner" disappears.

2. *Beggar scam:* The con poses as a down-and-out person, perhaps as someone who will work for food only. Often, he will carry photos of his "wife and kids back home" and give the mark a hard-luck story so the mark will feel sorry for him and give him money. A good con man can earn several hundred dollars a day this way.

3. *Coin game:* Also known as "pitching pennies," the con artist will weight his coins so that they have a better chance of staying against the wall.

4. *Currency con:* This involves asking a mark to make change for a $1 bill that has been altered on the corners with $10 bill markings. The con can go to a bank to exchange the partially mutilated bills for new ones.

5. *Dice con:* This is a favorite game for many con artists because the dice are smaller and can easily be hidden. The experienced con artist knows the odds of the game and the special techniques that can be used to gain an unfair advantage.

6. *Double shot:* Here, the mark is victimized at least twice. After the initial scam, the victim is contacted by another con artist who poses as a police officer investigating the con. The mark is told to give the rest of his money to the "police officer" for protection. The officer and the money are never seen again.

7. *Home repair scam:* The elderly homeowner is a favorite target for this scam. The con man, often wearing a company uniform, gives a low "free estimate" to the homeowner for work that needs to be done around the home. Once the estimate is accepted and a deposit laid down, the con man disappears.

8. *Merchandise swindle:* This involves the sale of "merchandise" in sealed boxes. For example, the con artist might show a "sample" TV to a mark, tell the mark that so-and-so is going out of business, and offer the mark a great deal on a TV. Later, the mark learns that the box contains nothing but rocks.

9. *Pigeon drop:* This is one of the oldest of all cons. One con artist approaches a mark on the street and chats for a few moments. Then an accomplice approaches the two and claims to have found a large amount of money. He offers to share this money with them if they will both put up some "good faith" money. The mark is driven to the bank and given the money to hold, which shows the con's "faith" in the mark. When the mark gives the cons his money, a switch is made. The mark will find that the "money" is only shredded paper.

10. *Shell game:* This is another old con game. The con man has three shells and a pea, which he places under one of the shells. After the pea is moved from one shell to another by rapid hand movements, the mark must guess which shell the pea is under, losing a bet, of course, if he is wrong. Actually, the shell game is a sleight-of-hand trick, and the mark never really has a chance of winning.

11. *Store clerk game:* In this particularly interesting scam, a well-dressed con artist, posing as a sales clerk, will approach a shopper waiting in line and offer to take the merchandise and the money (or credit card) to another register. Instructing the customer to remain in the line, the con artist disappears with the merchandise and the money. This con is particularly effective during busy shopping times.

Most of these con games play to the mark's perception of "easy money" to be had.

No one knows how much is lost each year through confidence games, but estimates run into the million of dollars. Even this may be a low esti-

Con games can take many forms, including door-to-door scams.

What scams could be conducted via the door-to-door method?

mate because many victims never report the incident. To avoid being the victim of a con game, it is important not to trust anyone who promises a deal that is too good to be true; do not put up "good faith money." In addition, individuals or businesses that promise an unusual return on an investment should be thoroughly investigated. Finally, individuals should be aware of scams in their area as they are reported by the media. Education is probably the best defense against con games.

Conclusion

This chapter covers a variety of property crimes, all of which have unique characteristics in terms of the way they are defined by law, the way in which they are committed, who commits them, and the response by law enforcement and other agencies. A common theme among the property crimes in this chapter is the instrumental motive of acquiring money or property through illegal means. Unfortunately, many property crimes are not high on the list of police priorities because they tend to be less serious than drug-related offenses and violent crimes. Research in the area of property crime is expanding and promises to help law enforcement track and stop offenders.

WRAP UP

Curbing Identity Theft

The task force should consist of state, local, and federal law enforcement agents. At the federal level, the FBI and the National White Collar Crime Center could provide important information about identity theft. Another possible member might be an ex-offender who had been convicted of identity theft. Such a person would know common techniques used to victimize citizens. The first line of activity is to study the nature of the problem in the location where you live. How has the crime been committed? Who have been the targets? What methods have been used to entrap them? A sting operation could be beneficial. Perhaps a member of the task force could pose as an unsuspecting victim to capture information about offenders operating in the area. Stings have the potential plus of catching offenders "red-handed." The drawback to sting operations is that they have to be carefully conducted so that the alleged offenders are not "entrapped" — that is, enticed to commit acts that they normally would not do.

Chapter Spotlight

- Major property crimes include burglary, arson, larceny-theft, and motor vehicle theft.

- Property crime rates have decreased since the 1980s; victimization rates have also declined. Property crimes are committed mainly by adult males.

- Home ownership and residential mobility play a role in the amount of victimization that takes place among households in the United States.

- Burglaries occur in both residential dwellings and businesses and most involve forceful entry. Research on burglary indicates that burglars may consider certain factors before carrying out the act itself. Included in these factors are the accessibility of the dwelling and a number of environmental factors (e.g., lighting, shrubbery, security devices). Burglary poses a challenge to law enforcement investigators and as a result has low clearance rates.

- Research on arson suggests that there are many motives for this crime. Arsonists are usually treated more harshly by the criminal justice system than other property crime offenders.

- Larceny-theft is one of the most prevalent forms of property crime and accounts for millions of dollars in money and property that is unlawfully taken each year. It includes acts of shoplifting, pocket-picking, and purse snatching.

- The major focus of research on larceny and theft is in the area of shoplifting. No evidence exists to suggest that there is one identifiable shoplifter based on age, race, or gender.

- Research on motor vehicle theft indicates that offenders steal cars for financial reward, but they may also do so for the thrill of the experience.

- Most instances of forgery, credit card fraud, and identity theft are motivated by the desire for financial gain. Identity theft has taken center stage in recent years as many unknowing people fall victim to the offense.

Putting It All Together

1. What may make a home or dwelling a less suitable target for burglars? How might this help law enforcement?

2. Discuss the idea that a relationship exists between the technology of a society and the character of its property crime. Can you think

of some examples that would substantiate this statement?

3. Why is it difficult to get a true picture of the extent of shoplifting that takes place in the United States?

4. Why are the clearance rates for burglary so low? What can law enforcement do to increase clearance rates?

5. Discuss the advantages and disadvantages of using the National Crime Victimization Survey to understand the extent of burglary.

6. What are the various forms of larceny-theft identified by the Uniform Crime Report? Is there anything that you think should be included or excluded? Explain.

7. Discuss the difference between dumpster diving and skimming. Which do you believe to be more common and why?

8. What common elements do con games share? Con game victims?

9. What accounts for the large percentage of women arrested for larceny-theft?

Key Terms

accessibility cues Indications such as an open window or an unlocked door that will allow burglars to enter the dwelling.

arson The unlawful use of fire or explosives to destroy property.

breaking and entering Synonymous with burglary; still used in certain criminal codes in the United States.

burglary The unlawful entry into any building or vehicle in order to commit a felony or larceny.

credit card fraud Counterfeiting plastics, altering stolen credit cards, or simply using a stolen credit card.

dumpster diving A low skill practice of identity thieves that involves sorting through garbage for other people's personal information to be utilized unlawfully.

fireplay Term used to describe the experimentation with fire out of curiosity and fascination.

firesetting Term used to describe the purposeful and willful setting of a fire that can have the potential for significant damage.

forgery The production of a false or altered document or other item in order to defraud another individual.

grand larceny Theft of property worth over a certain amount, usually $300.

hired torch A professional who is employed to set a fire for financial gain.

identity theft The unlawful acquisition and use of an individual's personal information.

kleptomania An obsessive impulse to steal; kleptomaniacs often steal objects that they do not need and could afford to pay for.

larceny-theft The unlawful taking or attempted taking of property from another person.

long con A scheme extending over a period of time; the "take" is typically much larger than in other cons.

motor vehicle theft The theft or attempted theft of a motor vehicle.

occupancy cues Indications for burglars that signal whether a dwelling is occupied.

petit larceny The theft of property worth less than $300.

pyromania The obsessive impulse to set fires with no conscious motivation.

shoplifting The taking and/or carrying away of goods without an intent to pay.

short con A scheme to take as much of a victim's money as possible at one time.

skimming The process whereby offenders use computers to read and store the information encoded on the magnetic strip of an ATM or credit card.

surveillability cues Indications to burglars they can proceed to the dwelling without being detected.

trespassing Knowingly entering a dwelling and remaining there unlawfully.

underground economy A social network that allows thieves and burglars to transform goods into cash.

Notes

1. Richard T. Wright and Scott Decker, *Burglars on the Job: Streetlife and Residential Burglary.* (Boston: Northeastern University Press, 1994): 60.
2. Federal Bureau of Investigation, U.S. Department of Justice (2005). *Crime in the United States, 2004* (Washington, DC: Government Printing Office).
3. Terance Miethe and Robert Meier, *Crime and Its Social Context: Toward an Integrated Theory of Offenders, Victims and Situations* (Albany: State University of New York Press, 1994); Terance Miethe, Michael Hughes, and David McDowall, "Social Change: An Evaluation of Alternative Theoretical Approaches," *Social Forces* 70 (1991): 165–185.
4. Federal Bureau of Investigation, 2005.
5. Ibid.
6. Shannon M. Catalano, *Criminal Victimization, 2004* (Washington, DC, U.S. Department of Justice, 2005).
7. Paul Cromwell, James Olson, and D'Aunn Wester Avary, *Breaking and Entering: An Ethnographic Analysis of Burglary* (Beverly Hills, CA: Sage, 1991).
8. Ibid.
9. Paul Cromwell, James Olson, and D'Aunn Wester Avary, "Decision Strategies of Residential Burglars," in Paul Cromwell, ed., *In Their Own Words: Criminals on Crime,* 2nd ed. (Los Angeles: Roxbury, 1999): 50–56.
10. Catalano, 2005.
11. Callie Rennison. U.S. Department of Justice, Office of Justice Programs, Bureau of Justice Statistics, *Criminal Victimization in the United States, 2002* (Washington, DC: U.S. Department of Justice, 2003).
12. Federal Bureau of Investigation, 2005.
13. Catalano, 2005.
14. Federal Bureau of Investigation, 2005.
15. Robert Davis, Arthur Lurigio, and Wesley Skogan, *Victims of Crime* (Thousand Oaks, CA: Sage, 1997).
16. Catalano, 2005.
17. Dean Dabney, *Crime Types* (Belmont, CA: Wadsworth, 2004): 174.
18. Neal Shover, "The Social Organization of Burglary," *Social Problems* 20 (1972): 499–514.
19. Scott Decker, Richard Wright, Allison Redfern, and Dietrich

Smith, "A Woman's Place Is in the Home: Females and Residential Burglary," *Justice Quarterly* 10 (1993): 143–162; Christopher Mullins and Richard Wright, "Gender, Social Networks, and Residential Burglary," *Criminology* 41 (2003): 813–839.
20. Ibid.
21. Paul Cromwell, James Olson, and D'Aunn Wester Avary, *Breaking and Entering: An Ethnographic Analysis of Burglary* (Beverly Hills, CA: Sage, 1991).
22. Dabney, 2004.
23. Stuart Henry, *The Hidden Economy: The Context and Control of Borderline Crime* (London: M. Robertson, 1978).
24. Carl Klockars, *The Professional Fence* (New York: Free Press, 1974).
25. Marilyn Walsh and Duncan Chappell, "Operational Parameters in the Stolen Property System," *Journal of Criminal Justice* 2 (1974):113–146.
26. Maine Criminal Code, Title 17-A, Section 359, available at http://janus.state.me.us/legis/statutes/17-A/title17-Ach0sec0.html, accessed January 30, 2006.
27. Uniform Crime Reports, *Crime in the United States, 2004.*
28. Ibid. p. 61.
29. U.S. Department of Justice, Office of Justice Programs, Bureau of Justice Statistics, *Federal Compendium of Federal Justice Statistics, 2002,* September 2004. NCJ 205368.
30. Uniform Crime Reports, *Crime in the United States, 2004.*
31. Ibid.
32. Adam Brett, "Kindling Theory in Arson: How Dangerous Are Firesetters?" *Australian and New Zealand Journal of Psychiatry* 38 (2004): 419–425.
33. Charles Putnam and John Kirkpatrick (2005). Juvenile Firesetting: A Research Overview. Juvenile Justice Bulletin, U.S. Department of Justice, Office of Justice Programs, Office of Juvenile Justice and Delinquency Prevention. (Washington, DC: Government Printing Office).
34. Wayne Bennett and Karen Hess, *Investigating Arson* (Springfield, IL: Charles C Thomas, 1984).
35. Anthony Rider, "The Firesetter: A Psychological Profile," *FBI Law Enforcement Bulletin* 49 (1980): 7–13.
36. Bennett and Hess, 1984.

37. American Psychiatric Association, *Diagnostic and Statistical Manual of Mental Disorders,* 3rd ed. (Washington, DC: American Psychiatric Association, 1980).

38. Uniform Crime Reports, *Crime in the United States, 2004.*

39. Richard Hollinger and Jason Davis, *2000 National Retail Security Survey, Final Report* (Gainesville, FL: University of Florida, 2002).

40. Uniform Crime Reports, *Crime in the United States, 2004.*

41. Bureau of Justice Statistics, *Criminal Victimization, 2004.*

42. Uniform Crime Reports, *Crime in the United States, 2004.*

43. Bureau of Justice Statistics, *Criminal Victimization, 2004.*

44. Ibid.

45. Lloyd Klemke, *The Sociology of Shoplifting: Boosters and Snitches Today.* (Westport, CT: Praeger, 1992); David Farrington, "Measuring, Explaining and Preventing Shoplifting: A Review of British Research," *Security Journal* 12 (1999): 9–27; Dean Dabney, Richard Hollinger, and Laura Dugan, "Who Actually Steals? A Study of Covertly Observed Shoplifters," *Justice Quarterly* 21 (2004): 693–728.

46. American Psychiatric Association, 1980.

47. Dabney, 2004.

48. Richard Moore, "Shoplifting in Middle America: Patterns and Motivational Correlates," *International Journal of Offender Therapy and Comparative Criminology,* 28 (1984): 53–64.

49. Dabney, 2004, 215.

50. Paul Cromwell, Lee Parker, and Shawna Mobley, "The Five-Finger Discount: An Analysis of Motivations for Shoplifting," in Paul Cromwell, ed., *In Their Own Words: Criminals on Crime,* 2nd ed. (Los Angeles: Roxbury, 1999): 57–70.

51. Robert Kraut, "Deterrent and Definitional Influences on Shoplifting, *Social Problems* 25 (1976): 358–68.

52. Erhard Blankenburg, "The Selectivity of Legal Sanctions: An Empirical Investigation of Shoplifting," *Law and Society Review* 11 (1976): 109–129; Michael Hindelang, "Decisions of Shoplifting Victims to Invoke the Criminal Justice Process," *Social Problems* 21 (1974): 580–593.

53. Gail Caputo, "Program of Treatment for Adult Shoplifters," *Journal of Offender Rehabilitation* 27 (1998): 123–137.

54. Uniform Crime Reports, *Crime in the United States, 2004.*

55. Bureau of Justice Statistics, *Criminal Victimization, 2004.*

56. Bureau of Justice Statistics, *Criminal Victimization, 2003.*

57. Ronald Clark and Patricia Harris. "Auto Theft and its Prevention," in Michael Tonry, ed., *Crime and Justice, An Annual Review of Research,* Volume 16 (Chicago: University of Chicago Press, 1995): 1–54.

58. Dennis Challinger, "Car Security Hardware — How Good is It?" in *Car Theft: Putting the Brakes on, Proceedings of Seminar on Car Theft* (Sydney: National Roads and Motorists' Association and The Australian Institute of Criminology, 1987); Zachary Fleming, "The Thrill of It All," in Paul Cromwell, ed., *In Their Own Words: Criminals on Crime,* 2nd ed. (Los Angeles: Roxbury, 1999): 71–79.

59. Ibid., 77.

60. Ibid., 78.

61. Office of National Drug Control Policy, *Pulse Check: Trends in Drug Abuse,* Washington, DC, 2001, NCJ 191248.

62. Hugh Barlow, *Introduction to Criminology,* 5th ed. (Glenview, IL: Scott Foresman/Little Brown, 1987).

63. Edwin Lemert, "An Isolation and Closure Theory of Naive Check Forgery," *Journal of Criminal Law and Police Science* 44 (1953): 297–298.

64. Joseph Sheley, *Exploring Crime: Readings in Criminology and Criminal Justice* (Belmont, CA: Wadsworth, 1987).

65. Joseph Sheley, *America's "Crime Problem": An Introduction to Criminology* (Belmont, CA: Wadsworth, 1985).

66. Katherine M. Jamieson and Timothy Flanagan, *Sourcebook on Criminal Justice Statistics* (Washington, D.C.: U.S. Government Printing Office, 1988).

67. Joseph Mele, *National Crime Prevention Institute* (Louisville, KY: 1992).

68. Sue Reid, *Criminology* (New York: Macmillan, 1992).

69. Hugh Barlow, 1987.

70. ABA Banking Journal (1986): 60-64.

71. Katherine Slosarik, "Identity Theft: An Overview of the Problem," *The Justice Professional* 15 (2002): 329–343.

72. Stuart Allison, Amie Shuck, and Kim Lersch, "Exploring the Crime of Identity Theft: Prevalence, Clearance Rates, and Victim/Offender Characteristics," *Journal of Criminal Justice* 33 (2005): 19–29.

73. Ibid., 20.

74. Federal Trade Commission, "Fraud Complaint and Identity Theft Victims by State," available at http://www.consumers.gov/sentinel/trends.htm, accessed January 6, 2006.

75. Federal Trade Commission, available at http://www.consumer.gov/idtheft, accessed January 6, 2006.

WWW.CRIMINOLOGY.JBPUB.COM

Interactivities
In the News
Key Term Explorer
Web Links

OBJECTIVES

Examine how moral entrepreneurship relates to public order offenses.

Understand the concept of "victimless" crime.

Discuss the broken windows theory as a method to explain public order offenses.

Examine how the moralistic perspective is used to examine both prostitution and gambling.

Examine how the law-and-order perspective is used to examine both prostitution and gambling.

Public Order Crimes

##

> *For the criminal law at least, man has an inalienable right to go to hell in his own fashion, provided he does not directly injure the person or property of another on the way. The criminal law is an inefficient instrument for imposing the good life on others.*
>
> — Norval Morris and Gordon Hawkins[1]

Combating Prostitution

In your community, a grassroots effort is being made to enforce the vice rules as they pertain to prostitution. Community leaders are committed to enforcing all laws. The religious community, which is a considerable force in your area, is demanding that law enforcement officials arrest all prostitutes and their customers, and make a special effort to notify the marriage partners of all "johns." Many others, including a core of politicians, have also voiced their approval of any and all efforts to carry out the plans for combating prostitution.

The leaders of this movement have asked you as a criminologist to offer a plan to fight the prostitution problem in your community.

What would be your basic plan from (1) the moral perspective? (2) the law-and-order perspective?

What would be the benefits and liabilities of notification of spouses or parties of the "johns"?

Introduction

It is not easy to precisely define public order crimes because the term is used to refer to a diverse collection of offenses. There is no standard list of public order crimes. Although these offenses are generally considered to be less serious than the major index crimes, they can have important effects on public health and safety, the economy, and public perception about the quality of life in a neighborhood or community.

In **TABLE 13-1**, examples of public order offenses are grouped by two basic perspectives: (1) morality and (2) law and order. Both aim to protect the public, but their concerns are different. The morality perspective seeks to use the criminal law to impose minimum standards of morality on citizens. Here, the laws defining offenses against public morality set standards for acceptable behavior. Examples include crimes of vice, such as prostitution, illegal gambling, and drug use. The law-and-order perspective views the enforcement of these laws as a way to maintain peace in the community. The enforcement of these laws sends a clear message that these dangerous behaviors will not be tolerated. These crimes make the public feel uneasy and unsafe and may even promote the occurrence of more serious offenses. However, these classifications are somewhat arbitrary. For example, driving while intoxicated (DWI) is a moral as well as a safety issue. Similarly, prostitution and illegal drug use constitute criminal offenses and also impact public health.

Another criminological perspective views public order offenses in a different way. Because the participants in these activities do not complain to the police, they are often referred to as **victimless crimes** — crimes that affect only the person committing them. Because of the absence of a complaining victim, some people question whether it is appropriate to label activities such as gambling and prostitution as crimes. However, the "victimless" label is controversial. Often, there are third parties who are harmed by these behaviors (e.g., the families of drug addicts). These acts affect a significant number of people and are disruptive to members of society. For example, the father who is a compulsive gambler hurts both himself and his family when he gambles away his weekly paycheck. Many people also feel that acts such as prostitution are a threat to the moral fabric of American society and thus are harmful to all.

In addition, questions exist about whether the participation of some (e.g., prostitutes) actually is completely consensual and whether prostitution is itself a form of victimization. In addition, many of these activities result in social ills, such as the spread of disease, addiction, and lost work productivity.[2] Historically, however, the laws prohibiting them originated with concerns about upholding moral standards.

Some criminologists feel that enforcement of public order offenses cause rather than prevent

TABLE 13-1	
Public Order Crimes	
Morality Perspective	**Law-and-Order Perspective**
Prostitution	Public intoxication
Gambling	Driving while intoxicated
Sodomy	Reckless driving
Obscenity (Pornography)	Selling alcohol to minors
Drug use and trafficking	Weapons possession
Incest	Public urination/defecation
Bigamy and polygamy	Disturbing the peace
	Unlawful assembly
	Disorderly conduct
	Panhandling
	Loitering
	Vagrancy
	Vandalism

problems for society. For example, Norval Morris and Gordon Hawkins believe that the "<u>overreach of the criminal law</u>" to attempt to govern such behaviors causes a number of secondary problems that aggravate the crime problem[3]:

1. Where the supply of goods or services is concerned (e.g., drugs, gambling, and prostitution), the criminal law acts as a "crime tariff," which makes the supply of such goods and services profitable for the criminal by driving up prices and at the same time discourages competition by those who might enter the market were it legal.

2. This leads to the development of large-scale organized criminal groups and provides them with the funds to expand other criminal enterprises in which they engage.

3. Criminal prohibition and law enforcement help to drive up the cost of drugs and thus cause persons to engage in crime in order to support their habit.

4. It leads to the growth of a criminal subculture that is subversive and does not support social order.

5. It depletes the time, energy, and manpower available for dealing with the crime problem.

6. The enforcement of such laws contributes to two major problems for the police. First, it promotes corruption because the police are bribed to ignore crimes such as drug use and prostitution. Second, the enforcement of these laws often leads the police to employ illegal means of law enforcement to capture offenders.

Therefore, Morris and Hawkins feel that the unwarranted extension of the criminal law into public order offenses is "expensive, unwarranted, and criminogenic." The law should not "intervene or attempt to regulate the private moral conduct of the citizen."[4]

In sum, public order offenses strain the relationship between law and morality more than other kinds of crimes. Here, the aim of enforcement is societal protection and crime prevention, but it is often difficult to establish and maintain a clear focus on these goals. With major crimes such as robbery or assault, it is evident that a victim has been harmed and violated by the offender. This relationship is less apparent in crimes such as prostitution, pornography, gambling, and drug use.

In addition to reviewing some of the various types of public order offenses, this chapter briefly discusses three issues relevant to criminal justice policy: the relationship between law and morality; the relationship between public order and more serious crime; and the question of whether enforcement of these laws amounts to discrimination against the poor. Consideration of the theoretical bases for the morality and law-and-order perspectives helps clarify the differences between them concerning the purpose of enforcing laws against public order offenses.

The Morality Perspective

Moral Entrepreneurs

It has often been repeated that "you can't legislate morality," yet people tend to assume that the law is grounded in and properly reflects moral standards for society. The major or index crimes tend to reflect a high level of agreement as to what is morally right and wrong. People generally agree that murder and robbery are illegal because they are morally wrong. Some research has even shown considerable consistency across such culturally different societies as the United States, India, Indonesia, and Iran.[5] Such widespread agreement is referred to as **consensus**. Compared with the index or major crimes, there is weaker consensus about the morality of public order crimes. Although some people question particular details of the law or disagree about whether a particular killing was justifiable, no one seriously advocates that murder should be legal.

In comparison, 34% of the public believes that marijuana use should be legal.[6] There is very little chance that a movement to decriminalize armed robbery will arise, but there are organizations that advocate for the decriminalization or legalization of marijuana.[7] The fact that some public order crimes are not universally condemned as immoral raises questions about the relationship between law and morality.

Religion, particularly the Judeo-Christian tradition in the West, has been the source of much of the morality expressed in legal codes. Thus, the criminal law against theft reflects the Biblical injunction "Thou shalt not steal." To some extent, the **legitimacy** of the law — the belief in the rightness of the law, public support for the law — was grounded in the presumed connection to religious ideas. However, most laws that originated in religious beliefs have purposes that can be identified and supported in secular terms.[8] Christians, Jews, Muslims, and atheists can all agree that murder is immoral and should be illegal — however, the direct connection between religion and law eroded as society became more secular and diverse.

Sometimes individuals or groups mobilize to create or enforce rules based on their particular values. Persons who take such a stance have been termed *moral entrepreneurs.* They concern themselves with the moral well-being of society, appointing themselves as watchdogs who seek to maintain "honorable" standards for all. They presume that they serve the community by protecting its virtue.[9] This situation causes considerable law enforcement problems. Moral entrepreneurs can have considerable influence because they help make the laws and determine their enforcement. However, enforcing morality poses tremendous, and perhaps insurmountable, problems for the police. Enforcing morality laws requires the police to use undercover operations that can lead to legal issues such as entrapment. Enforcing laws against prostitution requires police officers to pose either as clients or prostitutes and thus leads to the same legal and even ethical problems of enforcement. Unlike other crimes where there is a complaining victim, these crimes require the police to catch someone in the act and do more than simply respond to a call for service.

Moral entrepreneurs also raise public awareness about certain behaviors and demand that something be done about it. Mothers Against Drunk Driving (MADD) have publicized facts about alcohol-related

A Mothers Against Drunk Driving rally.

? *Are members of MADD moral entrepreneurs?*

automobile fatalities and pressured politicians to enact more stringent laws against driving while intoxicated. Laws requiring the use of seatbelts and prohibiting gambling largely resulted from the efforts of moral entrepreneurs and special interests rather than public demand. Such efforts have a long history in both North America and England.

The Puritans who settled the Massachusetts Bay Colony acted as moral entrepreneurs, writing their religious doctrine into law. They believed that the purpose of the law was to deter and punish sin and uphold the patriarchal family. Thus, Puritan law strictly regulated sexual behavior and criminalized nonproductive pleasurable pursuits such as gambling and sports. Many of these ideas were written into the statutes of the various states after the American Revolution. Perhaps most exemplary of the Puritan influence are the laws regulating sexual behaviors, such as fornication and sodomy, and the "blue laws" that prohibited or restricted certain activities and the sale of goods on Sunday. These persisted until recently; in fact, remnants exist in some states, notably the prohibition against selling alcohol on Sunday. Sometimes the law reflects the efforts of interest groups as well as moral entrepreneurs. For example, organized labor supported the laws prohibiting businesses from opening on Sunday. This was not so much for religious reasons as it was to shorten the workweek.[10]

LINK Moral entrepreneurs are also discussed in Chapter 7.

Another example of how public order crimes are shaped by interest groups is the evolution of vagrancy laws. Sociologist William Chambliss has described how the laws against vagrancy were used in England following the enclosure movement. *Enclosure* meant that peasants were forced from the land as feudal landlords converted farmland to pasture in order to produce wool for the fast-growing textile industry. Arresting those without work or "any visible means of support" was a way of maintaining social order and encouraging those displaced persons to become part of the emerging industrial working class. Thus, in the early stages of the industrial revolution, vagrancy law was adapted to meet the needs of landlords to control displaced peasants and the need of industrial capitalists for laborers. As the need for laborers was met, vagrancy law was used to control surplus labor. During the Great Depression, California used the tactic of arresting people for vagrancy to discourage migration. Gradually, the focus of vagrancy law shifted from controlling labor to the control of "the undesirable, the criminal, and the nuisance."[11]

The United States has become a morally diverse society, with a culture that defines many moral issues as a matter of personal preference. The puritanical tradition is only one theme in U.S. culture. Although it continues to shape the values of many, particularly conservative Christians, its dominance has been eroded by countervailing trends of individualism and hedonism. The erosion of the dominance of the puritanical tradition is revealed in the declining enforcement of laws regulating sexual behavior such as fornication, sodomy, and adultery.

Fornication is sexual intercourse between unmarried persons. *Adultery* is sexual intercourse between individuals when one of the participants is married to another person. *Sodomy* varies in definition. It refers to sexual acts that were once defined as "unnatural" or "crimes against nature", including oral and anal sex and bestiality (sex with animals). Most states have eliminated the laws that make fornication a crime. As of 2005, 11 states —

A homeless man sleeps on a park bench.

? *Should vagrancy be considered a crime?*

Georgia, Idaho, Illinois, Mississippi, Minnesota, North Carolina, South Carolina, Utah, Virginia, West Virginia, and Pennsylvania — still defined fornication as a misdemeanor. Adultery is a misdemeanor in 15 states and a felony in two (Wisconsin and Oklahoma). Consensual sex between adults is largely considered to be a private matter rather than a violation of public morals and these laws are rarely enforced. Even in earlier times, these laws were enforced normally only when the actions were "open and notorious"; they were intended to maintain *public* morality.[12]

In one famous case (*Bowers v. Hardwick*, 1986), the law against sodomy was enforced. Michael Hardwick was arrested when an Atlanta police officer who was attempting to serve a search warrant observed Hardwick and another man engaged in oral sex. The case went all the way to the Supreme Court, which ruled in a five-to-four decision that Georgia's sodomy law was constitutional.[13] The court ruled that Georgia could outlaw consensual homosexual intercourse. The religious basis of this belief was evident in Chief Justice Burger's concurring opinion, in which he stated "Condemnation of those practices is firmly rooted in Judeo-Christian moral and ethical standards." The court overturned this decision in 2003 in *Lawrence v. Texas* when the court cited a constitutional right to privacy.[14] Furthermore, the ruling specifically stated that because a governing majority traditionally believed a practice was immoral was not sufficient grounds for overriding the right to privacy, and antisodomy laws were struck down.

Ideally, most people expect law to reflect morals. As society diversifies, however, there is declining consensus on certain moral and ethical issues. If there is a diversity of morals, which group's values should the law represent? The example of sodomy laws illustrates this problem. Public order crimes often reflect the tension between values of individual liberty and community order. Furthermore, when some laws are believed to represent the values or interests of a particular group rather than a generally agreed-upon principle, the legitimacy of the rule of law may be eroded.

Drugs, Alcohol, Moral Entrepreneurs, and Interest Groups

Imagine that alcohol was illegal and marijuana was legal. This was the case in parts of the United States

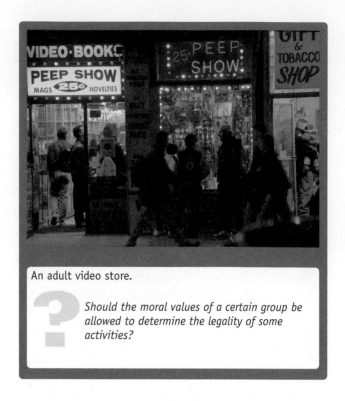

An adult video store.

? *Should the moral values of a certain group be allowed to determine the legality of some activities?*

in the 1920s. Marijuana was easily available and not outlawed in many parts of the country. The criminalization of marijuana was the result of efforts of moral entrepreneurs and interest groups. Their efforts culminated in the passage of the Marijuana Tax Act in 1937, which effectively criminalized the possession, sale, or distribution of the drug.

Ethnic conflict and prejudice were the background for the push to make marijuana illegal. In the western states, marijuana use was associated with migrant Mexican laborers, while in the South it was associated with African-Americans, especially jazz musicians. Newspapers and magazines of the time ran stories attributing outrageously exaggerated effects to the drug, such as claiming that "the man under the influence of hashish . . . runs through the streets hacking and killing everyone he meets," and stating that "you can grow enough marijuana in a window-box to drive the whole population of the United States stark, staring, raving mad."[15] During the 1930s, the nation was in the worst economic crisis in its history. Fearful of their poorly paid laborers turning violent under the influence of "Mexican opium," the land-owning classes in the western states began lobbying for marijuana to be made illegal. They had allies in the alcohol industry, which feared competition from marijuana as they returned to business following the repeal of Prohibition in 1933. A small group of legislators, newspaper editors, and concerned citizens pressured Congress to enact antimarijuana legislation.

Harry Anslinger, commissioner of the Bureau of Narcotics (1930–1962), took up their cause, even though he had previously testified before Congress that marijuana was a drug of little or no concern. Anslinger apparently changed his mind about marijuana, coming to believe it was the "assassin of youth" depicted in the popular press. Anslinger led the moral crusade, contributing his own hyperbole to the media accounts, mistakenly referring to marijuana as a narcotic, popularizing unsupported stories of murderous rampages committed by users, and playing on racial prejudice with references to such events as "colored students" using marijuana to seduce white female students.[16] Anslinger has been described as a shrewd bureaucrat who used the fear of marijuana to strengthen his agency's power and increase its budget.

Alcohol was banned in the United States from 1920 to 1933, the era known as Prohibition. The Eighteenth Amendment to the U.S. Constitution took effect in 1920. It outlawed the manufacture, sale, or transportation of intoxicating liquors for "beverage purpose." It is noteworthy that mere possession of alcoholic beverages was not mentioned and the phrasing of the law was widely interpreted as permitting alcohol for medicinal purposes. The passage of the Volstead Act (which defined intoxicating beverages as those containing more than 0.05% alcohol and laid out rules for enforcing the law) was the result of political pressure by a coalition of crusading groups collectively referred to as the Temperance Movement. The Temperance Movement originated in the Puritan/Protestant values of the New England elite middle class. Their values equated sobriety and abstinence with respectability, personal virtue, and social acceptance. The social dominance of the old middle class was threatened by the influx of immigrant groups whose values were different. The Temperance ideology merged with Protestant revivalism, and thus reflected ethnic and religious conflict.[17]

Probably the best-known organization of the Temperance Movement was the Women's Christian Temperance Union (WCTU) formed in 1873. The WCTU protested — sometimes violently — against saloons and bars, which the WCTU claimed were responsible for drunkenness and alcoholism, and therefore wife beating, child abuse, and the destruction of families.[18] Working with other temperance groups to elect congressional candidates who favored prohibition and pressuring other legislators, the Temperance Movement had enough votes by 1917 to enact Prohibition. The First World War was an important factor, as many feared that "liquor sapped the nation's strength and will power."[19]

The "noble experiment" of Prohibition is widely regarded as a failure of social policy. Although in its early years there were some positive effects, such as declining rates of alcohol-related deaths, these effects eventually rose again.[20] Many people continued to drink, often in illegal nightclubs known as *speakeasies*. Most importantly, the illegal liquor industry in the major cities was controlled by criminal gangs. The violence and corruption associated with organized crime created an intolerable situation.[21] Franklin D. Roosevelt included a promise to repeal Prohibition in his presidential campaign platform. Shortly after becoming president, he signed the legislation that became the Twenty-First Amendment, which was quickly ratified. Social policy toward alcohol shifted from prohibition to regulation, with criminal justice sanctions aimed at underage drinking, driving while intoxicated, and public drunkenness.

With the repeal of Prohibition and the enactment of the Marijuana Tax Act, alcohol became legal and marijuana illegal. The criminalization of each reflected the efforts of moral crusaders, interest groups, and class and ethnic conflicts. These factors also played a role in the criminalization of hard drugs, such as opiates and cocaine. These drugs were legal and widely used prior to the Harrison Narcotics Act enacted in 1914. When it was first marketed, Coca-Cola contained cocaine. It was intended to be a "temperance drink," a safe alternative to alcohol.[22]

Heroin was a brand name trademarked by the Bayer Company, the company better known today for their aspirin. Prior to 1914, opiates were legal and virtually unregulated. In fact, fortunes were made by British and American merchants who imported opium into China, where recreational use had become popular. Great Britain fought two wars with China in the first half of the 19th century to force the Chinese government to keep opium legal and remove trade restrictions on opium imports. When thousands of Chinese immigrated into the western United States, many brought the practice of smoking opium with them. When racial tensions flared, Chinese opium dens were frequently the target of vigilante and mob action by white

Americans. Just as marijuana was associated with Mexicans, opium smoking was associated with the Chinese. Moral panics surrounding the corrupting influences of these drugs emerged when they were feared to be spreading to white youths.

In the United States in the late 1800s, the typical narcotic addict was not smoking in Chinese opium dens but lived in average households. The drug could be acquired from family doctors and, often unbeknownst to the user, in so-called patent medicines. Opiates and alcohol were the active ingredients in numerous elixirs and syrups sold as miracle cures for all types of common ailments, including morphine addiction. At the time, manufacturers were not required to display the ingredients in their products.

Muckraking journalists began exposing the fraudulent claims of the patent medicines around the turn of the century. It was actually public outrage over the dangerous and unsanitary practices of the meat-packing industry, famously revealed in *The Jungle* by Upton Sinclair, that spelled the end of the patent medicines. In 1906, Congress passed the Pure Food and Drug Act, requiring the listing of ingredients. The press had waged an effective campaign against narcotics and the market for patent medicines declined.[23] Opiates were outlawed by the Harrison Narcotics Act of 1914. Originally, the Harrison Act was intended, like the Pure Food and Drug Act, to regulate drugs rather than criminalize the estimated 200,000 narcotics addicts. The Treasury Department, however, interpreted the law as making it criminal for doctors to prescribe narcotics to treat addiction.[24] Moral entrepreneurs like Charles B. Towns, who claimed to have a cure for addiction, and Mrs. William K. Vanderbilt, a member of the wealthy class, lobbied for legislation that further criminalized narcotic use. The typical addict as medical patient was replaced by the feared addict as criminal.[25] As with alcohol, the prohibition of narcotic drugs was followed by the creation of illegal black markets and the involvement of organized crime. Whether a return to legal status would break the drugs-crime connection remains a point of contentious debate.

LINK The relationship between drugs and crime is presented in Chapter 14.

In sum, the morality perspective calls for the enforcement of public order offenses to protect the public and to underscore the moral order that they seek to promote.

The Law-and-Order Perspective

From the law-and-order perspective, public order means the normal, peaceful conduct of social interaction conducted within social boundaries of decency and civility. Offenses against the peace are actions that interfere with the ability of the public to go about their daily business, utilize public space, or enjoy their private property. For example, aggressive panhandling (begging) can make sidewalks and subways uncomfortable and even threatening. Citizens typically want the police to deal with these behaviors to provide order and feelings of safety.

Wilson and Kelling: Broken Windows Theory

In 1982, two influential analysts of policing, James Q. Wilson and George L. Kelling, published their view of events in policing and offered their interpretation of them.[26] This article had a great impact on policing. It called for reform and change in policing operations in the United States.

Wilson and Kelling commented on studies on the return to foot patrolling as a method of policing. Although the research results revealed that foot patrol had no effect on crime rates, these studies also demonstrated that community residents felt safer when police officers patrolled their neighborhoods on foot. From their point of view, foot patrol had restored law and order to their community by controlling the street.

To support their views, they cited another study demonstrating that once one window was broken in an abandoned building, eventually all the remaining windows would be destroyed. The tolerance of one broken window led to the conclusion that no one cared. Wilson and Kelling carried this argument over to neighborhoods:

A piece of property is abandoned, weeds grow up, and a window is smashed. Adults stop scolding rowdy children; the children, emboldened, become more rowdy. Families move out, unmarried adults move in. Teenagers gather in front of the corner store. The merchant asks them to move, they refuse. Fights occur. Litter accumulates. People start drinking in front of the grocery, in time, an inebriate slumps to the sidewalk and is allowed to sleep it off. Pedestrians are approached by panhandlers.[27]

Thus, the failure to provide order leads to the deterioration of a neighborhood. Community controls break down and the police are unable to prevent crime.

Wilson and Kelling called for a return to the order-maintenance function of policing. This function was abandoned when policing emphasized professional crime fighting and moved away from direct contact with the community. Wilson and Kelling stressed that when the police maintain order, they reinforce the control mechanisms in the community. They stated that the police must return to their duty of protecting communities and preventing "broken windows."

> . . . the police must get out of their cars and spend more time in public spaces such as parks and plazas, confronting and assisting citizens with their private troubles. This is mundane, prosaic work, but it probably beats driving around in cars waiting for a radio call. Citizens would surely feel safer and, perhaps, might even be safer.[28]

In sum, Wilson and Kelling state that:

1. Disorder breeds fear among neighborhood residents.

2. If misbehavior is ignored, it signals that no one cares about the community and leads to more serious crime.

3. If the police are to deal with disorder to reduce both crime and fear, they must rely on citizens for assistance.

Their argument caught on. It is now one of the rationales for the development of police reforms such as Compstat. For example, criminologist Gary Sykes argues that police provide a functional role by dispensing "street justice." Responding to community demands, the officer often plays the role of judge, jury, and punisher. As a result, the officer is caught in a bind between the demands of the public and those of the due process-oriented, professional model of policing. He maintains that order maintenance is an important and vital role for police departments.[29]

George Kelling and Catherine Coles cite the development of the preventative model based on the tenets of the broken windows theory and community policing. This model features a partnership between the police and the community that recognizes that "citizens themselves must once again accept mutual responsibility for their own prudent, effective, and legally permissible involvement in crime prevention and order maintenance."[30] Kelling and Coles also cite research findings from New York City as evidence of the effectiveness of this approach (when the transit police and the entire department were under the direction of William Bratton)[31]:

> . . . robbery has been dramatically reduced in the subway, and murder is declining in the city. While we do not yet understand the precise nature of this linkage, and current police efforts extend beyond order maintenance activities alone, many police posit a direct correlation between restoring order and reducing violent crime in New York City. . . . the number of persons engaging in selling, buying, and using drugs decreased by 85%, and the number of people involved in "positive" activities increased by 79%. Furthermore, the presence of some officers, either stationed in one spot or on directed patrol, appeared more critical to affecting conditions than the absolute number of officers.

Central to these results was the establishment of the New York Police Department's Compstat program. Basically, Compstat formalized a crime control strategy for the NYPD that established clear and measurable goals for the department. Compstat stressed that:

1. The core function of the police is crime control, aimed at disorder, fear, and index crime.

2. The police have the capability to prevent crime.

3. Officers must be both aggressive and respectful in their activities — "being aggressive in crime control does not require being combative, nor does being respectful of citizens embody weakness."[32]

LINK Compstat is presented in Chapter 16.

One of the reasons that the broken windows theory became so popular was that it "gave police officers something to look out for and intervene about when they were on foot."[33] Because public order offenses are generally considered to be less serious than the index crimes, some question whether it is a waste of valuable resources to police and punish loiterers, johns, and panhandlers when communities are faced with high rates of murder, rape, robbery, and burglary. Again, the broken windows theory asserts that disorder and crime are causally linked. Put into practice, it implies that the police can reduce crime by cracking down on minor instances of disorder.[34]

For example, Kelling and Coles attribute the dramatic decrease in crime in New York City in the early

One of the great criminological controversies of recent years is whether the use of Compstat procedures based in part on the broken windows theory have had a significant impact on the crime rate in New York City. Many criminologists disagree that the declining New York crime rate can be attributed to the broken windows approach to community policing. They say that crime rates dropped nationally, even in communities that did not use the broken windows strategy. Therefore, the crime rate results from New York City could be attributed to the fact that many serious offenders also commit public order crimes. Therefore, aggressively policing specific forms of disorder may reduce crime by removing high-rate offenders from the community.

Yet, crime rates have fallen for 17 consecutive years in the Big Apple. During 2005, homicides fell to levels unseen since 1963. Nationwide, homicides rose by 2.1% in 2005, but in New York City they went down 14.4%. Other comparatively large U.S. cities, such as Boston, Houston, and Philadelphia, experienced increases in their homicide rates. Overall, here is how New York City ranked in the total index crime rate for the nation's 10 largest cities in 2005.

Rank	City	2005 Crime Rate per 100,000 Residents
1	Dallas	4270.6
2	Phoenix	3704.9
3	Detroit	3700.6
4	Houston	3430.4
5	San Antonio	3364.0
6	Las Vegas	2825.7
7	Philadelphia	2579.1
8	San Diego	2059.1
9	Los Angeles	1908.8
10	New York	1281.9

Criminologists are quick to note factors such as improved job opportunities, declining drug usage, and stricter prison sentencing rather than improved police work as the forces driving this "crime crash." However, David Kennedy, director of the Center for Crime Prevention and Control at the John Jay College of Criminal Justice in New York City, states: "The controversy remains. Is it something that law enforcement did, or isn't it? My thought is, you can't explain it without a very large contribution from law enforcement."

Do you think that the New York City crime rate drop is due to police operations or to other factors?

Sources: Al Baker, "Crime Dips Again in New York City," *The New York Times* (December 31, 2005): A1; B15; "Mayor Bloomberg and Police Commissioner Kelly Announce New York City Is the Safest Big City in America According to the FBI Uniform Crime Report," available at http://www.nyc.gov/cgi-bin/misc/pfprinter.cgi?action=print&sitename=OM, accessed January 3, 2006.

1990s to the implementation of these policies.[35] One example is the police crackdown on New York's infamous "squeegee men" (and women). Squeegeeing is the "unsolicited washing of car windows," with the expectation of receiving tips.[36] Many squeegee men conducted this activity in an aggressive, menacing style intended to intimidate drivers. Some spray soapy water or spit on car windows. Sometimes groups of three or four would surround a car, washing the windows whether the driver wanted them or not, and then refusing to get out of the way until they received their "tips." A 60-day study, during which squeegee men were observed, videotaped, and arrested revealed that, far from being homeless men down on their luck, most had residences, and half had prior convictions for felonies. In itself, squeegeeing was a minor infraction that was punishable only by a fine and community service. Therefore the action taken against squeegee men by police officers was usually to write them a desk appearance ticket (DAT). DATs were routinely ignored by the recipients. Although squeegeeing was not punishable by jail, failure to appear was. The police arranged to have warrants for nonappearance routed directly to the officer who issued the DAT. Thus the officer could make an arrest and the offender would serve jail time. Soon squeegeeing was a thing of the past and residents and commuters felt safer.

Gambling

Gambling is defined as the operating or playing a game for money in hopes of gaining more than the amount played or as a wager between two or more persons.[37] Historically, illegal gambling was one of the illicit goods and services provided by organized crime. The growth of legal gambling in the last 20 years has cut into the profitability, however. By 1992, it was estimated that the Mafia made "only" about $2 billion per year from illegal gambling operations. The Mafia's overall annual income was said to be around $60 billion. Arrests for running illegal gambling operations were an important part of a successful law enforcement campaign waged against the five New York Mafia families in the 1990s.[38]

LINK The business of organized crime is discussed in detail in Chapter 15.

Unlike pornography and drugs, gambling has been legalized, although restricted to certain forms and locations. As various state and local governments faced fiscal crises in the 1980s, many turned to gambling as a quick fix solution. For example, Charles Wellford determined that[39]:

It is now legal in all but three states, and 37 states have lotteries. More than 8 in 10 adults say they have played casino games, bet on races on and off the track, bought lottery tickets, or in some other way engaged in recreational gambling. In a single recent year, Americans collectively wagered more than half a trillion dollars.

In addition, Internet gambling has rapidly expanded with an estimated revenue of more than $4 billion in 2003.[40]

Also, gambling among college students is common. For many, gambling is part of a larger lifestyle pattern of risky behaviors that includes heavy drinking, tobacco use, and eating disorders.[41] There was a wave of illegal bookmaking on college campuses in the mid-1990s. Illegal bookmaking rings existed in eight different states. Studies of National Collegiate Athletic Association (NCAA) Division I student athletes found that 72% had gambled in some form since entering college, 25% had gambled on sporting events, and 3.7% had bet on games in which they played.[42]

States have become increasingly dependent on the tax revenues and employment benefits offered by legalized casinos. Due to the damage caused by Hurricane Katrina, it has been estimated that Mississippi will lose about $500,000 per day in tax revenue for each day that the legalized Biloxi-area riverboat casinos are closed, plus an additional $140,000 per day in tax revenue from the South River region casinos.[43]

The fact that legalized forms of gambling have become so widespread has not eliminated the harm caused by gambling.

The Morality Perspective: Compulsive Gambling

Compulsive or *pathological gambling* is seen as a symptom of a psychiatric disorder — the inability to resist the impulse to gamble that may grow progressively worse. It has a number of harmful consequences to both the gambler and his or her family.[44] These harms include[45]:

- Increasing indebtedness and bankruptcy
- Poor relationships with family and friends
- Suicide
- Committing crimes such as theft, embezzlement, domestic violence, and child abuse and neglect
- Drug abuse
- Alcoholism

The extensiveness of these problems underscores the moralistic view that gambling is wrong because it is injurious to the individual and others.[46] Gamblers Anonymous is one organization designed to help pathological gamblers; this organization is "a fellowship of men and women who share their experience, strength and hope with each other that they may solve their common problem and help others to recover from a gambling problem."[47]

One of the leading antigambling organizations is the National Coalition Against Legalized Gambling (NCALG). Their mission is to "provide resources to assist citizens in making an informed decision that all forms of legalized gambling are detrimental to economic, political, social, and physical well-being of individuals, the community, and the nation."[48] NCALG contends that the revenues generated by legalized gambling are simply not worth the costs to the fabric of society.

The Law-and-Order Perspective: Casinos and Crime

States that have or are considering having legalized gambling are confronted with other negative consequences. For example, do casinos increase the amount of crime in a community? Routine activities theory suggests that casinos are likely hot spots

Gamblers enjoying a night at the casino.

? At what point does gambling become harmful to an individual or society?

for crime for both residents and tourists who frequent the casinos. Research findings are inconsistent. For example, a major study by Grant Stitt, Mark Nichols, and David Giacopassi examined the effects of casino gambling on crime and the quality of life in seven communities (Alton and Peoria/East Peoria, IL; Sioux City, IA; St. Joseph, St. Louis, and St. Louis County, MO; and Biloxi, MS) that had introduced riverboat gambling over a 10-year period and a set of control communities for comparative purposes. The research findings were mixed: Three casino communities experienced an increase in crime while three others had a crime decrease and one had few significant differences in either direction.[49] Similarly, Wilson found that the establishment of a riverboat casino failed to significantly affect the crime rate (e.g., driving while intoxicated, disorderly conduct, prostitution) in two nearby Indiana communities.[50]

LINK Routine activities theory was presented in Chapter 3.

On the other hand, a study of Wisconsin counties determined a link between the presence of a casino and increased crime — an impact that spilled over to adjacent counties as well.[51] A study of persons seeking admission to Niagara Falls, Ontario, following the opening of Casino Niagara found that the number of criminally inadmissible individuals increased during this period. Thus, the study offered some support for the idea that casinos attract the criminal element.[52]

Despite these mixed findings, police chiefs in casino communities have said that law enforcement agencies must be aware of the possible effect of a new casino on crime in the area. They believe that police agencies should establish good working relationships with casino security and keep accurate track of crime rates in the area.[53]

Prostitution

Prostitution is the practice of engaging in sexual activities for hire.[54] Sometimes referred to as the world's oldest profession, prostitution continues to flourish around the globe. In some cultures, prostitution is tolerated or even condoned. It is legal in Thailand, where it is a major draw for tourism. Several European countries, most notably the Netherlands, have legalized prostitution. It remains illegal in the United States, except in several counties in Nevada. Prostitutes are usually women, but there are also substantial numbers of male and transsexual prostitutes.[55]

Prevalence of Prostitution

In spite of its illegal status, millions, perhaps billions, of dollars are spent each year on prostitution. Although there is no definitive answer to the question of how widespread the practice is, there are a number of indicators. These include arrest data, surveys, data from health care agencies, and other service providers and social agencies.

One way to estimate the extent of prostitution is to survey people, asking how often they had indulged in sex for pay. Early studies tended to overestimate the number of men who used the services of prostitutes. Recent studies based on scientifically designed representative samples yield much lower estimates. Three national surveys asked respondents if they had ever paid or been paid for

Sex workers in Amsterdam.

? *Because prostitution does not result in "complaining victims," should the United States consider legalizing this practice?*

sex: the General Social Survey (GSS), conducted biannually by the National Opinion Research Center; the National Health and Social Life Survey (NHSLS) conducted in 1992 by Robert Michael and colleagues[56]; and the Janus Report, conducted in 1991. Janus and Janus found that 20% of their male respondents had ever paid for sex.[57] The NHSLS survey found that 16% of the men had visited a prostitute and the yearly rate was only 0.6%. In other words, less than 1% of the men visited a prostitute in the previous year.[58] The 2002 GSS data yield an even lower lifetime rate of 3.4%. Although the survey method may undercount the number of people who have paid for sex, the data strongly suggest that the number is much lower than once thought and may be declining.

It is even more difficult to estimate the number of working prostitutes. Not surprisingly, prostitutes are underrepresented in the household surveys described previously. A large percentage of prostitutes live in institutional settings, such as jails or homeless shelters, or in residences such as motels that are not included in the sampling frame of the survey. No one knows for sure how many people work in the business of prostitution. Estimates of how many prostitutes there are in the United States range from 84,000 to 4.2 million. Janus and Janus (1993) estimate 4.2 million by projecting the percentage of women in their survey who had ever had sex for money.[59] In a much more sophisticated

analysis, John Potterat and colleagues and Brewer et al. used data from a decades-long study of prostitutes in Colorado Springs to estimate a national rate.[60] These researchers calculated a prevalence rate of 23 prostitutes per 100,000 persons in the population. This translates into 56,355 "full-time" prostitute women working per year. These authors admit that this is a conservative estimate, because it misses many part-time and short-term entries into the world of prostitution.

The FBI Uniform Crime Report (UCR) data include arrests for prostitution and commercialized vice. This category combines selling sex with related offenses such as soliciting, pimping, or transporting prostitutes. In 2004, the FBI estimated that there were more than 90,000 arrests for prostitution. This makes the Brewer estimate of 56,355 prostitutes seem far too small, even if it is taken into account that only 69.2% of the arrests were of women, some of whom were arrested more than once.

The numbers included in **TABLE 13-2** are based on a smaller total than 90,000 because they are the actual number of arrests reported. Not all law enforcement agencies participate in the UCR program. The data contradict the assumption that male customers and pimps are seldom targeted by law enforcement. Roughly one-third of prostitution arrests are of men.

It might be tempting to conclude that prostitution declined in the 10 years ending in 2004; however, it is important to remember that these are arrest data and reflect police activity as much, if not more, than the actual prevalence of illegal activity. During the same period, for example, arrests for drug abuse violations increased by 21.7%, even though there is no evidence that illegal drug use increased by a similar amount.

LINK The strengths and weaknesses of different sources of crime statistics were discussed in Chapter 2.

TABLE 13-2			
Arrests for Prostitution (1995 and 2004)			
	1995	**2004**	**Percent Change**
Males	25,098 (38.2%)	17,725 (30.8%)	−29.4
Females	40,680 (61.8%)	39,893 (69.2%)	−1.9
Total	65,778	57,618	−12.4

Source: Federal Bureau of Investigation, *Crime in the U.S. 2004* (Washington, DC: U.S. Department of Justice, 2005): 285.

Types of Prostitutes

Prostitutes are often classified into different types, related to the setting in which business is transacted. Most researchers who study prostitutes place the types into a status hierarchy within the profession. The amount of freedom in choice of clients, working conditions, hours, safety, and freedom to leave the business vary with status.

Streetwalkers occupy the lowest status. As the label suggests, they ply their trade on the streets, approaching potential customers who cruise by in automobiles or walk on the sidewalks. They may also work in hotel lobbies, bars, and nightclubs. Streetwalkers are the prostitutes most frequently arrested, for obvious reasons: They are more visible and therefore more likely to be reported as a nuisance by the public, plus they are more vulnerable to police sting tactics. They are likely to be members of minority groups. They are also the most likely to be studied. Some argue that the research literature is disproportionately based on streetwalkers and thus misrepresents the facts about prostitution as a whole.[61]

Higher status is afforded those who work indoors in massage parlors, brothels, escort services, or as "call girls."[62] *Call girls* are the elite of the profession, charging much more than streetwalkers. One of the women who worked for Heidi Fleiss, the Hollywood Madam, was said to have charged $10,000 for a single "date."[63] They are more selective with their clients and more discreet in the conduct of their business.

An exception to the status hierarchy appeared with the epidemic of crack cocaine in the 1980s. Prostitutes who worked in crack houses frequently exchanged sex for drugs rather than money and were disparaged even by the streetwalkers.[64] Where prostitution is legal or condoned, it typically occurs indoors in a brothel or club. In the "Wild West" frontier period, brothels (or "cat houses") were often multipurpose community institutions.

Farley and Kelly downplay the significance of the status hierarchy, arguing that: (1) many women engage in several types of prostitution and (2) there are more similarities in the lives of the different types of prostitutes, such as the risk of violence, than are commonly acknowledged.[65] Women who engage in prostitution at any level experience stigmatization and take the chance that others will see them as legitimate targets, responsible for their own victimization.

Entry to the Profession

Why do some women (and men) become prostitutes? Obviously, there is an economic motive, but most people who need money do not turn to prostitution. In a classic article, sociologist Kingsley Davis asserted that prostitutes essentially trade the chance to have a reputable social status for the opportunity to make money selling sex.[66] Consider the emotional impact of the word *whore*. The social stigma attached to prostitution prevents most women from even considering sex work. Women whose social identity has already been spoiled may find prostitution more attractive than other lines of work available to them. Many "working girls" (prostitutes) would dispute the claim that prostitution is "easy money."

Reasons for becoming a prostitute can be sorted into attracting, predisposing, and precipitating factors. *Attracting factors* are beliefs about prostitution that lead someone to consider it as an option — for example, the belief that it is an easy way to make money or that it is a glamorous or adventurous lifestyle. *Precipitating factors* refer to the circumstances that immediately precede entry into the trade. For example, many adolescents are recruited into prostitution following a family crisis such as running away from home. *Predisposing factors* are characteristics or experiences that increase the probability of an individual engaging in prostitution. Sometimes referred to as *risk factors*, these characteristics are not present in the lives of all prostitutes nor does their occurrence automatically mean that an individual will become a prostitute. For example, dropping out of school increases the chances of entry into prostitution, but most high school dropouts do not become prostitutes.

The Morality Perspective

The Dangers of Prostitution

Dozens of studies conducted in the last 40 years have identified drug use, violence, sexual abuse, and homelessness as important precursors of prostitution. Studies based on interviews with women currently or formerly in prostitution often reveal unusually high rates of physical and sexual abuse in childhood. For example, in a study of 123 women attempting to exit prostitution, 85% reported a history of incest and 90% reported a history of physical abuse.[67] Many of these studies are limited by the absence of a comparison sample of nonprostitutes. In one study, current and former prostitutes were compared to a sample of women clients of a community clinic for sexually transmitted diseases. These researchers found that, compared with nonprostitutes, women in prostitution were much more likely to have had sexual intercourse before age 11 and much more likely to have started using injection drugs at a young age.[68] There are exceptions, however. Susan Nadon, Catherine Koverola, and Eduard Schludermann compared 45 adolescent prostitutes with a sample of 37 nonprostitute adolescents and found no differences between the two groups in sexual abuse experienced.[69]

Drug use, violence, and homelessness are linked to prostitution in different combinations. A typical pathway to prostitution goes something like this: A young girl is sexually abused by a family member or associate such as her mother's boyfriend. As she matures, she becomes sexually promiscuous, either in search of intimacy or out of rebellion. She may begin experimenting with drugs. Unable to get along with the family, she runs away from home or is kicked out. Lacking the skills to support herself in legitimate work, she drifts into turning tricks.[70] Most of the studies that suggest this "typical" story are based on samples of women who worked the streets. Some suggest that an understanding of the role of these risk factors may be biased, because only 10% to 20% of prostitutes are streetwalkers.[71] Drawing heavily on the international literature, Vanwesenbeeck argues that predisposing and motivating factors are different for other forms of prostitution, particularly where it is legal.[72] Although some prostitutes are adolescent runaways, sexual abuse survivors, or drug addicts, some are also housewives, students, and secretaries attracted to the perceived flexibility, freedom, and enjoyment of sex work.

Violence is not only a precursor to prostitution, it is also a fact of everyday life for women in prostitution. Prostitutes risk violence from pimps and customers. Almost all of the women in one study had been sexually assaulted; 75% had been raped by one or more customers.[73] In addition to the sexual assaults, prostitutes are frequently physically assaulted and robbed.[74] Face-to-face interviews with 59 street prostitutes in an East Coast city determined that most of them had been raped, robbed, and or hospitalized while working.[75] On the other hand, one study of 2300 arrested customers concluded that most customers were nonviolent and that a relatively small proportion are responsible for most of the violence.[76] Although they may take

steps to protect themselves, prostitutes almost never report the victimization to the police.[77]

The risk of violence is not restricted to streetwalkers. Some researchers reject the claim that life is different and safer for the high-class call girl, asserting that women in all forms of sex work report high rates of sexual violence.[78] Perhaps it is the illegal status of prostitution that links it to violence and victimization. Although illegality enables both bosses and customers to abuse women who prostitute, as yet there are no convincing data that life is significantly better for sex workers in legal settings such as Nevada or the Netherlands. However, a number of studies conducted in England, Canada, Australia, and the United States report significantly lower rates of victimization for indoor compared with street prostitutes.[79]

Other dangers faced by prostitutes are endemic to the job. Of course, arrest and conviction is a possibility when anyone engages in an illegal business. Socially, prostitutes face the risk of social stigma once their status is public. Perhaps the most severe risk faced by prostitutes is the increased exposure to sexually transmitted diseases, including HIV/AIDS.[80] This risk is enhanced by the typically unprotected sex for drugs (especially crack cocaine) transactions in which street prostitutes often engage.[81]

Exploitation or Sex Work?

Two schools of thought exist regarding the nature of prostitution: (1) prostitution as exploitation and (2) prostitution as sex work. Those who view prostitution as exploitation emphasize the coercive aspects of the business: They see prostitution as part of a continuum of abuse, the ultimate form of gender discrimination.[82] Adherents of this view generally do not favor legalization, although they advocate for more lenient treatment of prostitutes who they see as victims. Citing a "growing moral panic over prostitution and sex trafficking," Ronald Weitzer summarizes this victimization pattern[83]:

1. Prostitution involves male domination and exploitation of women regardless of historical time period, societal context, or legal status.

2. Violence is omnipresent in prostitution.

3. Female prostitutes are victims because they do not actively make choices to enter or remain in prostitution.

4. Legalization or decriminalization will only make the situation worse because it would

grant the blessing of the state to a despicable institution, increase the supply and demand for services, and thus amplify the victimization of female prostitutes.[84]

Policing prostitution is thus viewed as a form of gender discrimination, because prostitutes are arrested more frequently than their customers or their managers and pimps. One leader in this fight against sexual exploitation is the international Coalition Against Trafficking in Women (CATW). Its main premise is that freedom from all forms of sexual exploitation is a fundamental human right and that women and girls have the right to sexual integrity and autonomy.[85]

The prostitution-as-sex-work perspective views prostitutes as exercising control over their lives.[86] As the label suggests, this viewpoint defines prostitution as work that is similar in important ways to legitimate jobs. One study concludes that, as sex workers, prostitutes actually shape their urban environment so that it facilitates the selling of sex.[87] This position is more common among those who favor legalization. The negative aspects of prostitutes' lives are attributed to its illegal status. Each of these perspectives emphasizes different aspects of the research literature. The sex-work perspective emphasizes the differences among types of prostitution, whereas the exploitation perspective downplays those differences.

The Law-and-Order Perspective

Policing Street Prostitution

The enforcement of laws against prostitution is typically promoted as both crime prevention and a public health initiatives.[88] Consistent with the premises of the broken windows theory, street prostitution creates an environment where other crimes can occur. For example[89]:

- The site of street prostitution can also become a marketplace for the sale of illegal drugs.
- Street prostitution may generate profits that eventually attract members of organized crime.
- Prostitution attracts strangers and criminals to a neighborhood. Bringing these two groups into close contact opens up the possibility of more crime, such as assault and robbery.
- Prostitutes create parking and traffic problems where they congregate.

Police crackdowns on street prostitution are thus viewed as an example of problem solving.

LINK Problem-oriented policing is discussed in Chapter 16.

Several methods have been proposed to deter both prostitutes and their clients. Law enforcement methods against street prostitution may thus include[90]:

1. **Enforcing laws prohibiting soliciting, patronizing, and loitering for the purposes of prostitution.** However, this is often a costly strategy because each prostitution arrest costs thousands of dollars to process. It also opens the police up to the possibility of corruption and civil rights abuse charges. It may also be ultimately ineffective because it may result in the moving of the market to another area.

2. **Enhancing fines/penalties for prostitution-related offenses committed within a specified high-activity**

zone. Here again, the intention is to close down the marketplace and the problem remains that it may be displaced somewhere else.

3. **Banning prostitutes or clients from geographic areas.** This option is typically used as a condition of probation for convicted prostitutes or their clients. They are ordered to stay out of certain areas where street prostitution is prevalent.

4. **Encouraging community members to publicly protest against prostitutes and/or clients.** Here, the intention is to mobilize community residents against prostitution in their neighborhood, thus disrupting the marketplace. However, if the citizens are overzealous, they may violate the rights of the prostitute and their client or even be retaliated against.

5. **Identifying and targeting the worst offenders.** This is an attempt at a high-impact strategy to remove the most active offenders and also discourage the lower level players operating in the area.

Thus, the enforcement of laws against prostitution is viewed as a method of containing a public nuisance that is tied to other serious social problems and preventing the creation of a site that can act as a haven for other types of crime.

Conclusion

Public order crimes present the criminologist with a number of interesting issues. Prostitution and gambling are mostly voluntary transactions between adults. The participants not only do not complain to the police, in many cases they also perceive their activities to be equivalent to legal pursuits. Some citizens ask: "Why is it a good thing to buy a state lottery ticket but a crime to place a bet in a numbers game?" or "Why can I drink alcohol and get drunk but get arrested for doing essentially the same thing with a marijuana joint?" Outlawing these activities does not eliminate the demand for them and organized crime is inevitably associated with the resulting illegal markets. Granted, there are serious social and personal harms associated with public order crimes — but how far should society go in using the criminal law to protect people from themselves?

The moral perspective brings attention to the social stigma often attached to public order offenses as well as the harm caused by them. Thus, the moral entrepreneurs pressure lawmakers and the law enforcement system to "do something" about public order offenses. They also stress that these crimes represent threats to the broader public — that prostitution spreads sexually transmitted diseases and gambling leads to compulsive behavior that can harm families. The law-and-order perspective stresses the ties between public order offenses and their tendency to be associated with other, often more serious, criminal activity. Perhaps the answer lies in the continued scientific and empirical study of the exact role and influence of public order offenses.

WRAP UP

Combating Prostitution

From the moral perspective, prostitution is morally wrong and should not be tolerated in society. Moral entrepreneurs emphasize the stigma attached to practicing prostitution and also to those who seek out prostitutes. Customers are viewed as blameworthy. They also stress the harms of prostitution, especially the public health threats posed by the spread of sexually transmitted diseases such as HIV/AIDS.

From the law-and-order perspective, prostitution represents a crime that is dangerous not only for the public health and moral threat that it represents but also because it attracts other more serious types of crime, such as assault, robbery, and drug trafficking. Police crackdowns, supported by public efforts by neighborhood residents, would be one method of combating prostitution from the law-and-order perspective.

Notifying spouses that their significant other had been arrested for soliciting a prostitute would create meaningful consequences for the customer. Shame can be a powerful deterrent to and social control over such behavior. However, this type of penalty may have some unintended consequences for the john, including divorce or loss of employment.

Chapter Spotlight

- The term *public order crimes* refers to a diverse collection of offenses. Generally considered to be less serious than major index crimes, they still can have important effects on public health and safety, the economy, and public perception about the quality of life in a neighborhood or community.

- Many consider public order crimes to be "victimless" because they affect only the person committing them. The absence of a complaining victim causes some people to question whether it is appropriate to label activities such as gambling and prostitution as crimes.

- Public order offenses strain the relationship between law and morality more than other kinds of crimes. Here, the aim of enforcement is societal protection and crime prevention, but it is often difficult to establish and maintain a clear focus on these goals.

- Two basic perspectives can be used to classify public order crimes: the morality perspective and the law-and-order perspective. The morality perspective seeks to use the criminal law to impose minimum standards of morality on citizens. The law-and-order perspective views the enforcement of these laws as a way to maintain peace in the community.

- A central question associated with crimes such as drug use, gambling, prostitution, and pornography is how far society should go in using the criminal law to protect people from themselves.

Putting It All Together

1. Why do public order crimes generate such a controversy? Do moral entrepreneurs reflect the attitudes of most Americans?

2. How can public order offenses be characterized as "victimless crimes"? Do you agree or disagree with this concept? Why or why not?

3. Morris and Hawkins decry the "overreach of the criminal law" regarding the enforcement

of public order offenses. Do you agree or disagree with their position? Why or why not?

4. Construct a debate between a moral entrepreneur and a law-and-order advocate on the issue: "Do casinos contribute to crime?"

5. What are the public costs of prostitution?

6. Which perspective on prostitution do you find more persuasive: exploitation or sex work?

Key Terms

consensus Widespread agreement in society that laws against crimes such as murder should be strictly enforced.

legitimacy The belief in the rightness of and public support for a law.

overreach of the criminal law Norval Morris and Gordon Hawkins contend that the attempt to govern public order offenses like prostitution causes a number of secondary problems that aggravate the crime problem.

victimless crimes Crimes that affect only the person committing them. Because of the absence of a complaining victim, some people question whether it is appropriate to label activities such as gambling and prostitution as crimes.

Notes

1. Norval Morris and Gordon Hawkins, *The Honest Politicians' Guide to Crime Control* (Chicago: University of Chicago Press, 1970): 2.
2. Edwin M. Schur and Hugo Adam Bedau, *Victimless Crimes: Two Sides of a Controversy* (Englewood Cliffs, NJ: Prentice Hall, 1974); Robert F. Meier and Gilbert Geis, *Victimless Crime? Prostitution, Drugs, Homosexuality, Abortion* (Los Angeles: Roxbury, 1997).
3. Morris and Hawkins, 1970, 5–6.
4. Ibid., 2: 4.
5. Graeme Newman, *Comparative Deviance* (New York: Elsevier, 1976).
6. *Sourcebook of Criminal Justice Statistics, 2003 — On Line*, available at http://www.albany.edu/sourcebook/pdf/t267.pdf, accessed January 5, 2006.
7. For example, NORML (The National Organization for the Reform of Marijuana Laws) advocates the decriminalization of marijuana laws and the medical use of marijuana. Available at http://www.norml.org.
8. John M. Scheb and John M. Scheb II, *Criminal Law* (Belmont, CA: Wadsworth, 1999).
9. Howard Becker, *The Outsiders* (New York: Macmillan, 1963).
10. Lawrence M. Friedman, *A History of American Law* (New York: Simon & Schuster, 1985); Kai T. Erikson, *The Wayward Puritans: A Study in the Sociology of Deviance* (New York: John Wiley and Sons, 1966).
11. William J. Chambliss, "A Sociological Analysis of the Law of Vagrancy," *Social Problems* 12 (1964): 67–77.
12. Friedman, 1985.
13. *Bowers v. Hardwick*, 478 U.S. 186, 1986.
14. *Lawrence v. Texas,* 539 U.S. 558, 2003.
15. Larry Sloman, *Reefer Madness: A History of Marijuana in America* (Indianapolis, IN: Bobbs-Merrill, 1979): 26.
16. James A. Inciardi, *The War on Drugs III* (Boston: Allyn and Bacon, 2002): 36.
17. Joseph Gusfield, *Symbolic Crusade* (Champaign, IL: University of Illinois Press, 1963).
18. Mark E. Lender and James R. Martin, *Drinking in America: A History* (New York: Free Press, 1982):107.
19. David F. Musto, *The American Disease* (New York: Oxford University Press, 1987): 68.
20. Jean-Charles Sournia, *A History of Alcoholism* (Cambridge, MA: Basil Blackwell, 1990): 122.
21. Ibid.
22. Inciardi, 2002, 21.
23. Ibid., 26–29.
24. Ibid., 29.
25. Musto, 1987, 101–109.
26. James Q. Wilson and George L. Kelling, "Broken Windows: Police and Neighborhood Safety," *Atlantic Monthly* 249 (March 1982): 29–38.
27. Ibid., 32.

28. Mark H. Moore and George L. Kelling, "'To Serve and Protect': Learning from Police History," *Public Interest* 70 (1983): 65.

29. Gary W. Sykes, "Street Justice: A Moral Defense of Order Maintenance Policing," *Justice Quarterly* 3 (1986): 497–512.

30. George L. Kelling and Catherine M. Coles, *Fixing Broken Windows: Restoring Order and Reducing Crime in Our Communities* (New York: The Free Press, 1996): 106–107.

31. Ibid., 111.

32. Ibid., 145. See also William Bratton with Peter Knobler, *Turnaround: How America's Top Cop Reversed the Crime Epidemic* (New York: Random House, 1998).

33. Ralph B. Taylor, "'Broken Windows' or Incivilities Thesis," in Larry E. Sullivan and Marie Simonetti Rosen, eds., *Encyclopedia of Law Enforcement, Volume 1: State and Local* (Thousand Oaks, CA: Sage, 2005): 31.

34. Wilson and Kelling, 1982.

35. Kelling and Coles, 1996.

36. Ibid., 141.

37. Dean John Champion, *The American Dictionary of Criminal Justice* (Los Angeles: Roxbury, 2005): 108.

38. Bonni Angelo, "Wanted: A New Godfather," *Time* (April 13, 1992): 30; Richard Corliss and Simon Crittle, "The Last Don," *Time* (March 29, 2004): 44–52.

39. Charles Wellford, "When It's No Longer a Game: Pathological Gambling in the United States," *National Institute of Justice Journal* (April 2001): 15.

40. U.S. General Accounting Office, *Internet Gambling: An Overview of the Issues,* available at http://www.gao.gov/cgi-bin/getrpt?GAO-03-89, accessed October 31, 2005; Mark Griffiths, "Internet Gambling and Crime," *The Police Journal* 73 (2000): 25–30.

41. Douglass Engwall and Robert Hunter "Gambling and Other Risk Behaviors on University Campuses," *Journal of American College Health* 52 (2004): 245–256.

42. Ibid.

43. "Gambling Industry," available at http://www.en.wikipedia.org/wiki/gambling, accessed October 31, 2005.

44. Wellford, 2001, 15.

45. Ibid., 16–17.

46. Marc N. Potenza, Marvin A. Steinberg, Susan D. McLaughlin, et al., "Illegal Behaviors in Problem Gambling: An Analysis of Data from a Gambling Helpline," *Journal of the American Academy of Psychiatry and the Law* 28 (2000): 389–403.

47. Gamblers Anonymous, "Gamblers Anonymous," available at http://www.gamblersanonymous.org/about.html, accessed January 9, 2006.

48. The National Coalition Against Legalized Gambling, available at http://www.ncalg.org/about_us.htm, accessed January 9, 2006.

49. B. Grant Stitt, Mark Nichols, and David Giacopassi, "Does the Presence of Casinos Increase Crime? An Examination of Casino and Control Communities," *Crime and Delinquency* 49 (2003): 253–284; B. Grant Stitt, David Giacopassi, and Mark Nichols, "The Effect of Casino Gambling on Crime in New Casino Jurisdictions," *Journal of Crime and Justice* 23 (2000): 1–23.

50. Jeremy M. Wilson, "Riverboat Gambling and Crime in Indiana: An Empirical Investigation," *Crime and Delinquency* 47 (2001): 610–640.

51. Ricardo C. Gazel, Dan S. Rickman, and William N. Thompson, "Casino Gambling and Crime: A Panel Study of Wisconsin Counties," *Managerial and Decision Economics* 22 (2001): 65–75.

52. Franco Piscatelli and Jay S. Albanese, "Do Casinos Attract Criminals? A Study at the Canadian–U.S. Border," *Journal of Contemporary Criminal Justice* 16 (2000): 445–456.

53. Wellford, 2001, 18.

54. Champion, 2005, 208.

55. Thomas C. Calhoun, "Male Street Hustling: Introduction Processes and Stigma Containment," *Sociological Spectrum* 12 (1992): 35–52; Jacqueline Boles and Kirk W. Elifson, "The Social Organization of Transvestite Prostitution and AIDS," *Social Science and Medicine* 39 (1994): 85–93; Kerwin Kay, "Male Prostitution in the Twentieth Century: Pseudohomosexuals, Hoodlum Homosexuals, and Exploited Teens," *Journal of Homosexuality* 46 (2003): 1–77.

56. Robert T. Michael, John H. Gagnon, Edward O. Laumann, and Gina Kolata, *Sex in America: A Definitive Survey* (Boston: Little, Brown and Company, 1994).

57. Samuel S. Janus and Cynthia L. Janus, *The Janus Report on Sexual Behavior* (New York: Wiley. 1993).

58. Michael, et al., 1994.

59. Janus and Janus, 1993.

60. John J. Potterat, D.E. Woodhouse, J.B. Muth, and Stephen Q. Muth, "Estimating the Prevalence and Career Longevity of Prostitute Women," *Journal of Sex Research* 27 (1990): 233–243.

61. Ine Vanwesenbeeck, "Another Decade of Social Scientific

Work on Sex Work: A Review of Research, 1990–2000," *Annual Review of Sex Research* XII (2001): 242–288. Also see Ronald Weitzer, "Flawed Theory and Method in Studies of Prostitution," *Violence Against Women* 11(2005): 934–949.

62. Ronald Weitzer, "Why We Need More Research on Sex Work," in Ronald Weitzer, ed., *Sex for Sale: Prostitution, Pornography, and the Sex Industry* (New York: Routledge, 2000): 1–16.

63. R. Barri Flowers, *The Prostitution of Women and Girls* (Jefferson, NC: McFarland, 1998).

64. James A. Inciardi, Dorothy Lockwood, and Anne E. Pottieger, *Women and Crack Cocaine* (New York: Macmillan, 1993).

65. Melissa Farley and Vanessa Kelly, "Prostitution: A Critical Review of the Medical and Social Sciences Literature," *Women and Criminal Justice* 11 (2004): 29–64.

66. Kingsley Davis, "The Sociology of Prostitution," *American Sociological Review* 2 (1937): 744–755.

67. S.K. Hunter, "Prostitution Is Cruelty and Abuse to Women and Children," *Michigan Journal of Gender and Law* 1 (1994): 1–14.

68. John J. Potterat, Richard B. Rothenberg, Stephen Q. Muth, William W. Darrow, and Lyanne Phillips-Plummer, "Pathways to Prostitution: The Chronology of Sexual and Drug Abuse Milestones," *Journal of Sex Research* 35 (1998): 333–340.

69. Susan M. Nadon, Catherine Koverola, and Eduard H. Schludermann, "Antecedents to Prostitution: Childhood Victimization," *Journal of Interpersonal Violence* 13 (1998): 206–222.

70. Leon E. Pettiway, *Workin' It: Women Living Through Drugs and Crime* (Philadelphia: Temple University Press, 1997).

71. Ine Vanwesenbeeck, 2001, 242–288.

72. Ibid.

73. Jody Miller and Martin D. Schwartz, "Rape Myths and Violence Against Street Prostitutes," *Deviant Behavior* 16 (1995): 1–23.

74. Jody Miller, "Your Life Is On the Line Every Night You're on the Streets: Victimization and Resistance Among Street Prostitutes," *Humanity & Society* 17 (1993): 422–446.

75. Charisse Coston and Lee E. Ross, "Criminal Victimization of Prostitutes: Empirical Support for the Lifestyle/Exposure Model," *Journal of Crime and Justice* 21 (1998): 53–70.

76. Martin A. Monto, "Female Prostitution, Customers, and Violence," *Violence Against Women* 10 (2004): 160–168.

77. Richard Tewksbury and Patricia Gagné, "Lookin' for Love in All the Wrong Places: Men Who Patronize Prostitutes," in Ronald M. Holmes and Stephen T. Holmes, eds., *Current Perspectives on Sex Crimes* (Thousand Oaks, CA: Sage, 2002): 88–89.

78. Farley and Kelly, 2004.

79. VanWesenbeeck, 2001; Weitzer, 2005.

80. Tewksbury and Gagné, 2002, 89; Nancy Romero-Daza, Margaret Weeks, and Merrill Singer, "Conceptualizing the Impact of Indirect Violence on HIV Risk Among Women Involved in Street-Level Prostitution," *Aggression and Violent Behavior* 10 (2005): 153–170.

81. Clyde B. McCoy, Lisa R. Metsch, and Robert S. Anwyl, "Dual Epidemics: Crack Cocaine and HIV/AIDS," in Dale D. Chitwood, James E. Rivers, and James A. Inciardi, eds., *The American Pipe Dream: Crack Cocaine and the Inner City* (New York: Harcourt Brace, 1996): 95.

82. Farley and Kelly, 2004.

83. Ronald Weitzer, "The Growing Moral Panic Over Prostitution and Sex Trafficking," *The Criminologist* 30 (September/October 2005): 1: 3.

84. Barbara G. Brents and Kathryn Hausbeck, "Violence and Legalized Brothel Prostitution in Nevada: Examining Safety, Risk, and Prostitution Policy," *Journal of Interpersonal Violence* 20 (2005): 270–295.

85. Coalition Against Trafficking in Women, available at http://www.catwinternational.org, accessed January 10, 2006.

86. Ann M. Lucas, "The Work of Sex Work: Elite Prostitutes' Vocational Orientations and Life Experiences," *Deviant Behavior* 26 (2005): 513–546.

87. Phil Hubbard and Teela Sanders, "Making Space for Sex Work: Female Street Prostitution and the Production of Urban Space," *International Journal of Urban and Regional Research* 27 (2003): 75–89.

88. Sherry Plaster Carter, Stanley L. Carter, and Andrew L. Dannenberg, "Zoning Out Crime and Improving Community Health in Sarasota, Florida: Crime Prevention Through Environmental Design," *American Journal of Public Health* 93 (2003): 1442–1445.

89. Michael S. Scott, *Street Prostitution — Problem-Oriented Guides for Police Series,* No. 2 (Washington, DC: U.S. Department of Justice, Office of Community Oriented Policing Services, 2002): 3.

90. Ibid., 16–21.

WWW.CRIMINOLOGY.JBPUB.COM

Interactivities
In the News
Key Term Explorer
Web Links

CHAPTER 12

OBJECTIVES

Discuss the relationship between drugs and crime.

Compare the research findings on drug use among the general public and persons in jail and prison.

Describe the Goldstein models of drug use and how they explain drugs and criminal behavior.

Discuss research findings on the effectiveness of treatment, especially the drug court model.

Discuss the economic impact of both the illegal drug trade and drug abuse.

Explain the arguments for and against the legalization of drugs such as marijuana.

Drugs and Crime

"

Is criminal behavior antecedent to addiction, or does criminality emerge subsequent to addiction? More specifically, is crime the result of a response to a special set of life circumstances brought about by addiction to narcotic drugs? Or conversely is addiction per se a deviant tendency characteristic of individuals already prone to offense behavior? Moreover . . . does the onset of chronic narcotics use bring about a change in the nature, intensity, and frequency of deviant and criminal acts? Does criminal involvement tend to increase or decrease subsequent to addiction? . . . What kinds of criminal offenses do addicts engage in? Do they tend toward violent acts of aggression? Or are their crimes strictly profit-oriented and geared toward violation of the sanctity of private property? Or is it both?

— James A. Inciardi[1]
Director, Center for Drug and Alcohol Studies,
University of Delaware

"

Crack Cocaine Breeds Violence

As many as 40% of the River City homicides last year involved drugs, especially crack cocaine. One example was the deaths of Harvey Johnson and James Foster; they were shot in the head last July by three men who didn't want to pay for a gram of cocaine. According to one of the suspects, "Everything was cool until . . . the dope didn't show right."

Another homicide case was the death of Shannon Bell, who was beaten and strangled. Her body was dumped in a trash container, allegedly by two of her public housing complex neighbors, Erwin Hayes and Charles Calvin. They are charged with her murder. They told homicide investigators that the three used crack cocaine and a drug deal had gone awry. Hayes said he was high when Bell was killed.

Often, determining the role of crack cocaine in a homicide case is pure guesswork. "The only person whose motive is ever clear to us is the murderer and they are usually not talking," said chief homicide detective Walter Holmes.

River City police say that crack, the highly addictive form of cocaine, arrived in this city later than other cities. According to police records, crack-related arrests are up 36% from last year. "Crack cocaine breeds violence," said Sam Elliot, head of River City Treatment Programs. "It is a strong stimulant narcotic. When you come off that drug, there is a strong feeling of belligerence and hostility, anger and frustration."

A national rise in homicide rates during the second half of the 1980s and early 1990s was attributable to the development of the crack trade and fierce competition between drug dealers competing for control of the market. Drug traffickers employed gun-toting salespeople who then squared off with their competitors. Scores of murders followed. The following table presents data on the number of drug-related homicides nationwide from 1991 to 1998.

Year	Number of Homicides	Drug Related (in %)
1991	21,676	6.2
1992	22,716	5.7
1993	23,180	5.5
1994	22,084	5.6
1995	20,232	5.0
1996	15,848	4.9
1997	15,289	5.1
1998	14,088	4.8

Source: Drug Policy Information Clearinghouse, Office of National Drug Control Policy, *Drugs & Crime Data — Fact Sheet: Drug-Related Crime* (Washington, DC: U.S. Department of Justice, 2000): 4.

In River City, this pattern was evident following the closing of two public housing areas last year. Cosair Homes was a major drug bazaar and its closing dispersed those dealers across the city, searching for other appropriate markets in public housing areas. Those areas experienced a subsequent increase in shootings and homicides in disputes over crack cocaine territories and customers.

In other cities such as Chicago, this trend subsided after turf issues had been settled. Cooling of the crack cocaine market is one reason why homicide rates declined in the late 1990s but some cities are behind the times.

Use the three Goldstein models to explain the phenomenon just described. Which of the three models offers the best explanation of why homicide rates have risen in River City?

Introduction

Drugs, although never completely absent from American life, have varied in the type and level of use throughout history. The U.S. Constitution has profoundly influenced the evolving interpretation of, and the legal response and consequences to, drugs. State and police powers now regulate the health professions and drug availability. Results to this have been mixed, producing a free economy in drugs until the late 19th century, when state anti-drug laws were enacted.

The questions posed by James Inciardi in the opening quote capture the nature of the relationship between drugs and crime. Answering these questions often drives research on drugs and criminal behavior. This chapter offers a brief overview of the history of drug abuse in the United States; explores the research evidence concerning criminal behavior and substance abuse; examines trends in drug use by juveniles; discusses specific drugs and their classification; and considers key policy issues, such as treatment and legalization, and analyzes their strengths and weaknesses.

Drug Use: A Historical Perspective

Narcotic drugs, introduced in the mid-19th century, offered promising applications for pain relief. However, by 1900, there were deep misgivings about the overuse of such drugs.

Opium, widely available to Americans in the 18th and 19th centuries, was used in a variety of medicines and concoctions.[2] Morphine, first isolated from opium in 1805, could be taken orally, applied topically, and injected.[3] Such extraction of purified active ingredients and their direct injection led to careless overprescription, because physicians incorrectly believed that, because the amount given by injection was so much smaller than the dosage given by mouth, there was little chance of addiction.

When cocaine was introduced in 1860, no restrictions were imposed on its sale or distribution. Alcohol extracts were marketed as tonics that provided energy and endurance. Indeed, an early formulation of Coca-Cola (minus the alcohol) was modeled after such a tonic.[4] However, concerns about cocaine mounted. The Shanghai Opium Commission of 1909 and a 1911 conference in The Hague were international responses to the growing problem of opium and cocaine.[5]

Marijuana, although regarded by many as benign, became the target of increasing scrutiny in the 1930s. In 1937, the Marijuana Tax Act became law.

In the United States, laws against narcotics at all levels reflected a growing antagonism toward their use.[6] Ironically, as the use of drugs decreased, the severity of punishment increased; indeed, by 1955, the federal penalty for providing heroin to anyone under the age of 18 years was death.[7]

In the 1960s, the recreational use of drugs increased. Marijuana and hallucinatory drugs such as LSD, peyote, depressants, barbiturates, and opiates (particularly heroin) were widely used. The Comprehensive Drug Abuse Act of 1970 led to softer penalties for federal drug violations, offsetting punitive laws of the Harrison Narcotic Act of 1914.

A tolerance of drug use continued to rise until the late 1970s. However, in the decades since, this tolerance has decreased while the fear of drug use has risen. Extensive antidrug campaigns were conducted in the 1980s and the motto "Just say no" was underscored by programs such as DARE (Drug Awareness Resistance Education).

During the 1980s, the war on crime became primarily a war on drugs as public concern over the problem increased dramatically.[8] In January 1985, only 2% of a national sample identified drug abuse as the most important problem facing the country. By November 1989, that figure had risen to 38%[9]; however, this percentage marked the peak for this fear. By February 2003, the percentage of Gallup poll respondents who considered drug abuse the most serious problem facing the country plummeted to 1%.[10]

This decline in concern about drug abuse matched the decrease in reported substance abuse in the country. Between 1979 and 2001, the percentage of persons reporting any illicit drug use declined for younger persons. For example, the percentage of persons age 12–17 who had ever used an illicit drug was 31.8% in 1979 and 28.4% in 2001; in the most recent reported past year (24.3% to 20.8%) and in the most recent reported past 30 days (14.3% to 10.8%). However, persons 26 and over reported increased use across all categories between 1979 and 2001. For example, persons aged 26–34 who had ever used an illicit drug rose from 49% in 1979 to 53.3% in 2001.[11]

Some indications of serious drug problems remain. These survey results also indicated that the earlier in life people initiate drug use, the more likely they are to develop a drug problem.[12] In addition, surveys of prisoners revealed that drug users are more likely than nonusers to commit crimes. Arrestees were frequently under the influence of drugs at the time of their offense, and these drugs were likely to generate violent behavior.[13]

As a result, the debate on what to do about drug abuse has generated a number of different policy suggestions.[14] Since 1980, there have been four major antidrug bills:[15]

1. The Comprehensive Crime Control Act of 1984 broadened the criminal and civil asset forfeiture laws and increased the federal criminal sanctions for drug offenses.

2. The 1986 Anti-Drug Abuse Act: Although it provided money for treatment and prevention, it also restored mandatory prison sentences for large-scale distribution of marijuana and imposed new sanctions for money laundering.

3. The 1988 Anti-Drug Abuse Amendment Act primarily increased the sanctions for crimes related to drug trafficking and put new federal sanctions into place.

4. The Crime Control Act of 1990 doubled the appropriation for drug law enforcement grants to states and strengthened forfeiture and seizure statutes.

All have a specific focus on reducing the supply of drugs. Although other reduction strategies had been tried in the past, history went forward without a demonstration of lessons learned.

Historic attempts to reduce drug use include:

1. *Prohibition*: Focused on banning illegal drugs by meting out severe penalties for use, distribution, and sale. Here illegal substance abuse is seen as a primary cause of crime. Therefore, the transport, possession, and sale of certain drugs are illegal. It also includes "hard-line" solutions such as interdiction and enhanced criminal sentences for offenders. The expectation is that these methods would force potential sellers to seek out other economic pursuits. In addition, the violence generated by the drug marketplace and the crime committed by persons to support their habit would be eliminated.

2. *Legalization*: Calls for the elimination of drug laws and the institution of government regulation on the use of now-illegal drugs.

3. *Decriminalization*: The removal of criminal penalties for the possession of illegal drugs.

4. *Medicalization*: Giving physicians the responsibility for treating drug abusers, including the decision to maintain some users on the drug on which they have become dependent.

5. *Harm reduction*: Emphasizes the use of a public health model to reduce the risks and consequences of drug abuse.

These different methods have attracted the attention of criminologists and policy makers in the United States and elsewhere. When discussing marijuana and its history in the United States, it is clear that the legal sanctions and control — not treatment, prevention, and education — have dictated policy. By attempting to keep marijuana from being imported, the United States has inadvertently encouraged domestic cultivation of new, more potent strands of marijuana. As a drug favored by youth and a gateway drug (one whose use leads to that of other more serious substances), it is unlikely that marijuana will become decriminalized.[16]

Drugs and Criminal Behavior

The Incidence of Substance Abuse Among Offenders

"Does drug use cause crime or does crime cause drug use?"[17] This is a classic chicken-or-the-egg question that appears to go both ways. Drug use may increase criminal behavior but it may do so by introducing the user to a high-risk subculture that promotes crime over legitimate, low-paying jobs to raise money. Criminals may be more likely to use drugs because they already are part of this subculture.[18] Thus, it is difficult to separate these two behaviors and determine which causes the other. The drugs–crime relationship is summarized in TABLE 14-1.

Research evidence reveals a strong link between substance abuse and criminal behavior. Bernard Gropper summarized research showing that offenders with a substance abuse problem commit a high percentage of the violent crimes (e.g., robbery; 75%). Drug addicts commit more crimes while they are under the influence — some four to six times more than when clean.[19] Research on heroin addicts in treatment uncovered a small group of "violent predators" responsible for a disproportionate amount of crime even when they were not addicted.[20] In his analysis of the relationship between drugs and crime, Inciardi concluded that "narcotics use freezes its users into patterns of criminality that are more acute, dynamic, violent, unremitting and enduring than those of other drug-using offenders."[21]

Substance-abusing offenders are typically cited as the most plausible explanation for high levels of property crime.[22] In 1997, more than 80% of state and 70% of federal prisoners reported past drug use. This report also noted that[23]:

TABLE 14-1

Summary of the Drugs–Crime Relationship

Drugs–Crime Relationship	Definition	Examples
Drug-defined offenses	Violation of laws prohibiting or regulating the possession, use, distribution, or manufacture of illegal drugs	Drug possession or use; marijuana cultivation; methamphetamine production; cocaine, heroin, or marijuana sales
Drug-related offenses	Offenses in which a drug's pharmacologic effects contribute; offenses motivated by the user's need for money to support continued use; offenses connected to drug distribution itself	Violent behavior resulting from drug's effects; stealing to get money to buy drugs; violence against rival drug dealers
Drug-using lifestyle	Drug use and crime common aspects of a deviant lifestyle; likelihood and frequency of involvement in illegal activity increased because drug users may not participate in the legitimate economy and are exposed to situations that encourage crime	Life orientation with an emphasis on short-term goals supported by illegal activities; opportunities to offend resulting from conflicts with offenders and illegal markets; criminal skills learned from other offenders

Source: Drug Policy Information Clearinghouse, Office of National Drug Control Policy, *Drugs & Crime Data — Fact Sheet: Drug-Related Crime* (Washington, DC: U.S. Department of Justice, 2000): 1; see also http://www.whitehousedrugpolicy.gov/publications/factsht/crime/index.html.

- About one in six prisoners overall reported committing their present offense to obtain money to buy drugs.
- Three out of four state and four out of five federal prisoners may be characterized as alcohol- or drug-involved offenders.
- Half of all prisoners were under the influence of alcohol and drugs at the time of their offense.
- The majority of state (72%) and federal (66%) prisoners were under the influence of cocaine or crack at the time of their offense.
- Assault, murder, and sexual assault were most closely tied to alcohol use at the time of the offense.
- Among drug offenders, 70% of state and 86% of federal prisoners were convicted of drug trafficking.

Nearly 75% of federal and more than 60% of state prisoners had used drugs in the past — a 60% increase in use over prisoners surveyed in 1991.[24]

Eric Wish and Brian Johnson also found that greater levels of illicit drug use are related to higher rates of drug distribution offenses and other serious offenses. In 1984, in fact, more than half of those charged with murder, manslaughter, robbery, and burglary in Manhattan tested positive for one or more drugs upon arrest.[25] Similarly, J.J. Collins reports that offenders who are problem drinkers are disproportionately involved in violent crime.[26]

Research further shows that offenders with active drug or alcohol abuse problems are likely to continue their criminal behavior.[27] In 1997, half of the state inmates and a third of the federal inmates surveyed reported that they committed their present offense while under the influence of drugs and/or alcohol.[28] The survey also revealed[29]:

- For both groups of prisoners, alcohol use was specifically related to violent crime: assault, murder, manslaughter, and sexual assault.
- Almost one-third of these prisoners were under the influence of drugs at the time of their offense. Marijuana was the most common drug abused by inmates while on the street, followed by crack cocaine, heroin, and stimulants.
- About one in six prisoners said that they committed their offense to get money for drugs.
- Prisoners were as likely to experience problems with alcohol as with drugs. Three quarters of all prisoners reported involvement with drug or alcohol abuse at the time of their offense.
- Female state prisoners reported higher levels of past drug use; levels were higher for male federal prisoners.
- Prisoners age 44 and younger report more prior drug use than older prisoners.
- Prior drug use of state prisoners varied little by race. Hispanics reported the lowest levels of abuse in federal prisons.

This level of involvement is clearly related to criminal behavior. A long-term study of addicts involved in treatment programs determined that

Police arrest a suspect in a drug bust.

? *What does the research on drug use among prisoners demonstrate about the relationship between drug abuse and crime?*

Similarly, Ball compared crime rate findings on three groups of male heroin addicts enrolled in methadone-maintenance programs in New York City, Philadelphia, and Baltimore. Addicts from these three cities had comparable offense rates. During an average addiction year, these offenders committed 603 (New York City), 631 (Philadelphia), and 567 (Baltimore) offenses. In each city, the most frequent offense was trafficking in drugs, followed by thefts from stores and forgery (checks). There were no differences in either the volume or pattern of offenses committed by the heroin addicts across the three cities.[35]

Heroin addicts do not specialize in one type of crime.[36] A study of 105 New York City addicts, for example, showed that during a single day, they committed 46 robberies (average take: $79), 22

dependence on cocaine and/or heroin was related to a greater diversity in offending and a specialization in violent, predatory crimes.[30]

Much of the crime committed by heroin addicts is devoted to obtaining funds to purchase more drugs. Research shows that the crime rate among heroin addicts is higher during periods of active addiction.[31] This pattern apparently holds true for both blacks and whites.[32] Another study found that most heroin addicts began committing minor property crimes before becoming addicted. Then, as their drug use increased, their rate of property crime increased as well. They also engaged in drug dealing to support their habit.[33]

John Ball and his colleagues interviewed a sample of 243 heroin addicts from a population of 4069 males arrested by the Baltimore Police Department between 1952 and 1971. Over an 11-year period, these addicts committed over 473,000 crimes — averaging 178 crimes per offender per year. The dominant offense was larceny-theft, but over 60% of the sample had been arrested more than once for violent crimes. Clearly, arrest and incarceration had little deterrent effect on their criminal careers.[34]

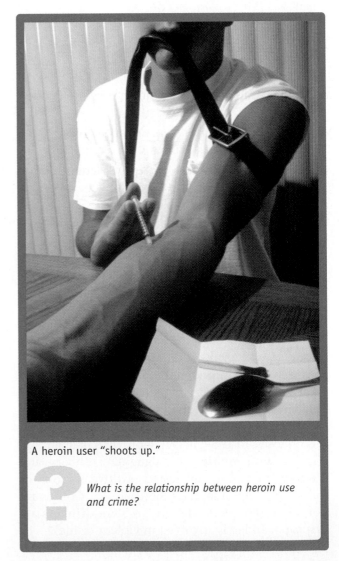

A heroin user "shoots up."

? *What is the relationship between heroin use and crime?*

burglaries ($112), and 41 thefts ($51). On average, addicts managed to hold onto only 5% of their money a day later. Robbers were the ones most likely to spend their funds on cocaine and heroin.[37]

Another argument is that drug use fuels crime because heroin addicts need money to purchase additional drugs. However, Inciardi strongly questions this **enslavement theory of addiction**: that monopolistic control over the heroin black market forces addicts into lives of crime to support their habit.[38] The research on the crime rates among heroin and other drug addicts has "convincingly documented that while drug use tends to intensify and perpetuate criminal behavior, it usually does not initiate criminal careers."[39] Similarly, the Chaikens assert that among predatory (violent) offenders, drug use only enhances the continuation and seriousness of a criminal career.[40]

One might expect to find that toughened drug laws led to a reduction in drug use. In fact, from the 1980s to 1999, drug use did not decline. Measures of the extent of drug use in the United States may be found in:

- National Household Survey on Drug Abuse
- Monitoring the Future Survey
- Survey of Health Related Behavior Among Military Personnel
- Drug Abuse Warning Network
- Survey of Inmates in State Correctional Facilities
- Arrestee Drug Abuse Monitoring

Drugs are related to crime in multiple ways, as reported in the Drug-Related Crime Survey of 2000. It is a crime to use, possess, manufacture, or distribute drugs classified as having a potential for abuse (e.g., cocaine, heroin, marijuana, and amphetamines). Drugs are also related to crime through the effects they have on the user's behavior and by generating violence and other illegal activity in connection with drug trafficking.

Drug-related offenses and drug-using lifestyles are also major contributors to the U.S. crime problem. The U.S. Department of Health and Human Services (HHS) conducts an annual National Household Survey on Drug Abuse (NHSDA) that asks individuals living in households about their drug and alcohol use and their involvement in crimes. In the year 2000, illicit drug users were about 16 times more likely than nonusers to report being arrested and booked for larceny or theft; more than 14 times

more likely to be arrested and booked for such offenses as driving while under the influence, drunkenness, or liquor law violations; and more than nine times more likely to be arrested and booked on an assault charge.[41]

The annual Bureau of Justice Statistics National Crime Victimization Survey asks victims of violent crimes who have reported seeing the offender, whether they "perceived" the offender as being under the influence of drugs or alcohol. According to the 1998 survey, 30% of victims reported they could not determine whether the offender was under the influence of drugs or alcohol. Of those who felt they could make a determination, about 31% percent noted that the offender was under the influence of alcohol and/or drugs.[42]

LINK The National Crime Victimization Survey (NCVS) was discussed in Chapter 2.

The Goldstein Models

Paul J. Goldstein offers an explanation of how drug abuse sponsors violent behavior that focuses on the effect of the drug and the motivation for the violent crime. There are three different models[43]:

1. **The psychopharmacological model:** Violent crime is a result of the effect of the drug on the offender and/or the victim. In short, the drug sponsors irrational and violent behavior.[44]

2. **The economic-compulsive model:** The offender commits a violent crime (e.g., murder or assault) during the course of a robbery. The addict commits crime to obtain money to support a drug habit.[45]

3. **The systemic model:** Some violent crimes are committed as a result of the pattern of drug use and distribution. These crimes represent an outgrowth of the system of drug dealing (e.g., gang wars) or reflect disputes between dealers and consumers (e.g., poor-quality drugs, failure to make payment) within a black market, elimination of informers, and robberies of drug dealers followed by retaliation.

Inciardi states that heroin use promotes psychopharmacological violence. For example, heroin-using prostitutes often engage in violence against their customers due to the irritability caused by withdrawal. It leads them to rob, rather than service, their clients.[46] He also believes that all three of the Goldstein models explain the impact of crack cocaine. First, the chronic use of crack leads to the "cocaine psychosis-paranoia that may lead to violent behavior against imagined persecutors." Cocaine-related violence may thus fit the psychopharmacological model. Second, crack addicts may commit robberies and muggings to support their drug habit (the economic-compulsive model). Third, systemic violence between cocaine traffickers is a byproduct of the crack trade.[47] This type of violence is so common that it has a street name: <u>tweaking</u>. Studies in New York and Miami report that cocaine is the "most frequently identified illegal drug in the bodies of homicide victims."[48] **TABLE 14-2** demonstrates the norms that have sprung up in this criminal subculture. For a case study that can be analyzed using the Goldstein models, see the **You Are the Criminologist** feature in this chapter.

However, data from the FBI's Uniform Crime Reporting program demonstrate that, nationwide, the percentage of drug-related homicides is declining and has leveled off since the peak year of 1989 (see **TABLE 14-3**).

LINK The strengths and weaknesses of the FBI's Uniform Crime Reporting system are presented in Chapter 2.

TABLE 14-3

Drug-Related Homicides by Year

Year	Number of Homicides	Drug Related (in %)
1987	17,963	4.9
1988	17,971	5.6
1989	18,954	7.4
1990	20,273	6.7
1991	21,676	6.2
1992	22,716	5.7
1993	23,180	5.5
1994	22,084	5.6
1995	20,232	5.1
1996	16,967	5.0
1997	15,837	5.1
1998	14,276	4.8
1999	13,011	4.5
2000	13,230	4.5
2001	14,061	4.1
2002	14,263	4.7
2003	14,408	4.6

Source: Bureau of Justice Statistics, *Drugs and Crime Facts: Drug Use and Crime,* available at http://www.ojp.usdoj.gov/bjs/dcf/duc.htm, accessed December 15, 2005.

TABLE 14-2

Norms of the Criminal Underclass Subculture

The criminal underclass subculture appears to have several norms that facilitate the drug trade:

- Illegal means are better than legal means for earning money. Legal money is "chump change." Hustlers are admired for their ability.
- Other people are to be manipulated and their goods or money taken for the offender's benefit. For example, women are "hos" valued only for sexual favors and the family is expected to provide basic necessities without any financial input from the criminal.
- Violence should be used to gain funds and maintain one's reputation.
- Illegal income should be spent on luxury items (e.g., gold jewelry, fancy clothes), drugs, and parties rather than basic necessities (e.g., food, shelter, and savings).
- Criminals should remain unknown to public officials (police and tax authorities).

Source: Based on Bruce D. Johnson, Terry Williams, Kojo A. Dei, and Harry Sanabria, "Drug Abuse in the Inner City: Impact Upon Hard-Drug Users and the Community," in Michael Tonry and James Q. Wilson, eds., *Drugs and Crime: Crime and Justice,* 13th ed. (Chicago: University of Chicago Press, 1990): 26–28.

Women, Drug Abuse, and Crime

To what extent do males and females differ when it comes to substance abuse and crime? In 1997, women (62%) in state prisons were more likely than male inmates (56%) to have used drugs in the month prior to their present offense. They were also more likely to commit this offense while under the influence of drugs (40% vs. 32%).[49] Researchers studying women, crime, and drug abuse usually have focused on females as a separate group in treatment programs (e.g., methadone maintenance) or in jail or prison. They usually do not make comparisons between male and female addicts, but they do try to analyze the relationship between specific drugs and the onset of criminality.

One study examined the results of drug testing on probationers and parolees and found that females had a more pronounced and persistent addiction problem than males, finding that females were more likely to be cross addicted to both drugs and alcohol. Women had higher long-term rates of substance abuse and were more likely to inject substances and engage in prostitution to acquire hard drugs. Of course, both of these behaviors put them at greater risk for contracting HIV/AIDS. Females had more problems finding jobs due to their lack of training and experience and their need for child care and referrals for Aid to Dependent Children (ADC).[50] Therefore, women face significantly different treatment needs to overcome substance abuse and to successfully return to society. Similarly, it has been recommended that therapeutic communities for female offenders should include dealing with abusive relationships and domestic violence as well as anonymous HIV and TB testing.[51] It may be that prison is the best site to provide substance-abuse treatment for substance-abusing, criminally involved females.[52] Prison provides an opportunity to offer services to a group in need while they are incarcerated.

In California, M. Douglas Anglin and Yih-Ing Hser studied 328 Anglo and Chicana female methadone-maintenance clients from 1976 to 1978. Although most of the women had committed property crimes before becoming addicted, their activity increased with their level of substance abuse.[53] Jose Sanchez and Brian Johnson found a similar pattern among drug-abusing women at New York's Rikers Island prison. The women who were daily users of heroin and cocaine had higher crime rates (e.g., property and drug crimes, fraud, and prostitution) than those who limited their drug use to marijuana, depressants, stimulants, or illegal methadone.[54]

Research reveals no clear distinction between the level of substance abuse and the types of crime committed by female substance abusers. Inciardi and Pottieger compared interview data from two Miami female cohorts. The first cohort was heavily involved with a variety of drugs and committed a great number of property crimes, vice offenses, and drug sales. The second cohort was more likely to abuse heroin and cocaine daily and committed more vice and drug sale crimes but fewer property crimes than the first cohort.[55] Inciardi and his colleagues also found that black female heroin addicts had "productive" criminal careers. Sixty-three women reported that they were responsible for over 32,000 offenses in the past year (median = 332) with prostitution, drug sales, and shoplifting accounting for most of the crimes.[56] Crack cocaine use caused street criminal women to engage in intense patterns of criminality and high-risk sexual behaviors.[57] Again, it was determined that these substance-abusing women lacked job skills and did not have funds from legal sources to obtain social and health services, making them more vulnerable to their street-addict lifestyle.[58]

A female drug addict smoking heroin.

? *How are substance abuse and female crime related?*

A related question is how women form drug partnerships (for the possession and/or sale of illegal drugs) with men. Leon Pettiway examined the effect of domestic arrangements, drug use, and criminal involvement on participation in crime partnerships by women. He found drug partnerships with men caused women to engage in a greater number of crimes. Also, these crimes were more likely to be vice and predatory crimes when women partnered with men.[59]

These studies show that addicted women engage in higher rates of crime when they are abusing drugs. However, instead of violent crimes, they more often commit property and vice crimes. The studies also confirm that female offenders with drug problems have different treatment needs that should be addressed to protect the community from further victimization. Programs must address these differences and not simply treat males and females in the same fashion. Because the impact of addiction is so dissimilar for males and females, treatment programs must consider the special problems that women, particularly mothers, face.[60]

Delinquency and Drug Abuse

Drugs also appear to play a crucial role in delinquency. Chaiken and Johnson reported that adolescents who used multiple drugs were more likely to be seriously delinquent. Young men and women who drank and used marijuana were likely to be truant and to steal. Juveniles who distributed drugs were responsible for 60% of all teenage felony thefts. In addition, they were more likely to continue their criminal careers as adults.[61]

In Florida, youths who tested positive for marijuana/hashish use had more juvenile court referrals for nondrug felony offenses.[62] Interviews with New York City youths revealed that seriously delinquent youths were regular users of drugs and alcohol. Furthermore, the most delinquent youths had the most significant substance-abuse histories.[63] An important source of information on substance-abuse rates among juveniles is the National Youth Survey conducted by the Institute of Behavioral Studies at the University of Colorado. An analysis of these data revealed that a very small proportion of drug-abusing delinquents (less that 5% of American youths) accounted for up to 60% of felony crimes committed. However, these reported crimes were not usually the result of an attempt to obtain drug money.[64] Findings from the Pittsburgh Youth Study of 1987 and 1988 indicate that drug-abusing youths often commit violent crimes and offenses with others and are likely to be arrested.[65] The 1995 Youth Risk Behavior Survey determined that school violence was related to the availability of drugs and increased with the number of drugs used.[66]

Other studies on drug abuse and delinquency failed to establish any direct relationship between the two. In one study, there was some indication that alcohol played a role in sexual assault and that serious drug abuse led to prolonged involvement in serious delinquency.[67] Factors influencing drug abuse among juveniles included age (older) and peer group influence, yet these factors were not related to delinquency.[68] A survey of male and female adolescents revealed that marijuana use was related to property offenses but was not associated with aggressive delinquency.[69] Here, as with adults, it is difficult to determine whether drug abuse drives criminal behavior or vice versa.

Studies also show that drug use is related to childhood physical and sexual abuse.[70] A study of juvenile drug abusers and their families revealed that juvenile self-esteem and perception of parental behavior, as well as parental attitudes toward child rearing, influenced levels of drug use.[71] Put simply, juveniles who are physically and sexually abused and who are raised in a laissez-faire atmosphere about drugs in the absence of strict parental supervision were more likely to abuse illegal drugs.

Gang involvement also plays an important role in the link between delinquency and drug abuse. In examining drug use and dealing among juvenile gang members in Los Angeles, San Diego, and Chicago, Fagan found that the level of gang-crime activity was related to the amount of drug use within the gang.[72] The link to violent crime was not directly related to substance abuse. Gangs have been found to be closely involved in the sale of drugs but their involvement was not as organized as would be expected. Predominately male gangs who had and were willing to use guns were more likely to engage in drug trafficking.[73]

However, the nature of the drug used may play a role in this relationship. For example, Inciardi and Pottieger interviewed 254 Miami delinquents concerning their involvement with crack cocaine. The youths in the crack business used marijuana, depressants, or crack on an almost daily basis. These dealers also spent more money on crack than other delinquents and had a longer and more serious delinquent career at a younger age.[74]

In her review of the literature on delinquency and drug use, White concludes that these behaviors are not causally related, but rather are independent manifestations of the deviant behavior in which juveniles engage. She also found that the majority of adolescents, despite their level of substance abuse, have little or no involvement with delinquency. Peer-group influences appear to be the best predictors of both delinquency and drug abuse.[75]

Types of Illegal Drugs: Drug Abuse and Trends

Controlled substances are usually grouped by pharmacological and legal criteria, and they fall into several categories: anabolic steroids, cannabis, depressants, hallucinogens, inhalants, and stimulants. The Drug Enforcement Agency (DEA) offers one more catch-all category, "dangerous drugs," which "includes illicitly manufactured as well as legitimate pharmaceutical stimulants, depressants, hallucinogens, and narcotics. Each class of substance is generally unlike other classes in its primary action and effect on the user."[76] Accountability and understanding the federal message about drugs and punishment have driven the federal trafficking penalties and controlled substances regulatory requirements.[77] Since 1970, the Controlled Substance Act places all substances that are in some way regulated under existing federal law into categories. The act also provides a mechanism for substances to be controlled, decontrolled, removed from control, and rescheduled or transferred from one schedule to another (See Section 201 of the Substance Controlled Act, 1970, 21 U.S.C. 811).

Trends in Use

Since 1975, the Monitoring the Future (MTF) survey annually studies the extent of drug abuse among high school 12th graders. The survey, expanded in 1991, also now includes 8th and 10th graders. Funded by the National Institute on Drug Abuse, the survey is conducted by the University of Michigan's Institute for Social Research. The goal of the survey is to collect data (30 day, annual, and lifetime) for drug use among students. **TABLE 14-4** lists the key findings from the 2004 Monitoring the Future survey.

In addition to studying drug use among 8th, 10th, and 12th graders, the MTF survey collects information on three attitudinal indicators related to drug use. These are the perceived risk of harm in taking a drug, disapproval of others who take drugs, and the perceived availability of drugs.

▌ The Impact of Treatment

Treatment for drug-abusing offenders can be effective. A research compendium of 41 treatment programs reported significant decreases in heroin and cocaine use among clients in treatment.[78] In their review of the treatment literature, Paul Gendreau and Richard Ross found that "addicts who stay the course of treatment or re-enroll after initial failure can decrease their drug intake and reduce criminal offenses."[79] Reviewing drug-abuse treatment programs, Anglin and Hser conclude that the longer a client remains in treatment, the greater the probability of success.[80]

These findings underscore the value of effective offender treatment programs. For example, a New York City study of a methadone maintenance program discovered that those clients who stayed with the treatment were less involved in criminal activity.[81] Research on the Kentucky Substance Abuse Program (KSAP) found that parolees who completed the program had substantially lower reincarceration rates during the first and second year of operations (3.6% and 9.7%) than those who did not complete treatment (35.2% and 36.6%).[82] Similarly, other research tracked clients referred to KSAP as a result of a positive drug test. Clients who completed treatment had a 3% reincarceration rate compared with 17.5% of persons who were referred but did not complete treatment and 6% for members of a comparison group.[83]

Drug courts have also been adopted as another method of dealing with offenders convicted of drug offenses. Beginning in Miami in 1989, a drug court is an intensive, community-based treatment and supervision program that is supervised by a judge, coupled with interaction between treatment, law enforcement, and court personnel.[84] Overall, studies have demonstrated that drug courts can effectively reduce both substance abuse and recidivism.[85] Their use is continuing to expand across the country.

John P. Walters, Director of the National Drug Control Policy, at City Hall in St. Louis on March 25, 2004. Walters traveled to 25 cities in the United States that were facing significant substance abuse problems.

? *What are the research findings on the effectiveness of Drug Courts?*

TABLE 14-4

Key Findings from the 2004 Monitoring the Future Survey (2003–2004)

Any illicit drug	30-day use of any illicit drug decreased significantly among 8th graders, from 9.7% in 2003 to 8.4% in 2004.
Inhalants	Lifetime use of inhalants increased significantly among 8th graders, from 15.8% in 2003 to 17.3% in 2004, continuing an upward trend in use noted among 8th graders in 2002, after several years of decline.
Prescription drugs	Annual use of Ritalin and Rohypnol remained statistically unchanged for all grades; annual use of Vicodin and OxyContin remained stable among all grades, but at somewhat high levels; annual use of Vicodin was at 2.5% for 8th graders, 6.2% for 10th graders, and 9.3% for 12th graders; annual use of OxyContin was at 1.7% for 8th graders, 3.5% for 10th graders, and 5.0% for 12th graders.
Marijuana	30-day use of marijuana was down significantly among 8th graders, from 7.5% in 2003 to 6.4% in 2004; some strengthening of attitudes against marijuana use also occurred among 8th and 10th graders.
MDMA (Ecstasy)	Lifetime use of MDMA decreased significantly for 10th graders, from 5.4% in 2003 to 4.3% in 2004; some strengthening of attitudes against use was seen among 10th and 12th graders.
Methamphetamine	Use decreased significantly among 8th graders, from 3.9% in 2003 to 2.5% in 2004 for lifetime use; from 2.5% in 2003 to 1.5% in 2004 for annual use; from 1.2% in 2003 to 0.6% in 2004 for 30-day use.
GHB and Ketamine	Significant decreases in annual use were seen among 10th graders for GHB, from 1.4% in 2003 to 0.8% in 2004; Ketamine from 1.9% in 2003 to 1.3% in 2004.
LSD	Lifetime use of LSD decreased significantly among 12th graders, from 5.9% in 2003 to 4.6% in 2004, continuing the pattern of decreases in LSD use noted in 2002 and 2003.
Anabolic steroids	Use of steroids decreased significantly among 8th graders, from 2.5% in 2003 to 1.9% in 2004 for lifetime use and from 1.4% in 2003 to 1.1% in 2004 for annual use; among 10th graders, lifetime use decreased significantly, from 3.0% in 2003 to 2.4% in 2004, continuing the decrease in use among 10th graders seen in 2003; steroid use among 12th graders remained stable at peak levels.
Cocaine (other than crack)	Significant increase in use of cocaine among 10th graders, from 1.1% in 2003 to 1.5% in 2004 for 30-day use
Cigarettes/Nicotine	Cigarette smoking decreased significantly among 10th graders, from 43.0% in 2003 to 40.7% in 2004 for lifetime use and from 4.1% in 2003 to 3.3% in 2004 for those smoking one-half pack or more per day; perception of harm from smoking one or more packs per day increased significantly among 8th and 10th graders from 2003 to 2004.
Alcohol, heroin, crack cocaine, hallucinogens other than LSD, PCP, amphetamines, tranquilizers, sedatives, and methaqualone	Remained stable among all grades from 2003 to 2004

Source: National Institute on Drug Abuse, 2004 Monitoring the Future Survey, available at http://www.drugabuse.gov, accessed December 14, 2005. For the 2004 MTF survey, 49,474 students in a nationally representative sample of 406 public and private schools were surveyed about lifetime, annual, 30-day, and daily use of drugs, alcohol, cigarettes, and smokeless tobacco.

These findings underscore the need for effective offender treatment. Punitive sanctions should be coupled with treatment to prevent crime.[86] For example, a therapeutic community can be combined with work release to treat offenders while helping the community.[87] Diverting felons convicted of drug offenses to residential treatment is a demonstrated method of handling these crimes.[88] Drug testing can also be combined with treatment while offenders are incarcerated to more accurately assess the effectiveness of programs.[89] In sum, drug treatment is a promising method to deal with drugs and crime.

The Economics of Drugs and Crime

Drug selling is a lucrative business. The United Nations Office for Drug Control and Crime Prevention estimated that the international illicit drug business generated approximately $400 billion in trade in 1998 or about 8% of all international trade worldwide.[90] High profitability attracts sellers to the drug marketplace. For example, according to the Office of National Drug Control Policy, in 2001, wholesale cocaine prices nationwide ranged from $12,000 to

$35,000 per kilogram. The price of heroin per kilogram ranged from a low of $13,200 (for the Mexican product) to $200,000 (South American products). Retail methamphetamine prices ranged from $400 to $3000 per ounce. The price of marijuana ranged from $400 to $6000 (sinsemilla) per pound.[91]

Purity levels vary by the type of drug. According to the Office of National Drug Control Policy, in 2001, the average purity level of cocaine was 73%. In 2000, the overall purity level (regardless of source) for heroin was 37%, compared with 7% 20 years ago. The average purity of methamphetamine seized by the U.S. Drug Enforcement Administration was 40% in 2001, down from its peak of 72% in 1994.[92]

A number of economic costs are associated with illicit drug use. Americans spent over $63 billion on illegal drugs in 2000 — ranging from $36.1 billion on cocaine to $2.2 billion on methamphetamines.[93] In 1998, the overall societal cost of drug abuse (lost productivity, health, and others, including criminal justice costs) was estimated at $143.4 billion, an increase over the 1992 figure of $102.2 billion.[94] Between 1980 and 1997, the number of drug arrests tripled. In 1997, four out of five drug arrests were for possession. Seventy-six percent of prison admissions between 1978 and 1996 were for nonviolent (mostly drug) offenses, while the amount of space housing violent offenders declined from 55% to 47%.[95] In 2000, it was estimated that the cost of incarcerating the approximately 485,000 drug offenders in the United States exceeded $9 billion annually.[96]

Of course, the crimes that drug abusers commit also cost society dearly. Official estimates of the crime-related costs of drug abuse increased to over $100 billion in 2000, up from about $61 billion in 1992.[97] A 1985 study estimated that the average heroin abuser committed about 100 crimes per year (especially robbery, burglary, larceny, and shoplifting). The average addict supplemented an annual legal income of $1000 with an illegal income of $12,000 and contributed more than $20,000 annually to the underground economy.[98] Addicts also increased their illegal income as their daily use of heroin and cocaine increased.[99]

Evidence concerning the link between employment, drug abuse, and levels of criminal activity is mixed. Interviews with 318 narcotic addicts revealed that they derived most of their income during periods of heavy use from illegal activities.

When they were not engaged in heavy use, their illegal income plummeted to less than 30% of their total income.[100] Similarly, 544 heroin users from five U.S. cities reported that they had lower rates of criminality while they were employed. However, employment did not have an impact on the rate of property crimes committed by women, nor did it slow drug sale offenses.[101]

The profits associated with the cocaine trade show similar effect on the economies of developing nations. For example, it is estimated that cocaine dealing added between $2 and $4 billion to the Columbian economy in the 1980s and 1990s. It also generated a real estate boom, revalued the Columbian peso, and encouraged contraband imports. However, it also became a source of income for left- and right-wing guerilla groups and the corruption of the government.[102]

Legalization of Drugs

Some argue that the best way to deal with the drug problem is to legalize drugs. Norval Morris and Gordon Hawkins, for example, propose that neither the acquisition nor the purchase, possession, or use of any drug should be a criminal offense as

An anti-narcotics officer surveys cocaine seized from a lab in Columbia.

? *How does the production of cocaine affect the Columbian economy?*

Max was an 18-year-old organizer and leader of a drug crew dealing in a major eastern city in the mid-1980s, before the advent of crack cocaine. Max's supplier "loaned" him three to five kilos of pure cocaine (the street value of which was between $180,000 and $360,000 at the time) for distribution. Max was responsible for returning about $100,000 a week.

When the crew was first formed in 1983, Max supplied each member with the amount of cocaine that they needed. They were responsible for sales to customers. After a designated time, they would return either money or unsold cocaine to Max and he would pay their supplier. It was estimated that, in the mid 1980s, Max and his top dealer could easily make a tax-free income of $100,000 or more after expenses.[1]

Thus, Max and his crew chose the benefits they could derive from their illegal activities and were selling their labor and sales skills in spite of the risk of receiving a substantial prison sentence upon apprehension and conviction. By selling high-quality cocaine to middle-class buyers (who would seldom interact with them other-

wise), Max and his crewmembers were taking advantage of the benefits of an illicit economy. The profits they could realize from the cocaine market were unlikely to present themselves elsewhere.

In particular, Max was able to benefit from the cocaine economy. He regularly sent a trusted relative back to Santo Domingo with $5000 in cash, which they converted at a very favorable exchange rate to the national economy. Max's otherwise destitute relatives were thus able to purchase comfortable homes in their homeland. Upon their arrival in the Unites States, several of his relatives also benefited by purchasing grocery stores (*bodegas*) and other cash businesses with Max's drug profits.

By the end of the 1980s, Max retired from the cocaine business at the request of his wife. He is reported to be living comfortably in Florida.

Use Robert Merton's theory of anomie and Messner and Rosenfeld's institutional anomie theory to analyze Max's involvement in the cocaine trade. Do these theories explain his involvement?

[1] According to the U.S. Office of Drug Control Policy, the 2003 wholesale price for powder cocaine in 2001 ranged from $400 to $1800 per ounce. Crack cocaine (which was not yet conceived of in Max's dealing days) prices typically ranged from $10 to $20 per rock. The price of these different types of cocaine can make drug selling a lucrative temptation for inner-city youths.

Sources: Executive Office of the President, Office of National Drug Control Policy. "Cocaine," *ONDCP Drug Policy Information Clearinghouse Fact Sheet* (November 2003), available at http://www.whitehouse drugpolicy.gov, accessed December 17, 2005; Bruce D. Johnson, T. Williams, K.A. Dei, and H. Sanabria, "Drug Abuse in the Inner City: Impact upon Hard-drug Users and the Community," in Michael Tonry and Norval Morris, eds., *Drugs and Crime* (Chicago: University of Chicago Press, 1990): 25–26.

---

long as it is bought from a licensed druggist through a prescription.[103] Others, however, have markedly different viewpoints.

LINK Robert Merton's theory of anomie and Messner and Rosenfeld's theory of institutional anomie are presented in Chapter 6.

Arguments in Favor of Legalization

Proponents of legalization argue that today's drug laws contribute to the problem in the following ways[104]:

- In the illegal narcotic trade, the criminal law operates as a "crime tariff" (a tax or duty) that makes the supply of narcotics profitable for the dealers by driving up prices. Simultaneously, it

discourages competition by keeping other vendors out of the market.

- Enhanced profits draw organized crime into the drug trade; these crime families grow, diversify, and promote other criminal activity.

- The high price caused by criminalization has a secondary criminogenic effect because it causes people to resort to crime to obtain the money for drugs.

- Harsh drug laws sponsor and enhance the growth of an extensive criminal subculture. Moreover, they give drug addiction the romantic aura of rebellion against authority, whereby the addict is somehow viewed as heroic. The rebellious image may have a particular appeal to juveniles and encourage experimentation with dangerous drugs.

- The attempts to enforce drug statutes consume disproportionate amounts of the time, energy, and resources of the criminal justice system, making it more difficult to deal with other types of crime.
- The drug trade promotes the corruption of the criminal justice system, particularly law enforcement officers. The availability of funds makes it possible to bribe officials.
- The drug trade promotes racial injustice. There are five times as many white drug users, yet black men are imprisoned at a rate that is 13.4 times greater than that of white men. In seven states, blacks constitute 80% to 90% of all drug offenders sentenced to prison.[105]

In short, current laws against drugs cause rather than deter crime. Therefore, according to these points, current illegal drugs should be legalized and addiction treated as a medical condition. This action would undercut the illicit traffic and largely eliminate the profit incentive supporting that traffic.

Similarly, Ralph Weisheit challenges the "criminalizers" of drugs by attacking a number of their basic assumptions. He makes the following points[106]:

- Criminalizers rely on deterrence theory to provide answers to the drug problem but fail to identify the most effective level of punishment. Extreme penalties are morally offensive and probably ineffective.
- It is impossible to "take back the streets" and halt the flow of illegal drugs. If law enforcement cannot keep drugs out of prisons, how can interdiction be effective in the free world?
- Criminalizers have been "shamefully silent" on whether the supervised use of drugs for the treatment of some medical problems should be permitted.
- It is difficult to assess the effectiveness of the war on drugs.
- Legal drugs, particularly alcohol and tobacco, are harmful. If some drugs deserve criminal penalties to combat their use, why don't these?
- There are problems associated with drug testing. First, drug tests measure use in the recent past, not current impairment. Second, they violate basic legal principles by presuming guilt until subjects can prove their innocence.

- Increasing the legal stigma attached to drug abuse and trafficking makes it more difficult for offenders to enter legitimate occupations following arrest.
- Law enforcement consumes the bulk of resources available to the neglect of alternatives such as treatment and prevention.
- Criminalizers assert that controlling the drug problem is the province of social institutions such as the family and the school systems. However, the use of classmates, teachers, and family members as informants may weaken, not strengthen these institutions.

Criminalization works against society in a variety of other ways as well.[107] First, it introduces the lower-class juvenile to the illegal drug market because of the vast profits available. Second, it leads to the corruption of law enforcement for the same reason. Third, it exposes police officers to increased risk of death and injury battling organized crime and juvenile gangs involved in the drug trade. Fourth, drug investigations bend civil liberties in the name of crime control. Fifth, the war on drugs is waged primarily against the poor and thus obscures the rate and type of substance abuse in the middle and upper classes. It also ignores the money that legal enterprises like banks (money laundering) and real estate agencies (the purchase of real estate by drug dealers for cash) gain from the illegal drug trade. Finally, criminalization promotes disrespect for the law and leaves the door open to extreme, totalitarian penalties such as work camps for drug offenders.

Another proponent of legalization, Arnold Trebach makes several "policy resolutions"[108]:

- The war on drugs should end everywhere. Experiments should be encouraged in various nations and localities that include different forms of decriminalization, legalization, and medicalization.
- Small dealers and simple users should be virtually ignored by the police unless they commit other crimes, such as robbery or burglary or create public nuisances by interfering with the normal flow of street traffic in the drug dealing area.
- The federal government should provide leadership as well as funds for treatment.
- AIDS treatment should be a special priority, given that it is a greater threat to survival than all drugs combined. Intravenous drug abuse is

Activists at the second annual Millenium Marijuana March in Seattle to support the legalization of marijuana.

? *What are some of the arguments that support making marijuana legal?*

directly linked with the passage of the AIDS virus.

- Society should not forget alcohol and tobacco, because abusers of these legal drugs are in the greatest need for affordable treatment.

Trebach calls for consideration of the Dutch approach to drug abuse. This approach features "flexible enforcement," which seeks to ensure that drug users are not caused more harm by prosecution and imprisonment than by using drugs. Addicts are viewed as patients who cannot be helped by being put in jail. In Holland, all drugs remain illegal but peaceful users and small-scale sellers are left alone. Arrest is reserved for blatant sellers and those who are violent or connected with organized crime. Trebach predicts that by following the Dutch model, the United Sates could reduce overcrowding in the criminal justice system.[109]

Arguments Against Legalization

The nation's first drug czar, William Bennett, viewed the legalization arguments as "a call to surrender" with social costs "too great to contemplate."[110] In a similar fashion, James Q. Wilson takes a moral stand against legalization[111]:

I believe that the moral and welfare costs of heavy drug use are so large that society should bear the heavy burden of law enforcement, and its associated corruption and criminality, for the sake of keeping the number of people regularly using heroin and crack as small as possible. I also believe that children should not be raised in communities in which heroin and cocaine are sold at the neighborhood drugstore. Obviously, there is some point at which the law enforcement costs might become too great for the gains they produce, but I do not think we are at that point yet.

To the criminalizers, the costs of enforcement are worthwhile burdens to prevent the greater and graver evils that the legalization of drugs would create.

Inciardi and McBride assert that the drug legalizers are offering a quick solution to a complex problem. Legalization is not a panacea and would require a great deal of thought. The policy questions surrounding legalization include the following[112]:

- What drugs should be legalized and according to what criteria? Who should determine the criteria?
- What potency level should be permitted?
- As with alcohol, should there be age limits on drug use?
- Should certain drugs be made available only to those already dependent on them?
- Where should drugs be sold?
- Will certain establishments be permitted to serve drugs (which ones) to their customers the way bars serve alcohol? Will there be separate drug-using sections in planes, restaurants, and public areas?
- Should it be necessary to obtain a prescription from a physician? How often should prescriptions be refillable?
- Where should the raw material for the drugs originate? Would cultivation be restricted to U.S. lands or would foreign sources be permitted?
- What kinds of advertising should be permitted?
- If drugs are to be legalized, what types of restrictions on their use should be enacted?
- Which government bureaucracy should be charged with the enforcement of the legalization statutes?

No evidence suggests that government regulation of illegal drugs would be more effective than current law enforcement efforts to reduce sub-

Supreme Court Allows Prosecution of Medical Marijuana

On June 6, 2005, the U.S. Supreme Court ruled that doctors can be blocked from prescribing marijuana for patients suffering from pain caused by cancer or other serious illnesses. In a 6–3 vote, the justices ruled that the Bush Administration can block the backyard cultivation of pot for personal use, because such use has broader social and financial implications. "Congress' power to regulate purely activities that are part of an 'economic class of activities' that have a substantial effect on interstate commerce is firmly established," Justice John Paul Stevens wrote for the majority. The decision means that federal antidrug laws trump state laws that allow the use of medical marijuana, according to CNN senior legal analyst Jeffrey Toobin.

At issue was the power of the federal government to override state laws on the use of "patient pot." The Controlled Substances Act prevents the cultivation and possession of marijuana, even by people who claim personal, "medicinal" use. The government argues its overall antidrug campaign would be undermined by even limited patient exceptions.

The U.S. Drug Enforcement Agency began raids in 2001 against patients using the drug and their caregivers in California — one of 11 states that legalized the use of marijuana for patients under a doctor's care. Among those arrested was Angel Raich, who has brain cancer, and Diane Monson, who grew cannabis in her garden to alleviate chronic back pain. A federal appeals court concluded use of medical marijuana was noncommercial and therefore not subject to congressional oversight of "economic enterprise."

However, lawyers for the U.S. Justice Department argued to the Supreme Court that homegrown marijuana represented interstate commerce, because the garden patch weed would affect "overall production" of marijuana, much of it imported across U.S. boarders by well-financed, often violent drug gangs.

Lawyers for the patients countered with the claim that the marijuana was neither bought nor sold. After California's referendum passed in 1996, "cannabis clubs" sprung up across the state to provide marijuana to patients. They were even-tually shut down by the state's attorney general.

In its hard-line stance in opposition to medical marijuana, the federal government invoked a larger issue. "The trafficking of drugs finances the work of terror, sustaining terrorists," said President Bush in 2001. Tough enforcement, the government told the justices, "is central to combating illegal drug possession."

In their defense, marijuana users argued, "Since September 11, 2001, defendants (the U.S. DEA) have terrorized more than 35 Californians because of their use of medical cannabis." California's Compassionate Use Act permitted patients with a doctor's approval to grow, smoke, or acquire the drug for "medical needs."

Should the government dedicate resources to prosecuting people who use small amounts of marijuana to relieve the symptoms of illness?

stance abuse. The civil lawsuits that would be filed against the government, similar to the suits now being filed against alcohol and tobacco companies by users, would be extremely costly. The government has been arguing for years that these drugs are dangerous. The costs necessary to cover these legal expenses would be passed on to the consumer, making a black market attractive.

Present societal norms are moving toward better health practices, improved diets, more exercise, and a restricted use of alcohol and tobacco. By making harmful substances more readily available, the government would be violating these norms.

Even marijuana, long viewed as on a par with alcohol and tobacco in terms of effects and health consequences, has some very damaging side effects. Smoking marijuana delivers more carcinogens to the system than tobacco. Moreover, THC (tetrahydrocannibinol) is stored in the parts of the body that have a high-fat content (e.g., brains, lungs, liver, reproductive organs) and thus is more difficult to "flush out."[113] In addition, there is no indication

An Australian tourist smoking marijuana in a coffee shop in Amsterdam.

? Do the damaging health effects of smoking marijuana justify keeping it classified as an illegal drug?

of what the long-term effects of such a buildup might be. The potency of marijuana has risen dramatically over the years. Inciardi notes that heavy use affects the behavior of users, such that they tolerate life's problems rather than confront them and thus problems magnify.[114] For these reasons, Inciardi believes marijuana should also be classified as a dangerous drug.

Inciardi also points out that legalization would include cocaine (crack in particular) — the drug that is responsible for much of the drug-related violence (psychopharmacologic, economic, and systemic). It would thus add to and compound the present levels of violence associated with another legal, regulated drug: alcohol.[115]

Most dramatically, proponents of legalization ignore the impact it would have on the lower classes, especially minorities living in ghetto areas. Again, Inciardi notes that drug use is one mode of adaptation to ghetto life. Consequently, the legalization of drugs would be a nightmare. Inciardi feels that it is an "elitist and racist policy that supports the neocolonialist views of underclass population control" and "legalization would initiate a public health problem of unrestrained proportions."[116] Legalization would serve to legitimize the chemical destruction of an urban generation and culture. In place of legalization, Inciardi argues that

more attention should be paid to treatment and education of drug users, particularly to ghetto youth.

The War on Drugs

It is abundantly clear that there is no easy solution to this country's drug problems. Perhaps it is time to drop the call for war while continuing more restrained enforcement efforts. The combat analogy has several weaknesses[117]:

1. **The lack of a clear-cut enemy.** The drug war assumes that there are two kinds of people: good and bad. Either one is a drug user or one is drug free, which dehumanizes drug offenders.

2. **The lack of a clear-cut front.** If it is a civil war, this country is the front. If U.S. citizens are concerned with halting production, the front is in foreign countries.

3. **The lack of consensus as to what type of warfare is acceptable.** Force can have some unintended effects. For example, New York's strict Rockefeller laws led to overcrowding of the courts and jails. It also introduced juveniles into the drug business (because they could avoid the penalties through the juvenile justice system).[118] At the same time, education and treatment are difficult to implement with a high degree of success.

4. **The lack of total mobilization and unlimited resources.** Although the federal drug budget for fiscal year 2004 was over $12 billion, these expenditures do not compare to those of an actual war.[119]

5. **The lack of expendable personnel and a willingness to take casualties.**

6. **The lack of strategic leadership by professionals.**

7. **The lack of a national will for victory at any cost.**

Beyond increased efforts at education and treatment, a peace policy (to use Trebach's phrase) could be pursued.[120] Drugs and crime are intertwined but an emphasis on enforcement has damaging hidden costs. A balanced approach to these problems is clearly in order. Enforcement efforts should be related to treatment, but the public should be protected from the harmful effects of illegal drugs. One attempt to deal differently with the drug–crime problem is California's Proposition 36 (see **TABLE 14-5**). It proposes to deal with drug offenders by treating them in the community, rather than putting them in prison.

California's Proposition 36

In 1996, California led the nation in the incarceration of drug offenders — 134 per 100,000 citizens — an increase of over 260% over the 1986 rate. In 1999, California spent over $1 million per year to imprison over 45,000 drug offenders. In an attempt to reverse these trends, California voters passed Proposition 36 — the Substance Abuse and Crime Prevention Act (SACPA) — in 2000. Based on an Arizona initiative, this act gives drug offenders the opportunity to participate in community drug treatment programs in place of incarceration or probation.

However, initial research on the impact of the law is mixed. Relative to other comparable groups of drug users, clients of SACPA were more likely to be rearrested for a drug crime, even after controlling for drug use severity and treatment modality. However, it was also determined that the demand for treatment among drug offenders under this act was inadequately met. In other words, there were more offenders than available placements. Despite these findings, the California method holds great promise and should be examined in the future. In fact, other states are looking for methods to handle the same problem. In 2004, New York State Governor George E. Pataki signed a law that reduced penalties under the so-called Rockefeller drug laws to dramatically reduce sentence lengths for drug offenders.

Sources: Deborah Baskin, "Proposition 36: Editorial Introduction," *Criminology and Public Policy* 3 (2004): 561–562; David Farabee, Yih-Ing Hser, M. Douglas Anglin, and David Huang, "Recidivism Among an Early Cohort of California's Proposition 36 Offenders," *Criminology and Public Policy* 3 (2004): 563–584; Judith Appel, Glenn Backes, and Jeremy Robbins, "California's Proposition 36: A Success Ripe for Refinement and Replication," *Criminology and Public Policy* 3 (2004): 585–592; James A. Inciardi, "Proposition 36: What Did You Really Expect?" *Criminology and Public Policy* 3 (2004): 593–598; Vincent Schiraldi, Barry Holman, and Phillip Beatty, *Poor Prescription: The Costs of Imprisoning Drug Offenders in the United States* (Washington, DC: Justice Policy Institute, 2000): 7–9; Michael Cooper, "New York State Votes to Reduce Drug Sentences," *The New York Times* (December 8, 2004): A1, A28.

A study of Arizona's Proposition 200 (the Drug Medicalization, Prevention and Control Act of 1996) revealed that the "hardening" of punishments produces an incarcerated offender, leading to more severe and extensive criminal records, and making offenders ineligible for treatment.[121]

Conclusion

Drug abuse has a varied history in the United States. A view of drug policy reveals an equally diverse approach. Illicit drug abuse may be declining in the United States, but there is evidence that a strong population of users still exists. Strategies to reduce the flow or trafficking of illicit drugs into the United States have been supplemented with education and treatment with the goal of reduction of crime.

There appears to be a strong connection between adult criminality and substance abuse. Efforts that combat drug abuse have stressed deterrence and interdiction even though the research evidence suggests that treatment must be a strong component of any attempt to break the cycle of substance abuse and crime.

Females and juveniles who abuse drugs have different links to crime than adult males. Women are more likely to commit crimes to support their habit, while self-esteem and gang involvement appear to be key factors in juvenile involvement with drugs. Here, again, treatment seems to offer more promise than a hard-line approach.

As David Musto suggests, drug use and abuse in the history of the United States is cyclical: "at the beginning phase of a drug epidemic, we are filled with hopeful fantasies about drugs; in the decline phase, we are caught up in anger, scapegoating, and excessive punishment."[122] In fact, the American public goes through a learning process on drug use. It ranges from seeking shortcuts through the use of a new drug to developing awareness by experiencing the unfortunate consequences of drug abuse.

Although the drug market is lucrative and interdiction appears to be ineffective in stopping the flow of drugs, legalization is no panacea to the drug problem. As Inciardi states, "treating drug abuse as a medical problem" is the logical solution.[123] Because treatment is more effective in reducing drug abuse and crime than is generally believed, a more balanced approach toward solving the problems of substance abuse and crime appears to be in order — one that addresses the "common underlying initiating and sustaining causes" of both drug abuse and criminal behavior, including increasing treatment services for drug-using, criminally involved populations to reduce drug demand, providing educational and economic development opportunities, and ensuring that civil rights are protected when enforcement practices are increased.[124]

WRAP UP

Crack Cocaine Breeds Violence

The three Goldstein models offer different frameworks within which drug-related homicides can be examined. Two models seem to offer the best explanations. First, the psychopharmacological model states that crack cocaine can promote homicide because the drug itself promotes violent behavior. In fact, drug treatment director Elliot stated that crack cocaine is a "strong stimulant narcotic" whose withdrawal symptoms include "belligerence, hostility, anger and frustration." Second, the statistical pattern of drug-related homicides reflects the possibility that the "fierce competition between drug dealers competing for control of the market" is fueling the rising tide of murders as fits Goldstein's "systemic model." There is also evidence that the closing of public housing properties has led to a competitive search for new sites for drug sales and has led to disputes over both territories and customers. The remaining "economic-compulsive" model does not seem to fit this situation because the homicides do not seem to be occurring during the course of robberies committed by crack addicts for the purpose of obtaining funds to purchase drugs.

Chapter Spotlight

- The war on drugs is a well-publicized effort waged on several "fronts." Proposed solutions to the drug problem include education, interdiction, and treatment.

- There is a strong link between substance abuse and criminal behavior. Offenders with a substance abuse problem are involved in a high percentage of violent crimes. Drug addicts commit more crime when under the influence of drugs than when they are clean and sober. High levels of illicit drug use are related to greater rates of drug trafficking offenses and other serious crimes.

- Offenders with active drug problems are likely to continue their criminal activities. Prisoners with the most serious criminal records reported a substantial involvement in drug abuse. The crime rate among heroin addicts is higher during periods of active use than in periods of abstinence.

- There is debate as to whether drug use causes crime or crime causes drug use. The enslavement theory of addiction argues that drug abuse fuels crime because heroin addicts need money to purchase more drugs. Others argue that the research has documented that, although drug use tends to intensify and perpetuate criminal behavior, it usually does not cause it. Others believe that among violent offenders, drug use only enhances the continuation and seriousness of a criminal career.

- The Goldstein models offer an explanation of how drug abuse sponsors violent behavior through the effect of the drug and the motivation for the violent crime. The psychopharmacological model asserts that violent crime is a result of the effect of the drug on the offender and/or the victim — that it supports irrational and violent behavior. The economic-compulsive model explains that the offender commits a violent crime during the course of a robbery; the offender commits crime to obtain money to support a drug habit. The systemic model maintains that some violent crimes are committed as a result of the drug use and distribution system.

- There are differences between males and females when it comes to substance abuse. Male inmates abuse drugs more often. Women prisoners are more likely to have used heroin, cocaine, PCP, LSD, or methadone. Women who were daily users of heroin and cocaine had higher crime rates than those who limited their drug use to marijuana, depressants, stimulants, or illegal methadone. Women form drug partnerships with men in a variety of ways. Addicted women engage in higher rates of crime when they are abusing drugs.

- Drugs appear to play a crucial role in delinquency. Adolescents who use multiple drugs are more likely to be seriously delinquent. Young men and women who drink and use marijuana are likely to be truant and to steal. They are more likely to continue their criminal careers as adults. Seriously delinquent youth are regular users of drugs and alcohol. The active delinquent youths had the most significant substance abuse histories.

- Treatment for drug abusing offenders can be effective. Addicts who stay the course of treatment or re-enroll after initial failure can decrease their drug intake and reduce criminal offenses. The longer a client remains in treatment, the greater the probability of success. Research findings emphasize the need for effective offender treatment coupled with punitive sanctions to prevent crime — as specified by the drug court model.

- Drug selling is a lucrative business that establishes underground economy. High profitability attracts sellers to the drug marketplace. The crimes that drug abusers commit also cost society dearly. Evidence concerning the link between employment, drug abuse, and levels of criminal activity is mixed. The profits associated with the cocaine trade affect the economies of drug-producing countries such as Columbia.

- There appears to be a strong connection between adult criminality and substance abuse, and the efforts to combat drug abuse have stressed deterrence and interdiction. Research suggests that treatment must be a strong component of any attempt to break the cycle of substance abuse and crime.

- Females and juveniles who abuse drugs have different links to crime than adult males. Self-esteem and gang involvement appear to be key factors in juvenile involvement with drugs.

- Legalization is not an easy solution to the drug problem. Treatment is more effective in reducing drug abuse and crime than is generally believed. A more balanced approach toward solving the problems of substance abuse and crime appears to be in order.

Putting It All Together

1. List the arguments for and against the legalization of drugs. Which arguments do you agree with and why?

2. Which approach has the most promise to combat drug abuse: enforcement or treatment? Explain.

3. How does substance abuse promote crime? Is it more accurate to say that crime promotes substance abuse? Compare and contrast these ideas.

4. Discuss the role of violence in drug trafficking.

5. Create a model for a program that will be implemented on campus to deal with substance abuse. What specific needs does your campus have? List the drug issues and outline how to approach each. Which elements would you include in your plan and why?

Key Terms

enslavement theory of addiction This theory assumes that addicts are "slaves" to their habit and are driven to crime by the high cost of drugs.

tweaking The violence that cocaine dealers routinely engage in against each other in an attempt to control the drug market.

1. James A. Inciardi, *The War on Drugs III: The Continuing Saga of the Mysteries and Miseries of Intoxication, Addiction, Crime, and Public Policy* (Boston: Allyn & Bacon, 2002): 182.

2. R.L. Dupont, *The Selfish Brain: Learning from Addiction* (Hazelden Center City, MN: The American Psychiatric Press, 1997).

3. C. Kuhn, S. Swartzwelder, and W. Wilson, *Bussed: The Straight Facts About Drugs Used and Abused from Alcohol to Ecstasy* (New York: The Hadden Craftsmen, 2003).

4. Ibid.

5. J.H. Lowinson, P. Ruiz, R.P. Millman, and J.G. Langrod, *Substance Abuse: A Comprehensive Textbook* (Philadelphia: Lippincott Williams & Wilkins, 1997).

6. R. Laing and J. Siegal, *Hallucinogens: A Forensic Drug Handbook* (San Diego, CA: Academic Press, 2003).

7. E. Foner and J.A. Garraty, *The Reader's Companion to American History* (New York: Houghton Mifflin Books, 1991).

8. Inciardi, 2002; Steven Wisotsky, *Breaking the Impasse in the War on Drugs* (Westport, CN: Greenwood Press, 1986).

9. Bureau of Justice Statistics, *Drugs and Crime Facts, 1990* (Washington, DC: U.S. Department of Justice, 1991).

10. Bureau of Justice Statistics, *Drugs and Crime Facts—Public Opinion About Drugs* (Washington, DC: U.S. Department of Justice, 2004), available at www.ojp.usdoj.gov/bjs/dcf/poad.htm, accessed December 10, 2005.

11. Ibid.

12. Office of National Drug Control Policy, *Juveniles and Drugs* (Washington, DC: Executive Office of the President, 2002): 2.

13. Office of National Drug Control Policy, *Drug Related Crime* (Washington, DC: Executive Office of the President, 2000): 4.

14. Inciardi, 2002, 297.

15. Bureau of Justice and Statistics, *Crime and the Justice System* (Washington, DC: U.S. Department of Justice, Office of Justice Programs, 1992).

16. Inciardi, 2002.

17. Cynthia S. Gentry, "Drugs and Crime," in Joseph F. Sheley, ed., *Criminology: A Contemporary Handbook* (Belmont, CA: Wadsworth, 1991): 423–440; Helene R. White, "The Drug-Use Delinquency Connection in Adolescence," in Ralph Weisheit, ed., *Drugs, Crime and the Criminal Justice System* (Cincinnati, OH: Anderson, 1990): 215–256.

18. Duane C. McBride and Clyde B. McCoy, "The Drugs-Crime Relationship: An Analytical Framework," in Larry K. Gaines and Peter B. Kraska, eds., *Drugs, Crime & Justice* (Prospect Heights, IL: Waveland Press, 2003): 109–110; David Deitch, Igor Koutsenok, and Amanda Ruiz, "The Relationship Between Crime and Drugs: What We Have Learned in Recent Decades," *Journal of Psychoactive Drugs* 32 (2000): 391–397.

19. Bernard A. Gropper, *Probing the Link Between Drugs and Crime* (Washington, DC: National Institute of Justice, 1985).

20. David N. Nurco, Thomas E. Hanlon, Mitchell B. Balter, Thomas W. Kinlock, and Ellen Slaght, "A Classification of Narcotic Addicts Based on the Type, Amount and Severity of Crime," *Journal of Drug Issues* 21 (1991): 440.

21. Inciardi, 2002, 190.

22. George Speckhart and M. David Anglin, "Narcotics and Crime: An Analysis of Existing Evidence for a Causal Relationship," *Behavioral Science and the Law* 3 (1985): 259–282.

23. Christopher J. Mumola, *Substance Abuse and Treatment, State and Federal Prisoners, 1997* (Washington, DC: Bureau of Justice Statistics, 1999): 1.

24. Ibid.

25. Eric D. Wish and Brian D. Johnson, "Impact of Substance Abuse on Criminal Careers," in Alfred Blumstein, Jacqueline Cohen, Jeffrey A. Cohen, and Christy A. Visher, eds. *Criminal Careers and Career Criminals,* Volume II (Washington, DC: National Academy Press, 1986): 52–88.

26. J.J. Collins, "Relationship of Problem Drinking to Individual Offending Sequences," in Alfred Blumstein, Jacqueline Cohen, Jeffrey A. Cohen, and Christy A. Visher, eds., *Criminal Careers and Career Criminals,* Volume II (Washington, DC: National Academy Press, 1986): 89–120.

27. M. David Anglin and George Speckart, "Narcotics Use and Crime: A Multisample, Multimethod Analysis," *Criminology* 26 (1988): 197–231.

28. Mumola, 1999, 1.

29. Ibid., 2–8.

30. David Farabee, Vandana Joshi, and M. Douglas Anglin, "Addiction Careers and Criminal Specialization," *Crime and Delinquency* 47 (2001): 196–220.

31. David N. Nurco, John C. Ball, John W. Shaffer, and Thomas E. Hanlon, "The Criminality of Narcotic Addicts," *Journal of Nervous and Mental Disease* 173 (1985): 94–102.

32. John W. Shaffer, David N. Nurco, John C. Ball, and T.W. Kinlock, "The Frequency of Nonnarcotic Drug Use and Its Relationship to Criminal Activity Among Narcotic Addicts," *Comprehensive Psychiatry* 26 (1985): 558–566.

33. George Speckart and M. Douglas Anglin, "Narcotic Use and Crime: An Overview of Recent Research Evidence," *Contemporary Drug Problems* 13 (1986): 741–769.

34. John C. Ball, Laurence Rosen, J.A. Flueck, and David N. Nurco, "Lifetime Criminality of Heroin Addicts in the United States," *Journal of Drug Issues* 21 (1982): 225–239.

35. John C. Ball, "The Similarity of Crime Rates Among Male Heroin Addicts in New York City, Philadelphia, and Baltimore," *Journal of Drug Issues* 21 (1991): 413–427.

36. Charles E. Faupel, "Heroin Use and Criminal Careers," *Qualitative Sociology* 10 (1987): 115–131; Charles E. Faupel and Carl B. Klockars, "Drugs-Crime Connections: Elaborations from the Life Histories of Hard-Core Heroin Addicts," *Social Problems* 34 (1987): 54–68.

37. Bruce Johnson, Eric D. Wish, and Kevin Anderson, "A Day in the Life of 105 Drug Addicts and Abusers: Crime Com-

mitted and How the Money Was Spent," *Sociology and Social Research* 72 (1988): 185–191.

38. Inciardi, 2002, 287.

39. Ibid., 288.

40. Jan M. Chaiken and Marcia R. Chaiken, "Drugs and Predatory Crime," in Michael Tonry and Norval Morris, eds., *Drugs and Crime* (Chicago: University of Chicago Press, 1990): 203–240.

41. Office of National Drug Control Policy, *Drug Policy Information Clearinghouse: Fact Sheet*, available at http://www.whitehousedrugpolicy.gov/publications/pdf/ncj181056.pdf, accessed December 14, 2005.

42. Ibid.

43. Paul J. Goldstein, "The Drugs/Violence Nexus: A Tripartite Conceptual Framework," *Journal of Drug* 15 (1985): 493–506.

44. Paul J. Goldstein, Patricia A. Bellucci, Barry J. Spunt, and Thomas Miller, "Volume of Cocaine Use and Violence: A Comparison Between Men and Women." *Journal of Drug Issues* 21 (1991): 345–367.

45. Henry H. Brownstein and Paul J. Goldstein, "A Typology of Drug-Related Homicides," in Ralph Weisheit, ed., *Drugs, Crime and the Criminal Justice System* (Cincinnati, OH: Anderson, 1990): 171–192.

46. Inciardi, 2002, 192.

47. James A. Inciardi, *The War on Drugs II* (Palo Alto, CA: Mayfield, 1991): 246–249.

48. Duane C. McBride and James A. Swartz, "Drugs and Violence in the Age of Crack Cocaine," in Ralph Weisheit, ed., *Drugs, Crime and the Criminal Justice System* (Cincinnati, OH: Anderson, 1990): 153.

49. Mumola, 1999, 7; Neal P. Langan, and Bernadette M.M. Pelissier, "Gender Differences Among Prisoners in Drug Treatment," *Journal of Substance Abuse* 13 (2001): 291–301.

50. Gennaro F. Vito and Richard Tewksbury, "Gender Comparisons in Drug Testing Probationers and Parolees," *Corrections Compendium* 25 (2000): 5.

51. Dorothy Lockwood, Jill McCorkel, and James A. Inciardi, "Developing Comprehensive Prison-Based Therapeutic Community Treatment for Women," *Drugs and Society* 13 (1998): 193–212.

52. James W. Marquart, Victoria E. Brewer, Janet Mullings, et al., "The Implications of Crime Control Policy on HIV/AIDS-Related Risk Among Women Prisoners," *Crime and Delinquency* 45 (1999): 82–98.

53. M. Douglas Anglin and Yih-Ing Hser, "Addicted Women and Crime," *Criminology* 25 (1987): 359–397.

54. Jose E. Sanchez and Brian D. Johnson, "Women and the Drugs-Crime Connection: Crime Rates Among Drug-Abusing Women at Rikers Island," *Journal of Psychoactive Drugs* 19 (1987): 205–214.

55. James A. Inciardi and Anne E. Pottieger, "Kids, Crack, and Crime," *Journal of Drug Issues* 21 (1991): 257–270.

56. James A. Inciardi, Anne E. Pottieger, and Charles E. Faupel, "Black Women, Heroin and Crime: Some Empirical Notes," *Journal of Drug Issues* 12 (1982): 241–250.

57. James A. Inciardi and Hilary L. Surratt, "Drug Use, Street Crime, and Sex-Trading Among Cocaine Dependent Women: Implications for Public Health and Criminal Justice Policy," *Journal of Psychoactive Drugs* 33 (2001): 379–388.

58. H. Virginia McCoy, James A. Inciardi, Lisa R. Metsch, et al., "Women, Crack, and Crime: Gender Comparisons of Criminal Activity Among 'Crack' Cocaine Users," *Contemporary Drug Problems* 22 (1995): 435–451.

59. Leon E. Pettiway, "Participation in Crime Partnerships by Female Drug Users: The Effects of Domestic Arrangements, Drug Use, and Criminal Involvement," *Criminology* 25 (1987): 741–766.

60. M. Rosenbaum, *Women on Heroin* (New Brunswick, NJ: Rutgers University Press, 1981).

61. Marcia R. Chaiken and Brian D. Johnson, *Characteristics of Different Types of Drug-Involved Offenders* (Washington, DC: National Institute of Justice, 1988).

62. Richard Dembo, Mark Washburn, Eric Wish, et al., "Heavy Marijuana Use and Crime Among Youths Entering a Juvenile Detention Center," *Journal of Psychoactive Drugs* 19 (1987): 47–56; Richard Dembo, Mark Washburn, Eric Wish, et al., "Further Examination of the Association Between Heavy Marijuana Use and Crime Among Youths Entering a Juvenile Detention Center," *Journal of Psychoactive Drugs* 19 (1987): 361–373.

63. Cheryl Carpenter, Barry Glasner, Bruce D. Johnson, and Julia Loughlin, *Kids, Drugs and Crime* (Lexington, MA: Lexington Books, 1988).

64. Brian D. Johnson, Eric D. Wish, J. Schmeidler, and David Huzinga, "Concentration of Delinquent Offending: Serious Drug Involvement and High Delinquency Rates," *Journal of Drug Issues* 21 (1991): 229.

65. Helene R. White, Peter C. Tice, Rolf Loeber, et al., "Illegal Acts Committed by Adolescents Under the Influence of Alcohol and Drugs," *Journal of Research in Crime and Delinquency* 39 (2002): 131–152.

66. Richard Lowry, Lisa R. Cohen, William Modzeleski, et al., "School Violence, Substance Use, and the Availability of Illegal Drugs on School Property Among U.S. High School Students," *Journal of School Health* 69 (1999): 347–355.

67. David H. Huizinga, Scott Menard, and Delbert S. Elliott, "Delinquency and Drug Use: Temporal and Developmental Patterns," *Justice Quarterly* 6 (1988): 419–455.

68. Helene White, Valerie Johnson, and Carole Garrison, "The Drug-Crime Nexus Among Adolescents and Their Peers," *Deviant Behavior* 6 (1985): 183–204.

69. William E. Thornton, "Marijuana Use and Delinquency: A Reexamination," *Youth and Society* 13 (1981): 23–37.

70. Richard Dembo, Linda Williams, Lawrence LaVoie et al., "Physical Abuse, Sexual Victimization, and Illicit Drug Use," *Violence and Victims* 4 (1989): 121–138.

71. Constance D. Rees and Bobbie L. Wilborn, "Correlates of Drug Abuse in Adolescents: A Comparison of Families of Drug Abusers with Families of Nondrug Abusers," *Journal of Youth and Adolescence* 12 (1983): 55–63.

72. Jeffrey Fagan, "The Social Organization of Drug Use and Drug Dealing Among Urban Gangs," *Criminology* 27 (1989): 633–669.

73. Scott H. Decker and Barrik Van Winkle, "'Slinging Dope': The Role of Gangs and Gang Members in Drug Sales," *Justice*

Quarterly 11 (1994): 583–604; Finn A. Esbensen and David Huizinga, "Gangs, Drugs, and Delinquency in a Survey of Urban Youth," *Criminology* 31 (1993): 565–589; Avelardo Valdez and Stephen J. Sifaneck, "Getting High and Getting By: Dimensions of Drug Selling Behavior Among Mexican Gang Members in Southern Texas," *Journal of Research in Crime and Delinquency* 41 (2004): 82–105; Alan C. Turley, "Female Gangs and Patterns of Female Delinquency in Texas," *Journal of Gang Research* 10 (2003): 1–12.

74. Inciardi and Pottieger, 1991.

75. White, 1990, 240.

76. National Narcotics Intelligence Consumers Committee, *The NNICC Report: The Supply of Illicit Drugs to the United States*, available at www.fas.org/irp/agency/doj/dea/product/nnicc97.htm, accessed December 9, 2005.

77. U.S. Department of Justice, *Drug of Abuse, 2005*, available at http://www.usdoj.gov/dea/pubs/abuse/doa-p.pdf, accessed December 14, 2005.

78. Robert L. Hubbard, Mary Ellen Marsden, J. Valley Rachel, Henrick J. Hartwood, Elizabeth R. Cavanaugh, and Harold Ginzburg, *Drug Abuse Treatment: A National Study of Effectiveness* (Chapel Hill: University of North Carolina Press, 1989).

79. Paul Gendreau and Richard R. Ross, "Revivification of Rehabilitation: Evidence from the 1980s," *Justice Quarterly* 4 (1987): 385.

80. M. Douglas Anglin, and Yih-Ing Hser, "Treatment of Drug Abuse," in Michael Tonry and Norval Morris, eds., *Drugs and Crime* (Chicago: University of Chicago Press, 1990): 439.

81. D.E. Hunt, Douglas S. Lipton, and Barry Spunt, "Patterns of Criminal Activity Among Methadone Clients and Current Narcotics Users Not in Treatment," *Journal of Drug Issues* 14 (1984): 687–702.

82. Gennaro F. Vito, "The Kentucky Substance Abuse Program: A Private Program to Treat Probationers and Parolees," *Federal Probation* 53 (1989): 65–72.

83. Gennaro F. Vito, Deborah G. Wilson, and Thomas J. Keil, "Drug Testing, Treatment, and Revocation: A Review of Program Findings," *Federal Probation* 54 (1990): 37–43; Gennaro F. Vito, Steven T. Holmes, Thomas J. Keil, and Deborah G. Wilson, "Drug Testing in Community Corrections: A Comparative Program Analysis," *Journal of Crime and Justice* 15 (1992): 63–90; Gennaro F. Vito, Deborah G. Wilson, and Steven T. Holmes, "Drug Testing in Community Corrections: Results from a Four Year Program," *The Prison Journal* 73 (1993): 343–354; Gennaro F. Vito, "What Works in Drug Testing and Monitoring," in Edward J. Latessa, ed., *Strategic Solutions: The International Community Corrections Association Examines Substance Abuse* (Latham, MD: American Correctional Association, 1999): 137–150.

84. Office of National Drug Control Policy, *Drug Treatment in the Criminal Justice System* (Washington, DC: Executive Office of the President, 2001a): 4.

85. Gennaro F. Vito and Richard Tewksbury, "The Impact of Treatment: The Jefferson County (Kentucky) Substance Abuse Program," *Federal Probation* 62 (1998): 46–51; Faye S. Taxman, "Unraveling 'What Works' for Offenders in Substance Abuse Services," *National Drug Court Institute Review* 2 (1999): 93–134.

86. Sam Torres, "A Continuum of Sanctions for Substance-Abusing Offenders," *Federal Probation* 62 (1998): 36–45.

87. Amie L. Nielsen, Frank R. Scarpitti, James A. Inciardi, et al., "Integrating the Therapeutic Community and Work Release for Drug-Involved Offenders," *Journal of Substance Abuse Treatment* 13 (1996): 349–358; Kathryn E. McCollister, Michael T. French, James A. Inciardi, et al., "Post-Release Substance Abuse Treatment for Criminal Offenders: A Cost-Effectiveness Analysis," *Journal of Quantitative Criminology* 19 (2003): 389–407.

88. Paul Dynia and Hung En Sung, "The Safety and Effectiveness of Diverting Felony Drug Offenders to Residential Treatment as Measured by Recidivism," *Criminal Justice Policy Review* 11 (2000): 299–311.

89. Michael L. Prendergast, Michael Campos, David Farabee, et al., "Reducing Substance Use in Prison: The California Department of Corrections Drug Reduction Strategy Project," *The Prison Journal* 84 (2004): 265–280; M. Douglas Anglin, Douglas Longshore, and Susan Turner, "Treatment Alternatives to Street Crime: An Evaluation of Five Programs," *Criminal Justice and Behavior* 26 (1999): 158–195.

90. United Nations Office for Drug Control and Crime Prevention, *Economic and Social Consequences of Drug Abuse and Illicit Trafficking* (New York: UNODCCP, 1998): 3.

91. Office of National Drug Control Policy, *Drug Data Summary* (Washington, DC: Executive Office of the President, 2003): 6.

92. Ibid.
93. Office of National Drug Control Policy, *What America's Users Spend on Illegal Drugs, 1988 to 1998* (Washington, DC: Executive Office of the President, 2000): 3.
94. Office of National Drug Control Policy, *The Economic Costs of Drug Abuse in the United States, 1992–1998* (Washington, DC: Executive Office of the President, 2001b): 2.
95. Vincent Schiraldi, Barry Holman, and Phillip Beatty, *Poor Prescription: The Costs of Imprisoning Drug Offenders in the United States* (Washington, DC: Justice Policy Institute, 2000): 3.
96. Ibid., 18.
97. Office of National Drug Control Policy, 2001b, 9.
98. Bruce D. Johnson, Paul J. Goldstein, E. Preble, J. Schmeidler, Douglas S. Lipton, Barry Spunt, and T. Miller, *Taking Care of Business: The Economics of Crime by Heroin Users* (Lexington, MA: Lexington Books, 1985).
99. James J. Collins, Rachel L. Hubbard, and J. Valley Rachal, "Expensive Drug Use and Illegal Income: A Test of Explanatory Hypotheses," *Criminology* 23 (1985): 743–764.
100. David N. Nurco, Ira H. Cisin, and John C. Ball, "Crime as a Source of Income for Narcotic Addicts," *Journal of Substance Abuse Treatment* 2 (1985): 113–114.
101. Charles E. Faupel, "Heroin Use, Crime, and Employment Status," *Journal of Drug Issues* 18 (1988): 467–479.
102. Francisco E. Thoumi, "Illegal Drugs in Columbia: From Illegal Economic Boom to Social Crisis," *The Annals of the American Academy of Political and Social Science* 582 (2002): 102–114.
103. Norval Morris and Gordon Hawkins, *The Honest Politicians Guide to Crime Control* (Chicago: University of Chicago Press, 1969).
104. Ibid., 5–6.
105. Schiraldi, Holman, and Beatty, 2000, 4.
106. Ralph Weisheit, "Challenging the Criminalizers," *The Criminologist* 15 (1990a): 1, 3–5.
107. Peter B. Kraska, "The Unmentionable Alternative: The Need For, and the Argument Against, the Decriminalization of Drug Laws," in Ralph Weisheit, ed., *Drugs, Crime and the Criminal Justice System* (Cincinnati, OH: Anderson, 1990):118–126.
108. Arnold S. Trebach, "Tough Choices: The Practical Politics of Drug Policy Reform," *American Behavioral Scientist* 32 (1989): 249–258.
109. Ibid., 257.
110. William Bennett, "Should Drugs Be Legalized?" *Reader's Digest* (March 1990): 90–96.
111. James Q. Wilson, "Drugs and Crime," in Michael Tonry and James Q. Wilson, eds., *Drugs and Crime: Crime and Justice,* Volume 13 (Chicago: University of Chicago Press, 1990): 527.
112. James A. Inciardi and Duane C. McBride, "Legalization: A High-Risk Alternative in the War of Drugs," *American Behavioral Scientist* 32 (1989): 261–262; Inciardi, 2002, 279–281; Ralph Weisheit, personal correspondence with the authors, 1991.
113. Ken Liska, *Drugs and the Human Body with Implications for Society* (Upper Saddle River, NJ: Prentice Hall, 2000): 49.
114. Inciardi, 2002, 282–283.
115. Inciardi, 2002, 289.
116. Inciardi, 2002, 297.
117. Ralph Weisheit, "Declaring a 'Civil' War on Drugs," in Ralph Weisheit, ed., *Drugs, Crime and the Criminal Justice System* (Cincinnati, OH: Anderson, 1990): 1–10.
118. Kraska, 1990, 126.
119. The White House, *National Drug Control Strategy: Update* (Washington, DC: Office of Drug Control Policy, 2004): 51.
120. Arnold Trebach, *The Great Drug War: And Rational Proposals to Turn the Tide* (Bloomington, IN: Unlimited Publishing, 2005).
121. K. Jack Riley, Nancy Rodriguez, Greg Ridgeway, et al., *Just Cause, or Just Because: Prosecution and Plea-Bargaining Resulting in Prison Sentences on Low-Level Drug Charges in California and Arizona*, available at http://www.rand.org/pubs/monographs/2005/RAND_MG288.sum.pdf, accessed December 14, 2005.
122. David F. Musto, "The American Experience with Stimulants and Opiates," in Larry K. Gaines and Peter B. Kraska, eds., *Drugs, Crime & Justice* (Prospect Heights, IL: Waveland Press, 2003): 43–44.
123. Inciardi, 2002, 247.
124. McBride and McCoy, 2003, 113–114.

WWW.CRIMINOLOGY.JBPUB.COM

Interactivities
In the News
Key Term Explorer
Web Links

CHAPTER

15

OBJECTIVES

Explain the similarities between organized crime and legitimate business enterprises.

Describe the characteristics of organized crime groups in the United States.

Recognize the difficulties in using current criminological theories to explain white-collar criminals.

Understand the complexities in defining white-collar crimes.

Identify different categories of white-collar crimes.

Identify societal impacts of white-collar crimes.

Explain white-collar crimes with historic and present examples.

Describe factors that influence sentencing for white-collar criminals.

Crimes of the Powerful: Organized and White-Collar Crime

> *Modern crime, like modern business, is tending toward centralization, organization, and commercialization. Ours is a business nation. Our criminals apply business methods. The men and women of evil have formed trusts.*
>
> —Colonel Henry Barrett Chamberlain[1]
> Director, Chicago Crime Commission (1919)

YOU ARE THE CRIMINOLOGIST

Organized Crime Sleeps with the Phishes

Two alleged Mafia members in the Gambino crime family pled guilty to charges that they used the Internet to defraud customers out of more than $650 million. They also used telephones to attract victims by making offers of free pornography, psychic readings, dating services, and sports betting tips to obtain their credit card numbers. Under a plea bargaining agreement, RICO charges were dropped and the two men pled guilty to one count of conspiracy to commit mail fraud and one count of extortion for trying to force a porn industry rival to pay them $1 million. They both face a 10-year prison term and fines of $15 and $10 million respectively. Seven of their associates also pled guilty and face five-year prison terms and fines of $1.7 to $30 million.

The technique they allegedly used, phishing, involves sending e-mail messages to Internet users that appear to be from a legitimate source (e.g., banks, credit card companies, online merchants, or Internet service providers). These notes promise some free service or lottery winnings or "warn" the recipient of problems with their Internet financial accounts. They then ask the victim to provide personal and financial information such as birthdates, Social Security numbers, and PIN codes. They are then subject to identity theft, credit card fraud, and loss of funds.

With the involvement of organized crime (not only La Cosa Nostra families but also Russian, Eastern European, and Asian organized crime groups), phishing scams have become more concentrated and more sophisticated. To send their e-mail messages, phishers also use computer worms that spread from one computer to another, making it impossible to trace the original source. They also build armies of "zombie machines." Zombies are created through the use of computer viruses that allow remote control of computers. These machines are then used to send out the messages as spam and to spread the viruses to other computers, starting the cycle over and over again.

This type of spam is very sophisticated. Typically, the messages carry announcements for low mortgage rates and products such as Viagra. The e-mails carry viruses that can infect computers even if the user does not click on the attachments. The viruses tend to go unnoticed by the user, but they track Internet use, keystrokes, and login passwords. Thus, more than a computer crash is at stake.

In this case, the victims were attracted by 1-800 phone numbers that offered free samples of phone sex, psychic hotlines, and dating services that became recurring charges on their monthly phone bills. On the Internet, porn users were asked to enter their credit card numbers for a "free tour" and were then billed for monthly charges of $20 to $90. The scammers routinely changed their corporate names and processed their transactions in foreign countries to avoid detection.

Using our discussion of the attributes, methods, and aims of organized crime as a template for analysis, what is new about this crime event? How is it consistent with the goals of organized crime and how is it different?

Sources: Michael Cohn, "Phishers Are Offshore Organized Crime Rings," available at http://www.messagingpipeline.com/showArticle.jhtml?articleID=22104317&_loopback=1. Dennis McCafferty, "Organized Cyber-Crime," available at http://www.thewhir.com/features/organized-cybercrime.cfm; MSNBC, "Crime and Punishment," available at http://useractive.com/proxycgi.cgi?par2=http://msnbc.msn.com/id/6928696/; Kate Stoodley, "In 2005, Organized Crime Will Back Phishers," available at http://itmanagement.earthweb.com/secu/print.php/3451501.

Introduction

"Crimes of the powerful" refers to offenses committed by influential persons or groups in society. These offenses are also characterized as "organized," "white-collar," and "enterprise" crime. In addition to the fact that both <u>organized crime</u> groups and white-collar criminals have power, they also share other common characteristics. First, they strive for economic control of financial markets, both legal and illegal. Typically, they desire monopolistic control of a market so that they can control prices. Second, they work to circumvent not only criminal law but also governmental regulations that are aimed at governing the market and protecting consumers. Third, the crimes that they commit are costly to society in both human and financial terms. Finally, their goal is to accumulate wealth and exercise power for the benefit of the organization and its members, regardless of the cost to others in society.

To this point, we have concentrated on "crimes of the street": murder, rape, robbery, burglary, and theft. Thus, our focus generally has been on the less affluent, more disenfranchised people in society. Although members of the middle and upper classes also commit these kinds of street crimes, their position in society creates opportunities for them to commit other kinds of crimes. In some cases, crimes of the powerful are committed by individuals, but large and small groups are just as capable of this sort of criminal activity.

Criminologists have devoted a great deal of attention to these forms of crime. This chapter provides an introduction to crimes of the powerful and examines the methods, motives, patterns, and extent of organized and white-collar crime in this country.

Organized Crime

A considerable number of criminal groups, including street and prison gangs, exist in American society at this time. Some of these groups are organized along racial and ethnic lines. Almost every group of immigrants to American society has developed some form of organized crime, including the Irish, Jewish, African-Americans, Puerto Ricans, Vietnamese, and Chinese. This chapter focuses specifically on two such organized crime groups. The first, the Sicilian Mafia, became a model for others to follow. The second, Russian organized crime, reveals how the Sicilian model has been altered to fit the expanding operations of new organized crime groups.

Similarities Between Organized Crime and Legitimate Business Enterprises

Some marked similarities exist between organized crime and legitimate businesses. Some common attributes are historical. Abadinsky points out that "robber barons" (e.g., John Jacob Astor, Cornelius Vanderbilt, and John D. Rockefeller) founded many of America's foremost businesses but made their fortunes in questionable ways.[2] Nevertheless, they all rose to the very top of American society, enjoying not only great wealth but also legitimate status and power. Bell suggested that organized crime provides a similar function — a "queer ladder of social mobility" by providing an opportunity for

achievement for immigrant groups.[3] In other words, it provides a method that is otherwise denied to immigrants because of societal prejudice and bias. In a classic example of Merton's theory of anomie, talented individuals gained access to the commonly held societal goals of wealth, status, and power through illegitimate means because their access to them by legitimate methods was blocked. Merton believed that upper- and lower-class persons adapt to societal goals (i.e., emphasizing money and materialism), whether legitimately or illegitimately, based on the opportunities to achieve those goals. In a capitalist society, the opportunities to achieve goals are not equally distributed. If a person has access to numerous legitimate opportunities to achieve wealth (e.g., the more successful that person becomes, higher expectations become harder and more difficult to achieve), illegitimate means may be more enticing as barriers arise to those higher expectations. Merton would also point out that the difficulties in prosecuting white-collar crimes might add to an environment of anomie for privileged persons.

LINK   Merton's theory of anomie is presented in Chapter 6.

Organized crime attempts to gain monopolistic control over illegal markets. As with legitimate businesses, the goal is to maximize profit, minimize risk, and meet the public demand for goods and services. Illegal markets follow the same market forces that legitimate businesses routinely deal with (e.g., supply and demand) with the exception that they seek monopolistic control, eliminating competition to secure an absolute advantage in the marketplace[4] (see TABLE 15-1).

Jay Albanese also argues that corporations often use the same tactics as organized crime families. For example, the "captains of industry" — industry leaders throughout American history — have employed violent tactics to break strikes and maintain their control over a particular market or industry. In the early 1970s, Lockheed Corporation made payments to Japanese officials to obtain lucrative business contracts and gain a clear advantage over the competition.[5] In order to hide their financial operations and transactions, organized crime often attempts to enter legal markets. Albanese maintains that these "takeovers" can be predicted (see TABLE 15-2). Organized crime is most likely to enter a market in which businesses are small and weak, the markets are open and easy to enter, demand is

TABLE 15-1

Elements of Organized and White-Collar Crime

Element	Organized Crime	White-Collar Crime
Goal	Money and power. Will attempt to fix elections to manipulate the political system. Bribery and corruption of public officials (i.e., police, judiciary) to control the criminal justice system.	Profit to amass economic and political power. Will make illegal campaign contributions to gain favor with politicians.
Product	Provides illegal goods and services (drugs, prostitution, gambling, etc.) Use of "muscle" to squeeze out competitors.	Provides legal goods and services but will engage in illegal methods to make a profit.
Monopoly	Aim is to dominate an industry or product (often in a limited geographic area). Will often attempt to enter and control legal markets in order to protect funds generated from illegal ventures.	Aim is to control an entire market (good or service) to fix prices and insure profit.
Violence and harm	Violence is used and/or threatened and is a common element. Is typically direct (i.e., murder with firearms), but illegal services (like the drug trade) also produce great harm indirectly through the product sold. Economic harm is also produced through the manipulation of pension funds and creating a "crime tariff" on construction and other legal goods and services.	Violence is indirect — both physical: providing unsafe products, pollution of the environment, and economic: the destruction of jobs and pensions, raising prices.
Organizational structure	Vertical and hierarchical with "Positional Power" — power resides in the position rather than the person who holds it. Specialization and a division of labor are present as are rules and regulations to govern the organization. Organization is designed to last into the future (i.e., many crime families, like the "Gambino" family, outlive their namesake).	Dependent on the business involved but often bureaucratic and hierarchical. Specialization and a division of labor are present as are rules and regulations to govern the organization. Organizations are designed to outlive their founders.
Membership	Limited based on expertise ("Expert Power") and often exclusive based upon race or ethnic background.	Also based on expertise (specialized knowledge, advanced degrees), background, and ability.

Source: Michael Bobellian, "Ebbers Sentenced to 25 Years for Role in WorldCom Fraud," *Law.com* (July 14, 2005), available at http://www.law.com.

inelastic, and the persons in charge are not well trained.[6]

For example, criminological studies have documented organized crime involvement in the solid and toxic waste disposal industries.[7] Szasz reported that corporations and the government made it possible for organized crime families to become involved in these businesses. Lax implementation and enforcement of government regulations were responsible for opening the door to this market. Corporations sponsored further participation by claiming that they were either ignorant of organized crime activity or powerless to take an active role against it.[8] When they attempt to enter legal markets, it is typical that violence need only be threatened, not actually used.

James Jacobs documents the control that organized crime families had over New York City's legitimate businesses, including the garment district, the Fulton Fish Market, John F. Kennedy Airport,

Genovese crime family members indicted for attempting to control the trash hauling industry.

? *How does such involvement in legitimate business by organized crime affect us all?*

TABLE 15-2

Organized Crime Risk Assessment Tool

Risk Factors	Measurement Methods
Economic	
Local standard of living is low, encouraging illegal activity.	Local economic indicators.
High demand for product or service: specific drug, business protection, prostitution, etc.	Addiction levels, arrests, surveys.
Affordable supply of product or service (i.e., availability)	Research estimates, seizures.
Competitive market: Is it favorable for entry/low barriers for criminal groups?	Research and intelligence on the market.
Government	
Local government weak in enforcing laws and contracts: The effectiveness of government and courts in enforcing the law.	Comparative assessment of effectiveness.
Corruption level among local government leaders and businesses: the extent to which local institutions abuse their authority or engage in misconduct.	Reports and indicators of corruption.
Laws that create or expand the illicit market (e.g., changes in drug laws, and tax laws)	Analysis of new and existing laws.
Law enforcement	
Level of training of local law enforcement in organized crime investigation (e.g., application of conspiracy laws, fraud and financial crime investigation, use of informants, undercover operations, multijurisdictional task force investigations, witness protection methods, conflict of interest, ethics training).	Comparative assessment of police training in these areas.
Working conditions of local law enforcement (to encourage loyalty to profession: e.g., salary level, nature of work assignments, promotional opportunities based on merit).	Comparative assessment of conditions.
Level of government interference in police agency(s): Do other government agencies interfere with police investigations or personnel?	Assess known past cases where this occurred.
Social/technological change	
Social change? Do recent social changes create or expand illegal opportunity in the market (e.g., local immigration wave, major political upheaval, and cross-boarder travel)?	Research and intelligence on impact of social changes.
New technology? Creates or expands illegal opportunities for a product or service (e.g., level of Internet access, cell phones, and availability of weapons).	Research on impact of current changes in technology.
Criminal history and special skills	
Have criminals existed in this market in the past? (increasing the likelihood of future involvement)	Police records, victimization surveys.
Have criminal groups existed in this market in the past? (increasing the likelihood of organized crime group involvement in the market)	Police records, victimization surveys.
Are technical or language skills or other special access required to participate in the illicit activity (i.e., barriers to entry for new offenders)?	Comparative level of skills/access needed.
Harm	
How serious is the potential harm? Estimate the financial and human costs of the activity upon this jurisdiction.	Projections of cost and social impact.

Source: Jay S. Albanese, "The Prediction and Control of Organized Crime: A Risk Assessment Instrument for Targeting Law Enforcement Efforts," Research Partnership with Ukraine: Teaming U.S. Researchers and Practitioners with Ukrainian Counterparts to Research High Priority Crime Topics, available at http://www.ojp.usdoj.gov/nij/international/programs/ukr_pred_text.html. Reproduced with permission from the U.S. Department of Justice.

the Javits Convention Center, and the waste hauling and construction industries. He notes that the Italian Mafia had several assets that made it attractive to legitimate businesses. First, the threat of violence deterred would-be competitors and helped maintain control over union labor. Second, they were a reliable business partner who could protect them from other criminals or opportunists. Finally, the organized crime families had "an entrepreneurial world view and an aptitude for business." One of their prescribed methods was to take a cut of a business rather than take it over. This method is consistent with the Mafia norm "to wet its beak" (*fari vagnari u pizzu*) and also an attribute noted in a study of America's excellent companies — "sticking to the knitting" — concentrating on one's specialty and avoiding overextension.[9]

In any event, organized crime is undoubtedly entrepreneurial, opportunistic, and adaptable.[10] Moreover, organized crime activities have become

The Yakuza of Japan are one of the world's powerful organized crime groups. Their members trace their origins back to the 17th-century samurai warrior outsiders (*kabuki-mono* — the "crazy ones") or the underdog, folk heroes (*machi-yokko* — "servants of the town") who stood up like Robin Hood for the poor and defenseless against marauders. After the collapse of the Japanese government after World War II, another Yakuza precursor (the *gurentai*) patterned themselves after America's Al Capone-like gangsters and used violence and threats to extort money.

The Yakuza follow a typical pyramid power structure with the patriarch in charge and his followers below him in an *oyabun* ("father-role") and *kobun* ("child-role") relationship. After admittance to the Yakuza, the member must accept this role and pledge unquestioning loyalty and obedience to the boss. In return, the boss must provide protection and good counsel.

The formal organizational structure of the Yakuza is complex. The *kumicho* ("supreme boss") is counseled by the *saiko komon* ("senior advisor") and followed by the *so-honbucho* ("headquarters chief"). Immediately after them is the regional boss (*wakagashira* or "number two man"), who runs several local gangs and is assisted by the *fuku-honbucho* who also operates several local gangs. Typically, a Yakuza family is made up of dozens of *shatei* (younger brothers) and *wakashu* (junior leaders).

Yakuza members typically have two prominent physical attributes. Often they are heavily tattooed over their entire torso, demonstrating their proud status as "outsiders" as well as their ability to withstand pain. If they have committed an offense against the boss, parts of their little finger are often missing. This punishment (known as *yubizume*) is self-inflicted and is symbolic of the loss of their ability to wield a samurai sword skillfully.

The Yakuza are heavily ensconced in Japanese society. Through violence and intimidation, they established their presence in legitimate businesses. In terms of criminal enterprises, they are involved in gun, drug (heroin and methamphetamines), and human trafficking (foreign women as sex slaves and foreign workers), prostitution, gambling, and white-collar crime (investment fraud and money laundering) activity in both Japan and the United States.

With regard to these attributes, do the Yakuza follow the alien conspiracy or the local, ethnic group model?

Sources: Anthony Bruno, "The Yakuza, the Japanese Mafia," The Crime Library, available at http://www.crimelibrary.com/gangsters_outlaws/gang/yakuza/1.html?sect=25; David E. Kaplan and Alec Dubro, *Yakuza: Japan's Criminal Underworld* (Berkeley, CA: University of California Press, 2003); Michael D. Lyman and Gary W. Potter, *Organized Crime* (Upper Saddle River, NJ: Prentice-Hall, 2004), 346–347.

---

diversified, moving beyond the traditional "rackets" (e.g., from prostitution to pornographic video cassettes). Like corporations, organized crime has developed into a conglomerate, franchising markets and firms — "the McDonald's-ization of the Mafia."[11] Indeed, evidence shows that the Mafia crime families have become involved in white-collar crime scams in health insurance fraud, prepaid telephone cards, and victimization of small Wall Street brokerage houses with loans to stockbrokers who are in debt or need capital to expand their business. Thus, the Mafia has diversified into legal markets through the use of their traditional illegal methods.[12]

Theories of Organized Crime

The Alien Conspiracy Model

According to the <u>alien conspiracy model</u>, foreign criminals (i.e., Sicilians) imported the crime values and family structures and secretly control crime activities in this country. In terms of structure, organized crime is a business-like hierarchy based on a system of formally defined relationships, obligations, and duties. FIGURE 15-1 presents the organizational hierarchy of the Philadelphia organized crime family in 1990. The head of the family (*capo*) is the key leader. He receives advice from his coun-

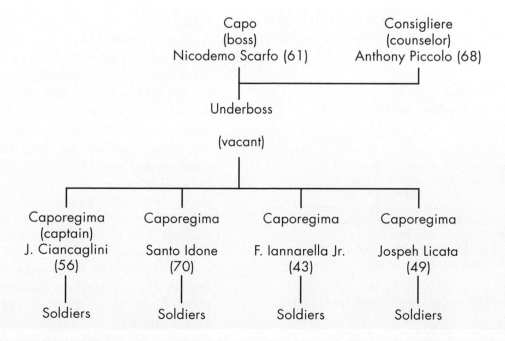

THEORY IN ACTION — The Fuk Ching

The Fuk Ching gang is an example of Chinese transnational organized crime. One of the most powerful Chinese gangs in the United States, the Fuk Ching gang primarily operates in New York City, where it operates extortion and protection rackets that victimize businesses in Chinatown neighborhoods. It also engages in human (illegal movement of migrants) and drug (heroin and methamphetamines) trafficking and ownership of legitimate businesses.

In terms of organizational structure, one of the key features of the Fuk Ching is its relationship to Chinese adult organizations known as tongs. The Fuk Ching are affiliated with the Fukein American Association, giving them a physical hangout and also a legitimate reason to operate in the community served by the tong. In some cases, the tong may protect the gang's gambling operations and supply them with necessities such as guns and money.

Their internal structure follows a family model. The grandfather (*ah kung*) or uncle (*shuk foo*) is the leader of the tong. The head of the gang is the *dai dai lo* (the "big, big brother") who communicates with the head of the tong. In descending order, the gang leader is followed by *dai los* ("big brothers"), the *yee lo/sam lo* (clique leaders), and the *mai jai* ("little horses") at the bottom of the organizational pyramid. Gang norms include respecting the *ah kung*, beating up members of other gangs on one's turf, not using drugs, following the orders of the *dai lo*, and not betraying the gang. Punishment for violators includes beating and death.

With regard to these attributes, do the Fuk Ching follow the alien conspiracy model or the local, ethnic group model?

Sources: James O. Finckenauer, "Chinese Transnational Organized Crime: The Fuk Ching," National Institute of Justice International, available at http://www.ojp.usdoj.gov/nij/international/chinese.html; William Kleinknecht, *The New Ethnic Mobs* (New York: The Free Press, 1996), 166–174; Michael D. Lyman and Gary W. Potter, *Organized Crime* (Upper Saddle River, NJ: Prentice-Hall, 2004), 345.

selor (*consigliere*) and delegates authority to the underboss. In turn, the underboss supervises the activities of the captains (*caporegimas*), who are responsible for the activities of their soldiers. Soldiers are typically employees of the family, not "made members" (those who have killed in the name of

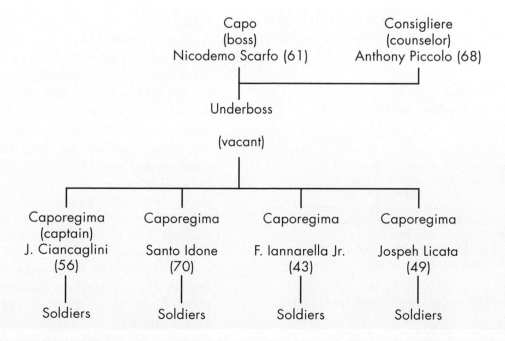

FIGURE 15-1 Chart from Pennsylvania Crime Commission, 1991
Source: Courtesy of the Commonwealth of Pennsylvania.

the family and undertaken a secret oath). According to the Task Force on Organized Crime of the President's Commission, this organized crime structure is national in scope, with several families operating across the country. These bosses formed a commission to govern activities across the United States.[13] **TABLE 15-3** summarizes the key elements of the alien conspiracy model.

Central to the alien conspiracy model is the **Mafia Code**, which is a list of secret oaths and norms that govern behavior within the family. This code includes the following elements:

1. *Omerta*: Family members must maintain the secrecy of the organization, its operations, and membership.

2. *Loyalty*: The organization comes before the individual and his family.

3. *Respect*: Members must respect other members of the organization and never harm them in any way. In addition, members must be honest in all relationships with one another. Reputed Mafia head Joseph Bonanno referred to Sicilians who follow "The Tradition" as "Men of Honor" (*uomo di rispetto*) who arbitrated disputes with both diplomacy and violence.[14]

4. *Discipline*: Orders are to be carried out and strictly obeyed. The "stand-up guy" who lives by the rules and will die for them is the hero of this social system.[15]

Although these norms have been popularized by films and novels, the alien conspiracy model is also exaggerated. Joseph Albini offers several reasons for the persistence of this traditional conspiracy view:[16]

- Belief in a secret society (especially Sicilians) allows Americans to ignore the fact that they are responsible for the great demand for illegal goods and services.

- It creates the image of an all-powerful menace that the government must take the necessary steps to destroy.

- The Mafia has served to provide entertainment and excitement for a public that does not fear its existence and wants to believe in it.

The Local, Ethnic Group Model

Several scholars disagree that organized crime represents a unified, national conspiracy.[17] Rather, they suggest that crime bodies are independent, local entities, often centered in major cities, with no formal national ties. Here, "organized criminality occurs in an informal, loosely structured, open system."[18] Function, not rational bureaucratic action, determines structure. Still, most families share some "cultural underpinnings," including the following:

- Strong familial ties and obligations and a heritage of kinship, ethnicity, and clannishness

- A distrust of outsiders and government

- A proclivity for sanctioned violence and private revenge (e.g., the Sicilian vendetta or "blood feud")

- A capacity for effective organization, including a pragmatic recognition of the need for cooperation and coordination with competing crime groups.[19] Haller notes that Al Capone's gang was most effective in organizing and effectively using the talents of nonmembers.[20]

- The savvy is to cultivate the goodwill of local residents and simultaneously exploit them for personal advantage. For example, the estate of the late New York City boss, Carlo Gambino, donated money to construct a new wing of a cancer hospital. Also in New York, reputed boss John Gotti regularly staged a Fourth of July celebration, complete with a fireworks display, in his neighborhood. When he was sentenced to life in prison for murder, a crowd of people protested.

Unlike the alien conspiracy model, the **local, ethnic group model** maintains that the locus of control is limited to certain cities or areas of the country. Here, the level of organization is rational

---

TABLE 15-3
Organized Crime: The Alien Conspiracy Model

- Organized crime groups exhibit many structural features of legitimate corporate enterprises. For example, they are rationally and bureaucratically structured to maximize profits gained from illegal enterprise. Nevertheless, they also feature feudal elements of a "Mafia code."
- Like businesses, they seek to monopolize criminal enterprises by expanding in size and forming large cartels of national and international scope.
- Ethnic or racial identity (especially Sicilian Italian) is the key to determining group membership in organized crime.
- Organized crime groups undermine the very foundations of democracy by corrupting public servants and professionals.

Source: Based on Stephen Mastrofski and Gary Potter, "Controlling Organized Crime: A Critique of Law Enforcement Policy," *Criminal Justice Policy Review* 2 (1987): 270–272.

John Gotti, nicknamed the "Teflon Don" because of his ability to elude prosecution. He was eventually convicted and died in prison of cancer.

? How do the "Dons" obtain and maintain their power?

but not bureaucratic. For example, Ianni noted that kinship played a significant role in the recruitment of crime family members but that expertise was also a factor.[21] Albini stressed the cohesive nature of the patron–client relationship as a central element in family formations.[22] An individual's connections enable him to get things done — the social network.[23] These roles shift depending on the nature of the transaction and the ability of the individual to meet obligations.

Mark Haller maintains that organized crime families often act in the same manner as organizations such as the Rotary Club. They can provide members with contacts, mutual assistance, and partnership opportunities.[24] Similarly, Alan Block has argued that the conspiracy model must be abandoned. The term *illegal enterprise* should be used in place of organized crime.[25] Instead of following strict organizational lines, families are decentralized. The boss

must be consulted, not only out of respect, but also because he can make schemes work and provide protection. For example, "Donnie Brasco" (an undercover FBI agent who infiltrates the Mafia in the 1997 movie by the same name) details the steps that he had to take to start a vending machine operation in the territory of Milwaukee crime family boss Frank Balistrieri. Although the final deal never materialized, Brasco had to arrange to pay tribute money to Balistrieri before any plans could be put in place.[26] All members are permitted to engage in any type of money-making activity, as long as the boss receives tribute.[27] Small, fragmented enterprises, not large corporate syndicates, tend to dominate illegal markets.[28]

These values may, of course, contradict one another and thereby set up inconsistencies in Mafia behavior. For example, the traditional notion is that Mafia dons were disinterested in drug trafficking, regarding it as too dangerous and as intolerable to the public. This position allowed these gangsters to engage in moral posturing. Nevertheless, there is strong evidence of long and deep Mafia involvement in drug sales. Family leaders were unable to keep their associates out of this large, lucrative market. Moreover, as Peter Lupsha noted, such organized crime luminaries as Charles "Lucky" Luciano and Vito Genovese had official criminal records for heroin trafficking. Luciano started the infamous "French Connection" heroin route to the United States. Many dons who opposed drug sales tried to keep their people out of it through threats (Bonanno) or bribes (Accardo).[29] In fact, Capeci states that Joseph Bonanno used his legitimate businesses in the United States, Canada, and Haiti to smuggle heroin and make millions of dollars with his partner, Carmine Galante.[30] Others, such as Philadelphia's Angelo Bruno, franchised the drug trade to others, such as the Greeks and motorcycle gangs (the Outlaws). Lupsha contends that Mafia dominance of the drug market faded with the drop in demand for heroin.[31] Obviously, the Mafia will not simply abandon the drug trade for moral or any other reason while consumer demand and vast profits remain.

The Mafia: La Cosa Nostra

The Mafia (also known as "La Cosa Nostra") offers a powerful and recurring image of crime in America. *La Cosa Nostra,* which literally means *our thing* in Italian, it is a "shorthand" term used by Mafia members. The federal government made further use of shorthand when it reduced this term to the acronym "LCN." Italian organized crime groups are also referred to as the Mob, the Outfit, and the Office.

Organized crime is a favorite Hollywood theme, as evidenced by films such as the *Godfather* series and *Goodfellas* and the television series *The Sopranos.* Both the President's Commission report (1967) and Donald Cressey's influential *Theft of a Nation* cited the existence of an all-powerful secret organization that controlled crime in this country.[32] This view was also perpetuated by events like the 1957 discovery of a meeting of organized crime leaders in Apalachin, New York, and the testimony of La Cosa Nostra member Joseph Valachi before the U.S. Senate in 1963.[33] These common threads formed a portrait of an omnipotent national crime syndicate known as the Mafia. Although the organization did indeed exist, its all-powerful nature was often exaggerated.

Indeed, La Cosa Nostra is either the prototype for other organized crime models or it has the same critical features. Jacobs asserts that La Cosa Nostra "stands apart" for several reasons:[34]

> No other organized-crime group has shown anything resembling the business sophistication and acumen of the Italian American organized-crime families. No other group has demonstrated the ability to control labor unions, much less play the roles of peacemaker, cartel enforcer, and "fixer" for entire industries. None has become a political force by underwriting campaigns and taking control of grassroots party organizations. Cosa Nostra is distinctive, even unique, because it has successfully penetrated labor unions to seize control of legitimate industries.

Thus, La Cosa Nostra is a unique example of organized crime.

Yet, there is some controversy over the proper definition of organized crime.[35] For example, to what extent and in what manner is crime "organized?" Generally, elements of the definition consider the breadth of organized crime operations, the markets and products they deal in, and their typical methods of operation.

Organized crime families seek to establish and maintain monopolistic control over various profitable

TABLE 15-4

Organized Crime Activities

Legitimate Industry	Illegal Activities
Food products	Gambling (e.g., numbers,
Realty	policy, dice, bookmaking)
Restaurants	Narcotics
Garbage disposal	Loan sharking
Produce	Labor racketeering
Garment manufacturing	Extortion
Bars and taverns	
Waterfront	
Securities	
Labor unions	
Vending machines	

Source: President's Commission on Law Enforcement and the Administration of Justice, *The Challenge of Crime in a Free Society* (Washington, DC: U.S. Government Printing Office, 1967): 164.

activities, both legal and illegal (see **TABLE 15-4**). They use violence as an instrument: first, to gain monopoly control over an enterprise by eliminating or discouraging competitors and, second, as a means of internal discipline to maintain control over family members. They also attempt to elude the criminal justice system by bribing and corrupting government officials. The existence and survival of organized crime groups are based on societal demand for the illegal goods and services that are provided by them.[36] Thus, the profit motive drives organized crime families. They seek the same goals of any business enterprise. They provide goods and services for which there is a well-established public demand but that are not widely available because they are illegal (e.g., narcotics, gambling, and prostitution). **TABLE 15-5** gives two official definitions of organized crime, as well as its elements as defined by criminologists.

Lupsha argues that organized crime in America is a reflection of American values and a twist on rational choice theory. The supposedly easy money draws people to organized crime — only "suckers" work.[37]

LINK Rational choice theory is discussed in Chapter 3. Rational choice theory holds that all persons, even criminals, reason and weigh their actions and the consequences. If humans are rational creatures, then individuals who are privileged or highly educated would have an advantage in weighing pros and cons of an action, including a criminal action. They have more knowledge and opportunities to make more informed decisions on whether to engage in illegal activities.

TABLE 15-5

Two Definitions of Organized Crime

Pennsylvania Crime Commission Definition:

The unlawful activity of an association trafficking in illegal goods and services, including but not limited to gambling, prostitution, loan sharking, controlled substances, labor racketeering or other unlawful activities or any continuing criminal or other unlawful practice that has as its objective large economic gain through fraudulent or coercive practices or improper governmental interest.

Federal Bureau of Investigation Definition:

Any group having some manner of formalized structure whose primary objective is to obtain money through illegal activities. Such groups maintain their position through the use or threat of violence, corrupt public officials, graft or extortion and generally have a significant impact on the people in their locales or region or country as a whole. One major crime group epitomizes this definition — La Cosa Nostra.

Elements and Attributes of Organized Crime:

Organized crime is defined by three elements: a criminal monopoly — total control of a market — that is gained through the threat of the use of violence and corruption of the legal and political systems. The violence aims to create and maintain the monopoly through an atmosphere of fear and intimidation. Corruption supports the creation of the monopoly by using legal authorities to help eliminate competitors. The third element, harm, is widespread as the integrity of the entire legal system is compromised and citizens fail to support what they see as corrupted processes.

The attributes of organized crime include the following:

- Specializing in entrepreneurial enterprises that may also extend into the legal economy
- A hierarchical organizational structure
- Abnormally high rates of return relative to other criminal organizations

Sources: Pennsylvania Crime Commission, *Organized Crime in Pennsylvania: A Decade of Change — 1990 Report* (Conshohocken: Commonwealth of Pennsylvania, 1991): 3; United Nations Office on Drugs and Crime, *Results of a Pilot Survey of Forty Selected Organized Criminal Groups in Sixteen Countries* (New York: United Nations, 2002): 4; James O. Finckenauer and Elin Waring, "Challenging the Russian Mafia Mystique," *National Institute of Justice Journal* (April 2001): 5.

Law Enforcement Methods to Combat Organized Crime

Headhunting: The Racketeer Influenced and Corrupt Organizations Statute

Given their insistence that the Mafia is a nationwide conspiracy, law enforcement officials traditionally have sought to control organized crime by apprehending and prosecuting family members, especially the bosses. In other words, they engage in headhunting. Heads of criminal families are targeted, and a "scorched earth" policy is followed: "freezing or seizing the assets used in or obtained through criminal enterprise."[38]

Since 1970, several specific law enforcement strategies to combat organized crime have been designed. The central issue surrounding them is that they may pose a threat to civil liberties. Primarily, they are based on Packer's "crime control model": the idea that certain harsh methods are necessary to capture criminals and that if abuses occur they will be corrected later in the criminal justice process.[39] The best example of this approach is the Organized Crime Control Act, passed by Congress and signed by President Nixon in 1970. One segment of this law is the Racketeer Influenced and Corrupt Organizations Act (RICO), which has been criticized as being too inclusive of individuals and groups that would not traditionally be labeled as organized crime. Here, again, the problem lies in how to define organized crime. According to RICO, organized crime consists of the acquisition, operation, or income from an "enterprise" through a "pattern" of "racketeering activity." An enterprise is defined as any individual or group. A pattern is two or more offenses within a 10-year period, and racketeering activity is any offense punishable by a year or more in prison.[40]

There are some problems with the headhunting approach. Stephen Mastrofski and Gary Potter suggest that successful headhunting causes long-term problems for society because organized crime becomes more decentralized and less visible.[41] New tactics are needed to discover information about organized crime activities: following large bank transactions, real estate sales, and transfers of funds to foreign bank accounts. Pagano argues that organized crime-control strategies must focus on systems because they remain intact when the bosses are removed. More attention must be paid to illicit markets and how they operate.[42]

Other strategies used to prosecute organized crime from 1980 to 1990 included the use of court-appointed trustees to oversee the operation of businesses (e.g., garment and construction industries) and unions that had been infiltrated by organized crime and regulatory strategies to monitor businesses and markets targeted by organized crime (e.g., New York City Trade Waste Commission).[43]

The Federal Witness Protection Program (WITSEC)

This program was developed by the Organized Crime and Racketeering section of the U.S. Department of Justice by Attorney General Robert F. Kennedy and U.S. Attorney Gerald Shur. It was formally authorized by the Organized Crime Control Act of 1970 and again by the Comprehensive Crime Control Act of 1984. The 1970 act granted the Attorney General the authority to provide witnesses protection for their testimony against alleged offenders who could retaliate against them. Thus, La Cosa Nostra members such as Joseph Valachi and Sammy "the Bull" Gravano broke their oath of silence (*omerta*) and testified against bosses like John Gotti in court.[44] The program provided not only protection while testifying but also a new identity for witnesses, relocation of themselves and their families, and housing, medical care, job training, employment, and subsistence funding until they became self-sufficient.[45]

Since its inception, more than 7500 witnesses and 9500 family members have entered WITSEC, were given new identities, and were protected by the U.S. Marshal's Service. The testimonies of WITSEC witnesses have generated an 89% conviction rate. None of the witnesses who have followed program guidelines has been harmed while under the protection of the U.S. Marshals, and less than 17% of the participants have been arrested and charged with a new crime after joining the program.[46]

Impact of Law Enforcement Methods on Organized Crime

In 1986, *Fortune* magazine published an article on the top 50 Mafia bosses, similar to its famous list of the top 500 legitimate companies.[47] By the end of 2004, only six of the "Top 50" Mafia leaders were out of prison, and the extent of their illegal activities is doubtful. One of the leaders, Michael Franzese, has become an author and a motivational speaker based on his experiences. Two of the leaders could not be located with Internet sources. As Finckenauer notes, it is apparent that La Cosa Nostra has been "severely crippled by law enforcement."[48]

Russian Organized Crime

Despite inroads against La Cosa Nostra, organized crime has arisen in other forms. For example, motorcycle gangs such as Hells Angels and the Outlaws have become involved in drug dealing, especially methamphetamines.[49] In addition, organized crime has become "transnational" in nature, crossing boarders and continents to control illegal markets in all sorts of goods and services.[50] For example, Russian organized crime groups in the United States have become involved in such markets as drugs, arms trafficking, stolen automobiles, trafficking in women and children, and money laundering.[51]

Russian organized crime groups have similarities to and differences from La Cosa Nostra families. Although Russian groups are often linked under the all-encompassing label of "Mafia," they do not look anything like La Cosa Nostra. Their structure is highly flexible — groups come together to commit a crime for the financial gain and do not answer to a boss or head. Their loyalty is not based on shared ethnicity or culture. Their partnerships are more opportunistic, and they do not seek monopolization or the systematic use of corruption.[52] Both the Italian Mafia and Russian organized crime groups began by extorting their fellow immigrants but quickly moved on to major enterprise offenses in mainstream American society. In addition to using violence as a means to an end, both groups possess high-tech equipment, including military weapons.[53]

The characteristics of the organization of the Russian Mafia are attributable to the political and economic structure of the former Soviet Union. Because of the rigid class structure under the czars and later the state-run Soviet economy, the Russian populace developed a "connive to survive" attitude in which stealing from the nobility (or the government) was not considered a crime, but "fit for the taking." Also, the black market was the normal vehicle to obtain the basic necessities of life. It was under the control of a professional criminal class (the *vory v zakone*) who were career criminals completely devoted to a life of crime. These elements combined to form a milieu of lawlessness that has aided the development of Russian organized crime.[54]

These norms also account for the way in which their crimes blend legal and illegal operations. In the United States, the Russian Mafia has moved into legitimate areas such as the textile industry and the movie business, although these areas are also used to launder money.[55] Other fraudulent activities conducted by the Russian Mafia include fuel tax evasions and staged automobile accidents. However, they are no strangers to extreme violence. Officials estimate that at least 65 murders in the New York–New Jersey area alone are attributable to the Russian Mafia. Their financial abilities are also evident. In 1999, a Russian organized crime case involved laundering more than $7 billion through legitimate channels.[56] Thus, Russian Mafia members have experience in complex areas of business and technology and may thus represent an even greater threat to society in the future.

White-Collar Crime

As with organized crime, the desire for profit drives most __white-collar crime__, and individuals or groups who wield considerable power perpetrate the crimes. Unlike organized crime, however, well-respected members of society who enjoy high social status commit white-collar crime. In fact, it is precisely the offender's prominent status that provides the opportunity for the crime.

The Sutherland Definition of White-Collar Crime

Building on the work of other criminologists and social commentators, Edwin H. Sutherland provided the breakthrough appraisal of white-collar crime; he defined a white-collar crime as "a crime committed by a person of respectability and high social status in the course of his occupation."[57] Sutherland gave three reasons why such actions are criminal. First, the law states that these crimes harm the public. For example, misrepresentation in advertising, unfair labor practices, financial fraud,

Members of the Russian Mafia are escorted from FBI Headquarters.

? *How do the methods of La Cosa Nostra and the Russian Mafia compare?*

violations of war regulations, and infringements of patents, trademarks, and copyrights are all crimes. Second, penalties for practices such as forming monopolies (or "combinations in restraint of trade") were already on the books. Third, these activities are willful and intentional, and the motive (profit, personal gain) is usually clear.

Sutherland called for a change in public values so that respectable white-collar offenders would be viewed as being equally as criminal as their street-level counterparts. He claimed that white-collar crime is not treated as seriously as street crime because the upper classes have the power to influence the creation and administration of the law. He also questioned criminological theories that focused exclusively on the lower classes. Specifically, he recommended the use of his theory of differential association to study white-collar crime. Like other criminals, Sutherland believed that white-collar offenders learned their methods, motives, and drives through interaction in small personal groups.

The Impact of White-Collar Crime

Unquestionably, white-collar offenses are as harmful to the public as street crimes. For example, estimates suggest that the bailout required by the savings and loan scandal will cost taxpayers as much as $500 billion by the year 2021.[58] Moreover, as Bohm states, white-collar crimes are not always nonviolent[59]:

> Conservative estimates show that each year at least 10,000 lives are lost due to unnecessary surgeries, 20,000 to errors in prescribing drugs, 20,000 to doctors spreading diseases in hospitals, 100,000 to industrial disease, 14,000 to industrial accidents, 200,000 to environmentally caused cancers, and an unknown number to lethal industrial products.

These deaths dwarf the number of murders recorded each year.

LINK Sutherland's theory of differential association is outlined in Chapter 7. Differential association applies to all criminal activities. In reference to white-collar crimes, differential association states that these criminals engage in illegal activities by learning from others they associate with, on a regular basis, who engage in these practices. Privileged persons interact with others of their same status, which allows for the transmission of skills, motives, attitudes, and behaviors necessary to commit the crime, to be learned by others.

The impact of white-collar and economic crime on American society is considerable and alarming[60]:

The Exxon Valdez accident resulted in massive environmental damage.

? *Do such accidents constitute crimes? How do environmental disasters like this affect the American public?*

- Almost 3.25 million adult Americans discovered that their personal information had been misused through identity theft in the past year.
- The total cost of identity theft approaches $50 billion per year, with an average loss of $4800 per victim.
- According to the U.S. General Accounting Office, healthcare fraud totals 10% of the total healthcare expenditures each year — approximately $100 billion.
- Check fraud is estimated to cost businesses $10 billion per year.
- Internet fraud losses were over $14 million in 2002.

The American public clearly understands that white-collar crimes represent severe threats to the community. The seventh highest ranking crime listed by a national survey of crime severity, which included 1169 U.S. citizens contacted by phone, was "a factory [that] knowingly gets rid of its waste in a way that pollutes the water supply of a city [and] 20 people die."[61] Nevertheless, a similar survey found that, among categories of white-collar crime, the public considers those that involve physical harm and price fixing the most serious.[62] The public also felt that white-collar offenders deserved to be punished, including incarceration.

In 1999, the National Public Survey on White Collar Crime determined that more than one in three households had been victimized by white-collar crime in the previous year. Although there are many white-collar crime victims, a significant number of them did not report their victimization to the authorities. Even more surprising is that, of those victimized, 95% claimed they would report the offense to police, although 41% did not report their incident. The majority of the survey respondents believed that white-collar crimes are important and that there is great need to increase apprehension, sanctioning, and resource allocations.[63]

Official figures on white-collar crime victimization are difficult to estimate for several reasons. First, white-collar crime offenses usually fall under the jurisdiction of several different federal agencies (such as the Food and Drug Administration or the Internal Revenue Service). Second, the investigation of corporate crime is often left to regulatory and professional organizations (such as the American Medical Association or the American Bar Association) rather than law enforcement agencies. Therefore, corporate crime is usually handled by regulatory sanctions (such as "cease and desist" orders) or in civil law cases.[64] The NIBRS system (Chapter 2), however, is making an attempt to compile and count white-collar offenses as they do other crimes. An estimate of white-collar victimization for selected offenses and limited jurisdictions for 1997 to 1999 is presented in **TABLE 15-6**. According to

Family members of a man who died while taking the prescription painkiller Vioxx appearing at their wrongful death civil trial. The man's widow was awarded $253.4 million by the jurors.

? *Do corporations have the responsibility to provide safe products and thoroughly test them before they are marketed?*

these figures, individuals were most likely to be the victims of property and bribery offenses, whereas businesses were most likely to be victimized in crimes of fraud, counterfeiting, and embezzlement.

LINK The NIBRS System is presented in Chapter 2.

Coleman also documents the impact of white-collar crimes. Ivan Boesky, the Wall Street financier

TABLE 15-6

Victims of White-Collar Crime Reported to NIBRS, 1997–1999

Victims	Property	Fraud	Bribery	Counterfeiting	Embezzlement	Total
Individual	2,621,843	47,826	143	45,270	3,006	2,718,088
Business	934,469	47,907	16	55,676	17,627	1,055,695
Financial institution	11,378	2,989	0	5,310	182	19,859
Government	73,623	3,844	36	2,949	260	80,712
Religious organization	10,794	70	0	104	35	11,003
Society or other	417,217	1,357	3	1,236	246	420,059
Totals	**4,069,324**	**103,993**	**198**	**110,545**	**21,356**	**4,305,416**

and convicted inside trader, agreed to pay over $100 million in fines — far more than the cost of the total number of robberies each year. Although the A. H. Robbins Company filed bankruptcy to prevent additional lawsuit filings, approximately $2.3 billion is in a trust fund to compensate victims who used the "Dalkon Shield" (a dangerous birth control device).[65]

White-collar crime differs from the street-level variety in that it is more complex in method and impact. In addition, the nature, degree, and volume of victimization are more substantial.[66] Victims of white-collar crimes suffer greatly at the hands of their "assailants," even though the results of the crime may take years to become evident. For example, exposure to unsafe working conditions can cause long-term, progressively debilitating illnesses. Victims of crimes such as the savings and loan scandal may have a diminished faith in a free economy and business leaders, as well as a lower standard of living. The public may withhold financial support and economic investment. Such crimes also cause a loss of confidence in political institutions, processes, and leaders and an erosion of public morality.[67] Victims of identity theft experience increased psychological and physical distress that is maintained over time, much like the victims of violent and traditional property crimes.[68] In terms of public policy, the boundaries between organized and white-collar crimes will continue to blur because of inconsistent definitions of these terms and the increasing number of new crimes (such as cyber crimes) that add to the complexities of enforcement. The public demands stricter enforcement of these crimes and punishment of these offenders, although allocated resources continue to be limited and focus more on street crimes.[69]

Expanded Definitions of White-Collar Crime

Sutherland's original definition of white-collar crime has been criticized. Indeed, criminologists have had some problems with accurately defining white-collar crime and in adequately capturing all its nuances and describing its many forms.[70] Although his sample included 70 of the largest manufacturing, mining, and mercantile corporations in 1929 and 1938, Sutherland's definition focused on the individual white-collar criminal and did not consider corporations or organizations acting as a whole. This creates a dichotomy in the definition of white-collar crime: crimes committed by (for) and against the organization.[71]

The earliest studies of white-collar criminality feature crimes committed by organizations. For example, Clinard's study of pricing and rationing violations during World War II found that businesses committed 338,029 violations during 1944 alone. Although agreeing that differential association could explain some violations, Clinard argued that the personality of the violator also accounted for the crime.[72]

Similarly, Hartung's investigation of the wholesale meat industry in Detroit,[73] Quinney's analysis of the violations of retail pharmacists,[74] and Geis' study of antitrust violations by manufacturers of heavy electrical equipment[75] all examined crimes committed by organizations. Studies that followed dealt with this dichotomy directly by expanding the definition of white-collar crime to include corporate criminality.

Shapiro argues that white-collar crime should be viewed as an abuse of trust. From this perspective, white-collar criminals typically hold monopolies of information that cannot be verified by their clients. Clients are separated from the perpetrators both physically and socially. Often, they act in a collective fashion as a bank, charity, or company. Usually, their activities are hidden and difficult to follow. Thus, lying, stealing, misappropriation, self-dealing, and corruption are violations of a relationship based on trust.[76]

In effect, the definition of white-collar crime has been split in two: <u>occupational crime</u> and <u>corporate crime</u>.

Occupational Crime

Gary Green defines occupational crime as "any act punishable by law that is committed through opportunity created in the course of an occupation that is legal."[77] He also sets up a typology that focuses on the beneficiary of the crime and separates the offenders motivated by a desire for individual gain from those who act on behalf of the organization. Occupational crime can be divided into four major types:[78]

1. *Crimes committed for the benefit of an employing organization.* Here, the employers, not the individuals, benefit directly from the offense. Insurance fraud in auto body repair is an example of this type of crime. Paul Tracy and James Fox conducted an experiment in which four drivers took their damaged autos to 96 repair shops in Massachusetts. Repair estimates were about one third higher for drivers who said they were covered by insurance than for those who said they were not. This finding held despite the type of car, the extent of the damage, the sex of the driver, and the location of the shop.[79]

2. *Crimes committed as the result of state-based authority.* To commit this type of crime, the offender must be "legally vested with governmental powers to make or enforce laws or to command others."[80] Chambliss defines <u>state-organized crime</u> as acts defined by law as criminal and committed by state officials in the pursuit of their job as representatives of the state. For example, CIA support of opium-growing feudal lords in the mountains of Vietnam, Laos, Cambodia, and Thailand during and after the Vietnam War represented occupational crime. Chambliss also includes arms smuggling (e.g., U.S. government arms sales to the Nicaraguan Contras) and state-organized assassinations (e.g., a CIA-sponsored coup in Chile that resulted in the assassination of socialist President Salvador Allende) in this category.

3. *Crimes committed by professionals in their professional capacity.* These crimes are a direct result of the trust that others have vested in certain indi-

viduals, usually an elite group (e.g., physicians, attorneys, and psychologists). Several studies have detected high levels of fraud committed by physicians against the Medicare and Medicaid programs. For example, doctors have submitted bills for procedures (e.g., x-rays and blood and urine tests) that were either unnecessary or never performed.[81] Psychiatrists have been sanctioned for charging the cost of individual therapy for patients treated in a group, billing for "therapy" that involved sexual contact between patient and physician, and generally inflating the cost of treatment.[82] In these offenses, the victim was not only the individual but also the taxpayer. It is difficult to detect and effectively sanction crimes committed under the veil of professional confidentiality by autonomous practitioners.[83]

4. *Occupational crimes committed by individuals for personal gain.* Put simply, these individuals have the same motives as armed robbers or muggers. Another study of auto repair shops revealed that they may misrepresent the need for a new car battery. Honesty was related to the presence of the owner, the economic health of the shop, incentive or commission payment procedures, and the longevity of the current management.[84] Interventions (e.g., public service announcements, filing of a suit against a major dealer, and a letter from the California Bureau of Automobile Repair) did not deter dishonest dealers.[85] Clearly, the individual salesperson was attempting to gain through the sale of a new battery.

Corporate Crime

Kramer defines corporate crime as[86]:

> crimes committed by corporate organizations. They are the result of deliberate decision making by persons who occupy structural positions within the organization. The organization makes decisions intentionally to benefit itself.

Two of the most infamous examples of corporate crime are the Ford Pinto case and the savings and loan scandal.

Ford Pinto Scandal

An article in *Mother Jones* magazine brought the Ford Pinto case to the attention of the public. Mark Dowie accused Ford Motor Company of ignoring a life-threatening defect in its profitable subcompact, the Pinto. Ford crash tested the Pinto and discovered that in every test performed at over 25 miles per hour, the fuel tank ruptured. Although inexpensive modifications ($11 per car) would have prevented any threat of fire, Ford decided not to issue a recall. An internal cost–benefit analysis estimated that the recall would cost Ford approximately $137 million, although 180 burn deaths would result in a company loss of only $49.5 million.[87] In August of 1978, three Indiana teenagers died when a rear-end collision caused their Pinto to burst into flames. In 1980, Ford Motor Company was indicted and brought to trial in Indiana under the reckless homicide provision of a state law. It was charged with building a dangerous vehicle and ignoring the company's duty to protect its customers from known dangers.[88] The trial resulted in a jury verdict of not guilty. Nevertheless, the case clearly established that a corporation could face criminal liability because of its actions.[89]

Savings and Loan Scandal

The savings and loan (S&L) crisis introduced a new form of corporate criminality: <u>collective embezzlement</u> — the siphoning of company funds for personal use by top management at the expense of the institution itself and with the implicit or explicit sanction of its management.[90] In effect, the S&L executives robbed their own banks.

During the 1970s, stagflation, high interest rates, and slow growth plagued the S&L industry. In addition, the development of money market mutual funds led to massive withdrawals from S&Ls. The Reagan administration pushed deregulation as the cure for the ills plaguing these institutions. The belief was that loosening restraints would make S&Ls more competitive under the "self-regulating mechanisms of the free market." Thus, restrictions on interest rates paid by S&Ls were phased out. Simultaneously, the federal protection offered by the Federal Savings and Loan Insurance Corporation was raised from a maximum of $40,000 to $100,000 per deposit.

The loosening of federal restrictions permitted such practices as linked financing ("daisy chains") to occur. Here, deposits were made and loans were made to the depositors. The brokers defaulted on the loans, essentially obtaining free cash ("drag loans"). Middlemen received a generous "finder's fee," and S&L operators recorded hefty deposits and inflated assets, which spelled extra bonuses and dividends for S&L executives.

These practices developed under the S&L-sponsored "casino economy." Speculative ventures led to windfall profits. "Junk" bonds transformed debt into wealth — one of the greatest fortunes in Wall Street history. This "fiddling with money," however, only produces capital gains — not jobs or products. The S&L corporate executives had little to lose by reckless behavior: The taxpayers would foot the bill for this casino extravaganza.

Thus, the S&L scandal is an example of a new form of corporate crime: crime by the corporation against the corporation with state complicity. Deregulation and the ideologies that fueled it gave birth to this fraud epidemic. Deregulation unleashed the temptation and the opportunity to commit fraud, and the systematic embezzlement of company funds became company policy.[91]

The Criminal Careers of Corporations

In Chapter 9, we considered the idea of career criminality in which the focus was the individual criminal. Here, we shift our concern to the criminal careers of organizations. Again, the centerpiece of the analysis is how frequently the same corporations commit a crime. Is there a pattern to this level of offending? These questions go back to Sutherland's original study.

LINK The elements of career criminality and research findings are presented in Chapter 9.

Sutherland found that every corporation in his sample had at least one judgment against it, but the maximum number was 50. A total of 980 decisions were levied. Specifically, 60 corporations had decisions for restraint of trade, 53 for infringement, 44 for unfair labor practices, and 43 for miscellaneous offenses, 28 for misrepresentation in advertising, and 26 for rebates. From the beginning, apparently, there was a career-like pattern to corporate criminality.[92]

Clinard and Yeager conducted a large, sophisticated examination of the pattern of corporate criminality. Their study encompassed criminal actions initiated or completed during 1975 and 1976 by 25 federal agencies. It examined the 477 largest publicly owned manufacturing corporations and 105 of the largest wholesale, retail, and service corporations in the United States. The corporations in the sample account for 1,553 federal cases filed by government agencies, or an average of 2.7 cases per corporation. Over 60% of these corporations had at least one federal case initiated against them. Almost half of them had multiple violations and multiple cases during 1975 to 1976. A few corporations

(13%) accounted for a disproportionate number (52%) of offenses. Thus, "street" thugs are not the only type of career criminals. Clinard and Yeager speculated that these corporations had developed a subculture favorable to unethical and illegal behavior. Their executives and employees may have become socialized to violate the law.[93]

Certain businesses had higher rates of offending. For example, the motor vehicle industry accounted for half of the hazardous product violations. Oil corporations committed violations far in excess of their size. Together, they accounted for over 90% of the financial and over 70% of the water pollution violations.

Another possible predictor of corporate crime is the "financial strain thesis": corporations in depressed industries and those with poor performance records tended to violate federal laws more frequently than those that performed well. The study also revealed that larger corporations, in terms of sales, were more likely to commit violations than were smaller ones.[94]

TABLE 15-7 presents a compilation of the "Top 50 Criminal Corporations" of the 1990s. How does this list compare with the presentation of the Top 50 Mafia Bosses presented earlier?

The Enron Scandal

The now infamous Enron scandal was one of the greatest securities frauds in American history. Based in Houston, Texas, the Enron Company was created in 1985 when Houston Natural Gas merged with a company called InterNorth. It grew quickly and entered into the energy and commodities trading markets. It became one of the 10 largest companies in America and profited mightily from the 2001 energy crisis in California by selling electricity at inflated prices.

Enron became involved in a number of such complicated deals and contracts that plunged the company into massive debt that was hidden from its stockholders and lower-level employees. By October 2001, Enron was worth $1.2 billion less than publicly reported. An investigation by the Federal Securities and Exchange Commission revealed illegal practices by high-ranking executives (such as CEO Kenneth Lay), investment banking partners, and even the company's accounting firm (Arthur Anderson).[95] The indictment and prosecution of Enron officials is well under way. The Enron experience represents "a corporation whose recklessness and dishonesty has devastated thousands of

TABLE 15-7

The Top 50 Criminal Corporations of the 1990s

Name of Corporation	Type of Crime	Criminal Fine
1. F. Hoffman — LaRoche Ltd.	Antitrust	$500 million
2. Daiwa Bank Ltd.	Financial	$340 million
3. BASF Aktiengesellschaft	Antitrust	$225 million
4. SGL Carbon Aktiengesellschaft	Antitrust	$135 million
5. Exxon Corp. & Shipping*	Environmental	$125 million
6. UCAR International Inc.	Antitrust	$110 million
7. Archer Daniels Midland	Antitrust	$100 million
8. (tie) Banker's Trust	Financial	$60 million
8. (tie) Sears Bankruptcy Recovery Management Services	Fraud	$60 million
10. Haarman & Reimer Corporation	Antitrust	$50 million
11. Louisiana-Pacific Corporation	Environmental	$37 million
12. Hoechst AG	Antitrust	$36 million
13. Damon Clinical Laboratories	Fraud	$35.2 million
14. C.R. Bard Inc.	Food and Drug	$30.9 million
15. Genetech Inc.	Food and Drug	$30 million
16. Nippon Gohsei	Antitrust	$21 million
17. (tie) Pfizer Inc.	Antitrust	$20 million
17. (tie) Summitville Consolidated Mining Co. Inc.	Environmental	$20 million
19. (tie) Lucas Western Inc.	False Statements	$18.5 million
19. (tie) Rockwell International Corporation	Environmental	$18.5 million
21. Royal Caribbean Cruises Ltd.	Environmental	$18 million
22. Teledyne Industries Inc.	Fraud	$17.5 million
23. Northrop	False Statements	$17 million
24. Litton Applied Technology Division and Litton Systems Canada	Fraud	$16.5 million
25. Iroquois Pipeline Operating Company	Environmental	$15 million
26. Eastman Chemical Company	Antitrust	$11 million
27. Copley Pharmaceutical Inc.	Food and Drug	$10.65 million
28. Lonza AG	Antitrust	$10.5 million
29. Kimberly Home Health Care Inc.	Fraud	$10.08 million
30. (tie) Ajinomoto Inc.	Antitrust	$10 million
30. (tie) Bank of Credit and Commerce International	Financial	$10 million
30. (tie) Kyowa Hakko Kogyo Co. Ltd.	Antitrust	$10 million
30. (tie) Warner-Lambert Company*	Food and Drug	$10 million
34. General Electric	Fraud	$9.5 million
35. (tie) Royal Caribbean Cruises Ltd.	Environmental	$9 million
35. (tie) Showa Denko Carbon	Antitrust	$9 million
37. IBM East Europe/Asia Ltd.	Illegal Exports	$8.5 million
38. Empire Sanitary Landfill Inc.	Campaign Finance	$8 million
39. (tie) Eklof Marine Corporation	Environmental	$7 million
39. (tie) Colonial Pipeline Company	Environmental	$7 million
41. (tie) Rockwell International Corporation*	Environmental	$6.5 million
41. (tie) Chevron	Environmental	$6.5 million
43. Tokai Carbon Ltd. Co.	Antitrust	$6 million
44. (tie) Allied Clinical Laboratories Inc.	Fraud	$5 million
44. (tie) Northern Brands International Inc.	Fraud	$5 million
44. (tie) Ortho Pharmaceutical Corporation	Obstruction of Justice	$5 million
44. (tie) Unisys	Bribery	$5 million
44. Georgia Pacific Corporation	Tax Evasion	$5 million
49. Kanzaki Specialty Papers Inc.	Antitrust	$4.5 million
50. ConAgra Inc.	Fraud	$4.4 million

* These are "criminal recidivist companies" that committed more than one crime during the 1990s.

Source: Russell Mokhiber and Robert Weissman, "The Top 100 Corporate Criminals," *Alter Net* (April 26, 2000), available at http://alternet.org/module/printversion/1075, accessed November 11, 2005.

innocent victims and has hung a cloud of public distrust over American financial markets."[96] It is hoped that this example will lead to the promotion of ethical conduct and more socially responsible behavior by corporations who place less emphasis on profit making and more stress on the establishment of economic democracy.[97]

Other Categories of White-Collar Crimes

White-collar crimes include a multitude of dimensions that continue to expand and complicate this area of study. Several crimes are studied and classified as white-collar crimes, although some researchers are questioning whether they should still be "housed under this umbrella." Such crimes include environmental crimes, cyber crimes, and money laundering. These crimes also expand national boundaries to the international arena. These specific crimes may be broad concepts themselves that encompass a wide variety of crimes that extend beyond the focus of white-collar crimes. These illegal activities fall into more than one area of criminology, but to date, they are still part of the discussion of white-collar crimes.

Environmental Crimes

Environmental crime refers to a broad range of illegal actions that endanger natural resources and the health of all living creatures. One of the first environmental problems to gain governmental attention in the 1970s was the issue of water pollution because of its relationship to public health and diseases.[98] Since then, political and public attention to violations of environmental standards allowed environmental crimes to be a staple within the study of white-collar crimes.

Businesses and corporations were the first perpetrators investigated and prosecuted under the category of white-collar crimes. Although environmental crimes cause more damage and harm to greater numbers of people, this area is still limited in existing research of the causes and consequences of these actions. Consistent with white-collar crimes in general, little attention is given to environmental crimes. Limited resources exist for investigations, and few cases are criminally prosecuted because of the status and power of those committing these illegal acts. Civil suits against corporations are more likely to occur than criminal prosecution. In the United States, the Environmental Protection Agency is responsible for protecting the environment and public health by developing laws, supporting research, conducting environmental testing, and educating the public on these issues. This agency is not responsible for prosecuting violators (U.S. Department of Justice has taken this position), which adds to the difficulty in resources, enforcement, and sanctions for these activities.

Today, this concept includes crimes related to dumping toxic waste, air pollution, dangerous consumer products, aquatic pollution, environmental racism, selling hazardous chemicals, employee exposure to hazardous materials, and unsafe work areas. Globally, environmental terrorism includes poaching, trafficking of illegal substances, and diverting rivers for water consumption.[99] The FBI prioritizes its work on environmental crimes to focus on hazards that place workers at risk, environmental catastrophes, chronic violators of federal environmental laws, and actions of organized crime groups in the waste industry.[100] Many of these crimes have transitioned into their own areas of study (i.e., employee safety) and within other areas of study (i.e., organized crime and racism), but all of them still hold a place in the discussion of white-collar crimes.

Cyber Crimes

Cyber crimes or Internet crimes have still not been strictly classified; criminologists are still trying to determine where to place them in the field of criminology and specifically in white-collar crimes. The predecessor to Internet crimes — computer crimes — has always been considered a white-collar crime. Although many definitions exist, computer crimes encompass any crime that involves the use of a computer, whether suffering occurs for the victim or gain is made for the perpetrator. This crime falls under white-collar crimes because persons who tended to have access to computers, beginning in the 1960s, were professional, higher status individuals. Cyber crimes have a shorter history under this field of study.

The term *cyberspace* came out of a science fiction book from the 1980s to address space, without a physical location.[101] Today, cyberspace is used extensively to address crimes that occur on the Internet. Although limited research exists on the motivations of perpetrators, effects of victimization, and the perpetuation and extent of these crimes, new information emerges on a daily basis. Internet crime information is also complex because cyberspace has no boundaries; for this reason, Internet crime is inherently a global issue.

Crimes committed in cyberspace fall into several different categories. Many of the crimes committed offline are not finding their way to the online world and would not be traditionally defined as white-collar crimes. Such crimes include fraud, social engineering, identity theft, stalking, harassment, copyright infringements, denial of service attacks, and other crimes that are constantly evolving.

Current studies are finding that many of the cyber criminals are not the privileged, upper-class persons who are traditionally sought in white-collar crimes.[102] Although computer crimes are addressed in white-collar crimes discussions, cyber crimes may earn a place in criminology all to themselves.

Money Laundering

The complexity of money laundering does not counter the simplicity of the practice: converting monies obtained from illegal activities into the appearance of legitimate funds. Money laundering allows criminals to go undetected by law enforcement and other officials, and thus, they can spend and enjoy the profits that they made by committing crimes. Although participants of organized crime commit a variety of acts, money laundering has been a classic practice within this criminal group. Today, money laundering is associated with drug-related crimes, computer hackers, and terrorists groups.

Money laundering has been classified as a white-collar crime for a variety of reasons. Organized crime groups, such as Russian groups and Al-Qaeda, have a history of laundering money.[103] These groups use their privilege and status to hide illegally acquired funds from detection. Bankers have used their position and social trust to launder money to enhance their profitability.[104] Large investment corporations (e.g., J. P. Morgan and Chase) have been investigated for their role in the financial devastation with the Enron Corporation.[105] In all of these situations, individuals, groups, and corporations used their privilege and status to process illegal funds into legitimate monies.

As with other white-collar crimes, few individuals or groups are actually prosecuted. Federal acts have been in place since the 1970s with the Bank Secrecy Act requiring banks to produce reports to justify their money processes. Enforcing these acts requires collaboration and cooperation from various agencies at the local, state, and federal levels. Since September 11, 2001, terrorist activities and the funding of these activities have brought national and international attention to money laundering. The USA Patriot Act of 2001 even has provisions to combat terrorism and terrorist activities that impact the U.S. financial system.[106] Money laundering, like cyber crimes and environmental crimes, has traditionally been placed under the heading of white-collar crime, although increasing attention and globalization may allow these crimes to venture into their own category of crime or expand to include a multitude of other crimes that extend well beyond the scope of traditional white-collar crime research.

The Careers of Individual White-Collar Criminals

Some evidence suggests that white-collar offenders also have criminal careers. A study of white-collar criminals revealed that they began their criminal careers later and at a lower rate of offending than street criminals.[107] More than a quarter of tax offenders had two or more prior arrests, and more than 10% of bank embezzlers and bribery offenders had multiple prior arrests. Many of these repeat white-collar offenders, ranging from 19% of bribery offenders to 46% of credit fraud offenders, had prior convictions. Among a subset of offenders who held elite positions or owned significant assets, over 25% had criminal records (10% had felony convictions; 6% had been previously incarcerated). In short, white-collar criminals are often repeat offenders and as such are not much different from persistent street criminals.

Prosecution of White-Collar Criminals

Several studies have examined how the criminal justice system deals with white-collar offenders. Prosecutors are the gatekeepers of the sentencing process and the prosecutorial process always involves selection, meaning that cases are chosen for prosecution because of their severity but also because of the strength of the evidence against the accused. Joan Gurney's study of economic crime cases (e.g., fraud, embezzlement) determined that roughly one third of 1,000 incidents were prosecuted in one midwestern city over a 6-year period.[108]

Adelphia founder John Rigas was sentenced in federal court to 15 years in prison for looting the cable company and defrauding its investors. His son, Tim Rigas, the company's former CEO, received a 20-year sentence. They were previously ordered to give up 95% of their assets (approximately $1.5 billion) to set up a compensation fund for the defrauded investors of the company.

Adelphia went bankrupt, and the Rigases were suspected of lying about the company's financial health while they stole funds and assets from the business. They were accused of conspiring to hide $2.3 billion in debts, stealing $100 million, and lying to investors about the financial health of the corporation. Federal prosecutors had asked for 215-year sentences under federal sentencing guidelines, noting that the Rigases had driven the company into bankruptcy.

Adelphia is in the process of selling its cable assets to Time Warner and Comcast for $17.6 billion.

Which criminological theory could explain the reasons why John and Tim Rigas engaged in fraud? What information is needed to assist in making this determination?

Is monetary compensation punishment enough for the Rigases? Is jail time needed? How will their punishment deter others from committing these same crimes?

Sources: "Adelphia Founder Gets 15-Year Term; Son Gets 20: Rigases Were Convicted of Stealing $100 Million in Company Funds," MSNBC (June 20, 2005), available at http://www.msnbc.msn.com/id/8291040/; "Adelphia Founder Sentenced to 15 Years," *CNN Money* (June 20, 2005), available at http://money.cnn.com/2005/06/20/news/newsmakers/rigas_sentencing/.

Several factors frame the decision to prosecute white-collar crimes. Individuals were more likely to be prosecuted than organizations, although the probability of prosecution increased when the *victim* was an organization. A survey of California prosecutors revealed that the primary obstacle to prosecution was the level of resources available to them.[109] Political influence was also evident: Prosecutors from small districts were less likely to take on a corporate prosecution that would have a major impact on the local economy.

Prosecutorial decisions also vary by the type of crime. Scott's study of corporate collusion between 1946 and 1970 determined that price fixing was the most common charge. On average, cases spanned 7 years and required 21 months to investigate and 23 months to litigate. There was no clear concentration of cases by industry. Most cases began with negotiations that start before charges were actually filed. Although the penalties levied were often weak, Scott believes that they did have a deterrent effect.[110]

Sentencing typically follows the traditional rationales for the punishment of crime: retribution, deterrence, and just deserts.[111] In terms of retribution, white-collar offenders tend to be treated more leniently than street criminals, although they may inflict more harm and affect more people than other crimes. White-collar criminals use their position to violate public trust and should be punished as any criminal would be. Punishment in the criminal justice system is a way of getting back at them for violating the public trust of their position in society. General deterrence theory demands that we punish these offenders severely to send a message that these crimes are intolerable. Just deserts theory stresses that the offender deserves to be punished because they have committed a crime.

Sentencing of White-Collar Criminals

White-collar criminals are not always sentenced severely. Some officials, including judges, believe that these offenders have "suffered enough."[112] The process of arrest and conviction causes them to lose their high place in society and "fall from grace."[113] They are also especially sensitive to imprisonment because of their lack of experience with the criminal justice system.[114] A survey of New York judges revealed their belief that prison was more severe punishment for a white, middle-class offender than the same sentence was for a black or Hispanic lower-class offender.[115] These feelings mirror the concept of just deserts, which focuses on the disgrace that the commission of the offense brings to the offender. Obviously, the public feels strongly that these offenses are a threat and deserve severe punishment. With just deserts, punishment causes stigmatization. The criminal is branded and labeled as an "offender."

The sentencing of white-collar offenders, however, appears to be affected by bias. In a study of offenders charged with the violation of federal security laws, David Eitle discovered that offenders who had positions of authority and control in the workplace were less likely to receive a punitive sanction. The differences in outcome may not be entirely due to bias but to prosecutorial resources and expertise.[116] There is also some evidence that female white-collar offenders sanctioned under federal sentencing guidelines received more lenient sentences than males.[117] Based on this evidence, it appears that white-collar sanctions are subject to the same pressures that plague the sentencing of other offenders.

Shaming

John Braithwaite has suggested that punishing organizational criminals should take the more constructive approach of **shaming**.[118] Shaming involves the attempt to reintegrate offenders by confronting them with the seriousness of their conduct while forgiving those who reform. Stigmatization is largely counterproductive:[119]

> Criminal subcultures are less likely to develop when potent shaming is mobilized against both guilty individuals and the organization itself by the general community, professional or industry peers, and government regulatory officials.

Shaming thus involves all aspects of the community acting together. It promotes self-regulation by the professional community in place of a subculture of organizational criminality and it fosters both crime prevention and improved public service.

Does shaming have an impact on white-collar offenders? What is the impact of conviction and sentencing on individuals convicted of white-collar crimes? Michael Benson determined that not all offenders suffer in the same fashion. He interviewed 70 white-collar offenders drawn from the Chicago Federal District Courts in 1979 and 1980. Professionals (e.g., lawyers, doctors) had different experiences than businesspeople because of their conviction, especially loss of or changes in their occupational status. Professionals and public sector employees were more likely to change their

Martha Stewart leaving court following her securities fraud conviction in March 2004.

? How can conviction "shame" white-collar offenders?

status and experience a greater loss than private business executives or employees. Large-scale offenders were most likely to lose their jobs.[120]

These offenders held the media (especially the newspapers) particularly responsible for holding them up for public ridicule. They felt that the media focused on their crime and ignored any good deeds in their life. They also blamed the criminal justice system for treating them "just like another criminal" and ignoring their status and public service record. Like Braithwaite, Benson condemns this process of stigmatization as counterproductive. Although it separates the offender and begins the process of punishment, it brands the offender and hinders repentance and reintegration.

Bernard Ebbers, 63-year-old former CEO of WorldCom, was sentenced to 25 years in prison for masterminding an $11 billion fraud that put 17,000 employees out of work and cost stockholders an approximated $2.25 billion. The tearful defendant was visibly shaken and responded with difficulty to questions from the sentencing judge.

Under federal sentencing guidelines, Ebbers was eligible for a sentence of 30 years to life for his crime. The prosecution had requested a life sentence. The judge noted that, given Ebbers' age, heart condition, and philanthropic activities, a 30-year sentence was "excessive" and reduced the punishment by 5 years. He must serve 85% of his sentence; thus, he will be eligible for parole release in about 20 years.

Ebbers' defense attorney pleaded that Ebbers "had an unblemished record" with "endless numbers of people who attest to" his goodness. "Doesn't that count?" More than 160 letters were sent to the judge on behalf of Ebbers asking for leniency in sentencing.

The prosecution contended that Ebbers directed former WorldCom executive, Scott Sullivan (the prosecution's chief witness), to manipulate the company's books to make it appear that the company was continuing to grow and prosper. The government argued that the manipulation led to WorldCom's bankruptcy in June 2002 from which it emerged as MCI — a unit that WorldCom had purchased previously.

Criminologists discuss how individuals tend to age out of crime, although Ebbers is in his sixties. How do the demographics of white-collar criminals influence profiles of "criminals" and trends of aging out of crime?

Source: Michael Bobellian, "Ebbers Sentenced to 25 Years for Role in WorldCom Fraud," *Law.com* (July 14, 2005), available at http://www.law.com, accessed November 11, 2005.

Severity of Sentencing

There is some evidence that judges are following public sentiment when sentencing white-collar offenders. Some judges may apply harsher sentences on white-collar criminals that violate public trust.[121] Federal judges with heavy white-collar crime caseloads have been outraged by these crimes. They believed that upper-class persons should display a higher level of responsibility because of their status and all the privileges that it brings. For that reason, some white-collar criminals, because of their higher status, may receive a greater penalty levied by judges (i.e., prison time).[122]

These judges may be reflecting a post-Watergate morality — a growing intolerance for offenses committed by upper-class individuals."[123] One outcome of the Watergate Scandal is a growing intolerance, especially among judges, for offenses committed by upper-class and powerful individuals. The question is this: Are white-collar offenders being sentenced more severely than in the past? If this is true, then white-collar offenders should be receiving more punitive sentences now than before the Watergate scandal. Hagan and Palloni found that white-collar offenders had a higher rate of imprisonment after Watergate.[124] Nevertheless, judges were giving these offenders short prison sentences.

Thus, the newly incarcerated white-collar offenders received somewhat light sentences that counterbalanced the increased use of imprisonment.

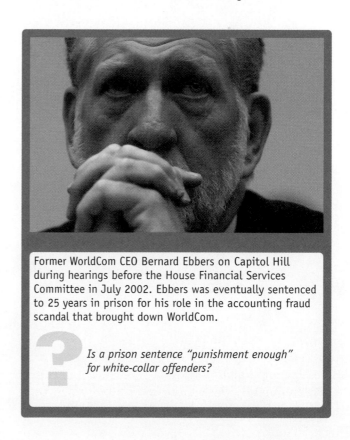

Former WorldCom CEO Bernard Ebbers on Capitol Hill during hearings before the House Financial Services Committee in July 2002. Ebbers was eventually sentenced to 25 years in prison for his role in the accounting fraud scandal that brought down WorldCom.

? *Is a prison sentence "punishment enough" for white-collar offenders?*

Benson and Walker reconsidered the question of severity or leniency in white-collar sentencing. They examined the sentences given to 189 white-collar criminals in a midwestern federal court between 1970 and 1980. They determined that higher status offenders were no more likely to be incarcerated or to receive a longer sentence than lower status ones. Neither status nor post-Watergate morality played a role in the type or length of sentence levied. Nevertheless, the impact of a criminal case extends far beyond the sentence itself.[125] Conviction is damaging to white-collar offenders, often setting other punishments in motion (e.g. fines, restitution, disbarment, civil penalties, tort suits, and lost business/reputation).[126]

Punishing corporations, however, is a different matter. Arriving at a punitive sanction in a corporate criminal case requires a certain amount of creativity, especially when the offender is an or-ganization.[127] Schwartz and Ellison have offered several suggestions. First, fines could be set to the level of profit generated by the corporation. Second, the offending organization could be punished by putting it under the control of a state-appointed receiver. The corporation would pay the salaries of the individual taking over the company and the probation officer assigned to the case.[128]

When the white-collar offender is an individual, some punishments can be more severe than a prison sentence. These punishments strike at the heart of the motive: greed and the desire for greater profits. One example is corporate disqualification. Typically, this action blocks offenders for a limited time from conducting managerial functions that are comparable to those that led to the initial offense. Here, the punishment can fit both the crime and the criminal. Union officials, physicians, security dealers, and police officers who abused their position for personal gain have received this sanction.[129] During the probation period, they were forbidden to hold their former position. It may be the most severe punishment available, since the offender suffers the financial costs of lost work opportunities.

Conclusion

Crimes of the powerful have a massive impact on society: Their damage far exceeds that of street-level crime. The power yielded by organized crime families, white-collar criminals, and corporate offenders makes it more difficult to apprehend, prosecute, and punish these individuals.

Organized crime is an evolving entity taking different forms than originally perceived. However, as Abadinsky notes, these different perceptions have several common threads. Organized crime families follow a hierarchy and seek both profit and power.[130] They strive for monopolistic control of illegal markets and limit competition through bribery or the threat or use of violence. They have a restricted membership based on either kinship or skill. They attempt to keep their structure and operations secret. They are similar to legitimate business in that they provide services (illegal) to meet public demand with the ultimate goal of wealth and power. As Albanese maintains, organized crime has less to do with ethnic conspiracies than with entrepreneurial activity.[130]

White-collar crimes are harmful and just as dangerous to society as street crimes. White-collar crimes, whether occupational or corporate, are willful and intentional.

WRAP UP

Organized Crime Sleeps with the Phishes

Apparent differences and consistencies exist in the methods of these mobsters. In terms of the similarities with organized crime models, they are branching out into a new area to make a profit using monopolistic control. They are meeting the public's demand for a service and are exploiting their victims' trust (the belief that the source of the messages is legitimate). The difference is that they did not have to engage in violence to get and maintain control over this enterprise and did not have to bribe officials. These Mafia members have adopted a new method to achieve their traditional goals. Of course, they have violated multiple laws in the process.

Chapter Spotlight

- "Crimes of the Powerful" are those offenses committed by influential persons or groups in society. These offenses are also characterized as "organized," "white-collar," and "enterprise" crime.

- Organized crime groups and white-collar criminals share characteristics: They both strive for economic control of financial markets, both legal and illegal; they work to circumvent not only criminal law but also governmental regulations that are aimed at governing the market and protecting consumers; the crimes that they commit are costly to society in both human and financial terms; and their goal is to accumulate wealth and exercise power for the benefit of the organization and its members, regardless of the cost to others in society.

- The alien conspiracy model and the local, ethnic group model constitute the major theories of organized crime. The alien conspiracy model contends that organized crime is a business-like hierarchy based on a system of formally defined relationships, obligations, and duties. The local, ethnic group model maintains that the locus of control is limited to certain cities or areas of the country; in this model, the level of organization is rational but not bureaucratic.

- The Mafia Code refers to a list of secret oaths and norms that govern behavior within an organized crime family. This code includes omerta (secrecy), loyalty, respect, and discipline.

- Law enforcement officials have employed "head-hunting," or targeting high-level family members for apprehension and prosecution as a means of controlling organized crime activities. In addition, the Racketeer Influenced and Corrupt Organizations Act (RICO) was enacted as part of the Organized Crime Control Act of 1970 and enabled law enforcement to seek greater penalties for certain crimes; according to this act, organized crime consists of the acquisition, operation, or income from an "enterprise" through a "pattern" of "racketeering activity." An enterprise is any individual or group.

- White-collar crime can be classified as either occupational (a crime committed in the course of doing business that is legal) or corporate crime (crimes committed by corporate organizations).

- The scope of white-collar crimes continues to expand with the inclusion of crimes such as environmental crimes, cyber crimes, and money laundering. Although these illegal activities fall into more than one area of criminology, they are currently part of the discussion of white-collar crimes.

Putting It All Together

1. The cliché "only in America" has been applied to organized crime. What elements or norms of American society allow organized crime to flourish?

2. What do organized and white-collar criminals have in common? How do they differ?

3. Is "shaming" a useful way to combat white-collar crime?

4. Use a current newspaper to find an example of organized crime. Use the material in this chapter to analyze your selected case.

5. Use a current newspaper to find an example of white-collar crime. Use the material in this chapter to analyze your selected case.

Key Terms

alien conspiracy model Assumes that foreign criminals (e.g., Sicilians) imported the crime values and family structures into the United States and secretly control crime activities in this country.

collective embezzlement Refers to company funds siphoned off for personal use by top management at the expense of the institution itself.

corporate crime Illegal acts by corporate officials to benefit the corporation.

headhunting Method of combating organized crime that focuses on the heads of criminal families and also seeks to freeze or seize the assets used in or obtained through organized crime.

local, ethnic group model Maintains that organized crime families have a decentralized structure and focus on operating businesses.

Mafia Code Secret oaths and norms that govern behavior within organized crime families by main-

taining secrecy and promoting loyalty, respect, and discipline.

occupational crime Illegal acts arising from opportunities created in the course of a legal occupation.

organized crime Criminal activity conducted by any group with some manner of formalized structure. The primary objective of organized crime groups is to obtain money through illegal activities.

shaming Punishment of white-collar criminals by confronting them with the seriousness of their conduct while forgiving and reintegrating those who reform.

state-organized crime Illegal acts committed by state officials in the course of their job as representatives of the state.

white-collar crime Deliberately harmful, illegal acts committed by persons of respectability and high social status in the course of their occupation.

Notes

1. Lawrence Bergreen, *Capone: The Man and the Era* (New York: Touchstone, 1994): 86.

2. Howard Abadinsky, *Organized Crime* (Belmont, CA: Wadsworth, 2003).

3. Daniel Bell, *The End of Ideology* (Glencoe, IL: The Free Press, 1964).

4. Dwight C. Smith, *The Mafia Mystique* (New York: Basic Books, 1975).

5. Jay S. Albanese, "What Lockheed and La Cosa Nostra Have in Common," *Crime and Delinquency* 28 (1982): 211–232.

6. Jay S. Albanese, "The Prediction and Control of Organized Crime: A Risk Assessment Instrument for Targeting Law Enforcement Efforts," Research Partnership with Ukraine: Teaming U.S. Researchers and Practitioners with Ukrainian Counterparts to Research High Priority Crime Topics,

available at http://www.ojp.usdoj.gov/nij/international/programs/ ukr_pred_text.html.

7. Peter Reuter, *Racketeering in Legitimate Industries: A Study in the Economics of Intimidation* (Santa Monica, CA: Rand Corporation, 1987); Frank R. Scarpitti and Alan Block, "America's Toxic Waste Racket: Dimensions of the Environmental Crisis," in Timothy S. Bynum, ed. *Organized Crime in America: Concepts and Controversies* (Monsey, NY: Willow Tree Press, 1987): 115–128.

8. Andrew Szasz, "Corporations, Organized Crime, and the Disposal of Hazardous Waste: An Examination of the Making of a Criminogenic Regulatory Structure," *Criminology* 24 (1986): 1–28.

9. James B. Jacobs with Coleen Friel and Robert Radick, *Gotham Unbound: How New York City Was Liberated from the Grip of Organized Crime* (New York: New York University

Press, 1999): 116–118; Tom Peters and Robert Waterman, *In Search of Excellence* (New York: Harper and Row, 1982).

10. Ibid., Smith.

11. Howard Abadinsky, "The McDonald's-ization of the Mafia," in Timothy S. Bynum, ed., *Organized Crime in America: Concepts and Controversies* (Monsey, NY: Willow Tree Press, 1987): 43–54.

12. James O. Finckenauer, "La Cosa Nostra in the United States," United Nations Activities: Participating in the U.N.'s Crime Prevention Program, available at http://www.ojp.usdoj.gov/nij/international/lcn_text.html, accessed October 5, 2005.

13. President's Commission on Law Enforcement and the Administration of Justice, *Task Force Report: Organized Crime* (Washington, DC: U.S. Government Printing Office, 1967): 33.

14. Joseph Bonanno and Sergio Lalli, *A Man of Honor: The Autobiography of Joseph Bonanno* (New York: Simon and Schuster, 1983): 40–41; Diego Gambetta, *The Sicilian Mafia: The Business of Private Protection* (Boston: Harvard University Press, 1993): 139.

15. A complete description of a Mafia membership induction is given by Joseph Valachi, the first to break the oath of omerta. Peter Maas, *The Valachi Papers* (New York: G.P. Putnam's Sons, 1968): 94–98.

16. Joseph L. Albini, "Reactions to the Questioning of the Mafia Myth," in Israel L. Barak-Glantz and C. Ronald Huff, eds., *The Mad, the Bad and the Different* (Lexington, MA: Lexington Books, 1981): 125–134.

17. Albanese, "Organized Crime," 210.

18. Stephen Mastrofski and Gary Potter, "Controlling Organized Crime: A Critique of Law Enforcement Policy," *Criminal Justice Policy Review* 2 (1987): 275.

19. Pennsylvania Crime Commission, *Organized Crime in Pennsylvania: A Decade of Change — 1990 Report* (Conshohocken: Commonwealth of Pennsylvania, 1991): 103–104.

20. Mark H. Haller, "Organized Crime in Urban Society: Chicago in the Twentieth Century," *Journal of Social History* 5 (1971): 210–234.

21. Francis A. Ianni, *A Family Business: Kinship and Social Control in Organized Crime* (New York: Russell Sage Foundation, 1972).

22. Joseph L. Albini, *The American Mafia: Genesis of a Legend* (New York: Appleton-Century-Crofts, 1971).

23. Jeffrey S. McIllwain, "Organized Crime: A Social Network Approach," *Crime, Law and Social Change* 32 (1999): 301–323.

24. Mark H. Haller, "Bureaucracy and the Mafia: An Alternative View," *Journal of Contemporary Criminal Justice* 8 (1992): 1–10.

25. Alan Block, "History and the Study of Organized Crime," *Urban Life* 6 (1978): 455–474.

26. Joseph D. Pistone with Richard Woodley, *My Undercover Life in the Mafia: Donnie Brasco: A True Story of an FBI Agent* (New York: New American Library, 1987): 202–225.

27. Pennsylvania Crime Commission, 1991, 105.

28. Mastrofski and Potter, 1987, 276.

29. Peter Lupsha, "La Cosa Nostra in Drug Trafficking," in Timothy S. Bynum, ed., *Organized Crime in America: Con-*

cepts and Controversies (Monsey, NY: Willow Tree Press, 1987): 31–42.

30. Jerry Capeci, *The Complete Idiot's Guide to the Mafia* (Indianapolis, IN: Alpha Press, 2002): 310.

31. Lupsha, "La Cosa Nostra in Drug Trafficking" 31–42.

32. President's Crime Commission on Law Enforcement and the Administration of Justice, *The Challenge of Crime in a Free Society* (Washington, DC: U.S. Government Printing Office, 1967); Donald R. Cressey, *The Theft of a Nation* (New York: Harper and Row, 1969).

33. Jay S. Albanese, "Organized Crime: The Mafia Mystique," in Joseph F. Sheley, ed., *Criminology: A Contemporary Handbook* (Belmont, CA: Wadsworth, 1991): 204–205.

34. James B. Jacobs with Colleen Friel and Robert Radick, *Gotham Unbound: How New York City was Liberated from the Grip of Organized Crime* (New York: New York University Press, 1999): 128.

35. Timothy S. Bynum, "Controversies in the Study of Organized Crime," in Timothy S. Bynum, ed., *Organized Crime in America: Concepts and Controversies* (Monsey, NY: Willow Tree Press, 1987): 3–12.

36. James O. Finckenauer, "La Cosa Nostra in the United States," United Nations Activities: Participating in the U.N.'s Crime Prevention Program, available at http://www.ojp.usdoj.gov/nij/international/lcn_text.html, accessed October 5, 2005.

37. Peter A. Lupsha, "Individual Choice, Material Culture, and Organized Crime," *Criminology* 19 (1981): 3–24.

38. Mastrofski and Potter, 1987, 280–281.

39. Herbert L. Packer, *The Limits of the Criminal Sanction* (Palo Alto, CA: Stanford University Press, 1968).

40. Albanese, "Organized Crime," 213.

41. Mastrofski and Potter, 1987, 285.

42. C.L. Pagano, "Organized Crime Control Efforts: A Critical Assessment of the Past Decade," *The Police Chief* 48 (1981): 20–25; John Dombrink and James W. Meeker, "Racketeering Prosecution: The Use and Abuse of RICO," *Rutgers Law Journal* 16 (1985): 633–654; James D. Calder, "RICO's Troubled Transition: Organized Crime, Strategic Institutional Factors, and Implementation Today," *Criminal Justice Review* 25 (2000): 31–76; William R. Geary, "The Legislative Recreation of RICO: Reinforcing the 'Myth' of Organized Crime," *Crime, Law and Social Change* 38 (2002): 311–356.

43. Jacobs, 1999, 223–233.

44. Pete Early and Gerald Shur, *WITSEC: Inside the Federal Witness Protection Program* (New York: Bantam Books, 2003).

45. United States Marshals Service, "Witness Security Program," available at http://www.usmarshall.gov/witsec/index.html, accessed October 5, 2005.

46. Ibid.; Risdon N. Slate, "The Federal Witness Protection Program: Its Evolution and Continuing Growing Pains," *Criminal Justice Ethics* 16 (1997): 20–35.

47. Robert Rowan, "The 50 Biggest Mafia Bosses," *Fortune* (November 10, 1986): 25–28.

48. Finckenauer, "La Cosa Nostra," 1.

49. James F. Quinn, "Angels, Bandidos, Outlaws, and Pagans: The Evolution of Organized Crime Among the Big Four 1% Motorcycle Clubs," *Deviant Behavior* 22 (2001): 379–399; James Quinn and D. Shane Koch, "The Nature

of Criminality Within One-percent Motorcycle Clubs," *Deviant Behavior* 24 (2003): 281–305; Tom Barker, "Exporting American Organized Crime: Outlaw Motorcycle Gangs," *Journal of Gang Research* 11 (2004): 37–50.

50. Adam Edwards and Pete Gill, "Crime as Enterprise? The Case of Transnational Organized Crime," *Crime, Law and Social Change* 37 (2002): 203–223; Sheldon Zhang and Ko Lin Chin, "Enter the Dragon: Inside Chinese Human Smuggling Organizations," *Criminology* 40 (2002): 737–768.

51. James O. Finckenauer and Yuri A. Voronin, *The Threat of Russian Organized Crime* (Washington, DC: U.S. Department of Justice, 2001): 1.

52. James O. Finckenauer and Elin Waring, "Challenging the Russian Mafia Mystique," *National Institute of Justice Journal* (April 2001): 6–7.

53. Robert J. Rush and Frank R. Scarpitti, "Russian Organized Crime: The Continuation of an American Tradition," *Deviant Behavior* 22 (2001): 516–540.

54. Finckenauer and Voronin, 2001, 5; Finckenauer and Waring, 2001, 4–5.

55. James O. Finckenauer, "Russian Organized Crime in the United States," available at http://www.ojp.usdoj.gov/nij/international/russian.html, accessed November 2, 2005.

56. Finckenauer and Voronin, 2001, 27.

57. Edwin H. Sutherland, *White Collar Crime* (New York: Dryden, 1949): 9.

58. Kitty Calavita and Henry N. Pontell, "'Other People's Money' Revisited: Collective Embezzlement in the Savings and Loan Insurance Industries," *Social Problems* 38 (1991): 94.

59. Robert M. Bohm, "Crime, Criminal and Crime Control Policy Myths," *Justice Quarterly* 3 (1986): 195.

60. Victims' Rights–America's Values, available at http://www.ojp.usdoj.gov/ovc/ncvrw/2004/pg5i.html, accessed October 5, 2005.

61. Marvin E. Wolfgang, Robert M. Figlio, Paul E. Tracy, and Simon I. Singer, *The National Survey of Crime Severity* (Washington, DC: U.S. Department of Justice, 1985): vi.

62. Francis T. Cullen, Bruce G. Link, and Craig W. Polanzi, "The Seriousness of Crime Revisited: Have Attitudes Toward White-collar Criminals Changed?" *Criminology* 20 (1982): 82–112.

63. Donald J. Rebovich, Jenny Layne, Jason Jiandani, et al., *The National Public Survey on White Collar Crime* (Morgantown, WV: National White Collar Crime Center, 2000).

64. Cynthia Barnett, "The Measurement of White-Collar Crime Using Uniform Crime Reporting (UCR) Data," *NIBRS Publication Series* (Washington, DC: U.S. Department of Justice, Federal Bureau of Investigation, 2005): 6.

65. Richard B. Sobol, *Bending the Law: The Story of the Dalkon Shield Bankruptcy* (Chicago: University of Chicago Press, 1993).

66. Stanton Wheeler, David Weisburd, Nancy Bode, and Ellen Waring, "White Collar Crime and Criminals," *American Criminal Law Review* 25 (1988): 331–357.

67. Elizabeth Moore and Michael Mills, "The Neglected Victims and Unexamined Costs of White Collar Crime," *Crime and Delinquency* 36 (1990): 408–418.

68. Tracy Sharp, Andrea Shreve-Neiger, William Fremouw, et al., "Exploring the Psychological and Somatic Impact of Identity Theft," *Journal of Forensic Sciences* 49 (2004): 131–136.

69. James W. Meeker, John Dombrink, and Henry N. Pontell, "White Collar and Organized Crimes: Questions of Seriousness and Policy," *Justice Quarterly* 4 (1987): 73–98.

70. Marshall B. Clinard and Peter C. Yeager, Corporate Crime (New York: The Free Press, 1980); Gilbert Geis and Colin Goff, "Edwin H. Sutherland's White Collar Crime in America: An Essay in Historical Criminology," in Louis A. Knafla, James Cockburn, and Ellen Dwyer, eds., *Criminal Justice History: An International Annual* (Westport, CT: Meckler, 1986): 1–31; Ronald C. Kramer, "Corporate Criminality: The Development of an Idea," in Ellen Hochstedler, ed., *Corporations as Criminals* (Beverly Hills, CA: Sage, 1984): 13–38; Stephen M. Rosoff, Henry N. Pontell, and Robert H. Tillman, *Profit Without Honor: White Collar Crime and the Looting of America* (Upper Saddle River, NJ: Pearson-Prentice Hall, 2004).

71. Marshall B. Clinard and Richard Quinney, *Criminal Behavior Systems: A Typology* (New York: Holt, Rinehart and Winston, 1973); Herbert Edelhertz, "White Collar and Professional Crime: The Challenge for the 1980s," *American Behavioral Scientist* 27 (1980): 109–128.

72. Marshall B. Clinard, "Criminological Theories of Violations of Wartime Regulations," *American Sociological Review* 11 (1946): 258–270.

73. Frank E. Hartung, "White-Collar Offenses in the Wholesale Meat Industry in Detroit," *American Journal of Sociology* 56 (1950): 25–34.

74. Richard Quinney, "Occupational Structure and Animal Behavior: Prescriptions Violations by Retail Pharmacists," in Gilbert Geis, ed., *White Collar Criminals* (New York: Atherton Press, 1968): 190–221.

75. Gilbert Geis, "The Heavy Equipment Antitrust Cases of 1961," in Marshall B. Clinard and Richard Quinney, eds., *Criminal Behavior Systems: A Typology* (New York: Holt, Rinehart and Winston, 1973): 139–150.

76. Susan P. Shapiro, "Collaring the Crime, not the Criminal: Reconsidering the Concept of White Collar Crime," *American Sociological Review* 55 (1990): 346–365.

77. Gary Green, *Occupational Crime* (Belmont, CA: Wadsworth, 1996): 12.

78. Ibid., 15–16.

79. Paul E. Tracy and James A. Fox, "A Field Experiment on Insurance Fraud in Auto Body Repair," *Criminology* 27 (1989): 589–603.

80. William J. Chambliss, "State-organized Crime," *Criminology* 27 (1989): 184.

81. Henry N. Pontell, Paul D. Jesilow, and Gilbert Geis, "Policing Physicians: Practitioner Fraud and Abuse in a Government Medical Program," *Social Problems* 30 (1982): 116–125.

82. Gilbert Geis, Paul Jesilow, Henry Pontell, and Mary Jane O'Brien, "Fraud and Abuse by Psychiatrists Against Government Medical Benefit Programs," *American Journal of Psychiatry* 142 (1985): 231–234.

83. Paul D. Jesilow, Henry N. Pontell, and Gilbert Geis, "Medical Criminals: Physicians and White Collar Offenses," *Justice Quarterly* 2 (1985): 149–158.

84. Paul Jesilow, Gilbert Geis, and Mary Jane O'Brien, "Is My Battery Any Good? A Field Test of Fraud in the Auto Repair Business," *Journal of Crime and Justice* 8 (1985): 1–20.

85. Paul Jesilow, Gilbert Geis, and Mary Jane O'Brien, "Experimental Evidence that Publicity Has No Effect in Suppressing Auto Repair Fraud," *Sociology and Social Research* 70 (1986): 222–233.

86. Kramer, 1984, 31.

87. Mark Dowie, "Pinto Madness," *Mother Jones* 2 (1977): 24.

88. Francis T. Cullen, William J. Maakestad, and Gray Cavender, "The Ford Pinto Case and Beyond: Corporate Crime Under Attack," in Ellen Hochstedler, ed., *Corporations as Criminals* (Beverly Hills, CA: Sage, 1984): 120.

89. Francis T. Cullen, William J. Maakestad, and Gray Cavender, *Corporate Crime Under Attack: The Ford Pinto Case and Beyond* (Cincinnati: Anderson, 1987).

90. Calavita and Pontell, 1991, 94.

91. Kitty Calavita and Henry N. Pontell, "'Heads I Win, Tails You Lose': Deregulation, Crime and Crisis in the Savings and Loan Industry," *Crime and Delinquency* 36 (1990): 309–341.

92. Sutherland, 1949.

93. Clinard and Yeager, 1980.

94. Ibid.; Marshall B. Clinard, Peter C. Yeager, John M. Brissette, Dennis Petrashek, and Ellen Harries, *Illegal Corporate Behavior* (Washington, DC: U.S. Government Printing Office, 1979).

95. "How Did Enron Defraud Shareholders," Securities FraudFYI.com, available at http://www.securitiesfraudfyi.com/enron_fraud.html, accessed January 4, 2005.

96. Rosoff, Pontell, and Tillman, 2004, 292.

97. Raymond Michalowski and Ronald Kramer, "Beyond Enron: Toward Economic Democracy and a New Ethic of Inclusion," *Risk Management: An International Journal* 5 (2003): 37–47.

98. James W. Coleman, *The Criminal Elite: The Sociology of White Collar Crime,* (New York: St. Martin's Press, 1985).

99. Environmental Crimes, available at http://www.interpol.int/Public/EnvironmentalCrime/Default.asp, accessed January 30, 2006.

100. "Facts and Figures 2003: Environmental Crimes", available at http://www.fbi.gov/libref/factsfigure/enviro.htm, accessed January 30, 2006.

101. Angelia DeAngelis, *Cyber Crimes* (Philadelphia: Chelsea House Publishers, 2003).

102. Dan Verton, *The Hacker Diaries: Confessions of Teenage Hackers* (Dubuque, Iowa: McGraw-Hill Osbourne Media, 2002).

103. K. Eichenwald, "Terror money hard to block, officials find" *The New York Times* (December 10, 2001: A1).

104. John K.Villa, *Banking Crimes* (New York: Clark Boardman, 1998).

105. R. Urban, "2 Banks Slammed for Enron Activities," *Philadelphia Inquirer* (December 10, 2002):D1.

106. Office of the Comptroller of the Currency, *Money Laundering: A Banker's Guide to Avoiding Problems*, 2002, available at http://www.occ.treas.gov/moneylaundering 2002.pdf, accessed January 30, 2006.

107. David Weisburd, Ellen Chayet, and Elin Waring, "White-collar Crime and Criminal Careers: Some Preliminary Findings," *Crime and Delinquency* 36 (1990): 342–355; David Weisburd, Ellen Chayet, and Elin Waring, *White-collar Crime and Criminal Careers* (Cambridge, UK: Cambridge University Press, 2001).

108. Joan N. Gurney, "Factors Influencing the Decision to Prosecute Economic Crime," *Criminology* 23 (1985): 609–628.

109. Michael L. Benson, William J. Maakestad, Francis T. Cullen, and Gilbert Geis, "District Attorneys and Corporate Crime: Surveying the Prosecutorial Gatekeepers," *Criminology* 26 (1988): 505–518.

110. Donald W. Scott, "Policing Corporate Collusion," *Criminology* 27 (1989): 559–587.

111. Kip Schlegel, "Desert, Retribution, and Corporate Criminality," *Justice Quarterly* 5 (1988): 615–634.

112. C. Leaf, "Enough is Enough" *Fortune* (March 18, 2002): 61–76.

113. Michael L. Benson, "The Fall from Grace," *Criminology* 22 (1984): 573–594.

114. Michael L. Benson and Francis T. Cullen, "The Special Sensitivity of White-collar Offenders to Prison: A Critique and a Research Agenda," *Journal of Criminal Justice* 16 (1988): 207–215.

115. Harriet S. Pollack and Alexander B. Smith, "White Collar v. Street Crime Sentencing Disparity: How Judges See the Problem," *Judicature* 67 (1983): 164–182.

116. David Eitle, "Regulatory Justice: A Re-examination of the Influence of Class Position on the Punishment of White-collar Crime," *Justice Quarterly* 16 (2000): 809–839.

117. Celesta A. Albonetti, "The Role of Gender and Departures in the Sentencing of Defendants Convicted of White Collar Offenses Under the Federal Sentencing Guidelines," in Jeffrey T. Ulmer, ed., *Sociology of Crime, Law and Deviance,* vol. 1. (Stamford, CT: Jai Press, 1998): 3–48.

118. John Braithwaite, *Crime, Shame and Reintegration* (Oxford, United Kingdom: Cambridge University Press, 1989).

119. John Braithwaite, "Criminological Theory and Organizational Crime," *Justice Quarterly* 6 (1989): 346.

120. Michael L. Benson, "The Influence of Class Position on the Formal and Informal Sanctioning of White-collar Offenders," *Sociological Quarterly* 30 (1989): 465–479; Michael L. Benson, "Emotions and Adjudication: Status Degradation Ceremonies Among White Collar Criminals," *Justice Quarterly* 7 (1990): 515–528.

121. H. Croall, *Understanding White Collar Crime* (Buckingham, UK: Open University Press, 2001).

122. Stanton Wheeler, Kenneth Mann, and Austin Sarat, *Sitting in Judgment: Sentencing the White-collar Offender* (New Haven, CT: Yale University Press, 1988); Stanton Wheeler, David Weisburd, and Nancy Bode, "Sentencing the White-collar Offender: Rhetoric and Reality," *American Sociological Review* 47 (1982): 641–659; D. Glater, "Mad as Hell: Hard Time for White Collar Criminals," *The New York Times* (July 28, 2002: wk 5); John Hagan and P. Parker, "White-collar Crime and Punishment: The Class Structure and Legal Sanctioning of Securities Violations," *American Sociological Review* 50 (1985): 302–316.

123. John Hagan and Alberto Palloni, "'Club Fed' and Sentencing of White-collar Offenders Before and After Watergate," *Criminology* 24 (1986): 615.

124. Ibid, 603–621.

125. Michael L. Benson and Esteban Walker, "Sentencing the White Collar Offender," *American Sociological Review* 53 (1988): 294–302.

126. Mark A. Cohen, "Corporate Crime and Punishment: A Study of Social Harm and Sentencing Practice in the Federal Courts," *American Criminal Law Review* 26 (1989): 605–660.

127. Thomas J. Bernard, "The Historical Development of Corporate Criminal Liability," *Criminology* 22 (1984): 3–15.

128. Martin Schwartz and Charles Ellison, "Criminal Sanctions for Corporate Misbehavior: A Call for Capitalist Punishment," *Humanity and Society* 6 (1982): 267–292.

129. Martin F. McDermott, "Occupational Disqualification of Corporate Executives: An Innovative Condition of Probation," *Journal of Criminal Law and Criminology* 73 (1982): 628.

130. Abadinsky, 1987.

131. Albanese, "Lockheed and La Cosa Nostra," 1982.

OBJECTIVES

Recognize and understand future trends in crimes, policing, corrections, and criminological theory.

Discuss new approaches to crime and criminological theory, such as community policing, problem-oriented policing, and Compstat.

Discuss future trends in correction.

Explain the impact and promise of evidence-based research.

Discuss promising trends in criminological theory, such as the General Theory of Crime, criminology as peacemaking, coercion and social support, and the social development model.

The Future of Criminal Justice and Criminology

The future ain't what it used to be.

—Yogi Berra[1]

Introduction

Predicting the future of crime and criminology is a precarious business, particularly given how dramatically the nature of crime has changed since the early 1970s. Then, for example, serial murders were not even mentioned in any text, nor were narcoterrorism or computer crimes. Child abuse and other forms of family violence were not yet widely recognized as serious social problems; drug-related crime was only beginning to become a major law enforcement concern. As society moves through this 21st century, what new trends in crime will emerge? How will criminology change? What function will criminology perform in the future?

In this final chapter, changes in the world of crime in the last few decades, as well as how society has responded to the new forms of crime, are examined. Several promising trends in criminological theory will also be reviewed.

The Changing Character of Crime

What kinds of criminals will dominate the news in the coming years? Steven Egger, Professor of Criminal Justice at the University of Illinois, is an internationally known expert on serial murder and its investigation. He has made several predictions. First, because U.S. inner cities continue to deteriorate, gang activity is expected to increase. There are now more than 2200 gangs in the United States.[2] Some operate according to an organized crime model, while others are oriented toward violence. A new form of gang activity, **wilding**, combines theft and violence in an atmosphere of racial hatred — a threatening blend of gang violence and hate crimes:[3]

> Wilding is a street term signifying new dimensions in public concern over teenage violence. Seemingly without instrumental purpose, wilding is described as "running amok" in the community, as the senseless perpetuation of violence for fun and amusement.

Thus, wilding is a form of gang activity that includes mugging, robbery, assault, murder, and attacks on designated ethnic and racial groups. The psychology of wilding is described by a juvenile offender in Scott Cummings' classic work *Left Behind in Rosedale*.[4]

> It starts out just drinking and messing around. He's liable to do something. Go break in a store or something. His partner see that he stole something. I ought to go in and rob something to make myself look good, you know; all of them try to race to be the leader. It just keeps going and going just like a chain. I guess they figure out who's the toughest. It don't ever stop, you know.

> Kids don't get into trouble by theyselves. It mostly happens in a crowd. Like one being encouraged by the other. Just to be on top, like, you know, 'You're a punk if you don't do that.'

On the basis of such interviews, Cummings concluded that "adolescent crime is as great a threat to the stability of interracial neighborhoods as are traditional forms of racism."[5]

> **LINK** Theories related to delinquency are presented in Chapter 7. Cumming's interviews with delinquents also indicated that they drifted toward drugs, violence, and illegal enterprises as a response to the absence of legitimate work opportunities in their neighborhoods.

Second, as computers become the key information source of everyday and business life, technological crime is certain to increase. Identity theft, electronic transfer of funds, computer crime, and credit card and telemarketing fraud are all made possible through technology. These forms of finan-

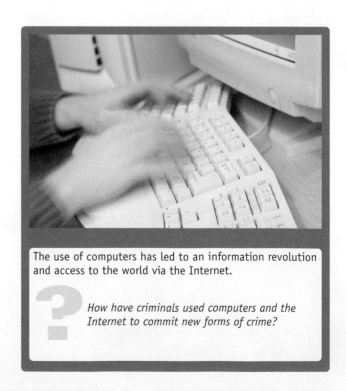

The use of computers has led to an information revolution and access to the world via the Internet.

? *How have criminals used computers and the Internet to commit new forms of crime?*

cial transactions, including simple buying and selling of goods, used to be done with paper or in person. These opportunities for criminal behavior simply did not exist in 1980; now, an entire agency, the National White Collar Crime Center, is devoted to the prevention of these crimes. This center is designed to provide nationwide support for law enforcement agencies involved in the prosecution of economic, high-tech crimes, and violations of homeland security. It conducts research and provides training to help related agencies combat these offenses.[6]

Third, crimes involving and related to illegal drugs will crop up as new methods of transportation and marketing of drugs are developed. Criminals are quick to take advantage of the demand for new drugs.

Identity Theft

As noted above, the World Wide Web can facilitate criminal activity, including fraud and other economic crimes. Identity theft occurs when someone wrongfully obtains and uses another person's personal data (e.g., name, Social Security number, credit card number, bank account number, telephone calling card number, or other identifying information) to commit fraud or deception for economic gain.[7] According to the Identity Theft Clearinghouse of the Federal Trade Commission (FTC), the most common types of identity theft are[8]:

- Using or opening a credit card account fraudulently
- Opening telecommunications or utility accounts fraudulently
- Passing bad checks
- Making fraudulent withdrawals from or opening a new bank account
- Getting loans in another person's name
- Working in another person's name
- Using another person's identification information if stopped by the police
- Taking over or hijacking the existing account of another person
- Obtaining other goods or privileges that might be denied if the criminal applied in his or her name

The costs of identity theft are substantial. Estimates from 2003 indicate that thieves who used personal information to establish new credit and bank accounts cost victims and financial institutions over $33 billion.[9] The victims of these crimes not only face financial losses, but also must contend with the loss of identity and restoration of their good financial standing (in terms of credit rating).

To combat these crimes, the U.S. Congress passed the Identity Theft and Assumption Deterrence Act of 1998, which prohibits[10]:

> knowingly transfer[ing] or us[ing], without lawful authority, a means of identification of another person with intent to commit, or to aid and abet, any unlawful activity that constitutes a violation of federal law, or that constitutes a felony under any applicable state or local law.

The act also provides for a maximum prison term of 15 years, a fine, and criminal forfeiture of any personal property used or intended to be used to commit identity theft. If the offense also involves credit card, computer, wire, or financial institution fraud, penalties of up to 30 years imprisonment plus fines and criminal forfeiture can be levied.

Identity thieves obtain personal data in a number of creative ways. One method is *shoulder surfing* where criminals watch from a nearby location as victims give their credit card number or other identification to an automated teller machine. Another technique is *dumpster diving*. Thieves dig through the trash to find discarded documents (e.g., checks, credit card or bank statements, preapproved credit card applications) that contain valuable personal identification data. *Phishing* occurs when unsuspecting victims respond to offers over the Internet and give credit card numbers or other information to scammers.[11]

LINK The connection between organized crime and phishing is presented in Chapter 15. Credit card fraud is discussed in Chapter 12.

Some evidence exists that identity theft is on the rise. Overall, complaints of identity theft received by the FTC increased from 161,896 in 2002 to 246,570 in 2004. In 2004, the most common forms of identity theft were credit card fraud (28%), phone or utilities fraud (19%), bank fraud (18%), and employment fraud (13%). In addition, complaints concerning fraudulent electronic fund transfers more than doubled between 2002 and 2004.[12]

Narcoterrorism

One of the more startling crime mergers of recent times is that between drug trafficking and terrorism — a crime genre known as *narcoterrorism*. The

U.S. Drug Enforcement Administration (DEA) defines narcoterrorism as a "subset of terrorism in which terrorist groups, or associated individuals, participate directly or indirectly in the cultivation, manufacture, transportation, or distribution of controlled substances and the monies derived from these activities."[13] It may also be characterized by "the participation of groups or associated individuals in taxing, providing security for, or otherwise aiding and abetting drug trafficking endeavors in an effort to further, or fund, terrorist activities."[14]

Cocaine cartels have sponsored revolutionary movements through armaments and cash.[15] Several South American insurgent groups (e.g., The Revolutionary Armed Forces of Colombia [FARC] and M-19 in Colombia; Sendero Luminoso in Peru) have used the enormous profits from the drug business to carry out political assassinations, kidnappings, and other violent crimes.[16] In short, they use the drug trade to generate the funds they need to destroy political systems and achieve their political goals. It has been estimated that the FARC receives up to $300 million annually from the drug trade and trades cocaine for weapons to use in its war against the Colombian government.[17]

TABLE 16-1 provides a list of characteristics that terrorist and drug trafficking organizations have in common.

TABLE 16-1
Common Characteristics of Terrorist and Drug Trafficking Organizations

- Both operate globally and benefit from trends associated with globalization and an open, deregulated environment.
- Terrorists and drug traffickers thrive in countries and regions lacking strong government control.
- Both exploit porous U.S. borders and seek loopholes in U.S. immigration controls.
- Terrorists and drug traffickers rely heavily on technology to network and avoid detection, including use of the Internet, encryption technology, satellite and cell phones, global positioning systems, surveillance, and eavesdropping technology.
- Both utilize individual cell operations, allowing them to change tactics and personnel literally overnight.
- Terrorists and drug traffickers rely on the services of the criminal underworld. They need forged documents, safe houses, stolen cars, guns, and money laundering.
- Both are long-term phenomena for which there are no quick fixes.
- Terrorists and drug traffickers target civilian populations with violence and killings. Traffickers compound the violence by targeting civilian populations with drugs.
- Both types of organizations target youth — either for recruitment into drug use or recruitment into terrorist cells.

Source: Drugstory, Terror, Violence and the Drug Trade, 2005, (Washington, DC: The Office of National Drug Control Policy), available at http://www.drugstory.org/pdfs/DandT_Fact_Sheet.pdf, accessed September 21, 2005.

Methamphetamine-Related Crimes

A derivative of amphetamine, methamphetamine is a drug that is having a great and deleterious effect on the public. A powerful central nervous system stimulant, its use increases energy and alertness while decreasing appetite. When used, the drug produces a short, intense "rush" due to the release of high levels of dopamine from the brain. Methamphetamine can be smoked (in its granulated, crystal form known as "ice"), snorted, orally ingested, or injected.[18]

A unique aspect of this drug is that its deleterious effects are felt by users, by innocent bystanders to its manufacture, and by law enforcement agents closing meth labs. According to the Office of National Drug Control Policy, chronic abuse of methamphetamine can lead to psychotic behavior — intense paranoia, visual and auditory hallucinations (including the feeling that "crank bugs" — imaginary bugs caused by delusions from the drug — are crawling under the user's skin), and out-of-control violent rages. Physically, the drug can result in inflammation of the heart lining, rapid heart rate, irregular heartbeat, increased blood pressure, damage to the small blood vessels of the brain, and even acute lead poisoning (lead acetate is commonly used in the production of the drug).[19]

Because the "cooking" of methamphetamine involves the brewing of several toxic chemicals, its manufacture has a severe effect on the environment. Brewing one pound of methamphetamine releases poisonous gas and produces five to seven pounds of toxic waste that is typically carelessly dumped into the lab's environment without regard for its impact. Thus, persons living in or near the lab (including children of the lab's owners) and first responders raiding meth labs often suffer physical injury, including respiratory and eye irritations, headaches, dizziness, nausea, and shortness of breath. The chemicals used to create the drug are highly volatile and can cause explosions and fire. The DEA's estimates from 2001 reported 12,715 methamphetamine laboratory incidents in 46 states. Missouri, California, and Washington had the highest incidence of meth lab incidents.[20]

The contents of a seized methamphetamine lab.

? *What harmful effects do methamphetamine labs have on the environment and neighborhoods?*

National data from the 2003 Arrestee Drug Abuse Monitoring Program (ADAM — 39 states) determined that 4.7% of adult males and 8.8% of adult females tested positive for methamphetamine upon entry to jail. Between 1992 and 2002, yearly rates of admission to drug treatment for methamphetamine abuse increased from 1% to 5.5%.[21] During the same time frame, U.S. hospitals reported a 69% increase in methamphetamine-induced emergency department visits (from 10,447 to 17,696).[22]

During 2001, the DEA made over 7000 methamphetamine-related arrests — about 22% of the total number of drug arrests the agency made. In 2003, federal courts sentenced almost 4500 offenders on methamphetamine-related charges. Of these offenders, the majority were white (59.3%) and male (85.9%). Over 11% of these offenders had a weapon involved in their drug offense.[23]

Control over trafficking in methamphetamines has changed in recent years. Traditionally, outlaw motorcycle gangs and independent operators ran meth labs and sold the drug. Beginning in 1994, other crime groups entered the methamphetamine market. Mexican drug trafficking organizations now dominate this drug market. Their established drug-trafficking routes and smuggling methods coupled with the establishment of "super labs" (labs capable of producing in excess of 10 pounds of methamphetamines in one 24-hour production cycle) made this takeover possible.[24]

Future Trends in Policing

Community Policing

Because of the changing nature of crime, policing methods have changed as well. In Chapter 1, community policing was introduced as a new method of law enforcement. Not just a program, community policing is an operational and organizational philosophy designed to promote police-citizen-community–based problem solving.

Community policing implies a partnership between the police and the people they serve. This partnership is designed to improve the quality of life in the community through the introduction of strategies designed to enhance neighborhood solidarity and safety. Thus, the police and the community should work together to offer solutions to social problems faced by the community. The creation of a social bond between the police and the community is encouraged. Officers are given time and authorization by their department to get to know the community's habits, wishes, and customs. The belief is that unless the police are able to truly relate to a community, they will not be able to offer creative responses to local problems.

Community policing demands that officers and their departments adopt proactive strategies and tactics to repress crime, fear, and disorder within local neighborhoods.[25] In turn, community residents are expected to take a proactive stance in helping the police and other government entities set policy at both the macro and micro level. It is through this exchange process that the citizens provide real input into setting organizational goals, objectives, and departmental values. This partnership can take many forms, but it requires a shared understanding of the problems that require attention, as well as some degree of joint responsibility for their resolution.

Problem-Oriented Policing

Problem-oriented policing (POP) is often used as the framework to enact community policing. POP recognizes that the role of the police as law enforcers is overrated. Herman Goldstein notes that an analysis of the problems handled by the police will indicate how they can be managed in the long run.[26] As defined in San Diego, POP[27].

> emphasizes identifying and analyzing problems (criminal, civil, or public nuisance) and implementing solutions to resolve the underlying causes of the problem. It emphasizes proactive intervention rather than reactive responses to calls for service, resolution of root causes rather than symptoms, and use of multiparty, community-based problem solving rather than a unilateral police response. POP focuses on a problem in a long-term, comprehensive manner, rather than handling the problem as a series of separate incidents to be resolved via arrest or other police action.

POP requires that the police develop a systematic process for examining and addressing the problems that the public expects them to handle. It requires identifying these problems in more precise terms, researching each problem, documenting the nature of the current police response, assessing its adequacy and the adequacy of existing authority and resources, engaging in a broad exploration of alternatives to present responses, weighing the merits of these alternatives, and choosing from among them.

LINK The theoretical basis for community policing is presented in Chapter 1.

The Effectiveness of Community Policing and Problem Solving

As community policing evolved as the dominant police organizational philosophy in the latter part of the 20th century, a debate regarding the appropriate way for police managers to direct their organization's service delivery function emerged. Some administrators still favored the traditional bureaucratic organizational model with its emphasis on efficiency and control. Others believed that community-and/or problem-oriented policing was a more appropriate way to address the needs of the nation's diverse communities for public safety.

Research findings do confirm positive results from community policing programs. In their literature review on community policing, Arthur Lurigio and Dennis Rosenbaum consolidated research findings over an 18-year period covering 11 cities. They concluded that community policing has exerted a positive influence on the both the police and on citizens' views of the police.[28] Police officers engaged in community policing report increases in job satisfaction and motivation, a broadening of their role, improvements in relationships with coworkers and citizens, and greater expectations regarding community participation in crime prevention efforts.[29] Citizens feel that community policing officers are more visible, helpful, polite, and effective in a variety of job activities.[30] For example, in Madison, Wisconsin, Mary Ann Wycoff and Wesley Skogan found that even senior officers' attitudes can shift from more traditional views of policing to ones that are more in line with community policing.[31] Madison officers also reported that increased contacts with citizens led to an increase in citizen requests for assistance. Wycoff reported that four policing strategies tested in Houston, Texas, and Newark, New Jersey, appeared to reduce citizens' fear of crime, improve citizens' views of crime and disorder problems in their neighborhoods, and improve citizens' evaluations of the police.[32] A review of National Crime Victimization Survey data from 12 cities served by community policing programs determined that satisfaction with police service and citizens' crime prevention behaviors increased while fear of crime was largely unaffected.[33]

Finally, an assessment of the impact of COPS (community policing grants from the federal government) found a positive effect of police hiring on arrest rates between 1995 and 1999. COPS grants were positively associated with arrests for violent, drug, and social order offenses.[34] These results indicate that, under community policing, police departments altered their emphasis and operations.

Despite these findings, many criminologists feel that community policing has not developed into the major reform that its advocates had hoped for. Today, almost every specialized program developed by a police department is labeled community policing. Although many police departments claim they are engaged in some form of community policing, the majority of them are still bureaucratically structured, not decentralized. Thus, they are delivering their services in the same traditional style.[35] Research also indicates that police departments were slow to adopt community policing as an across-the-board, organizational strategy. In some police departments, community policing is the responsibility of an organizational subunit, rather than the whole department.[36]

In fact, problems in adopting community policing appear to be widespread across departments. For example, a representative survey of police chiefs in cities of over 25,000 in population revealed that 67% of them had implemented community policing programs in the last three years. The departments with the greatest interest in training and education were more likely to implement community policing programs.[37] An analysis of the survey responses revealed three basic types of impediments to the implementation of community policing: organizational, community, and transitional. The analysis revealed that police agencies were more concerned with internal organizational barriers than obstacles in their community. Internally, the top factors were resistance from middle management and line officers. Such departments were less likely to implement community policing. Another analysis discovered that, although interest in community policing had risen and impediments to implementation had been identified, the institutionalization of community policing was far from certain.[38]

Similar research findings have been attributed to POP. For example, Cordner and Biebel interviewed and surveyed 320 San Diego police officers to determine how POP had been implemented. San Diego was selected because its police department was one of the pioneers in the adoption of POP. Seventy percent of the officers reported that they had used POP principles to cope with crime, particularly drug and disorder problems. However, their tactics in assessing problems were most often based on "personal observation" and thus did not reflect a full crime analysis assessment in the initial identification of problems. In other words, they tended to think differently about crime but did not strictly follow the POP method.[39]

Compstat

Community policing and problem solving are not the only change in police management thought.

Another key change is the Compstat paradigm (or model). Police departments are designed to provide public safety through certain services (responding to calls for service from citizens, preventing crime, rendering first responder aid, enforcing laws and ordinances, resolving disputes, regulating traffic, investigating crime scenes, and arresting offenders).[40] Compstat is an effort to get police departments to effectively provide services by measuring performance and holding police executives accountable for meeting agency objectives.

In the mid-1990s, a group of police executives in New York City proposed that crime prevention, order maintenance, and community safety could be achieved through integrated problem solving, strategy development, and intense managerial oversight of the entire organizational process.[41] William Bratton, then New York City Police Commissioner, and his command staff developed a goal-oriented strategic management process that uses information technology, operational strategy, and managerial accountability to effectively control crime. This process evolved out of the weekly Crime Control Strategy meetings the New York City Police Department (NYPD) began holding as a means to increase the flow of information between the agency's executives and the commanders of operational units. These meetings placed particular emphasis on the dissemination and analysis of crime and quality-of-life enforcement information. Bratton and his command staff designed these "Compstat" meetings as a way to make his 76 precinct commanders and their officers accountable for the crime rate. During these meetings, Compstat combined a comprehensive, continuous analysis of current crime with strategy development and assessment.

There are four key elements to the Compstat model[42]:

1. **Accurate and timely intelligence**: To reduce crime, you must know about it.
   - What type of crime is it (e.g., drug sales, robbery, burglary)?
   - Where is crime occurring (e.g., areas, specific locations)?
   - When is crime happening (e.g., day of week, hour of day)?
   - Why is crime happening (motive — e.g., drug-related shootings)?

2. **Rapid deployment**: By providing weekly crime statistics, the Compstat process allows admin-

istrators to assess this intelligence. Commanders can then deploy their resources as rapidly as possible to address crime conditions in the areas where they are most needed.

3. **Effective tactics**: Focusing specific resources in a directed manner on specific problems. Operational commanders are encouraged to develop strategies that focus resources as rapidly as possible to address crime conditions in the areas where they are most needed.

4. **Relentless follow-up and assessment**: The first three steps are only effective if commanders constantly follow up on what is being done and assess their results. If results are not what they should be, changes need to be made. The primary assessment of these commanders and their tactics takes place at the Compstat meetings. These meetings provide the arena for instant assessment, analysis, and redirection.[43]

Here, holding managers accountable for performance is the crucial aspect of the process.

Computer technologies allow for the mapping of crime patterns and of causal relationships among different crime categories. This information is disseminated to operational managers (the precinct commanders) in a Compstat report. This report contains crime complaint and arrest activity at the precinct, patrol borough, and citywide levels, as well as a concise summary of these and other important performance indicators. During these meetings, crime patterns and selected strategies are discussed and analyzed, results evaluated, and resources allocated. Compstat has transformed the NYPD from a reactive organization that settled for the status quo to a vigorous, motivated police department that works actively to achieve its mission. Operational managers are held accountable for addressing the crime and disorder issues and trends associated with the Compstat report's data for their areas. Under Compstat, operational managers are empowered to focus, manage, and direct their unit's problem-solving process. A principle objective of the Compstat process is not to just displace crime but to reduce it and create a permanent change in the community.

Compstat and Accountability

The underlying principle of Compstat is that police officers and police agencies can have a substantial positive impact on crime and the problems facing

While serving as police commissioner in New York City, William Bratton implemented the Compstat model.

? *What are the key features of the Compstat model?*

the communities they serve. Again, accountability for performance is the heart of the process.

> . . . the word accountability holds the promise of bringing someone to justice, of generating desired performance through control and oversight, of promoting democracy through institutional forms, and of facilitating ethical behavior.[44]

Accountability challenges police executives and managers to take a different approach to the way they manage police organizations and police activities. Because of its emphasis on accountability, Compstat is radically different from the accepted concepts and practices that have guided police administration through most of its existence. It points the way to new methods and strategies police agencies can use to fulfill their mission. Compstat emphasizes the vital link between command accountability, information, operational decision making, and crime-control objectives. For example, police commanders are held accountable for the quality of their plans (strategy and tactics), managerial oversight of their operations (efficiency), and the result of their efforts in terms of crime reduction (effectiveness). Compstat is a management tool; its impact extends well beyond crime fighting and can be applied to any organizational setting. Baltimore Mayor Martin O'Malley adopted this method as the primary management process for city government and renamed it "Citystat."[45] It is a management process that can adapt to constantly changing conditions.

Compstat is a strategic leadership model similar to those found in business organizations. This leadership style represents a change in how police organizational managers conceive of their department's vision, mission, values, goals, engagement, empowerment, accountability, outcomes, and evaluation. These new strategic leaders are police executives who proactively develop and implement an organizational direction that allows their departments to successfully initiate and reshape activities to effectively meet the demands of their operational environment. By this process, the strategic leader seeks to align his or her external and internal environments in order to fulfill the organization's mission. They are creating an open system adaptive-learning organization.

To date, Compstat has been deemed by some as the single most successful crime-fighting management tool in the nation.[46] The NYPD is credited with turning the city around from a place that once represented the ultimate in urban lawlessness to a city now safer than any of the 23 other largest cities in the United States. Police statistics for New York City indicate that serious crime has decreased by double-digits since the police department changed its operational strategy in 1994. A study by Kelling and Sousa (2001) reports a number of positive outcomes associated with the creation of Compstat in the NYPD. First, they consider its impact on crime rates, concluding that the average NYPD precinct during the 10-year period (1989–1999) studied could expect to suffer one less violent crime for approximately every 28 additional misdemeanor arrests made.[47] They also re-

port that, after an initial increase in complaints filed against NYPD officers from 1994 to 1995, the number of complaints actually declined over the rest of the decade — from 5618 in 1995 to 4903 in 1999 (the last year in the study) — even though the size of the force increased by more than 9000 officers during this period.[48] In 1996, Compstat won the prestigious Innovations in American Government Award from the Ford Foundation and the John F. Kennedy School of Government. Compstat is in the process of being replicated and evaluated by a number of police departments across the country, including Indianapolis, Indiana; Louisville, Kentucky; Boston, Massachusetts; Baltimore, Maryland; Newark, New Jersey; New Orleans, Louisiana; and others.[49]

Critics of Compstat

Commissioner Bratton was adamant that he would use crime rates as an indicator of police performance — that both preventing and solving crime constituted the "bottom line" for policing. In fact, Bratton and Kelling cite the impact of Compstat methods on the crime rate in the New York City subways, before Bratton became Commissioner of the NYPD. Although the city had adopted a number of programs to clean up the subways (graffiti eradication) and prevent crime (target hardening — i.e., making fare stations more difficult to rob), crime was not controlled until the police directly confronted illegal disorderly behavior (e.g., "fare jumping" — jumping over turnstiles rather than paying the fare) and disorder (e.g., panhandling) under Bratton's leadership. From this point of view, the impact on subway crime became a pre-test of what happened when Bratton took over the NYPD.[50]

The view that the police were responsible for the crime rate was a dramatic reversal in thinking about this relationship. The dominant view in criminology is that crime is such a multicausal, multifactorial phenomenon that no one agent, the police or another element of society, could have an effect on it. Joel Conklin's examination of crime rates in New York City and elsewhere is an example of this school of thought[51]:

> The per capita size of a city's police force does not affect its crime rate, nor do the number of patrol cars or foot patrols. Community policing has no demonstrated impact on crime rates, though the strategic target can curb crime under some circumstances. The perception of an increased threat of being stopped or arrested

might reduce serious crime by deterring facilitating offenses, such as the unlicensed carrying of firearms or the possession and sale of drugs. New York City's decline in firearm homicides and firearm robberies in the mid-1990s could have been due, at least in part, to the quality-of-life initiative, which raised the risk that people carrying guns would be stopped by the police for minor infractions such as turnstile jumping or drinking alcoholic beverages in public. However, other than New York, cities where the police did not deal aggressively with quality-of-life offenses also saw their crime rates drop.

Accordingly, criminologists examined this decline in the crime rate and attributed it to factors other than changes in police operations, such as demographic changes (the aging of the population), economic factors (low unemployment rates in the 1990s), and related crime factors (the rise and fall of the crack cocaine market). John Eck and Edward Maguire concluded that although Compstat may have had a subtle and indirect effect on violent crime rates in New York City, it would be better to "attempt to craft crime-reduction tactics that are effective and yet do not rely heavily on the application of force."[52] Other authors have determined that other cities also experienced downturns in homicide rates during the same time period as New York City.[53]

However, a substantial amount of literature on police operations demonstrates that when the police concentrate their efforts on a particular crime, they are effective and the crime rate drops. For example, a congressionally mandated evaluation of state and local crime prevention programs funded by the federal government determined that "extra police patrols in high-crime hot spots reduce crime in those places."[54] Often when criminologists examine the impact of the police on the crime rate, they use an aggregate measure (the number of police officers) to determine police effectiveness.[55] This method assumes that the number of police, regardless of what they are doing, will impact the crime rate. But, if they target a certain crime like drug sales, arrests for this crime should go up in the short run. Over a longer period of time, such a strategy could reduce drug sales and the number of arrests will go down. Such a measure fits the other independent variables used to analyze the causes of the crime-rate decline (i.e., the size of the prison population) but it fails to truly consider the nature of police operations. It is not the number of officers but how they are used that determines whether they are effective.

Still, it remains to be seen if Compstat will have a long-term effect on crime rates. Creating responsive and effective police organizations will require organizational changes that demand more than quick adaptations and limited structural changes. A properly designed Compstat process will establish accountability at all managerial levels of the organization under the direction of the executive staff and focuses the entire organization on the department's mission. Thus, by involving the whole organization, Compstat goes beyond the incremental structural changes that occurred during the adaptation of community policing but retains an organizational leadership style.[56]

Future Trends in Corrections

How will the correctional system operate in the future? It has been predicted that jails will deteriorate to a two-tier system: The public sector will serve the economic underclass and private-sector jails will handle the more affluent suburbs or jurisdictions that can afford to offer improved services to inmates.[57] Prisons will become more technologically advanced with electronic monitoring, video recording, and computerized data collection to enhance both the accountability and safety of staff and inmates.[58]

The character of treatment must also change to reflect the different types of criminals as well as the probable increase in jail and prison populations. The nature of the treatment provided must be individualized to meet the problems of the inmates. There will have to be more use of community-based corrections, with electronic devices used to monitor offenders. Since drug use is so closely linked to crime, drug treatment in prison and drug testing will continue to be a key feature of community-based programs. Drug treatment will continue to prove to be an effective way to deal with the crime problem posed by offenders — an example of an effective rehabilitation and treatment program.[59]

At the same time, the more punitive aspects of corrections will stay in place.

Longer sentences will be given for violent crimes, and career criminal statutes will continue to be applied. Finally, use of the death penalty will increase.[60] These trends suggest that the punitive approach to crime will continue to influence corrections.[61]

The future trends in policing and corrections have two promising elements in common:

1. **Community involvement is the key to crime prevention.** Simply put, crime is committed within communities where both offenders and victims reside. Particular attention must be paid to the needs and problems faced by communities. For example, gang monitoring by community workers and probation and police officers are a promising method of reducing gang violence.[62]

2. **Accountability for effective performance as determined by evidence-based research is the standard for the future.** For example, Edward Latessa makes a strong argument that, like police practices under Compstat, correctional programs have become more evidence based — that correctional research can be used to implement change and improve programs while holding both offenders and administrators accountable for performance.[63]

Thus, both police and correctional programs will be driven by community needs and interests. The effectiveness of policies and programs will be determined by scientific research that is designed to measure the achievement of program goals and objectives.

Criminological Theory

The Utility of Criminological Theory

A good deal of frustration exists over the apparent inability of criminology to solve the crime problem. Indeed, serious questions about the utility of criminological theory have arisen. As Mary Tuck asserts[64]:

> Many argue that criminological theories have changed so wildly over the years — that criminologists have often provided "the wrong" advice about policies now claimed to be "right." They have argued for rehabilitative custody and against it, for longer sentences and against them; criminology both created the treatment model and destroyed it. As for "the causes of crime" — you are as aware as I am that "you pay your money and you take your choice." Even on supposedly narrow practical ques-

tions . . . criminologists speak with no single voice.

As Austin indicates, when Congress and state legislatures consider crime legislation, their first question is not, "What do the criminologists think?"[65] However, Tuck also suggests that policies cannot proceed directly from any one criminological theory. They emerge from debate — "the gradual working out of disagreement and contradiction."[66]

Similarly, Joan Petersilia believes that this problem stems from the development of criminology into an academic discipline. As academics, she argues, criminologists have lost touch as they pursue theories rather than deal with day-to-day realities. As a result, they often lose sight of the value of practical applications. Like Tuck, Petersilia asserts that research can be an unimpeachable guide to policy. She argues that criminologists should strive for "research [that] is more likely to influence the way policymakers think about problems than to provide solutions 'off the shelf.'"[67] Furthermore, she urges criminologists to make clear the policy implications of their research findings. As noted throughout this text, this is not an easy task, but it is certainly essential if criminology is to stay relevant.

Criminology must also abandon the pretense of value-free research and state how findings can be best applied in real-world situations. There is a rich tradition to draw from in this regard. From Beccaria and Bentham, Shaw and McKay, to Cloward and Ohlin, criminologists have developed theories to meet the problems of the day and sought to apply them. As James Gilsinan has aptly noted: "criminological theory has never been confined to the ivory tower."[68] Policy and criminology have a symbiotic relationship that forms a significant link with research. Clearly, each cannot function effectively in isolation. Theory organizes thoughts about crime and its causes; research tests the validity of theory. Policy is fed by both theory and research.

For example, in Chapter 1, Jack Gibbs' conception of the four major questions in criminology was discussed. The fourth major question is: "What are the means of controlling criminality?" Gibbs declares that criminologists must take up this question for the following reasons[69]:

> No scientific enterprise will be supported indefinitely unless it benefits someone other than the scientists, and perhaps much of criminology's support stems from a concern with crime

prevention. There is simply no justification for the indifference of theorists to attempts to prevent criminality, including delinquency.

Criminology must return to its roots as an applied social science. The complex nature of the crime problem demands that policy implications be developed through criminology.

> **LINK** Gibbs' four major questions in criminology are presented in Chapter 1.

Future Trends in Criminological Theory

Demise of the Criminological Imagination?

Frank Williams has decried the "demise of the criminological imagination." He cites three major reasons for this decline. First, there is a lack of critical analysis of both issues and actions; for example, a theory that explains homicide may not apply to serial or mass murder. How can social learning theory provide an explanation for such disparate crimes as computer theft, insider stock trading, and spouse abuse? Is it possible that the nature of crime is changing so rapidly that some criminological theories are no longer applicable without modification or even replacement?[70]

Second, Williams criticizes the overconcentration of criminology on empiricism — quantitative, multivariate analyses of large data sets. The recent training of criminologists emphasizing quantitative skill "has raised methodology and large data sets above theory development." Intuitive skills — the very skills needed to determine the policy implications of any given research findings — are thus not developed. One wonders how well the work of Sutherland, Sykes, Matza, and other qualitative analysts would be accepted today. Is quantitative analysis the only route to scientific validity?

Like Petersilia, Williams blames the demise of criminological theory on the emergence of criminal justice as an academic discipline. Williams claims that the discipline emphasizes how the criminal justice system responds to crime — therefore, it ignores the behavior of criminals. Naturally, one can take exception to this characterization. Academicians in criminal justice programs may be more concerned with questions of management (efficiency and effectiveness of policies and programs) but many of them are or were practitioners or have their academic training in applied areas (e.g., public administration).[71]

Similarly, L. Edward Wells notes that research and policy seem to "control the development of limited theories chosen to suit practical contingencies."[72] New models that promote deterrence and incapacitation have not been supported by research but they are still favored because they "are closer to political sensibilities and more consistent with what people feel *should* be true."[73]

However, the following theories have shown particular promise and should continue to do so in the future.

Gottfredson and Hirschi's General Theory of Crime

Gottfredson and Hirschi developed a general theory of crime that explains the bulk of criminal behavior from petty theft to insider trading. It is an example of theory integration that combines key features of Walter Reckless' containment theory and social bond theory. To these theorists, the key feature that accounts for crime is a lack of self-control, and the absence of self-control is a direct result of ineffective child rearing. Therefore, these researchers believe that parents must pay particular attention to the preschool years of their children. Attachment to parents and effective supervision (including the ability to recognize poor behavior when it occurs and to administer punishment) can bolster self-control.[74] A healthy self-concept and its sponsorship by the family and community agencies such as schools and churches are now recognized as a piv-

A father spends time with his daughter.

? *What theories support the development of a strong social bond between parents and children?*

Criminology as Peacemaking— Sister Helen Prejean, *Dead Man Walking*

The death penalty is the ultimate weapon in the war on crime — it personifies the violent response of the criminal justice system to crime. Sister Helen Prejean, a Roman Catholic nun in Louisiana, has committed herself to stand against the death penalty. Her actions demonstrate the commitment that criminology as peacemaking requires — service to both offenders and victims. Her work as a spiritual advisor to condemned men was documented in her book, *Dead Man Walking*, and in an Academy Award–nominated movie by the same name. The book was on the *New York Times* Best Seller List for 31 weeks and was nominated for a Pulitzer Prize. Over the span of 15 years, she has witnessed five executions and accompanied three men to the electric chair. One received a life sentence on appeal.

Her personal journey has encouraged many people to rethink their position on the death penalty. To Sister Helen, the death penalty embodies "the three deepest wounds of our society: racism, poverty, and violence." It led her to consider not only the plight of the death row inmate but also that of the families of their victims. She recognized that the families of the victims and the inmates shared one element: They were abandoned by friends and family. As a result, she founded Survive, a victim's advocacy group, and works closely with other groups such as Murder Victim's Families for Reconciliation.

She has received two of the highest honors bestowed on American Catholics: the Vision 2000 Award from Catholic Charities USA and the Laetare Medal from the University of Notre Dame for illustrating the ideals

Sister Helen Prejean speaking at an anti–death penalty rally.

How can criminology as peacemaking change the nature of the criminal justice system?

of the church. Her latest book, *The Death of Innocents*, analyzes how flaws in the death penalty system allow innocent people to be executed.

Sources: Helen Prejean Official Website, available at http://www. prejean.org, accessed November 28, 2005; Sister Helen Prejean, *Dead Man Walking* (New York: Vintage, 1994); Sister Helen Prejean, "Would Jesus Pull the Switch?" http://salt.claretianpubs.org/issues/deathp/ prejean.html, accessed November 28, 2005; Sister Helen Prejean, *The Death of Innocents* (New York: Random House, 2004).

---

otal factor in child development.[75] Other criminologists are emphasizing the link between child-rearing practices and subsequent delinquency.[76]

LINK Containment and social bond theory are presented in Chapter 7.

Criminology as Peacemaking

The criminal justice system has been criticized for its warlike nature. Weapons and the threat of incarceration have long been key themes in criminal justice operations. They emphasize the need to confront and control people directly and coercively. They ig-

nore or dismiss the social factors that contribute to crime and emphasize the dual themes of deterrence and incapacitation.

LINK Deterrence is discussed in Chapter 3 and incapacitation is a key element of career criminal prosecution and sentencing policies presented in Chapter 9.

The underlying theme of criminology as peacemaking is that individuals can contribute to the solution to problems by handling their personal lives differently. For example, they can counter racism and sexism when and where they occur. Crime is considered another form of human suffering —

perhaps if more people took the time to work for justice in society, less crime would occur.

Criminology as peacemaking also directs offenders to sponsor their own rehabilitation by working on their self-concept. For example, meditation and self-reflection have been proposed as ways for offenders to find inner peace and promote peacekeeping.[77] A call for such personal and demanding involvement by all citizens is absent from other theories.

The Theory in Action feature, **Criminology as Peacemaking — Sister Helen Prejean,** *Dead Man Walking*, presents a profile of Sister Helen Prejean, an exemplar of criminology as peacemaking.

Coercion and Social Support: An Example of Integrative Theory

Chapter 1 considered Francis T. Cullen's theory of social support; that theory has been integrated with another theory: crime and coercion.[78] This integrated theory, developed by Mark Colvin, has several central premises. As discussed under criminology as peacemaking, coercion is a central component of the criminal justice system. It is also manifested in society (structural unemployment, poverty, competition between groups) and interpersonal relationships (creates anxiety, desperation, and anger). However, coercion has negative consequences, whether it is maintained erratically or consistently. If coercion is erratic, individuals learn that they cannot control the consequences of life because negative occurrences happen randomly and are unpredictable. Thus, it leads to anger directed at others, low self-control, and weaker bonds to society. If coercion is consistent, it produces low levels of criminal behavior and even health problems, such as chronic depression and a strong sense of anger that is self-directed. This anger can become manifest in predatory crime.

LINK Cullen's theory of social support is presented in Chapter 1.

Social support is offered as an antidote to destructive aspects of coercion. The crucial difference between the two is that they are inversely related: coercion promotes crime and social support prevents it.

In terms of a criminal justice policy, the clear implication here is that "to reduce crime, societies must enhance the legitimate sources of social support and reduce the forces of coercion."[79] A consistent level of social support must emerge at two levels: (1) social support to families (e.g., parent-effectiveness training, paid family leave, health care insurance, nutrition programs) and schools (e.g., preschool Head Start programs with educational spending a high government priority, mentoring) and (2) more democratic workplace management (e.g., participatory management, expanded collective bargaining, worker participation in ownership and control of industries and businesses).

In the criminal justice system, programs and policies must emphasize offender rehabilitation and crime prevention. Get-tough policies often backfire and lead to anger and a sense of injustice. The value of freedom must not only be strongly promoted but also combined with social support and the absence of coercion.[80] This combination has a strong potential to prevent and reduce crime.

The Social Development Model

The social development model is a comprehensive approach to preventing youth crime. Consistent with social control theory, the model is based on the premise that the most important units of socialization (i.e., family, schools, peers, and community) influence behavior in a sequential fashion. When youths have the opportunity to engage in the conforming behavior within each of them, law-abiding behavior is the result. To accomplish this, youths must develop necessary skills and be rewarded for positive behavior. These conditions will sponsor the development of the social bonds listed by Reckless and Hirschi. These social bonds inhibit association with delinquent peers and prevent delinquent behavior.[81]

The social development model is based on social bond theory. J. David Hawkins and Richard Catalano present data on <u>risk factors</u> associated with a number of problem behaviors, such as violence, drug abuse, teen pregnancy, and school drop-out. These risk factors are conditions that increase the likelihood that a child will develop one or more behavior problems in adolescence — the greater the exposure to these factors, the greater the likelihood that juveniles will engage in these negative behaviors.

Community risk factors and the behaviors they sponsor include[82]:

- Availability of drugs (substance abuse)
- Availability of firearms (delinquency, violence)
- Community laws and norms favorable toward drug use, firearms, and crime (substance abuse, delinquency, and violence)

- Media portrayals of violence (violence)
- Transitions and mobility (substance abuse, delinquency, and drop out)
- Extreme economic deprivation (substance abuse, delinquency, violence, teen pregnancy, and school drop out)

Family risk factors and the behaviors they sponsor include:

- A family history of high-risk behavior (substance abuse, delinquency, violence, teen pregnancy, and school drop out)
- Family management problems (substance abuse, delinquency, violence, teen pregnancy, and school drop out)
- Family conflict (substance abuse, delinquency, violence, teen pregnancy, and school drop out)
- Favorable parental attitudes and involvement in the problem behavior (substance abuse, delinquency, and violence). Children whose parents engage in violent behavior inside or outside the home are at greater risk for exhibiting violent behavior.

School risk factors and the behaviors they sponsor include:

- Early and persistent antisocial behavior (substance abuse, delinquency, violence, teen pregnancy, and school drop out)
- Academic failure beginning in elementary school (substance abuse, delinquency, violence, teen pregnancy, and school drop out)
- Lack of commitment to school (substance abuse, delinquency, violence, teen pregnancy, and school drop out)

Individual/peer risk factors and their indicators consist of:

- Alienation and rebelliousness (substance abuse, delinquency, and school drop out). It may be a more significant risk for young people of color. Discrimination may cause these youths to reject the dominant culture and rebel against it.
- Friends who engage in the problem behavior (substance abuse, delinquency, violence, teen pregnancy, and school drop out). This factor has proven to be a consistent predictor of problem behaviors.
- Favorable attitudes toward the problem behavior (substance abuse, delinquency, teen pregnancy, and school drop out). Here, the middle school years are particularly significant. If youths are involved with peers who demonstrate favorable attitudes to these behaviors, they are more likely to engage in them.
- Early initiation of the problem behavior (substance abuse, delinquency, violence, teen pregnancy, and school drop out). The research review demonstrates that youths who begin to use drugs before age 15 are twice as likely to have drug problems as those who wait until after the age of 19.
- Constitutional factors (substance abuse, delinquency, and violence). These factors are biological or psychological in nature. Youths who have problems with sensation-seeking behavior, low harm avoidance, and lack of impulse control are more likely to engage in these problem behaviors.

Hawkins and Catalano assert that these risks occur in multiple domains; that is, multiple risks can be present at the same time in a person's life. Therefore, the most effective way to combat them is a multifaceted approach across the community. Hawkins and Catalano suggest that neighborhood residents and community agencies of all types join together to deal with these problems. The aim is to provide protection against the sponsorship of risk factors and the spread to problem behaviors that result from them; the goal is to use the public health model to prevent crime. Awareness of these factors is the first step in the development of plans and programs to deal with them in an effective manner.

A program that uses this theory as its basis has been developed. The Safe Futures Initiative is an extension of the U.S. Office of Juvenile Justice and Delinquency Prevention's Comprehensive Strategy for Serious, Violent, and Chronic Juvenile Offenders. The strategy focuses on[83]:

1. Youth who are at high risk of future delinquent behavior
2. Youthful offenders who have already exhibited delinquent behavior and are at risk of, or already are, engaging in serious, violent, or chronic law breaking

Within demonstration communities, Safe-Futures is based on nine components[84]:

1. Afterschool Programs (Pathways to Success)
2. Juvenile Mentoring Programs (JUMP)
3. Family Strengthening and Support Services
4. Mental Health Services for At-Risk and Adjudicated Youth
5. Delinquency Prevention Programs

6. Comprehensive Community-Wide Approaches to Gang-Free Schools and Communities

7. Community-Based Day Treatment Programs (Outpatient drug treatment offered to clients who are uninsured and unable to pay)

8. Continuum-of-Care Services for At-Risk and Delinquent Girls

9. Serious, Violent, and Chronic Juvenile Offender (SVCJO) Programs (with an emphasis on enhancing graduated sanctions)

This program is presently in the implementation stage, but it offers great promise by incorporating the principles of social control theory and bringing them into operation. It is also an excellent example of a program that reduces coercion and increases the levels of social support available to the public.

Taken together, these theories demonstrate recognition of the complexity of the causes of crime. The interaction of different variables in the crime equation is acknowledged and a deeper understanding of their impact on crime and criminals is clearly in order. They represent the current emphasis on both community- and evidence-based programs to combat crime — the trends of the future.

Conclusion

Unfortunately, the scope of criminal enterprises will continue to expand. New forms of criminal behavior will occur and attempts at explanation will follow. Although there is no panacea, criminologists are making progress toward understanding the origin and nature of many of the crimes that plague society. With that understanding, both citizens and researchers can hope that something can be done to reduce the rate and severity of crime in the future.

The emphasis on evidence-based programs that are well designed and include the community and its resources are truly the wave of the future. As Samuel Walker notes[85]:

> The evidence-based policy movement defines very specific standards. . . . it demands empirical evidence of the effectiveness of a policy. This rules out hope, wishful thinking, good intentions, and even policies whose assumptions are extrapolated from other evidence.

The link between theory, policy, and research is clearly established. If they are based on these premises, the crime programs and policies of the future hold promise.

WRAP UP

Chapter Spotlight

- Evidence suggests that gang violence, computer crimes, and drug-related crimes are on the rise. New crimes of special concern include wilding, identity theft, narcoterrorism, and methamphetamine use.
- The changing nature of crime has necessitated new forms of policing, such as community policing, problem-oriented policing, and Compstat.
- Trends in corrections suggest that the system will deteriorate to a two-tier system: The public sector will serve the economic underclass and private-sector jails will handle the more affluent suburbs or jurisdictions that can afford to offer improved services to inmates. Prisons will also become more technologically advanced with electronic monitoring, video recording, and computerized data collection to enhance both the accountability and safety of staff and inmates.

- The future trends in policing and corrections have two promising elements in common:
  - Community involvement is the key to crime prevention.
  - Accountability for effective performance as determined by evidence-based research is the standard for the future.
- A good deal of frustration exists over the apparent inability of criminology to solve the crime problem. In spite of serious questions about the utility of criminological theory, several theories have shown promise: Gottfredson and Hirschi's general theory of crime, criminology as peacemaking, Colvin's coercion and social support theory, and the social development model. Taken together, these theories demonstrate recognition of the complexity of the causes of crime.

Putting It All Together

1. It has been said that the crime issue elects presidents. How valid is that statement?
2. How might the role of policing change in the next 20 years to reflect the changing scope of crime in American society?
3. How might the classical criminological theories be changed to explain the crimes of the future?
4. Discuss the role of theory and crime causation and how this should affect crime policy in this country. What should be the role of government in implementing policy in trying to control crime?

Key Terms

risk factors Conditions that increase the likelihood that a child will develop one or more behavior problems in adolescence — the greater the exposure to these conditions, the greater the likelihood that juveniles will engage in these negative behaviors.

wilding The behavior of gangs of youths "running amok" in the community and committing senseless acts of violence for fun and amusement.

1. Yogi Berra, *The Yogi Book* (New York: Workman Publishing, 1998): 118–119.
2. Steven Egger, "The New Predators: Crime Enters the Future," *The Futurist* 19 (1985): 15–16; Steven Egger, *The Killers Among Us: An Examination of Serial Murder and Its Investigation* (Englewood Cliffs, NJ: Prentice-Hall, 1998).
3. Scott Cummings, "Anatomy of a Wilding Gang," in Scott Cummings and Daniel J. Monti, eds., *Gangs: The Origins and Impact of Contemporary Youth Gangs in the United States* (Albany: State University of New York Press, 1992): 51.
4. Scott Cummings, *Left Behind in Rosedale* (Boston: Westview Press, 1998): 119.
5. Ibid.
6. National White Collar Crime Center, available at http://www.nw3c.org, accessed November 21, 2005.
7. U.S. Department of Justice, "Identity Theft and Fraud," available at http://www.usdoj.com/criminal/fraud/idtheft.html, accessed July 25, 2005; Federal Trade Commission, "ID Theft Home," available at http://www.consumer.gov/idtheft/, accessed July 25, 2005.
8. Federal Trade Commission, Consumer Sentinel's Identity Theft Data Clearinghouse, "Facts for Consumers," available at http://www.ftc.gov/bcp/conline/pubs/general/idtheftfact.htm, accessed July 25, 2005; Tad Hughes, George E. Higgins, Melissa L. Ricketts, and Brian D. Fell, "Student Perception and Understanding of Identity Theft." Paper presented at the annual meeting of the Academy of Criminal Justice Sciences in Chicago, IL, March 2005.
9. Synovate, *Federal Trade Commission — Identity Theft Survey Report* (Washington, DC: Federal Trade Commission, 2003): 6.
10. Federal Trade Commission.
11. U.S. Department of Justice, 2005.
12. Consumer Sentinel, Identity Theft Data Clearinghouse, *National and State Trends in Fraud & Identity Theft* (Washington, DC: Federal Trade Commission, 2005): 3–4.
13. Drugstory, *Terror, Violence and the Drug Trade,* 2005, available at http://www.drugstory.org/pdfs/DandT_Fact_Sheet.pdf, accessed August 8, 2005.
14. Ibid.
15. Duane C. McBride and James A. Swartz, "Drugs and Violence in the Age of Crack Cocaine," in Ralph Weisheit, ed., *Drugs, Crime and the Criminal Justice System* (Cincinnati, OH: Anderson, 1990): 151.
16. James A. Inciardi, "Narcoterrorism: A Perspective and Commentary," in Robert J. Kelly and Donal E. J. MacNamara, eds., *Perspectives on Deviance: Dominance, Degradation, and Denigration* (Cincinnati, OH: Anderson, 1991): 89–104.
17. Drugstory, 2005.
18. ONDCP Drug Policy Clearinghouse Fact Sheet, *Methamphetamine* (Washington, DC: Executive Office of the President, Office on National Drug Control Policy, 2003): 1; Office of National Drug Control Policy, *Drug Facts — Methamphetamine,* available at http://www.whitehousedrugpolicy.gov/drugfact/methamphetamine/index.html, accessed July 6, 2005.
19. Ibid.
20. ONDCP Drug Policy Clearinghouse Fact Sheet, *Methamphetamine*, 2003, 4.
21. Office of National Drug Control Policy, *Drug Facts*, 2005.
22. Ibid.
23. Ibid.
24. Ibid.
25. Robert Trojanowicz and Bonnie Bucqueroux, *Community Policing: A Contemporary Perspective* (Cincinnati: Anderson, 1990).
26. Herman Goldstein, *Problem Oriented Policing* (Philadelphia, PA: Temple University Press, 1990).
27. George E. Capowich and Janice A. Roehl, "Problem Oriented Policing: Actions and Effectiveness in San Diego," in Dennis P. Rosenbaum, ed., *The Challenge of Community Policing: Testing the Promises* (Thousand Oaks, CA: Sage, 1994): 127–128.
28. Arthur Lurigio and Dennis Rosenbaum, "The Impact of Community Policing on Police Personnel: A Review of the Literature," in Dennis P. Rosenbaum, ed., *The Challenge of Community Policing: Testing the Promises* (Thousand Oaks, CA: Sage, 1994): 147–163.
29. Jack Greene, "Police Officer Job Satisfaction and Community Perceptions: Implications for Community Oriented Policing," *Journal of Research in Crime and Delinquency*, 26 (1989): 168–183.
30. David Hayeslip and Gary Cordner, "Effects of Community-Oriented Patrol on Police Officer Attitudes," *American Journal of Police* 6 (1987), 95–119.
31. Mary Ann Wycoff and Wesley Skogan, "Community Policing in Madison: An Analysis of Implementation and Impact," in Dennis P. Rosenbaum, ed., *The Challenge of Community Policing: Testing the Promises* (Thousand Oaks, CA: Sage, 1994): 75–91.
32. Mary Ann Wycoff, "The Benefits of Community Policing: Evidence and Conjecture," in Jack R. Greene and Stephen Mastrofski, eds. *Community Policing: Rhetoric or Reality* (New York: Prager, 1988): 103–121.
33. Matthew C. Scheider, Tawandra Rowell, and Veh Bezdikan, "The Impact of Citizen Perceptions of Community Policing on Fear of Crime: Findings from Twelve Cities," *Police Quarterly* 6 (2003): 363–386.
34. Jihong "Solomon" Zhao, Matthew C. Schneider, and Quint Thurman, "A National Evaluation of the Effect of COPS Grants on Police Productivity (Arrests) 1995–1999," *Police Quarterly* 6 (2003): 402.
35. Jack R. Greene and Stephen Mastrofski, eds. *Community Policing: Rhetoric or Reality* (New York: Prager, 1988); Howard Safir, "Goal-Oriented Community Policing: The NYPD Approach," *The Police Chief* (December 1997): 31–58; Wesley Skogan, *Disorder and Decline: Crime and the Spiral of Decay in American Neighborhoods* (New York: Free Press, 1990).
36. Jihong "Solomon" Zhao, Ni He, and Nicholas P. Lovrich, "Community Policing: Did It Change the Basic Functions of Policing in the 1990s? A National Follow-up" *Justice Quarterly* 20 (2003): 697–724.

37. Jihong Zhao, Quint C. Thurman, and Nicholas P. Lovrich, "Community-Oriented Policing Across the U.S.: Facilitators and Impediments to Implementation," *American Journal of Police* 14 (1995): 11–28.

38. Jihong Zhao, Nicholas P. Lovrich, and Quint C. Thurman, "The Status of Community Policing in American Cities," *Policing: An International Journal of Police Strategies and Management*, 1 (1999): 74–92; Jihong S. Zhao, Ni He, and Nicholas P. Lovrich, "Community Policing: Did It Change the Basic Functions of Policing in the 1990s? A National Follow-up," *Justice Quarterly* 20 (2003): 697–724.

39. Gary Cordner and Elizabeth Perkins Biebel, "Problem-Oriented Policing in Practice," *Criminology and Public Policy* 4 (2005): 155–180.

40. William F. Walsh and Gennaro F. Vito, "The Meaning of Compstat: Analysis and Response," *Journal of Contemporary Criminal Justice* 20 (2004): 51.

41. Vincent Henry, *The Compstat Paradigm: Management Accountability in Policing, Business and the Public Sector* (Flushing, NY: Looseleaf Law Publications, 2002); Eli Silverman, *NYPD Battles Crime: Innovative Strategies in Policing* (New York: Northeastern University Press, 1999).

42. The name Compstat arose from "Compare Stats" (a computer file name at NYPD). Eli B. Silverman, "Compstat," in Larry E. Sullivan and Marie Simonetti Rosen, eds. *Encyclopedia of Law Enforcement, Volume 1 — State and Local* (Thousand Oaks, CA: Sage, 2005): 83.

43. Walsh and Vito, "Meaning of Compstat," 59.

44. H. George Fredrickson, "Accountability: The Word that Ate Public Administration," *PA Times* (November 2005): 11.

45. William F. Walsh, "Compstat: An Analysis of an Emerging Police Managerial Paradigm," *Policing: An International Journal of Police Strategies & Management* 24 (2001): 347–362.

46. Henry, *The Compstat Paradigm*.

47. George L. Kelling and William H. Sousa, *Do Police Matter? An Analysis of the Impact of New York City's Police Reforms* (New York: Center for Civic Innovation at the Manhattan Institute, 2001): 9.

48. Ibid., 19.

49. Walsh and Vito, "Meaning of Compstat," 58.

50. George L. Kelling and William J. Bratton, "Declining Crime Rates: Insiders' View of the New York City Story," *Journal of Criminal Law and Criminology* 89 (1998) 1217–1231.

51. Joel E. Conklin, *Why Crime Rates Fell* (Boston: Allyn and Bacon, 2003): 193.

52. John E. Eck and Edward R. Maguire, "Have Changes in Policing Reduced Violent Crime? An Assessment of the Evidence," in Alfred Blumstein and Joel Wallman, eds., *The Crime Drop in America* (Cambridge, UK: Cambridge University Press, 2000): 251.

53. Ana Joanes, "Does the New York City Police Department Deserve Credit for the Decline in New York City's Homicide Rates? A Cross-City Comparison of Policing Strategies and Homicide Rates," *Columbia Journal of Law and Social Problems* 33 (1999-2000): 265–311; Richard Rosenfeld, Robert Fornango, and Eric Baumer, "Did *Ceasefire*, *Compstat*, and *Exile* Reduce Homicide," *Criminology and Public Policy* 4 (2005): 419–450.

54. Lawrence W. Sherman, Denise C. Gottfredson, Doris L. MacKenzie, John Eck, Peter Reuter and Shawn D. Bushway, "Preventing Crime: What Works, What Doesn't, What's Promising," *National Institute of Justice Research in Brief* (Washington, DC: U.S. Department of Justice, 1998): 8; see also Larry T. Hoover, ed., "Rationale for Police Program Evaluation," *Police Program Evaluation* (Washington, DC: Police Executive Research Forum, 1998): 1–14.

55. Thomas B. Marvell and Carlisle E. Moody, "Specification Problems, Police Levels, and Crime Rates," *Criminology* 34 (1996): 609–646.

56. William F. Walsh and Gennaro F. Vito, "The Meaning of Compstat: Analysis and Response," *Journal of Contemporary Criminal Justice* 20 (2004): 51–69.

57. David Kalinich and Paul Embert, "Grim Tales of the Future: American Jails in the Year 2010," in John Klofas and Stan Stojkovic, eds., *Crime and Justice in the Year 2010* (Belmont, CA: Wadsworth, 1995): 172.

58. Lucien Lombardo, "The Pen and the Pendulum," in John Klofas and Stan Stojkovic, eds., *Crime and Justice in the Year 2010* (Belmont, CA: Wadsworth, 1995): 194.

59. Sherman, Gottfredson, MacKenzie, Eck, Reuter, and Bushway, *Preventing Crime*, 8: see also Francis T. Cullen, "Rehabilitation and Treatment Programs," in James Q. Wilson and Joan Petersilia, eds., *Crime: Public Policies for Crime Control* (Oakland, CA: ICS Press, 2004): 272–275 .

60. Gennaro F. Vito, "The Penalty of Death in the Next Century," in John Klofas and Stan Stojkovic, eds., *Crime and Justice in the Year 2010* (Belmont, CA: Wadsworth, 1995): 251–266.

61. Harry E. Allen, Edward J. Latessa, and Gennaro F. Vito, "Corrections in the Year 2000," *Corrections Today* (April 1987): 92–96.

62. Sherman, Gottfredson, MacKenzie, Eck, Reuter, and Bushway, *Preventing Crime*, 9.

63. Edward J. Latessa, "The Challenge of Change: Correctional Programs and Evidence-Based Practices," *Criminology and Public Policy* 3 (2004): 554–558.

64. Mary Tuck, "Is Criminology Any Use?" *The Criminologist* 16 (1989): 1.

65. James Austin, "Why Criminology is Irrelevant," *Criminology and Public Policy* 2 (2003): 557.

66. Tuck, "Is Criminology Any Use?," 6.

67. Joan Petersilia, "Policy Relevance and the Future of Criminology," *Criminology* 29 (1991): 1–16.

68. James F. Gilsinan, "Public Policy and Criminology: An Historical and Philosophical Reassessment," *Justice Quarterly* 8 (1991): 202, 204.

69. Jack P. Gibbs, "The State of Criminological Theory," *Criminology* 25 (1989): 824.

70. Frank Williams, "The Demise of Criminological Imagination: A Critique of Recent Criminology," *Justice Quarterly* 1 (1984): 91–106.

71. Ibid.

72. L. Edward Wells, "Explaining Crime in the Year 2010," in John Klofas and Stan Stojkovic, eds., *Crime and Justice in the Year 2010* (Belmont, CA: Wadsworth, 1995): 45.

73. Ibid., 53.

74. Michael Gottfredson and Travis Hirschi, *A General Theory of Crime* (Stanford, CA: Stanford University Press, 1990). See also James Q. Wilson, "Raising Kids," *The Atlantic Monthly* (October 1983): 45–56.

75. D.C. Briggs, *Your Child's Self-Esteem* (New York: Doubleday, 1975).

76. Robert M. Regoli and John D. Hewitt, *Delinquency in Society: A Child-Centered Approach* (New York: McGraw-Hill, 1991).

77. Michael Braswell, John Fuller, and Bo Lozoff, *Corrections, Peacemaking and Restorative Justice* (Cincinnati, OH: Anderson, 2001); John R. Fuller, *Criminal Justice: A Peacemaking Perspective* (Needham Heights, MA: Allyn and Bacon, 1998).

78. Mark Colvin, *Crime and Coercion: An Integrative Theory of Chronic Criminality* (New York: St. Martin's Press, 2003).

79. Mark Colvin, Francis T. Cullen, and Thomas Vander Ven, "Coercion, Social Support, and Crime: An Emerging Theoretical Consensus," *Criminology* 40 (2002): 33.

80. Ibid., 36–37. See also Francis T. Cullen, John Paul Wright, and Mitchell B. Chamlin, "Support and Social Reform: A Progressive Crime Control Agenda," *Crime and Delinquency* 45 (1999): 178–207.

81. J. David Hawkins and Joseph Weis, "The Social Development Model: An Integrated Approach to Delinquency Prevention," *Journal of Primary Prevention* 6 (1985): 73–97.

82. J. David Hawkins and Richard F. Catalano, *Communities That Care* (San Francisco: Jossey-Bass, 1990). See also J. David Hawkins, "Controlling Crime Before It Happens: Risk-Focused Prevention," *National Institute of Justice Journal* (August 1995): 10–16. In addition, visit the Web site for the Hawkins-Catalano model at http://www.preventionscience.com/.

83. Elaine Morley, Shelli B. Rossman, Mary Kopczynski, Janeen Buck, and Caterina Gouvis, *Comprehensive Responses to Youth at Risk: Interim Findings from the SafeFutures Initiative* (Washington, DC: Office of Juvenile Justice and Delinquency Prevention, 2000): 3.

84. Kathleen Coolbaugh and Cynthia J. Hansel, *The Comprehensive Strategy: Lessons Learned from the Pilot Sites* (Washington, DC: Office of Juvenile Justice and Delinquency Prevention, 2000).

85. Samuel Walker, *Sense and Nonsense About Crime and Drugs: A Policy Guide* (Belmont, CA: Thomson Wadsworth, 2006): 10.

GLOSSARY

accessibility cues Indications such as an open window or an unlocked door that will allow burglars to enter the dwelling.

adult social bonds An extension of Hirschi's social control theory from adolescence to adulthood. Adult social bonds include quality marriage and quality employment. They are a form of indirect control (something risked in order to engage in crime).

aggravated assault The unlawful attack by one person on another for the purpose of inflicting severe or aggravated bodily injury. Aggravated assaults usually involve a weapon or other means likely to produce death or serious bodily harm.

alien conspiracy model Assumes that foreign criminals (e.g., Sicilians) imported the crime values and family structures into the United States and secretly control crime activities in this country.

altruism According to Bonger, altruism was a characteristic of primitive societies. In these societies, social solidarity was high, and individuals were more selfless and looked after each other's needs.

altruistic criminal Defined by Durkheim as a person somehow offended by the rules of society who wishes to change those rules for the better. This "criminal" is motivated by a sense of duty to improve society.

anomie Term coined by Durkheim to describe a state of affairs in which the norms and values of society weaken and are no longer able to control behaviors.

arson The unlawful use of fire or explosives to destroy property.

Aryan Nations Organization founded on the notion of white supremacy that preaches violent anti-Jewish and antiminority messages. The Aryan Nations' stated goal is the "establishment of a White Aryan homeland on the North American continent."

atavism Term used by Lombroso to describe people whom he believed were "evolutionary throwbacks" to a more primitive line of human beings.

aversion therapy The use of classical conditioning to reverse an unwanted relationship between a stimulus (e.g., alcohol) and response (e.g., pleasure).

behavioral genetics The scientific study of how genes and heredity affect particular behaviors.

bourgeoisie Within the Marxist theory, those who hold salaried and management positions.

breaking and entering Synonymous with burglary; still used in certain criminal codes in the United States.

brutalization effect A concept used by researchers who find that executions actually increase some forms of homicide.

burglary The unlawful entry into any building or vehicle in order to commit a felony or larceny.

capitalists Within Marxist theory, capitalists are the owners of the means of production.

case law Law that is created when judges interpret constitutional provisions, statutes, or regulations created by administrative agencies.

Chicago Area Projects (CAP) A large-scale delinquency prevention program developed by Shaw and McKay. The projects targeted high-crime neighborhoods and created "community committees" to promote community organization, assigned "detached" local adults to neighborhood gangs, and made efforts to improve sanitation, traffic control, and physical decay.

child abuse Physical, emotional, or sexual abuse or maltreatment of a child.

chivalry hypothesis The idea that females are treated leniently by the criminal justice system because police, prosecutors, and judges are predominately male and have a gracious attitude toward women.

chronic offenders Persons who habitually engage in crime; in both Philadelphia Birth Cohorts (all persons born in 1945 and then 1958), the small group of offenders who were responsible for the bulk of serious crimes committed by the entire array.

classical conditioning By pairing an unconditioned stimulus (e.g., meat) with a conditioned stimulus (a bell), over time a conditioned response (e.g., salivation) is reproduced using only the conditioned stimulus.

coercive rape Unlawful sexual intercourse by force or without legal or factual consent. This is a more inclusive definition of rape; it does not require force.

cognitive restructuring A rehabilitation technique for which criminal-thinking errors (cognitive distortions) are identified and contested.

cognitive skills programs Rehabilitation programs that attempt to build thinking skills, such as moral reasoning, empathy, and anger management.

cohort A group of individuals who share the same experience in time. Birth cohorts are often tracked to determine the groups that have the highest rates of offending.

collective efficacy The combination of social cohesion and informal social control within a neighborhood.

collective embezzlement Refers to company funds siphoned off for personal use by top management at the expense of the institution itself.

common criminal Defined by Durkheim as a person who rejects all laws and discipline and purposely violates the law without concern for the rightness of the acts.

concentrated disadvantage The idea that poverty and unemployment have become concentrated within certain neighborhoods, leaving isolated pockets of "truly disadvantaged" citizens.

concordance rate Focus of twin studies. The outcome (criminal behavior) is concordant if both twins exhibit the same behavior.

conflict model The belief that the law is the result of a battle between people or groups that have different levels of power. Control over the state (including the law and the criminal justice system) is the principal prize in the perpetual conflict of society.

conflict perspective View that criminal law is the result of constant clashes between groups with different levels of power. Those groups that win the clashes define the legal code in a manner consistent with their values.

conflict theory Theories that emphasize a pluralistic perspective — multiple groups within a society wield different levels of power.

consensus Widespread agreement in society that laws against crimes such as murder should be strictly enforced.

consensus model The belief that the law reflects common agreement over the fundamental values held by society.

consensus perspective View that criminal law is the result of widespread agreement among members of society as to what should be legal and illegal.

constitutional law The law as expressed in the U.S. Constitution, as well as the constitutions of individual states. Constitutions are the supreme law of the land.

contingency contract A tool to promote parental use of operant conditioning. Parents and children sign a contract that lays out expected behaviors, reinforcements, and consequences.

corporate crime Illegal acts by corporate officials to benefit the corporation.

correctional boot camps Like their military counterparts, these programs emphasize physical training and military drill. Research suggests that most of these programs have little effect on criminal behavior.

countertransference A term from psychoanalysis; when the client "pushes the buttons" of the counselor so that the resulting anger and hostility interferes with treatment.

credit card fraud Counterfeiting plastics, altering stolen credit cards, or simply using a stolen credit card.

crime displacement The idea that when crime is suppressed in one geographical area, it may simply shift to a new location.

crime prevention through environmental design (CPTED) A policy implication of routine activities theory. The way an environment is designed can promote or prevent crime.

criminal event In rational choice theory, decisions about the how, when, and where of a particular crime.

criminal involvement In rational choice theory, decisions about whether to engage in crime in general, as opposed to satisfying needs and wants with noncriminal alternatives.

cyberstalking A specialized form of stalking that occurs when the perpetrator uses a computer and the Internet to follow and harass their victim.

defense mechanisms Psychological ploys that individuals use (often unconsciously) to reduce or eliminate anxieties.

delinquent ego Application of Freudian principles to describe an ego that effectively blocks any potential restraint from the conscience (superego) and permits the delinquent to rationalize criminal behavior.

delinquent superego Application of Freudian principles to describe a superego that is guided by a delinquent code of behavior, rather than appropriate values.

distributive justice Campaign theme of liberal Democrats that increased economic opportunity is the best defense against crime.

diversion programs Programs designed to divert juveniles away from official juvenile justice processing. A policy derived largely from labeling theory.

dizygotic (DZ) twins Fraternal twins who share the same amount of genetic similarity as non-twin siblings.

domestic violence Term used to describe abuse or violence that occurs in the context of the home or family. It includes spouses, co-habiting partners, former intimates, children, and parents.

dramatization of evil Phrase coined by Frank Tannenbaum to characterize the process whereby the primary deviance of certain people is singled out and labeled as "bad."

dumpster diving A low skill practice of identity thieves that involves sorting through garbage for other people's personal information to be utilized unlawfully.

ego The conscious part of Freudian personality; the "psychological thermostat" that regulates the savage wishes and demands of the id and the social restrictions of the superego.

egoism A lack of consideration for others. According to Bonger, capitalism encourages selfishness, greed, and insensitivity to others.

enslavement theory of addiction This theory assumes that addicts are "slaves" to their habit and are driven to crime by the high cost of drugs.

eugenics The goal of improving the human race through selective breeding. In the 20th century, eugenics led to limitations on the immigration of southern and eastern Europeans into the United States and the institutionalization or forced sterilization of the poor, deviant, and disabled.

extra-legal factors Characteristics such as race, class, and gender that can impact criminal justice decision making.

felony murder A homicide committed during the course of another felony offense. For example, an offender burglarizes a house and kills one of the occupants of the house during the crime.

fetal alcohol syndrome (FAS) A well-documented condition caused when pregnant women ingest high levels of alcohol. FAS is defined by a host of characteristics, including central nervous system dysfunction, growth retardation, and organ anomalies.

fireplay Term used to describe the experimentation with fire out of curiosity and fascination.

firesetting Term used to describe the purposeful and willful setting of a fire that can have the potential for significant damage.

forgery The production of a false or altered document or other item in order to defraud another individual.

free association A technique used in psychoanalysis in which the patient verbalizes, uncensored, anything that comes to mind.

gender-ratio problem A key issue for criminologists is to explain the empirical observation that males account for the vast majority of delinquent and criminal offending.

general deterrence Punishing criminals so that the general public will get the message that crime doesn't pay.

generalizability problem Because most criminology theorists are male, mainstream criminological theories may not be applicable (they may not generalize) to female offending.

grand larceny Theft of property worth over a certain amount, usually $300.

grand theories Sweeping theories that attempt to explain all types of criminal behavior.

hate crime Crime in which a person intentionally selects a victim because of the race, color, religion, national origin, ethnicity, gender, or sexual orientation.

headhunting Method of combating organized crime that focuses on the heads of criminal families and also seeks to freeze or seize the assets used in or obtained through organized crime.

hedonistic calculus Jeremy Bentham used this term to describe human nature — humans seek pleasure (hedonism) in a rational, calculating manner.

hired torch A professional who is employed to set a fire for financial gain.

homicide The unlawful taking of life by another human. Types of homicide include first- and second-degree murder and voluntary and involuntary manslaughter.

Human Genome Project (HGP) Begun formally in 1990 and completed in 2003, the HGP was a coordinated effort by the U.S. Department of Energy and the National Institutes of Health to map the entire human genome. *Genome* is the term used to describe an organism's complete set of DNA.

hypoglycemia Low blood sugar. Some studies suggest that hypoglycemia triggers violent behavior. Recent research casts some doubt on this proposition.

hypotheses Testable statements about the relationship between variables in a scientific study.

id The unconscious, instinctual aspect of the Freudian personality. Id wishes often include the immediate gratification of basic drives (e.g., sex, aggression).

Identity Church Organization of churches that believes in the supremacy of the white race and preaches a message of hate, particularly toward Jews.

identity theft The unlawful acquisition and use of an individual's personal information.

incapacitation The use of prison and the death penalty to prevent crime by removing offenders from society.

index offenses The most serious crimes in the Uniform Crime Report: murder, rape, assault, burglary, larceny-theft, motor vehicle theft, and arson.

informal social control The perspective that inadequate or incomplete socialization leads to criminal behavior.

inner containment A form of internal control (good self-concept) from Walter Reckless' containment theory.

instrumental Marxism This type of theory argues that the law and criminal justice system are always instruments to be used by the capitalist class.

intensive supervision Practice based on the assumption that probation/parole officers with reduced caseloads can better monitor and supervise high-risk offenders more effectively. This practice has also been touted as a potential solution to jail and prison-crowding problems.

intensive supervision probation (ISP) Offenders are supervised in the community under strict conditions, including frequent drug testing, curfews, and contacts with a probation officer. These programs were designed to increase the punishing aspect of probation. Research suggests that ISP programs do not reduce criminal behavior any more than traditional probation.

intergenerational transmission of violence The process by which children who observe or experience violence themselves become violent or abusive later in life.

intimate partner abuse Abuse that occurs between current or former, heterosexual or homosexual intimates. Includes physical, sexual, and emotional abuse and violence.

just deserts A justification for punishment (e.g., prison) that emphasizes the pain caused and thus earned by the criminal. Punishment serves as a collective expression of society's disapproval for criminal acts.

Kansas City Preventative Patrol Study An experimental study of police patrols. The main conclusion from this finding was that increased police presence has little effect on crime. Later research suggests that more dramatic increases in police presence can suppress crime.

kleptomania An obsessive impulse to steal; kleptomaniacs often steal objects that they do not need and could afford to pay for.

Ku Klux Klan (KKK) Fraternal organizations that promote the "white rights movement" and anti-Semitism. Known for terrorizing minority groups, especially blacks and Jews.

mass murder The killing of a number of people, usually three or more, in one place at one time.

labeling The perspective that a change in a person's self-concept, caused by criminal justice actions, may increase criminal behavior.

larceny-theft The unlawful taking or attempted taking of property from another person.

law and order Campaign theme of conservative Republicans that a "hard line" is the best defense.

laws of imitation An early form of social learning theory. Gabriel Tarde identified three laws to explain how criminals learned to engage in crime.

legal factors Factors such as offense seriousness and prior record that play a role in criminal justice decision making.

legitimacy The belief in the rightness of and public support for a law.

local, ethnic group model Maintains that organized crime families have a decentralized structure and focus on operating businesses.

Lombrosian fallacy The use of incarcerated persons to reach conclusions about the influence of biology in the general population. This type of research is problematic because those who end up in prison might not reflect the true population of criminals.

long con A scheme extending over a period of time; the "take" is typically much larger than in other cons.

looking-glass self The idea that self-concept is formed based on how other people respond to a person.

low self-control The key form of internal control in Gottfredson and Hirschi's "general theory of crime." The authors believe that effective parenting produces self-control in children.

lumpenproletariat Within Marxist theory, the dispossessed, unorganized workers.

Mafia Code Secret oaths and norms that govern behavior within organized crime families by maintaining secrecy and promoting loyalty, respect, and discipline.

mala in se Crimes that are considered as "evil in themselves" (e.g., homicide).

mala prohibita Crimes that are forbidden by laws that attempt to regulate behavior (e.g., drug abuse, gambling, prostitution).

marginal deterrence The idea that incremental increases in the certainty or severity of punishment should produce decreases in criminal behavior.

market society A country (e.g., the United States) where the capitalist economy dominates all other spheres of life. This is a sink-or-swim society that does not provide a strong safety net for citizens.

mass murder The killing of a number of people, usually three or more, in one place at one time.

mechanical solidarity Term used by Durkheim to describe rural societies, which are homogeneous, cohesive, and self-sufficient.

middle-class measuring rod Term used by Cohen to describe a school system that favored middle-class dress, mannerisms, and etiquette. Cohen argued that lower-class boys were often unable to meet these standards, and therefore experienced strain or "status frustration."

Mobilization for Youth Program (MFY) A program that Cloward and Ohlin actively supported. MFY attempted to attack the root causes of crime in New York City's Lower East Side by securing social services and establishing political structures in lower-class neighborhoods. The program became embroiled in political struggles with city officials, was investigated by the FBI (but exonerated of any wrongdoing), and ultimately disappeared.

monozygotic (MZ) twins Identical twins who are products of a single egg and sperm and thus are exactly the same genetically.

moral entrepreneurs Describes individuals (in the context of labeling theory) who seek to pass laws that prohibit particular behaviors.

motor vehicle theft The theft or attempted theft of a motor vehicle.

murder The unlawful, premeditated taking of another human's life.

National Crime Victimization Survey (NCVS) A survey conducted since 1972 by the U.S. Bureau of Justice Statistics that attempts to uncover unreported crime by seeking victims. The NCVS is a representative sample drawn of about 60,000 U.S. households that is renewed every year.

National Incident-Based Reporting System (NIBRS) A system designed to collect a greater number of details than the UCR about crimes reported to the police. The NIBRS will contain information on both reported crime and arrests. It will eventually replace the UCR as the official source of crime information from police departments as reported to the FBI.

    NIBRS will contain information on 46 Group A offenses that represent 22 categories, rather than concentrate on the eight index offenses from the UCR. Unlike the UCR, NIBRS will:
- make a distinction between attempted and completed crimes.
- provide more inclusive definitions of crime (i.e., the definition of rape has been expanded to include male victims).
- count all offenses that occur during an incident rather than concentrating upon only the most serious crime.

negative reinforcement The removal of a noxious stimulus (e.g., bad smell) to increase a target behavior.

observational learning Learning behavior by observing and modeling the behavior of others.

occupancy cues Indications for burglars that signal whether a dwelling is occupied.

occupational crime Illegal acts arising from opportunities created in the course of a legal occupation.

operant conditioning The use of reinforcement and punishment to shape behavior.

organic solidarity Term used by Durkheim to describe industrial societies, which are more complex and based on exchanges of goods and services.

organized crime Criminal activity conducted by any group with some manner of formalized structure. The primary objective of organized crime groups is to obtain money through illegal activities.

outer containment A form of indirect control (supervision) from Walter Reckless' containment theory.

overdeveloped superego Application of Freudian principles to describe a superego that causes a person to seek out punishment.

overgeneralization Jumping to sweeping conclusions based on the results of a single study.

overreach of the criminal law Norval Morris and Gordon Hawkins contend that the attempt to govern public order offenses like prostitution causes a number of secondary problems that aggravate the crime problem.

panaceas Cure-alls. Applied to criminology, the term refers to the search for simple solutions to the crime problem.

pedophilia The unnatural desire for sexual relations with children.

personality The sum of personality traits that define a person.

personality trait A characteristic of an individual that is stable over time and across different social circumstances.

petit larceny The theft of property worth less than $300.

policy analysis Focuses on the condition the government wishes to create, rather than on the root causes of crime.

positive reinforcement The use of rewards (e.g., praise, money, tokens) to increase a target behavior.

prefrontal cortex The part of the brain responsible for "executive functions" (i.e., abstract reasoning, the ability to sustain attention, self-monitoring, and the inhibition of impulsive behavior). Biological studies suggest that deficiencies in this region of the brain may lead to a criminal disposition.

primary conflict A concept from Thorsten Sellin's culture-conflict theory. Primary conflict may arise between an established culture and a less-powerful culture. For example, recent immigrants may conduct themselves based on codes from the old country that may be criminal in the dominant culture.

primary deviance Term that describes deviant behavior that occurs prior to any official reaction. Labeling theorists portray primary deviance as sporadic and relatively unimportant.

procedural law The portion of the criminal law that dictates the type of behaviors in which criminal justice actors can legally engage.

proletariat Within Marxist theory, the working class.

punishment The presentation of a noxious stimulus (e.g., spanking, scolding) to decrease a target behavior.

pyromania The obsessive impulse to set fires with no conscious motivation.

racial profiling Racially biased law enforcement; targeting individuals for law enforcement based primarily on their race.

racial threat hypothesis The idea that as minority populations increase relative to the white population, they will be viewed as a threat and punitive measures will increase.

radical theory Theoretical perspective that emphasizes conflict between the wealthy elite and the rest of society.

rape Unlawful sexual intercourse against another's will, by using force or the threat of force.

rape myths Cultural beliefs or stereotypes that justify or condone rape and sexual assault. Rape myths include thinking that women secretly desire to be raped and that women who dress or act seductively are asking to be raped.

recidivism Repeat offending.

Repeat Offender Projects (ROP) Projects that selectively focus police resources on career criminals and take a proactive approach. Police target offenders and try to catch them in the act.

restorative justice A general philosophy that the proper role of the criminal justice system is to repair the harm caused by an offense. Victim-offender mediation is a central program in this perspective.

retribution Similar to just deserts, retribution is a justification for punishment that suggests that criminals deserve punishment because they have violated the legal code from which everyone benefits.

risk factors Conditions that increase the likelihood that a child will develop one or more behavior problems in adolescence — the greater the exposure to these conditions, the greater the likelihood that juveniles will engage in these negative behaviors.

robbery Taking or attempting to take anything of value from the care, custody, or control of a person by force or threat of force or violence.

Seattle Social Developmental Project (SSDP) A project that implements many of the policy implications from the social control theory in an attempt to prevent childhood aggression and delinquency. The project attempts to increase direct control over youth, as well as build attachment to parents and teachers and a commitment to education.

secondary conflict Concept from Thorsten Sellin's culture-conflict theory. Secondary conflict occurs within a single culture that has different subcultures, each with their own conduct norms.

secondary deviance Deviance that is caused by the adoption of a delinquent self-concept. Without an official reaction to crime, secondary deviance would not be possible.

serial murder The killing of a number of people, usually three or more, at different times.

Serious Habitual Offender/Drug-Involved (SHODI) Program Program that targets serious, habitual juvenile crime and enhances the system response to drug-related, juvenile crimes. It emphasizes a system-wide effort to coordinate records and services to apprehend and treat the habitual juvenile offender.

serotonin A neurotransmitter that helps conduct the electrical impulses in the brain; low levels of serotonin hinder communication between cells. Research links low levels of serotonin with criminal behavior.

sexual assault Any forced or coerced sexual intimacy (including unwanted touching with no consent).

shaming Punishment of white-collar criminals by confronting them with the seriousness of their conduct while forgiving and reintegrating those who reform.

shoplifting The taking and/or carrying away of goods without an intent to pay.

short con A scheme to take as much of a victim's money as possible at one time.

skimming The process whereby offenders use computers to read and store the information encoded on the magnetic strip of an ATM or credit card.

skin conductance A method for measuring how an individual's fingers sweat. Although research is mixed, some studies find that criminals have lower skin conductance than noncriminals.

skinheads Originally, a group of rebellious working-class youths from England. The movement spread to the United States where youths have adopted a message of group hatred directed typically at minorities.

social bond From Hirschi's control theory. The social bond ties individuals to society, so that they are not free to engage in crime. Elements of the bond include attachment, commitment, involvement, and belief.

social ecology The study of how human relationships are affected by a particular environment (the Chicago School is based on social ecology).

social learning The perspective that socialization toward the *wrong* norms and values produces criminal behavior.

socialization The gradual process whereby a person learns the "proper" way to live, including the norms and values that guide human behavior.

somatotype The classification of human body types into three categories. Sheldon argued that body type was related to a person's personality or disposition. Endomorphs are fat, soft, and round, and they tend to be extroverts. Ectomorphs are thin and wiry, and are easily worried, sensitive, and introverted. Mesomorphs are muscular, gregarious, aggressive, assertive, and action oriented. Some research suggests that the mesomorph is the dominant body type among delinquents.

specific deterrence Punishing criminals so that they will be less likely to commit crimes in the future.

stalking The act of willfully, maliciously, and repeatedly following or harassing another person and making threats with the intent of placing that person in imminent fear of death or serious bodily injury.

state-organized crime Illegal acts committed by state officials in the course of their job as representatives of the state.

statutory law Criminal code created by legislatures and governing bodies.

structural Marxism This type of Marxist analysis grants the government (at least in the short run) a degree of political autonomy. Some laws may run counter to the desires of the capitalists.

subculture of violence Wolfgang and Ferracuti's theory that some segments of society hold values that legitimatize or justify violence. Violent subcultures are characterized by a high level of gun ownership, stories or songs that glorify violence, and rituals that stress macho behavior.

superego The conscience of the Freudian personality — the keeper of prohibitions ("Stealing is wrong") and wishes about what one wants to be ("I am going to be just like my father when I grow up").

superstructure The system of social institutions (e.g., law, education, and politics) that lend legitimacy to capitalist arrangements.

surveillability cues Indications to burglars that they can proceed to the dwelling without being detected.

symbolic interactionism A general perspective within sociology that emphasizes communication through symbolic labels and gestures.

techniques of neutralization Common excuses for delinquency identified by Sykes and Matza. These excuses neutralize the guilt associated with criminal behavior. This represents one of the first attempts to measure Sutherland's concept of "definitions favorable to law violation."

terrorism The instilling of fear through violence or threats of violence. Terrorist groups worldwide seek to achieve often political goals and objectives.

testosterone The male sex hormone responsible for the fetus carrying a Y chromosome. Testosterone influences secondary sex characteristics (e.g., body hair, muscle mass). Research consistently demonstrates a relationship between levels of testosterone and aggression.

theory of differential association Edwin Sutherland's influential learning theory. He proposed that crime is learned in intimate groups through communication.

token economy Application of operant conditioning to corrections. Individuals are reinforced and punished using "tokens" that can be exchanged for privileges.

transference A term from psychoanalysis to describe when the client uses the counselor as a "stand in" from the past.

trespassing Knowingly entering a dwelling and remaining there unlawfully.

tweaking The violence that cocaine dealers routinely engage in against each other in an attempt to control the drug market.

typology A framework and theoretical construct that is used to describe and compare different forms of criminal behavior.

underground economy A social network that allows thieves and burglars to transform goods into cash.

Uniform Crime Report (UCR) An annual report, published by the FBI since 1930, consisting of crimes reported to and uncovered by the police. Currently, the UCR is the major source of nationwide crime data, containing information from most U.S. jurisdictions.

value free The belief that researchers should keep their personal views out of their study and the interpretation of its findings. Objectivity is the goal.

victimless crimes Crimes that affect only the person committing them. Because of the absence of a complaining victim, some people question whether it is appropriate to label activities such as gambling and prostitution as crimes.

violent crime index The Uniform Crime Report creates this measure of serious violent crime based on four crimes: homicide, robbery, aggravated assault, and rape.

Violent Juvenile Offender (VJO) Program Program that places chronically violent juvenile offenders in an intervention program designed to halt their criminal career.

weed-and-seed strategy A federal initiative designed to reduce violent crime, drug abuse, and gang activity in targeted high-crime neighborhoods across the country. The "weeding out" involves targeting chronic violent offenders for incapacitation. The "seeding" consists of programs designed to bring human services to the area and promote economic and physical revitalization to neighborhoods.

white-collar crime Deliberately harmful, illegal acts committed by persons of respectability and high social status in the course of their occupation.

wilding The behavior of gangs of youths "running amok" in the community and committing senseless acts of violence for fun and amusement.

XYY A rare chromosome abnormality in which a male (typically XY) has an extra Y chromosome. Early research suggested these individuals were unusually aggressive ("supermales"). Later research indicates that they are no more violent than others, but perhaps slightly more crime prone.

zone in transition In Burgess' concentric zone theory, this is the geographical area just outside the business district. Research by Shaw and McKay confirmed that the zone in transition had consistently high crime rates from 1900 to 1930.

A

Challinger, Dennis, 338–339, 349
Chamberlain, Henry Barrett, 399
Chambers, J. M., 170
Chambliss, William J.
    citations, 108, 110, 234, 235, 236, 369, 429
    conflict theory and, 209, 210, 212, 218
    historical analysis of law and control systems, 222–223
    on state-organized crime, 415
    on vagrancy laws, 355
Chamlin, M. B., 77, 78, 171, 204, 453
Champion, D. J., 370
Chandler, C., 170
Chaney, James, 313
Chappell, D., 348
Chayet, E., 430
Check forgeries, 340
Check fraud, 412
Chemical castration, 286
Chen, E., 267
Cherek, D., 109
Chesney-Lind, Meda, 227, 237
Chicago Area Projects (CAP), 152
Chicago, murder rate in, 274
Chicago School of Crime, 6, 147, 177, 178
Chiesa, J., 60, 267
Child abuse, 310–311
Child Abuse Prevention and Treatment Act (1974), 311
Child labor laws, 224
Chin, K. L., 429
Chiricos, T. G., 78
Chitwood, D. D., 371
Chivalry hypothesis, 229–230
"Choices" program, Chicago, 65
Christian Defense League, 314
Christian-Patriot Defense League, 314
Christiansen, K. O., 108
Christianson, S., 90
Chronic offenders, 240. *See also* Career criminals
Cincinnati Lead Study (CLS), 97
Cisin, I. H., 397
Citystat program, Baltimore, Md., 441
Civil law, criminal law *versus,* 8
Clark, R., 349
Clarke, Ronald V., 67–69, 72, 79
Class, State and Crime (Quinney), 221
Class-based society
    Bonger on crimes of wealthy and, 220
    crime, the state and, 221
    criminal justice system and, 222–224
    strain/anomie theory and, 154–156
Classical conditioning, 118–119
Classical School, of crime, 15–16, 17, 21–22, 56
Clearance rates, general deterrence and, 61
Cleckly, Hervey, 128, 135, 139
Cleland, C. M., 139, 203
Clinard, M. B.
    on career criminals, 246
    citations, 266, 429, 430
    on corporate criminality, 417
    on pricing and rationing violations
        during WWII, 415

Clinton, Bill, 21
Cloward, Richard A., 161–162, 165, 171
Coalition Against Trafficking in Women (CATW), 366, 371
Cobb, J., 170
Coca-Cola, cocaine in, 357
Cocaine. *See also* Drugs and drug abuse
    violent crime and increased use of, 293
Cocaine cartels, 436
Cocaine psychosis-paranoia, 380
Cochran, J. K., 77, 78, 171, 203, 204
Cockburn, J., 429
Code of Hammurabi, 7
Coercion. *See also* Peacemaking
    social support and, 446
Coercive rape, 280
Coffee, John, 223
Cognitive content, 124–125
Cognitive distortion, rape and, 285
Cognitive psychology, 123–125
Cognitive restructuring, 125, 135
Cognitive skills programs, 125
Cognitive structures, 124
Cognitive-behavioral rape treatment programs, 286
Cohen, Albert K., 23–24, 31, 160–161, 165, 171
Cohen, E. G., 30, 78
Cohen, J., 265, 394
Cohen, J. A., 394
Cohen, L. R., 395
Cohen, Lawrence E., 69–70, 79
Cohen, M. A., 431
Cohen, P., 139
Cohn, M., 400
Cohort, definition of, 247
Coin games, 343
Colburn, J., 267, 268
Cold checks, forgery using, 340
Cole, David, 215, 235
Cole, R., 268
Cole, U.S.S., bombing of, 316
Coleman, F., 308, 324, 325
Coleman, J. W., 413–414, 430
Coles, Catherine M., 359–360, 370
Collective efficacy, 149, 152
Collective embezzlement, 416
Collective incapacitation, 58
College students
    gambling among, 361
    violent victimization of, 41
Colletti, P., 109
Collins, D. J., 30, 78
Collins, G., 301
Collins, J. J., 377, 394, 397
Columbine High School Massacre, 42, 120
Colvin, C. M., 139
Colvin, Mark, 446, 453
Commitment costs, arrests and, 66
Commitment, social bonds and, 186–187
Committee of the States, 315
Common criminals, 145
Communism, failure of, radical theory and, 224

Inverarity, J., 235
Involuntary manslaughter, 273
Involvement, social bonds and, 186–187
IQ tests, 131–132, 135. *See also* Intelligence theories
Irrational choices, 68
Irwin, J., 267
Israelites, Mosaic Code of the, 7

J

Jackson, Jerome E., 245, 266
Jacobs, B. A., 299, 300
Jacobs, D., 235
Jacobs, James B.
  citations, 298, 326, 427, 428
  on effectiveness of gun control laws, 277
  on La Cosa Nostra, 408
  on organized crime in New York City, 402–403
Jacobs, Patricia, 86, 108
Jacobson, J. M., 266
Jacoby, J. E., 108
Jail population statistics, 44–45
Jamieson, K. M., 349
Janjaweed (Sudanese government militia), 272
Janus, C. L., 363, 370
Janus Report, 363
Janus, S. S., 363, 370
Janzen, W. B., 139
Japan, Yakuza of, 404
Jarjoura, G. R., 141, 171
Jeffrey, C. Ray
  citations, 17, 29, 30, 79, 108
  on crime prevention through environmental design, 72
  on Sheldon's somatotype theory, 85
  on theoretical relevance, 20
Jenson, G. F., 237
Jesilow, P. D., 429, 430
Jesperson, Keith, 128
Jiandani, J., 429
Jim Crow laws, 218
Joanes, A., 452
Johnson, Brian D., 377, 381, 382, 394, 395
Johnson, Bruce D.
  citations, 301, 380, 386, 394, 395, 397
  on illicit drugs and inner-city violence, 293
Johnson, E. H., 235
Johnson, J. G., 139, 203
Johnson, Lyndon B., 21, 163
Johnson, R. E., 203
Johnson, V., 395
Johnston, N., 139
Jones, M., 30
Jones, P. R., 266
Joseph, R., 109
Joshi, V., 394
Joyriding, motor vehicle theft and, 338–339
Jukes, Ada, descendants of, 89, 90
Jungle, The (Sinclair), 358
Jurik, N. C., 298
Just deserts concept, 56, 421–422
Justifiable homicide(s), 273

Juvenile Justice and Delinquency Prevention act (1974), 196
Juveniles, chronically violent, 246–254

K

Kaczynski, Ted, 156
Kadish, S. H., 326
Kaduce, L. L., 234
Kahan, J., 30
Kahl, Gordon, 314
Kakar, S., 324
Kalinich, D., 452
Kallikak, Martin, descendants of, 89
Kallinger, Joseph, 321
Kanarek, R. B., 110
Kandel, B., 326
Kandel, D., 203
Kandel, E., 109
Kania, R. R. E., 31
Kanka, Megan, 312
Kansas City Preventative Patrol Study, 61
Kaplan, D. E., 404
Kappeler, V. E., 171
Karberg, J. C., 51
Kasen, S., 139
Katz, Jack, 288
Katz, Janet, 108, 110
Kaufman, P., 50
Kay, B., 203
Kay, K., 370
Kazdin, A., 139
Keeney, B. T., 321, 327
Keil, T. J., 205, 235, 396
Kelling, George L.
  broken windows theory of, 358–360
  citations, 78, 369, 370, 452
  on Compstat program, 441
Kelly, A., 235
Kelly, R. J., 326, 451
Kelly, S. J., 109
Kelly, V., 364, 371
Kelson, G. A., 235
Kempf, Kimberly L., 248, 266, 267
Kennedy, David, 360
Kennedy, L. W., 79
Kennedy, M. C., 234
Kennedy, Robert F., 410
Kentucky Substance Abuse Program, 383
Kerr, Philip, 82, 106
Kerstetter, Wayne, 316, 317, 326
Ketamine, as date rape drug, 281
Khat, East African immigrants' use of, 217
"Killer Clown," 320
Kilpatrick, D. G., 325
Kinlock, T. W., 394
Kinsey, R., 236
Kirchheimer, Otto, 220, 235
Kirkham, George L., 20, 30, 31
Kirkpatrick, J., 293, 348
Kitzma, H., 269
Klaas, Polly, 262

Tice, P. C., 395
Tilley, N., 79
Tillman, Robert, 261, 267
Tillman, Robert H., 429, 430
Time ordering, definition of, 11
Tingle, D., 325
Tittle, C. R., 78, 141, 171
Tjaden, P., 298, 299, 310, 324, 325
Toby, Jackson, 224, 236
Toch, H., 138
Token economy, 123, 135, 184
Tong, R., 323
Tonry, Michael
  on career criminals, 257
  citations, 171, 235, 236, 266, 324, 349,
    380, 386, 396, 397
  on crime control policies' effects on minority communities,
    153
  on war on drugs effects on black communities, 215
Torres, S., 396
Tort law, criminal law *versus*, 8
Towns, Charles B., 358
Toxic Substance Control Act, 211
Tracy, Paul E., 234, 266, 267, 415, 429
Transference, 118
Travis, L. F., 29, 31
Trebach, Arnold S., 387–388, 390, 397
Tremblay, Pierre E., 256, 267, 268
Tremblay, R. E., 204
Trespassing, use of term, 333
Trial by ordeal, 14
Trick, K., 336
Triplett, R. A., 170
Trojanowicz, R., 171, 202, 451
Tsai, Y-M., 170
Tuck, Mary, 443, 452
Tuma, A. H., 139
Tunnel, K. D., 79
Turk, Austin T., 209, 210–212, 234
Turley, A. C., 396
Turner, M. G., 298
Turner, S., 29, 30, 78, 234, 396
Turpin-Petrosino, C., 65
Tweaking, definition of, 380
Twenty-First Amendment, 357
Twin studies, 89, 90–91
"Twinkie Defense," 98
Typologies
  of crime, 221
  of criminal behavior, 245–246
  of female offenders, 229
  of rapists, 283–284
  of robbers, 288, 290

U

UCLA Center for Communication Policy, 138
Uggen, C., citations, 265
Uhlmansiek, M. H., citations, 324
Ulmer, J. T., citations, 431
Umbreit, M., 197, 205

Underclass. *See also* Class-based society
  concentrated disadvantage for, 150
Underground economy, burglars and, 334
Uniform Crime Report (UCR), 35–36
  on aggravated assault, 290–291
  on arson, 335–336
  on burglaries, 333
  citations, 348, 349
  on drug-related homicides, 380
  on female offenders, 258
  gender ratio in, 227
  on hate crimes, 312
  on homicides, 274, 275
  on larceny-theft, 336–337
  limitations, 36–37
  NCVS *versus*, 39–40, 44
  NIBRS *versus*, 37–39
  police performance assessments and, 34
  on property crimes, 330–331
  on prostitution and commercialized vice, 363
  radical critique on scope of, 224
  on rape, 279
  on robbery, 287, 288
  on violent crimes, 273
United Kingdom. *See also* England
  career criminal, Rochdale, 259
  leftist realism in, 225
  murder rate, 274
  Securitas Depot Robbery, 288, 289
  situational crime prevention in, 73
  war on crime in, 258
United Nations Office for Drug Control and Crime
  Prevention, 384, 396
United Nations Office on Drugs and Crime, 409
United States
  homicides in, 276–279
  violent crime trends in, 273
U.S. Department of Health and Human Services
  citations, 325
  National Household Survey on Drug Abuse by, 379
U.S. Department of Homeland Security, 319
  citations, 326
U.S. Department of Justice, 8. *See also* Bureau of Justice
  Statistics
  citations, 29, 324, 396, 451
  on property crimes, 330–332
  on secure confinement rates, 58
  on stalking, 308, 309
U.S. Department of Justice Violence Against Women Office,
  324, 325
U.S. Environmental Protection Agency, 98, 109
U.S. General Accounting Office, 216–217, 235, 370, 412
United States Marshals Service, 428
U.S. National Crime Survey, 71
United States, regional differences in homicide rates, 274
Universalism, institutional anomie theory and, 158
University of Chicago, sociology department, 6
Unnever, J. D., 203
Urban, P., 430
Urban renewal projects, 153. *See also* Cabrini-Green
  housing development, Chicago

Front Matter

Cesare Lombroso photograph © Stock Montage, Inc.; Sigmund Freud photograph © Popperfoto/ Alamy Images; Emile Durkheim portrait © British Centre for Durkheim Studies, Oxford; Robert K. Merton portrait Courtesy of Columbia University; Karl Marx photograph © The National Archives.

Chapter 1

Opener © Marty Lederhandler/AP Photos; p. 5 © Cora Reed/ShutterStock, Inc.; p. 11 © Robert Deal/ ShutterStock, Inc.; p. 13 © BananaStock/age foto-stock; p. 21 © Jim Cole/AP Photos.

Chapter 2

Opener © Charles Rex Arbogast/AP Photos; p. 36 © Debra Reid/AP Photos; p. 37 © SuperStock/ Alamy Images; p. 42 © HO/AP Photos; p. 43 © Orlin Wagner/AP Photos; p. 45 © Visions of Amer-ica, LLC/Alamy Images.

Chapter 3

Opener © Bill Fritsch/Brand X Pictures/Alamy Images; p. 54 © Jim Mone/AP Photos; p. 55 © Paul Connors/AP Photos; p. 61 © Bob Child/AP Photos; p. 62 © Adam Nadel/AP Photos; p. 64 © Erik Daily, La Cross Tribune/AP Photos; p. 74 © Keith Curtis/ Adams Picture Library/Alamy Images.

Chapter 4

Opener © John Foxx/Alamy Images; p. 84 (left) © Stock Montage, Inc.; p. 84 (right) © Douglas C. Pizac/AP Photos; p. 86 © Phil McCarten/ PhotoEdit; p. 87 © CWH/AP Photos; p. 88 © Steve Helber/AP Photos; p. 91 © David Young-Wolff/ PhotoEdit; p. 93 © Elise Amendola/AP Photos; p. 97 © Tom McCarthy/PhotoEdit; p. 98 © Tony Freeman/PhotoEdit.

Chapter 5

Opener © Al Golub, Pool/AP Photos; p. 114 © Jeff Tuttle/EPA/Landov; p. 116 © Popperfoto/Alamy Images; p. 119 © Michael Newman/PhotoEdit; p. 122 © D. Hurst/Alamy Images; p. 128 © Don Ryan/ AP Photos; p. 133 © Sangjib Min, Daily Press/AP Photos.

Chapter 6

Opener © John Sohm/Visions of America, LLC/ Alamy Images; p. 144 © Beth A. Keiser/AP Photos; p. 146 © British Centre for Durkheim Studies, Oxford; p. 149 © Bill Fritsch/Brand X Pictures/ age fotostock; p. 151 © Charles Rex Arbogast/AP Photos; p. 153 © Josh Reynolds/AP Photos; p. 155 Courtesy of Columbia University; p. 156 © Eric Miller/Reuters/Landov.

Chapter 7

Opener © Michael Newman/PhotoEdit; p. 179 © Jason Horowitz/Alamy Images; p. 182 © Doug Menuez/Photodisc/Getty Images; p. 186 © Photos.com; p. 188 © Robert Harding Picture Library Ltd./Alamy Images; p. 190 © Ingram Publishing/Alamy Images.

Chapter 8

Opener © Tom Uhlman/AP Photos; p. 210 © Eric Gay/AP Photos; p. 214 © Mark Richards/ PhotoEdit; p. 215 © Janine Wiedel Photolibrary/ Alamy Images; p. 216 © Brett Coomer/AP Photos; p. 219 © The National Archives; p. 222 © Louis Lazano/AP Photos; p. 228 © Ron Chapple/ Thinkstock/Alamy Images.

Chapter 9

© Ben Margot/AP Photos; p. 241 © Banana Stock/ age fotostock; p. 243 © AbleStock; p. 245 © SuperStock/Alamy Images; p. 249 © Don Ryan/ AP Photos; p. 251 © Bob Child/AP Photos; p. 255 © Jakub Mosur/AP Photos; p. 262 © Damian Dovarganes/AP Photos.

Chapter 10

Opener © Tim Vizer, Belleville News-Democrat/AP Photos; p. 275 © Ron Romanski, Reading Eagle/ Times/AP Photos; p. 277 © J. Scott Applewhite/AP Photos; p. 282 © Vstock/agefotostock; p. 283 © Jack Carey/Alamy Images; p. 288 © FBI/AP Photos; p. 292 © Design Pics/age fotostock.

Chapter 11

Opener Courtesy of Andrea Booher/FEMA; p. 307 © Patrick Schneider, The Charlotte Observer/AP Photos; p. 309 © Nick Ut/AP Photos; p. 312 © Brian Branch-Price/AP Photos; p. 313 © Mike Williams/UPI/Landov; p. 314 © Tom Davenport, File/AP Photos; p. 315 © Marcus Fuehrer/EPA/Landov; p. 317 © Mark Mobley/AP Photos; p. 318 © Al Jazeera/AP Photos.

Chapter 12

Opener Courtesy of District Chief Chris E. Mickal/New Orleans Fire Department, Photo Unit; p. 335 © Eric Parsons, The Tennessean/AP Photos; p. 337 © Mauritius/age fotostock; p.339 © Corbis; p. 340 © image100/Alamy Images; p. 345 © Paul Risdale/Alamy Images.

Chapter 13

Opener © Matthew Cavanaugh/EPA/Landov; p. 354 © Roger L. Wollenberg/UPI/Landov; p. 355 © Kevin R. Williams/ShutterStock, Inc.; p. 356 © Bebeto Matthews/AP Photos; p. 362 © Stewart Cohen/Getty Images; p. 363 © Peter Dejong/AP Photos.

Chapter 14

Opener © AbleStock; p. 378 (left) © Jack Dagley Photography/ShutterStock, Inc.; p. 378 (right) © Tony Freeman/PhotoEdit; p. 381 © Janine Wiedel Photolibrary/Alamy Images; p. 383 © Bill Greenblatt/UPI Photo/Landov; p. 385 © Ricardo Mazalan/AP Photos; p. 388 © Jay Drowns/AP Photos; p. 390 © Michel Porro/AP Photos.

Chapter 15

Opener © Nick Ut/AP Photos; p. 402 © Mike Derer/AP Photos; p. 407 © Mark Lennihan/AP Photos; p. 411 © Monika Graff/AP Photos; p. 412 © AP Photos; p. 413 © Pat Sullivan/AP Photos; p. 422 © Louis Lanzano/AP Photos; p. 423 © Dennis Cook/AP Photos.

Chapter 16

Opener © Jane Tyska, The Argus/AP Photos; p. 434 © AbleStock; p. 437 © Joel Andrews, The Lifkin Daily News/AP Photos; p. 440 © Nick Ut/AP Photos; p. 444 © AbleStock; p. 445 © Paul Vathis/AP Photos.